Readings for the Economics of Money, Banking, and Financial Markets 1993 Edition

Edited by

James W. Eaton
Bridgewater College

Frederic S. Mishkin
Columbia University

HarperCollins*CollegePublishers*

READINGS FOR THE ECONOMICS OF MONEY, BANKING, AND FINANCIAL MARKETS, 1993 Edition by James W. Eaton and Frederic S. Mishkin

ISBN: 0-673-52286-5

93 94 95 96 9 8 7 6 5 4 3 2

Credits:

William Power, "Small Investor Continues to Give Up Control of Stocks," *The Wall Street Journal*, May 11, 1992. Reprinted by permission of The Wall Street Journal, © 1992 Dow Jones & Company, Inc. All Rights Reserved Worldwide.

Fred R. Bleakley and David Wessel, "Treasury Bond Rates Defy Best-Laid Plans of the Federal Reserve," *The Wall Street Journal*, February 28, 1992. Reprinted by permission of The Wall Street Journal, © 1992 Dow Jones & Company, Inc. All Rights Reserved Worldwide.

Constance Mitchell and David Wessel, "Will 30-Year T-Bond Become Extinct Species?" *The Wall Street Journal*, January 6, 1992. Reprinted by permission of The Wall Street Journal, © 1992 Dow Jones & Company, Inc. All Rights Reserved Worldwide.

Kenneth H. Bacon, "The New Banking Law Toughens Regulation, Some Say Too Much," *The Wall Street Journal*, November 29, 1991. Reprinted by permission of The Wall Street Journal, © 1991 Dow Jones & Company, Inc. All Rights Reserved Worldwide.

Lindley H. Clark Jr. and Alfred L. Malabre Jr., "Belying Forecasts, U.S. Prints More Cash," *The Wall Street Journal*, October 4, 1990. Reprinted by permission of The Wall Street Journal, © 1990 Dow Jones & Company, Inc. All Rights Reserved Worldwide.

Alan Murray, "Inflation Hawks: Fed Banks' Presidents Hold Private Positions But Major Public Role," *The Wall Street Journal*, August 1, 1991. Reprinted by permission of The Wall Street Journal, © 1991 Dow Jones & Company, Inc. All Rights Reserved Worldwide.

Alfred L. Malabre Jr., "Fed Assumes Bigger Share of U.S. Debt," *The Wall Street Journal*, March 17, 1992. Reprinted by permission of The Wall Street Journal, © 1992 Dow Jones & Company, Inc. All Rights Reserved Worldwide.

"Shapely Curves," *The Economist*, March 7, 1992. © 1992 The Economist Newspaper Group, Inc. Reprinted with permission.

"The Worship of Basle," *The Economist*, May 2, 1992. © 1992 The Economist Newspaper Group, Inc. Reprinted with permission.

"Big MacCurrencies," *The Economist*, April 18, 1992. © 1992 The Economist Newspaper Group, Inc. Reprinted with permission.

"Currencies on the Verge of a Nervous Breakdown," *The Economist*, May 2, 1992. © 1992 The Economist Newspaper Group, Inc. Reprinted with permission.

CONTENTS

PART THREE *FINANCIAL INSTITUTIONS* 75

ACKNOWLEDGEMENTS

Reading 1 "*Progress in Retail Payments*," Elizabeth Laderman, Federal Reserve Bank of San Francisco *Weekly Letter*, February 7, 1992.

Reading 2 "*Monetary Aggregates*", John R. Walter, Federal Reserve Bank of Richmond *Macroeconomic Data: A User's Guide* (1990), 36-44.

Reading 3 "*Small Investor Continues to Give Up Control of Stocks*," William Power, *The Wall Street Journal*, May 11, 1992.

Reading 4 "*Auctioning Treasury Securities*," E. J. Stevens and Diana Dumitru, Federal Reserve Bank of Cleveland *Economic Commentary* June 15, 1992.

Reading 5 "*Treasury Bond Rates Defy Best-Laid Plans of the Federal Reserve*," Fred R. Bleakley and David Wessel, *The Wall Street Journal*, February 28, 1992.

Reading 6 "*Recent Views of Viewing the Real Rate of Interest*," Rosemary Thomas Cunningham and Thomas J. Cunningham, Federal Reserve Bank of Atlanta *Economic Review*, July/August 1990, 28-37.

Reading 7 "*The Truth about Junk Bonds*," Sean Becketti, Federal Reserve Bank of Kansas City *Economic Review*, July/August 1990, 45-54.

Reading 8 "*Will 30-Year T-Bond Become Extinct Species?*" Constance Mitchell and David Wessel, *The Wall Street Journal*, January 6, 1992.

Reading 9 "*Shapely Curves*," *The Economist*, March 7, 1992, 83.

Reading 10 "*Solving the Mystery of High Credit Card Rates*," Randall J. Pozdena, Federal Reserve Bank of San Francisco *Weekly Letter*, November 29, 1991.

Reading 11 "*Is There Too Much Corporate Debt?*" Ben Bernanke, Federal Reserve Bank of Philadelphia *Business Review*, September/October 1989, 3-13.

Reading 12 "*Lessons on Lending and Borrowing in Hard Times*," Leonard I. Nakamura, Federal Reserve Bank of Philadelphia *Business Review*, July/August 1991, 13-21.

Reading 13 "*Credit Flows and the Credit Crunch*," Steven Strongin, Federal Reserve Bank of Chicago *Chicago Fed Letter*, November 1991.

Reading 14 "*Banking and Commerce: The Japanese Case*," Sun Bae Kim, Federal Reserve Bank of San Francisco *Weekly Letter*, March 29, 1991.

Reading 15 "*Interest Rate Risk: What's a Bank to Do?*" Sherrill Shaffer, Federal Reserve Bank of Philadelphia *Business Review*, May/June 1991, 17-27.

Reading 16 "*Investigating the Bank Consolidation Trend,*" John H. Boyd and Stanley L. Graham, Federal Reserve Bank of Minneapolis *Quarterly Review*, Spring 1991, 3-15.

Reading 17 "*Bank Branching and Portfolio Diversification,*" Elizabeth Laderman, Ronald H. Schmidt, and Gary C. Zimmerman, Federal Reserve Bank of San Francisco *Weekly Letter*, September 6, 1991.

Reading 18 "*The Worship of Basle,*" *The Economist*, May 2, 1992, pp. 5-6 of "*World Banking Survey.*"

Reading 19 "*Risk-Based Capital Standards and Bank Portfolios,*" Jonathan A. Neuberger, Federal Reserve Bank of San Francisco *Weekly Letter*, January 10, 1992.

Reading 20 "*Is Banking Really Prone to Panics?*" Randall J. Pozdena, Federal Reserve Bank of San Francisco *Weekly Letter*, October 11, 1991.

Reading 21 "*Too Big to Fail: Origins, Consequences, and Outlook,*" Robert L. Hetzel, Federal Bank of Richmond *Economic Review*, November/December 1991, 3-15.

Reading 22 "*The New Banking Law Toughens Regulation, Some Say Too Much,*" Kenneth H. Bacon, *The Wall Street Journal*, November 29, 1991.

Reading 23 "*Deposit Insurance: Recapitalize or Reform?*" Mark E. Levonian, Federal Reserve Bank of San Francisco *Weekly Letter*, October 18, 1991.

Reading 24 "*Securitization: More Than Just a Regulatory Artifact,*" Charles T. Carlstrom and Katherine A. Samolyk, Federal Reserve Bank of Cleveland *Economic Commentary*, May 1, 1992.

Reading 25 "*Path-Dependent Options,*" William C. Hunter and David W. Stone, Federal Reserve Bank of Atlanta *Economic Review*, March/April 1992, 29-34.

Reading 26 "*Managing Interest Rate Risk with Interest Rate Futures,*" Charles S. Morris, Federal Reserve Bank of Kansas City *Financial Market Volatility and the Economy* (1990), 131-49.

Reading 27 "*Will Increased Regulation of Stock Index Futures Reduce Stock Market Volatility?*" Sean Becketti and Dan J. Roberts, Federal Reserve Bank of Kansas City *Economic Review*, November/December 1990, 33-46.

PREFACE

This *Reader* is designed to make *The Economics of Money, Banking, and Financial Markets* a unique teaching package that meets the current needs of both the professor and the students. A basic problem of textbooks in the Money and Banking or Financial Markets and Institutions field is that current events and financial innovation make many of the facts in the textbooks obsolete soon after they are published. To minimize this problem, *The Economics of Money, Banking, and Financial Markets* focuses less on a set of facts, but rather stresses a few basic economic principles that never go out of date to understand the role of money in the economy and the structure of financial markets and institutions. To make this economic approach to teaching Money and Banking or Financial Markets and Institutions even more effective, it is important to keep the textbook analysis up to date by supplementing it with current articles on money, financial markets and institutions. This is what this *Reader* does.

UNIQUE FEATURES OF THIS READER

This *Reader* is unique in the Money and Banking and Financial Markets and Institutions field because of features such as its being the most up-to-date, its use to provide a new way to teach financial markets and institutions, its pedagogical aids and its low price when purchased with the textbook.

Most Up-to-date

In contrast to other readers in the Money and Banking or Financial Markets and Institutions field, this *Reader* will be updated annually, with over half the articles new each year. In this edition the number of articles has expanded from forty to forty-five; nearly three-fourths of these are new to this edition. Thirty of the forty-five articles — two-thirds — have been published since July 1991. These include articles on Treasury security auctions, the steepening of the yield curve, credit card interest rates, banking and deposit insurance reforms legislated by Congress in late 1991, securitization, international comparisons of central bank independence, debt monetization, Latin American currency pegging, the relative effectiveness of monetary and fiscal policies, and stock market efficiency. No other reader in the field is as current, and this will continue to be the case with the appearance of a new edition of the *Reader* every year.

A New Way to Teach Financial Markets and Institutions

The third edition of *The Economics of Money, Banking, and Financial Markets* develops a unifying economic framework to organize students' thinking about financial markets and institutions so that they can make sense of, rather than be confused by, all the facts about our financial system. The strength of this approach, in contrast to the approach used in other textbooks which focus on a set of facts about financial institutions, is that it will not go out of date. Because this approach stresses lasting economic concepts, it allows instructors to discuss the latest developments in financial markets and institutions. As part of this approach to teaching financial markets and institutions, instructors will want to use current articles in class to illustrate the economic forces that are driving changes in financial markets. This *Reader* has been designed to make it easier for instructors to do this and keep their teaching current. Over half of the readings are devoted to financial markets and institutions, and two-thirds of these articles have been published since July 1991. Because the need for current discussion of financial markets and institutions is so important to teaching Money and Banking or Financial Markets and Institutions, future annual editions will make a special effort to have a similarly high percentage of current articles in the *Reader* focus on financial markets and institutions.

The numerous, current readings on financial markets and institutions that will appear annually in this and future editions of the *Reader* and the stress on economic analysis in the textbook provide a whole new way of teaching financial markets and institutions. This new approach will make it less likely that students will memorize a mass of facts that will be forgotten after the final exam and that soon become obsolete because of the rapid pace of financial innovation. Instead, they will have an understanding of the dynamism of our financial markets and institutions and will see that what they have learned applies to current developments in financial markets, illustrating the relevance of their coursework.

Pedagogical Aids

Each of the *Reader*'s seven parts begins with an introduction (written by James Eaton) which provides the student with a brief summary of each article. In addition, the introduction provides suggestions for which chapter(s) the reading might be assigned to, thus helping instructors decide how they might like to organize their course.

James Eaton has also written several discussion questions which follow each reading in order to encourage students to think about how the reading relates to material in the text. Instructors may find these questions useful for class discussions of the reading or as written assignments in problem sets.

Low Price

Because we believe that this *Reader* is such an important supplement to courses in Money and Banking or Financial Markets and Institutions, it will be sold with the text at a particularly low price. This should give students the benefit of the *Reader* without making its cost prohibitive.

SUGGESTIONS AND ACKNOWLEDGMENTS

It is hoped that instructors and students who use this *Reader* will indeed find it an effective pedagogical tool. The editors look forward to receiving any comments or suggestions concerning the articles in this edition of the *Reader* or ones which would be appropriate for its next edition. Your comments and suggestions may be sent to:

James W. Eaton
Box 110
Bridgewater College
Bridgewater, Virginia 22812

We owe sincere thanks to several people for their help in preparing this *Reader*. Our thanks go first to Elizabeth Middleton, whose retyping of each article accounts for the

Reader's uniform, polished appearance; and to Dan Spitzer, Jr., Ted Flory, and Scott Moomaw, who on many occasions shared helpful hints about word processing; and to Bruce Kaplan, economics editor at HarperCollins, and Evelyn Owens, supplements editor at HarperCollins, for their advice and encouragement. Above all, we would like to thank our wives Mary and Sally, and our children, Amanda, Elizabeth and Matthew (for Eaton) and Matthew (for Mishkin), who put up with us while this project claims a large share of our time. We hope they know that they are infinitely more important to us than a book.

James W. Eaton
Frederic S. Mishkin

Readings for the Economics of Money, Banking, and Financial Markets 1993 Edition

PART ONE

INTRODUCTION

The four readings for Part I introduce several basic issues related to money and the financial system: alternative means of making payments, the definition and measurement of the money supply, ownership of financial instruments and the distinction between direct and indirect finance, and the operation of a financial market.

Reading 1 is "Progress in Retail Payments" by Elizabeth Laderman. Laderman asks why electronic alternatives to checks haven't become more widely used in making retail payments. She suggests that the answer lies in the benefits of check float and difficulties in pricing the new payments services. This reading is recommended for use with Chapter 2's discussion of the evaluation of the payments system.

"The Monetary Aggregates" by John R. Walter is Reading 2. Walter reviews the origin and evolution of the monetary aggregates and describes how they are prepared and released and how the monetary data is used by economists. This reading provides an extended look at the monetary aggregates and the theoretical and empirical definitions of the money supply which are covered in Chapter 2. (Because this reading also discusses the money supply process, some instructors might wish to save it for discussion with Chapter 15.)

Reading 3 is "Small Investor Continues to Give Up Control of Stocks" by William Power. Power looks at the long term decline in individual stock ownership and the concomitant rise in the proportion of stocks held by pension funds, mutual funds and other institutions. His discussion of the causes and implications of these trends can be a springboard for the coverage of direct and indirect finance, financial instruments, and financial intermediaries in Chapter 3.

Reading 4 is "Auctioning Treasury Securities" by E.J. Stevens and Diana Dumitru. Much attention has been focused on Treasury auctions since attempts by Salomon Brothers to control specific Treasury note issues in 1991. Stevens and Dumitru contrast the current multiple price, sealed bid auction format with alternative formats which might eliminate the incentives and opportunities for market manipulation. This reading is recommended for use with Chapter 3's discussion of Treasury securities and financial markets.

READING 1

Progress in Retail Payments

Elizabeth Laderman

Technological innovation has introduced new retail payment methods that have the potential to replace, to varying degrees, the traditional methods of cash, check, and credit card. If widely adopted, these new methods could increase retail payments efficiency by replacing paper-based systems, especially checks, with computer- and electronic-based systems. However, certain characteristics of the check system and of payments systems generally may inhibit the widespread adoption of such systems. In this issue of the *Weekly Letter*, I discuss these characteristics and the prospects for increased efficiency in retail payments.

THE AUTOMATED CLEARING HOUSE AND DIRECT DEBIT

The most familiar and popular small value, or "retail," payment instruments are cash, check, and credit card. As of 1987, approximately 83.4 percent of the total number of transactions in the United States were conducted using cash, 14.1 percent were made by check, and 1.5 percent were conducted using a credit card.

Relatively new and perhaps unfamiliar types of retail payment methods include the Automated Clearing House (ACH) and debit cards at the point of sale. Together, these payment methods account for only about 0.3 percent of payments made in the United States, the remainder consisting of travelers checks, money orders, wire transfers, and automated teller machine bill payment.

ACH. The ACH was established in the early 1970s, with the goal of providing an electronic alternative to checks for regularly scheduled, relatively low-value payments. There are two types of ACH transactions—credit and debit. ACH credit transactions are initiated by the recipient of the funds, the payee. For debit transactions, the payor has to agree beforehand that the payee will be permitted to initiate such transfers. Credit and debit transfers can be originated via diskette, magnetic tape, or electronic transmission.

At present, the ACH is relatively underused by the private sector. Less than 10 percent of U.S. private sector employees receive their salaries through the ACH, while about 46 percent of Social Security recipients receive their benefits and 67 percent of government employees receive their salaries by this means.

Debit Cards at the Point of Sale. Debit cards are magnetically encoded, machine-readable plastic cards, like credit cards in appearance. They enable a customer to make a payment at the point of sale that more or less automatically debits the customer's deposit account and credits the merchant's account. Some point of sale (POS) systems are "off-line" in the sense that using a debit card creates a paper sales draft which is used for posting to accounts. Other POS systems are "on-line" in the sense that customers' accounts are debited completely electronically, either immediately or in a day or two. Gas stations, supermarkets, convenience stores, and fast food restaurants, where purchases typically are made with cash or checks, are beginning to adopt POS systems, but only gradually.

Debit POS would seem to offer several advantages to customers, over checks at least. For example, a debit POS transaction often is faster than a check transaction. Retail customers have to handwrite checks and often provide identification information that the merchant must then examine and perhaps transcribe onto the check. In contrast, an on-line debit POS transaction requires the customer only to swipe a card through a slot and key in transaction information and a personal identification number on a keypad. Also, many consumers appreciate the automatic balancing and written record of purchases that debit POS provides. In addition, balances can be checked and cash can easily be obtained in conjunction with a debit POS transaction.

RELATIVE COSTS

As noted above, the ACH and debit POS systems account for only 0.3 percent of transactions in the United States and are used much more infrequently than checks for retail payments. However, economists Allen Berger and David Humphrey have suggested that ACH and debit POS transactions are significantly more efficient than check transactions. The processing and accounting costs that payees incur and the processing and transportation costs that the banking system and the Federal Reserve incur in collecting these pieces of paper account for a significant portion of the cost disadvantage of checks over electronic payment methods. Berger and Humphrey estimate that the cost of an ACH transaction is $0.29 and that of a POS transaction is $0.47. (The POS transaction cost figure is probably more representative of on-line than of off-line POS transactions.) A check transaction, on the other hand, uses up $0.79 in real resources.

If checks are so inefficient and costly, then why are they so popular? According to Berger and Humphrey, the answer is that payors benefit from check "float," but don't pay enough for this benefit. Float is the interest the payor saves due to good funds not being debited from his or her bank account until some time after the good or service has been transferred. Float arises because it takes time to process, transport, and clear checks and because the check recipient, the payee, may not immediately deposit or cash the check. Berger and Humphrey explain that people who use checks don't pay enough for the benefit of float in the sense that they don't fully compensate payees for their float costs—costs that arise because payees don't *receive* good funds until some time after the transaction occurs (although often before the payor's account is debited). This "underpricing" of float is at least partially due to the constraints of custom, law, and logistics that make it difficult to charge a different price if payment is made by check than if it is made by some other means.

Prospects for reducing float anytime soon and thereby encouraging the use of the ACH and debit POS are dim. Float is not likely to be significantly reduced without the widespread adoption of technological innovations such as digital image processing that have the potential to speed up check processing and collection. Unfortunately, sufficiently high-speed systems are still a few years off.

Eventually, though, a significant reduction in float would likely be effective in reducing households' and businesses' check usage. Dollar amounts for business checks are large enough that the interest saved due to float is significant. For businesses, if float were substantially reduced, the relevant alternative to checks would likely be the ACH.

Consumers, on the other hand, probably benefit from float not because of the interest savings, but rather because of the liquidity benefits of the delayed debiting of their account. For example, anecdotal evidence indicates that a significant fraction of supermarket shoppers who pay for their groceries with checks are awaiting an account credit (perhaps a paycheck deposit) but in fact have insufficient funds in their accounts at the time they write the check. For consumers, the relevant alternative to checks would probably be debit POS.

THE PRICING BUGABOO

In both check payment systems and electronic payment systems, the pricing of the payment service itself is somewhat complicated. This complexity may also be contributing to the somewhat slow growth of debit POS; pricing arrangements are well-established for checks, but must still be worked out for debit POS.

Payment system pricing can be complex because there are at least *three* supply and demand relationships, and therefore three prices, involved. The first is the usual one—the price the buyer is willing to pay the seller for the product, say, tomatoes. The second price is the one the consumer's bank charges for debiting the consumer's account. The third price is the one the merchant's bank charges for crediting his account. All of these prices are tied to one another because given the price of tomatoes, the more the customer has to pay for his payment service, the fewer tomatoes he'll want to buy; similarly, the more the merchant has to pay for his payment service, the fewer tomatoes he'll want to sell.

Just as institutional and other constraints may make it difficult for float to have the correct price, they may also contribute to the complexity of pricing in payment systems that involve multiple parties. This complexity is evident in the variety of types of prices and fees that can exist. For example, in certain systems, buyer's and seller's banks may pay each other. In addition, a bank may have to pay a third-party processor several different types of fees.

Because debit POS is relatively new, participants still have to work out appropriate structures. Observers comment that myriad pricing schemes now are used by regional POS networks and that feasible pricing schemes for national POS networks are being debated. For example, there is some controversy surrounding the structure of one type of fee paid by merchants' banks. The national on-line POS network, Interlink, has reportedly instituted a 45-basis point "interchange fee," a side payment to be paid by the merchant's bank to the customer's bank. This type of interchange fee is a percentage of the dollar value of a transaction. Apparently, many merchants believe that percentage interchange rates, as opposed to flat interchange fees per transaction, will potentially lead to prohibitive costs for them, and therefore vehemently oppose the percentage rates.

The brief discussion above hints that we should not be surprised if pricing issues are a sticking point in the early stages of growth of debit POS. It will naturally take time and experience to work out pricing arrangements in these new systems. The pricing of check services in the early days of widespread check usage in the nineteenth and beginning of the twentieth centuries also was characterized by controversy.

CONCLUSION

For more than a century, the check has been a very popular means of retail payment. Today, electronic and computer technologies offer us the opportunity to replace checks, to a large degree, with more efficient retail payment methods such as the ACH and debit POS.

However, businesses and individuals will not take advantage of this opportunity on a wide-spread basis at least until check float is somewhat diminished. This may happen if technology significantly reduces the need for the physical transport of checks, but such developments are unlikely in the near future.

In addition, consumer use of debit POS will require the solution of problems entailed in working out mutually agreeable and beneficial pricing arrangements. But, as long as POS network participants recognize the complications inherent in the pricing of payments services and are not bound by custom and past practice, more and more debit POS terminals should begin showing up at merchant locations over the next several years.

REFERENCES

Humphrey, David B., and Allen N. Berger. 1990. "Market Failure and Resource Use: Economic Incentives to Use Different Payment Instruments." In *The U.S. Payment System: Efficiency, Risk and the Role of Federal Reserve*, edited by David B. Humphrey. Boston: Kluwer Academic Publishers.

QUESTIONS

1. What alternative retail payment methods does Laderman identify? What is the relative importance of each?

2. What are the relative costs of ACH, POS, and check transactions?

3. Why does the use of checks remain more popular than lower-cost electronic payment methods?

READING 2

Monetary Aggregates

John R. Walter

The monetary aggregates are measures of the nation's money stock. The most narrowly defined monetary aggregate, M1, is the sum of the dollar amounts of currency and nonbank travelers checks in circulation, plus checkable deposits. M2 includes M1 plus overnight repurchase agreements, overnight Eurodollar deposits, general purpose and broker/dealer money market fund balances, money market deposit accounts, and savings and small time deposits. M3 is the sum of M2 and large time deposits, term repurchase agreements, term Eurodollar deposits, and balances in money market funds employed solely by institutional investors. Analysts study the relationships among these monetary measures and other macroeconomic variables, such as national income, employment, interest rates, and the price level. These relationships are then used to forecast changes in economic activity, interest rates, and inflation. The Board of Governors of the Federal Reserve System defines the aggregates and calculates and reports their values.

This article explains the origin and evolution of the monetary aggregates and discusses how they are prepared and released, how they are used, and when and why they are revised. Information on the monetary base is also included.

HOW THE MONETARY AGGREGATES EVOLVED

Over the years economists have proposed many different groupings of financial assets into something called "money." No single definition of money has been universally acceptable. Two approaches have been used to define money. The first is to identify what financial assets are commonly used for certain purposes. Analysts using this approach generally include as money financial assets serving (1) as a medium of exchange, i.e., assets widely acceptable in payment for goods, services, and debts, and (2) as a store of value. A second approach to defining money is to find the groupings of financial assets the movements of which are most closely correlated with the movements of certain macroeconomic variables such as national income, employment, and prices. Both approaches have contributed to the development of the monetary aggregates constructed by the Federal Reserve. A brief chronology of the evolution of these measures is given below.

In 1944 the Board of Governors of the Federal Reserve System began reporting monthly data on two types of exchange media, (1) currency outside of banks, and (2) demand deposits at banks, i.e., non-interest-bearing deposits transferable by check or convertible into cash "on demand." It also reported the sum of these two. The Board's expressed intent in reporting the data was "to increase the information available to the public on current changes ... in the nation's money supply." In time the sum of currency outside banks and demand deposits came to be called M1, the narrowest of the Fed's monetary aggregates.

Until 1971 M1 was the only monetary aggregate for which estimates were published by the Board of Governors. In that year, however, the Board began reporting data for two additional aggregates, M2 and M3. Interest in these latter variables reflected the growing importance of the monetary aggregates in formulating monetary policy. It also reflected the view among some economists that the appropriate definition of money should include assets capable of providing a temporary store of value. Accordingly, M2 was defined to include M1 plus savings deposits at commercial banks and time deposits at commercial banks except large negotiable certificates of deposit. Similarly M3 was defined as the sum of M2 and deposits at mutual savings banks and savings and loan associations.

In 1975, the Board began publishing data for even broader collections of financial assets, namely M4 and M5. M4 included M2 plus large negotiable certificates of deposit. M5 was the sum of M3 and large negotiable certificates of deposit.

The decade of the 1970s witnessed the development of many financial instruments. Some of the new assets were close substitutes for demand deposits, namely negotiable order of withdrawal (NOW) accounts which are interest-bearing checkable accounts, savings accounts featuring automatic transfer to checking accounts (ATS accounts), credit union share draft accounts, and money market mutual funds with checking privileges. These new accounts began to be used as exchange media but were not counted in M1 until 1980.

The introduction of these new assets also coincided with what some economists interpreted as changes in the relationships between the monetary aggregates and economic variables such as income, employment, and prices. These apparent changes provided some of the Fed's motivation for modifying its definitions of the aggregates in 1980.[1] At that time the Fed replaced its M1 definition of money with M1A and M1B. M1A was equivalent to the old M1, including only currency and demand deposits; M1B included all of M1A plus NOW and ATS balances at banks and thrifts, credit union share draft balances, and demand deposits at mutual savings banks.[2] At the same time old M2 through M5 were replaced with new measures of M2 and M3. New M2 included all of M1B and a number of other assets that are easily convertible to transaction account deposits or that can be used in transactions to a limited degree. These were overnight repurchase agreements (RPs) issued by commercial banks and certain overnight Eurodollars held by nonbank U.S. residents, money market mutual fund shares, and savings and small-denomination time deposits at all depository institutions.[3] New M3 added to M2 large-denomination time deposits at all depository institutions and term RPs at commercial banks and savings and loan associations.

In January 1982 the Board of Governors stopped reporting M1A and redesignated M1B as M1. Since then the definitions have been modified only slightly. Table I shows the current magnitudes of M1, M2 and M3.

MONETARY BASE

The monetary base is composed of currency held by the public and in vaults of depository institutions, plus reserves of depository institutions. In 1968 the Federal Reserve Bank of St. Louis began publishing figures on the monetary base. In 1979 the Board of Governors of the Federal Reserve System also began publishing data on a somewhat different version of the monetary base.

The base can be viewed as the foundation upon which the superstructure of deposits is erected. An increase in the reserves component of the base allows the system of depository institutions to expand deposits. Initially, an increase in reserves—resulting from open market operations or loans by the Fed—leads to an increase in "excess" reserves, that is, reserves beyond the amount needed to meet reserve requirements at depository institutions. These institutions use the excess reserves to make loans and investments which soon become deposits. When these deposits are spent and redeposited, they create additional excess reserves and lead to the extension of more loans. Through a multiplicative process the money supply is increased by a multiple of the Fed's original addition to the monetary base. The extent to which the money stock increases upon an increase in the monetary base depends on the percentages of required and excess reserves held by depository institutions and on the public's holdings of cash relative to deposits.[4]

As noted above, the Board of Governors' and the St. Louis Federal Reserve Bank's estimates of the monetary base differ, and do so in three respects. First, the Board and St. Louis adjust the base differently to cleanse it of changes that are simply the result of changes in reserve requirements.[5] Second, the Board and St. Louis account for vault cash differently. Third, they seasonally adjust their estimates differently.[6]

Table I

COMPONENTS OF THE MONETARY AGGREGATES AND MONETARY BASE AND THEIR LEVELS

August 1988

Billions of dollars

M1	**782.5**
Currency	207.2
Travelers checks	7.2
Demand deposits	290.0
Other checkable deposits	278.1
M2	**3032.0**
M1	782.5
Overnight RPs	64.9
Overnight Eurodollars	15.8
MMF balances (general purpose and broker/dealer)	231.2
MMDAs	517.1
Savings deposits	433.8
Small time deposits	985.2
M3	**3847.3**
M2	3032.0
Large time deposits	514.7
Term RPs	121.0
Term Eurodollars	102.4
MMF balances (institution only)	84.0
Monetary Base	**271.2**
Currency	207.2
Reserves	61.1

Sources: Data for M1, M2, M3 and their components are from Board of Governors of the Federal Reserve System H.6 release, "Money Stock, Liquid Assets, and Debt Measures," dated October 6, 1988. Data for Monetary Base are from Board of Governors of the Federal Reserve System H.3 release, "Aggregate Reserves of Depository Institutions and the Monetary Base," dated October 6, 1988. The Currency figure shown below Monetary Base is from H.6 while the Reserves figure is from H.3.

Explanation: M2 and M3 both differ from the sums of their components because these aggregates are seasonally adjusted by adjusting the non-M1 components of M2 and the non-M2 components of M3 as blocks. Several of these components are not reported in seasonally adjusted form while those that are have been adjusted individually. Monetary Base differs from its components because the currency component the Board uses in its Monetary Base computation includes some adjustments excluded from the H.6 currency figure. The Board does not publish the currency portion of Monetary Base separately.

Other checkable deposits are negotiable order of withdrawal (NOW) accounts, automatic transfer service (ATS) accounts, credit union share draft accounts, and demand deposits at thrift institutions.

RPs, repurchase agreements, are loan arrangements in which the borrower sells the lender securities with an agreement to repurchase them at a future date.

Eurodollars are dollar-denominated deposits issued to U.S. residents by foreign branches of U.S. banks worldwide.

MMF, money market mutual funds, are funds investing in money market instruments, offered by investment companies.

MMDA, money market deposit accounts, are savings deposits on which only a limited number of checks can be drawn each month.

Savings deposits are liabilities of depository institutions that do not specify a date of withdrawal or a time period after which deposited funds may be withdrawn, although depository institutions must reserve the right to require at least seven days written notice before withdrawal of savings deposits.

Time deposits are liabilities of depository institutions payable on a specified date, or after a specified period of time or notice period, which in all cases may not be less than seven days following the date of deposit.

Term, as in Term RPs and Term Eurodollars, means maturities of greater than one day.

The *Reserves* component of Monetary Base is total reserves of depository institutions with Federal Reserve Banks plus vault cash used to satisfy reserve requirements and is adjusted for reserve requirement changes.

For a detailed description of each of the components of M1, M2, and M3 see any recent H.6 release or footnotes to the table entitled "Money Stock, Liquid Assets, and Debt Measures," in the statistical section of a recent *Federal Reserve Bulletin*. For a detailed description of the Reserves component of Monetary Base see the footnotes to the H.3 release, or footnotes to the table entitled "Reserves and Borrowings, Depository Institutions" in the statistical section of a recent *Federal Reserve Bulletin*. The Federal Reserve Bank of Richmond's *Instruments of the Money Market* includes a chapter for each of the major money market instruments, including Eurodollars, RPs, and MMF, listed above.

The Federal Reserve, in its H.6 release and in the tables of its *Federal Reserve Bulletin*, publishes estimates of liquid assets and total debt of nonfinancial sectors with the monetary aggregates even though these are not considered monetary aggregates. The liquid assets measure is called L and is made up of M3 plus U.S. savings bonds, short-term Treasury securities, commercial paper, and bankers acceptances. The aggregate labeled "Debt" includes the debt of the U.S. government, state and local governments, and private nonfinancial sectors. L first appeared in the *Federal Reserve Bulletin* in 1980, with Debt following in 1984. Items in L and Debt fall outside of the category of assets that most economists would call money.

PREPARATION AND RELEASE OF MONETARY DATA

The Board of Governors constructs its estimates of the monetary aggregates from information supplied by depository institutions, the U.S. Treasury, money market mutual funds, New York State investment companies, nonbank issuers of travelers checks, and foreign central banks. Some of these institutions report every week, others report less frequently. Some report in an abbreviated form not available to larger institutions. To produce weekly and monthly estimates of the aggregates, the Board estimates missing data where detail or frequency of reporting are lacking. Table II lists, by component, sources of data used by the Board to calculate the monetary aggregates.

The Board of Governors reports figures for M1, M2, and M3 each week (usually on Thursday afternoon at 4:30 eastern time). Reported values are weekly averages of daily figures for the week ending ten days earlier. The Board publishes both seasonally adjusted and not seasonally adjusted data. Revisions of the seasonally adjusted aggregates can be large due to changing seasonal patterns over time.[7]

The Board of Governors releases its most recent estimates of the monetary base every two weeks. These figures are two-week averages of daily figures for the two weeks ending eight days earlier. The Board publishes a seasonally adjusted monetary base figure adjusted for changes in reserve requirements, a not seasonally adjusted base figure adjusted for changes in reserve requirements, and a not seasonally adjusted figure not adjusted for reserve requirement changes. The St. Louis Federal Reserve Bank also releases a new estimate of the average monetary base every two weeks. It provides only a base figure adjusted for reserve requirement changes and for seasonal change.

The Board of Governors publishes historical series of the monetary aggregates and many of the components making up the aggregates. These series are periodically updated to reflect revisions or redefinitions of the aggregates. Both the Board and the St. Louis Fed produce historical series for the base. Table III lists the monetary aggregates and their component series as well as the monetary base and its component series available from the Board and St. Louis.

HOW DATA ON MONETARY AGGREGATES ARE USED

The Fed's legislative mandate is to set a monetary policy consistent with high employment, stable prices, and moderate long-term interest rates. In semiannual testimony to Congress, the Chairman of the Board of Governors of the Federal Reserve System reports the targets set by the Federal Open Market Committee (the Fed's monetary policy making body)[8] for growth of the monetary aggregates. The Chairman also relates these targeted growth rates to forecasted rates of unemployment, output growth, and inflation. Because of concern with the instability of the behavior of M1, the Federal Open Market Committee has not specified an M1 target range since 1986, although it has continued to set target ranges for M2 and M3.

The Federal Reserve cannot directly control the quantity of money. It can, however, control variables that influence short-term interest rates, namely the quantity of reserves held by depository institutions and the monetary base, and thereby influence the growth rate of the aggregates. Greater provision of reserves through Federal Reserve open market purchases of securities tends to push down the federal funds rate and other short-term interest rates. Lower interest rates, in turn, help determine the quantities of the

Table II

SOURCES OF DATA USED BY THE BOARD OF GOVERNORS IN THE ESTIMATION OF THE MONETARY AGGREGATES AND THE MONETARY BASE

Component	Description of Component	Source of Data on Component and Frequency
M1		
Currency	Currency and coin in the hands of the nonbank public.	Consolidated Statement of Condition of All Federal Reserve Banks (H.4.1)—weekly; vault cash data from Report of Transaction Accounts, Other Deposits and Vault Cash (FR 2900)—weekly, and Quarterly Report of Selected Deposits, Vault Cash, and Reservable Liabilities (FR 2910Q).
Nonbank travelers checks	Travelers checks issued by institutions other than banks. Included in M1 because they can be used directly for purchases.	Report of Travelers Checks Outstanding (FR 2054)—monthly.
Demand deposits and Other checkable deposits	Checkable deposits including regular non-interest-bearing checking accounts, NOW balances, ATS balances, and credit union share draft balances.	FR 2900; FR 2910Q; Reports of Condition and Income (Call Reports)—quarterly; internal Federal Reserve float data; Weekly Report of Assets and Liabilities for Large Banks (FR 2416).
M2		
M1		
Overnight repurchase agreements	Overnight and continuing contract repurchase agreements (RPs) issued by commercial banks. Included in M2 because they are generally considered short-term investments used in managing demand deposit balances.	Report of Selected Borrowings (FR 2415)—weekly; Annual Report of Repurchase Agreements (FR 2090A); Weekly Report of Assets of Money Market Mutual Funds (FR 2051A); Weekly Report of Assets for Selected Money Market Mutual Funds (FR 2051C).
Overnight Eurodollars	Overnight Eurodollars issued to U.S. residents by foreign branches of U.S. banks worldwide. Short-term investments like RPs.	Report of Selected Deposits in Foreign Branches Held by U.S. Residents (FR 2050)—weekly; FR 2051A; FR2051C.
Money market mutual fund (MMF) balances (general purpose and broker/dealer)	Often checkable, but included in M2 rather than M1 because turnover rates are more like savings instruments than transactions instruments.	Investment Company Institute (ICI) gathers FR 2051A and FR 2051C for Fed covering all MMFs.
Money market deposit accounts (MMDAs)	Limited check writing features and turnover rates like savings rather than transactions accounts cause Fed to include this asset in M2 rather than M1.	FR 2900; FR 2910Q; Call Reports.
Savings deposits	Passbook and telephone transfer accounts.	FR 2900; FR 2910Q; Call Reports; FR 2416.
Small time deposits	Time deposits at depository institutions with denominations less than $100,000. Includes RPs with denominations less than $100,000.	FR 2900; FR 2910Q; Call Reports; Monthly Survey of Selected Deposits and Other Accounts (FR 2042); Report of Repurchase Agreements on U.S. Government and Federal Agency Securities (FR 2090Q)—quarterly; FR 2090A.
M3		
M2		
Large time deposits	Time deposits at depository institutions with denominations of $100,000 or more. Held largely by institutions.	FR 2900; FR 2910Q; Call Reports; FR 2416; FR 2051A; FR 2051C.
Term RPs	Denominations $100,000 or greater with more than one day maturity. Held largely by institutions rather than individuals.	FR 2415; FR 2090A; Call Reports; FR 2051A; FR 2051C.
Term Eurodollars	More than one day maturity, held largely by institutions rather than individuals.	Weekly Report of Foreign Branch Liabilities to, and Custody Holdings for, U.S. Residents (FR 2077); information from Bank of Canada and Bank of England; FR 2051A; FR 2051C.
MMF balances (institution only)	Balances held by institutions rather than individuals.	FR 2051A; FR 2051C.
Monetary Base		
Currency	Currency and coin in the hands of the nonbank public plus currency and coin in bank vaults not used to satisfy reserve requirements.	H.4.1; FR 2900; FR 2910Q; Call Reports.
Reserves	Reserves of depository institutions held with Federal Reserve Banks plus vault cash used to satisfy reserve requirements.	FR 2900; H.4.1.

Table III

AVAILABILITY OF TIME SERIES ON MONETARY AGGREGATES AND COMPONENTS MAKING UP MONETARY AGGREGATES

Series	Weekly Averages Available Beginning: sa	nsa	Monthly Averages Available Beginning: sa	nsa
Aggregates				
M1	1/75	1/75	1/59	1/47*
M2	1/81	1/81	1/59	1/59
M3	1/81	1/81	1/59	1/59
Monetary Base—Board				
Adjusted	1/59**	1/59**	1/59	1/59
Unadjusted		1/59**		1/59
Monetary Base—St. Louis				
Adjusted	1/72**	1/72**	1/50	1/29
Unadjusted		1/72**		1/19
Components of Ms				
Currency	1/75	1/75	1/59	1/47*
Demand deposits	1/75	1/75	1/59	1/47*
Other checkable deposits	1/75	1/75	1/63	1/63
Overnight RPs		1/75		11/69
Overnight Eurodollars		12/79		2/77
MMMF (general purpose and broker/dealer)		2/80		11/73
MMMF (institution only)		2/80		4/74
Nonbank travelers checks	1/75	1/75	1/59	1/59
Savings deposits	1/81	1/81	1/59	1/59
Small time deposits	1/81	1/81	1/59	1/59
Large time deposits	1/81	1/81	1/59	1/59
MMDA		12/82		12/82
Term RPs		1/75		10/69
Term Eurodollars		12/79		1/59
Components of Base				
Reserves—Board				
Adjusted	1/59**	1/59**	1/59	1/59
Unadjusted		1/59**		1/59
Reserves—St. Louis				
Adjusted			1/50	1/47
Currency—St. Louis		1/72**		1/50

Sources: Board of Governors of the Federal Reserve System, H.6, "Historical Money Stock Data," March 1988; Board of Governors of the Federal Reserve System, H.3, "Reserves of Depository Institutions, Historical Data," June 1988; *Banking and Monetary Statistics, 1941-1970*, Board of Governors of the Federal Reserve System, 1976; The Federal Reserve Bank of St. Louis.

* Data from 1/47 until 12/70 can be found in *Banking and Monetary Statistics, 1941-1970*, Board of Governors of the Federal Reserve System, 1976, while data for 1/59 to current are available from Board of Governors of the Federal Reserve System, H.6, "Historical Money Stock Data," March 1988. Definitions used in these two sources differ.

** Weekly data are available until 2/84, after which only biweekly data are available.

sa = Seasonally adjusted

nsa = Not seasonally adjusted

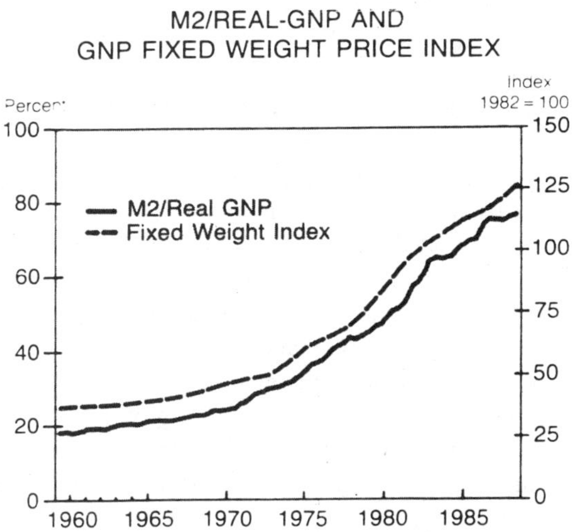

monetary aggregates demanded by the private sector. Downward pressure on federal funds and other rates makes holding money balances, which pay no or low rates of interest, less costly. The lower cost of holding money increases the quantity of money demanded. Assuming money supply equals money demand, the result is an increase in the level of monetary aggregates. Changes in the aggregates normally are followed by temporary changes in aggregate output and employment and by permanent changes in prices.[9] Chart 1 illustrates the relationship between M2 and the price level. As is conventional in such comparisons, M2 is shown per unit of real output, i.e., is divided by real GNP, to adjust for growth in the economy.[10]

The monetary aggregates have been watched closely by those attempting to predict Fed policy moves.[11] In periods when the Fed sought tight control of the growth rate of the aggregates, unusually fast or slow money growth has generated expectations of subsequent policy actions by the Fed to arrest or reverse these movements. In such periods, the financial markets react to the announcement of the weekly M1 figure. The announcement of a higher than expected M1 figure, for example, leads market participants to increase their estimate of the probability that the Fed will put upward pressure on the funds rate, and other short-term rates rise in reaction to these changed expectations.[12]

Many economists study the aggregates to improve their understanding of the links between monetary growth and changes in other macroeconomic variables. Prior to the 1980s empirical studies generally found stable relationships between M1 growth and inflation and GNP growth. These findings were important to the Fed's decision to place more emphasis on the monetary aggregates in monetary policymaking during the 70s and early 80s. With the financial deregulation and disinflation of the early 1980s however, studies began to find that the once stable relationships between M1 growth and inflation and GNP growth were breaking down. These findings led the Federal Reserve in 1982 to de-emphasize M1 in its monetary policymaking process.[13] Recent studies, however, suggest that changes due to disinflation and deregulation have had a smaller effect on M2 than on M1 growth, and that the relationship between M2 growth and inflation has remained fairly stable.[14] In his February 1989 testimony before Congress the Chairman of the Board of Governors stated that "over the long haul there is a close relationship between money [M2] and prices."

The Fed, consistent with the view that further reductions in the growth rate of M2 are necessary to achieve long-run price stability, reduced its target range for M2 in both 1988 and 1989.[15]

REVISIONS TO THE MONETARY AGGREGATES

Major revisions to the published data on the monetary aggregates occur for four reasons. First, the data are revised as reporting or processing errors are discovered. Second, the aggregates are revised annually to incorporate "benchmark" changes. Third, the seasonally adjusted data are revised annually to incorporate new seasonal adjustment factors. Finally, the historical series are revised whenever there is a redefinition of the aggregates.

With thousands of institutions reporting to the Federal Reserve System on a weekly basis, it is impossible for the Fed to find and correct all errors before the first release of monetary aggregate data. As errors are discovered the Board revises the data. Most revisions occur within the first month following initial release of a figure, although some can take place months later.

As noted above, to produce estimates of the monetary aggregates the Board of Governors must estimate the deposits held in financial institutions not reporting on a weekly basis. Most of these institutions do report data on a quarterly or annual basis, however. When these quarterly or annual figures become available, they provide points of reference, or "benchmarks," which the Board uses to make more accurate estimates for intervening dates. The Board makes these benchmark revisions to the aggregates each February.

The monetary aggregates are seasonally adjusted to remove those movements that tend to recur at the same time each year, such as the temporary increases in transactions balances before Christmas and before the due date for tax payments. To determine the proper seasonal adjustment factors to apply to a given month's or week's aggregates the Board normally uses data on the aggregates for three years before and three years after the month or week in question. No later data are available for the most recently released aggregates so the Board forecasts fifteen months of the data and appends it to the actual aggregate data. As time passes, the estimates of the seasonal factors can be made more accurately as forecasted data are replaced by actual data and as data errors are corrected and new benchmarks become available. Each February, the Board re-estimates the seasonal factors for the data series used in the monetary aggregates and revises the seasonally adjusted data accordingly.[16]

As discussed earlier, the Federal Reserve changes the definitions of its aggregates from time-to-time following financial market innovations and regulatory changes that affect the way money is held. Some definitional changes are minor and produce only small revisions in the aggregates; others, such as those occurring during the early 1980s, lead to major revisions. When the Fed changes the definitions of the monetary aggregates, it revises the historical data to be consistent over the whole period of the series. (For a list of the beginning dates of various series see Table III.) Previously published data, however, may not bear the same definitions. Thus when comparing data at different dates, users should take care to determine that the data definitions are consistent.

SOURCES OF DATA

Monetary aggregate data are available from many sources. On each Friday *The Wall Street Journal* publishes a table giving the money stock data released on Thursday afternoon. Historical data can be found in the *Federal Reserve Bulletin*, in the Board of Governor's H.6 release, in the Board's annual historical supplement to the H.6, "Historical Money Stock Data," in the Federal Reserve's *Banking and Monetary Statistics, 1914-1941*, *Banking and Monetary Statistics, 1941-1970*, and *Annual Statistical Digest* for years since 1970.

Historical data on the monetary base are available directly from the St. Louis Federal Reserve Bank and from the Board of Governors, or in the Board's H.3 release as well as the Board's historical supplement to the H.3, "Reserves of Depository Institutions, Historical Data." Normally, on Friday, *The Wall Street Journal* publishes a table including the most recent figures on the monetary base from the H.3 release.

SUGGESTIONS FOR FURTHER READING

Most college level money and banking texts discuss the monetary aggregates and the monetary base and their relationship to economic variables. James N. Duprey's "How the Fed Defines and Measures Money" in the Spring-Summer 1982 issue of the *Quarterly Review* of the Federal Reserve Bank of Minneapolis, examines the aggregates and discusses their construction. "Data Sources Used in Constructing the U.S. Monetary Aggregates," a 1984 monograph by Cynthia Glassman of the Board of Governors of the Federal Reserve System, details the sources used in the estimation of the monetary aggregates. The debate among economists over the best definition of money is discussed in Alfred Broaddus's "Aggregating the Monetary Aggregates: Concepts and Issues" in the *Economic Review* of the Federal Reserve Bank of Richmond, November/December 1975.

The footnotes found in the Board of Governor's weekly H.6 release provide detailed definitions of the aggregates. The H.6 release also describes components included in each of the aggregates and reports their estimated levels over time.

The February 1980 *Federal Reserve Bulletin* article "The Redefined Monetary Aggregates" by Thomas Simpson, describes the events and intellectual forces that led the Fed to redefine its aggregates in 1980 and specifies how the redefinition was accomplished. This article includes time series charts showing the growth of the pre-1980 aggregates and the post-1980 aggregates.

A Monetary History of the United States, 1867-1960, by Milton Friedman and Anna Schwartz provides a seminal discussion of how changes in growth of the money stock have affected the American economy. The authors discuss and make use of the Fed's monetary aggregates throughout much of the book. *Monetary Statistics of the United States*, also by Friedman and Schwartz, provides estimates of the quantity of money for the period 1867-1968 and discusses sources and methods of construction of historical money stock estimates. This volume also devotes more than 100 pages to alternative approaches to the definition of money.

The *Federal Reserve Bulletin* and the Board of Governors' *Annual Report* generally document and explain definitional changes in the monetary aggregates. *Banking and Monetary Statistics, 1941-1970*, published by the Board of Governors, includes a detailed discussion of the Fed's money stock measures.

"The Monetary Base—Explanation and Analytical Use," by Leonall C. Anderson and Jerry L. Jordon, in the August 1968 Federal Reserve Bank of St. Louis *Review*, explains the construction of the St. Louis version of the monetary base and points out why that concept is of importance to monetary economists. The Board of Governors' H.3 release gives a complete definition of the Board's monetary base in its footnotes. Carl M. Gamb's "Federal Reserve Intermediate Targets: Money or the Monetary Base?" in the January 1980 Federal Reserve Bank of Kansas City *Economic Review*, discusses the pros and cons of use of the monetary base in monetary control and provides a good review of the Board's and St. Louis' construction of the base.

ENDNOTES

1.See Board of Governors (June 1976) and Board of Governors (January 1979), p.24.

2.M1A excluded demand deposits held by foreign commercial banks and foreign official institutions while old M1 did not.

3.For a thorough discussion of RPs see Stephen A. Lumpkin's article "Repurchase and "Reverse Repurchase Agreements" in Cook and Rowe (1986), pp.65-80.

4.Humphrey (1987) describes the theory of deposit expansion and its history. Most introductory level college money and banking text provide a basic discussion of how monetary actions of the Fed affect the base and the money stock. Burger (1971) goes into great detail.

5.For example, when the reserve requirement against business time deposits with maturities of 2-1/2 to 3-1/2 years was dropped in April 1983, the amount of reserves banks were required to hold declined by $80 million. In order to prevent a corresponding increase in excess reserves the Fed concurrently withdrew this $80 million through open market operations, leading to an identical decline in the monetary base. The Board of Governors and the Federal Reserve Bank of St. Louis then eliminated this $80 million decline in their adjusted monetary base data.

6.Burger (1979) discusses the causes of the differences between the Board of Governors' and St. Louis' monetary base estimates.

7.For a discussion of the difficulties of seasonal adjustment see Hein and Ott (1983).
8.The President of the Federal Reserve Bank of New York is a permanent voting member of the Federal Open Market Committee while the other eleven Federal Reserve Bank presidents share four voting memberships on a rotating basis. All seven members of the Board of Governors are also permanent voting members.
9.See Board of Governors (July 1988), pp.419-20, and Broaddus (1988), pp.45-49.
10.Friedman (1969), p.177.
11.Loeys (1984).
12.Walter (1988), pp.222-25.
13.Friedman (1988) and Bernanke and Blinder (1988).
14.Hetzel and Mehra (1988), and Reichenstein and Elliot (1987).
15.Greenspan (April 1989) and Board of Governors (March 1989).
16.Lawler (1977), Hein and Ott (1983), pp.16-20, and Cook (1984), pp.22-25.

REFERENCES

Anderson, Leonall C., and Jerry L. Jordon. "The Monetary Base—Explanation and Analytical Use." Federal Reserve Bank of St.Louis *Review* 50 (August 1968): 7-11.

Bernanke, Ben S., and Alan S. Blinder. "Credit, Money, and Aggregate Demand." *American Economic Review* 78 (May 1988): 435-39.

Board of Governors of the Federal Reserve System. "A Proposal for Redefining the Monetary Aggregates." *Federal Reserve Bulletin* 65 (January 1979): 13-42.

___. *Banking and Monetary Statistics, 1914-1941*. Washington, 1976.

___. *Banking and Monetary Statistics, 1941-1970*. Washington, 1976.

___. "Implementing Monetary Policy." *Federal Reserve Bulletin* 74 (July 1988): 419-29.

___. "Improving the Monetary Aggregates." Report of the Advisory Committee on Monetary Statistics. June 1976.

___. "Monetary Aggregates and Money Market Conditions in Open Market Policy." *Federal Reserve Bulletin* 57 (February 1971): 79-95.

___. "Monetary Policy Report to the Congress." *Federal Reserve Bulletin* 74 (August 1988): 517-33.

___. "Monetary Policy Report to the Congress." *Federal Reserve Bulletin* 75 (March 1989), forthcoming.

___. "Money Stock Revisions." (Annual historical supplement to the Board of Governors of the Federal Reserve System release H.6, "Money Stock, Liquid Assets, and Debt Measures"). March 1988.

___. "New Monetary and Banking Statistics." *Federal Reserve Bulletin* 30 (February 1944): 134.

___. "Notes to Table 1.21." *Federal Reserve Bulletin* 72 (November 1986): A14.

___. "Reserves of Depository Institutions." (Annual historical supplement to the Board of Governors of the Federal Reserve System release H.3, "Aggregate Reserves of Depository Institutions and the Monetary Base"). June 1988.

___. *69th Annual Report*, 1982. Washington: Board of Governors, 1983.

___. *The Federal Reserve System: Purposes & Functions*. 7th ed. Washington: Board of Governors, 1984.

Broaddus, Alfred. Aggregating the Monetary Aggregates: Concepts and Issues." Federal Reserve Bank of Richmond *Economic Review* 61 (November/December 1975): 3-12.

___. *A Primer on the Fed*. Richmond: Federal Reserve Bank of Richmond, 1988.

Broaddus, Alfred, and Marvin Goodfriend. "Base Drift and the Longer Run Growth of M1: Experience from a Decade of Monetary Targeting." Federal Reserve Bank of Richmond *Economic Review* 70 (November/December 1984): 3-14.

Burger, Albert E. "Alternative Measures of the Monetary Base." Federal Reserve Bank of St. Louis *Review* 61 (June 1979): 3-8.

___. *The Money Supply Process*. Belmont, California: Wadsworth Publishing Co., Inc., 1971.

Cook, Timothy Q. "The 1983 M1 Seasonal Factor Revisions: An Illustration of Problems That May Arise in Using Seasonally Adjusted Data for Policy Purposes." Federal Reserve Bank of Richmond *Economic Review* 70 (March/April 1984): 22-33.

Cook, Timothy Q., and Timothy D. Rowe, eds. *Instruments of the Money Market*, 6th ed. Richmond: Federal Reserve Bank of Richmond, 1986.

Duprey, James N. "How the Fed Defines and Measures Money." Federal Reserve Bank of Minneapolis *Quarterly Review* (Spring-Summer 1982), pp.10-19.

Federal Reserve Bank of St. Louis. "Monetary Trends." Various dates.

___. "U.S. Financial Data." Various dates.

Friedman, Benjamin M. "Monetary Policy Without Quantity Variables." *American Economic Review* 78 (May 1988): 440-45.

Friedman, Milton. *The Optimum Quantity of Money and Other Essays*. Chicago: Aldine Publishing Company, 1969.

Friedman, Milton, and Anna Jacobson Schwartz. *A Monetary History of the Unites States, 1867-1960*. Princeton, N.J.: Princeton University Press, 1963.

___. *Monetary Statistics of the United States, Estimates, Sources, Methods*. New York: National Bureau of Economic Research, 1970.

Gambs, Carl M. "Federal Reserve Intermediate Targets: Money or the Monetary Base?" Federal Reserve Bank of Kansas City *Economic Review* 65 (January 1980): 3-15.

Glassman, Cynthia A. "Data Sources Used in Constructing the U.S. Monetary Aggregates." Paper presented at 21st Meeting of Technicians of Central Banks of the American Continent. Washington: Board of Governors of the Federal Reserve System, Division of Research and Statistics, Financial Reports Section, 1984.

Greenspan, Alan. "Statement before the Committee on Banking, Finance and Urban Affairs, U.S. House of Representatives, February 21, 1989." *Federal Reserve Bulletin* 75 (April 1989), forthcoming.

Hein, Scott E., and Mack Ott. "Seasonally Adjusting Money: Procedures, Problems, Proposals." Federal Reserve Bank of St. Louis *Review* 65 (November 1983): 16-24.

Hetzel, Robert L., and Yash P. Mehra. "The Behavior of Money Demand in the 1980s." Federal Reserve Bank of Richmond, June 1988. Photocopy.

Humphrey, Thomas M. "The Theory of Multiple Expansion of Deposits: What It Is and Whence It Came." Federal Reserve Bank of Richmond *Economic Review* 73 (March/April 1987): 3-11.

Lawler, Thomas A. "Seasonal Adjustment of the Money Stock: Problems and Policy Implications." Federal Reserve Bank of Richmond *Economic Review* 63 (November/December 1977): 19-27.

Lindsey, David E., and Henry C. Wallich. "Monetary Policy." In *The New Palgrave, A Dictionary of Economics*, edited by John Eatwell, Murray Milgate, and Peter Newman, vol.3. London: The MacMillan Press Limited, 1987, pp.508-15.

Loeys, Jan G. "Market Views of Monetary Policy and Reactions to M1 Announcements." Federal Reserve Bank of Philadelphia *Business Review* (March/April 1984), pp.9-17.

Mehra, Yash P. "The Forecast Performance of Alternative Models of Inflation." Federal Reserve Bank of Richmond *Economic Review* 74 (September/October 1988): 10-18.

McCarthy, F. Ward, Jr. "Basics of Fed Watching." In *The Handbook of Treasury Securities*, edited by Frank J. Fabozzi. Chicago: Probus, 1987.

Reichenstein, William, and J. Walter Elliot. "A Comparison of Models of Long-Term Inflationary Expectations." *Journal of Monetary Economics* 19 (May 1987): 405-25.

Simpson, Thomas D. "The Redefined Monetary Aggregates." *Federal Reserve Bulletin* (February 1980): 97-114.

Stone, Courtenay C., and Jeffrey B. C. Olson. "Are the Preliminary Week-to-Week Fluctuations in M1 Biased?" Federal Reserve Bank of St. Louis *Review* 63 (December 1978): 13-20.

Taylor, Herb. "What Has Happened to M1?" Federal Reserve Bank of Philadelphia *Business Review* (September/October 1986), pp.3-14.

Walter, John R. "How to Interpret the Weekly Federal Reserve Data." In *The Financial Analyst's Handbook*, 2nd ed., edited by Sumner N. Levine. Homewood, Illinois: Dow Jones-Irwin, 1988.

QUESTIONS

1. How was the M1 monetary aggregate originally defined? Why has its definition changed over time and why did the Fed begin reporting data on the aggregates M2 and M3?

2. How is the monetary aggregate data used by policymakers, economists, and participants in the financial markets?

3. How does Walter use the notion of an empirical definition of money in his discussion of monetary policy?

4. Why is the initial data reported for the monetary aggregates subsequently revised? How might this revised data be useful to policymakers and economists?

READING 3

Small Investor Continues to Give Up Control of Stocks

William Power

New York - The individual investor continues to give up control of the U.S. stock market, but that doesn't mean he has given up on investing in stocks.

While direct stock holdings of individuals dropped to a record-low 53.5% of the market last year, down from 84.1% in 1965, individuals continue to pour money into stock mutual funds that give them indirect access to the market's gains and losses.

Some analysts actually say last year's drop in direct investing in stocks by individuals is encouraging. They say that with the growth of mutual funds and other institutionalized pools of money, they had pictured the household number dropping even lower.

One day soon—probably in the next three years—the stock market will mark an historic moment: It will officially become dominated by pension funds, mutual funds and other large institutions, rather than mon-and-pop investors. That will be the day when institutions hold more than 50% of U.S. stocks, a level they have been moving toward for decades.

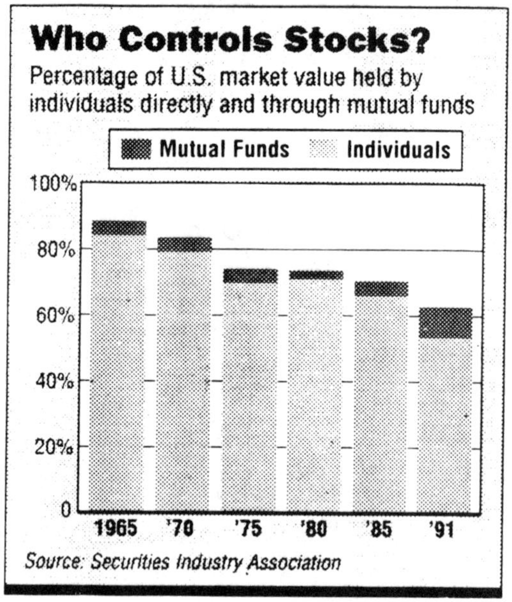

But the long pullback of stock ownership by households "certainly has slowed down," says Jeffrey Schaefer, research director at the Securities Industry Association, which compiled the latest numbers using Federal Reserve Board data. Households sold far fewer stocks in 1991—$14 billion more than they bought—compared with $77 billion more than they bought annually during the years 1970-1990, the Fed says. Some market analysts question how accurate the numbers are, but last year's slowdown in selling is clear.

Still, keeping control of the stock market is eventually going to be a losing battle for individuals. Mr. Schaefer concedes it is "inevitable" that individual ownership of stocks will fall below 50% in coming years. That is because individual investors are more comfortable turning over control of stock-picking to mutual funds and other institutions—thereby becoming part of the big institutions themselves.

The steady decline in the number of small investors who want to buy and sell stocks on their own—and the increased popularity of mutual funds—has major implications for the U.S. stock market and for Wall Street brokerage companies. As recently as 1980, households still owned 70% of U.S. stocks; in 1970, they had held 80%. Those levels will never be seen again, most analysts agree.

Households themselves have contributed to the explosion of stock investing by pension funds, mutual funds, insurance companies and foreign investors because they have been selling their individual stocks and reinvesting the money in mutual funds, which have risen nearly tenfold in size over the past decade. Mutual funds now hold nearly $400 billion of the market's total $4.37 trillion of stocks.

Wall Street brokerage firms know all about the pattern; that is why most have been rearranging themselves to stress money management for individuals rather than hawking individual stocks. For example, brokerage firms have heavily promoted "wrap" accounts, in which investors pay fees to brokers to have their money invested by professional money managers.

The drop in stock ownership by individuals "is a continuation of a trend, and it's something that obviously influences our strategy," says Donald Marron, chairman of PaineWebber Group Inc. Mr. Marron says PaineWebber's wrap accounts are growing by $100 million a month, to nearly $3 billion at present. He says the 1987 stock-market crash convinced many investors that they didn't necessarily want to own as many individual stocks anymore.

The crash didn't convince individuals that they should shun the stock market, but rather that "they shouldn't invest in stocks on their own," Mr. Marron says. "The market is more complicated and subject to different forces, like derivative products. It's gone from national to global. And needs of investors are long-term. All of those things combined means you need more professional guidance for your portfolio."

There is another school of thought on all this. Discount brokerage companies, not surprisingly, are holding out hope that individuals will continue to trade individual stocks; that is the main way the discount firms make money.

Leslie Quick III, president of discounter Quick & Reilly Group Inc., says he anticipates a "whole new generation" of younger investors wanting to buy individual stocks in the next few years. These are investors who have fled low-yielding certificates of deposit and saving accounts and have bought mutual funds, he says. But now, they might shift to stocks themselves.

Says Mr. Quick: "I think some of the newer people who are getting their feet wet in mutual funds will come over and buy stocks. They're going to do as well, or probably better, than mutual funds because of the fees that mutual funds are charging." Just in case, though, Quick & Reilly is planning to beef up its sales of mutual funds, firm officials say.

Of course, if individuals do start buying stocks again, Wall Street executives such as Mr. Marron won't mind; all brokerage firms still earn commissions when individuals trade stocks and bonds.

And any slowdown in the move toward institutional dominance of the stock market will cheer those on Wall Street who say that direct ownership of stocks by individuals—rather than indirect ownership through mutual funds—is crucial to keep the stock market healthy.

Individual investors who hold stocks for the long term help to offset the rapid zigs and zags of program traders and many large institutional investors. The New York Stock Exchange has emphasized individual-investor stock ownership as a "major source of liquidity in the stock market."

Institutional investors have more impact than individuals on the day-to-day stock market. Many small investors who buy stocks hold on to them for years, as market professionals advise them to. With so many individuals sitting on the sidelines, an estimated 75% to 80% of daily trading is done by institutions, rather than individuals.

Yet some analysts say that means that individual investors have more opportunities than ever to do well in stock trading; for example, they can invest in a good stock for the long term when it gets battered by seemingly pointless institutional selling. "If you've got a balanced portfolio, you're going to be OK, whether there are crashes or whatever," Mr. Quick says. "If you have all your eggs in one basket, hey, than you're going to get smashed."

QUESTIONS

1. Why are individual stockholdings on the decline? Who is picking up the stocks in terms of stock ownership? Explain these trends in terms of direct and indirect finance.

2. How are these changes in stock ownership likely to affect the stock market?

READING 4

Auctioning Treasury Securities

E.J. Stevens and Diana Dumitru

The U.S. Treasury expects to sell about a trillion dollars of new securities this fiscal year to finance a projected $400 billion budget deficit and to refinance maturing debt. Most of the securities will be issued through public auctions, where competition among bidders might be expected to minimize interest payments on the debt.

The competitiveness of Treasury auctions was called into question last August, however, when Salomon Brothers, a large securities dealer, admitted to having placed unauthorized bids in the names of customers during eight auctions. For example, in the May 22, 1991 note auction, the firm controlled more than 90 percent of the issue, far exceeding the 35 percent limit set by the Treasury. Rumors of a market "squeeze" had surfaced even before the notes were issued on May 31.[1] Disappointed bidders, with contracts to deliver the security after it was issued, had to pay an unexpectedly high price for the issue in the secondary market, where Salomon controlled most of the supply.

Two causes for concern emerge from this incident. First, of course, is simply that the market is not fair when auction rules are broken. Some investors might shun the Treasury securities market rather than be exposed to losses resulting from market manipulation. Thus, any short-term gain to the Treasury from an artificially high price at a single auction could be outweighed by lower demand and prices in all auctions. Second, as suggested here, is the possibility that the auction process itself may be at fault. Perhaps a different system of selling new issues of Treasury debt would reduce incentives for manipulation.

Following Salomon's admissions and other reported irregularities, the Treasury Department, the Board of Governors of the Federal Reserve System, and the Securities and Exchange Commission conducted a study in 1991 leading to a joint report on the government securities market. The report reaffirms that public auctions are the best means of issuing new Treasury debt and recommends some minor adjustments that have already been adopted to ensure public access to the existing auction process. It also recommends a more thorough exploration of alternative methods of conducting public auctions. This *Economic Commentary* examines the rationales for adopting a different system for determining the price paid by a winning bidder and a new technology for bidding.[2] Both of these changes could make public auctions of Treasury securities less susceptible to manipulation.

TODAY'S AUCTIONS: MULTIPLE-PRICE, SEALED-BID

The Treasury maintains a regular schedule of auctions in which it sells bonds, notes, and bills. Bonds and notes are sold in $1,000 denominations and pay interest every six months until maturity, which ranges from 10 to 30 years for bonds and from one to 10 years for notes. The recent schedule has included monthly auctions of two- and five-year notes and quarterly auctions of three-, seven-, and 10-year notes and 30-year bonds.

Treasury bills, in $10,000 denominations, have no coupon. An investor's return comes from the difference between the maturity value and the price paid—the "discount." Bills maturing in 13 weeks and 26 weeks are auctioned every Monday. Bills maturing in 52 weeks are offered every four weeks.

About a week before each auction, the Treasury announces the auction day, size, maturity, and the settlement day when successful bidders must make payment. From this announcement until settlement, the impending security actually trades in the market on a "when-issued" basis, with the promise of delivery on settlement day. When-issued trading thus may provide potential bidders with information about the likely price in the auction.

By 1:00 p.m. on auction day, bidders must submit tenders (written, sealed bids) at Federal Reserve Banks or their branches. Two kinds of tenders can be used: Competitive tenders state the amount of securities desired (as much as several billion dollars) and either a yield bid (for bonds and notes) in one-basis-point increments or a price bid (for bills) on the basis of 100 (for example, 98.995). Noncompetitive tenders can be placed only for smaller amounts (up to $5 million for notes and bonds, or $1 million for bills), with the yield or price determined by the average of awards in competitive bidding.

At 1:00 p.m. on the day of an auction, bids are tabulated and transmitted to the Treasury. Securities are awarded to all noncompetitive bidders; the remainder of the issue is awarded to competitive bidders in descending order of price bid (increasing yield bid).[3] A bidder may submit tenders up to a maximum of 35 percent of the amount being auctioned, with bids at various prices. The exception is that if too many bids are received at the lowest accepted "stop-out" price, these awards are made in proportion to the total of all bids received at that price.

The process can be summarized as a sealed-bid auction, open to anyone, with awards at multiple prices. Modifications already adopted address the openness of the process, to ensure that any financially responsible party can participate in a Treasury auction. Some drawbacks are nevertheless associated with multiple prices and sealed bidding.

THE WINNER'S CURSE

Making auction awards at multiple prices means that the highest bidders must follow through, actually paying the prices they offered even though others are paying less for the identical security. This may seem only fair. After all, if the high bidders didn't think the securities were worth so much, they shouldn't have bid so much. This view assumes that the item's value to the winner may be largely independent of the lower value placed on the item by unsuccessful bidders.

In the case of Treasury auctions, however, the value of a security is not independent of the market. A dealer wants the security being auctioned only in order to sell it, but must compete with other dealers who may have paid less in the auction; an investor wants the securities for portfolio purposes and could wait to buy in the post-auction market. No matter how fair it may seem, paying a high price for an award of securities that others have bought more cheaply truly involves a "winner's curse."

The winner's curse has serious implications for Treasury auctions. While a high bid will increase the chances of an award, it also raises the possibility of paying more than the post-auction market value of the security. The auction process might reveal something about that value, but only the smallest-volume bidders can benefit by submittingnoncompetitivetenders; competitive bidders cannot take advantage of the information revealed in the auction. The winner's curse dampens the aggressiveness of their bidding, resulting in a lower auction price received by the Treasury. Bids may be lowered to cover the costs of gathering information about what others are likely to bid. Alternatively, customers may submit their bids through a small number of well-informed dealers, where bidding might tend to become concentrated. Thus, a winner's curse may dampen all competitive bidding and lower multiple auction prices relative to market values.

Sealed bidding, one the other hand, when coupled with multiple prices, enables a single bidder to corner the post-auction market, transforming the auction-winner's curse into a post-auction blessing. A well-informed and well-financed bidder or group of bidders could deliberately submit a high bid to ensure receiving a dominant share of auction awards. Because of the substantial volume of when-issued trading, controlling the post-auction supply of a Treasury security places the high bidder in a position to squeeze unsuccessful bidders who had contracted to deliver the security after the auction. While not a necessary outcome, the current auction setup does contain the seeds of market manipulation that can discourage demand. The winner's curse places a premium on discovering how others will bid, creating the basis for a bid that will corner an auction and squeeze the post-auction market.

SAFEGUARDS AGAINST MANIPULATION

Treasury auctions contain an important safeguard against cornering the supply of a new issue: A single bidder is prohibited from acquiring more than 35 percent of an issue. As the Salomon example attests, enforcing this rule is not easy. For example, winning bidders must be contacted to ensure that customers' names are not used improperly by a dealer trying to control more than his share of an issue. Moreover, 35 percent is an arbitrary limit that may restrict demand and unnecessarily lower auction prices when there is no threat of manipulation.

One alternative to this rule is to reopen the issue whose supply has been cornered. Augmenting supply would drive down an artificially high price and eliminate profits expected by the perpetrators of the squeeze. Knowing that the Treasury would respond in this way would eliminate the incentive to manipulate the market. Of course, this approach is simply the price equivalent of the 35 percent rule, reducing the high bidder's market share by increasing total supply. It would involve an equally arbitrary judgment about the permissible range within which the post-auction price could vary without triggering a reopening, as well as arbitrary judgments about whether prices reflected manipulation or a change in market fundamentals.

A SINGLE-PRICE AUCTION

Changing to a single-price auction has been proposed as an alternative to enforcing arbitrary rules on the current auction process.[4] This procedure would be identical to the current one, except that all competitive awards would be made at the stop-out price, which is the price that clears the market. The winner's curse would disappear because winning bidders would receive their awards at the stop-out, even if they bid higher.

Resistance to a single-price auction centers around its implication for the cost of servicing government debt. With a single-price auction, the Treasury would forgo revenue now received from the difference between successful price bids and the stop-out price. Actually, however, Treasury auction revenues might increase, although auction theory is ambivalent on this matter.[5] Revenue foregone by shifting from a multiple- to a single-price auction might be more than offset by an increase in demand as participants bid more aggressively in the absence of a winner's curse, as illustrated in figure 1. Whether the gain would actually exceed foregone revenues, though, depends in part on the *size* of the increase in demand. It could be slight if most participants are already so averse to the risk of not getting an award that they bid aggressively in multiple-price auctions, despite the winner's curse. So, a single-price auction will increase demand, but might not reduce the interest cost of financing the debt.

More to the point, a single-price auction also might or might not produce a less fertile environment for market manipulation. A high bid could garner a dominant market position

FIGURE 1 SINGLE-PRICE AUCTIONS: GAINS AND LOSSES

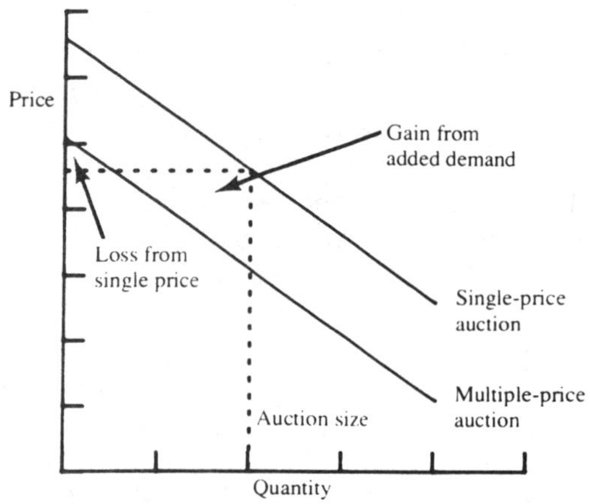

SOURCE: Authors.

without requiring the successful bidder to pay any more than the stop-out price. But other incentives to corner the market might be weaker, because bidders would no longer conduct as intensive a pre-auction search for information about others' bids. Thus, a bidder would have to make special efforts to gather information; cornering the market would become more costly. Chances of pre-auction detection by other bidders, who might raise their own bids by enough to defeat an attempted corner, would also increase.

AN AUCTION BY OPEN OUTCRY

Perhaps the most intriguing alternative presented in the joint report is that of conducting Treasury auctions by open outcry, rather than by sealed bid. The disadvantage of sealed bidding is that participants cannot be certain of the distribution of all other bids. In the multiple-price auction, winning with a bid higher than the stop-out implies that your estimate was too high, and the risk of this winner's curse leads to conservative bidding. In a single-price auction, your winning bid is lowered to the stop-out, based on the auctioneer's information about the actual distribution of bids, all of which will be less conservative than in a multiple-price auction. In an open-outcry auction, which is typically used to sell antiques or works of art, information about the distribution of bids is revealed gradually to all bidders before the auction closes. As the auction process drives the bidding higher and higher, low prices become irrelevant.

An attempt to gain a dominant share of Treasury auction awards seems unlikely to succeed with this system, because the auction process reveals more information about the actual distribution of bids. If the distribution of bids initially contains an unusually large bid at a high price, the ascending price reveals that a large number of bidders underestimated the value of the security and therefore can raise their bids. While the final auction price may be unusually high, the individual who attempted to corner will not gain a large share of awards.

In the past, formidable obstacles have stood in the way of conducting Treasury auctions by open outcry, obstacles mostly absent from the typical auction of a unique art object. At one time, it might have been difficult even to assemble all bidding in a single place, but today, open communication lines to Federal Reserve offices and to individual bidders could overcome that geographic problem, just as telephone bidding does in major art auctions.

More difficult, and unlike an auction of a single work of art, bidders must cry out not just a price, but a *quantity* at each price. Bidding must ascend from low prices, where the demand for securities exceeds the supply, to the market-clearing price, where demand exactly equals supply. As envisioned in the joint report, bidding would have to proceed in discreet "rounds," starting from a low price and rising by small increments. As the results of each round were announced, participants could drop out, resubmit the same quantity, or adjust the quantity in light of information gained from the previous round.

Auctioning Treasury securities by open outcry would consume too much time to be feasible with current auction technology. Each round of bidding probably would take more than an hour using today's paper tenders, manual tabulation, verification of payment status, transmission to the Treasury, and final compilation. Each open-outcry auction might consume most of a day, during which unfolding world events might be moving market fundamentals enough to change bidding decisions and to prevent the process from moving smoothly toward an equilibrium market-clearing price.

The Treasury expects to automate the current sealed-bid, multiple-price auction process this year, allowing telecommunication of tenders and computerized compilation of bids. Going any further toward auctions by electronic open out-cry would require substantial investments, both in hardware and software and, before that, in design. One critical design question would involve the information feedback provided at the end of each round of bidding. Simply announcing the amount of excess demand might not be sufficient for bidders to detect an aggressive effort to dominate the awards. On the other hand, a complete (anonymous) list of all bid quantities received might prove too cumbersome for rapid rounds of bidding. Another design question involves the computer and telecommunications capacity required to receive large numbers of bids virtually simultaneously. Too little is known at this time, but automation could conceivably reduce the turn-around time between successive rounds of bidding to a matter of minutes, with an entire auction lasting perhaps less than an hour.[6] Given the information benefits of open outcry, serious further exploration seems warranted.

CONCLUSION

The U.S. Treasury securities market is the largest and most efficient market in the world today. Nonetheless, the events of 1991 demonstrated that concerted strong bidding in the primary market for an issue could result in a squeeze in the secondary market. More aggressive policing of the current rule against control of more than 35 percent of a new issue promises to reduce chances of similar episodes in the future.

Embedded in the current sealed-bid, multiple-price auction process are both incentives and opportunities for a bidder to seek a dominant share of awards. New methods of conducting auctions are worth serious consideration if they would reduce the need for arbitrary policing of the market. A single-price, sealed-bid auction would reduce the current incentive of each bidder to discover the price at which other bidders will make tenders. With less of their activity focused on discovering one another's intentions, bidders would have less opportunity and incentive to corner an issue. Perhaps more promising would be to enlist telecommunications and computer technology in conducting auctions by electronic open outcry, relying on competition among the bidders themselves to limit the share of auction awards controlled by any single bidder.

ENDNOTES

1A squeeze occurs when there is an unexpected restriction of supply relative to demand for a particular security, manifested by an unusually high price of that security relative to prices of comparable securities.

2See *Joint Report on the Government Securities Market*. Washington, D.C.: Department of Treasury, Securities and Exchange Commission, and Board of Governors of the Federal Reserve System, January 1992. A somewhat more technical examination of these matters appeared recently in Vincent Reinhart, "Theory and Evidence on Reform of the Treasury's Auction Procedures," Federal Reserve Board, Finance and Economics Discussion Series No. 190, March 1992.

3Federal Reserve Bank and government tenders are also awarded in full at the price established for noncompetitive bidders, but the amount of these awards is added to the amount being auctioned.

4Milton Friedman has been a long-time proponent of this procedure. For references, see *Joint Report on the Government Securities Market*, p. B-22.

5See Robert J. Weber, "Multiple-Object Auctions," in Richard Engelbrecht-Wiggins, Martin Shubik, and Robert M. Stark, eds., *Auctions, Bidding, and Contracting: Uses and Theory*. New York: New York University Press, 1983.

6An alternative to rounds of bidding might be to conduct auctions on an interactive, open-screen basis: Qualified bidders would have access directly (or at a Federal Reserve Bank) to a telecommunications terminal. Beginning hours (or days) before the close of an auction, a screen would display an instantaneously updated list of all (anonymous) bids received and their implied auction stop-out price. Bidders would have the right to alter their bids up until the close of the auction, when the final stop-out price would be determined, with awards made to all who bid at or above that price.

QUESTIONS

1. How are Treasury auctions conducted? What are competitive and noncompetitive bids?

2. What auction rule did Salomon Brothers violate? How did it stand to benefit from controlling the market?

3. What is the "winner's curse" inherent in the present Treasury auction method?

4. How would a single price auction affect the Treasury's auction revenues and the incentives to corner the market?

PART TWO

FUNDAMENTALS OF INTEREST RATES

Interest rates are among the most important variables in the economy. For this reason, explaining how they are determined is an essential part of most courses on money, banking, and financial markets. The readings for Part II provide illustration and examples for key aspects of interest rate determination.

Reading 5 is "Treasury Bond Rates Defy Best-Laid Plans of the Federal Reserve" by Fred R. Bleakley and David Wessel. Although the Fed has succeeded in pushing short-term interest rates down, the rates in 30-year Treasury bonds remain stubbornly high. Bleakley and Wessel assess the effects high long-term interest rates have on the economy and survey the factors responsible for keeping the long-term rates up. This reading provides several opportunities for applying the bond supply and demand analysis presented in Chapter 6.

"Recent Views of Viewing the Real Rate of Interest" by Rosemary Thomas Cunningham and Thomas J. Cunningham is Reading 6. The authors consider alternative explanations of how the real rate of interest is determined, including the loanable funds and liquidity preference frameworks developed in Chapter 6, and investigate the question of whether the monetary authorities have any influence over real, as distinct from nominal, interest rates. (Instructors who want to emphasize applications of rational expectations might alternatively want to wait until their students have read Chapter 29 to discuss this reading.)

Readings 7, 8 and 9 deal with aspects of the risk and term structure of interest rates covered in Chapter 7. Reading 7 is "The Truth About Junk Bonds' by Sean Becketti. After defining junk bonds, Becketti examines whether junk bonds are responsible for the rise in corporate mergers, corporate debt, and financial market volatility. His treatment of junk bonds may be discussed with the material in Chapter 7 on risk structure of interest rates and corporate bond ratings, or instructors who plan to include the appendix to Chapter 8 on corporate restructuring in their reading assignments could use this reading then.

Reading 8 is "Will 30-Year T-Bond Become Extinct Species?" by Constance Mitchell and David Wessel. In light of the sizable spread between long-term and short-term interest rates, many economists and members of Congress are proposing to eliminate or reduce the sales of long-term Treasury bonds. Mitchell and Wessel sample a variety of opinions on how this would affect interest rates and the government's borrowing costs.

Reading 9, "Shapely Curves", suggests that the shape of the yield curve may be seen as a leading indicator of economic activity and that the large gap between long-term and short-term interest rates in the U.S. could mean the American economy is set for a strong recovery.

READING 5

Treasury Bond Rates Defy Best-Laid Plans of the Federal Reserve

Fred R. Bleakley and David Wessel

Why can't the Federal Reserve Board get long-term interest rates down?

After jolting the financial markets with a big rate cut in late December, the central bank thought interest rates would continue slowly drifting downward, breathing life into the economy. But the Fed's grand plan is being threatened by bond investors.

Although short-term rates—less than a year in maturity—have remained low, rates on longer-range debt, which tumbled in late December and early January, have since crept back up. The yield on the bellwether 30-year U.S. Treasury bond (known on Wall Street as the long bond) edged close to 8% early this week, compared with 7.40% in early January. After the Fed cut in December, economists thought it might drop as low as 7%.

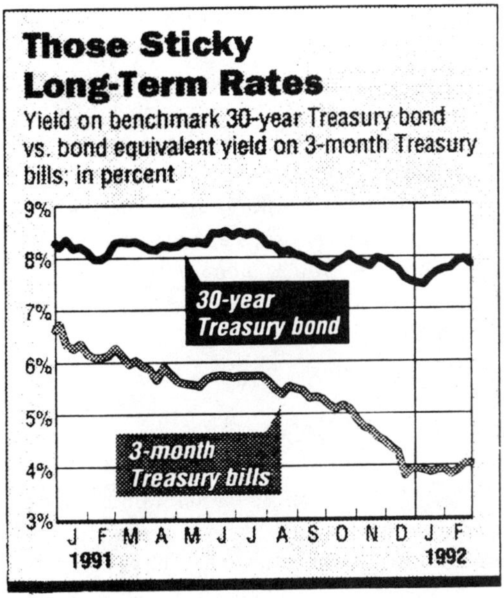

The current long-bond rate of 7.86% is too high to keep the fire lit under home sales and long-range business spending, economists say. Rates on mortgages and corporate securities are directly affected by long-term Treasury yields.

EFFECTS ON THE ECONOMY

"If long-term interest rates do not come back down, the economy will remain in a perpetual funk," says Lacy Hunt, chief economist of Carroll, McEntee & McGinley Inc., a government-securities dealer.

Trouble is, the Fed says there's little it can do about the long-bond rates. Although it can relatively easily adjust short-term rates, it can't directly manipulate the long ones. So it relies on long-term investors to reflect economic reality. That's what many analysts, including the Fed, expected would happen this time: Longer-maturity notes and bonds would also fall because the economy was so weak.

But the long side of the bond market has a mind of its own. It's driven by the supply of new bonds, competition from foreign bond markets and expectations about inflation. On each of those fronts, bond investors found fewer reasons to buy U.S. Treasurys, forcing rates higher.

A BIG THREAT

"Long-bond rates approaching 8% pose an enormous dilemma for the economy, financial markets, the Federal Reserve and government policy in general," says Henry Kaufman, the former Salomon Brothers Inc., economist, who now runs his own money management firm. Besides crimping big-ticket spending, rising rates strengthen the dollar, and that hurts exports, another economic catalyst. And high rates could end the surge in refinancing of mortgages and corporate debt that is injecting billions of dollars of spending power into the U.S. economy.

The lack of buyers for 30-year bonds, even at these higher rates, is evident throughout Wall Street. Fearing that yields will continue to rise (and prices fall), firms are carrying smaller inventories of bonds. And there's more uncertainty over day-to-day pricing.

Also, dealers are "stripping" far fewer of the 30-year bonds for truly long-term investors. When a bond is stripped, its corpus, or principal due upon maturity, is sold separately without interest payments. Investors buy such "zero-coupon" bonds at a steep discount and expect to hold them until maturity.

Finding that he has little power to force long-term rates down, yet pressed by Congress to offer some hope, Chairman Alan Greenspan said Wednesday the Fed was willing to consider the unusual tactic of buying long-term Treasury securities to try to force long-term rates down. Higher demand would spell higher prices—and thus lower yields.

Fed officials deny market rumors that the central bank has already been doing this, and officials privately say they aren't seriously entertaining the idea. From the first of the year through this Wednesday, in fact, the Fed says it decreased its Treasury-bond holdings by $288 million.

Even Mr. Greenspan said there's no assurance buying long bonds would have any material effect on interest rates. Investors evidently feel the same way; when he was quoted on news wires that buying long bonds was "worth a shot," the report barely rippled bond yields.

Fed officials maintain the Treasury itself can do whatever is needed by reducing the amount of long-term debt it issues. In past years, sporadic attempts by the Fed to influence long-term bond rates directly were overwhelmed by the Treasury's increased offerings, these officials note.

That doesn't let the Fed off the hook for the spike in rates, some economists say. "The Fed missed an opportunity to be more accommodating in early January," says Mr. Kaufman. He and some others believe the Fed should have cut the federal-funds rate—the rate banks charge one another for overnight loans—by another quarter or half percentage point to match the full-point cut it made Dec. 20 in the discount rate, another closely watched barometer of short-term rates. But Mr. Greenspan said in early January that there was enough stimulus in the pipeline for recovery, indicating no further cuts were imminent.

"We were surprised at the Fed's rhetoric over the past month," adds John Costas, managing director in charge of government securities sales and trading at First Boston Corp. "We've been maintaining all along that the economy is weak and rates should come down."

GOOD NEWS, BAD NEWS

The prospect of economic recovery meant higher rates and lower bond prices, enough to drive investors to the sidelines, says Neal Soss, chief economist at First Boston Corp. "The market has become habituated to think that if bonds are bought below a yield of 8%, there will be a capital loss. No one today has made money buying bonds at current yields," he told clients in January.

A host of other factors added to the push on rates, however. Competing with government securities for investors, a record $106 billion in new corporate debt was brought to market from early January through Wednesday, according to IDD Information Services Inc.

At the same time, Wall Street was bracing for a record number of new Treasury securities to finance the budget deficit. If President Bush's budget and tax plan are carried out, the current fiscal year budget deficit would grow to $399.2 billion, $30 to $40 billion more than expected in the bond market and up from $268 billion last year.

"There was a humongous supply of $36 billion of new Treasury securities in February and more is due in May," notes Stephen Axilrod, a former top Fed official who is now vice chairman of Nikko Securities in New York. He and others also say the bull market in stocks is drawing money away from long bonds.

Treasury Secretary Nicholas Brady blames the tax policy stalemate, which causes investors to worry that the budget deficit will widen from too much fiscal stimulus. "When people watch the debate...they get a little depressed," he says. "The 30-year bond rate is a little bit like a consumer-confidence number."

The bond market believes "that in an election year, politicians will do what is politically expedient, rather than what is fiscally prudent," says Eugene McInerney, chief executive of Deutsche Bank Government Securities Inc. He adds that the push up in rates is a protest—like "the market's Buchanan vote in New Hampshire."

BOND BEARS

To bond investors, such as William Gross, managing director of Pacific Investment Management Co. in Newport Beach, Calif., higher interest rates abroad, particularly in Germany, were a more compelling investment than similar U.S. Treasury maturities. He moved about $2 billion of his firm's $35 billion abroad over the past few months. At 7.9%, the German 10-year bond is yielding as much as the U.S. 30-year Treasury and half a percentage point more than the 10-year Treasury.

Another drain on demand for U.S. securities has been the withdrawal of Japanese investors. Last year, for the first time in 11 years, Japan drew more capital in from the rest of the world than it invested outside the country.

Despite those pressures, economists and the bond market were caught by surprise by the wide range of interest rates. "it's a bit of a mystery," says Lyle Gramley, chief economist of the Mortgage Bankers Association. "I see continued improvement on inflation and the economy struggling to recover." With long-term mortgage rates climbing half a percentage point from the 8.3% level in early January, he expects that the increase in home sales will be squelched before long.

Normally, long-term interest rates hover at three to four percentage points above the inflation rate. Now, with the long bond trading near 8% and the annual inflation rate in the 3% range, the norm is being ignored. It's odd for rates to rise at this stage of the economy, Mr. Hunt says. "Historically, rates decline in the first third of a business cycle expansion," he says. If there is a rise during that period, it's usually temporary.

PAST EXPERIENCE

Typically, when the Fed eases short-term rates to stimulate loan demand, long bond yields fall, though not as steeply as money-market rates. After the 1973-74 recession, says Robert DeClemente, a Salomon Brothers economist, the Fed kept easing at the same time as inflation fears abated. That led to a decline in long yields as well as short. Then, the inflation problem was viewed as temporary; today, "the low inflation is viewed as temporary," he adds.

Although the Fed's emphasis on recovery has gotten the market thinking about renewed inflation, the Fed's own comments have been just the opposite. It told Congress in its semi-annual report on monetary policy earlier this month, "An underlying disinflationary trend has now been established." Fed policy makers forecast that consumer prices will rise somewhere between 2.5% and 3.5% this year.

Moreover, a new survey of 40 professional economic forecasters, conducted by the Philadelphia Fed, shows they expect consumer prices to rise at a 3.7% annual rate over the next decade; three months earlier, the median forecast was 4.0%.

But investors remain skeptical about inflation and even about the fact that short-term rates will stay low. Although the Fed's actions have pounded the three-month London Interbank Offered Rate, a key international short-term rate, Eric Rosenfeld, managing director in charge of government bond trading at Salomon Brothers, noted that the current 4¼% level is probably only good for the next six months. Trading in the Eurodollar futures market, he says, shows the rate climbing to 5.5% by December and 7.30% by the end of next year.

The Fed is getting some help from the Treasury in its frustrating battle against high long-term rates. After months of deliberation, the Treasury said in February it would reduce its reliance on 30-year and 10-year debt securities—but only slightly. The Treasury cut the size of its quarterly sale of 30-year bonds to $10 billion from about $12 billion; it trimmed the 10-year note issue to $11 billion from about $12 billion.

The decision caused interest rates to decline when it was announced, but traders say the reduction would have had to be billions of dollars more to move rates down very far. "A drop to $10 billion in long-bond sales isn't much," says one. "When I came into this business a few years ago, $6 billion auctions of 30-year bonds were typical."

Jay Powell, Treasury's assistant secretary for domestic finance, says the amount of long- or medium-term securities in the May refunding will remain steady. "We don't want to surprise the marketplace," he says. "The market charges for uncertainty, and we try to avoid" that.

TAKE ACTION

But the pressure to take action is intense. Sen. Alfonse D'Amato yesterday told the Senate that he believes the Fed and Treasury "must act together to more aggressively lower the bond rates."

Many economists maintain long-term rates will fall before midyear. "My hope is that when investors realize fears of a big blowup in the federal deficit is unfounded, that economic recovery is moderate with inflation under control, some of the pressure on rates over the past six weeks will be relieved," says Mr. Gramley. He doubts the long-bond yield will drop as low as levels in early January.

Joseph Petri, chief executive of Merrill Lynch Government Securities, adds that "the best you can hope for is a re-test of the rally that brought bonds to the 7.4% level." But he adds that "there will be a lot of bonds sold before you get there, and if our rates are to remain competitive globally, the long bond can't go much below 7.5%."

Yet some stalwart investors are betting long-bond yields will fall sharply. Mr. Gross has doubled his usual holdings of long-term government securities to more than $10 billion. He calls that "a pretty bold statement," underlying his belief that German interest rates will keep falling, making U.S. securities more appealing. He expects the long bond to "challenge the 7% level in the next six months."

But shaken by the course of rates this year, most forecasters of lower yields are not as sure of themselves as usual. "How much confidence do I have in my forecast?" asks Mr. Gramley. "Not much, considering what's happened in the past few months."

QUESTIONS

1. How are high long-term interest rates affecting the economy's recovery?

2. List all the factors Bleakley and Wessel identify as responsible for keeping the long-term interest rates up. For each factor, illustrate its effect on interest rates with a diagram of bond supply and demand.

3. How did long-term real interest rates in early 1992 compare with their usual level? What does this imply about the relationship between actual and expected inflation?

READING 6

Recent Views of Viewing the Real Rate of Interest

Rosemary Thomas Cunningham and Thomas J. Cunningham

Interest rates play a pivotal role in determining economic activity, and thus the behavior of the real, or inflation-adjusted, rate of interest is central to understanding macroeconomic dynamics. Investment expenditures, consumer durable expenditures, and saving are particularly sensitive to movements in real rates of interest.

This article is an attempt to understand recent developments in economic theory relating to the real rate of interest and, in particular, the ability of the monetary authority to influence it. Several perspectives deserve attention. If real processes and preferences within the economy give rise to the real rate, the real rate then conveys information about the economy's preference for consumption now rather than in the future (that is, it represents the intertemporal marginal rate of substitution). If the real rate is thought of as the marginal product of capital, it provides information about the potential profitability of investment. In either case the monetary authority has no influence over the real rate process. If the real rate is viewed as being the outcome of a market for loanable funds, however, monetary policy does gain some influence over its behavior. Finally, if the economy is small relative to the rest of the world and open to international capital flows, the real rate may be influenced by, and indicate something about, relevant world conditions.

Understanding the real rate of interest has been quite problematic ever since Irving Fisher (1930) made the distinction between the ex ante and the ex post real rate of interest. Because the ex post real rate of interest is simply the nominal rate of interest less the rate of inflation, it can be observed. In contrast, the ex ante real rate cannot be observed because it is the nominal rate of interest minus the expected rate of inflation. The ex ante real rate is the one that influences economic decisions and should be thought of as the real rate of interest even with the obvious problem it presents.

A recent solution to the dilemma posed by the ex ante real rate's being unobservable focuses on the problem of expectation formation and imposes some restrictions on that process in order to approximate an ex ante real rate of interest series. This article provides an overview of the theory behind the problem, followed by a discussion of the proposed solution and the implications of the restrictions it imposes. The concluding sections present applications of the solution, including recent research based on a small, opening economy, and summarize the role of the monetary authority in relation to real interest rates.

ECONOMIC THEORY AND THE REAL RATE OF INTEREST

In Fisher's (1930) division of nominal interest rates, he claimed that the nominal (observed) rate of interest, i, was composed of the real rate of interest, rr; an adjustment for the inflation (denoted by π) that was expected to occur over the relevant time period, π^e; and the cross product of the two, π^e x rr. Thus the basic Fisher equation is

$$i=rr+\pi^e+(\pi^e)(rr)$$

Most empiricists ignore the cross-product term since it is quite small under conditions of modest inflation and real rates of interest.[1] The resulting equation for the real rate of interest is

$$rr=i-\pi^e$$

There are two prevalent misuses of the Fisher equation. First, assuming that the real rate is constant (usually 2 or 3 percent), any change in nominal interest rates could be interpreted as a change in expected inflation. Although many claim that the real rate of interest may be constant over the long run, drawing inferences about expected inflation in short-run analysis frequently results in error.

A more problematic misapplication of Fisher's work is the substitution of *observed* rates of inflation (as in ex post real rates of interest) for *expected* rates (as in ex ante rates) in the construction of a real rate of interest series. Although the two are not interchangeable, the substitution is frequently made because of the problem associated with observing the expected rate of inflation.[2] The difference between the ex post and ex ante rate is the forecast error for inflation during the period in question, and this error can be substantial, as may have been the case of fixed-rate mortgages in the 1960s. During that time, the ex post rate of return on mortgages seemed to be negative, by a large margin and it seems unlikely that lenders would have made fixed-rate loans on the basis of negative ex ante rates.

Before developing the issue of the substitutability of the ex post for the ex ante real rate and the assumptions and restrictions that the substitution implies, an overview of various theories of the real interest rate's behavior is in order. The theories provide alternative approaches to interpreting movements in the real interest rate and to assessing the effectiveness of policy, particularly monetary policy, in influencing the real rate.

The most familiar class of model wherein monetary policy—the actions of the central bank—has any influence over the real interest rate is the Keynesian "liquidity effect," which views the rate of interest as representing the price of holding on to money. From this perspective, it follows that a relative increase in the money supply should lower interest rates.

A problem with this approach, however, is that the Keynesian paradigm has trouble accounting for inflation. The Keynesian world is one in which prices are essentially fixed. In a fixed-price world—without inflation and thus without any inflation premium—a decrease in "the rate of interest" is equivalent to a decrease in the real interest rate. The idea of fixed prices may be a useful assumption in certain situations but clearly is inappropriate for contemporary thinking about the effects of money supply increases. Because of this shortcoming, the Keynesian model has fallen out of favor for policy analysis.[3]

The monetary authority also has some influence over the real rate of interest in the loanable funds model, according to which the real rate of interest is the outcome of market interaction between savers, who supply funds, and borrowers, who demand funds. The real interest rate is the price that adjusts to clear the market, with aggregate inflation expectations simply added to the real rate outcome.

In this model the monetary authority exerts its influence over the real rate in two ways. First, by conducting open market operations the central bank directly enters the market to purchase or sell securities. Second, to the extent that the central bank can influence the operations of other financial intermediaries, usually through reserve requirements, it can induce others to provide funds to the market, thereby influencing the real rate.

A more prevalent way of thinking about the real interest rate centers on the real side of the economy and equates the real interest rate with the marginal product of capital (the output associated with adding one additional unit of capital to the economy). The argument is that if this marginal product of capital is greater than the real rate of interest, borrowing the money to add to the capital stock is profitable. The agent making the investment must pay the real rate of interest on the debt created to purchase the capital but receives the additional output, the real return, from that added capital. The difference is profit to the investing agent. As long as the profits are positive—that is, as long as the real interest rate is less than the real return on that investment (the marginal product of capital)—additional investment will continue because it is profitable.

As the additional investment occurs, two things happen. First, the demand for capital bids up the real interest rate. At the same time, the additional investment drives down the marginal product of capital, decreasing the profitability of added capital. The investment process ends when real profitability reaches zero (that is, when the marginal product of capital equals the real rate of interest).

The marginal product of capital model has gained popularity because of its explanatory power. It results from general equilibrium models, which attempt to describe an entire economy and can portray the interaction among various markets and potential transmission of disturbances from one sector to the rest of an economic system. For example, any disturbance to individuals' saving preferences will show up as disturbances in the real interest rate and thus in the amount of investment undertaken in the aggregate economy. Similarly, technological innovations that raise the marginal product of capital would stimulate investment, and disturbances to the supply of production inputs (oil supply shocks, for example) would alter the productivity of capital, affecting investment and the real rate.

In the marginal product of capital model only real factors influence the real rate of interest. Purely nominal disturbances have no effect. In Keynesian terminology, it is as if the economy suffered no "money illusion." What matters is not money prices but real prices, as though everyone in the economy could immediately understand the distinction between general changes in the price level—simple inflation—and relative changes in the price of goods, representing some real difference in the economy.

Modifications to the marginal product of capital model give the monetary authority some influence, albeit temporary, over the real rate of interest by assuming that economic agents cannot make the above distinction correctly and instantaneously. During the period in which economic agents are sorting out relative price changes from general price level changes, the monetary authority may influence the real rate. Ultimately, when agents understand the changes and have full and complete information, the monetary authority loses control over any real facet of the economy and has influence over only the nominal price level.

The central theme of this "policy ineffectiveness" result is that the monetary authority has no influence over real activity except what these informational disparities make possible.[4] Additional assumptions about how the economy learns over time could make these informational disparities quite short-lived and reduce the monetary authority's control to that of the inflation rate only.

If in fact the monetary authority influences only the inflation rate, the Fisher equation indicates that there will be a somewhat perverse effect on the observed nominal interest rates: a policy of monetary ease (supplying relatively more money) would result in higher nominal interest rates as the markets translate the faster growth rate of money into higher expected inflation.

In principle, the difference between this model and the Keynesian model can be tested empirically. Thomas J. Cunningham (1987) described the difficulties of detecting liquidity effects and concluded that models allowing the monetary authority its perverse influence on interest rates are generally the most appropriate for describing the economy; that is, it is largely accepted that the real rate of interest is beyond the influence, even in the short run, of the monetary authority. Some recent evidence challenges this view, however, and will be discussed below.

An alternative way to view the real interest rate in a general equilibrium setting is to envision the real return on saving as a reward for abstaining from consumption. Imagine that at the end of the production cycle there exists a set of goods that can either be consumed directly or invested in the next production cycle. Firms want the output to be invested productively and are willing to offer a real reward to consumers willing to forgo some consumption. The reward is the real rate of interest. As discussed earlier, firms will be willing to offer a real return up to the value of the marginal product of capital.

The consumer, on the other hand, must weigh the value of consumption now against its value later. Because future consumption is less desirable to consumers, they must be induced to delay some consumption by being given the potential for greater consumption in the future—the real return on savings.

From the consumption standpoint, this real rate of interest represents consumers' rate of time preference for consumption now versus consumption later. If the real interest rate is higher than a consumer's rate of time preference, the consumer will save more because the ultimate reward for saving is considered relatively large. By the same token, if the real interest rate is less than the rate of time preference, the consumer will save less.

Ultimately the real rate of interest must coincide with the economy's aggregate rate of time preference—a real factor over which the monetary authority has no effect. Taken with the demand for capital discussed above, the real interest rate grows out of the interaction between the marginal product of capital and the aggregate rate of time preference, neither of which the central bank influences. The real rate of interest is, according to the logic of this model, exogenous to monetary policy.

Thus far the discussion of the behavior of real interest rates has assumed an economy that is not open to international capital flows. Particularly as the economies of the world are becoming increasingly integrated, this assumption can be misleading. The implications of an open economy for monetary policy and the real rate of interest hinge on the type of exchange rate regime to which the monetary authority commits itself: a fixed exchange rate, tying the value of the currency to that of another currency, a basket of currencies, or some commodity; or a flexible exchange rate, whereby market forces determine the international value of domestic money.

Operating under a fixed exchange-rate system, the monetary authority will use monetary policy to stabilize the currency's international value.[5] Committed to this exchange-rate regime, monetary policy cannot deviate from a course of keeping exchange rates constant. Consequently, many questions concerning the influence of the monetary authority become moot. Problems of the domestic economy's price level stability and movements in the real interest rate are beyond the immediate concern of the monetary authority and are resolved by interaction with the rest of the world. Any difference in the domestic real rate of interest from the world real rate would immediately be arbitraged away by a sufficiently large flow of capital toward the relatively higher return.

Flexible exchange rates, on the other hand, allow monetary authorities to pursue a monetary policy independent of pure exchange-rate considerations. Because the monetary authority does not have to conduct policy in a manner exclusively designed to stabilize the exchange rate, it is free to pursue other goals. Indeed, a major impetus for the breakdown of the post-World War II Bretton Woods agreement (establishing a fixed-rate regime) was the difficulty of coordination among the major central banks with differing policy goals.

Under a flexible exchange-rate system, currencies are traded on an open market, much as any other financial instrument. Relative supply and demand will determine a currency's international value. Interest rates can differ among countries without engendering a large capital flow because the international return on domestic investments is no longer simply the domestic interest rate but the domestic interest rate plus the change in the currency's international value during the period the investment is held. Thus any difference in real returns between domestic economies can be equalized by a real change in the relative value of the currencies.

In the framework of the models discussed above, opening the economy to international financial markets simply shifts the level of discussion from that of the nation to that of the world. World real rates of return tend to equalize, and, if a nation's economy is sufficiently small and open relative to the rest of the world, its adjustment process can be quite quick. At the extreme, the small open economy has no ability to control independently its domestic real rate of interest, price level, and exchange rate. The three must simultaneously adjust to equate (among other things) real rates of return with the rest of the world.

With the exception of the work discussed below, there is little evidence that the monetary authority can influence real interest rates. Indeed, what evidence there is to support the notion that the monetary authority has any influence over even nominal interest rates suggests that the effect is to raise, not lower, nominal interest rates; an increase in the money supply (or money supply growth rates) will lead to an increase in nominal interest rates so that an "easy money" policy actually is associated with higher, not lower, nominal interest rates.

Two hypotheses have been put forth to explain this result. The "policy anticipations" or "expected liquidity" hypothesis suggests that a liquidity effect does exist but that an unexpected increase in the money supply today leads to expectations of lower money growth rates in the future; nominal interest rates rise because of an expected liquidity effect in the future. This is a popular explanation for results during the period from 1979 to 1982, when the Federal Reserve System had an operating procedure focused on targeting monetary growth rates, thus giving the central bank a motive to ensure that deviations in the expected path of money growth were eventually offset. A second hypothesis, the inflation expectations hypothesis, argues that an increase in current money supply growth causes expectations that inflation will rise, thereby pushing up nominal interest rates according to a straightforward Fisher effect.[6]

Two important conclusions follow from the foregoing empirical analysis. First, there is substantial evidence that an easing of monetary policy will lead to higher nominal interest rates. The second, and more important, point is that monetary policy cannot claim to influence the real rate of interest. The problem, however, discussed above, is that the relevant measure of real rates of interest is unobservable and thus out of the reach of simple econometric models. It is to the solution of this problem that attention is now turned.

HOW TO SOLVE THE PROBLEM: AN APPLICATION OF RATIONAL EXPECTATIONS

Fredric Mishkin of Columbia University has recently exploited rational-expectations restrictions to construct a real interest-rate time series useful for econometric inquiry. "Rational expectations" theory maintains simply that economic agents cannot systematically be fooled in forming expectations; that is, people may be continuously incorrect in their expectations, but the mistakes they make are unpredictable. Stated simply, people learn enough from their mistakes that they do not repeat the same error.

This simple insight turns out to be rather powerful in practice. Consider the real interest rate equations described above. The goal is to be able to derive the ex ante real rate of interest, which, to repeat with added notation, is

$$rr_{ea}=i-\pi^{e}.$$

However, we are able to observe only the ex post real rate of interest,

$$rr_{ep}=i-\pi^{a},$$

where π^a represents the actual rate of inflation. The difference between these two measures of the real rate is simply the inflation forecast error:

$$\begin{aligned} rr_{ep}-rr_{ea} &= (i-\pi^{a})-(i-\pi^{e}) \\ &= \pi^{e}-\pi^{a} \\ &= \textit{forecast error}. \end{aligned}$$

According to the rational expectations hypothesis, the mathematical expectation of the forecast error is zero. Thus, as long as the notion and implications of rational expectations theory are acceptable, the observable ex post real rate of interest series can be directly substituted for the unobservable, but economically important, real rate of interest.

APPLICATIONS OF THE SOLUTION

Mishkin has used rational expectations to investigate, among other things, the effects of monetary policy changes on real interest rates, the economic effects of high real interest rates in the United States during the 1980s, and the equality of real interest rates across countries. The approach and work is relatively new. While the rational expectations restrictions discussed above seem rather simple and innocuous, the notion of empirically estimating real rates of interest is quite controversial.

Mishkin's work with John Huizinga (1986) indicates that monetary policy has been the source of the high real interest rates of the 1980s in the United States. In particular, the researchers conclude that the high real interest rates of that decade were the result of the regime change adopted by the Fed in order to disinflate the U.S. economy.

Huizinga and Mishkin focus not only on the high level of real interest rates in the early 1980s and its relation to the Fed's policy changes of October 1979 and October 1982 but also on what they term the significant shift in the stochastic process of real interest rates—the behavior of the real rate series as it bounces around over time.

In October 1979 the Federal Reserve System changed its policy from one of targeting interest rates to targeting nonborrowed reserves. In October 1982 the Fed switched to a borrowed reserve target. Huizinga and Mishkin explored the possibility that, after the policy changes of 1979 increased uncertainty about interest rates, money supply growth and inflation played a role in real interest-rate movements. In addition, they investigated a similar regime change that took place in 1920 when, in response to high inflation rates, the Fed dramatically increased the discount rate twice.

Using data from 1953 to 1984, Huizinga and Mishkin employ rational expectations theory to describe the ex ante real rate of interest as a linear function of a constant, the one-month nominal interest rate, the one-month inflation rate lagged one and two months, and a supply-shock variable (measured as the logarithm of the relative price of fuel and related products in the producer price index) lagged one month. In substituting the ex post real rate for the ex ante real rate, they substituted the nominal interest rate on the one-month bill less the rate of inflation calculated from the consumer price index.

To test whether or not monetary policy regime changes influence the manner in which these variables affect the real rate of interest, Huizinga and Mishkin tested for the equality of the coefficients during various time periods. They found that a shift did indeed occur in these coefficients in October 1979 and October 1982. While in all sample periods a significant negative relationship exists between real rates and expected inflation, the relationship between real and nominal interest rates in the 1979-82 period differs from those in the pre-1979 and the post-1982 periods. In the 1953-79 and 1982-84 periods, there is a significant negative relationship between real and nominal interest rates, whereas in the 1979-82 period the relationship is significantly positive.

Huizinga and Mishkin hypothesized that if a break occurred during the early 1980s in the stochastic process of real interest rates, there should also be breaks in the process during other periods of monetary policy regime changes. Although the exact data series used for the latter time periods were not available in the 1916-27 period, Huizinga and Mishkin worked using comparable data and again tested for the equality of coefficients before and after the monetary policy change in 1920. The results of their tests indicate that, similar to the effect of the monetary policy regime changes of the early 1980s, there was a significant shift in the stochastic process of real interest rates.

Mishkin (1988) explains that because there is not one real rate of interest, monetary policy may affect various sectors of the economy differently. In particular, he claims that during the 1980s agriculture bore a disproportionate share of the disinflationary burden. This situation occurred not only because farmers depended heavily on debt markets in financing production but also because real interest rates were much higher in that sector than in the economy as a whole.

According to Mishkin the relevant real interest rate for the agricultural sector is not one that should be calculated with a broad-based price index such as the consumer price index but rather with one that reflects the prices of farm products. To do this, he constructed a real rate of interest series by subtracting the rate of increase in the farm products component of the producer price index from the one-month Treasury bill rate for the period from January 1953 to December 1986.

Using the relevant real interest rate for the agricultural sector for the periods from January 1953 to October 1979 and from November 1979 to December 1986, Mishkin then estimated essentially the same equation as in Huizinga and Mishkin (1986). The results indicated that the only significant explanatory variable in either period was the one-month Treasury bill rate.

Mishkin also compared his estimates of real interest rates in the agricultural sector with real interest rates for the economy as a whole. In his plot of the two graphs, the real rate for the farm sector appears to be an amplified movement of the real rate for the overall economy. Mishkin confirms this conclusion by regressing the estimated agricultural real rate with the overall real rate and finds that there is a statistically significant comovement between the two and that the agricultural real rate moves more than one-for-one with the overall real rate. From this information, he concludes that the agriculture sector bore much of the burden of the disinflationary period of the early 1980s.

Using data from the Eurodeposit market for seven industrialized nations, Mishkin (1984) also investigated the equality of real interest rates across countries. Again, if a nation is engaging in free trade and there are no restrictions on the mobility of capital, then real interest rates should be equal across countries. If his theory is correct, domestic monetary authorities have no control over real interest rates and their ability to use expansionary or contractionary monetary policy to influence economic activity is therefore constrained.

Mishkin investigated the equality of real interest rates across the United States, Canada, the United Kingdom, France, West Germany, the Netherlands, and Switzerland from the second quarter of 1967 to the second quarter of 1979. He calculated the ex ante real rate of interest two ways: the three-month Eurodeposit rate less the rate of change in the consumer price index and the three-month Eurodeposit rate less the rate of change in the wholesale price index for a particular country. The results indicated that these nations' real interest rates were not equal. Mishkin asserts that real interest rates may differ across countries because risk premiums may differ and because transactions costs and the lack of perfect substitutability of goods implies the violation of purchasing power parity; it does not necessarily imply that real rate arbitrage opportunities exist.

He also asked whether real rates at least moved similarly over time from economy to economy even if they were not strictly equal among nations. The results imply that real rates of interest do not move in similar ways across nations. Mishkin's results indicate that, although capital markets may be integrated, real rates may differ across countries and the domestic monetary authorities may therefore be able to employ monetary policy to influence economic activity.

REAL INTEREST RATES IN A SMALL, OPEN ECONOMY

We recently began some work that has been in part motivated by Mishkin's work concerning real rates of interest and adopts his restrictions (Cunningham and Cunningham 1990). It centers, though, on the theoretical conformity of the behavior of real rates of interest in a small, open economy. Although real rates of interest may not be equal or move similarly over time across the developed nations that Mishkin studied, the situation may be quite different for a small, open economy with which a relatively large economy such as the United States is a major trading partner.

For a small, open economy the actions of the domestic monetary authorities may determine real rates of interest, or world (U.S.) real interest rates may be the primary influence on real interest rates. The idea that domestic monetary forces control real interest rates simply extends Huizinga and Mishkin's work to small, open economies. The possibility that world real interest rates have the greater influence is in accord with standard open economy macroeconomic theory and, if true, would indicate that U.S. monetary policy has not only domestic effects but also influence over economic activity in at least some other nations.

To investigate the behavior of real interest rates in a small open economy, we looked at the case of the Republic of China on Taiwan from October 1985 through January 1990. Taiwan is an interesting subject because in July 1987 the country moved from a functionally closed economy to one that is essentially open. Prior to financial liberalization, foreign investment was limited to certain types of direct investment in manufacturing, and domestic investment in foreign firms was restricted. In July 1987 reforms were enacted that opened capital markets, relaxing foreign exchange restrictions and permitting international capital flows.

To examine the relative influences of domestic monetary policy and the U.S. real rate of interest on the real interest rate in Taiwan, we regressed the real rate of interest in Taiwan on the growth rate of the domestic money supply, growth in industrial production, and the real rate of interest in the United States. The results could indicate one of three situations. First, the real interest rate in Taiwan could have been affected by the U.S. real rate of interest even before the economy was opened financially because of the fact that the real side of the economy was relatively open, thereby potentially bringing the domestic marginal product of capital in line with the world (U.S.) marginal product of capital. Second, the real rate of interest could have been influenced by the action of the domestic monetary authorities before July 1987 and influenced by U.S. real interest rates thereafter, with the domestic monetary authority's having lost whatever control it had had prior to the financial opening. And third, the primary influence on real interest rates both before and after financial liberalization could have been the domestic monetary authority only.

Our preliminary results are consistent with standard economic theory. They provide some evidence of conditions similar to a liquidity effect and are consistent with Mishkin's work in that, both before and after the financial opening of the economy, the change in the domestic money supply is a significant explanatory variable of real interest rates in Taiwan. The results, however, also indicate that after financial liberalization, U.S. real rates of interest influenced real interest rates in Taiwan.

Overall, our results have intuitive appeal. There is some evidence that before the financial opening of an economy, the domestic monetary authority can influence real rates of interest. After the financial opening, the monetary authority still has some influence, but world real interest rates also become important. The significance of the study is tempered by a somewhat small data set, however, and preliminary results should best be considered simply suggestive. At the same time, the validity of the results is supported by their consistency with standard open-economy macroeconomic theory.

CONCLUSION

The question of whether the monetary authority may have some influence over real interest rates is far from settled. A substantial body of empirical work shows a direct relationship between money growth rates and nominal interest rates.

Nevertheless, the work discussed above intimates an avenue of influence for the monetary authority over real interest rates. Mishkin's work suggests a liquidity effect (in the real interest rate) for developed economies, and our work extends that result to a newly industrialized economy. Our work also suggests that the overall influence of the monetary authority in a small, open economy may be tempered substantially by real rate movements in the rest of the world. Nonetheless, economies with financial markets in a limited state of development may find the judicious use of monetary policy effective in influencing real rates of interest.

ENDNOTES

1. This article's analysis also ignores tax complications and the term structure. The information about economic expectations contained in the term structure is a separate issue from that discussed here, which relies on the convenient conventional assumption that there is "an" interest rate.
2. Some surveys are attempting to address this issue and can be expected, eventually, to provide a potentially useful source of data for certain countries during certain times.
3. An early attempt to solve this problem came, independently, from Robert Mundell and James Tobin. The Mundell-Tobin effect allowed for the incorporation of inflation into the Keynesian IS-LM model, and the effect of this inflation was to reduce marginally the real rate of interest while raising the equilibrium level of income. See Blanchard and Fischer (1989, 546).
4. The concept is now pervasive enough to show up in undergraduate economics texts.
5. One of the most frequently forgotten rules of economic policy is the assignment principle, which says that for each and every policy target there must be a policy instrument--that is , for every economic variable to be influenced (inflation, unemployment, exchange rates, and so forth), the policymaker needs to have a policy instrument (such as money growth or government spending) to manipulate. The dilemma facing the monetary authority is that it is limited to using the policy instrument to target one economic variable at a time. For example, suppose the monetary authority wishes to target a specific rate of inflation. If it adopts a policy of money growth designed to engender the desired effect, it cannot respond to nominal interest rate movements without abandoning the initial policy. Having chosen the rate of inflation as the target, the policymaker must accept whatever happens to other economic variables, including perhaps undesired consequences.
6. These hypotheses are described in Cunningham and Cunningham (1991), Cunningham and Hardouvelis (1987), and an excellent review by Sheehan (1985) and touched on in Cunningham (1987).

REFERENCES

Blanchard, Olivier Jean, and Stanley Fischer. *Lectures on Macroeconomics. Cambridge, Mass.: MIT Press, 1989.*

Cumby, Robert E., and Frederic S. Mishkin. "The International Linkage of Real Interest Rates: The European U.S. Connection." National Bureau of Economic Research Working Paper 2876, 1987.

Cunningham, Thomas J. "Observations about Observations about Liquidity Effects: The Difficulties of Exploring a Simple Idea." Federal Reserve Bank of Atlanta *Economic Review* 72 (September/October 1987): 14-22.

Cunningham, Thomas J., and Rosemary Thomas Cunningham. "The Behavior of Real Rates of Interest in a Small, Opening Economy." Federal Reserve Bank of Atlanta working paper, forthcoming 1990.

___. "Another Source of Money Supply Announcement Surprises." *Journal of Macroeconomics* (forthcoming 1991).

Cunningham, Thomas J., and Gikas A. Hardouvelis. "Temporal Aggregation, Monetary Policy, and Interest Rates." Federal Reserve Bank of Atlanta Working Paper 87-4, May 1987.

Fisher, Irving. *The Theory of Interest.* New York: Macmillan Publishing Company, 1930.

Huizinga, John, and Frederic S. Mishkin. "Inflation and Real Interest Rates on Assets with Different Risk Characteristics." *The Journal of Finance* 39 (July 1984): 699-712.

___. "Monetary Policy Regime Shifts and the Unusual Behavior of Real Interest Rates." National Bureau of Economic Research Working Paper 1678, 1985.

___. "Monetary Policy Regime Shifts and the Unusual Behavior of Real Interest Rates." *Carnegie-Rochester Conference Series on Public Policy* 10 (Spring 1986): 231-74.

Kuo, Shirley W.Y. *The Taiwan Economy in Transition.* Boulder, Co.: Westview Press, 1983.

Mishkin, Frederic S. "Are Real Interest Rates Equal Across Countries? An Empirical Investigation of International Parity Conditions. *The Journal of Finance*. 39 (December 1984): 1345-57.

___. "The Real Interest Rate: A Multi-Country Empirical Study." National Bureau of Economic Research Working Paper 591, 1985.

___. "Understanding Real Interest Rates." National Bureau of Economic Research Working Paper 2691, August 1988.

Sheehan, Richard G. "Weekly Money Announcements: New Information and Its Effects." Federal Reserve Bank of St. Louis *Review* (August/September 1985): 25-34.

Tauchen, George. "Statistical Properties of Generalized Method-of-Moments Estimators of Structural Parameters Obtained from Financial Market Data." *Journal of Business and Economic Statistics* 4 (October 1986): 397-416.

White, Halbert. "A Heteroskedasticity-Consistent Covariance Matrix Estimator and Direct Test for Heteroskedasticity." *Econometrica* 48 (1980): 817-38.

QUESTIONS

1. Distinguish between the real and nominal interest rate and between the ex ante and ex post real rate of interest. Why are these distinctions important?

2. How are the concepts of marginal product of capital and consumers' rate of time preference used to argue that real economic factors rather than the monetary authorities determine the real interest rate?

3. Cunningham and Cunningham refer to evidence which suggests that an increase in the money supply or in money supply growth rates will raise nominal interest rates rather than lower them. How do they explain this result? Compare their explanation to the one given in the "Application: Money and Interest Rates" section of Chapter 6 of the text.

READING 7

The Truth about Junk Bonds

Sean Becketti

Junk bonds have been a common element in some of the country's worst financial wrecks this year. The Campeau retailing conglomerate collapsed in January under a heavy debt burden, much of it junk bonds. First Executive Corporation, one of the nation's largest insurance companies, announced a fourth-quarter 1989 loss of $859 million on its junk bond holdings. And Drexel, Burnham, Lambert, the investment bank responsible for the growth of the junk bond market, filed for bankruptcy in February 1990.

These corporate casualties are only the most recent of the problems blamed on junk bonds. For years, some critics have claimed junk bonds are responsible for a host of broader financial market ills. According to these critics, junk bonds fueled the merger mania of the 1980's, caused the rapid growth in the level of corporate debt in recent years, and more generally increased financial market volatility.

If these serious charges are accurate, it may be time for laws or regulations to restrict the use of junk bonds. But if the charges are not accurate, restricting the use of junk bonds would unnecessarily increase the cost of funds for many businesses.

The truth is that the evidence does not support these extreme charges against junk bonds. To be sure, there may be other concerns about junk bonds, such as whether junk bonds are suitable investments for banks and thrifts. This article does not address concerns such as these. Instead, the article examines whether junk bonds should be blamed for the rise in corporate mergers, corporate debt, and financial market volatility. The first section of the article defines junk bonds. The second section explains why some critics make these accusations against junk bonds, and the third section shows why these charges are not well-founded.

I. WHAT ARE JUNK BONDS?

A corporation can obtain funds in many ways. It can raise funds by retaining earnings, issuing equity, or floating debt. If it chooses to take on debt, the corporation faces further choices. For short-term finance, it can issue commercial paper or take out bank loans. For intermediate and long-term finance, it can take out bank loans, mortgage property, privately place bonds, or issue marketable corporate bonds. If the corporation chooses to issue marketable bonds, the bonds might be junk bonds.

Junk bonds are corporate bonds with low ratings from a major ratings service. Bond ratings are letter grades that indicate the rating services' opinions of the likelihood of a default. High-rated bonds are called investment-grade bonds, low-rated bonds are called speculative-grade bonds or, less formally, junk bonds.

A bond may receive a low rating for a number of reasons. If the financial condition or business outlook of the company is poor, bonds are rated speculative-grade. Bonds also are rated speculative-grade if the issuing company already has large amounts of debt outstanding. Some bonds are rated speculative-grade because they are subordinated to other debt—that is, their legal claim on the firm's assets in the event of default stands behind the other claims, so-called senior debt.

Junk bonds are traded in a dealer market rather than being listed on an exchange. A small group of investment banks makes a market in these securities; that is, they stand ready to buy or sell junk bonds.[1] Participating investment banks typically make a market in the issues they underwrite and in a limited number of relatively heavily traded issues considered "good credits."

Institutional investors hold the largest share of junk bonds. At the end of 1988, insurance companies, money managers, mutual funds, and pension funds held three-quarters of the face value of the outstanding junk bonds (SEC 1990, p.2). Individual investors held only 5 percent of the outstanding bonds.

II. WHY ARE JUNK BONDS CRITICIZED?

Junk bonds have been blamed for three financial market ills in recent years: the merger boom, the rise in corporate debt, and the increase in financial market volatility. Critics connect junk bonds with these developments because they occurred simultaneously during the 1980s.

The market for junk bonds was revitalized in the late 1970s and the 1980s after decades of inactivity.[2] In 1977, the investment banking firm of Drexel, Burnham, Lambert began underwriting original-issue junk bonds. From 1977 through 1981, new issues never exceeded \$1.5 billion (Chart 1). Then, starting in 1982, junk bond issues enjoyed five years of explosive growth. New issues peaked in 1986 and receded slightly in the last few years to between \$25 billion and \$30 billion a year. The face value of outstanding junk bonds is currently in the neighborhood of \$200 billion, up almost twentyfold over ten

Chart 1
New Issues of Junk Bonds

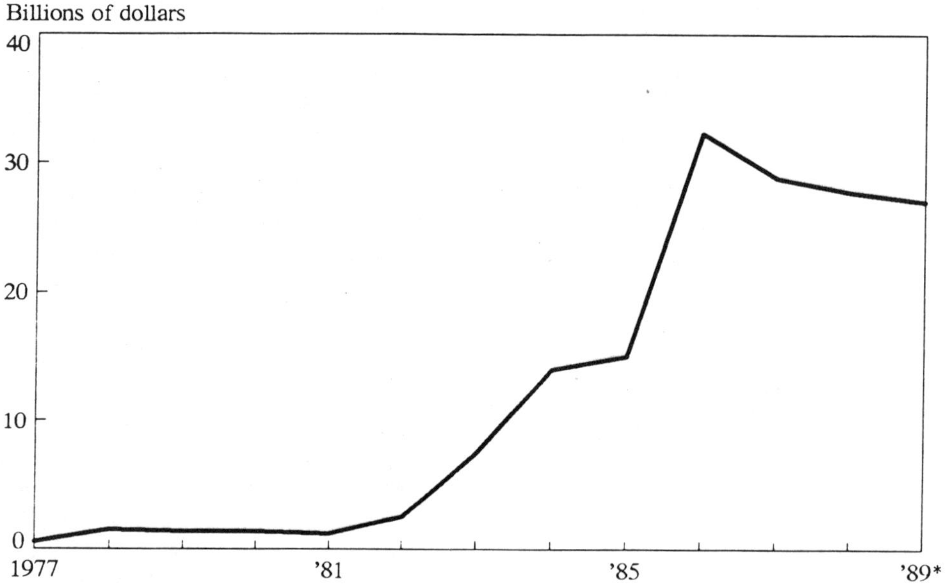

*Annualized estimate from data for the first nine months of 1989.

Sources: Perry and Taggart, Jr. 1990 (1977-80); SEC 1990 (1981-89).

years ago.[3]

As the junk bond market flourished during the last decade, mergers, corporate debt, and financial market volatility also grew. From the end of 1979 through the end of 1989, the value of U.S. mergers grew more than 300 percent.[4] Corporate debt grew over 270 percent.[5] Volatility in U.S. bond markets reached an all-time high in the 1980s. In addition, notable episodes of financial market volatility were the stock market collapses of October 1987 and October 1989.

More than mere coincidence, however, is needed to blame the financial market ills of the 1980s on the growth of the junk bond market. The decade of the 1980s saw the rise of many financial market innovations besides junk bonds—financial futures, program trading, portfolio insurance, and asset-backed securities to name just a few.[6] Why single out junk bonds as the cause of the merger boom, the growth in corporate debt, and financial market volatility?

Some observers suggest that junk bonds caused both the merger boom and the growth in corporate debt by extending credit too freely. According to this argument, corporations unable to borrow in traditional debt markets obtained funds by issuing junk bonds. Some potential acquirers found it easy to float junk bonds to raise the funds for their corporate takeovers. Similarly, some corporate borrowers took advantage of lower credit standards in the junk bond market to go on a debt "binge."[7]

Observers also suggest that the unusual volatility and unpredictability of junk bonds led to higher financial market volatility. This argument is related to the previous one. If, as some critics believe, junk bonds are the result of declining credit standards, then the market for junk bonds is prone to collapse. Investors may initially enjoy high returns, but the borrowers' failure to generate enough earnings to redeem the bonds leads inevitably to defaults. The prospect of these defaults caused frequent shifts in investor portfolios, from junk bonds to safer assets and back again, as investor confidence in junk bonds ebbs and flows with every change in the financial news. These shifts into and out of junk bonds increase the volatility of returns in other markets, such as the market for investment-grade corporate bonds and the market for equities.[8]

These arguments about the links between junk bonds and other financial market developments imply that junk bonds are qualitatively different from other securities and forms of debt. No one claims that such conventional securities as investment-grade bonds or equity extend funds too freely. Nor are these conventional forms of finance accused of causing excessive financial market volatility. Thus, if junk bonds are responsible for the growth in corporate debt, the merger boom, and the increase in financial market volatility, they must have some special characteristic that sets their behavior very much apart from that of other forms of finance.

III. THE TRUTH ABOUT JUNK BONDS

This section disputes the idea that junk bonds have special characteristics-the key assumption behind the charges against junk bonds. The section then discusses specific flaws in each of the claims and draws the following conclusions: First, junk bonds played a relatively small role in financing the merger boom of the 1980s. Second, junk bonds are too small a part of the debt market to account for the growth in corporate debt. Third, the timing of the growth in junk bond issues is not closely related to financial market volatility.

Junk Bonds Are Similar to Conventional Investments

Junk bonds are similar to other, familiar investments with respect to the four principal characteristics of investments: risk, return, liquidity, and control over corporate management.[9] When measuring investments along each of these four dimensions, junk bonds lie between such conventional investments as equities, investment-grade bonds, bank loans, and private placements.[10]

Junk bonds are *riskier* than investment-grade bonds but less risky than equities. Altman (1988) finds that the junk bond default rate, a key component of risk, was 2.2 percent for the years 1970 through 1986, compared with just 0.2 percent for all publicly issued corporate bonds.[11] A more comprehensive measure of risk is the standard deviation of returns. Perry and Taggart (1990) find the standard deviation of monthly returns of junk bonds is greater than that of investment-grade bonds but less than that of equities and of the capital market as a whole.

Junk bond *returns* lie between those of investment-grade bonds and equities. Blume and Keim (1990) find that from January 1977 through December 1988 average monthly junk bond returns were 0.89 percent, higher than the 0.71 percent earned by investment-grade bonds and lower than the 1.14 percent earned by stocks. Perry and Taggart examined the relative performance of various portfolios in the quarters just preceding, during, and just after the seven post- World War II recessions. They found, again, that junk bond returns were intermediate between those of investment-grade bonds and equities.[12]

Junk bonds are more *liquid* than bank loans and private placements but less liquid than equities. Loan contracts and private placements typically contain customized clauses protecting the rights of the investors and restricting the actions of the borrowers. These clauses reduce the marketability of loans and private placements by increasing the cost to third parties of analyzing and valuing the debts and by increasing the frequency of renegotiation. Junk bonds, in contrast, are relatively standardized securities with an established secondary market. Even issues in default have a limited secondary market allowing investors to cut their losses and avoid protracted bankruptcy proceedings.[13] Recent disruptions in the junk bond market, however, are a reminder that the junk bond secondary market is neither as developed nor as liquid as the secondary market for equities.

Junk bonds offer investors more *control over corporate management* than investment-grade bonds but less control than bank loans, private placements, and equities. Some junk bonds contain "equity kickers," that is, options or conversion privileges that let investors obtain an equity share in the borrowing firm. These features give investors the option to participate in the management of the firm.[14] In addition, some junk bonds are sold in strip financing deals, where both bonds and stocks are sold in fixed proportions to investors. In this case, bond holders have voting rights in the management of the firm.[15]

Since junk bonds are not markedly different from other securities, it is hard to understand why they should have any special ability to trigger corporate borrowing sprees. Junk bonds may have cost or tax advantages that allow for some marginal increase in debt. But these advantages are not likely to induce bondholders to invest in junk bonds more recklessly than they do in other debt instruments that are not materially different from junk bonds. Indeed, the bulk of junk bonds are purchased by the same institutional investors who purchase the bulk of private placements, investors who presumably apply the same credit standards to both types of investment.

Again, because junk bonds are similar to traditional financial instruments, it is doubtful they have any special ability to disrupt financial markets. As in any new financial market, the junk bond market may endure brief periods of somewhat greater volatility than average as the market matures and as investors learn how to analyze the investment characteristics of junk bonds. This extra volatility in the junk bond market may be transmitted to other markets as investors adjust their holdings of junk bonds and other securities. However, the fundamental investment characteristics of junk bonds are similar to those of other well-understood securities, such as equities and investment-grade bonds. All of these markets endure episodes of turbulence: the junk bond market does not stand alone in this regard.

In sum, the similarity of junk bonds to conventional financial instruments casts doubt on claims that junk bonds are responsible for the financial market ills of the 1980s. Furthermore, there are specific reasons why junk bonds should not be blamed for these events.

Junk Bonds and the Merger Boom of the 1980s

The junk bond market is too small to have caused the 1980s merger boom. Although a large fraction of the junk bonds issued in the late 1980s were used to finance corporate takeovers, junk bonds accounted for only a small share of merger finance.[16] Even if all junk bonds issued had been used to finance mergers, junk bonds would have accounted for less than 8 percent of the value of U.S. mergers each year. Because not all junk bonds are used to finance mergers, this ratio is a generous upper bound on the junk bond share of merger finance. Moreover, a General Accounting Office study (1988) found that the bulk of the initial financing for tender offers came not from junk bonds but from bank loans. Thus, junk bonds appear to have played a minor role in financing mergers in the 1980s.

Some critics argue that junk bonds were the catalyst for many mergers and, in this way, caused the merger boom despite their small share in merger finance. It is true that junk bonds played a prominent role in several well-publicized mergers, and it is likely that the availability of junk bonds made a few more mergers possible than would have been the case without junk bonds. However, there are many ways to finance a merger. If junk bonds had not been available, mergers that made economic sense would probably have found other forms of finance. Indeed, previous merger booms have occurred without the aid of junk bonds. For example, during the merger wave of the late 1960s—the most recent merger wave prior to the current one and by some measures as significant as the wave of the 1980s—there was no market for original-issue junk bonds. This lack of junk bond financing in no way restrained the 1960s merger wave.

In fact, the merger boom of the 1980s may have helped establish the junk bond market rather than the other way around. The surge in new issues of junk bonds in the late

1980s coincided with the peak in the merger boom. Some part of the demand for debt generated by the merger boom may have increased interest in junk bonds and other innovative debt instruments.

Junk Bonds and Corporate Debt

There is a striking coincidence in the growth of corporate debt and the revitalization of the junk bond market. However, the growth in outstanding junk bonds in the 1980s is not large enough to account directly for the growth in corporate debt. Junk bonds outstanding increased $189 billion from the end of 1979 to the end of 1989. Over the same period, corporate debt increased $1,322 billion. Thus, junk bonds accounted for only 14 percent of the growth in corporate debt.

Furthermore, it is difficult to say that junk bonds were more responsible for the growth in total corporate debt than any another component. During the 1980s, investment-grade bonds increased more than 100 percent, bank loans grew more than 150 percent, and commercial paper outstanding increased more than 300 percent (Board of Governors of the Federal Reserve System 1990, pp.35-36). These three forms of debt account for two-thirds of the growth in corporate debt. Clearly, all of these forms of debt played a part in the growth.

Indeed, it is possible that the growth in corporate debt contributed to the growth of the junk bond market, rater than the other way around. A prominent trend in financial markets in the 1980s was the move toward securitization of debt, that is, a move away from intermediated, nonmarketable forms of debt, such as bank loans, and toward marketable securities, such as corporate bonds.[17] Many of the financial innovations of the 1980s came to popularity as part of this trend. Junk bonds may be just another reflection of the securitization phenomenon.

Junk Bonds and Financial Market Volatility

Financial markets in the late 1980s endured some difficult times—particularly the stock market collapse of October 1987. Some observers claim the growth of the junk bond market increased financial market volatility.

One problem with this claim is the lack of an apparent relationship between the growth of the junk bond market and stock market volatility. Chart 2 shows new issues of junk bonds and stock market volatility from 1981 through 1989.[18] Junk bond issues grew rapidly through 1986 and then leveled off. Stock market volatility was very high in 1987, thanks to the October market collapse, but was unexceptional other wise.[19] If there were a connection between stock market volatility and the growth of the junk bond market, stock volatility would be high throughout the late 1980s instead of just in 1987.

Furthermore, the growth of the junk bond market and volatility in high-grade corporate bond returns are inversely related. Chart 3 shows new issues of junk bonds again, but this time with the volatility of the Salomon Brothers index of long-term, high-grade corporate bonds.[20] Bond market volatility beganthe 1980s at record levels and was lower thereafter. If there were a connection between

Chart 2
Junk Bond Issues and Stock Market Volatility

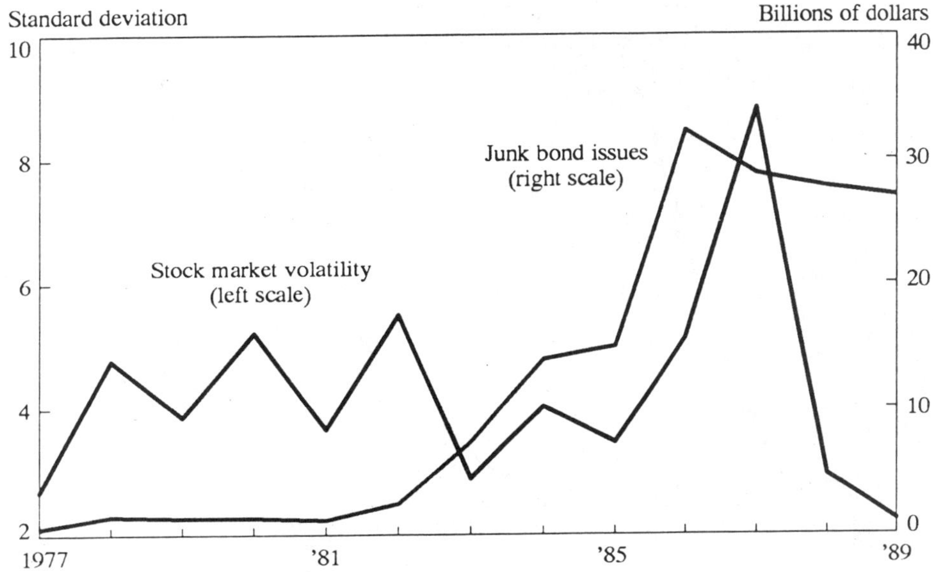

Note: In this chart, volatility is measured by the annual standard deviation of monthly stock returns of the Standard & Poor's index of 500 stocks.

Sources: See chart 1 (junk bond issues); Center for Research in Security Prices (stock market volatility).

bond market volatility and the growth of the junk bond market, bond volatility would have risen rather than fallen in the late 1980s.[21]

IV. CONCLUSION

For years, critics have blamed junk bonds for a variety of financial market ills. The merger boom of the 1980s, the rise in corporate debt, and financial market volatility in the 1980s are all traced, by some observers, to junk bonds.

The truth is that the evidence does not support these charges against junk bonds. The key premise in the case against junk bonds—the belief that junk bonds have special properties that upset financial markets—is questionable. While the junk bond market grew at the same time that financial market problems surfaced, this circumstantial link turns out to be unpersuasive. The junk bond market has accounted for only a small part of

Chart 3
Junk Bond Issues and Bond Market Volatility

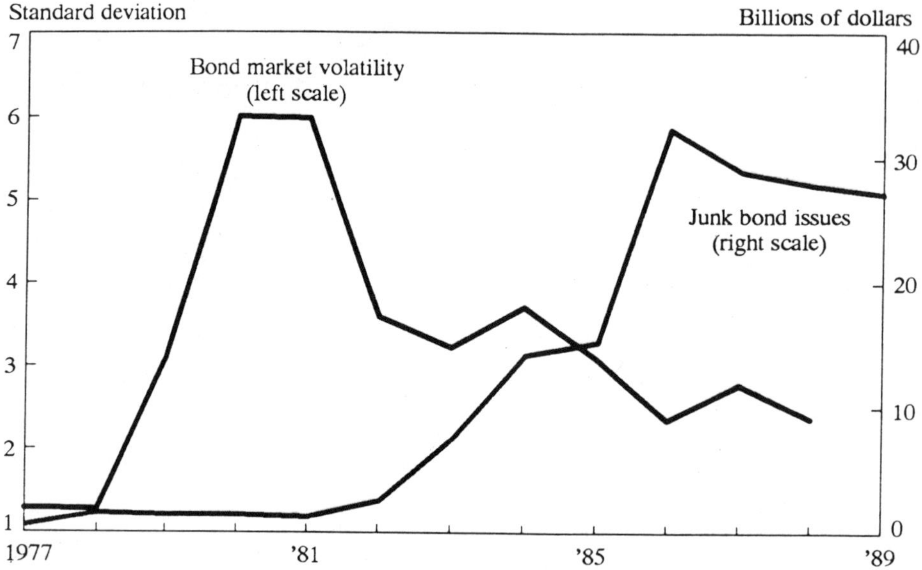

Note: In this chart, volatility is measured by the standard deviation of monthly returns of the Salomon Brothers' Long-Term High-Grade Corporate Bonds Index.

Sources: See chart 2.

the merger boom and of the growth in corporate debt, and the growth in the junk bond market is not closely associated with the trends in financial market volatility. Of course, there may be other concerns over junk bonds; for example, it may be inappropriate for banks and thrifts to hold junk bonds. Nevertheless, the three charges against junk bonds examined in this article are not supported by the evidence.

ENDNOTES

1. A small number of junk bonds, including some RJR Nabisco issues, are listed on the New York Stock Exchange (SEC 1990, p.1).
2. Junk bonds are just low-rated bonds, and low-rated bonds have always been a component of debt markets. In fact, in the 1920s and 1930s, junk bonds accounted for about 17 percent of new issues of corporate bonds on average (Hickman 1958, p.153). However, the high default rates of the 1930s soured investors on junk bonds, and the market lanquished until the late 1970s.
3. The SEC estimates that $204 billion par value registered securities were outstanding as of September 30, 1989. There are no reliable estimates of the market value of these securities (SEC 1990, p.1). Altman (1987) gives estimates of the value of outstanding junk bonds for earlier years.
4. This figure is from the database maintained by *Mergers & Acquisitions* magazine. This database tracks mergers of domestic firms with at least $1 million in assets. The value of each merger is recorded as the estimated value of all forms of consideration paid--cash, stocks, bonds, options, etc.--for the acquired company.
5. There are many ways to measure the increase in corporate indebtedness in the 1980s. Two thorough examinations of this issue are Bernanke and Campbell 1988 and Faust 1990.
6. Links have been suggested between financial market problems and some of these innovations. For example, program trading and portfolio insurance have been blamed for financial market volatility. However, none of these innovations has been connected with all three financial market developments.
7. A number of observers make these or similar claims. For examples on the connections between junk bonds and the merger boom, see the comments of Gail I. Hessol, Managing Director for Standard & Poor's, a major securities rating service (Hessol 1988 and *Wall Street Journal* 1990).
8. Hessol (1988) testified both to the current and prospective risk of junk bonds. In addition, if junk bonds caused the merger boom and the growth of corporate debt, then junk bonds may also have indirectly increased financial market volatility, because some analysts believe that both the merger boom and higher debt affected financial market performance. This point was made in a speech by Rand Araskog, the chairman of ITT Corporation (Clark and Malabre 1988). More recently, some market participants attributed the stock market disruptions of October 1989 to the collapse of the United Airlines buyout.
9. The similarity of junk bonds to conventional investments does *not* imply that junk bonds are appropriate investments for all investors. For example, junk bonds may not be appropriate for banks and thrifts, just as some other conventional investments--equities, for example--are considered inappropriate investments for banks and thrifts.
10. Private placements are essentially loans made by nonbanks, typically such institutional investors as insurance companies. They may take the form of either loan contracts or bonds. However, if they are bonds, they are not offered for sale on the public market. Private placements are underwritten by commercial and investment banks.
11. Junk bonds are, of course, expected to have a higher default rate than investment-grade bonds. That is why they are rated lower than investment-grade bonds. A number of studies attempt to quantify the default risk of junk bonds. Most report annual default rates in the 1 to 3 percent range. Asquith, Mullins, and Wolff (1989) find much higher annual default rates, in the 3 to 9 percent range.
12. Some observers argue that changes in the nature of junk bond issues make historical evidence on the risk and return of junk bonds an unreliable guide to their future behavior. If these observers are correct, junk bonds could be much riskier and could earn lower returns in the future.
13. Altman (1989) reports that, on average, junk bonds sell for slightly less than 40 percent of face value at the end of the month in which default takes place.
14. Equity kickers also allow investors to share in any unexpectedly high profits the firm might earn. This characteristic stands in contrast to traditional bonds where returns are limited to the coupons explicitly offered by the bond. These

features not only increase the expected return to bondholders but also serve as a form of call protection since borrowers are more likely to call bonds when profits increase.

15. Some observers argue that strip financing, along with other forms of junk bond finance, is chosen to reduce the double taxation of corporate dividends while retaining an equity relationship with investors. In other words, according to this view, junk bonds in strip financing function as though they were common stock. The interest paid on the junk bonds is tax deductible to the corporation, in contrast to any dividends paid. Since bondholders and stockholders are the same entities, the net tax burden can be decreased by paying out earnings as coupon payments on the junk bonds rather than as dividends on the common shares.

16. Drexel, Burnham, Lambert estimated that all forms of acquisition financing accounted for 79 percent of junk bond issues in 1987 and 83 percent in 1988. First Boston found that acquisition financing accounted for 76 percent of junk bond issues in 1989 (SEC 1990, p.20).

17. All forms of corporate debt grew in the 1980s. However, bank loans grew more slowly than bonds, causing them to lose market share to corporate bonds.

18. New issues of junk bonds are compared with the annual standard deviation of monthly returns to see if the growth of the junk bond market increased financial market volatility generally. It might be the case that very short-lived disruptions in the junk bond market caused similarly brief disruptions in other financial markets. That is not the kind of volatility considered here.

The rate of new issues is used to measure the size of the junk bond market in this chart. Essentially the same picture would be produced by using the value of outstanding junk bonds to measure the size of the market.

19. For the post-World War II period, the annual standard deviations of monthly stock returns averaged 3.9 percent. Excluding 1987, the annual standard deviation of monthly stock returns in the 1980s was again 3.9 percent.

20. The Salomon Brothers index includes AAA and AA corporate bonds with maturities of ten years or more. These data end in 1988. In the post-World War II era, the annual standard deviation of this index averaged 1.8 percent. In the 1980s the annual standard deviation averaged 3.7 percent.

21. Although bond market volatility fell during the 1980s, it remained above its post-World War II average throughout the decade. Some observers maintain that increased corporate leverage in the 1980s, that is, higher ratios of corporate debt to equity, is responsible for this generally higher bond market volatility. Even if this claim is correct, all forms of corporate debt grew in the 1980s, and there is no reason to single out junk bonds as the sole or most important debt component responsible for increased volatility.

REFERENCES

Altman, Edward I., ed. 1987. "The Anatomy of the High-Yield Bond Market," *Financial Analysts Journal,* July/August.

____. 1988. "Analyzing Risks and Returns in the High-Yield Bond Market," *Financial Markets and Portfolio Management.*

____. 1989. "The 'Junk Bond' Default Rate Debate," Working Paper 539, Salomon Brothers Center for the study of Financial Institutions, New York University, November.

Asquith,P., D. Mullins, and E. Wolff. 1989. "Original Issue High Yield Bonds: Aging Analyses of Defaults, Exchanges, and Calls," *Journal of Finance*. September.

Bernanke, Ben S., and John Y. Campbell. 1988. "Is There a Corporate Crisis?" *Brookings Papers on Economic Activity.*

Blume, Marshall E., and Donald B. Keim. 1990. "Risk and Return Characteristics of Lower-Grade Bonds, 1977-1987." in Edward I. Altman, ed., *The High-Yield Debt Market: Investment Performance and Economic Impact*. Homewood, Ill.: Dow Jones-Irwin.

Board of Governors of the Federal Reserve System. 1990. Balance Sheets for the U.S. Economy 1945-1989.

Clark, Jr., Lindley H., and Alfred Malabre, Jr. 1988. "Takeover Trend Helps Push Corporate Debt and Defaults Upward," *Wall Street Journal*. March 15.

Faust, Jon. 1990. "Will Higher Corporate Debt Worsen Future Recessions?" *Economic Review*, Federal Reserve Bank of Kansas City, March/April.

General Accounting Office. 1988. Financial Markets: Issuers, Purchasers, and Purposes of High Yield, Noninvestment Grade Bonds. Washington: Government Printing Office. February.

Hessol, Gail. 1988. *United States General Accounting Office Hearing on High Yield Bonds*, comments in appendix. General Accounting Office. May, p.177.

Hickman, W. Braddock. 1958. *Corporate Bond Quality and Investor Experience*. Princeton, N.J.: Princeton University Press.

Perry, Kevin J., and Robert A. Taggart, Jr. 1990. "Development of the Junk Bond Market and Its Role in Portfolio Management and Corporate Finance," in Edward Altman, ed., *The High-Yield Debt Market: Investment Performance and Economic Impact*. Homewood, Ill.: Dow Jones-Irwin.

U.S. Securities and Exchange Commission. 1990. *Recent Developments in the High Yield Market*. Staff Report, March.

Wall Street Journal. 1990. "Reactions to Milken: Villain or Victim?" April 25.

QUESTIONS

1. What are junk bonds? What characteristics or circumstances can lead bonds to be classified as "junk"? How are these bonds traded and what are notable features of the pattern of their ownership?

2. How do junk bonds compare with equities, investment-grade bonds, bank loans and private placements in terms of risk, return, liquidity, and control over corporate management? Which elements of this comparison can help explain the relatively high yields on junk bonds?

3. Why does Becketti conclude that junk bonds are not to blame for the rise in mergers, the growth of corporate debt, and increased financial market volatility?

READING 8

Will 30-Year T-Bond Become Extinct Species?

Constance Mitchell and David Wessel

Can the government really save taxpayers money and at the same time stimulate business activity by curbing sales of 30-year Treasury bonds?

In Washington and on Wall Street, government officials, economists and bond dealers are hotly debating the pros and cons of a move to eliminate—or at least sharply reduce—sales of long-term Treasury bonds.

What's behind the debate is the unprecedented gap between long-term and short-term interest rates at a time when the economy is slumping. Short-term rates have plunged; long-term rates haven't.

"It's foolish for the government to issue long-term bonds" at rates that are as much as 3½ percentage points higher than it costs the Treasury to sell short-term securities, says James Tobin, Nobel Laureate economics professor at Yale University and a former economic advisor to President John F. Kennedy. His advice: stop selling 30-year bonds, at least until the economy is back on track and the spread between long-term and short-term interest rates has narrowed.

'MISGUIDED' SHIFT

But on Wall Street, Robert Giordano, economist at Goldman, Sachs & Co., warns that abandoning sales of 30-year bonds would be "misguided." He says the Treasury "is about to get railroaded" into curtailing or eliminating the long bond "on dubious grounds."

The idea of curtailing sales of 30-year Treasury bonds surfaced more than a month ago when Treasury Secretary Nicholas Brady told Congress that the Treasury is "taking a look at" the amount of long-term bonds it sells, adding that "the question really is how much effect would you have on this huge market if you shifted your emphasis."

In the past two weeks, officials in Washington say the Treasury has grown increasingly serious about curtailing, though not eliminating, sales of 10-year and 30-year bonds, both to save the taxpayers' money and to nudge down long-term interest rates. It is being pressed to curb 30-year bond sales by members of Congress and academic economists who say the government should take every opportunity available to save borrowing costs. The Treasury is likely to make a decision before February's quarterly refunding of the federal debt, when the government is slated to sell more than $37 billion of Treasury notes and bonds.

SLOWLY FALLING YIELD

Since the Treasury began selling 30-year bonds in the early 1960s, the Treasury's long-term bond has become the most actively traded security in the world. It's considered the bellwether security for the entire bond market; its yield is used as a benchmark from which yields on other long-term securities are determined by the market. Because the long bond, as it is known on Wall Street, is far more volatile than other fixed-income securities—its price moves further up or down with swings in interest rates—it is a favorite for speculators who like to make big bets on interest rate changes.

But economists and the Bush Administration are frustrated at how slowly yields on 30-year Treasury bonds have fallen, even though the Federal Reserve has been aggressively pushing down short-term interest rates. In the past 12 months, for example, the Fed has driven down the federal funds rate, which banks charge each other for overnight loans, to 4% from 7%. In response, yields on three-month Treasury bills have fallen 2.7 percentage points to just under 4%.

But yields on the 30-year Treasury bond have fallen just three-quarters of a percentage point to about 7.5%. In fact, the gap between yields on short-term and long-term securities is now the widest it has ever been. Part of the problem is that long-term bonds reflect investors' inflation expectations. Long-term rates in turn directly influence mortgage rates and corporate borrowing costs.

Proponents of paring back sales of 30-year bonds argue that reducing the supply of long-term bonds would give them a scarcity value, causing their yield to decline and their price to rise.

Burton Malkiel, a Princeton University economist and a student of markets and interest rates, suggests that a substantial move by the Treasury to curb its sale of 30-year bonds could reduce long-term interest rates by as much as one-half a percentage point.

And since institutional investors are showing strong demand for short-term and intermediate-term Treasurys, the shift probably would not cause shorter-term rates to rise very much, says Maria Ramirez, president of Maria Ramirez Capital Consultants Inc. Ms. Ramirez adds that eliminating the 30-year bond would make U.S. debt management comparable to other major countries, where bonds with maturities longer than 10 years are rare.

Mr. Malkiel, like many others, believes that reducing sales of 30-year bonds might help stimulate economic activity, cutting long-term rates and thus allowing corporations and consumers to replace high-interest-rate debt with lower-rate debt. With lower debt service, consumers and corporations would have more to spend on goods and services. "It's the long rate that is important in terms of mortgage financing," he explains. "I am absolutely convinced if there were 7% mortgage rates, you'd get quite a pop in home sales. You might even see some residential construction."

Lacy Hunt, chief economist at Carroll McEntee & McGinley Inc., a bond dealer in New York, says that financing the budget deficit by having the government sell fewer long-term bonds and shifting Treasury sales to shorter-term securities could save taxpayers billions a year in financing costs.

Based on the Treasury's recent sales of $12 billion in long-term bonds each quarter, the Treasury should be offering about $50 billion of new 30-year bonds over the next 12 months. At current rates, those 30-year bonds would carry a 7.5% coupon.

Mr. Hunt estimates that if the Treasury instead halted its sales of 30-year bonds and took up the slack by selling more securities ranging from three-month bills to five-year notes—at an average interest rate of 5%—the Treasury could save $1.25 billion in interest payments in the first year. If the Treasury merely halved its 30-year bond issuance to $25 billion a year, taxpayers would save $625 million in the first year.

Mr. Hunt also recommends that the Fed simultaneously shift a portion of its $260 billion investment portfolio of U.S. Treasury securities from short-term bills to long-term bonds, while continuing to use monetary policy to keep short-term interest rates from rising. The Fed's increased purchases of long-term Treasury bonds would help drive down long-term interest rates, he says.

But opponents of the idea of eliminating 30-year bonds doubt that the Treasury would achieve its objectives. In a 15-page research report, Mr. Giordano of Goldman Sachs said that a shift away from long-term bonds is "unlikely to lower long-term interest rates appreciably, save the government much, if any, money or help the private sector." Goldman is one of the biggest government bond dealers on Wall Street. Many dealers oppose a curb on 30-year bonds, which they say would increase uncertainty about the Treasury's borrowing plans and, perhaps, reduce dealers' profits.

Among other things, Mr. Giordano notes that past efforts by the Treasury to influence interest rates by manipulating the supply of bonds failed. He notes that the last time the Treasury stopped selling long-term bonds, in 1967-72, the shape of the yield curve, or gap between long and short-term rates, "was only marginally flatter than in other periods."

At the time, the Treasury, by law, couldn't sell securities with a coupon higher than 4¼%. Since market rates were higher than that, the Treasury essentially was shut out of the long-bond market.

In the early 1960s, during the Kennedy Administration, the Fed tried to influence rates in an experiment that came to be called "Operation Twist." At the time, the U.S. economy looked soft, which argued for lower interest rates. But a high balance of payments deficit was putting pressure on the dollar; higher rates would help prop up the U.S. currency. In an effort to bring down long-term rates while nudging up short-term rates, producing a "twist" in the yield curve, the Fed purchased long-term notes and bonds and sold bills. Many viewed the plan as unsuccessful.

Other economists at Goldman Sachs argue that the Treasury should sell *more* 30-year bonds to take advantage of long-term interest rates they consider low by historical measures. They believe long-term yields won't fall much lower.

S.G. Warburg & Co., another primary dealer of government securities, also is against the idea of limiting sales of 30-year bonds. "We don't recommend it," says Lawrence Leuzzi, head of the firm's government securities group. "I don't believe that public debt management policies that reign over $3 trillion on debt should be based on interest-rate speculation."

Mr. Leuzzi says the Treasury's argument is flawed partly because the supply is just one of several reasons yields on the long-term bonds are relatively high. "I believe that more important than supply, they are a function of inflation expectations and global credit demand," he says. These are issues, he says, that can't be fixed by shifting supply.

QUESTIONS

1. What are the arguments in favor of curtailing the sales of 30-year Treasury bonds?
2. What are the arguments against curtailing the sales of 30-year Treasury bonds?
3. Which explanation of the term structure of interest rates—expectations hypothesis, segmented markets theory, or preferred habitat theory—gives primary justification for the claim that curtailing the sales of long-term bonds will help reduce long-term interest rates? Explain.

READING 9

Shapely Curves

Since early 1989 the Federal Reserve has pushed down America's short-term interest rates from 10% to just over 4%. It is powerless to reduce long-term ones, however. Yields on 30-year Treasury bonds are nudging 8%, barely one percentage point below their level of three years ago. Many Americans fret that high bond yields—which feed through into mortgage rates and the long-term cost of corporate borrowing—could stifle economic recovery. In fact, the large gap between short- and long-term interest rates could signal precisely the opposite—that recovery will be stronger than expected.

The yield curve, which traces yields on securities of varying maturities, normally slopes upwards because investors demand higher yields on long-term securities to make up for their greater risk. But the shape of the yield curve can change. For example, when short-term interest rates are raised, the curve can become inverted—ie, long-term rates can fall below short-term rates—as in America in 1989, or in Germany today. At the other extreme, America's yield curve now slopes up more steeply than at any time since the war.

Some economists reckon that the slope of the yield curve is a good measure of the tightness of monetary policy. It can certainly be more useful than money-supply measures, which often mislead. The shape of the yield curve reflects investors' expectations about inflation. When they expect higher future inflation, they demand bigger long-term yields on their money. So if the curve is steeply upward-sloping, it suggests that monetary policy is relatively loose. If the yield curve is inverted, it means that policy is tight.

America's broad measure of money, M3, fell by 1.3% in real terms in the 12 months to January. Some argue that this shows the Fed's monetary policy to be too tight. But the shape of the yield curve suggests, on the contrary, that monetary policy has not been so loose for 50 years.

Taking the argument a stage further, the shape of the yield curve might be seen as a leading indicator of economic activity. A steeply upward-sloping curve (ie, a loose monetary policy) could suggest that future output will rise, at least in the short term. The more the curve slopes downward, the greater the risk that tight monetary policy will choke off growth.

A recent study[1] concludes that the slope of the yield curve has been one of the best predicters of changes in activity between a year and 18 months ahead. Its forecasting record is better than that of three rivals: the index of leading indicators, real short-term interest rates and consensus GNP forecasts.

Between 1955 and 1989 there were six recessions in America. The study shows that all six were preceded by a flattening or inversion of the yield curve. Moreover, there was only one false alarm: an inversion of the curve in 1966 was not followed by recession. Periods when the curve switched to being upward-sloping were always followed by economic growth a year or so later.

The chart shows America's GNP growth plotted against the gap between short- and long-term interest rates a year earlier (so the interest-rate spread at the end of 1990 is plotted in the chart at the end of 1991). The inversion of the yield curve in 1989 heralded the recession that followed, though it arrived with a rather longer lag than most of its predecessors. More relevant to what happens next, in each of the past six business cycles the yield curve was at its steepest within a few months of the end of the recession. If such historical relationships hold now, today's record spread suggests that a strong rebound is imminent.

In Germany, by contrast, where the correlation between the yield curve and growth has been an even more reliable

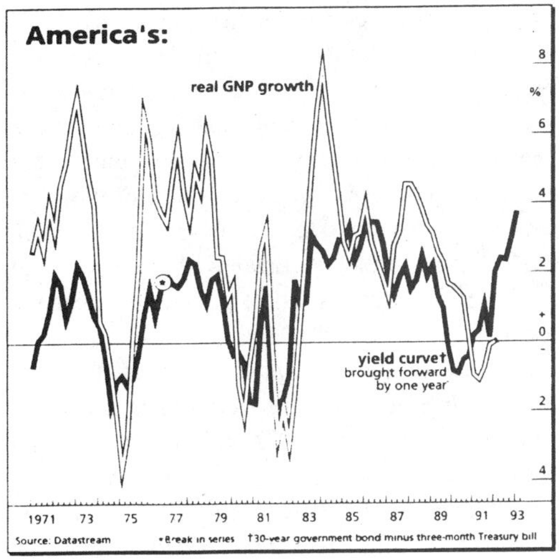

Source: Datastream *Break in series †30-year government bond minus three-month Treasury bill

indicator of coming economic activity than in America, the yield curve has been inverted for more than a year. On past experience, this means that Germany will see a full recession—that is, a year-on-year drop in output—in 1992.

Some argue that the unusually large spread between short- and long-term interest rates in America has been exaggerated by two related factors keeping bond yields high. The first is the huge increase in the supply of bonds needed to finance America's budget deficit, which is heading for a record $400 billion in the current fiscal year. And second, Japanese investors have lost their appetite for American Treasury bonds. In 1991 the Japanese spent a net $8.6 billion on Treasury bonds, far less than the $37.8 billion they bought in 1988.

A more significant reason for the steepness of the yield curve must be that investors do not believe inflation will remain low. American consumer prices rose by 2.6% in the 12 months to January, but the underlying inflation rate is still around 4%. Worse, the markets fear that in an election year Congress might over-stimulate the economy through tax cuts, while the Fed lowers interest rates too much. Such enthusiastic stoking means that the long-expected recovery could be powerful—perhaps too powerful—when it arrives.

It is of course possible that the old relationship between the yield curve and GNP has broken down. David Morrison, an economist at Goldman Sachs, an American investment bank, suggests that financial deregulation and the hangover from the borrowing binge of the 1980s may have severed the link. Even so, he says, the steep yield curve suggests that there has been a lot of monetary stimulus. If businesses and consumers start borrowing again, it will fuel a recovery.

In early 1989 most economists refused to believe that the inversion of the yield curve signalled a recession. They argued that the link with the business cycle was weaker, because deregulation had made the economy less sensitive to changes in interest rates. Now it seems that they were wrong: recession did follow, albeit with a longer lag than usual. Economists today ignore the yield curve at their peril.

ENDNOTES

1 "The Term Structure as a Predicter of Real Economic Activity". By Arturo Estrella and Gikas Hardouvelis. Journal of Finance, June 1991.

QUESTIONS

1. List all the reasons you find in the reading for why yield curves may slope upwards. For each reason, explain whether it is based on the expectations hypothesis, the segmented markets theory, or the preferred habitat theory.

2. The reading states that some economists think the slope of the yield curve reflects the looseness or tightness of monetary policy. Explain.

3. If the slope of the yield curve is a good predictor of future economic activity, what explanation is there for this?

PART THREE

FINANCIAL INSTITUTIONS

Because much of the dynamism associated with the field of money, banking, and financial markets is related to changes in the structure and operations of financial institutions and to the innovation of new financial instruments in response to changes in the economic environment, Part III is the longest and most important part of this *Reader*. Part III in the text develops an economic framework for analyzing financial markets and institutions and uses this framework to examine such topics as the financial structure of corporations, the importance of financial intermediaries as sources of finance for businesses, bank management, the structure of the banking industry and the regulatory crisis in which it is currently embroiled, and financial innovation. Several of these issues are treated in the readings for Part III.

Reading 10 is "Solving the Mystery of High Credit Card Rates" by Randall J. Pozdena. Pozdena seeks to explain why credit card interest rates have remained high and stable despite significant declines in market interest rates since the early 1980s. The answers he offers are that credit card debt is unsecured debt and is subject to moral hazard because the lender cannot closely monitor the borrower's net worth. This reading is suggested for use with Chapter 8's discussion of adverse selection problems.

Reading 11, "Is There Too Much Corporate Debt?" by Ben Bernanke, also fits well with Chapter 8. Bernanke explores this question from the micro perspective of efficiency and the macro perspective of financial and economic stability and concludes that choosing between higher and lower leverage involves a trade-off between efficiency and stability.

Reading 12 is "Lessons on Lending and Borrowing in Hard Times" by Leonard I. Nakamura. Nakamura examines the role of collateral in loan contracts. He argues that seizing collateral can harm lenders as well as borrowers by shutting down firms that have more value as going concerns and that problems of lending are magnified during recessions, resulting in tighter credit terms. This reading can be used with Chapter 8's discussion of the role of collateral or with the discussion of bank lending in chapter 9.

Reading 13 is "Credit Flows and the Credit Crunch" by Steven Strongin. Looking at trends in corporate funding, credit flows, and bank loans since the 1970s, Strongin argues that what many policymakers currently are calling a credit crunch is in large part the continuation of a longer term restructuring of financial flows and a decline in the importance of external funding of corporations. Because of this, basing policy on historical relationships between credit growth and economic growth may be unwise. This reading can be used with Chapter 8's discussion of the economics of financial structure or with Chapter 9's discussion of bank lending.

Chapter 9 in the text describes Japanese and German banking arrangements that deal with asymmetric information, a topic dealt with in Reading 14, "Banking and Commerce: The Japanese Case" by Sun Bae Kim. Kim looks at the costs and benefits of the Japanese system in which banks can both lend to and own stock in industrial firms and applies insights from the Japanese system to the policy choices currently facing the U.S. (This reading could also be tied in with the treatment of information asymmetries in Chapter 8, of regulatory reform in Chapter 11, or of separation of banking and the securities industry in Chapter 12.)

Reading 15 is "Interest Rate Risk: What's a Bank to Do?" by Sherrill Shaffer. Interest rate fluctuations over the past decade, with their potential impacts on banks' net worth, have made measuring and controlling interest rate risk a vital concern of bankers and regulators. Shaffer presents an introduction to maturity gap and duration gap analysis and considers various techniques for hedging interest rate risk, including the use of non-traditional financial instruments: loan sales, swaps, and interest rate futures. This reading is suggested for use with Chapter 9's discussion of interest rate risk or Chapter 13's discussion of financial innovation.

Reading 16 is "Investigating the Banking Consolidation Trend" by John H. Boyd and Stanley L. Graham. Boyd and Graham reject the view that consolidation will benefit the banking industry and the U.S. economy by allowing the capture of economies of scale, eliminating excess capacity, and reducing the risk of bank failure. In their view, banking consolidation is not primarily due to natural market forces but rather results from incentives to consolidate inherent in public policies such as the too-big-to-fail-policy and policies which discourage hostile takeovers of banks. They conclude that those looking for the benefits of consolidation likely will be disappointed. This reading is an excellent supplement to the discussion of banking industry structure in Chapter 10.

Reading 17 is "Bank Branching and Portfolio Diversification" by Elizabeth Laderman, Ronald H. Schmidt, and Gary C. Zimmerman. These authors examine the effects of *intrastate* branching on agricultural lending by urban and rural banks to gain insights into how *interstate* branching might affect bank asset diversification. They find that banks in states with unrestricted branching have more diversified loan portfolios than similar banks in states where branching is restricted. This reading is suggested for use with Chapter 10's discussion of bank branching and industry structure.

Readings 18-23 treat various aspects of the current bank regulatory crisis covered in Chapter 11 of the text. Reading 18, "The Worship of Basle," describes the new international capital standards for banking, why they were adopted, and what effects they likely will have on banking. (This reading also can be assigned with Chapter 10's discussion of capital standards.)

Reading 19, "Risk-Based Capital Standards and Bank Portfolios" by Jonathan A. Neuberger, also considers the new international capital standards. Neuberger identifies changes in the composition of bank portfolios since the adoption of the new standards and discusses the implications of these portfolio changes for the safety of the banking system and the allocation of credit in the economy. (This reading also can be assigned with Chapter 10.)

Reading 20 is "Is Banking Really Prone to Panics?" by Randall J. Pozdena. Recognizing that concern over contagious bank runs is a major justification for deposit insurance, Pozdena assesses the empirical importance of contagion effects among banks. Based on a study of stock returns at individual banks, he concludes that contagion effects are significant and strong and do indeed justify depositor protection and the regulation of bank capital.

In Reading 21, "Too Big to Fail: Origins, Consequences, and Outlook," Robert L. Hetzel presents a relatively brief but detailed overview of the myriad factors which have shaped present U.S. banking structure and policy. He claims that the too big to fail policy developed in part to remedy the absence of satisfactory bankruptcy arrangements for banks, but has the drawbacks of encouraging bank risk taking and obstructing efficient shrinkage of the banking industry. Hetzel concludes with an assessment of the 1991 Deposit Insurance Reform Act and how it will affect bank risk- taking and closures.

Reading 22 is "The New Banking Law Toughens Regulation, Some Say Too Much" by Kenneth H. Bacon. Bacon summarizes the key provisions of the 1991 Deposit Insurance Reform Act and speculates on the new law's effects on bank managers, shareholders, borrowers and regulators. He also explains why many of the original Bush administration proposals to strengthen the banking system did not make it through Congress and samples a variety of opinions regarding how effective the new law will be. This reading updates Chapter 11's discussion of the U.S. Treasury's plans to reform the banking system.

Reading 23 is "Deposit Insurance: Recapitalize or Reform?" by Mark E. Levonian. Levonian identifies two different types of problems besetting the Federal Deposit Insurance Corporation's Bank Insurance Fund: illiquidity and insolvency. Borrowing can remedy the illiquidity problem but successfully overcoming the insolvency problem requires reforms that will either reduce the expenditures or raise the income of the insurance fund. Levonian argues that recapitalizing the fund through borrowing must not be viewed as a substitute for needed reforms of the deposit insurance system.

Readings 24-27 deal with financial innovation, the topic of Chapter 13 of the Text. Reading 24 is "Securitization: More Than Just a Regulatory Artifact" by Charles T. Carlstrom and Katherine A. Samolyk. Securitization, the packaging of loans into marketable securities, reduces financial institutions' credit and interest-rate risks. Carlstrom and Samolyk find that the growth of securitization activities is the result of bank capital and deposit regulations and improvements in information technology.

Reading 25 is "Path-Dependent Options" by William C. Hunter and David W. Stowe. Path-dependent options are a relatively new and rapidly growing class of financial instruments. Hunter and Stowe review the origins of these options, give examples of their use by investors, and describe three frequently used types of path-dependent options—the lookback option, the barrier option, and the average-rate option.

Reading 26, "Managing Interest Rate Risk with Interest Rate Futures" by Charles S. Morris, examines the development and use of interest rate futures contracts to protect investors against interest rate volatility. Morris also identifies and discusses risks associated with hedging with interest rate futures. (Some instructors may wish to use this reading with Chapter 9 of the text if they cover interest rate risk.)

Reading 27 is "Will Increased Regulation of Stock Index Futures Reduce Stock Market Volatility?" by Sean Becketti and Dan J. Roberts. Becketti and Roberts describe how stock index futures are used and investigate whether this innovation has contributed to stock market volatility. They conclude that regulations to limit the use of stock index futures impose net costs on market participants.

READING 10

Solving the Mystery of High Credit Card Rates

Randall J. Pozdena

The behavior of credit card interest rates has befuddled many observers. The rates seem high, relative to other interest rates, currently averaging about 12 percentage points above the Treasury bill rate. In addition, whereas market interest rates have declined significantly since the early 1980s, credit card rates have not moved down significantly. Indeed, the spread between the Treasury bill rate and credit card rates has doubled in that time.

The credit card industry has not offered a good explanation of the behavior of credit card rates. In light of the high level of credit card rates, therefore, about half the states have imposed usury limits on credit card rates. While credit card issuers have been able to avoid these restrictions in many cases by moving their activities to other states, other policy makers recently have proposed national rate caps. It is important to know whether such usury laws are justified.

The purpose of this *Weekly Letter* is to present a simple view of credit card rate-setting that produces the high and insensitive rate structure observed. The model is used to reproduce the actual historical performance of credit card rates. The conclusion is that high and invariant credit card rates are not necessarily evidence of a failure of competition in the credit card market. This calls into question the advisability of usury restrictions.

THE CREDIT CARD MARKET

Credit cards are both payment and credit devices. Cardholders can use them in lieu of cash for a variety of retail transactions. At any given time, a bit fewer than half of all cardholders also use them to access a revolving credit line of a preset amount. The use of credit cards as a payments device is growing at the rate of about 10 percent per year. The amount of credit card debt outstanding is growing at about a 6 percent annual rate and represents about 30 percent of all consumer installment credit.

Providers of "interchange" services (such as MasterCard and Visa) transmit payment information between the cardholder's and the merchant's banks. However, the issuing institution sets the card's terms, including the interest rate, the grace period, annual fees, penalties, and most other card features. While there are relatively few suppliers of interchange services, according to the Nilson Report there are at least 5,000 credit card issuers in the United States (excluding private label variations of these cards). In addition, entry into the business is relatively easy, with individual retailers and other commercial entities of even modest size offering credit card plans.

RESOLVING A CONUNDRUM

The existence of this many suppliers normally would be expected to lead to aggressive price competition. Yet, credit card rates appear to be very sticky, responding sluggishly, if at all, to trends and fluctuations in other market interest rates. The volatility of credit card rates is less than one-fifth that of Treasury Bill rates, for example, and the correlation between the two interest rates over the past 10 years has been less than 0.1.

In addition, as pointed out by Ausubel (1991) and the Board of Governors (1991), the rate of return to banks on credit card assets appears to be high relative to the return observed for other bank assets. Yet actual loss (charge-off) rates do not appear to be very high, averaging below 3 percent for most of the past decade—seemingly too little to justify a 12 percent premium over riskless rates.

All of this evidence is seen as being consistent with abnormally high profits in credit card lending, in sharp contrast to what would be expected given the structure of the industry.

To resolve this conundrum, it is necessary to focus on the nature of the debt created by using the revolving credit feature of a credit card. In particular, credit card debt is unsecured debt; when a customer uses a credit card in a purchase and does not pay off the balance within the grace period, the issuing bank acquires an unsecured loan. That is, neither the merchandise purchased, nor any other asset of the cardholder, may be repossessed easily by the lender to ensure payment.

The obvious reason for this feature is that for small transactions, the additional contractual steps involved in establishing title as part of the loan agreement would be costly. (Such steps do make sense, on the other hand, for larger denomination installment credit, such as auto loans or home equity lines.)

The only avenue open to the lender to obtain repayment from delinquent cardholders is to proceed in court against the general assets or income of the cardholder and to report the delinquency to credit rating agencies. In the former case, the transactions costs conceivably could be large relative to outstanding balances, which average only about $1,200 per card in 1990 (using data from the market for credit card-backed securities). The threat of impaired credit ratings serves to discipline the user against excessive use of the card, but does not actually assist in recovery of outstanding balances.

MODELING CREDIT CARD DEBT

Finance theory provides a way of pricing risky debt using options pricing theory, by recognizing that the default potential of a loan essentially implies the existence of a financial option. Using such models, it can be shown that the value (to the lender) of such a loan depends on more than just the market interest rate; in particular, the loan value declines with increases in the riskiness of the cardholder's net worth (which provide the ultimate security of the loan) and with decreases in collateralization.

If the issuing bank can predict the risk accurately, of course, it can charge a higher initial interest rate on the credit to compensate for the additional risk. However, even if the bank knows the risk beforehand, its ability to control the riskiness of the borrower, once the borrower has the credit, is limited. Indeed, once the borrower has the funds at an agreed price, he has a strong incentive to use it under conditions that are most favorable to him—namely, when his net worth is impaired. The issuing bank has limited ability to identify when these conditions prevail and to exercise control over its exposure.

Banks can (and do) impose limits on credit card credit as a means of controlling exposure. In addition, credit card companies try to identify consumer segments that pose lower risks of default (and these selective issuers charge lower rates). But within any consumer segment, the lender can never be certain how leveraged the borrower has become because of other obligations, and because of the lack of collateralization, must assume "worst case" exposure within each segment.

IMPLICATIONS

The primary, practical solutions to this so-called "moral hazard of lending" dilemma are (1) to collateralize the loan (a possibility likely foreclosed because of the title cost considerations expressed above), or (2) to price the loan assuming maximum risk exposure. That is, credit card debt interest rate must be set very high in order to compensate the issuer for the fact that users will adjust their risk in response to the price of the credit.

Indeed, if there were no way to limit the moral hazard problem, no rate would be high enough. (As a practical matter, of course, the reputational costs associated with a bad credit rating help cap extreme behavior of borrowers.) The result is that under conditions of poor collateralization, lenders must charge considerably higher credit card rates than when lending is secured, even to "creditworthy" segments. (In addition, it can be shown theoretically that the rate on a poorly collateralized loan is insensitive to variations in riskless rates.)

The resultant use of high rates implies that credit card debt will be "overpriced" for households that pose low risks of default.

These households will tend not to use the revolving credit features of their cards, but rather to use them mainly as transactions devices. (In practice, slightly more than half of all cardholders use the cards without running credit balances.) They will be primarily sensitive to annual fees and the grace period, an implication consistent with observations of credit card marketers cited by Ausubel.

"Riskier" households, on the other hand, will self-select into using the credit feature of their cards because, for them, the rate premium is attractive given the costs to them of alternative credit. Although the charge-off rate for these borrowers will be accordingly high, the average across all outstanding balances is reduced by those who choose to pay at the end of the grace period, partly explaining the low, actual charge-off rates.

SIMULATING CREDIT CARD PRICING

The options pricing model described above can be stated mathematically, and its parameters estimated by varying them until they best fit the historical experience of credit card rates. Through such an exercise, we can determine (1) if it is possible for the model to match actual credit card pricing and (2) if the parameters are consistent with the assumptions of the nature of credit card debt. In particular, we can see whether it is priced assuming a low level of collateralization and high marginal risk.

Actual and Simulated Credit Card Rates

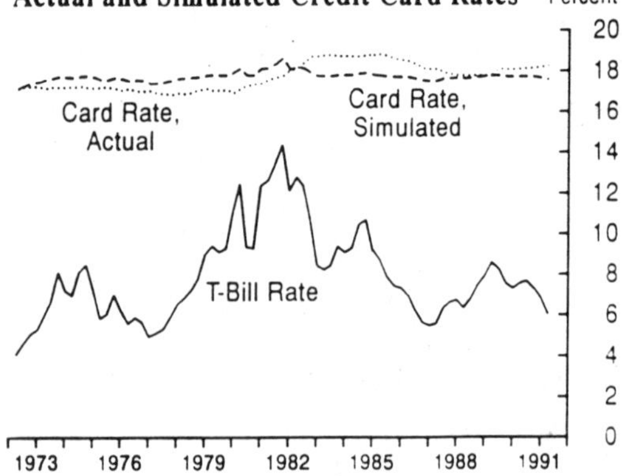

The author performed this exercise, using a simple Black-Scholes type representation of collateralized debt. Actual short-term interest rates were used, with all other parameters of the model selected using an optimization technique to find the best fit of the modeled rates to actual credit card rates. The results, present in the Chart, show that it was easy to fit the options-based model to the actual data, even if it is assumed that the risk exposure of the lender has not varied over this time period. (In addition, there is no attempt to control for the removal of interstate usury controls in 1982.)

More importantly, however, the parameters of the underlying model are consistent with the representation of credit card debt as costly-to-service, unsecured credit extended to relatively high-risk borrowers. Specifically, the loan seems to be priced as if the lender perceived the debt as poorly collateralized or costly to service, and the variance of the borrower's net worth as high. (As a point of reference, the implied variance is similar to the variance in the S&P 500 returns.) As a check on the internal consistency of the simulation exercise, the term of the credit card debt was also estimated, rather than assumed, as a part of the empirical exercise. The implied term of the credit card debt in the model is about four years, in the range of the terms implied in secondary market sales of credit card debt.

CONCLUSION

In Ausubel's very thorough study of the credit card market, he concludes that cardholders were "irrational," acquiring the cards with no intention of ever using them, but ending up incurring large credit card balances and debt service costs. The implication of the analysis here is that no such irrationality need be invoked. Rather, the high, and insensitive, credit card rates are consistent with the pricing of risky credits in an atmosphere of moral hazard and costly collateralization or service. The fact that credit card issuers that do offer lower rates do so only to more carefully selected consumer segments also is consistent with the risk management model employed here.

This alone, of course, does not prove that the credit card market is as competitive as it should be. However, the current performance of credit card rates is completely consistent with the model used in this *Letter*. This suggests that attempts to reduce credit card rates through usury legislation will have the effect of exposing banks to increased risk, and reducing the availability of consumer credit. This is a curious policy direction in an economy already plagued by weak financial institutions and sluggish credit growth.

REFERENCES

Ausubel, L. 1991. "The Failure of Competition in the Credit Card Market." *American Economic Review* (March) pp. 50-81.

Board of Governors of the Federal Reserve System. 1991. "Profitability of Credit Card Plans: Second Annual Report to Congress."

QUESTIONS

1. What is Pozdena's explanation for high credit card rates?

2. How do the high credit card rates affect low risk and high risk households? Does this represent an adverse selection problem?

3. Pozdena claims that usury limits on credit card rates will expose banks to more risk and reduce the availability of consumer credit. Is this the reaction you would expect to asymmetric information problems? Explain.

READING 11

Is There Too Much Corporate Debt?

Ben Bernanke

Borrowing by U.S. corporations has increased dramatically in recent years. The outstanding debt of nonfinancial corporations rose 70 percent between 1983 and 1988, more than two-thirds faster than growth of nominal GNP. Highly leveraged transactions, such as the $25 billion takeover of RJR Nabisco, routinely make the front pages.

Heavy borrowing such as this has raised the issue of whether corporate debt has become excessive. Congress has been considering whether changes should be made in the tax law to try to reduce the rate of corporate debt accumulation. The Federal Reserve has been studying the implications of debt growth for monetary policy and banking system oversight.

In evaluating the debt situation there are many issues to consider, but two questions lie at the heart of the debate. First is the "micro" issue: do high levels of debt increase the efficiency of firms, as some proponents of high leverage have claimed? Then there is the "macro" issue: does increased corporate debt reduce the stability of the country's financial and economic system?

THE MICRO ISSUE: DOES DEBT PROMOTE EFFICIENCY?

The traditional explanation for why corporations use debt as a source of finance is debt's tax advantage: interest payments made by a firm are tax-deductible, while dividend payments are not. Offsetting this advantage are the costs of bankruptcy and reorganization that may be incurred should the firm not be able to meet the stipulated interest payments. According to the traditional view, the optimal ratio of debt to equity is the one that just balances these two costs.

More recently, however, financial economists have gone beyond this traditional view to focus on the possibly beneficial effects of debt issuance on managerial performance.[1]

This point can be illustrated by a simple example.

A Tale of Two Twins. Suppose that there are two potential entrepreneurs, who (like the two characters in a well-known children's magazine) are named Goofus and Gallant.[2] Goofus and Gallant plan to start ice cream stands on opposite sides of town. The necessary equipment for a stand costs $1,000, and since the entrepreneurs each have only $100, they must obtain some outside finance.

Goofus finances his ice cream stand through stock issuance: that is, he finds some friends to put up $900, in exchange for which he promises them 90 percent of the profits. Gallant issues debt instead; he gets a friend to lend him $900, for which Gallant promises to pay $100 annual interest. Both boys thus have enough capital to get their businesses going.

Things go along well enough at first for both entrepreneurs. But the summer days are hot, and scooping ice cream is hard work. Goofus says to himself, "I've make $100 profit at my stand already this week. If I were to keep working through the weekend, I could make another $100. But I have to share 90 percent with my partners—so that extra $100 really means only $10 for me! I'm not really willing to work the weekend for less than a $25 personal profit, so I think I'll quit and go fishing."

On the other side of town, Gallant is also having a crisis of conscience; he is developing scooper's elbow from serving so much ice cream. He loves to fish as much as Goofus does. Should he quit working? He says to himself, "The $100 I have earned so far is enough to cover the interest payment on my loan. From now on, any profits the ice cream stand earns are mine to keep. If I worked through the weekend, I could earn another $100; that's more than the $25 I would be willing to pay to knock off and go fishing." So Gallant goes back to work.

The two entrepreneurs have faced the same quandary, but have made different decisions. It is important to understand that, in both cases, it is economically efficient to keep the ice cream stand in operation through the weekend, in that the $100 in extra profit that could be earned is greater than the $25 value the proprietor of each stand places on his leisure. Yet, of the two, only Gallant does the "right" thing and keeps working.

Incentives to Do the Right Thing. In the children's magazine, Gallant's decisions to do the right thing stem from his superior moral character. In this example, morality has nothing to do with it; both boys make their decisions based on their calculations of personal gain. The difference between Goofus and Gallant is the way in which they have financed their ventures. By financing with equity, Goofus has created a situation in which his personal rewards are relatively insensitive to the profits of the company; a $100 increase in profits increases his personal return by only $10. This reduces Goofus's incentive to work hard and make decisions that are in the interest of the company. In contrast, once the interest payment is made, Gallant's personal returns fluctuate dollar for dollar with the profits of the company; he thus has a strong incentive to take actions that maximize the company's profits.

Indeed, in this particular example, Gallant would do the right thing (keep working) as long as he was financed at least 60 percent by debt. With 60 percent ($600) in debt, there would be 40 percent ($400) in total equity. Gallant's $100 in original capital would give him 25 percent of that equity, giving him a 25 percent share of the firm's profits. With a 25 percent share, Gallant would be just indifferent between working through the weekend (which nets him an extra .25 x $100 = $25) or going fishing (which is worth $25 to him). With anything above 60 percent debt finance, he would keep working.

Changing the Mode of Financing. We can add another chapter to the story of Goofus and Gallant. At the end of the summer, both boys notice that the debt-financed ice cream stand is more profitable than the equity-financed stand, and that this extra profitability is due entirely to the way in which the stands are financed. This implies that pure profits can be earned by a capital restructuring—a change in the mode of finance—of Goofus's operation. This restructuring can be accomplished if someone takes out a loan and uses the borrowed money to buy back the shares from Goofus's shareholders; this changes the stand's financing from equity to debt. The share buyback is particularly attractive at the current market price for Goofus's company's shares, which—because Goofus is always going fishing—is low. But the buyback would be profitable even if the acquirers had to pay the current stockholders some premium for their shares; the acquirers would simply be sharing with the current shareholders some of the profits expected to be produced by the restructuring.

The capital restructuring of Goofus's stand would work equally well if performed by Goofus, by Gallant, or by someone else.[3] In any case, the swapping of debt for equity is called a *leveraged buyout*, or LBO. If done by Goofus, the current manager of the operation, it could also be called a *management buyout*; if done by Gallant, it wold be called a *takeover* (a hostile takeover, if Goofus resisted and tried to hold on to the company). The key point is that, in either case, the leverage of the company (its ratio of debt to equity) would increase, and this would lead to more efficient and profitable operations.

The Recent Explosion of Debt. The parable of Goofus and Gallant illustrates the idea that the financial structure of firms influences the incentives of "insiders" (managers, directors, and large shareholders with some operational interest in the business) and that, in particular, high levels of debt may increase the willingness of insiders to work hard and make profit-maximizing decisions. This incentive-based approach makes a valuable contribution to our understanding of a firm's capital structure. But while this theory might explain why firms like to use debt in general, does it explain why the use of debt has increased so much in recent years?

Michael Jensen, a founder and leading proponent of the incentive-based approach to capital structure, argues that it can.[4] Jensen focuses on a recent worsening of what he calls the "free cash flow" problem. Free cash flow is defined as the portion of a corporation's cash flow that it is unable to invest profitably within the firm. Companies in industries that are profitable but no longer have much potential for expansion—the U.S. oil industry, for example—have a lot of free cash flow.

Why is free cash flow a problem? Jensen argues that managers are often tempted to use free cash flow to expand the size of the company, even if the expansion is not profitable. This is because managers feel that their power and job satisfaction are enhanced by a growing company; so given that most managers' compensation is at best weakly tied to the firm's profitability, Jensen argues that managers will find it personally worthwhile to expand even into money-losing operations. In principle, the board of directors and shareholders should be able to block these unprofitable investments; however, in practice, the fact that the management typically has far more information about potential investments than do outside directors and shareholders makes it difficult to second-guess the managers' recommendations.

How More Leverage Can Help. The problem of free cash flow is precisely analogous to the problem in the Goofus and Gallant example. Just as Goofus was willing to sacrifice company profits in order to pursue his personal goals (going fishing), so the company manager with lots of free cash flow may attempt to use that cash to increase his power and perquisites, at the expense of the shareholders. Jensen argues that the solution to the free-cash-flow problem is the same as the solution to the Goofus-Gallant problem: more leverage. For example, suppose that management uses the free cash flow of the company, plus the proceeds of new debt issues, to repurchase stock from the outside shareholders—that is, to do a management buyout. This helps solve the free-cash-flow problem in several ways. First, as in the Goofus and Gallant example, the personal returns of the managers are now much more closely tied to the profits of the firm, which gives them incentives to be more efficient. Second, the re-leveraging process removes the existing free cash from the firm, so that any future investment projects will have to be financed externally; thus, future projects will have to meet the market test of being acceptable to outside bankers or bond purchasers. Finally, the high interest payments implied by re-leveraging impose a permanent discipline on the managers; in order to meet these payments, they will have to ruthlessly cut money-losing operations, avoid questionable investments, and take other efficiency-promoting actions.

According to Jensen, a substantial increase in free-cash-flow problems—resulting from deregulation, the maturing of some large industries, and other factors—is a major source of the recent debt expansion. Jensen also points to a number of institutional factors that have promoted increased leverage. These include relaxed restrictions on mergers, which have lowered the barriers to corporate takeovers created by the antitrust laws, and increased financial sophistication, such as the greatly expanded operation of takeover specialists like Drexel Burnham Lambert Inc. and the development of the market for "junk bonds."[5] Jensen's diagnosis is not controversial: it's quite plausible that these factors, plus changing norms about what constitutes an "acceptable" level of debt, explain at least part of the trend toward increased corporate debt.[6] However, the implied conclusion—that the debt buildup is beneficial overall to the economy—is considerably more controversial.

Criticisms of the Incentive-Based Rationale for Increased Debt. Jensen and other advocates of the incentive-based approach to capital structure have made a cogent theoretical case for the beneficial effects of debt finance, and many architects of large-scale restructurings have given improved incentives and the promise of greater efficiency as a large part of the rationale for increased leverage. The idea that leverage is beneficial has certainly been embraced by the stock market: even unsubstantiated rumors of a potential LBO have been sufficient to send the stock price of the targeted company soaring, often by 40 percent or more. At a minimum, this indicates that stock market participants *believe* that higher leverage increases profitability. Proponents of restructuring interpret this as evidence that debt is good for the economy.

There are, however, criticisms of this conclusion. First, the fact that the stock market's expectations of company profitability rise when there is a buyout is not proof that profits *will* rise in actuality. It is still too soon to judge whether the increased leverage of the 1980s will lead to a sustained increase in profitability. One might think of looking to historical data for an answer to this question. But buyouts in the 1960s and 1970s were somewhat different in character from more recent restructurings, and, in any case, the profitability evidence on the earlier episodes is mixed.

Even if the higher profits expected by the stock market do materialize, there is contention over where they are likely to come from. The incentive-based theory of capital structure says they will come from improved efficiency. But some opponents have argued that the higher profits will primarily reflect transfers to the shareholders from other claimants on the corporation—its employees, customers, suppliers, bondholders, and the government. For example, Andrei Shleifer and Lawrence Summers, in a soon-to-be-published study, present evidence that the premium received by shareholders of Trans World Airlines, when it was taken over, was paid for twice over by the wage concessions wrested from three TWA unions. Customers may be hurt if takeovers are associated with increased monopolization of markets.[7] Bondholders have been big losers in some buyouts, as higher leverage has increased bankruptcy risk and thus reduced the value of outstanding bonds. The government may have lost tax revenue, as companies, by increasing leverage, have increased their interest deductions (although there are offsetting effects here, such as the taxes paid by bought-out shareholders on their capital gains). The perceptions that much of the profits associated with re-leveraging and buyouts comes from "squeezing" existing beneficiaries of the corporation explains much of the recent political agitation to limit these activities.[8]

Another possible explanation for the effect of LBOs on stock prices is that the announcement of a buyout provides information about, but does not directly affect, the firm's future prospects. Suppose that the management of a publicly owned pharmaceutical firm has secret information about a revolutionary new drug discovered in its laboratories. This highly profitable new opportunity, being secret, is not reflected in the firm's stock price. The management of this company has a strong incentive to do a buyout, because it knows the stock is currently underpriced relative to the firm's future profits. But if the managers attempt a buyout, this will reveal to the public that the management thinks the stock is underpriced—which will cause the stock price to be bid up. This means that the managers will have to share some of the profits from their inside information with the shareholders. Profits may indeed rise after the buyout—reflecting the introduction of the new drug—but this increase in profits would not be in any way caused by the increase in leverage associated with the buyout. Similar arguments apply if the buyout is initiated by a competitor or someone else who might have better information about the firm than do stock market investors.

The debt buildup can also be criticized from the perspective of incentive-based theories themselves. Two points are worth noting: first, the principal problem that higher leverage is supposed to address is the relatively weak connection between firms' profits and managers' personal returns, which reduces managers' incentives to take profit-maximizing actions. But if this is truly the problem, it could be addressed more directly—without subjecting the company to serious bankruptcy risk—simply by changing managerial compensation schemes to include more profit-based incentives. Robert Vishny and Andrei Shleifer (1988) argue that the approach of tying managers' pay to profits is limited by legal precedents that allow shareholders to sue if managerial compensation is "excessive"; however, if managerial incentives are really the problem, it does seem that more could be done in this direction.

The Downside of Debt Financing. A second point, made by the original Jensen-Meckling (1976) article and many since then, is that increased debt is not the optimal solution to all incentive problems. For example, it has been shown, as a theoretical proposition, that managers of debt-financed firms have an incentive to choose riskier projects over safe ones; this is because firms with fixed-debt obligations enjoy all of the upside potential of high-risk projects but share the downside losses with the debt holders, who are not fully repaid if bad investment outcomes cause the firm to fail.

That high leverage does not always promote efficiency can be seen when highly leveraged firms suffer losses and find themselves in financial distress. When financial problems hit, the need to meet interest payments may force management to take a very short-run perspective, leading them to cut back production and employment, cancel even potentially profitable expansion projects, and sell assets at fire-sale prices. Because the risk of bankruptcy is so great, firms in financial distress cannot make long-term agreements; they lose customers and suppliers who are afraid they cannot count on an ongoing relationship, and they must pay wage premiums to hire workers.

These efficiency losses, plus the direct costs of bankruptcy (such as legal fees), are the potential downside of high leverage. In terms of the ice cream stand, if Gallant does not earn enough to make his interest payment, he may be tempted to skimp on the ice cream or even serve the cracked cones, sacrificing future sales to increase short-run income and avoid bankruptcy. Or he may simply choose to stop working, letting the stand go into default. Maybe a highly leveraged Gallant isn't so gallant after all!

THE MACRO ISSUE: SPILLOVERS AND MULTIPLIERS

Most discussion of corporate debt has focused on the microeconomic efficiency issues. However, the macroeconomic implications of debt are also important. There are several possible (although speculative) scenarios under which high corporate debt could contribute to macroeconomic dislocations.

One scenario is a "liquidity crisis." In 1970, the bankruptcy of the Penn Central railroad, and Penn Central's resulting default on its short-term borrowings, caused a temporary, sharp decrease in new lending in the commercial-paper market. Prompt action by the Federal Reserve stabilized the situation. However, the potential for a similar episode, possibly on a larger scale, exists.

This potential arises from the fact that many firms count on being able to "roll over" their short-term debt (that is re-borrow) as it comes due. If, for some reason, lenders became worried about bankruptcy risk and refused to roll over maturing debt, then these firms (even though they might be fundamentally solvent) would find themselves illiquid—that is, short of cash to make promised payments.

In most cases, firms would respond to this by taking loans on lines of credit previously negotiated with banks; however, that would spread the illiquidity problem to the banking system, as banks suddenly were subjected to large demands for credit. To ease such a liquidity crisis, the Federal Reserve would have to provide more funds to the financial system, either through the discount window, as it did during the Penn Central episode, or through open-market operations.

Perhaps a more disturbing scenario is a "solvency crisis." Suppose that, for reasons unrelated to financial structure, the economy were to enter a serious recession, leading to falling earnings and (perhaps) rising interest costs. Given high leverage inherited from the past, some firms might find it difficult to service their debt. Firms in financial distress are likely to retrench, cutting back employment, production, and investment. This would reduce total demand, worsening the recession and leading to financial problems in other firms. Thus, the initial recessionary shock could be magnified by high leverage; in the language of traditional Keynesian macroeconomic analysis, the "multiplier" relating the size of the initial disturbance to the size of the resulting recession will have increased.

Distressed Firms Can Have Far-reaching Effects. The difference between the microeconomic and macroeconomic perspective is that in the macroeconomic approach, we are concerned not only with the effects of financial distress on the distressed firm itself, but with the effects of the distressed firm's actions on other firms. If there are "spillovers" from one firm to another (for example, if the shutdown of a large employer in a town affects the town's economy more generally), then financial distress will increase the multiplier. Higher leverage thus has the potential to increase the vulnerability of the economy to destabilizing shocks. Importantly, the possible effects of spillovers and multipliers will not be taken into account by individual firms when they choose their preferred level of debt.

Are these scenarios likely? Nobody knows for sure, but there are several ways to argue that they are not very likely.

First, it should be pointed out that, despite the rapid increase in debt, corporate debt-to-equity ratios (measured in market-value terms) have not changed much during the 1980s. Indeed, Ben Bernanke and John Campbell (1988), using a sample of 1,400 large U.S. nonfinancial corporations, showed that debt-to-equity ratios in the 1980s remain well below their peaks, which occurred during the 1973-74 recession. The relative stability of the debt-to-equity ratio reflects the bull market in stocks of the 1980s, which allowed stock values to keep up with the high rate of debt issuance. From this perspective, debt burdens have not really increased.

However, even though debt-to-equity ratios have not increased, another measure of debt burden—the ratio of interest payments to total cash flow—has grown significantly. Bernanke and Campbell found this measure of interest burden to be about 50 percent higher in the mid-1980s than in the 1970s; several studies report that this ratio is currently close to its 1981-82 recession high, despite the long expansion that has occurred since the end of 1982.

How do we reconcile the fact that the interest-payments-to-earnings ratios (and debt-to-earnings ratios) have grown while debt-to-equity ratios have not? Mechanically, the answer is that both debt and stock values have grown much faster than earnings. The high ratio of stock prices to current earnings—sometimes called the P/E ratio—implies optimism on the part of investors about future earnings.[9] The stock market can be interpreted as saying that, even though current interest burdens are high, earnings are likely to rise enough in the future for firms to meet their debt obligations.

If we take the stock market's prediction at face value, then, a liquidity crisis or solvency crisis cannot be called a likely event; a reasonable expectation is that the corporate debt will be serviced. This doesn't mean that macroeconomic problems due to debt are not possible, however; it only means that they should be thought of as a sort of worst-case scenario. Nevertheless, good policymaking requires attention to worst-case as well as average outcomes. Indeed, it is during crisis situations in which good policies are most important.

The Likelihood of Macroeconomic Debt Problems. To get an idea of what might happen in a worst-case situation, Bernanke and Campbell (1988) simulated the effects of a recession in their sample of large firms. They asked what would have happened if the changes in cash flow, stock prices, and interest rates that actually occurred in the recessions of 1973-74 and 1981-82 had occurred again in 1986, affecting the very same firms in their sample. Those two recessions were found to have different effects in the simulations. In the 1973-74 scenario, the stock market declines sharply; the simulation shows that in this type of recession more than 10 percent of the large firms would become technically insolvent, in the sense that the market value of their assets would fall below the market value of their debt.[10] In the 1981-82 scenario the stock market is fairly stable, but cash flow falls and interest rates rise; in this case Bernanke and Campbell found that about 10 percent of their firms would be unable to meet interest obligations without further borrowing. In the terminology introduced above, a 1973-74-type recession would create the potential for a solvency crisis, while a 1981-82-type recession might lead to a liquidity crisis.

Overall, then, the high share prices of U.S. corporations—not to mention the willingness of lenders to accept the high leverage of borrowing corporations—suggest that knowledgeable investors consider a macroeconomic debt crisis unlikely. However, unlikely is not the same as impossible; the Bernanke-Campbell simulations suggest that macroeconomic debt problems could be triggered by recessionary shocks of a magnitude that has been experienced twice in the last decade and a half.[11] This risk could possible be ameliorated in the short run by aggressively expansionary monetary and fiscal policies, but only at the cost of higher inflation and potentially greater instability in the long run.

Has Debt Become Less Risky? An alternative way to question the possibility of a macroeconomic debt crisis is to argue that, because of changes in the financial environment, a given level of debt poses less risk in 1989 than it would have in, say, 1974. Here is a concrete example: a recent development is the use of what is called "strip financing," in which investors in a firm commit to holding a fixed combination of the firm's debt and equity instruments. The idea is to minimize conflict between debt holders and shareholders (who, under strip financing, are one and the same), thus reducing the potential cost of financial distress and reorganization. Another development, stressed by Jensen, is that financial firms involved in arranging buyouts are in some cases retaining some stake in the management of the LBO firm; thus, the financial firm will have an incentive to assist the reorganization process should the LBO fall into financial trouble.

It is certainly true that the safety of any given level of debt depends on the financial environment. Japanese corporations, for example, have borne much higher levels of debt than their U.S. counterparts without experiencing problems. This works because most Japanese corporate debt is in the form of bank loans, and large banks take an active role in the management of the firms to which they lend. Should a firm experience difficulties, the bank assists in obtaining new finance or in reorganization; at the same time, the bank is well placed to oversee whatever management or strategy changes the firm must make. These sorts of practices, which contrast with traditional "arm's length" lending in the United States, make high debt burdens safer.

Whether the U.S. financial environment has in fact moved substantially in the Japanese direction is an open question. Oversight of corporate management by the financial firm that arranged the LBO is a step toward the Japanese model; however, it is not clear at this point how widespread this practice is. Working in the other direction is the fact that increasing corporate reliance on below-investment-grade (junk) bonds has come at the expense of corporate use of bank loans. Since junk bonds tend to be held by mutual funds, insurance companies, and other institutions not directly involved in the management of the firms to which they lend, the use of junk bonds (in place of bank loans) may strengthen the traditional "arm's length" tendency of U.S. capital markets. This may make negotiated avoidance of bankruptcy more difficult and increase potential bankruptcy costs.

The contention that the risks of leverage have been reduced by institutional changes also raises a theoretical question: according to the incentive-based approach, the whole point of increased leverage is to impose discipline on corporate management. If, because of changes in the financial environment, failure to make contracted interest payments becomes a minor concern, then it would seem that the disciplinary impact of debt on management will be much reduced.

CONCLUSION

The argument for higher leverage is that it imposes discipline on the managers of the corporation, leading to greater efficiency. Effectively, this greater discipline is achieved by means of a threat: if the firm does not perform up to expectations, it may well suffer insolvency and reorganization. As with the discipline of children, the advantage of a draconian threat is the good behavior it may promote; the disadvantage is that the threat may have to be carried out.

Here is an analogy often used in discussing the costs and benefits of high leverage. Suppose we want people to drive more carefully. One way to do this would be to require every car to have a dagger in the steering wheel, the point aimed directly at the chest of the driver. This would certainly promote more careful driving, since even a fender bender might have ghastly consequences. But suppose there was a sudden worsening in driving conditions—a freak snowstorm, for example—that unexpectedly put even the most careful drivers at risk of accidents. Under these circumstances, the dagger-in-the-wheel policy might well lead to more deaths and injuries than if this "discipline device" had never been used.

In this story, the dagger in the wheel is supposed to represent high corporate leverage—which under normal circumstances promotes profit maximization ("safe driving") by managers. The snowstorm is an economy-wide recession (or perhaps some other disturbance, like a sharp increase in interest rates). The concern is that high leverage, while possibly a boon in good times, might become a destructive force in bad times.

This trade-off poses a quandary for policymakers. Despite the criticisms and existing uncertainties, few economists would completely dismiss the claim that higher leverage can be used to improve incentives and promote efficiency. Given the importance of improving the performance of U.S.

corporations in a competitive international marketplace, it would probably be a severe mistake for the government simply to ban buyouts or limit leverage. On the other hand, pro-debt biases in the tax code, the possibility that higher leverage can help shareholders "squeeze" employees and others, and the possibility of "spillovers" from financial distress all suggest that firms will take on more debt than is good for the economy as a whole.

Three types of policy responses might help the situation. First, the government should take actions to increase the accountability of managers to shareholders (for example, by eliminating legal barriers to paying managers profit-based compensation); this would reduce the need to improve incentives indirectly through high leverage. Second, banking, financial market, and antitrust regulators should carefully scrutinize highly leveraged deals that fall within their purview; it is particularly important that government-insured deposits not be the funding source for risky buyouts, unless the bank's capital is demonstrated to be adequate. Finally, biases in the tax code that favor buyouts and high leverage should be removed.

ENDNOTES

1.The classic article that introduced this approach is Jensen and Meckling (1976).

2.The characters Goofus and Gallant are copyrighted by *Highlights for Children*, and their names are used with permission.

3.This assumes, first, that Gallant has time to operate both stands and, second, that Gallant has enough profits from operating his own stand to buy out Goofus's share.

4.For a summary of Jensen's views, see Jensen (1988). Jensen's article is part of a *Journal of Economic Perspectives* special symposium on takeovers, which provides an excellent and balanced introduction to this subject.

5.Junk bonds, more properly called below-investment-grade or high-yield bonds, have been used in a number of large corporate restructurings. For a discussion of the junk bond market and the uses of junk bonds in takeovers, see Loeys (1986).

6.One important piece of evidence in favor of this explanation is that net equity issues have been substantially negative since 1983. This suggests that much of the proceeds of the new debt issues is being used to repurchase outstanding shares. This is what we would expect if corporations are attempting to re-leverage their existing assets, rather than using debt to expand their asset holdings.

7.McAndrews and Nakamura (1989) present a model in which increased leverage by existing firms can help deter potential competitors from entering the market.

8.Not much systematic empirical work on the "squeezing" hypothesis has been done to date. In a careful study of 76 companies' management buyouts, Kaplan (1988) found that most of the value gained from the buyout was due to increased operating income and tax benefits, and that the transfers from bondholders were small. However, the study considered only the first two years' experience of each firm after its buyout, and lack of data prevented measurement of the buyout's effects on employees, suppliers, and customers.

9.If the stock market is "efficient," then the price of a share should represent the present discounted value of current earnings and future expected earnings. If the P/E ratio is high, then either interest rates are low (which they currently are not), or future earnings are expected to be high relative to current earnings.

10.If the value of assets is less than the value of debt, then the debt cannot be repaid; the firm must either eventually go bankrupt or be reorganized.
11.Another quantitative objection to the possibility of a macroeconomic debt crisis is that much of the recent debt buildup has occurred in cyclically insensitive sectors, such as food processing and services (see Roach, 1988). While this is true, it is also true that debt burdens have increased in cyclically sensitive sectors, like durable goods, as well. The simulations reported in the text implicitly take into account any shifting sectoral composition of debt.

REFERENCES

Bernanke, Ben, and John Campbell. "Is There a Corporate Debt Crisis?" Brookings Papers on Economic Activity (1988:1) pp.83- 125.

Jensen, Michael C. "Takeovers: Their Causes and Consequences," *Journal of Economic Perspectives*, vol.2 (Winter 1988) pp.21-48.

Jensen, Michael C., and William H. Meckling. "Theory of the Firm: Managerial Behavior, Agency Costs and Ownership Structure," *Journal of Financial Economics*, vol.3 (1976) pp.305-60.

Kaplan, Stephen. "Management Buyouts: Efficiency Gains or Value Transfers?" University of Chicago, unpublished (1988).

Loeys, Jan. "Low-Grade Bonds: A Growing Source of Corporate Funding," Federal Reserve Bank of Philadelphia *Business Review* (November/December 1986) pp.3-12.

McAndrews, James J., and Leonard I. Nakamura. "Entry-Deterring Debt," Federal Reserve Bank of Philadelphia, Working Paper No. 89-15 (1989).

Roach, Stephen. "Living With Corporate Debt," *Economic Perspectives*, Morgan Stanley, November 11, 1988.

Shleifer, Andrei, and Lawrence Summers. "Breach of Trust in Hostile Takeovers," in Alan Auerbach, *Corporate Takeovers: Causes and Consequences*, Chicago: University of Chicago Press (forthcoming).

Vishny, Robert, and Andrei Shleifer. "Value Maximization and the Acquisition Process," *Journal of Economic Perspectives*, vol.2 (Winter 1988) pp.7-20.

QUESTIONS

1. How can an increased level of debt relative to equity promote efficiency? Does it follow that the growth of corporate debt during the 1980s has improved efficiency? Why?

2. What is the free cash flow problem? How does it help explain the growth of corporate debt?

3. What macroeconomic problems might result from the increased level of corporate debt? Describe scenarios in which these problems might unfold.

READING 12

Lessons on Lending and Borrowing in Hard Times

Leonard I. Nakamura

Problem loans and highly leveraged transactions have brought home a truth about lending that is easily forgotten in good times: loans sometimes fail, with sad consequences for both borrower and lender. Many existing loans have soured, causing lenders to tighten credit terms on new lending. Meanwhile, borrowers have complained—and policymakers have openly worried—that lenders are refusing sound loans.

New theories about lending and about loan contracts emphasize the difficulties lenders face in ensuring repayment of their loans. According to these theories, the collateral for a loan is not just a back-up source of repayment if the borrower defaults; collateral is also crucial for inducing payments from borrowers who can make them.

Cash-strapped borrowers, when their businesses sour, will often try to put off lenders and keep paying their employees, suppliers, and landlords. In response, lenders will threaten to seize collateral and declare loans in default to ensure they get their fair share of a distressed borrower's cash flows.

This threat is a blunt instrument that often harms the lender as much as the borrower. After all, the value of the borrower's collateral, particularly during a recession, may be insufficient to repay the loan. But there are other considerations, as well. A foreclosure causes valuable resources to be lost that would not be lost otherwise. Management may lose partial control over the firm because of bankruptcy rules, or spend too much time in court, struggling against creditors and other claimants, and too little time running the business. Customer relationships inevitably worsen as customers begin looking for alternative suppliers. And ultimately, if an otherwise viable borrower is liquidated, valuable relationships between management, employees, and customers are lost.

If a borrower's business is fundamentally sound, its longer-term profitability ought to be the best source to repay the loan. But if the lender forces the borrower out of business, this source of funds is lost.

THE DILEMMA OF FORECLOSURE

In the tale of the goose that laid the golden eggs, the owner foolishly tried to get the goose's prized eggs more quickly by killing it. Lenders are not so unwise; still, they might have to threaten foreclosure as a way to force borrowers to repay. When lenders must carry out their threats, they kill the golden goose—and this is the dilemma of foreclosure.

Unfortunately, standard economic theory had assumed away this dilemma, maintaining that the interests of borrowers and lenders could always be aligned through loan agreements. Consequently, economists believed that inefficiencies associated with loan default were small and that liquidation decisions were always sound. After all, wasn't it true that only firms having no value as going concerns were liquidated?

More recent theories offer less optimistic conclusions about lending. They show that firms having value as going concerns may well be liquidated and that inefficiencies associated with loan default can have important consequences for aggregate economic activity. In particular, the implication is that some loans that would ordinarily be made in good times would not be made in uncertain times. These newer theories are more realistic about the potential for conflicts between borrower and lender; accordingly, they are useful guides—to all parties—for anticipating, and thereby lessening, the pain associated with hard economic times.

Two theories in particular have emphasized the importance, and difficulty, of maintaining the borrower's incentive to repay. The idea is disarmingly simple: if given a choice of how much to repay, a borrower who wishes to maximize profits will always choose to repay the smallest amount. One theory, originated by Robert Townsend[1], underscores the lender's ignorance, relative to the borrower, of the borrower's net worth. The other theory, originated by Oliver Hart and John Moore[2], emphasizes the borrower's control over cash flows (the revenues that flow to the borrower from sales of products and services).

TOWNSEND: LOAN CONTRACTS REDUCE INFORMATION COST

Townsend's model stresses the cost to investors of obtaining financial information about borrowers. Before granting a loan, outside financial investors must first obtain detailed information about the firms seeking finance. This information extends to the firm's products and services, the customer base, marketing data, advertising plans, management, alternative financial resources, plant and equipment, labor resources and costs—in short, a detailed financial analysis and forecast. And until the financing is actually in hand, the firm has a strong incentive to provide investors with satisfactory information.

But once the investment is made, the investors may not be well positioned to keep informed about a firm's net worth. Information gathering is a costly procedure, requiring, at a minimum, an audit of current assets and liabilities, an explanation of variances between planned income and expenses and the results achieved, and an evaluation of future profit prospects.

The loan contract, according to Townsend, minimizes this informational cost by specifying a fixed dollar amount that the borrower agrees to pay; as long as repayment is made, no further financial investigation is required. If the borrower fails to repay, however, the lender investigates the borrowing firm, learns of its net worth, and seizes its assets up to the value of the debt plus the cost of the investigation. A solvent borrower will have a strong incentive to repay, as long as the costly investigation following default makes a solvent borrower worse off. The loan contract thus minimizes the cost of post-investment financial investigation while preserving the incentive to repay.[3]

The Defaulting Borrower Pays a Penalty. In practice, a borrower who fails to make timely repayments faces the threat of loan foreclosure and seizure of collateral. (See the box on p. 100 for a discussion of collateral.) Although the borrowing firm can partially protect itself by seeking bankruptcy protection, its business and plans become subject to legal restrictions and scrutiny by the lender. Such constraints, not to mention the loss of reputation and goodwill that bankruptcy may entail, can hurt the firm. The key consequence of default, as required by Townsend's theory, is that the borrower pays a penalty[4]: a loss of asset value. The penalty can be imposed on borrowers through various methods—loan workouts, liquidation, takeover of the firm by an outside administrator acting on behalf of creditors, or seizure and selling of collateral. (The practical steps on the road to liquidation are briefly defined in the box on p. 101).

Let's take, as an example, an investment in a fictitious computer chip manufacturer, Custom Chip. Custom Chip's value is only partially its factory and inventory of materials and chips; much of its value is its new *ideas* for chips. Only an expert in the computer chip business can know how much Custom Chip's value increased—or decreased—in a given period. One way to find out might be to auction off Custom Chip's patents, its chip-design department, and its manufacturing plant (as would happen in a liquidation). But doing that would destroy the firm.

If Custom Chip owes its lender $2 million, then as long as the firm's true value is greater than $2 million, the owners will have a strong incentive to repay the debt rather than risk having the firm thrust into bankruptcy. The threat of foreclosure enforces the loan repayment and means that the lender need not pay computer consultants to analyze Custom Chip's value. However, if Custom Chip cannot or will not repay the $2 million, the lender may have to declare a default and thrust Custom Chip into bankruptcy.

The high cost of default is most obvious when the lender seizes collateral. The

Are You Sure It's Collateral?

Collateral may be any asset of the borrower. Physical assets would be land, plant, equipment, and inventory. Financial assets would include receivables (customers' promises to pay) and financial securities (stocks and bonds).

However, collateral is of value only to the extent that the lender can actually claim, seize, and dispose of it in the event of default. For most borrowers, collateral is property that is a functional part of the business, and its value varies with the business's ups and downs. Then there are other important assets—customer goodwill and other future profit opportunities, for example—that are intangible and cannot be used as collateral because the lender cannot seize and sell them.

Establishing a clear claim to collateral is not always easy. Lenders must follow procedures, set forth in the Uniform Commercial Code, to ensure that their claim is valid. In essence, this requires clearly identifying the collateral, making sure that no one else has a prior claim to it, and making public the lender's claim. This process is called securing and perfecting collateral. If not crucial to the borrower's business, the collateral may actually be held by the lender. However, very often the collateral is integral to the borrower's business and cannot conveniently be held by the lender.

Numerous anecdotes attest to the problems that can arise with collateral. In one instance, the collateral was salad oil, held in vats. When default occurred, the vats turned out to contain water with a thin film of oil on top. In another instance, collateral was mineral rights and a car. But the borrower, it turned out, had never bought the mineral rights, and when the lender came to collect the car, he found that it had already been sold.

A cattle rancher pledged five steers as collateral for a loan, but none of the steers was specifically identified as such. Just before the rancher defaulted, five steers left the herd and, caught in a lightning storm, sought shelter under a tree. The tree was struck by lightning and the five steers died. The rancher was able to argue successfully that the bank's claim was to the five dead steers.

Collateral often deteriorates in value when the firm's lines of business deteriorate. When oil prices slumped in 1986, drilling rigs fell in value. When retail sales slumped in 1990, the value of unsold merchandise declined along with them. If a firm's sales falter because its customers are in financial straits, the firm's receivables will turn out to have little value.

collateral is then no longer available to the borrower, who was actively using it, and it goes to a lender, for whom it has no direct use. The borrower loses by not having use of the collateral, which is often necessary to doing business. In addition, the lender incurs

The Road to Liquidation: Some Terminology

Bankruptcy - A debtor is afforded relief from its debt under the provisions of the Bankruptcy Code either through a liquidation (Chapter 7 of the Code) or rehabilitation (Chapter 11 for commercial enterprises and Chapter 13 for individuals). In a liquidation proceeding, the assets are collected and distributed by a trustee. In a bankruptcy, lenders cannot seize assets or attempt to collect payments; secured lenders are entitled, eventually, to payments equal in value to their collateral, but unsecured lenders often receive little. Rehabilitation and emergence from bankruptcy proceedings typically involve the consent of creditors and equity holders.

Collateral - Any property of the borrower that secures the debt to a lender. In the event of a default, a lender may seize the borrower's collateral; in bankruptcy proceedings, a secured lender has first claim to proceeds from collateral.

Default - A borrower's violation of the loan's terms. Failure to make timely payments or to fulfill other terms, such as providing timely and accurate financial data, constitutes default. The lender's response—foreclosure of the loan—typically includes the right to demand full loan repayment and the right to seize any collateral specified in the loan contract.

Loan workout - A business plan by which a borrower tries to resolve a problem loan. The business plan is typically an agreement arrived at by the lender and the borrower in an effort to avoid bankruptcy proceedings. Renegotiation of loan payments is often a part of a loan workout.

Liquidation - The collection and disposal of a borrower's assets.

Renegotiation - Resetting the terms of a loan contract, typically involving a delay of payments and often a reduction in interest or principal.

costs in seizing, storing, and selling collateral. And as the lender has no special expertise with the collateral, its value may deteriorate further while in the lender's possession.

Lender Must Carry Out the Threat. In Townsend's model, the story ends there. Once default occurs, the lender must carry through the threat of foreclosure and seize the collateral. Thus, Townsend's theory predicts that costly bankruptcies will rise from the existence of debt contracts—and that firms having more value as going concerns than in liquidation may be liquidated solely because they cannot pay their debts. If lenders chose instead to renegotiate the terms of the loan, then borrowers would lose their incentive to repay. Unfortunately, by foreclosing on borrowers who are potentially viable, the lenders may lose their best source of repayment: the borrower's value as an ongoing business.

A partial parallel for the lender's dilemma can be found in the famous Bible story about King Solomon. The wise king was able to discern which of two women claiming to be a baby's mother was telling the truth when he threatened to cut the child in two. Similarly, the lender must threaten to destroy the firm in order to learn the owners' true assessment of its worth. In both cases, the threat must be made in order to learn information. King Solomon, at least, had the advantage of knowing that his threat was only a threat. But in Townsend's model, the lender may discover that the firm cannot repay and that the threat will have to be carried out. And so, a temporary cash shortage can result in business failure when the lender cannot verify that the borrower's problems are indeed temporary.

HART AND MOORE: COLLATERAL MAKES RENEGOTIATION POSSIBLE

A more recent model, by Hart and Moore, explores renegotiation as an alternative to liquidating the firm. But unlike Townsend's model, this one assumes that investors have no difficulty maintaining good information about borrowers—only trouble controlling them contractually.

Hart and Moore assume that investors and entrepreneurs begin with the same information and that they always learn new information simultaneously. However, entrepreneurs control cash flows and can always divert them from investors by, say, using cash to pay workers and suppliers instead.

The only commitment entrepreneurs can make is collateral—and lenders can seize collateral if fixed payments are not made. This collateral, however, is worth more when left in the hands of the entrepreneur. And if collateral falls in value, as often happens in recessions, the lenders' ability to collect payment decreases.

This theory rests on the idea that the variety of possible events that can affect a business is simply too large and complex to be captured in a contract. Moreover, as contract provisions become more complicated, both writing and interpreting the contract become increasingly expensive. Lenders thus keep financial contracts in a form as simple as possible in order to enforce them at low cost. This allows them control over specific types of collateral, but not over details about cash flows.

By Hart and Moore's reasoning, the owner of Custom Chip will repay the loan as long as the manufacturing plant and inventory of computer chips (as distinct from anticipated future profits) remain valuable. However, if the plant and inventory fall in value, the owner can divert cash and ideas to start up a new firm, defaulting on the original loan, even if current cash flows would suffice to repay it.

Threat of Loss Enforces Repayment. Another example of the role collateral plays in enforcing payment can be found in the mortgage market. Consider Robin House, who is buying a $200,000 house with a 10 percent down payment of $20,000; her debt is therefore $180,000. Initially, the value of the collateral—the house—exceeds the value of the debt by $20,000. The threatened loss of home easily enforces Robin's mortgage payments. But suppose the housing market deteriorates and the home falls in value to $150,000. If Robin values her credit reputation (including assets the mortgage lender might be able to seize) at only $20,000, she has an economic incentive to default on the mortgage: her debt exceeds the value of the collateral plus bankruptcy cost. She may refuse to make mortgage payments even though she can afford them.

Borrowers who lose their incentive to repay when their collateral falls in value frequently do default. It is also true that when borrowers are unable to repay, their collateral is often low in value—and both situations occur for the same reason: a weak economic environment. Consider inventory as collateral. When a firm fails, its inventory will consist of those goods it could not sell at close to the original price. Loans that are overcollateralized when made may be severely undercollateralized when foreclosed on. Yet, this does not mean that the collateral serves no purpose; indeed, it helps ensure repayment during periods in which the borrower *can* repay.

While lenders would prefer collateral with an unshakable value, it is extremely hard to find. Indeed, it is not always easy to put the proper value on collateral in the first place. Collateral may not be as difficult to evaluate as the value of an ongoing concern, but it still may not be straightforward. (See the box on p. 104 for difficulties in determining how much the home underlying a mortgage is worth.)

Collateral Is Key to Renegotiation. In Hart and Moore's model, lenders can renegotiate a loan instead of seizing collateral. In a renegotiation, lenders may allow payments to be stretched out or even reduced so as to avoid the losses from seizing collateral. But since only collateral can enforce repayment, the lender will be willing to do this only if the borrower can offer immediate cash and future collateral that are at least as good as what the lender can gain through immediate seizure. If future collateral is inadequate, the lender will foreclose and a viable firm may be lost. Thus, renegotiation only partially solves the dilemma.

Suppose Custom Chip is unable to repay a loan during a period in which profit margins decline because of a recession in the computer industry. The lender has two options. One, it could seize the plant and its inventory of chips. Or two, it could renegotiate—permit Custom Chip to stay in business, accept an incomplete payment of the loan, accept the owner's beach condo, say, for additional collateral, and agree to a partial write-down of the remaining debt. However, if Custom Chip cannot come up with some combination of current cash and future collateral that is more valuable than existing collateral, the lender will go with the first option and seize the collateral. So, in this case, although Custom Chip might have a good chance of

Who Assumes the Risk in Offers to Pay Closing Costs?

Real estate ads sometimes include the come-on "Seller will pay closing costs." This practice creates the innocent appearance of a generous home seller helping the prospective buyer who otherwise would have trouble making the down payment on the house. But is this practice innocent from the perspective of the mortgage lender? No, because the seller is really being generous with the lender's money.

An offer to pay closing costs actually inflates the house's selling price. To see this, consider a house priced by its owner at $100,000 but whose true market value has fallen to $92,000. In method 1, the standard method, the owner straightforwardly lowers the price by $8,000, to $92,000. In method 2, the owner offers to pay the borrower $8,000 up front by paying the buyer's closing costs.

	Method 1	Method 2
House price	$92,000	$100,000
Down payment	$9,200	$10,000
Mortgage loan	$82,800	$90,000
Closing costs	$8,000	$8,000
Buyer puts up	$17,200	$10,000
Seller gets	$92,000	$92,000

The only difference in the bottom line is that the lender has loaned $7,200 more to the borrower; in both cases, the seller winds up with exactly the same amount of money. But suppose the house falls in value by 10 percent, to $82,800. in the first case, the lender is fully protected, and the borrower has no incentive to default on the mortgage. But in the second case, the lender is likely to take a substantial loss if the borrower defaults on the mortgage—and now the borrower may have an incentive to default because the collateral that the borrower loses is less than the debt the borrower would otherwise have to pay.

substantial future earnings, it is unable to realize them because it cannot promise the lender an adequate share of future earnings.

Renegotiations preserve the firm's value. And loans that make renegotiation more possible by preserving repayment incentives are attractive to borrowers as well as lenders. In renegotiation, loans in which borrowers have uncommitted resources to offer the lender are preferable to loans in which borrowers have no negotiating room. In the Custom Chip example, the fact that the owner's beach condo can be put up as collateral helps keep the firm alive. If the owner lacked this resource, renegotiation would be less attractive to the lender.

In 1989, Michael Jensen[5] argued that highly leveraged transactions would not result in bankruptcies because lenders would always be better off renegotiating. In retrospect, Jensen's argument appears incorrect. One reason may be that in many highly leveraged transactions, the borrowers had very little cash margin, or extra collateral, with which to renegotiate.

LENDING DURING A RECESSION

Lenders' most difficult decisions are made during recessions. For the prospective borrower, access to additional financing may be crucial to survival. But for the lender, recession financing is treacherous. In recessions, the probability of bad economic outcomes is higher than at other times, and inefficient, costly bankruptcies and liquidation are more likely.

Unless lenders have established procedures for commanding cash flows from troubled borrowers, they will be unable to lend profitably during recessions, when cash flows become more questionable. Collateral is crucial—both as an ultimate source of repayment and as a threat to command repayment. But in recessions, collateral—unfortunately—becomes less reliable.

Loan Contracts Are Less Efficient in Recessions. According to both of the models just discussed, firms with going-concern value may be shut down if loan repayments cannot be made. This is more likely to occur during recessions, when demand falls and cash flows dry up. As a consequence, loan contracts are more likely to lead to inefficiency during bad times than in good times, since bankruptcies and liquidations are more likely. Thus, the practice of making fewer loans in a weak economy is consistent with these theories.

Several other points about lending during a recession fall out of these models:

1. *More collateral will be required to further ensure repayment, although this makes borrowing more difficult.* During a recession, the increased risk that collateral will fall in value means that lenders will need larger amounts of it to maintain the borrower's incentive to repay. Inevitably, more potential borrowers will find that they lack the collateral necessary for the loan they're seeking.

2. *More documentation will be presented, and past lender-borrower relationships will be more important.* Lenders should attempt to know more about borrowers during recessions because default is more likely—and more expensive—when lenders are relatively ignorant. This makes it doubly hard on borrowers whose normal lenders themselves become cash constrained; for borrowers to exchange a lender who knows them well for one who does not will be expensive, if not impossible. Detailed and accurate record-keeping may make the difference in whether new financing is obtained.

3. *Noncredit terms on loans will tighten.* Tightening noncredit terms for borrowers may make it harder for them to qualify for loans, but at least lenders will be able to continue making profitable loans in hard times. For example, in a weak real estate market, lenders should require higher down payments on mortgages and be particularly wary of techniques home sellers may use to foist greater risk on the lender.

In addition, lenders may demand more *covenants* to their loans. Loan covenants are legal conditions added to the loan contract that permit the lenders to declare loans in default. Some covenants constrain managerial discretion; others specify standards of continued creditworthiness. Covenants increase the lender's ability to seize collateral while it retains much of its value.

RENEGOTIATION IN RECESSION

Hart and Moore's model also has implications for what borrowers and lenders can expect from loan renegotiations during a recession. The lender's purpose in renegotiating a loan is to achieve new combinations of cash and collateral that leave the lender better off than under the previous agreement.[6] For example, a lender will write down an unsecured loan, forgiving part of the debt to obtain collateral and immediate cash under a new agreement.

Conversely, borrowers should realize that in times of a weak economy, failure to repay a loan is likelier to have serious consequences—collateral may be seized, for example. In assessing their possibilities for a successful renegotiation, borrowers should review those assets that may be used for cash and collateral.

Lenders are best off pushing for low-risk operation of the firm. A debt-burdened borrower has a strong incentive to divert funds at the lender's expense.[7] To counter this, the lender will—in what is called a "loan workout"—actively negotiate the borrower's business plan to maximize the probability of receiving cash flows. In the loan workout, the lender should push to err on the side of safety and carefully monitor the borrower's expenses and receipts to see whether the borrower is adhering to plan. (A bank that handles a borrower's transactions is often well positioned to conduct a loan workout because it can best observe the borrower's behavior.) Cutting costs to conserve cash should almost always be part of a workout plan. A borrower who must give up something during renegotiation is less likely to default frivolously.

Both parties to the renegotiation should recognize the fundamental importance of good information. A strong relationship between lender and borrower and full, open communication are crucial to sound loan renegotiations. In a renegotiation, lenders often demand more information than in the initial loan process. Borrowers should recognize that, lacking good information, lenders ought not to make concessions in a renegotiation.

A final but crucial point following from the logic of Hart and Moore's model is one more pertinent to planning for the next recession than surviving the current one. When embarking on a relationship with a lender, borrowers too often care only about the short term, believing that all will be fine if only the lender grants the loan request. But borrowers ought to be forward-thinking, too, and ask themselves whether the lender will be helpful in hard times or force them to turn elsewhere when loan funds tighten generally. Just as lenders must look for sound borrowers, so should borrowers seek out sound lenders.

CONCLUSION

Recent theories on lending and the loan contract build on the idea that borrowers may lack adequate incentives to repay lenders. One conclusion they share is that loan defaults can have important economic consequences and lead to the failure of otherwise viable businesses. Another conclusion is that noncredit terms of loans can be expected to tighten in recessions.

In a downturn, credit terms to new borrowers normally tighten. The models attribute this tightening to the inherent conflicts that intensify between lender and borrower during recessions. Consequently, lending becomes less efficient and is more likely to lead to foreclosures and real economic losses. By tightening up lending practices, lenders may be able to increase their confidence in repayment and perhaps avoid being excessively conservative in hard times. And by anticipating potential credit problems, borrowers may be better able to minimize them.

Tighter credit terms are unpleasant for the borrower and may reduce the borrower's activity from the original plan. But they may be crucial for borrowing to continue in a tough economic environment.

ENDNOTES

1.Robert M. Townsend, "Optimal Contracts and Competitive Markets With Costly State Verification," *Journal of Economic Theory* 21 (1979) pp. 265-93.

2.Oliver Hart and John Moore, "Default and Renegotiation: A Dynamic Model of Debt," MIT Working Paper (August 1989).

3.Townsend's model can best be understood by comparing the loan contract with a venture-capital contract, whereby the investor expects to receive a share of the venture's net worth. This financing contract repays the investor an amount depending on the firm's net worth; if the investor is ignorant of the firm's position, the owner, in an effort to minimize the repayment, will likely claim that the firm has net worth. As a result, this type of contract requires the investor to always know the firm's net worth—which is costly information to obtain—and is likely only when the investor takes a large stake in the firm and the venture shows potential for substantial returns. Venture capitalists invest relatively large stakes in small start-ups and follow them closely.

4.For a precise specification of how the losses of collateral associated with liquidation relate to the optimal debt contract, see Jeffrey M. Lacker, "Collateralized Debt as the Optimal Contract," Federal Reserve Bank of Richmond Working Paper 90-3 (March 1990).

5.Michael Jensen, "Is Leverage an Invitation to Bankruptcy? On the Contrary--It Keeps Shaky Firms Out of Court," *Wall Street Journal*, February 1, 1989.

6.This article assumes that a firm's lenders are acting in concert. A natural tension between lenders often emerges in loan renegotiations, and the presence of many independent lenders may complicate renegotiation outside the framework of bankruptcy court. A lender acting independently should be cautious about infringing on the rights of other lenders; indeed, obtaining a preference over other lenders can be reversed if bankruptcy actually occurs. Worse yet, if the borrower is viewed as being in a lender's control, that lender may become liable to other lenders for the borrower's debts.

7.See Leonard I. Nakamura, "Loan Workouts and Commercial Bank Information: Why Banks Are Special," Federal Reserve Bank of Philadelphia Working Paper 89-11 (February 1989).

QUESTIONS

1. What is the role of collateral in loan contracts.? What contributions do Townsend and Hart and Moore make to better understanding loan contracts and the role of collateral?

2. How does the seizure of collateral when default occurs harm the borrower and, potentially, the lender as well?

3. Why will credit terms tighten in a recession? What conflicts does the economic downturn create between lenders and borrowers?

READING 13

Credit Flows and the Credit Crunch

Steven Strongin

The U.S. economy underwent a debt explosion in the 1980s. Widespread denunciations of the leveraging of America have become grist for both serious commentary and political worry-mongering about the future of the U.S. economy. However, recent weakness in money and credit growth combined with the continuing lackluster performance of the U.S. economy have softened the general distrust of debt growth and generated significant pressures to ease monetary policy until the rate of money and credit growth returns to historically normal rates. What is not well understood in this debate is the degree to which the changes in the make-up of U.S. credit flows that began in the 1980s has obscured the reality of the situation. Innovative financing techniques and tax related intermediation, in combination with the continuing fall-out of the thrift bailout, have combined to conceal the meaningful movements in credit flows beneath a tidal wave of substantially larger, but less meaningful financial trends.

The credit crunch, as it is called, is the outgrowth of changes in private sector loan evaluation standards and in regulatory practices that occurred in the late 1980s. Tighter capital requirements, higher deposit insurance premiums and a substantial increase in market discipline have all made it harder for some types of borrowers to qualify for credit, both in regulated and non-regulated markets. Such pressures have been cited regularly by Chairman Greenspan and other senior policy officials as part of the justification for a number of interest rate reductions in the last two years. Today, even with short term interest rates at thirteen year lows, credit growth remains anemic, raising the question of whether interest rates should be lowered until money and credit respond.

The seriousness of the situation posed by the ongoing credit crunch is clear; however, before too much weight is placed on forcing

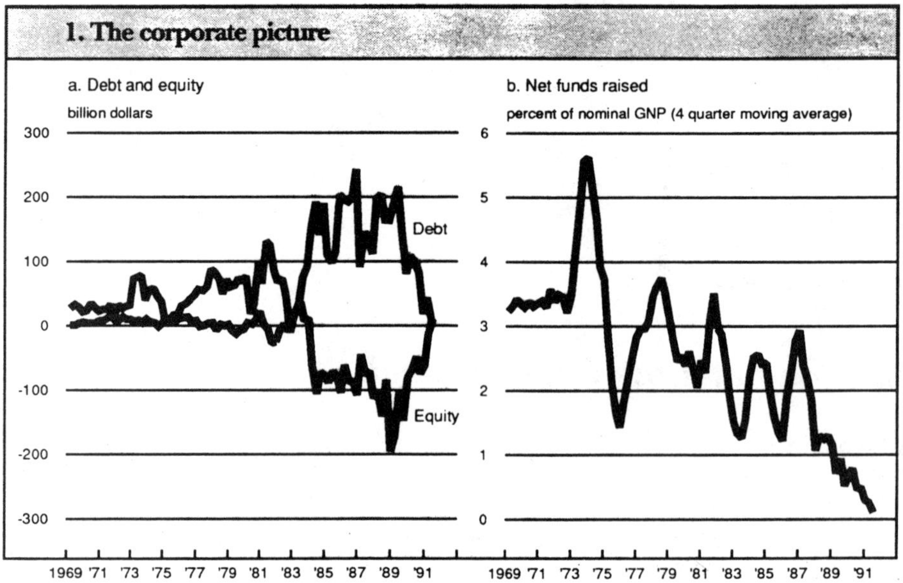

1. The corporate picture

money and credit growth to historically "normal" rates, it is important to understand just how distorted these numbers have become. The economy's need for credit is unquestioned, but those credit flows need to reflect the reality of today's financial and economic environment, not historical averages.

DISTORTIONS RUN AMOK

Probably the most discussed development in the credit markets in the 1980s was the massive build up of debt by American corporations. Between 1984 and 1990, U.S. corporations added $1.1 trillion of debt to their balance sheets. This helped generate an explosion not only in corporate debt, but also in total nonfinancial debt and total debt for the U.S. as a whole. During this same period, corporations were buying their own stock back at a rate of $90 billion a year. As can be seen in Figure 1a, these two phenomena were actually mirror images of each other.

Essentially, corporations were just crossing the word "stock" off their stock certificates and penciling in the word "debt." Very little growth related economic activity was involved in this process, just a lot of very expensive financial transactions. Nevertheless, it caused debt aggregates to soar relative to economic growth and destroyed what up until then had been a solid statistical relationship between nonfinancial debt and real growth. Today, the situation has normalized to some extent. Debt growth is down and equity growth is actually positive again. The reversal is causing debt aggregates to seem depressed relative to the go-go 1980s and, to some extent, even to the more normal periods in the 1960s and 1970s, as the excesses of the 1980s are unwound.

The economic reality underneath all the balance sheet gymnastics is startling, especially given all the hype about increased importance of the financial markets in the 1980s. Figure 1b shows total net funds raised by nonfinancial corporations from all sources as a share of nominal GNP
(stock buy-backs are netted out of the increase in debt instruments). This shows that, relative to overall economic growth, external funding of corporations has actually been of declining importance in the U.S. since the mid-1970s. This process may have accelerated somewhat beginning in 1986, but has not shifted appreciably since then. Thus, while corporate debt growth has been declining, it has done so along a 6 year trend.

There are a number of likely reasons for this trend. First, as corporations have become larger and more diversified, they are better able to finance investment out of current cash flow. Second, the high speed, highly imitative nature of modern international business practice favors large firms purchasing or licensing new technologies for rapid development over innovators acquiring external funding to build their own firms. Third, U.S. tax policy has consistently favored internal funding over debt and debt over equity, giving high cash flow firms that can invest their own cash flows a major competitive advantage, reinforcing the trend away from external finance and toward internal funding. The trend toward internal

2. U.S. government borrowing

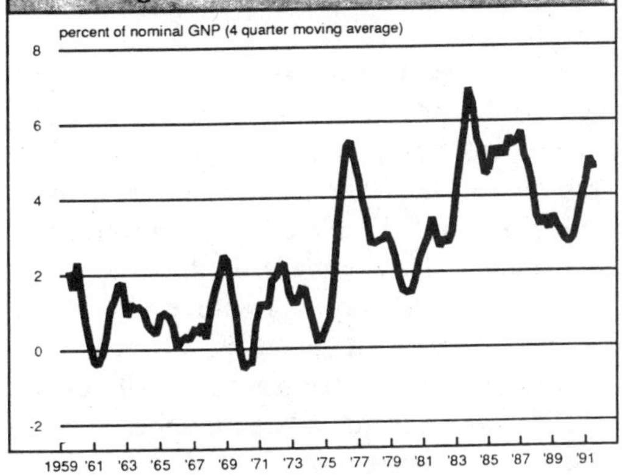

corporate funding is unmistakable and implies that corporate debt growth will in all likelihood either continue to decline or, at least, not grow as fast as historical averages would indicate. In fact, if U.S. corporations are going to reverse the leveraging of the 1980s, current downward trends may continue for some time, regardless of the growth level in the economy.

The path of government borrowing over this period provides another, no less cautionary, tale about the easy interpretation of credit numbers. The large run-up in government borrowing in the late 1970s and early 1980s shown in Figure 2 and the resulting increase in total borrowing in U.S. credit markets is well known. The recent trends and their implications are less well understood. Government borrowing began to fall as a percent of GNP beginning in 1986 and by 1989 had fallen to 3% of nominal GNP. While still sizable, this level of government borrowing was not large by international standards, putting less strain on the markets as well as damping the rate of overall credit growth relative to economic growth.

More recently, in large part due to the need to finance the thrift industry bailout, government borrowing has again exploded. This run-up, however, is very different from the earlier one. In this case, the government is assuming debts already in the economy. Very little in the way of resource allocation, the real meat and potatoes of economic growth, is actually happening. All that is really going on is that a large number of S&L liabilities are becoming (officially) liabilities of the U.S. government, damping financial debt growth and swelling nonfinancial debt. While this has significant consequences for taxpayers, it does not put any additional stress on the credit markets. Before the bailout, the S&Ls owed the money, now the government does. No new funds other than working capital for the Resolution Trust Corporation are actually required. In fact, as the government is not making the types of questionable loans that got many of the now defunct S&Ls in trouble, more funds rather than less may well be available for productive investment. Thus, nonfinancial debt growth has been pushed up relative to economic growth while financial aggregates and the savings component of the money supply are depressed. As before, much of what we observe in the credit numbers is not related to economic activity, but to large scale changes in labeling of assets.

IT'S NOT ALL BOOKKEEPING

Not all of the large movement in the credit aggregates are labeling changes. The 1981 and 1982 tax bills, building on previous tax laws, heavily favored certain types of offsetting financial transactions. Under these tax laws, it often paid to borrow money on which the interest was deductible and invest in some other, often complicated, financial shelter arrangement that paid tax free returns or produced tax write-offs. This often generated a host of offsetting financial transactions for one (and sometimes no) economic investment. The simplest examples are individuals who borrowed cash from banks to invest in IRAs in order to take advantage of the IRA tax deduction and the deductibility of interest on the bank loan. Some of the fastest growth in tax generated intermediation was in complicated Subchapter S corporations and limited partnerships arrangements that often, though not always, involved complicated real estate deals and leasebacks that could generate large numbers of off-setting financial transactions.

These tax laws generated a massive increase in purely financial credit activity that had little, if anything, to do with economic activity. This can be seen in Figure 3a, which shows as a percent of GNP the net funds flows into the nonfarm, noncorporate sector, which includes all the Subchapter S corporations and other tax shelter activity. Figure 3b shows the growth in commercial real estate mortgages, a particularly favored recipient of special tax treatments, and Figure 3c shows nonmortgage consumer debt, which includes all of the individual efforts to take

3. The tax effect

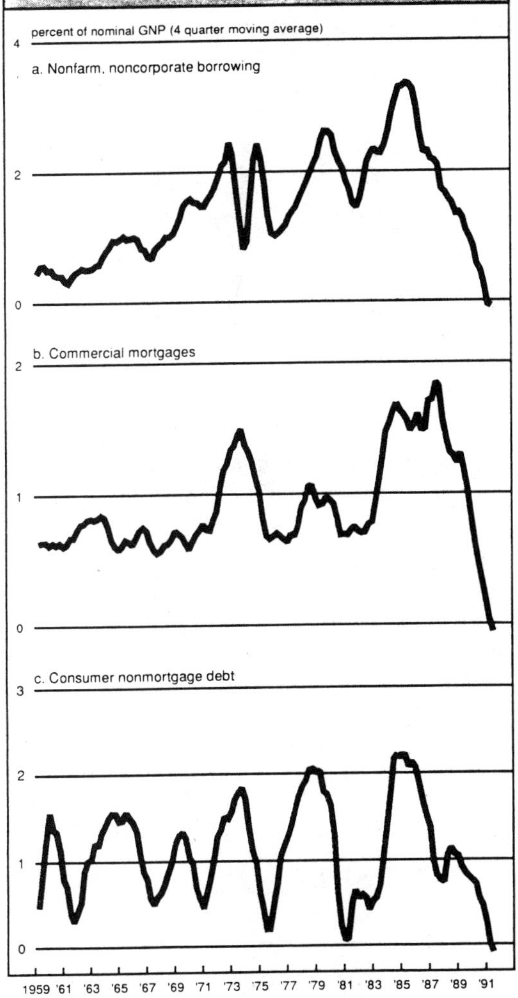

advantage of the tax laws. As can be seen, intermediation activity exploded in all of these sectors from 1981 to 1986, reaching historical highs. At their peak, the funding going into these sectors was immense. The nonfarm, noncorporate sector absorbed $129 billion in 1985. commercial mortgages peaked at $74 billion in 1986. Consumer nonmortgage debt peaked at $83 billion in 1985, for a total in the three sectors of $286 billion.

The Tax Reform Act of 1986 removed many of the incentives for purely financial transactions. Tax shelters were in large part eliminated. The special treatment of commercial real estate was severely reduced, and many of the individual incentives, such as the interest deductibility of nonmortgage consumer debt, were eliminated or phased out. The effect was enormous. By 1990, the flows into nonfarm, noncorporate credit, commercial mortgages, and consumer nonmortgage debt had dropped to $14 billion, $9 billion, and $14 billion a year, respectively, all historical lows. This means that these sectors are absorbing $249 billion a year less in credit than they did in 1985. Further, as can be seen in Figures 3a, 3b, and 3c, these changes did not occur overnight but rather constitute a continuing restructuring of credit flows. These shifts in basic trends clearly make detecting recent movements in credit creation virtually impossible.

One way to see this in terms of the overall market is shown in Figure 4, which shows net credit raised in all sectors, thus illustrating the full force of the explosion in purely financial transactions. The rapid rise from the 1981 tax bill and the equally dramatic reversal of trend that begins with the 1986 tax bill stand out in sharp relief. Credit flows peak in the fourth quarter of 1985 at an unbelievable 34% of GNP or $1.387 trillion and then descend steadily to a current level of 9% of GNP or $505 billion. It is equally apparent from this

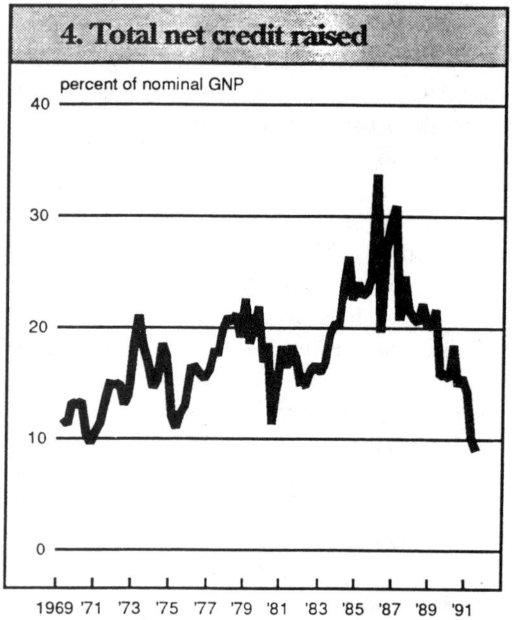

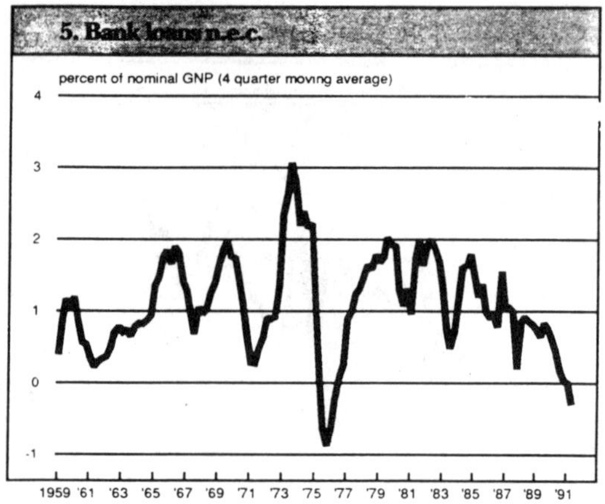

graph that detecting whether or not there has, in fact, been a decline in credit creation due to the credit crunch is much like trying to measure the effects of an electric fan in the midst of a hurricane.

Nor does it help, as some have suggested, to concentrate on the banking sector as a provider of business loans to measure the potential effects of the credit crunch. As Figure 5 shows, bank loans not elsewhere classified (where the bulk of business lending done by banks is counted) has been declining steadily as a percent of GNP since the 1970s. While the recent drop *may* be a bit faster, it is no more dramatic than other declines over this period, only some of which were in any way associated with economic slowdowns. This conclusion is further reinforced by the observation that banks were also engaged in the tax generated lending of the early 1980s as well as the subsequent decline. Consequently, bank loan numbers are subject to all of the same problems of interpretation as the numbers presented above. The fact is that, as worrisome as recent trends in money and credit growth have been in light of sluggish overall economic performance, they are, in terms of the credit numbers, at most a modest backwash in the midst of the ferocious riptides of financial restructuring.

CONCLUSION

This article has examined recent trends in credit creation and suggested that these trends are in large part the result of major shifts in intermediation patterns in the U.S. economy as well as the unwinding of the effects of the tax policies of the 1980s. These trends are so large that any evaluation of current credit numbers to determine the direction of current policy are subject to substantial uncertainty and should be treated as such. When there are major changes in financial structure, as so often has been the case in the 1970s and 1980s, policymakers must rely heavily on real economic numbers and exercise careful judgment concerning what constitutes reasonable economic performance. In such an environment, policymakers cannot rely on simple rules, or on limited sets of financial indicators. Given recent economic performance and known changes in the financial environment, concerns about the availability of credit are in all likelihood well-founded. Nevertheless, as this article has argued, we should examine the overall performance of the economy and the terms of credit availability rather than the credit flows for information to guide the future course of policy.

QUESTIONS

1. What reasons does Strongin suggest for a tightening of bank lending standards since the late 1980s?

2. What trends does Strongin identify in the issuance of corporate debt and equity and in net funds raised by corporations? Can you explain these trends in terms of the economic theory of financial structure?

3. What have been the trends in U.S. government borrowing? How does government borrowing to finance the thrift industry bailout affect economic growth?

4. How were credit flows affected by tax law changes in 1981-82 and 1986?

5. Does a decline in the relative importance of bank lending to business indicate the existence of a credit crunch? Why?

READING 14

Banking and Commerce: The Japanese Case

Sun Bae Kim

With the February 5 release of the Treasury's proposal, banking reform will be a high priority on the nation's agenda. Of the many reforms, several shatter Glass-Steagall restrictions on banks' powers, and expand the scope of banking in order to bolster the competitiveness of U.S. banks in an increasingly global market.

One example is that nonfinancial firms, such as plastics manufacturers, would be permitted to own banks. But the reverse situation, permitting banks to own shares in plastics manufacturers, is not part of the proposal and was not even debated. The notion of allowing banks to hold shares in nonfinancial firms is not without precedent. The European community plans to adopt the model of "universal" banking in 1992, and in Japan, banks have traditionally held shares in firms they lend to.

This *Letter* examines the experience of postwar Japan to identify some of the potential benefits as well as costs of a system that allows banks simultaneously to lend to an industrial firm and hold its equity.

A LITTLE FINANCE THEORY

To understand the costs and benefits of combining lending *and* shareholding requires a small dose of finance theory. The theory argues that a borrower knows more than a lender about his prospects or the actions he can take to affect his prospects. Because of this information asymmetry, the lender-borrower relationship is subject to *moral hazard*. More specifically, after obtaining funds from the lender, the borrower has an incentive to undertake investments of greater risk than originally stipulated in the contract. In other words, for the borrower, it's a version of "heads I win, tails you lose": If the gamble pays off, the borrower gets all of the "upside gain" while the lender just gets the fixed sum of interest; if the gamble goes sour, the lender and the borrower share the loss.

A lender anticipates such behavior when negotiating the terms of the loan in the first place and demands an interest rate commensurate with the highest amount of risk the borrower can undertake. This preempts any possible loss through risk-shifting by the borrower, but ultimately at a cost to society. Suppose that bankruptcies are costly; that is, the transfer of ownership of the firm's assets from the shareholders to the creditors in the event of default imposes some deadweight loss. Deadweight losses include legal costs as well as indirect costs such as internal losses due to disruption in production when the firm encounters financial distress. Since the lender demands a higher interest rate in anticipation of moral hazard, it implies a higher probability of bankruptcy and hence higher *expected* bankruptcy costs. In a competitive market, these expected deadweight costs will be passed on to the borrower in the form of a higher interest rate.

In principle, lenders can check borrowers' propensity for risk-taking by monitoring them and exercising restrictive covenants. But monitoring itself is costly, and that cost is ultimately borne by the borrower. Indeed, modern finance theory ascribes the very raison d'être of banks to their superior capacity to screen and monitor borrowers economically. However, the fact remains that the moral hazard problem will impose a deadweight loss to the economy in the form of higher financing costs faced by firms. Moreover, the potential magnitude of such deadweight losses will be greater the higher the corporate sector's leverage, since the greater will then be the severity of the moral hazard problem.

THE JAPANESE PUZZLE

According to the theory outlined above, the financing costs for the typical Japanese firm should have been very high in the 1950s and 1960s. Emerging from the ashes of World War II, Japanese firms typically had little accumulated profits to undertake investments; that is, their need to rely on outside financing was high. This was all the more so because growth during this period was concentrated in heavy and chemical industries. These industries were essentially being rebuilt, requiring investment in large increments, rather than being expanded, which requires only marginal increments that are more amenable to financing out of retained earnings. But judging from the performance of Japanese industries and the overall economy, the Japanese financial system appears to have been relatively unimpaired by the sort of information-related problems described above.

How were Japanese firms able to draw large and sustained flows of funds from the banks despite low collateral or net worth? Traditional explanations emphasized interest rate regulations. Interest rates on bank deposits were artificially suppressed to low levels so that industries, in turn, could borrow these funds at low rates. This explanation, however, has been seriously challenged by growing evidence that the legal and institutional attributes of the Japanese banking system were primarily responsible for

Corporate Shareholders

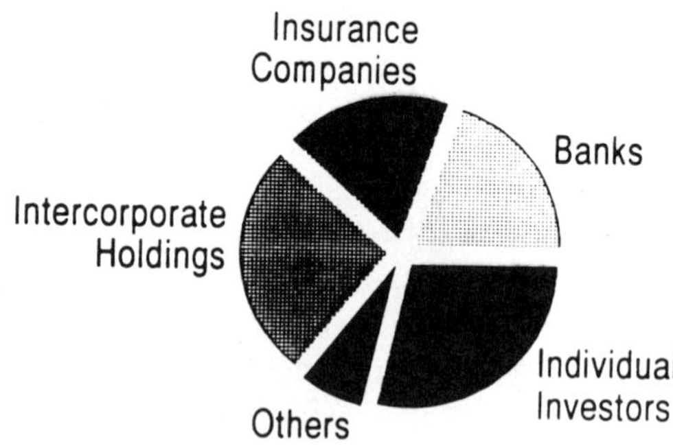

JAPAN

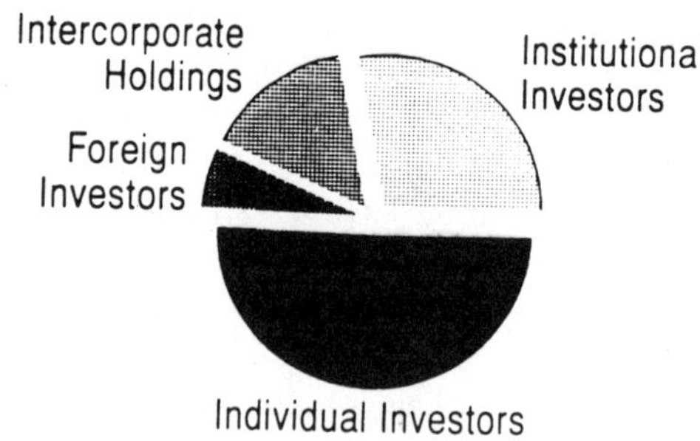

U.S.

attenuating the potentially high deadweight costs of an imperfect market.

Since the occupation era, Japan has had its own version of the Glass-Steagall Act, but with a notable difference. Throughout most of the postwar period, until 1987, Japanese banks were allowed to hold up to 10 percent of the outstanding shares in any single company. In effect, however, Japanese banks could hold more than 10 percent through cross-holding effects; that is, if the bank holds 10 percent in firm A and 10 percent in firm B, and firm A holds some shares, say 30 percent in firm B, then the bank effectively holds 13 percent of firm B (10 percent plus 10 percent of 30 percent). The effects of these intercorporate shareholdings have not been closely monitored. In this legal setting, the typical corporate financing arrangement in Japan featured the bank as the principal lender as well as major shareholder of industrial enterprises.

The chart illustrates the differences in corporate ownership structure between Japan and the U.S. In Japan, financial institutions have held close to 40 percent of corporate shares and constitute the largest shareholders. Out of this 40 percent, commercial and trust banks together account for about 20 percent; insurance companies hold roughly another 20 percent. In the U.S., where financial institutions cannot own shares, individual investors have been the largest group of shareholders, holding roughly one-half of the total corporate shares outstanding. Intercorporate shareholding is much more extensive in Japan, claiming over 25 percent of the total compared to 15 percent in the U.S. Because of these cross-shareholdings, the *effective* holding of corporate equity by Japanese banks are likely to be much larger than the reported figure.

...BOTH A LENDER AND A SHAREHOLDER BE...

If lenders are also shareholders, then finance theory argues that the costs of financing should be lower. A lender who holds equity is less likely than a pure lender to force a firm into bankruptcy when it encounters temporary financial problems. If the firm goes bankrupt, the value of its share held by the bank will go to zero, so the bank will have a greater incentive to behave as a "committed investor." Therefore, if a bank holds a firm's shares, the probability of bankruptcy is reduced and so is the expected cost of bankruptcy. This lower cost is passed on to the firm in the form of more favorable financing terms.

Likewise, if a major lender is also a significant shareholder, the cost of bankruptcy when it is declared actually is lower. When shareholders and creditors of a bankrupt firm are largely the same entities, the firm's assets need not change hands. This avoids much of the cost of protracted legal battles among the various claimants to the firm. Again, the saving from this lower expected cost is passed on to the firm.

The evidence seems to be consistent with these predictions. Large Japanese firms appear to avoid bankruptcies in predicaments that elsewhere would have placed them under receivership. When bankruptcies actually are declared, reorganizations are often swift and less disruptive than is usually the case in the U.S. In many cases, insolvency prompts the lead shareholder bank to orchestrate a rescue effort. The main bank would not only inject new loans into the firm, but, by guaranteeing existing debt claims by other creditors in the consortium, also would ensure their rollover. The most celebrated case is that of Sumitomo Bank's rescue of Mazda Motors in the early 1970s, turning the company around from the verge of bankruptcy to one of the industry's most profitable firms.

Finally, allowing banks to hold equity would reduce the bias in the lending or monitoring pattern typically associated with banks that cannot own shares. The conventional bank that cannot hold shares tends to be more concerned about the probability of bankruptcy than about the best or even the likeliest prospects of the firm. This "conservative" penchant is natural for a non-shareholding bank because it cannot share in the "upside return" of the firm; the best it can do is to recoup principal plus interest while the worst it can do is to lose the entire amount of investment. The scope of Japanese banks to share in the firm's upside return may explain their greater willingness to take calculated risks promising high payoffs.

WHY NOT U.S. BANKS?

The arguments in favor of a financial system that allows equity participation by banks must be tempered by at least two sets of considerations, one economic and the other political. The first relates to the issue of risk and the second to the concentration of economic power.

Equity is in general riskier than ordinary bank loans. Allowing banks to own equity shares, therefore, raises the problem that banks will assume undue levels of risk with depositors' funds. Under a system where banks' downside loss is protected by deposit insurance, banks' access to a risky security such as corporate equity may intensify the moral hazard of the banks themselves, a problem that has become all too familiar in the wake of the S&L crisis in the U.S. Therefore, systematic checks on the amount of risk banks may undertake need to be carefully considered. In the case of postwar Japan, the government took an active role in monitoring the banks. The task was feasible because of the small number of banks in the system—which takes us to the next consideration.

The efficiency gains from allowing banks to hold industrial securities may come at the cost of increased concentration of resources and power in the banking system. How much concentration to accept is, in the final analysis, a political decision. In Japan, the limit of bank equity holding was reduced from 10 percent to 5 percent, effective in 1987. The change reflected a policy shift in Japan in favor of decreased economic concentration. Given that the U.S. is traditionally much more wary of concentration of power than Japan is, the increased concentration likely to emerge if banks are given commerce powers will no doubt be met with greater resistance here.

CONCLUSION

Banking reform will likely remain at the fore of public debate in the coming months and years. Appraisal and comparison of foreign systems of bank regulation provide valuable insights into policy choices currently facing the U.S., despite differences in economic, social, and political context. In this regard, the experience of postwar Japan suggests the possible advantages, as well as the attendant costs, of giving banks the ability to lend to and hold equity shares in the same corporation. It bears noting that the Japanese system is neither unique, nor is its apparent success in supporting a vigorous economy an isolated event. As suggested in an earlier issue of this *Letter* (June 1, 1990), other major industrialized economies, such as France, Germany, and Italy, have allowed their banks similar latitude. With the European community's plan to adopt the universal banking model in 1992, the issue of expanded securities powers for U.S. banks will undoubtedly warrant public consideration and scrutiny.

QUESTIONS

1. How does allowing banks to hold corporate stock affect the pattern of shareholding in Japan and help alleviate the moral hazard problem inherent in bank lending?

2. What differences exist between the pattern of shareholding in Japan and the U.S.? Why do these differences exist?

3. What are the advantages of letting banks hold corporate stock? Should the U.S. alter its banking laws to enable its banks to hold stock in the corporations they lend to? Why?

READING 15

Interest Rate Risk: What's a Bank to Do?

Sherrill Shaffer

In today's competitive environment, banks and regulators alike must become more familiar with ways to measure and control interest rate risk, despite the complexities involved. Fluctuations in interest rates can either raise or lower the net worth of a financial institution when its assets and liabilities do not respond in the same direction or by equal amounts. True, gains and losses may tend to average out over time if interest rates move in both directions over the long term; nevertheless, the short-term losses from even temporary adverse conditions can be very costly. For example, the rise in interest rates in the early 1980s was a leading cause of losses in the savings and loan industry.

To do anything about interest rate risk, a bank must first measure how much it has. Unfortunately, traditional measures of such risk, while convenient, provide only rough approximations at best. Analysts have known better measures for years, but banks have been slow to adopt them because of their complexity and data requirements. Similarly, regulators to date have sometimes appeared ambivalent about encouraging banks in this direction.

Once it has adopted a reliable measure of interest rate risk, a bank must choose how to respond. Techniques now exist for hedging against interest rate movements, but those same techniques can just as easily be used for speculative purposes. Moreover, hedging involves direct costs, as well as the forgone profits that an unhedged bank would have earned had it gambled correctly on a change in rates. Gone are the days, however, when a bank can safely ignore the issue.

Recent losses and the current economic environment strongly suggest that many banks are exposed to more risk than is desirable and that at least some degree of hedging is essential. Interest rates have fluctuated much more over the past decade than in earlier periods, implying larger potential losses for an unhedged portfolio. Moreover, even though interest rates are currently lower than in the early 1980s, banks' operating margins tend to be thinner and more variable—and hence more vulnerable to losses due to interest rate risk—because financial markets are more competitive.

MEASURING INTEREST RATE RISK

The traditional measure of interest rate risk is the maturity gap between assets and liabilities, which is based on the repricing interval of each component of the balance sheet—that is, the period of time over which the interest rate is required by contract to remain fixed. The repricing interval of a fixed-rate account equals its maturity. For adjustable-rate assets or liabilities, the repricing interval is given by the date of the next adjustment.

To compute the maturity gap, an analyst would first group assets and liabilities according to their repricing intervals, such as less than three months, three months to one year, and so on. Within each category, the gap is then expressed as the dollar amount of assets minus liabilities. This approach, however, offers no single summary statistic that expresses the bank's interest rate risk.

Traditionally, depository institutions have had longer average maturities on the asset side than on the liability side. For example, smaller banks and thrifts, especially, often use deposit liabilities payable on demand to fund long-term assets such as fixed-rate mortgage loans. Such banks would have a large negative maturity gap in the shorter-maturity brackets (short-term liabilities exceed short-term assets) and a large positive gap in the longer-maturity brackets (long-term assets exceed long-term liabilities). In this situation, a rise in interest rates would lead to a higher cost of funds before loan rates could adjust, narrowing the bank's interest rate spread and lowering its profits.

Even though the maturity gap can suggest how a bank's condition will respond to a given change in interest rates, it omits certain important factors, including cash flow, unequal interest rates on assets and liabilities, and initial net worth. It is therefore more appropriate to view the maturity gap as an indicator of a bank's liquidity risk, not its interest rate risk: in the event of massive withdrawals of deposits, the rate of withdrawal is limited by the maturity of the deposit accounts; likewise, the rate at which assets can be liquidated to meet the withdrawals is limited by the maturity of loans and other assets. Liquidity risk is important and plays a valid role in maturity-gap management. However, we need a better measure of interest rate risk.

A Conceptual Alternative. The "right" theory for the problem was advanced at least as far back as 1938, when Frederick Macaulay formulated the concept of *duration*. Duration is usually presented as an account's weighted average time to repricing, where the weights are discounted components of cash flow. Originally, however, the technique was devised to determine what percentage change in present value would result from a 1 percent change in the interest rate.[1] In its simplest form, duration provides the correct answer to this question only under special conditions. The most restrictive conditions are that interest rate movements be small and that long-term interest rates be equal to short-term rates at all times. (See *A Simple Example of Duration Analysis*, p. 125.)

A bank is perfectly hedged against interest rate risk when the duration of its assets, *weighted by dollars of assets*, equals the duration of its liabilities, *weighted by dollars of liabilities*.[2] The difference between these two weighted durations is called the duration gap, distinct from the maturity gap discussed above. The larger the duration gap, the more sensitive the bank's net worth will be to a given change in interest rates.

The key element distinguishing duration from maturity is the cash flow, in terms of both its timing and its amount. For a zero coupon bond or a so-called "bullet" loan, the only payment comes at maturity; in such cases, the duration equals the maturity. However, when interim payments are scheduled, each payment received can be reinvested while each payment owed must be funded. Changes in interest rates that occur before the last payment will affect the value of all remaining payments and hence the net worth of the contract or the portfolio to which it belongs.

Likewise, when loan rates differ from deposit rates (as they must in order for the bank to earn a positive spread), the cash-flow amounts will differ between an asset and an otherwise identical liability. Duration incorporates this distinction, whereas the maturity gap does not.

In addition, the initial net worth also affects an organization's sensitivity to interest rate changes. When assets do not initially equal liabilities, then net worth can change with interest rates even when the duration of assets equals that of liabilities. That is, setting the duration of assets equal to that of liabilities does not by itself necessarily eliminate interest rate risk; these durations need to be weighted by dollars of assets and liabilities to achieve that goal.

Why have these additional factors not been universally incorporated into management and accounting practices more than half a century after their importance was first recognized? There are two reasons, one institutional and the other technical.

Until 1980, not only were interest rates in the U.S. relatively stable, but federal regulations also set the maximum interest rate that banks could pay on deposits. Banks consequently believed they had little reason to worry about interest rate risks. However, the success of money market mutual funds during the 1970s demonstrated that regulatory ceilings on interest rates provided false security to banks, as depositors simply shifted their funds from bank accounts to more lucrative investments. After 1980, the institutional environment shifted as regulatory rate ceilings were phased out just as market interest rates were rising to record levels.

Even though banks now have a stronger motive for measuring and managing interest rate risk than before, several technical factors make it difficult to apply duration analysis correctly. First, the detailed information on cash flows required for duration analysis presents a computational and accounting burden. Second, the true cash-flow patterns are not well known for certain types of

A Simple Example of Duration Analysis

To keep calculations as simple and clear as possible, let's look at a balance sheet in which a single-payment two-year loan of $100 is funded by two successive one-year $100 certificates of deposit. (Note that this assumes no initial equity or reserves.) We want to do two things: calculate the duration gap for this portfolio and examine the effect of changing interest rates on the present value of profits (which defines the market value of the portfolio).

Suppose initially that the interest rate is 6 percent for both the loan and the CD. (This means that the bank earns zero spread and, consequently, no profit—not a realistic scenario, but one easy to follow.) At the end of the first year, the bank pays $106 on the first CD and takes in $100 for the second CD for a net cash flow of -$6. In two years it pays out $106 more. The loan is a "bullet loan," requiring no repayment until it matures. At that time the entire loan, plus interest for two years at 6 percent, will be repaid: $100 x 1.06 x 1.06 = $112.36. So the bank's cash flows, both undiscounted and discounted at a 6 percent annual rate, can be summarized as follows:

Year	Income	(Discounted)	Expense	(Discounted)	Profit	(Discounted)
1	0	(0)	$6.00	($5.66)	-$6.00	(-$5.66)
2	$112.36	($100.00)	$106.00	($94.34)	$6.36	($5.66)
Total		($100.00)		($100.00)		(0)

The net present value of the portfolio is zero.

Duration for each side of the balance sheet is calculated as the weighted average time to repricing, where the weight in each period up to repricing is the discounted cash flow as a proportion of total present value. Since the loan has only a single payment coming at the end, the duration of assets is 1 year x ($0/$100) + 2 years x ($100/$100) = 2 years, the same as its maturity. Likewise, each CD has one payment coming at its maturity, so the duration of the liability side is 1 year x ($100/$100) = 1 year.

The duration gap for the entire portfolio is the *difference* between the asset duration, weighted by the present value of assets, and the liability duration, weighted by the present value of liabilities: $100 x 2 years - $100 x 1 year = 100 dollar-years. By comparison, the maturity gap is -$100 in the zero-to-one-year range and $100 in the one-to-two-year range, as seen from the outset.

Like that of the typical small bank, this portfolio has a positive duration gap. Consequently, duration theory tells us that an increase in interest rates will *lower* the present value of the portfolio. We can demonstrate this directly. Suppose there is an immediate, unanticipated increase in the market interest rate to 8 percent. Both the loan and the deposit are locked into the original 6 percent rate for the first year. But in the second year, the deposit rate adjusts to 8 percent while the loan rate is still fixed at 6 percent. Discounting at the new market rate of 8 percent, the cash flows become:

Year	Income	(Discounted)	Expense	(Discounted)	Profit	(Discounted)
1	0	(0)	$6.00	($5.56)	-$6.00	(-$5.56)
2	$112.36	($96.33)	$108.00	($92.59)	$4.36	($3.74)
Total		($96.33)		($98.15)		(-$1.82)

(Example is continued at top of next page)

The net present value of the portfolio declines from zero to -$1.82.

We can compare this drop in present value with that predicted by duration theory. As discussed by George Kaufman (1984), the change in the present value of the portfolio equals the negative of the duration gap, times the change in interest rates, divided by the original discount factor. In our example, this equals $-100 \times .02/1.06^2 = -$ $1.78, very close to the change of -$1.82 computed directly.

accounts, such as demand deposits or passbook savings accounts; they are likely to vary with the size or timing of a change in market interest rates, making it all the harder to quantify the associated interest rate risk. For example, during the 1970s and 1980s, demand deposits continued to pay zero interest while nonbank instruments paid increasingly high rates; in response, commercial firms devised new cash-management practices to economize on their demand balances, which led to lower, more volatile demand balances than previously seen. Prepayments similarly complicate the measurement or prediction of cash flows on home mortgages.

And finally, a more complex version of duration is needed to reflect the fact that long-term interest rates do not always equal short-term rates and indeed may move independently of each other. For these reasons, many institutions have thus far chosen either to retain the simpler, but less accurate, maturity gap methods, or to rely on computer scenarios without always acknowledging their linkage to duration. In the latter case, a better understanding of duration can safeguard against misuse of the simulation results.

A Numerical Approach. Some banks simulate the impact of various risk scenarios on their portfolios, asking, for example, "If interest rates rise by 2 percentage points, how much will my net worth fall?" When done properly, this technique essentially replicates the same bottom line as duration theory while bypassing the more sophisticated mathematical derivations. Indeed, a computer simulation can be made to yield a single summary statistic representing the bank's interest rate risk, which will then equal its duration gap. A useful way of thinking about both the level of risk and how to hedge it, this technique may be thought of as "brute force" duration analysis. (The box gives a simple example.) However, drawbacks remain.

The major complication is, again, the need for detailed cash-flow data for assets and liabilities. When loans are repaid monthly and interest payments accrue daily, for example, correct calculations are more difficult than in the simple example shown in the box. A computer scenario is only as useful as it is realistic, and either oversimplifying the cash flows or omitting them from the model entirely can lead to nasty surprises. As it happens, the inclusion of cash flows is an unavoidable complexity—a cost of doing business in today's market environment. One possible response to this cost is to simplify contractual payment schedules according to the trade-off between the benefits of such simplification (easier calculation of portfolio effects) and the costs (lumpier cash flows and other inconveniences).

Likewise, computers alone cannot solve the problem of forecasting cash-flow patterns for some assets and liabilities. Simulations often rely on historical data to estimate the duration of savings accounts, mortgages, and other types of accounts. This backward-looking approach may give good estimates of cash flow under the historical pattern of interest rates, but possibly not if the pattern changes in the future; for that, a more theoretical approach may provide a better forecast. Techniques to address these thorny questions have been under development for several years now. For example, several computer programs designed to model mortgage prepayments as interest rates change ar now commercially available, and even better answers can be expected in the future.

Choosing appropriate interest rate scenarios within which to explore portfolio effects remains more art than science. It is not enough to project a given rise or fall in rates across the board; the term structure may shift, with long rates changing either more or less than short rates, and each variation can have a different impact on overall net worth. The computer cannot tell an analyst how to do this. But even so, the computer-based scenario method can prove more flexible and require less effort than the strictly theoretical duration approach.

CONTROLLING INTEREST RATE RISK

Once a bank has measured its interest rate risk, what action should it take? Some theories of banking consider it essential that banks accept some degree of interest rate risk, and most bankers prefer not to hedge completely against such risk. However, for a bank to profit consistently from changes in interest rates requires the ability to forecast interest rates better than the rest of the market. Obviously, not everyone can be better than average all the time.

The experience of the 1980s suggests that more hedging would be an improvement for the banking industry, even if a complete hedge is not best. There are several ways of bringing a bank's duration gap near zero to construct a hedge. The various approaches generally involve some combination of adjusting the portfolio of assets and liabilities or using nontraditional financial instruments.

Adjusting the Portfolio. Possibly the simplest, most conventional solution is to adjust the maturity, repricing, and *payment schedules* of assets and liabilities. In its simplest form, this approach does not require exotic instruments or strategies; in fact, many banks already use it in a general way.

Consider the example of a small bank or thrift with long-term fixed-rate mortgages funded by short-term CDs. The bank may shorten its asset duration to reduce interest rate risk by holding adjustable-rate mortgages (ARMs) instead of fixed-rate ones, thereby changing the repricing interval of assets. A drawback here is that the demand for ARMs may be substantially weaker in some markets than that for fixed-rate mortgages. Accordingly, a bank may not be able to go as far with this strategy as it would like, and it may also have to accept a lower expected return or spread. A second drawback is that an ARM's cash-flow pattern itself may change following large movements in interest rates: if rates fall sharply, ARMs are frequently refinanced using fixed-rate mortgages; and if interest rates rise very much, ARMs may suffer a higher default rate. These changes in the cash-flow pattern would need to be modeled in order to choose the right amount of ARMs to provide the desired degree of hedging against interest rate risk. A third drawback is that most ARMs are sold with a cap on interest rates, leaving the bank exposed to risk if market rates rise above the cap.

Other actions that a bank can take to shorten its average asset duration include holding short-term securities and lending overnight—for example, in the interbank market. Moreover, early amortization by means of accelerated or fixed-amortization payment schedules can reduce the duration of loans.

Another element of portfolio adjustment involves matching the amounts of assets and liabilities within each duration category. For example, suppose a bank found that its savings accounts behave like a long-duration deposit, even though in principle depositors are free to withdraw at any time. Armed with this information, the bank could then try to match the amount of its savings deposits with the amount of its fixed-rate mortgages, relying on short-duration CDs and other deposits to fund any short-duration assets. In this way the overall weighted duration of liabilities can be brought close to that of the bank's assets, resulting in a hedged balance sheet.

As the example suggests, duration matching is often applied to the balance sheet on an item-by-item basis, where it can provide only an imprecise hedge. More exact hedging is possible if the approach is applied instead to the portfolio as a whole, taking advantage of the fact that a balance between durations of weighted assets and weighted liabilities does not require a perfect match between any subset of the assets and liabilities.

However, a portfolio that is perfectly matched ("immunized") at one set of interest rates will typically require rebalancing as soon as rates move. Such rebalancing can involve transactions costs, as well as more complicated calculations if individual components of the balance sheet are not matched. In addition, at some point greater precision in hedging may require more exotic instruments or techniques.

Using nontraditional Financial Instruments. Within the past decade, banks have increasingly turned to such hedging instruments as asset-backed securities, futures, options, and swaps.[3] Their adoption has been concentrated among the large banks, however, and has tended to meet with suspicion from small bankers (who view them as a costly and unnecessary complication) and even from regulators (who view them as another means by which banks can take on more risk.)

There is some truth in all these views. A wider range of instruments requires more resources to manage, but these instruments, if managed well, can save resources in the long run. And indeed, additional instruments can be used either to reduce or to increase overall portfolio risk, according to the intention and expertise of a bank's management and staff. Examiners would need special training to distinguish good from bad. But as with fire, informed use beats uninformed neglect.

Securitization. Traditionally, bankers have viewed the activities of originating and holding a loan as inseparable. More recently, however, they have recognized that the activities are truly distinct, such that the originating institution may differ from the institution that holds the asset to maturity. A bank may originate a loan, shortly thereafter sell the loan for a fee to a third party, and subsequently repeat the process.

When a loan is sold, it may be marketed alone or as part of a package of loans. A common approach is to bundle a number of similar loans, such as auto loans, credit-card loans, or home mortgages, and sell the package at a specified yield—a process called "securitization," since it converts loans into a contractual stream of payments resembling a bond or some other security. The similarity of loans within a bundle makes assessing its risk easier, while the multiplicity of loans allows some diversification of default risk.

Although fee income from the sale has drawn attention as a motivation for this activity, an equally important aspect is that the loan's effective maturity *to the bank* is only the interval between origination and sale. Therefore, securitization may substantially reduce the bank's average asset duration and, in the case of a typical small bank with long-term mortgages and short-term deposits, reduce its interest rate risk.

The success of this method requires, among other things, a demand for the securitized asset. If interest rates rise, a loan with a fixed rate suddenly below market is no longer an attractive purchase. It could be sold only at a discount, forcing the originating bank to realize an immediate loss.

Recent evidence also suggests that combining traditional banking with securitizing may tend to raise a bank's costs.[4] This result could be viewed as reflecting a cost of managing interest rate risk: you don't get something for nothing. Subject to these limitations, securitization offers an attractive opportunity for banks to shorten their asset duration.[5] Of course, misuse is possible. Banks can buy as well as sell securitized assets, and a bank that buys a package of securitized loans may lengthen its asset duration, increasing its interest rate risk. For this reason a bank should make sure that it ends up on the right side of a deal for its own portfolio needs; indeed, some banks have suffered losses by neglecting this principle.

Swaps. A swap is a contract that trades payment streams (but not the underlying principal or associated credit risk) between two parties. For example, a bank having a fixed-rate mortgage with 10 years remaining to maturity may prefer to receive a variable-rate payment stream in order to shorten its asset duration and reduce its interest rate risk. Suppose it finds another institution that has made a variable-rate commercial loan of equivalent principal amount with 10 years left to maturity. If that institution would prefer to receive fixed-rate payments, the bank can contract to pass through its mortgage payments to the second institution in return for receiving a pass-through of the variable-rate commercial loan payments. The mortgage itself remains on the bank's books, while the commercial loan stays on the books of the second institution. Such a contract is known as a swap.

Interest rate swaps can reduce interest rate risk either by converting a fixed-rate income stream to a variable-rate stream, as in the example, or by converting a variable-rate expense stream to a fixed-rate stream. Used in the first way, a swap shortens the duration of assets; used in the second way, it increases the duration of liabilities. Either or both approaches can help overcome the typical bank's mismatch between long-duration assets and short-duration liabilities.[6]

The arrangement has several shortcomings, however. First, if the commercial borrower defaults, then the variable-rate income stream stops and the bank must turn elsewhere if it desires to continue trading fixed-rate for floating-rate payments. By that time, interest rates may have changed, making it difficult for the bank to find another counterparty at the original terms. This possibility shows that the hedge is not perfect.

Second, the arrangement seemingly requires the bank to find an institution with repricing needs exactly opposite its own. However, approximate matches can be accommodated by more complicated contracts involving more than two assets or parties. A related problem is that if all banks want to be on the same side of the deal, there may not be enough counterparties willing to take the other side.

Futures. An interest rate futures contract is an agreement between two parties to buy (or sell) a fixed-income asset, such as a Treasury security, fora fixed price at a specified date. The holder of such a contract earns a positive or negative profit based on the difference between the specified delivery price and the price at which the underlying securities can be sold after taking delivery.[7]

Unlike securitization and swaps, which alter the repricing intervals of a bank's assets and liabilities, futures can be used to create cash flows that offset losses on the original portfolio. For example, a bank that would lose net worth if interest rates rise can reduce this risk by *selling* bond futures, locking in the current interest rate and, in effect, selling bonds short.[8] If interest rates rise before the futures contracts expire, bond prices will fall and the bank can close out its futures position at a profit by buying either the bonds or additional futures at a lower price. The profits on the futures offset losses due to declining interest rate spreads on the rest of the portfolio. If interest rates fall, losses on the futures are offset by increased interest rate spreads on the rest of the portfolio. However, it should be emphasized that futures, like any hedging device, cannot totally eliminate all risk; some sources of residual risk remain even after careful application of futures.[9]

Although any interest-rate futures contract can provide a hedge against interest rate risk, futures on U.S. Treasury instruments have special advantages: (1) there is negligible risk of default on the underlying instruments; (2) the relevant markets are highly liquid; and (3) the yields move more in line with market interest rates than with factors unique to the instrument, making them ideal for hedging diversified portfolios.[10]

WHAT NEXT?

Fundamental changes in the regulatory and market environment have made interest rate risk a vital issue. The importance of this risk underlies the explosive growth of banking's involvement in so-called derivative instruments (such as futures and options, which are "derived" from other financial contracts) and in new strategies over the past decade. In the period from 1980 to 1985, the volume of interest rate futures held by banks grew tenfold, as did the volume of loan sales by banks in the period from 1983 to 1988.[11] Interest rate swaps grew from an estimated world market of $3 billion in 1982 to well over $100 billion just three years later and to over $500 billion by 1987; the outstanding amount of pass-through securities backed by residential mortgages reached $769 billion by 1988.[12]

However, even though the aggregate volume has grown dramatically, these new activities have been concentrated in a relatively few large banks. For example, in the second quarter of 1989, nine money-center banks accounted for about 40 percent of total loan sales, and 54 banks accounted for more than 90 percent.[13] Most of the nation's 13,000 banks have remained hesitant about plunging in, some on the premise that the fundamental business of banking hasn't changed and therefore doesn't require new approaches, and others on the premise that the costs of learning and managing the new techniques would outweigh any benefit. Such arguments appear short-sighted in today's combination of thinner margins, aggressive competition, and volatile interest rates.

As more banks perceive the need to reduce their interest rate risk, regulators need to be trained in evaluating the use of the new techniques, since a debate inevitably arises when managers and regulators disagree on an institution's position. A recent dispute occurred in Kansas, where regulators argued that Franklin Savings Association was insolvent even though management (and eventually a federal court) held that it was solvent once its sophisticated hedging techniques were properly recognized.[14] Traditional accounting rules further cloud the issue: when the balance sheet is not marked to market, a gain on the portfolio will not be fully reflected on the books, whereas a corresponding loss on the hedge may have to be recorded. However, the Financial Accounting Standards Board allows a loss on futures or other hedging programs to be kept off the books if it "correlates with and offsets" an unbooked capital gain.[15]

To avoid such uncertainty and waste, regulatory guidelines must keep pace with the industry. The Basle accord on banks' risk-based capital requirements recognized this need by incorporating a commitment to augment guidelines over the next few years to account for interest rate risk. This resolve was reiterated in a recent Treasury Department proposal to reform the financial system.[16]

The only alternative would be to ban modern hedging techniques, a move that would have at least two unfortunate consequences. First, it would leave the burden of interest rate risk on the banks and the already strained federal safety net. Second, it would place U.S. banks at a further competitive disadvantage relative not only to major players from other nations, but also to other U.S. financial institutions.

In summary, we can't turn back the clock now. Regulators and banks alike need to become more familiar with measures of interest rate risk and the ways of hedging it.

ENDNOTES

1.Many people are surprised to realize that this response factor corresponds to units of time: percent, divided by percent per year, equals years. Excellent introductions to duration theory are provided by Kaufman (1984), French (1988), and, on a more academic plane, Grove (1974). To see that the duration of an asset need not equal its maturity, consider a two-year loan for $200 at 8 percent repaid in equal installments of $112.15 each year. The present values of the cash payments are $103.85 and $96.15, so the duration of the loan equals (1 x $103.85 + 2 x $96.15)/$200 = 1.48 years. More generally, the formula for duration is $[\Sigma^T_{t=1} tP_t/(1+r_t)^t]/[\Sigma^T_{t=1} P_t/(1+r_t)^t]$, where P_t is the cash flow in period t, r_t is the interest rate in period t (usually assumed in textbooks to be constant across t), and T is the maturity of the loan. The box on p. 125 explains in more detail how duration is calculated.

2.This implication of duration theory was first derived by Samuelson (1945) and Hicks (1946). The property is strictly true either under simplifying assumptions (if the simple concept of duration is used) or when an appropriate generalization of duration is used, as discussed in Kaufman et al. (1983). The requirement of weighting is discussed later.

3.A number of these instruments are described by Grumball (1987).

4.See Mester (1990).

5.See Nadler (1987) for an argument that even community banks can benefit from securitization.

6.Even community banks can benefit from this seemingly intricate arrangement; see Findlay (1987).

7.Morris (1989) provides an excellent introduction to the potential use of interest rate futures by banks, while Koppenhaver (1986) describes the role of options on such futures.

8.See Green (1986), p. 86.

9.Morris (1989) discusses several types of residual risk.

10.For a small, undiversified bank, a futures contract on the sector most heavily represented in its portfolio may also be an effective hedge, not only against interest rate risk but also against price or credit risk, if the futures market is liquid and default risk on the contract is low. Examples might be oil futures for Texas banks or commodities futures for agricultural banks.

11.See Parkinson and Spindt (1985), p. 226, and Boemio and Edwards (1989).

12.See Bank for International Settlements (1986), pp. 39-43; Smith et al. (1988); and Boemio and Edwards (1989).

13.See Mester (1990), p. 5.

14.See Labaton (1990) and Milligan (1991).

15.See Milligan (1991), pp. 54-55.

16.See U.S. Department of the Treasury (1991).

REFERENCES

Bank for International Settlements. *Recent Innovations in International Banking*. Basle: BIS, 1986.

Boemio, Thomas R., and Gerald A. Edwards, Jr. "Asset Securitization: A Supervisory Perspective," *Federal Reserve Bulletin* 75 (October 1989) pp. 659-69.

Findlay, David M. "Swap Applications for Community Banks," *Journal of Commercial Bank Lending* (December 1987) pp. 9-14.

French, George E. "Measuring the Interest-Rate Exposure of Financial Intermediaries," FDIC *Banking Review* 1 (Fall 1988) pp. 14-27.

Green, Edward J. "Financial Futures and Price-Level Variability," in Myron L. Kwast, ed., *Financial Futures and Options in the U.S. Economy*. Washington: Board of Governors of the Federal Reserve System (1986) pp. 79-89.

Grove, Myron A. "On 'Duration' and the Optimal Maturity Structure of the Balance Sheet," *Bell Journal of Economics* 5 (Autumn 1974) pp. 696-709.

Grumball, Clive. *Managing Interest Rate Risk*. New York: Quorum Books, 1987.

Hicks, John R. *Value and Capital*. Oxford: Clarendon Press, 1946.

Kaufman, George G. "Measuring and Managing Interest Rate Risk: A Primer," Federal Reserve Bank of Chicago *Economic Perspectives* (January 1984) pp. 16-29.

Kaufman, George G., Gerald O. Bierwag, and Alden Toevs, eds. *Innovations in Bond Portfolio Management: Duration Analysis and Immunization*. Greenwich, CT: JAI Press, 1983.

Koppenhaver, Gary D. "Futures Options and Their Use by Financial Intermediaries," Federal Reserve Bank of Chicago *Economic Perspectives* (January 1986) pp. 18-31.

Labaton, Stephen. "The Return of S&L Is Ordered," *New York Times*, September 6, 1990.

Macaulay, Frederick R. *Some Theoretical Problems Suggested by the Movements of Interest Rates, Bond Yields, and Stock Prices in the U.S. Since 1856*. New York: National Bureau of Economic Research, 1938.

Mester, Loretta J. "Traditional and Nontraditional Banking: An Information-Theoretic Approach," Federal Reserve Bank of Philadelphia Working Paper 90-3 (1990).

Milligan, John W. "Abuse of Power: How the Government Railroaded Franklin Savings," *Institutional Investor* (January 1991) pp. 50-60.

Morris, charles S. "Managing Interest Rate Risk with Interest Rate Futures," Federal Reserve Bank of Kansas City *Economic Review* (March 1989) pp. 3-20.

Nadler, Paul S. "Implications of Securitization for the Community Bank," *Journal of Commercial Bank Lending* (November 1987) pp. 19-25.

Parkinson, Patrick, and Paul Spindt. "The Use of Interest Rate Futures by Commercial Banks," in Myron L. Kwast, ed., *Financial Futures and Options in the U.S. Economy*. Washington: Board of Governors of the Federal Reserve System (1986) pp. 221-48.

Samuelson, Paul A. "The Effect of Interest Rate Increases on the Banking System," *American Economic Review* 35 (1945) pp. 16-27.

Smith, Clifford W., Jr., Charles W. Smithson, and Lee Macdonald Wakeman. "The Market for Interest Rate Swaps," *Financial Management* 17 (Winter 1988) pp. 34-44.

U.S. Department of the Treasury. *Modernizing the Financial System: Recommendations for Safer, More Competitive Banks*. Washington (February 1991).

QUESTIONS

1. What fundamental aspects of banking admit the possibility of interest rate risk? How would banks' profits and net worth be affected by a rise in interest rates?

2. Why was interest rate risk not of great concern to U.S. bankers before 1980?

3. How are the maturity gap and the duration gap measured and interpreted? Why don't all banks use these concepts in managing their balance sheets?

4. What techniques for controlling interest rate risk does Shaffer identify? How does each one work and what are its drawbacks?

READING 16

Investigating the Banking Consolidation Trend

John H. Boyd and Stanley L. Graham

Lately, the U.S. commercial banking industry has been consolidating. Although some firms have left the industry, many more have simply combined with other firms, resulting in fewer, bigger banks. Many legislators, regulators, bankers, and economists have roundly applauded this consolidation trend. In their view, consolidation is a laudable market response to industry changes that will bring significant benefits such as greater efficiency and a lower rate of bank failures. They also see consolidation as an effective way to shift resources out of banking, an industry they think is plagued with excess capacity.

We take exception to this widely held positive view of consolidation. After examining the available evidence, we do not think consolidation will deliver any of the benefits its proponents expect from it. That's because consolidation in banking does not appear to be primarily due to market forces. Although we cannot definitely explain why this trend is occurring, the data suggest that a major cause is incentives created by government policy. In fact, our investigation raises serious questions about the wisdom of certain bank regulatory practices.

THE TREND

The first step in our investigation of the recent banking consolidation trend is to define more precisely what we mean by *consolidation* and document that it is actually occurring. *Consolidation*, by our definition, means a decrease in the number of firms in the industry combined with an increase in their average size.

Chart 1

Although Still Healthy, Entries Have Lately Been Outweighed by Exits in the Banking Industry.

Changes in the Number of U.S. Insured Commercial Banks Annually, 1960–90

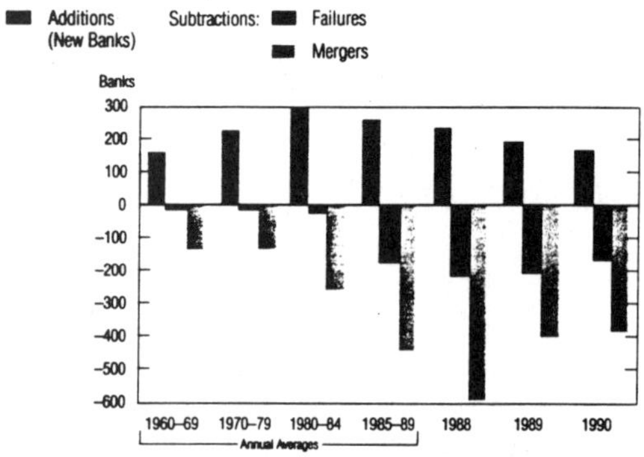

Source: Federal Deposit Insurance Corporation

Chart 2

. . . But Not, Primarily, the Top 10.

% of All U.S. Assets Held by the 100 Largest Banking Firms, 1977 vs. 1990

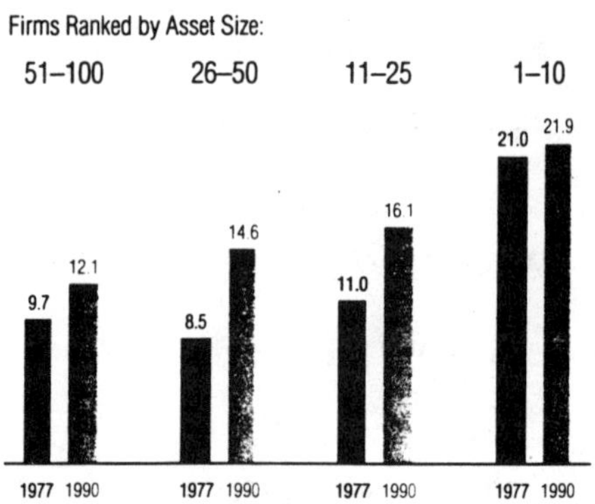

Source: Federal Reserve Board of Governors

Fewer Banks

There's no doubt that the number of banks has declined recently. After reaching a post-Depression high of about 14,500 in 1984, the number of U.S. insured commercial banks dropped to about 12,300 by 1990, a decline of 15 percent. As Chart 1 reveals, the decline partly reflects the exit of failed banks from the industry, but much more it reflects the absorption of both ailing and healthy banks into branch offices of other banks.[1] Chart 1 also reveals that the large decline in the number of banks does not necessarily reflect a sick industry, for the number of new banks has not dropped dramatically. In fact, in the pst five years, new banks have entered the industry at a 1.6 percent annual rate (newly chartered banks as a percentage of total banks). This is only slightly slower than in the first half of the 1980s, and it's faster than in the 1960s or the 1970s.

The evidence for consolidation is even more compelling when we shift from banks to banking organizations. A banking organization, such as a bank holding company, usually includes more than one bank. Changes in the number of these firms provide a better measure of banking consolidation because in them management decisions are generally made at the top; the true economic entity is the total organization. Between 1976 and 1990, the number of U.S. banking organizations declined 24 percent, roughly ten percentage points more than the number of banks declined. The larger contraction in the number of banking organizations reflects the acquisition and conversion of independent banks into bank holding company subsidiaries (which retain

Table 1

Bigger Banks Have Been Getting Bigger . . .

Number of U.S. Banking Firms and the Assets They Held, Grouped by Size of Firm, 1976 vs. 1987

	Number of Firms						Assets Held					
	Firms			% of All Firms			Billions of $			% of All Assets		
Asset Size of Firms	1976	1987	Deflated 1987*	1976	1987	Deflated 1987*	1976	1987	Deflated 1987*	1976	1987	Deflated 1987*
Less Than $50 Mil.	10,542	6,389	8,902	85.0	62.2	86.6	167.7	152.0	133.7	16.7	5.9	13.3
$50 Mil.–$100 Mil.	943	2,071	719	7.6	20.1	7.0	64.0	143.9	48.5	6.4	5.5	4.8
$100 Mil.–$1 Bil.	767	1,557	511	6.2	15.1	5.0	207.7	358.9	142.5	20.7	13.8	14.2
$1 Bil.–$5 Bil.	130	173	108	1.0	1.7	1.1	265.2	401.9	242.3	26.4	15.5	24.1
$5 Bil. or More	22	89	39	.2	.9	.4	299.1	1,540.6	436.7	29.8	59.3	43.5

*These columns represent the distribution after bank assets have been deflated by the change in total domestic banking assets between 1976 and 1987.

Source: Federal Reserve Board of Governors

their individual bank charters), rather than into branches. This multibank ownership structure largely reflects state branching restrictions.

Bigger Banks

Now let's complete our documentation of consolidation: While the number of banking firms has been shrinking, the average size of banking firms has been growing.

To see this, we can't look just at the changes in the share of all assets held by firms of different sizes; we must also look at the changes in the number of firms of each size. Between 1976 and 1987, the number of banking organizations with total assets less than $50 million dropped from 85 percent to 62 percent of all banking organizations, and their share of total assets dropped from 17 percent to 6 percent (Table 1). At the high end, firms with total assets of $5 billion or more, the number of firms rose from 0.2 percent to 0.9 percent of all banking organizations, and their share of total assets rose from 30 percent to 59 percent. Note that this group of large banks is the only size group that increased its share of assets between 1976 and 1987. This remains true even after the asset data are adjusted for inflation.

The growth in asset size, however, does not seem to be concentrated at the very top. Chart 2 shows the domestic market share of the 100 largest U.S. banking organizations. Between 1977 and 1990, it increased from 50 percent to 65 percent. Most of the gains, though, occurred at banks ranked 11th or lower.[2]

ARE MARKET FORCES BEHIND THE TREND?

Thus, the evidence reveals a recent rapid consolidation trend in the U.S. banking industry. Why is this trend occurring? The popular belief is that market forces are causing banking consolidation; the industry is adjusting to take advantage of economies of scale, to eliminate excess capacity, and to reduce the risk of bank failure. The available evidence, however, does not generally support this popular belief.

Scale Economies?

> Consolidation, particularly in-market mergers, will reduce the number of institutions chasing marginal business and running up the cost of funds. And it will allow substantial overhead reductions without impairing the ability of banks to serve their customers properly.

This comment (Isaac 1990, p. 4) reflects the popular view that banking is an industry which exhibits broad economies of scale. If that were true, then the recent consolidation in banking could be the result of natural market forces driving the industry toward bigger firms in order to achieve lower costs and higher profitability. Unfortunately, however, the popular view appears to be largely incorrect.

A firm is said to exhibit *economies of scale* when its average cost of production declines as the quantity of its output increases. In theory, such economies could extend indefinitely. In fact, however, the available data show something different for commercial banking: after banks reach a fairly modest size, there is no cost advantage to further expansion. Some evidence even suggests diseconomies of scale for the very largest banks.

Past Studies. Many researchers have studied scale economies among U.S. banking firms. Most such studies find significant scale economies in the industry, as predicted by theory, but they also suggest that these are exhausted below the relatively modest size of $100 million in deposits. (In 1988, for example, over 3,000 banks had total deposits between $50 million and $200 million.) Clark (1988) provides an excellent survey of this large literature. He reports that of 13 studies of economies of scale in banking, only 2 have found significant scale economies above $100 million in deposits. And since Clark's survey, several studies have actually found diseconomies of scale for very large banking firms, those in the multibillion-dollar range (for example, Berger and Humphrey 1990).

Although there is a general consensus in this literature, researchers have not been unanimous in their conclusions. Thus, it would be reassuring if we could explain why different researchers have obtained somewhat different results. And we can. A recent study by Humphrey (1990) considers these studies and concludes that different results can generally be explained by differences in assumptions, methodology, or both.[3] Humphrey (1990, p. 48) ends his study this way:

Tables 2 and 3

Bigger Doesn't Mean More Profitable . . .

Table 2

. . . Among All U.S. Banks . . .

Measures of Profitability and Leverage for All U.S. Commercial Banks by Size of Assets
Annual Averages, 1972–90†

		Asset Size			
		Less Than $25 Mil.	$25 Mil.–$100 Mil.	$100 Mil.–$1 Bil.	$1 Billion or More
Profitability	Return on Assets (Net Income as % of Total Assets)				
	1972–75	**.92**	.86	.75	.72
	1976–79	.97	**1.00**	.84	.59
	1980–83	1.01	**1.07**	.88	.59
	1984–87	.86	**1.02**	.98	.69
	1988–90‡	n.a.	.72	**.82**	.54
	Return on Equity (Net Income as % of Equity Capital)				
	1972–75	11.9	**12.2**	11.6	12.0
	1976–79	11.3	**12.9**	12.2	12.2
	1980–83	10.7	**13.0**	12.4	12.5
	1984–87	9.0	12.3	**13.9**	8.8
	1988–90‡	n.a.	8.2	**10.9**	10.0
Leverage	Equity/Asset Ratio (Equity Capital as % of Total Assets)				
	1972–75	**7.8**	7.0	6.5	6.0
	1976–79	**8.5**	7.7	6.9	6.5
	1980–83	**9.5**	8.7	7.1	6.3
	1984–87	**9.0**	8.0	6.9	5.2
	1988–90‡	n.a.	**8.9**	7.5	5.6

†Because of data irregularities, for 1972–75, bank size is based on total deposits; for all other periods, it is based on total assets. Annual averages are weighted (aggregate) averages of banks in each size class except those for 1984–87, which are medians of individual bank ratios. Where size classes have been combined, the 1984–87 measures are weighted averages of the median values.

‡Data for 1990 are preliminary. For banks with total assets less than $25 million, 1990 data are not available; these banks are included in the next largest size class.

Source: Federal Deposit Insurance Corporation

> Overall, a consensus conclusion of the preferred studies on bank scale economies suggest that the average cost curve in banking reflects a relatively flat U-shape at the firm level, with significant economies at small banks...but small and significant diseconomies at the largest....This relatively flat U-shape also holds even when large banks are viewed separately.

Another Look. Having examined what other researchers have found, we now look at the data ourselves. Rather than examining bank costs, though, we study bank profitability. Profits are a broader measure than costs, but obviously the two are closely related. Profits have the advantage of being a more readily available measure.

Table 2 displays two standard profitability measure for U.S. insured commercial banks over the period 1972-90: the rate of return on assets (ROA) and the rate of return on equity (ROE). Banks are grouped there in four size categories based (primarily) on their total assets. Weighted average annual rates of return are averaged in four-year intervals, except that median annual rates of return are averaged in the 1984-87 period. Of necessity, the final period is shorter than four years.

Key features of these data are consistent with the findings of the literature just reviewed: specifically, neither very small nor very large banks are the most profitable. In Table 2 profitability generally increases with bank size, but reaches a maximum before the largest. The single exception to the pattern of interior maximum is the ROA profitability measure for 1972-75, when the highest return was recorded by the *smallest* banks, those with assets less than $25 million.

You may notice an apparent discrepancy in the two profitability measures: the largest banks appear to have done much worse than the other bank groups according to the ROA, but not according to the ROE. This can be understood by examining the leverage measure that is also displayed on Table 2. The equity/asset ratio measures capital adequacy—what decline in asset values could be covered by a firm's equity. The smaller this measure is, the riskier is the firm (with other relevant factors held constant). As is clear in Table 2, larger banks tend to be more highly leveraged than other banks. Of course, the smaller equity is, the greater income will appear as a percentage of equity. Therefore, to compare banks across size classes, the ROE is a somewhat deceptive measure of profitability.[4] (The Appendix provides a more detailed analysis of the relationship between the ROA and the ROE.)

The published bank industry data are not very enlightening for very large banks—those with assets of $1 billion or more. That broad size category could be masking economies of scale at some very large size. Unfortunately, we cannot look for that in the published data; size categories have been changed repeatedly over the last two decades, making intertemporal comparisons difficult. However, we can study data for a sample of 131 large bank holding companies.

Table 3 shows for that sample the same profitability and leverage measures used for banks in Table 2. We've displayed these measures for the whole sample and for four size classes, all over the full period 1971-87.

Table 3

... Or Among the Largest.

Measures of Profitability and Leverage for a Sample of U.S. Bank Holding Companies by Size of Assets
Annual Averages (Group Means), 1971–87

		Full Sample	Asset Size: $1 Bil.– $2.5 Bil.	$2.5 Bil.– $5 Bil.	$5 Bil.– $10 Bil.	$10 Bil. or More	Test for Significant Differences†
Profitability	Return on Assets (Net Income as % of Total Assets)	1.0	**1.5**	.9	.9	.5	14.5*
	Return on Equity (Net Income as % of Equity Capital)	12.8	13.2	12.7	**13.5**	11.5	1.43*
Leverage	Equity/Asset Ratio (Equity Capital as % of Total Assets)	5.9	**6.6**	5.9	5.7	4.4	21.3
The Sample	Number of Firms	131	48	36	27	20	
	Average Total Assets ($ Bil.)	8.13	2.01	3.39	6.55	33.50	

†*F*-test for significance of difference of group means (one-way ANOV).
*Significant at 99% confidence level.
Source: Standard and Poor's Compustat Services, Inc.

The results of tests for the statistical significance of differences in group means are also provided.

The sample results are generally consistent with the published banking industry data. For the large banking firms, the ROE measure of profitability is not significantly different across size classes. But the largest size class does have the lowest average ROE, consistent with the finding of diseconomies of scale for very large firms. For the ROA measure, the differences among size classes are statistically highly significant, and they favor the smaller firms. Here, as in the bank data, there is a definite relationship between size and the use of financial leverage.

Summary. Our analysis of bank and bank holding company data over the last two decades is fully consistent with the main conclusions of the literature. Economies of scale are captured at a modest size, and once that size is reached, further increases do not improve profitability. In fact, there is some evidence that very large banking firms are less profitable than middle-sized ones. Thus, the evidence does not support the popular belief that a quest for economies of scale is behind the banking industry's consolidation.[5]

Chart 3

Is Banking a Declining Industry? . . .

% of All Financial Assets Held by Depository Institutions and the Rest of the Financial Sector*

Annually, 1974–89

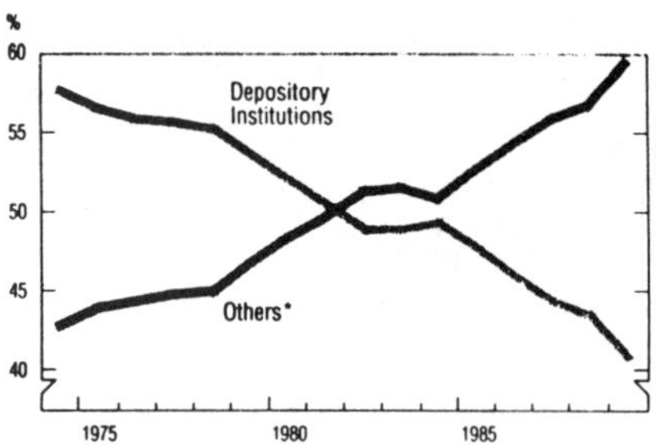

*Includes pension and retirement funds, insurance companies, agencies and mortgage pools, mutual and money market funds, and the monetary authority

Source: U.S. Treasury 1991

Chart 4

. . . Maybe Not.

Shares of U.S. Gross National Product Produced by Banking and by Other Finance and Insurance Industries*

Annually, 1947–87

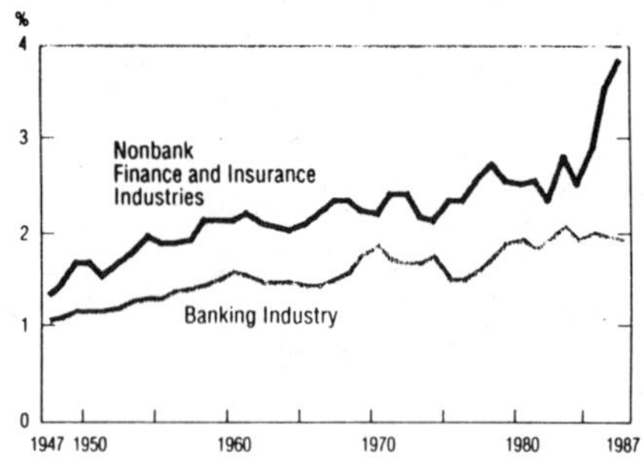

*The nonbank finance and insurance industries do not include real estate

Source: U.S. Department of Commerce

Excess Capacity?

> The U.S. banking system must wring out its excess capacity...The real driving force in the cutback in capacity will be an inevitable, sweeping consolidation. That alone should help U.S. banks compete with foreign banks.

This notion that the banking industry is sodden with excess capacity is another popular market explanation for the current consolidation trend (McColl 1991, p. 7). This explanation, like the first, does not stand up well to scrutiny.

A Fuzzy Picture. Some seem to think excess capacity in banking is an established fact. Chart 3, for example, is an illustration from the recent report describing the U.S. Treasury's (1991) proposals for reform of the banking industry. The picture it paints seems clear: The industry's share of financial intermediation has declined substantially over 15 years. Such seemingly irrefutable evidence suggests to some that resources need to be moved from banking to other industries, and that is why we see banks consolidating.

Actually, the picture is not nearly so clear.

First, much of the nonbank financial intermediary claims produce profits for commercial banks, even though banks don't hold them. One example is commercial paper borrowing. Although this borrowing is not in the form of bank loans, commercial paper issuers must have backup credit lines. These are usually issued by banks—which do not provide them for free. Another example is money market mutual funds, an important competitor to bank deposits. While these balances are not held by commercial banks, virtually every check written against them clears through the commercial banking system. And again, banks charge a fee for this service. Other examples abound.

A second reason the declining market share picture is not as clear as it may seem is that an increasingly substantial amount of the business done by commercial banks will not show up in the asset totals used to measure market share. The most rapidly growing product lines of banks are off-balance sheet activities that are invisible in these totals. Examples include standby letters of credit and other off-balance sheet guarantees, options, and forward contracts. Moreover, banks now originate billions of dollars of loans which are sold in the secondary market and don't appear on their balance sheets. That activity covers a wide spectrum of loans, including residential mortgages, credit card and other consumer loans, and commercial loans. Although banks may not be the ultimate holders of these loans, they are key players in originating and servicing them, and they earn substantial fee income in the process.

So, to a considerable extent, what pictures like Chart 3 reflect is not a loss of market share by commercial banks as much as a massive change in the way banks do business. In particular, it reflects the spectacular growth of off-balance sheet activity, fee income, and secondary-market loan sales.

Perhaps a better measure of market share change would be the disaggregation of the gross national product (GNP) by industry. This is assembled and published by the U.S. Department of Commerce. Chart 4 shows, for 1947-87, the share of GNP accounted for by the nonbank finance and insurance industries and the share accounted for by banking. Note that both banking and nonbank finance and insurance industries increased their share of GNP over this period. Moreover, they grew at almost the same rate over the period 1947-85. In 1986 and 1987, however, the nonbank sector grew much faster than the banks. Overall, this is a totally different picture than the 15-year decline shown by the balance sheet data. In particular, the GNP data suggest that both types of industries have been growing faster than the overall economy.

Some Fuzzy Economics. Determining if banks really are losing market share (and, if so, the timing and extent of that loss) is beyond the scope of this study. But, then, it's more than we need to do. For even if the aggregate demand for bank services is declining, it does not follow that consolidation in banking is inevitable or desirable.

Assume for a moment that banking is indeed a declining industry. If this is true, then redeployment of resources to other industries would be the expected and economically desirable response. However, that objective would not necessarily require consolidation. Nor would consolidation necessarily achieve that objective. Larger average firm size would not lower costs—it could raise them—and larger banks would be at a strategic disadvantage.

In and of themselves, combinations of banks merely shift resources around within the industry, resulting in larger average firm size. Obviously, after banks merge, some resources are often let go to other industries. However, banks can achieve that objective without merging: by increasing their dividend payout ratios to redeploy equity, firing some employees to redeploy labor, and so on. If all banks were to do this proportionally to size, resources would be appropriately shifted out of the industry, and the average size of banks would fall, not rise.

The idea that mergers are a natural and inevitable response of banks to a decline in demand follows from an invalid, often implicit, assumption that there are economies of scale to be captured by increasing firm size. As we have seen, economies of scale in banking are fully achieved at a modest size, and diseconomies may exist at very large banks.[6]

The relevant economic theory does not predict consolidation; it predicts exit by large banking firms. Ghemawat and Nalebuff (1985), for example, have studied structural changes in a model of an oligopoly industry which is experiencing declining demand. They find that when there are constant returns-to-scale, the largest firms exit first. This occurs for strategic reasons: as demand falls in an oligopoly market, the smaller firms can remain profitable longer, and this greater survivability allows them to drive larger firms out of business. Ghemawat and Nalebuff further show that under certain circumstances large firms will have an incentive to acquire small ones and simply eliminate their productive capacity. However, there is never an incentive to combine large firms, since size alone produces a strategic disadvantage.

Although Ghemawat and Nalebuff's study is theoretical, they cite case studies of declining industries which conform to the predictions of the theory. Among these are the U.K. steel casings industry and the U.S. machine tool industry. Research in business policy also emphasizes the advantage small plants have in industries experiencing declining demand (for example, Hall 1980). And commercial banking fits Ghemawat and Nalebuff's assumptions reasonably well, if we assume the industry is declining. As we have seen, all feasible economies of scale are attained by relatively small banks. If there are diseconomies for very large banks, as some believe, that would only sharpen the theory's predictions. Considerable evidence also exists that at least some bank loan and deposit markets are imperfectly competitive. Finally, the key prediction of the theory—that large firms will exit first—is consistent with the severe financial difficulty that many large banks have experienced recently.

However, what is totally inconsistent with predictions of the theory is the recent consolidation trend, which includes an increasing average firm size. There is no technical advantage in this trend, and there will be a technical disadvantage if scale diseconomies exist. In addition, theory suggests there is a strategic disadvantage to large size. Thus, it's difficult to explain consolidation as a market response to declining demand for banking services.

Summary. Is there excess capacity to wring out of the banking industry, as proponents of consolidation claim? The answer is far from obvious. The data used by proponents of consolidation are misleading, in part because of recent changes banks have made from asset-based to off-balance sheet activities. However, even if proponents are right and banking is a declining industry, that apparently cannot explain the recent wave of mergers. For that explanation to make sense, there would have to be economies of scale for large banks, which there are not; or consolidation would have had to primarily involve small banks, which it has not. Both theory and evidence from other industries suggest that in industries with excess capacity and constant returns-to-scale, it is the larger firms which exit first.

Safety?

> To save the banking system, reform of the banking laws must provide for: diversification of risk, larger institutions and a national regulatory scheme....It is instructive to note that of the 5,000 banks that failed in the 1920s...most were tiny and dependent on farm or real estate loans.

This is the last popular explanation for consolidation: that average-bank size increases reflect a natural attempt to "save" the banking industry (Chernow 1990, p. A14). Consolidation proponents applaud the trend they think will result in fewer bank failures, since very large banks can diversify their investments and so reduce their risk. Unfortunately, the applause is premature and, ultimately, inappropriate.

Of course, large banks are better able than small banks to diversify. Large banks can make a greater variety of different kinds of loans, each of which demands some unique expertise and specialized staff. They can lend in more geographic areas through branching networks, loan production offices, and the like. If they choose to invest in a branching network, they can obtain retail deposits from a wider geographic area. Finally, they can access liability markets unavailable to smaller banks, such as those for commercial paper, bank acceptances, Eurodollars, and Eurobonds.

All of this, however, describes what large banks *can* do, not what they necessarily *do* do. That's an important distinction because (as is well known) distortions caused by deposit insurance result in moral hazard, which reduces or eliminates banks' aversion to risk. As we have already seen, large banks use systematically more financial leverage than small banks, and (other things constant) financial leverage increases risk failure. Thus, it is not clear that because large banking firms are better able to diversify, they are less likely to fail.

Too Big to Fail. In a very narrow sense, very large banking firms are unquestionably less risky than smaller firms. But this is due to special regulatory treatment.

Under normal market conditions, when a corporation fails or goes into bankruptcy, it defaults on its debt obligations. Its creditors put the firm into bankruptcy proceedings, and they cannot do that unless the firm has defaulted.

Under a unique regulatory policy, this is not allowed to happen to very large banks. If a bank is so large that its failure might have consequences for the national economy, then the government considers that bank *too big to fail*. When such a bank is in serious financial trouble, the government always pays off its creditors. The government infuses public money into the bank and either operates it under government management (as was done with Continental Illinois) or arranges for a

Table 4

Bigger Doesn't Mean Less Risky.

Failures Among Small and Large Banks
As % of All U.S. Banks of Each Size, 1971–88*

Asset Size of Banks	Time Period 1971–79	1980–88	1971–88
Small (Less Than $1 Billion)	.49	5.71	6.18
Large† ($1 Billion or More)	2.19	8.00	12.55

*For each size class, percentages are based on the cumulative number of failures and the average annual number of banks of that size over the time period specified. Over this 18-year period, the average number of small banks was 14,301; the average number of large banks, 231. Failures of small banks averaged 49 per year; large banks, 1.61 per year. Failure data reported by the FDIC include federally insured savings banks.

†For a list of all large banks that failed during 1971–88, see footnote 7.

Source: Federal Deposit Insurance Corporation

shotgun-wedding merger with a healthier bank (as was done with First Republic of Texas).

Under these conditions, the too-big-to-fail bank has not failed in the sense that losses are realized by its debt holders. But it certainly has failed in the sense that it has experienced losses sufficient to wipe out its equity—and then some. Thus, from a creditor's perspective, too-big-to-fail banks are less risky than others. But from a public policy perspective (that of the Federal Deposit Insurance Corporation or the taxpayers who back it), that is a rather myopic point of view.

The Data. Do big banks actually fail less often than small banks? The data say, no—not when too-big banks that required government assistance are classified as *failures*.

A simple head count may be behind the popular misconception that larger banks are less risky than smaller banks. Over the 18-year period starting in 1971, many more banks with assets less than $1 billion have failed than larger banks: 884 vs. 29.[7] Counting bank failures by size of bank, however, is not good enough. On average during this period, the United States had about 14,300 small banks and only about 230 large banks. What we need to know is not just the number of failures, but what percentage of all banks of each size failed. This failure rate, as Table 4 shows, has been twice as great for the large banks as for the small ones.

Some may think that this difference has only appeared in the last decade, as the large banks have been hard hit by unusually high losses on loans to developing nations, the energy industry, and the commercial real estate industry. Note in Table 4, however, that the large bank failure rate was greater in both the 1970s and the 1980s.

Summary. The data do not support the notion that consolidation is occurring because larger banks are better positioned to diversify and are thus less risky. The empirical evidence shows that, contrary to popular belief, in recent years, larger banks have gotten into trouble more often than smaller banks.

IF NOT MARKET FORCES, WHAT?

The consolidation trend is real, but it is not (easily) explained by any natural market forces of which we are aware. What, then, can explain it? Why are large and medium-sized banks so eager to combine? If the explanation is not in private market forces, the natural place to look is in public policies.

Too Big to Fail, Revisited

The government's too-big-to-fail policy may produce an incentive for banks to increase their size. After all, if a bank gets big enough to be considered too big to fail, it gets implicit guarantees for all its liabilities, whether they are insured deposits or not. The bank does not have to pay for these guarantees, since deposit insurance premiums are only assessed against deposits. So, in essence, attaining a certain size provides a bank with some free insurance and more complete coverage than it would get otherwise.

The empirical evidence on this nonmarket incentive issue is mixed, however. Boyd, Graham, and Hewitt (1991) find no evidence that the equity shares of too-big banking firms are more highly valued than are shares of smaller banking firms. Such higher valuation might be expected if too-big firms were systematically benefiting by their status. Using modern option pricing theory, Kuester and O'Brien (1991) estimate the value of government insurance and find that it is not systematically related to size. However, O'Hara and Shaw (1990) report that equity investors did respond to an official pronouncement of the too-big-to-fail policy in 1984. Using an event testing approach, they find immediate price increases in the shares of the banks believed to be in that category.

Until more research is done, the size-incentive effects of the too-big-to-fail policy must be viewed as undetermined. Common sense suggests that this policy encourages large size, but so far the empirical results are mixed.

Too Hard to Take Over

Another government policy that might be encouraging increases in bank size is the (unintentional) regulatory protection from hostile takeovers that bank managers often enjoy. This protected position could be related to the banking consolidation trend because bank managers do seem to have an incentive to create bigger banks—an incentive that is unrelated to increased efficiency.

The data suggest that, regardless of bank profitability, the bigger the bank, the bigger the compensation package its top managers receive. We determined this by studying recent data for a sample of the 50 largest bank holding companies. Using standard statistical techniques, we investigated the relationship between managerial salaries (and bonuses) and three banking firm characteristics—total asset size, total asset growth, and profitability (measured by the ROA). The results: compensation is positively and significantly related to asset size, but not significantly related to either profitability or asset growth.[8]

Over the long haul, of course, any management will have a hard time pursuing its own objectives at the expense of shareholders. However, bank managers do have more freedom to do this than managers in other industries because one of the most effective tools for ousting bad management is essentially inoperative in banking: the hostile takeover. The regulated nature of banking makes hostile takeovers extremely difficult to execute (perhaps unintentionally). All bank mergers require time-consuming regulatory approval. In fact, hostile takeovers were unheard of in banking until a few years ago, and they still are rare.

More work needs to be done on the topic of managerial incentives in banking, and the results presented here (based on a small sample and a short time period) should be viewed as exploratory. Nevertheless, the data do suggest that, even without scale efficiencies, bank managers have a personal financial incentive to expand their firms and perhaps more latitude to do so because of the way their industry is regulated.[9]

Too Able to Increase Market Share

A final government policy that could be behind the banking consolidation trend is the policy of allowing—or even encouraging—banks in the same market to merge. These sorts of mergers often increase the market share of the merged banks and could increase their ability to earn monopoly rents.

General evidence on U.S. bank mergers supports the idea of a relationship between this bank behavior and the government's policy toward it. That many of the bank mergers of recent years have occurred among competitors in the same market is well known. However,

Chart 5

Bigger Does Mean More of the Market.

Average Annual % of Total Bank Deposits in U.S. Urban Markets Held by the 3 Largest Banks, 1976–89

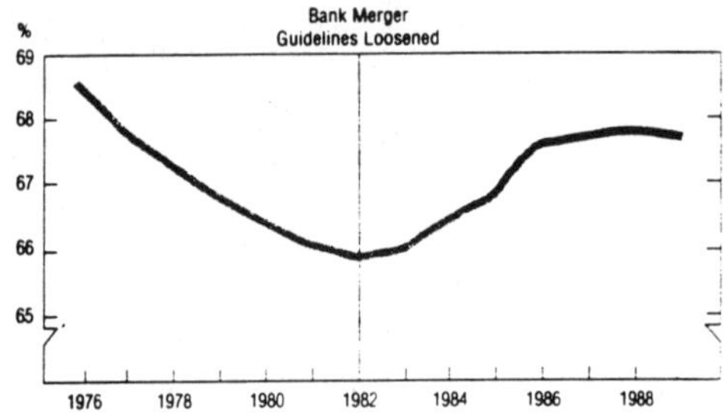

Source: Federal Reserve Board of Governors

we know of no source which categorizes bank mergers by whether or not the banks involved were in the same market. Still, the data in Chart 5 are highly suggestive. The chart shows the annual average share of total bank deposits held by the largest three banks in urban markets in the United States from 1976 to 1989. This concentration ratio declined from 68.45 percent in 1976 to a low point of 65.83 in 1982 and then climbed fairly steadily, reaching 67.65 in 1989. The general rise in this ratio since 1982 reflects a liberalized attitude toward within-market mergers adopted by the U.S. Justice Department and bank regulatory authorities. Indeed, the turn-around in the ratio dovetails with the Justice Department's loosening of its bank merger guidelines in 1982.[10]

Research on concentration in banking suggests a relationship between market structure and pricing. Higher loan rates and lower deposit rates are seen in more concentrated markets (Berger and Hannan 1989, Sharpe 1990). In other words, there is evidence of some ability for banks to earn monopoly rents, at least in some markets. If these findings are correct, they suggest an obvious incentive for banks to get bigger by merging with other banks in the same market, regardless of cost or risk efficiencies.

CONCLUDING REMARKS

Consolidation in banking is not all it seems, and those who have enthusiastically applauded it are likely to be badly disappointed by its results. Contrary to popular belief, large banks are not more profitable than middle-sized ones or less likely to impose costs on the Federal Deposit Insurance Corporation. In fact, according to the data, middle-sized banks have had the advantage on both counts for roughly the past two decades.

It's not even clear that banking is a declining industry, as many observers believe. That belief is hard to reconcile with the continued solid rate of new entries into the industry, for example. What is clear is that the nature of banking has changed so dramatically that market-share computations based on balance sheet data may be misleading. Much of the recent growth in commercial banking has been off-balance sheet and so invisible in such computations.

If competitive market forces are not behind this trend to consolidation, another likely candidate is public sector interventions. We have identified aspects of public policy which arguably do produce nonmarket incentives for consolidation, especially larger average bank size. Admittedly, our argument is not conclusive, and we may have overlooked some other significant causal factors. Nevertheless, our findings raise questions about current public policy toward banks.

Particularly serious is this one: Are competitive forces and policy forces pushing the banking industry in opposite directions? By this we mean, is the market slowly eliminating large banks, while the government systematically resuscitates some of them and encourages the formation of others? Just such a conflict has been described recently by Mayer (1991, p. 71), in a popular press article:

> These facts—the weakness of the big banks and the robustness of the smaller and regional banks—argue against the current wisdom that says the salvation of the system is even bigger banks....Using the taxpayers' money and credit in a futile effort to keep the whole herd alive could create another tragedy for the federal budget and for the future efficiency of financial intermediation in the U.S.

This is a stronger statement than we would make now—and an analysis of such policy issues is beyond the scope of this study. Nevertheless, our findings here are not inconsistent with Mayer's view. Like him, we see scant evidence that further banking consolidation will benefit either the U.S. banking industry or the U.S. economy.

APPENDIX
THE EFFECTS OF FINANCIAL LEVERAGE

In the profitability data discussed in the preceding paper, the largest banks did much worse than smaller banks when profits were measured by the return on assets (ROA), but not much worse when they were measured by the return on equity (ROE). Compared to the size groups with the greatest profits in each period, the largest banks had an average ROA 35 percent smaller, but an average ROE only 11 percent smaller.

This difference is traceable to the fact that, compared to smaller banks, larger banks operate with higher ratios of debt to assets, which is commonly known as *leverage*. Table 2 in the paper shows the equity/asset ratio, an inverse measure of leverage, for U.S. insured commercial banks between 1972 and 1990, grouped by size and by time period. In the table, leverage increases monotonically with bank size in every period.

The differing effects of leverage on the ROA and the ROE can be demonstrated with a few equations. Let Π be profits; A, assets; L, liabilities (or debt); E, equity; r, the gross rate of interest on assets; and i, the rate of interest on debt. An equation for profits, then, would be

(A1) $\Pi = rA - iL.$

With this notation, the return on assets (ROA) would be Π/A, and leverage, the debt/assets ratio, would be L/A. Then, if r is constant, the effect of a change in leverage on ROA would be

(A2) $\partial(\Pi/A)/\partial(L/A) = -i.$

Similarly, the return on equity (ROE) would be Π/E, and another measure of leverage, the debt/equity ratio, would be L/E. With r constant, then, the effect of a change in leverage on ROE would be

(A3) $\partial(\Pi/E)/\partial(L/E) = (r-i) - (L/E)[\partial i/\partial(L/E)].$

An increase in leverage results in a decrease in the ROA. This is understandable. A shift of one dollar from equity to debt financing produces an increase in interest expense and a concomitant decrease in profits. Since this shift doesn't change assets, the result will be a reduction in Π/A. However, an increase in leverage increases the ROE as long as the gross rate of return on assets exceeds the interest rate on debt ($r > i$) plus the increase in debt rate due to increased leverage $[\partial i/\partial(L/E)]$.

The point of all this is that large banks partially offset their lower ROAs by using systematically more financial leverage. However, if other relevant factors do not change, then increased leverage increases the risk of bankruptcy.

ENDNOTES

1.A high proportion of failed banks are absorbed by healthy banks under the Federal Deposit Insurance Corporation's (FDIC's) purchase and assumption option. The acquiring bank purchases some of the assets and assumes the deposits and other liabilities of the failed bank. The acquiring bank may also pay a premium to the FDIC representing in part the value of the failed bank's charter.

2.One explanation for the small gain in the industry share of the 10 largest banking firms is that they generally have been excluded from interstate banking expansion. Most state laws permitting entry by out-of-state banks restrict entry to banks from specified states, once reciprocity is established. All but one of the top 10 firms are domiciled either in New York or in California, and these states are not generally included in reciprocity agreements.

3.Humphrey (1990) makes three main points. First, some studies have examined just operating costs which, he argues, will bias their results in the direction of finding scale economies. The more appropriate variable to consider is total costs, including overhead and indirect costs. Second, early studies used linear (Cobb-Douglas) production functions, which are also biased in the direction of finding economies of scale. Humphrey argues for the use of nonlinear production functions in this research. Third, and finally, some studies have taken as their size measure individual office size instead of the overall size of the banking firm. Such studies also ignore overhead and administrative costs.

4.For that reason, many researchers prefer to use the ROA measure in such comparisons by size group.

5.In one situation, the merger of two banks seems bound to deliver substantial cost savings: when the banks both have large networks of branches which substantially overlap. By merging, it seems, the two banks can close many duplicating branches and reduce overhead costs considerably.

However, a recent study of such mergers (Savage 1991) concludes that the resulting costs savings are likely to be trivial. It offers several reasons for this conclusion. First, careful investigation reveals that, although U.S. banks have over 48,000 branches in this country, their branching networks don't overlap much. Thus, "even massive closings of overlapping branches would result in only a small percentage change in the national total of bank branches" (Savage 1991, p. 1). Second, indirect branch costs are not high relative to the direct costs of serving bank customers. And third, the study's estimates are based on a statistical cost function (developed by Berger and Humphrey 1990) which exhibits diseconomies of scale.

The merger study does not mention one significant point: when two banks have large, overlapping branching systems, they are (by definition) large banks and direct competitors. Merging them will necessarily reduce competition and may render the survivor more profitable simply because of its enhanced ability to earn monopoly rents (a subject we will discuss further later in this paper). For obvious reasons, bankers are loathe to mention rent-seeking as a possible motive for merging. But banking industry security analysts are less inhibited, and they clearly recognize the link between market concentration and profitability. For example, Alpert and Lynch (1991a, p. 68) state that "the lack of competition in Arizona, Nevada, and Oregon has allowed...[two banks]...to scrape by despite their horrendous losses in real estate lending" and that a "healthy Maine bank...also should benefit from the disappearance of so much competition." Elsewhere Alpert and Lynch (1991b, p. 35) state that "Ideally, the benefits of a large intramarket merger should include...reduction of competition. If enough competitors in a market consolidate, a resulting oligopoly should lead to more control over pricing. Deposit rates could be set low and consumer and middle-market lending rates set high."

6.Moreover, if scale economies were the principal explanation for the recent consolidation trend, it would have occurred mostly among the smaller banks, those with less than $100 million in total deposits, which is not where we have seen it.

7.The 29 commercial and savings banks with assets of $1 billion or more that required FDIC assistance during this period are listed here, grouped by the year they failed: 1972, Bank of the Commonwealth; 1973, United States NB; 1974, Franklin NB; 1980, First Pennsylvania NB; 1981, Greenwich SB and Union Dime SB; 1982, Western NY SB, NY Bank for Savings, and Western SB; 1983, Dry Dock SB and FNB Midland, Texas; 1984, Continental Illinois; 1985, Bowery SB; 1986, FNB Oklahoma City and BankOklahoma; 1987, BankTEXAS, Syracuse SB, and First City Bankcorp, Texas (2 banks); 1988, First Republic, Texas (4 banks), United Bank Alaska, MCorp., Texas (3 banks), Texas American Bankshares, and National Bankshares, Inc. (NBI), Texas.

8.We used an ordinary least-squares regression. Managerial salaries, M, are represented by the 1989 compensation (including bonuses) of corporate chief executives as reported in the October 19, 1990, *Business Week*. Bank size is represented by the log of total assets, A, at yearend 1988; bank growth, by the average annual growth in total assets $\Delta A/A$, in 1986-88; and profitability, by the average annual ROA, Π/A, in 1986-88. The data on the independent variables come from quarterly reports submitted by bank holding companies to the Federal Reserve. The time lag between the independent variables and the dependent variable reflects the assumption that managerial salaries are partly based on past performance. Our sample consisted of the 50 largest domestic bank holding companies, but incomplete data reduced the number of firms in the regression to 42.

The results of the regression (with t-values in parentheses):

$$M = 136.5 + \underset{(5.05)}{265.9[\ln(A)]} - \underset{(0.10)}{0.52(\Delta A/A)} + \underset{(0.32)}{26.3(\Pi/A)}.$$

$$R^2 = 0.40$$

These results are not materially affected by different averaging periods for the explanatory variables or different specifications of the regression.

9. Many industries besides commercial banking exhibit a positive relationship between firm size and management compensation. This does not necessarily argue against the existence of a pro-size incentive for bank managers; it may instead suggest that other industries share this incentive. See, for example, Brown and Medoff 1989.

A recent fascinating study by Allen and Cebenoyan (1991) sheds additional light on the issue of managerial incentives and acquisition strategies in commercial banking. This study finds that most acquisitions are made by banks with *entrenched managers*, banks with a high fraction of inside equity ownership by the management group and diffuse holdings otherwise (spread among outside investors). The study further finds that stock prices respond negatively (on average) to such announcements by other banks. Taken together, these findings suggest that when management groups have sufficient control, they may pursue acquisition strategies inconsistent with shareholder wealth maximization.

10. Under the U.S. Department of Justice 1982 Merger Guidelines, as revised in 1984, a market in which the post-merger Herfindahl-Hirschman Index (HHI) is above 1800 is considered highly concentrated, and the Justice Department is likely to challenge a merger that increases the HHI by more than 50 points unless other factors indicate that the merger will not substantially lessen competition. In a subsequent change, in mergers involving commercial banking, the Justice Department has indicated that in a market where the post-merger HHI is at least 1800, the merger generally will not be challenged unless it increases the HHI by at least 200 points. The higher than normal HHI threshold for bank mergers implicitly recognizes the competitive effect of limited-purpose lenders and other nondepository financial entities.

Perhaps nowhere is this policy shift more apparent than in the Minneapolis-St. Paul area, a market dominated by two large bank holding companies. For several decades, there was essentially a regulatory moratorium on within-market acquisitions by those two large firms. Beginning in the 1980s, however, this policy changed markedly, and both firms were allowed to launch aggressive acquisition campaigns.

From the passage of the Bank Holding Company Act of 1956 until 1988, the Board of Governors of the Federal Reserve System invoked the concentration issue in denying all applications for within-market acquisitions in the Minneapolis-St. Paul banking market by First Bank System and Norwest, the two largest banking organizations. Since 1988, the Board has approved seven within-market acquisitions by these two firms. Today, they control about 65 percent of total bank deposits in the market.

REFERENCES

Allen, Linda, and Cebenoyan, A. Sinan. 1991. Bank acquisitions and ownership structure: Theory and evidence. *Journal of Banking and Finance* 15: 425-48.

Alpert, Mark, and Lynch, Mark. 1991a. Bank shots—Unusual perspectives on banking: Market share shifts. *Research Highlights* (June 21): 67-69. Bear, Stearns & Co. Inc.

__. 1991b. Banking industry outlook: Will NCNB and C&S/Sovran herald a new era of mergers? *Research Monthly* (July 5): 35-37. Bear, Stearns & Co. Inc.

Berger, Allen N., and Hannan, Timothy H. 1989. Price rigidity and market structure: Theory and evidence from the banking industry. Finance and Economics Discussion Series 59. Board of Governors of the Federal Reserve System.

Berger, Allen N., and Humphrey, David B. 1990. The dominance of inefficiencies over scale and product mix economies in banking. Finance and Economics Discussion Series 107. Board of Governors of the Federal Reserve System.

Boyd, John; Graham, Stanley; and Hewitt, Shawn. 1991. Size and performance in banking firms: Testing the predictions of theory. Manuscript. Research Department, Federal Reserve Bank of Minneapolis.

Brown, Charles, and Medoff, James. 1989. The employer size-wage effect. *Journal of Political Economy* 97 (October): 1027-59.

Chernow, Ron. 1990. The menace of the small bank. *Wall Street Journal* (October 31): A14.

Clark, Jeffrey A. 1988. Economies of scale and scope at depository financial institutions: A review of the literature. *Economic Review* 73 (September/October): 16-33. Federal Reserve Bank of Kansas City.

Ghemawat, Pankaj, and Nalebuff, Barry. 1985. Exit. *Rand Journal of Economics* 16 (Summer): 184-94.

Hall, W.K. 1980. Survival strategies in a hostile environment. *Harvard Business Review* 58 (September/October): 75-85.

Humphrey, David B. 1990. Why do estimates of bank scale economies differ? *Economic Review* 76 (September/October): 38-50. Federal Reserve Bank of Richmond.

Isaac, William M. 1990. Comment: Outmoded policies thwart needed bank consolidation. *American Banker* 155 (December 6): 4.

Kuester, Kathleen A., and O'Brien, James M. 1991. Market-based deposit insurance premiums: An evaluation. Finance and Economics Discussion Series 150. Board of Governors of the Federal Reserve System.

Mayer, Martin. 1991. Too big not to fail. *Forbes* (April 15): 68-71.

McColl, Hugh L., Jr. 1991. Required reading: Updated recipe for international success. *American Banker* 156 (February 14): 4,7.

O'Hara, Maureen, and Shaw, Wayne. 1990. Deposit insurance and wealth effects: The value of being "too big to fail." *Journal of Finance* 45 (December): 1587-1600.

Savage, Donald T. 1991. Mergers, branch closings, and cost savings. Manuscript. Board of Governors of the Federal Reserve System.

Sharpe, Steven A. 1990. Switching costs, market concentration, and prices: The theory and its empirical implications in the bank deposit market. Finance and Economics Discussion Series 138. Board of Governors of the Federal Reserve System.

U.S. Treasury Department. 1991. *Modernizing the financial system: Recommendations for safer, more competitive banks*. Washington D.C.: U.S. Government Printing Office.

QUESTIONS

1. How do Boyd and Graham define consolidation? What evidence of consolidation do they present?

2. What are economies of scale? Do they exist in banking? How do Boyd and Graham test for their existence?

3. Is banking a declining industry? If it is, will consolidation into larger organizations help? Why?

4. Why might larger banks be less likely to fail than smaller banks? Why might they be more likely to fail? What data do Boyd and Graham present on this issue?

5. What public policies may be promoting the consolidation trend in banking? Why is it a problem if this trend is counter to competitive market forces?

READING 17

Bank Branching and Portfolio Diversification

Elizabeth Laderman, Ronald H. Schmidt, and Gary C. Zimmerman

In recent months, banking powers reform has become a major congressional policy issue. One option under consideration would permit a bank to operate branches in different states. The hope is that this would enhance banks' ability to diversify their assets. Potentially, this approach could lead to consolidation of the banking industry with a smaller number of large banks operating national branch networks.

Would interstate branching increase bank asset diversification? To answer this question, we can begin by examining the historical experience of *intrastate* branching. In this *Letter*, we focus on the effects that intrastate branching has had on agricultural lending. Our evidence suggests that banks in states with unrestricted branching typically have developed more diversified loan portfolios than similar banks in restricted states. By extension, *interstate* branching could lead banks to choose to broaden the set of industries to which they lend. Specifically, we can expect that banks headquartered in urban areas would devote more of their loan portfolios to agriculture, while banks headquartered in rural areas would concentrate less on agricultural lending.

PORTFOLIO CHOICE

For banks, diversification presents both benefits and costs. The major benefit is that banks can distribute their loans across a broad range of customers, which helps insulate them from the effects of individual loan defaults. By not "putting all their eggs in one basket," banks can reduce the chance of insolvency.

The costs are largely due to the increased need for information-gathering. In particular, lending to customers in a greater variety of industries requires the bank to learn about those industries to evaluate their loan potential. Economists usually argue that banks specialize in evaluating and monitoring the creditworthiness of their borrowers—borrowers whose projects and prospects cannot be as easily evaluated by other creditors.

Banks' special, customer-specific expertise may stem from their access to information, including information about transactions activity, gained from deposit relationships with borrowers. Thus, banks may find that, despite potential diversification benefits, it is more attractive to take advantage of knowledge specific to existing customers than to bear the cost of acquiring expertise in new areas.

This trade-off between diversifying a portfolio and acquiring expertise about new borrowers and their projects also has a geographic component. Banks may recognize the benefits of diversification, but may find that it requires some lending to borrowers in geographically dispersed areas. If evaluating and monitoring distant borrowers is too costly, diversification may suffer.

EFFECTS OF REGULATION

To the extent that it is hard to learn about and monitor borrowers at a distance, lifting branching restrictions enhances banks' efforts to diversify their portfolios. Setting up a branch in an area can provide a bank with a local observation post to gather information. For example, by having a branch in the area, a bank may be able to learn more about the potential returns to a local investment than could a bank outside the area. A branch may also provide the bank with information gained through a relatively long-term relationship with the borrower, both in the bank and in the community. Although banks without branches in the area may still make loans there, their evaluation and monitoring costs will very likely be relatively high.

Regulations limiting branching, therefore, may tend to restrict the market area of a bank to the region that is close to the bank's headquarters. Thus, states that allow branching may have banks that lend across wider markets. To the extent that different locales in the potential market area have different industrial structures, banks in branching states may have more diversified portfolios.

EVIDENCE IN AGRICULTURE

Examining agricultural lending in bank portfolios offers one test of this hypothesis. Agriculture is by its nature restricted to low-density rural areas. Moreover, the nation's agricultural land is present in both states that allow branching and those that do not, making comparison possible.

We examined data on lending by individual banks taken from the Federal Reserve's "Survey of Terms of Bank Lending to Agriculture" over the period 1981 to 1986. Our statistical model sought to explain the ratio of a bank's agricultural loans to its total loan portfolio. Variables to explain this agricultural share included bank characteristics, such as its size (assets) and its aggressiveness in lending (deposit-to-loan ratio).

The model also accounted for differences in the characteristics of the agricultural economy, taking into account average farm size, government payments to agriculture, and agriculture's share of the gross state product. Competition from other institutional lenders also was included, using the Farm Credit System's share of total agricultural lending in the preceding year in the bank's state as an explanatory variable.

Finally, to get at the central point, variables were included to indicate whether the bank was in a restricted or unrestricted branching state, and whether the particular bank was in an urban or rural area.

FINDINGS

Results from the regression analysis found that branching restrictions were associated with important variations in bank portfolios. Moreover, the effects of the restrictions worked in the expected direction: Banks in states that allowed branching had more diversified loan portfolios than similar banks in states without branching restrictions.

Not surprisingly, urban banks had significantly smaller portfolio shares in agricultural lending than did rural banks, in both restricted and unrestricted states. However, in unrestricted states, urban banks had agricultural shares only 5.3 percentage points below those in rural areas. Restricted urban banks, in contrast, had agricultural shares 19.3 percentage points below the portfolio shares of their rural counterparts.

Simple simulations indicated that eliminating branching restrictions would boost the diversification of rural and urban banks. We found that if all other explanatory variables were held constant and branching restrictions were eliminated, urban banks would increase their agricultural portfolio shares by 4.3 percentage points, while rural banks would decrease their shares by 9.7 percentage points.

IMPLICATIONS

The empirical results suggest that geographic limitations on banking may limit a bank's ability to diversify its lending portfolio. A more comprehensive branching system, therefore, may produce a different lending pattern from the one we now observe.

Although the model predicts a decrease in the rural banks' agricultural portfolio share, the net effect on agricultural lending may be positive for two reasons. First, because urban banks in restricted states hold 98 percent of total loans in those states, urban banks' modest increase in agricultural lending predicted by the model would swamp the decrease implied for the rural banks. The model predicts a net increase of 4.2 percentage points in average agricultural portfolio shares in restricted states.

Second, branching could help agricultural communities by increasing diversification and reducing costs of bank services. First, by encouraging greater portfolio diversification, branching can enhance rural bank (and urban bank) stability. Because the health of many agricultural banks is at present tied so closely to the fortunes of the area's agricultural economy, a few bad years in a row can put the bank in jeopardy. For example, Smith (1987) found empirical evidence that intrastate branching restrictions increase the incidence of bank closure.

The failure of a local bank can have a serious effect on an agricultural community. Calomiris, Hubbard, and Stock (1986) have argued that, since agricultural lending depends heavily on the information a bank has acquired about the borrower, other banks cannot quickly step in to take the place of rural banks that fail. In fact, they found a statistically significant negative relationship between bank failures and farm output.

Branching also may be more efficient. Encouraging too many banks to operate by restricting branching may make bank costs higher than necessary. Mergers of small banks can result in reduced overhead and lower costs of service to bank customers. Moreover, if rural banks have access to broader credit markets, they may be able to invest in loans yielding higher returns. At present, many agricultural banks lend a sizable portion of their assets at low rates in the federal funds market because of their limited ability to identify other, more profitable investment opportunities. Thus, interstate branching may well increase the supply of agricultural loans at a given price. Moreover, rural customers may benefit in other ways, perhaps through increased interest on their deposits, enhanced services, or decreased service charges.

CONCLUSIONS

Increased banking activity is likely to allow banks to compile more diversified portfolios. Current restrictions on branching appear to have limited banks' portfolios to the industries geographically close to the bank. Specifically, an examination of agricultural lending reveals that banks in states that allow branching had more diversified lending patterns than those that restricted branching.

Reform that allows more branching activity may increase loan availability to agriculture from commercial banks. Contributing to an increase in supply would be increased lending by urban banks as they establish branch networks. In addition, such reform would strengthen the health of the banking system through diversification and possibly would lead to an increase in bank operating efficiency.

REFERENCES

Smith, Hilary H. 1987. "Agricultural Lending: Bank Closures and Branch Banking." Federal Reserve Bank of Dallas *Economic Review* (September) pp. 27-38.

Calomiris, Charles W., R. Glenn Hubbard, and James H. Stock. 1986. "The Farm Debt Crisis and Public Policy." *Brookings Papers on Economic Activity* 2, pp. 441-485.

Laderman, Elizabeth S., Ronald H. Schmidt, and Gary C. Zimmerman. 1991. "Location, Branching, and Bank Portfolio Diversification: The Case of Agricultural Lending." Federal Reserve Bank of San Francisco *Economic Review* (Winter) pp. 24-38.

QUESTIONS

1. What are the benefits and costs of loan diversification for banks? How can the elimination of branching restrictions lower the costs of loan diversification?

2. Why do the authors choose agricultural lending as a test of their hypothesis? In their study, what variable are they trying to explain and what other variables do they examine to explain it?

3. What do the authors conclude about the effects of branching restrictions on loan portfolios? What are the public policy implications of their findings?

READING 18

The Worship of Basle

If banks have come to their senses, the first sobering splash of cold water came from the "Basle ratios", which tell banks how much capital they must hold against loans of varying riskiness. At a stroke the Basle accord of 1988 made bank capital a scarce commodity. Banks that had sought to grow by piling as much lending on top of as little capital as possible had to revise their strategies. Banks have slowed the growth of their loans; the cost of borrowing has shot up and economies have slumped. For all this, the new capital standards get more than their share of credit and blame.

Central bankers devised the Basle ratios to solve two problems. The level of capital in the world's banking system relative to loans had been falling for decades. That worried them, because capital is the cushion that protects depositors by absorbing losses when loans go bad. Americans fretted about something else: that Japanese banks were trouncing their competitors in international markets partly because they put up scant capital to back their loans. In 1988 Peter Cooke, a Bank of England official, and regulators from 11 other central banks unveiled a proposal for "International Convergence of Capital Measures and Capital Standards".

The Basle ratios (mistakenly called the BIS ratios because the authors took tea and advice from the Bank for International Settlements) are simple in outline, but intricate enough in detail to open plenty of loopholes for banks that are short of capital. They require banks to hold $8 of capital for every $100 of lending. At least half of that capital must be equity or near-equity ("tier 1" capital). The rest can consist of subordinated (ie, riskier) debt, provisions against unexpected loan losses and other elements of "tier 2" capital. Although all commercial loans require the full $8 of capital backing, less-risky activities have lower weightings. Home mortgages, for example, usually require half the capital backing of ordinary loans; loans to governments of industrialised countries consume no capital.

Whether the accord achieved its primary aims—safer banks competing on more equal terms—is a subject of hot dispute. Banks have boosted their capital ratios since 1988, though not uniformly. Strong ones have done so by issuing equity and debt in the capital markets. Weaker banks, facing prohibitive prices for capital, improved their ratios by selling loans and restricting new lending. (At some banks bad loans have wiped out the capital thus gained.) Even though the 8% ratio will not be in force until the end of 1992, banks were required to meet a 7¼% transitional ratio at the end of 1990.

Critics of the Basle accord, and they are many, point out that the ratios are at war with themselves. The weightings set by Basle rules have little to do with market risks and may encourage banks to put the wrong price on the risks they take. Robert Maxwell and IBM would have been equally risky borrowers in the eyes of the Basle accord. A yield-hungry bank with a taste for risk has every incentive to lend to the disgraced publisher rather than the blue-chip computer-maker. A recent survey by Price Waterhouse, an accounting firm that is Mr. Cooke's new employer, found little evidence that the distortion had prompted banks to funnel capital into higher-risk loans. But the danger is there.

Basle has fired the banks' enthusiasm for activities deemed low-risk by the accord. That is fine, as long as the risks are as low as the rules imply. Some may not be. Dealing in swaps and options has surged in the past few years, in part because the Basle rules require less capital for such off-balance-sheet transactions than for normal loans. Bankers do not fully understand the risks of such derivatives; regulators may eventually require greater capital backing for them.

Higher capital ratios do not guarantee safer banks. Most failed banks in the past few years met regulatory capital standards in their final published accounts. Yet there is good reason for making capital the centrepiece of regulation. Consider this: if the Basle ratios had applied to America's thrifts when they found themselves in difficulty, they might have sought solvency by shrinking instead of courting bankruptcy in a game of double or quits. Strongly capitalised banks are not only safer on average but more profitable than under-capitalised ones. According to a study of banks in 1983-89 by Allen Berger, an economist at the Federal Reserve Board, returns on capital rose after banks raised capital, mainly because their funding costs fell.

Having levelled the international playing-field, the Basle accord pocked it with exceptions and loopholes. National authorities, especially those overseeing under-capitalised banks and weak economies, have not hesitated to exploit them. Japan is the best-known exploiter. Its banks count 45% of unrealised gains on their securities portfolios as tier 2 capital. That puts the capital ratios of Japanese banks at the mercy of the country's plunging stockmarket. When the Nikkei index is below 20,000 most big commercial banks do not meet the 8% minimum, which will be enforced on March 31st 1993, the end of their fiscal year.

Japan is not the only country to trifle with the spirit of the Basle accord. American regulators want banks to be able to count certain intangible assets, such as rights to administer portfolios of credit cards and mortgages, as tier 1 capital. Tier 1, purists insist, should be equity and nothing but. France's state-owned banks goose their capital ratios by swapping shares with other state-owned companies. British banks converted unrealised profits on their vast property holdings into tier 1 capital.

The Basle accord has two virtues that compensate amply for its faults:

- It blunted the drive for asset growth and spurred banks to seek profitability instead.
- It encourages governments to supervise banks rather than regulate them by setting needless restrictions on their activities.

QUALITY CONTROL

The post-Basle banker tends to be more cautious and thoughtful than his predecessor. He is stingy with capital, and demands a higher return for putting it at risk. Bankers credit Basle (along with the recession) for mopping up the glut of lending and raising its price. "Competition in lending is now disappearing due to the BIS regulations," says Tatsuro Itoh, a senior managing director of Japan's Kyowa Saitama Bank. "We have shifted our priority from volume to quality sales."

Thanks to the Basle rules, banks are just beginning to lend money sensibly on the basis of a risk-adjusted return on capital (RAROC). RAROC, a technique pioneered by Bankers Trust and other American banks, measures systematically the expected return on an investment of capital adjusted for risk. Banks deploy their capital when the return on a particular transaction meets the bank's risk-adjusted profit target, usually 12-20% on equity. Like much that sounds elementary in banking, RAROC is a novelty to most banks. A 1989 Price Waterhouse survey of banks operating in London found that none of the six Japanese banks questioned used risk-adjusted measures of profitability to make business decisions.

Under the lash of Basle, RAROC and techniques like it are spreading. The "great benefit" of Basle, Mr. Cooke believes, is that it "focused banks' own thinking on how to price capital and how it should be allocated". There is an irony in this. As bankers adopt more objective formulas for judging risk, they will undermine the age-old justification for banking: a banker's unique insight into the creditworthiness of each customer. Once a risk can be priced systematically, it can be traded. Once traded, it can be brokered by firms more efficient than banks and held by investors. The better banks manage, the less like bankers they are.

QUESTIONS

1. What capital standards do the Basle ratios impose on banks? How do they differentiate between categories of bank assets and bank capital?

2. Why were the new standards adopted? How will they affect bank portfolio decisions?

3. What criticisms have been levied at new standards? What overall evaluation of them is presented in this reading?

READING 19

Risk-Based Capital Standards and Bank Portfolios

Jonathan A. Neuberger

Banks in the U.S. must meet several regulatory standards for minimum levels of capital. The primary purpose of bank capital is to serve as a cushion to absorb losses. Traditionally the size of this cushion has been set as a fixed percentage of bank assets. In recent years, capital requirements have been changed to reflect certain dimensions of bank risk. By year-end 1992, U.S. banks must satisfy the international risk-based standards promulgated by the Basel Committee on Banking Regulations and Supervisory Practices.

In contrast to fixed capital requirements, the risk-based standards establish a variable capital cushion based on the risk of a bank's assets. These standards assign risk weights to different categories of assets, and thus create incentives for banks to shift their portfolios toward assets that receive favorable risk weights and away from less favored asset categories. These portfolio shifts are desirable as long as the weights accurately reflect the true risk of the assets. If the weights are inappropriate or arbitrary, however, the risk-based standards could actually increase bank risk. In this *Weekly Letter*, I describe recent changes in the composition of bank portfolios and consider some of the consequences of these portfolio shifts.

Conceptually, risk-based capital standards are an improvement over fixed capital regulations because they explicitly acknowledge the heterogeneity of bank assets. Under traditional regulations, two banks with the same quantity of assets, but with different asset risks, are required to maintain the same minimum capital cushion. Risk-based guidelines, in contrast, recognize that the riskier bank has a higher probability of default, and require it to hold a larger capital cushion against losses.

The variable capital requirement is especially important in the presence of fixed-price deposit insurance. The two banks considered above pose significantly different risks to the deposit insurer. Under fixed capital regulations, the bank with the riskier asset portfolio receives a larger subsidy from deposit insurance. Properly administered risk-adjusted capital requirements can eliminate the insurance subsidy, and thus reduce the incentive to exploit that subsidy by assuming more risk.

RISK-BASED CAPITAL STANDARDS

While bank capital regulation is not new, risk-based capital standards are a recent phenomenon. In 1988, the so-called Basel Committee, under the aegis of the Bank of International Settlements, presented an agreement among regulators from Europe, North America, and Japan describing a risk-based system of minimum capital standards that all banks should satisfy. Though the Committee has no official jurisdiction, regulators in the different countries issued domestic capital guidelines that largely accord with the Basel agreement. These guidelines must be met in full by the end of 1992.

Under these standards, banks are required to maintain capital equal to at least 8 percent of *risk-adjusted* assets. Capital is divided into two components which are ranked according to the availability of the funds to buffer losses. So-called Tier 1 capital consists primarily of common equity, while Tier 2 can include subordinated debt and such instruments as cumulative perpetual preferred stock. Tier 1 capital must comprise at least 4 percent of risk-adjusted assets.

The risk-adjusted aspect of the capital standards involves allocating bank assets to different categories, each of which has a risk weight. These weights were determined by considering the *credit risk* of assets. For example, the asset category considered to have the lowest credit risk includes cash and central government securities (like Treasury bonds). This category receives a zero risk weight. This means that banks are not required to hold capital against these safest of assets.

In contrast, the highest risk category includes most loans to private entities (such as commercial and industrial loans) and receives a 100 percent risk weight. Against these assets, banks must maintain the full 8 percent capital support. In between these extremes, there is a 20 percent risk weight category, which in the U.S. includes securities issued by the Federal National Mortgage Association (FNMA) and the Federal Home Loan Mortgage Corporation (FHLMC), and a 50 percent risk weight category which includes residential mortgage loans. The standards also account for credit risk associated with off-balance sheet activities like interest rate swaps and standby letters of credit. Total risk-adjusted assets are the totals in each category, multiplied by the corresponding risk weight. Note that a bank could have zero risk-adjusted assets if it holds only the safest assets. According to the risk-based capital guidelines, such a bank would be required to hold no capital. To avoid anomalies like this, U.S. regulators issued an additional requirement that banks must hold at least 3 percent capital to *unadjusted* assets.

SOME PROS AND CONS OF RISK-BASED CAPITAL GUIDELINES

The risk-based capital standards have been criticized for arbitrarily assigning risk weights to different asset categories. For example, the standards treat every home mortgage held by banks as being half as risky as every commercial loan. Undoubtedly, this is not correct in all cases, even though home mortgages historically have tended to be less risky than commercial loans.

The risk weighting scheme used in the capital standards also ignores variations in asset quality *within* categories. This means that a short-term bank loan to a blue chip corporate borrower is considered just as risky and requires just as much capital support as a long-term loan to a high-risk startup venture. The capital standards thus ignore information relevant to individual asset risk.

The risk-based capital standards overlook potentially important interactions between individual assets. The standards establish the relative risk weights based on an asset's risk *in isolation* of other assets. Portfolio theory suggests, however, that the relevant risk of an asset is its risk *in portfolio*. Thus, an individual asset's contribution to portfolio risk depends not only on its own variability but also on its covariation with other assets in the portfolio. These latter effects are ignored in the risk-based standards.

Finally, the risk-based capital guidelines consider only credit risk in differentiating bank assets while ignoring other risks, such as interest rate risk. Thus, any Treasury security, regardless of term to maturity, is treated as if it poses no risk to the bank holding it. While this may be true for default risk, long-term bonds are far more sensitive to changes in interest rates than short-term Treasury bills.

These criticisms suggest that the risk-based capital guidelines may not present an accurate picture of bank risk, and thus may require banks to hold an inappropriate amount of capital. Defenders of the standards, however, counter these arguments by suggesting that the different risk categories are broadly consistent with the perceived riskiness of bank assets. While exceptions can always be found, central government debt is less risky than obligations of government-sponsored enterprises, which in turn are safer than claims against private sector borrowers. A recent study by Avery and Berger (1991) provides further support for the risk-based standards, finding statistical evidence that risk-based capital is more informative about bank performance and risk than unadjusted capital ratios.

Proponents of the risk-based capital standards also admit that the failure to incorporate interest rate risk is a real limitation. However, most bank regulators believe that credit risk is the primary risk facing banks. While some banks may have significant interest rate risk in their portfolios, the major cause of bank failures is more likely bad management and poor asset quality, and *not* excessive interest rate risk. Moreover, bank examiners continue to rely on subjective evaluations of bank portfolio diversification, loan quality, and interest rate risk management practices. While the risk-based capital guidelines do not formally address these factors, they still receive considerable scrutiny from bank examiners.

SHIFTING PORTFOLIOS

A bank regulatory system that establishes preferential treatment for certain types of assets relative to others creates incentives for banks to alter the composition of their portfolios. A look at bank balance sheets over the past few years confirms that significant portfolio shifts have occurred that are consistent with such incentives. For these comparisons, I use data from the reports of condition on insured commercial banks (Call Reports) for the fourth quarter of 1987 (before the risk-based guidelines were announced) and the fourth quarter of 1990.

During this three-year period, banks maintained their securities portfolios at a constant 19 percent of total assets. However, they altered the composition of these portfolios. Commercial bank holdings of U.S. government securities rose from 65 percent of total securities in 1987 to 74 percent of securities holdings in 1990. Similarly, bank holdings of government sponsored, mortgage-backed securities, so-called Ginnie Maes, Fannie Maes, and Freddie Macs, rose from 15 percent of bank securities portfolios in 1987 to 25 percent in 1990. These figures indicate that while banks maintained the relative size of their securities portfolios, they shifted about 20 percent of their holdings into assets with the lowest risk weights under the Basel accord.

Significant shifts also have occurred in bank loan portfolios. While total loans were stable at approximately 62 percent of total bank assets, the proportion of these loans to finance residential real estate rose from 17 percent of total loans in 1987 to 22 percent by the end of 1990. In contrast, commercial and industrial loans fell from 30 percent of bank loans in 1987 to less than 27 percent in 1990, and loans to individuals held steady at 20 percent of bank loan portfolios in both years.

These portfolio shifts are undoubtedly due to additional factors besides implementation of the risk-based capital standards. The decline in business loans, for example, is partially the result of the recession that began in July 1990 as well as intensified competition from nonbank sources of finance. Similarly, the greater share of real estate finance in bank portfolios has been aided by the decline of the thrift industry. While all of these influences affect the behavior of lenders and borrowers, the portfolio shifts that have occurred are consistent with banks increasing their holdings of risk-preferred assets under the risk-based capital guidelines.

If the asset categories under the new standards truly reflect the risks of broad groups of bank assets, then the shift toward risk-preferred categories means that banks have reduced the credit risk of their portfolios. As bank holdings of assets in the zero, 20, and 50 percent risk weight groups increase, then a given level of industry capital supports a safer portfolio of assets. Viewed in this light, the portfolio shifts are a desirable outcome of implementing the Basel agreement.

While these shifts may be beneficial for the safety of the banking system, they likely will alter the allocation of credit in the economy. The risk-based capital standards make real estate loans and certain securities more attractive to hold while increasing the relative cost of business loans. As banks respond by raising their holdings of Treasury and mortgage-backed securities, and home mortgage loans, it may become more difficult for some businesses to obtain bank finance. This implies that future borrowers and lenders may operate in a different financial environment than currently exists.

INTEREST RATE RISK

Regulatory agencies are aware that exposure to interest rate risk should be considered in bank regulation. The Basel Committee has been debating this issue since the late 1980s, although no formal proposals on this subject have been offered to date. The Office of Thrift Supervision proposed early in 1991 a model for incorporating interest rate risk into thrift capital regulation. This proposal was withdrawn pending action by other U.S. bank regulatory agencies. Staff at the Federal Reserve Board of Governors recently suggested a system to measure the interest rate risk exposure of banks, but not to impose a specific capital charge for this risk. Instead, the measure would be used by examiners to evaluate banks' risk management policies and to suggest ways for banks to reduce this risk exposure.

The banking reform bill recently signed into law requires regulators to broaden the risk-based capital standards in the next few years by considering additional elements of bank risk, including interest rate risk. This raises an interesting policy question: will unilateral action by U.S. bank regulators to stiffen capital standards further impair the competitiveness of U.S. banks relative to foreign banks? The answer to this question could be important for the future of the U.S. banking system.

REFERENCES

Avery, Robert, and Allen Berger. 1991. "Risk-based Capital and Deposit Insurance Reform." *Journal of Banking and Finance* 15, pp. 847-874.

QUESTIONS

1. How do risk-based capital standards differ from and improve upon fixed capital requirements?

2. Describe the risk-based capital standards agreed to by the members of the Basle Committee in 1988.

3. On what grounds are the risk-based capital standards criticized? How do proponents of the new standards defend them?

4. What bank portfolio shifts does Neuberger detect since the adoption of the new standards? Are these shifts consistent with expected bank behavior under the new standards?

READING 20

Is Banking Really Prone to Panics?

Randall J. Pozdena

Much of the social justification for deposit insurance springs from concerns over contagious bank runs, or "panics." In a panic, a run at one bank (justified or not) precipitates runs at other, inherently healthy banks. When a panic occurs, it may result in a significant, and costly reduction in total banking capacity and an attendant burden on the economy.

The private market may not adequately protect against contagious runs (through, for example, higher capital and liquidity levels). This is because individual bank managers are concerned only about their own profitability, and have no incentive to limit the negative burdens or "externalities" they impose on other banks. Deposit insurance and the regulation of bank capital thus can be justified as a means of controlling the externality problem by limiting the tendency to run and increasing the protection against runs.

Despite its importance to bank policy, the theory and empirical evidence of contagious runs is scanty. In this *Letter*, we discuss the notion of contagious runs as a consequence of rational "signal extraction," and use data from the behavior of bank stock returns to demonstrate that there may, indeed, be a tendency for banking to be prone to contagious runs.

CONTAGIOUS RUNS

Policymakers' concern about contagious runs or "panics" in banking has its roots in the turbulent, early history of U.S. banking. According to Klebaner (1974), for example, about 25 percent of all banks that had ever existed had failed by 1861, most during a panic. Significant banking panics also occurred in 1873, 1884, 1890, 1893, and 1907. And in all cases but one (1890), the panic was followed by a deep depression.

The banking panics of this early period were often regional and often involved the largest banks first. The panic of 1907, for example, began with runs on the third largest and then the second largest banks in New York City. The panic spread first to smaller New York institutions, and only later to country banks and other communities, a pattern repeated in the 1930s.

While this experience was, and still is, frequently taken as evidence of the importance of controlling bank runs, there have been recent challenges to this interpretation. Benston, et al. (1986), for example, believe that the rate of bank failures was often much less than reported. In addition, it is possible that the episodes of bank runs and failures occurred because of widespread economic weakness, and not the other way around; hence, the widespread runs were not the result of a "contagion," but simply runs on many individually weak banks.

A THEORY OF CONTAGION

To help resolve the issue of the relevance of contagious runs, we need a testable, theoretical justification for a banking panic. That is, can we posit a situation in which the depositors of banks are well-informed and rational, yet still will tend to "panic" and run on healthy banks?

King and Wadhwani (1990) recently presented a model of contagion of stock market crashes that seems to offer a relevant framework for a "rational panic" in financial markets. This author has adapted their model to study the case of banking panics. The model assumes that investors (depositors or equity holders) in a particular bank recognize that the value of their investments depends upon two general types of factors. The first are factors that affect the banking industry, such as general economic conditions, or conditions in particular asset markets that banks have in common. Second are factors that are idiosyncratic to individual banks, such as the behavior of assets peculiar to an individual bank.

At any point in time, of course, the depositors and other investors in the individual banks can make only imperfect estimates of the behavior of these factors, because their information is imperfect. In so doing, the behavior of Bank B may be of interest to depositors in Bank A because of common factors. Consequently, one task of the depositors in Bank A is to efficiently extract useful information from the behavior of Bank B, while recognizing their mutual dependence on common factors. In economic parlance, this involves rationally deriving an "efficient signal extraction" rule.

A consequence of this signal extraction process is that depositors in Bank A will react to the idiosyncratic factors that affect Bank B. That is, it can be shown that information that should only be "bad news" for Bank B can propagate to Bank A. This is because the efficient search for common information tends to be contaminated by idiosyncratic effects.

MEASURING THE CONTAGION EFFECT

Whether this contagion effect is important empirically depends upon the validity of the assumptions of imperfect information, and the tendency of depositors in Bank A to look to Bank B for insight on common factors. Thus, it is important to test the strength of the contagion effect empirically.

Information on the behavior of depositors in individual banks is not easily available. The behavior of equity holders, on the other hand, is easily observed for those banks with traded stocks. The approach taken here, therefore, is to examine the behavior of stock returns at various individual banks for evidence of a contagion effect. Presumably, equity holders are better informed than depositors so, if anything, their tendency to be affected by idiosyncratic information should be less than for depositors.

The empirical implementation of such a study involves regressing the returns to stockholders of Bank A in each period on the returns to stockholders of Bank B in the same period. That is, the theory predicts that the greater the contagious propagation of idiosyncratic information, the greater should be the regression coefficient linking the two returns.

From a statistical viewpoint, such a regression is plagued by an important problem. Since contemporaneous returns data are used for both banks, a simple regression would not be able to distinguish the effect of A on B from that of B on A. (This is called simultaneous equations bias.) As it turns out, this problem can be resolved in the estimation process using the lagged return on A as a statistical "instrument."

STATISTICAL FINDINGS

Using this statistical method, regressions were run using daily returns data from the 54 banks whose stocks have been traded continuously for the past 10 years. Each bank's return was regressed on every other bank, resulting in 2862 regressions, each with about 2500 observations. The contagion coefficients were extracted from each of these regressions, and examined for relationships to the characteristics of the individual banks involved.

The findings are interesting, and support the notion that contagion effects between banks are significant and strong. For the entire sample of contagion regressions, the contagion coefficient averaged 12 percent. That is, 12 percent of an idiosyncratic factor affecting Bank B will be picked up by Bank A.

The contagion coefficients were much higher between certain pairs of banks and at certain times. First, everything else being equal, big banks had much larger effects on other big banks that they did on small banks (and a bigger effect than small banks had on each other). This result is depicted in Chart 1. This finding is consistent with the notion that investors in big banks are monitoring closely the behavior of other big banks.

Second, the contagion effect is greater for banks that are physically close to one another. If the two banks are separated by the length of the country, for example, the contagion effect is weaker by about 50 percent than if the banks are in the same region. This suggests that investors expect fewer common factors to affect distant banks, thereby weakening the

Chart 1
The Contagion Coefficient By Bank Asset Size: 1980-1990

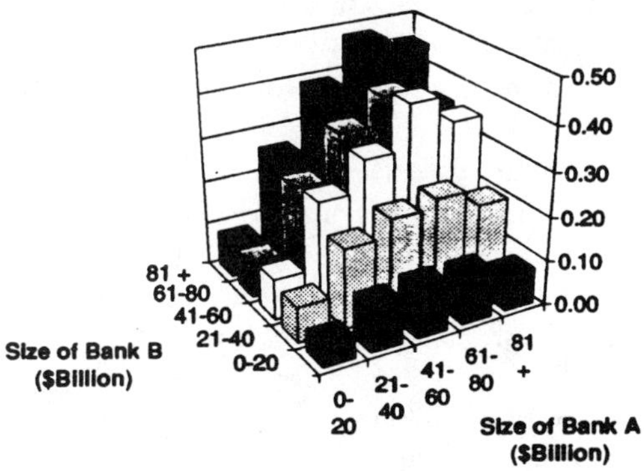

transmission of idiosyncratic effects. This is consistent with the "regionalization" of contagions historically.

Third, the contagion effect rises very dramatically during period of uncertainty. In our case study, such a period was proxied by the time period around the stock market crash of October 1987. The average contagion coefficient was over five times as large during this period as for the sample as a whole. This finding is predicted by the signal extraction models, and implies that propensity to run can accelerate significantly during times of financial stress.

Fourth, bank stock contagion effects are smaller if the affected bank has a high capital/asset ratio. That is, equity investors in a bank worry less about transmitted effects from other banks if their bank has a sizable capital buffer. This follows from the concern that depositors are more likely to run, and impose costs on the bank, if there is insufficient capital to shield them from adverse events. In our sample, an increase in the capital asset ratio at a bank from 5 percent to 15 percent decreases the contagion coefficient by about 35 percent in normal circumstances, and by 80 percent during the 1987 crash period. This suggests that higher capital ratios provide considerable protection against contagion, particularly during times of financial stress.

Finally, contagion coefficients among bank stocks appear higher than those estimated for nonbank stocks. Using a sample of stock returns from ten randomly selected, broker-defined industry categories, contagion coefficients were estimated for the largest firms in the industry category. The contagion coefficients estimated were three to five times smaller for these nonfinancial firms than for similarly ranked banking firms. One explanation for this finding is that the performance of a bank's assets is difficult for outside investors to assess, causing them to rely more on signals from peer performance than is the case for nonbank firms. This, in turn, is consistent with the notion that banks exist precisely because the risk of certain credits is too difficult for the marketplace to assess directly, requiring a very closely monitored, bank-type relationship.

CAVEATS

Before translating these results on stock returns into implications for depositor runs, several caveats must be offered. First, it must be recognized that the stock return contagion coefficients were estimated in an environment in which flat-premium deposit insurance existed. With this policy in place, "bad news" is less likely to result in higher deposit costs for a bank, thereby cushioning equity holders. This means that the contagion coefficients I have estimated may understate the degree of contagion that would exist in an uninsured banking system.

Second, the reaction of the value of equity to a piece of bad news is likely to be more pronounced than the reaction of the value of deposit liabilities; this is because equity is the junior security, and thereby cushions debt holders somewhat from deterioration in portfolio value. On the other hand, because bank depositors hold debt that is, by definition, redeemable on demand at low cost, even small decreases in the perceived value of those deposits may precipitate "runs."

CONCLUSIONS

Addressing these caveats is beyond the scope of this *Letter*. In addition, we have not provided any evidence that bank panics are costly to the economy. However, the results of our study are consistent with a tendency of the banking system to experience contagious runs. And the pattern of contagion effects accords nicely with the historical record of regionalized panics, and the tendency for panics to propagate among big banks. This suggests that if bank panics are costly, a policy of high capital requirements and deposit protection may be justified as a means of stabilizing a run-prone banking system.

REFERENCES

Benston, G., et al. 1986. *Perspectives on Safe and Sound Banking*. Cambridge: MIT Press.

King, M.A., and S. Wadhwani. 1990. "Transmission of Volatility between Stock Markets." *The Review of Financial Studies* 3, pp. 5-33.

Klebaner, B.J. 1974. *Commercial Banking in the United States: A History*. Hinsdale: Dryden Press.

QUESTIONS

1. What are the justifications for deposit insurance and bank capital regulation?

2. Are episodes of widespread bank failures necessarily an indication of contagious bank runs? How else might these episodes be explained?

3. Describe Pozdena's study to test empirically the strength of the contagion effects. What significant findings does he report? What does he conclude about contagion effects?

READING 21

Too Big to Fail: Origins, Consequences, and Outlook

Robert L. Hetzel

I. INTRODUCTION

The General Accounting Office estimates the cost of the thrift industry bailout to be around $150 billion. George Benston, professor at Emory University, helps his students grasp the immensity of this number by asking them to imagine how hard it is to become a millionaire. He then asks them to imagine 150,000 millionaires being made paupers (*New York Times*, 6/10/90). The most important lesson of the thrift debacle is the need to close insolvent and nearly insolvent financial institutions promptly [Kane (1989); Bartholomew (1991)].

"Too big to fail" refers to the practice followed by bank regulators of protecting creditors (uninsured as well as insured depositors and debt holders) of large banks from loss in the event of failure. In this article, attention is focused on the resulting transfer of the decision to close a troubled bank from its creditors to bank regulators. The paper argues that the policy of too big to fail created in banking the same kinds of problems of timely closure that existed in the thrift industry.

The policy of too big to fail resulted from a fundamental deficiency in bankruptcy arrangements for banks. In banking there is no arrangement analogous to that existing for nonfinancial corporations unable to meet their debts, where the troubled corporation continues to operate while its creditors determine whether it is viable. It is usually undesirable to liquidate a large corporation immediately following a failure to pay its debts. The corporation may be viable if restructured. Also, an orderly, rather than an immediate, liquidation can increase the salvageable value of its assets. For non-financial corporations, therefore, Chapter 11 of the bankruptcy law provides a procedure under which a bankruptcy judge supervises the operation of a corporation that cannot pay its debts. Creditors and existing management then negotiate whether to liquidate or restructure.

Banks are not subject to bankruptcy law. For banks, there is no Chapter 11 administered by the courts. In its absence, the Federal Deposit Insurance Corporation (FDIC) and the Federal Reserve have come to run an informal Chapter 11 for banks. Particularly since the early 1980s, deposit insurance and the discount window have been used to keep in operation banks that otherwise would have been closed by the market.[1] This arrangement has been useful in that it prevents the abrupt closing of large banks. In contrast to corporate bankruptcy proceedings, however, the decision to allow a bank to fail is made by public officials rather than the bank's creditors. This arrangement has delayed the resolution of insolvencies.

Section II relates the genesis of the policy of too big to fail. Section III examines how it encourages risk taking. Section IV advances a reform that would provide deposit insurance while leaving the decision to close a troubled bank to bank creditors. Using this reform as a benchmark, Section V asks whether the changes in bank regulation mandated by the Comprehensive Deposit Insurance Reform and Taxpayer Protection Act of 1991 will ensure that banks are closed neither too soon nor too late and that banks take neither too much nor too little risk.

II. THE DEVELOPMENT OF TOO BIG TO FAIL

A. A Brief History of Restrictions on Bank Competition

Free entry, the sine qua non of competition, has never had the constitutional protection in banking that it has in other industries. The Constitution prohibits states from interfering with trade across their boundaries. The commerce clause (Article I, Sec. 9) states, "No tax or duty shall be laid on articles exported from any state." In 1869, in Paul v. Virginia, the Supreme Court extended the protection of the interstate commerce clause to corporations by ruling that a state could not exclude an out-of-state corporation from doing business in it. [See Butler (1982), especially Ch. IV.] Banks are engaged in commerce in the sense that they are middlemen. They make money on the difference between the rates at which they borrow and lend. It has never been acceptable politically, however, to extend to banking the constitutional protection of free entry across state boundaries accorded other corporations.[2]

The ability of states to exclude out-of-state banks allowed state legislatures to organize their intrastate banking industries into a large number of small banks, each of which enjoyed some local monopoly power. Around the turn of the century, when the demand for banking services grew in rural areas, state legislatures passed laws prohibiting banks from meeting this demand through branching. By 1929, almost all states had laws either prohibiting or restricting intrastate branching. Along with low capital requirements for establishing a bank, the result was a banking industry consisting of large numbers of unit banks. The National Banking Act included ambiguous language that was often interpreted as forbidding interstate branching by national banks. In 1927, the McFadden Act eliminated any ambiguity by specifically prohibiting national banks from branching across state lines. As a result, banks could not diversify geographically their loans and the sources of their deposits. [For a history of prohibitions on branching, see Mengle (1990)].

Competition in banking was further restricted during the Depression. At the time, many blamed the Depression on excessive competition. It appeared plausible that individual insolvent firms could be made solvent by restricting competition. In many industries, consequently, government regulation attempted to raise prices by restricting competition. The government divided financial intermediation into separate industries that could not compete with each other. Glass-Steagall separated fund-raising for corporations into banking and securities industries. Insurance companies, savings and loans, and credit unions were assigned their own regulators and spheres of influence. The Banking Act of 1933 prohibited the payment of interest on demand deposits, and Regulation Q limited the interest banks could pay on time and savings deposits. Later, the 1956 Bank Holding Company Act restricted the ability of banks to operate nationally through multibank holding companies. Justice Department antitrust guidelines restricted competition by limiting the ability of banks to acquire other banks.

B. Increased Competition for Banks

Beginning in the late 1960s, innovations in communications and computer technology eroded restrictions on competition in banking by making it possible for nonbank institutions like money market mutual funds to offer bank-like services to bank customers. By lowering the cost of bookkeeping and disseminating information, this technology lessened the advantage that banks had possessed formerly in gathering deposits and monitoring the credit risk of borrowers. The emergence of new competitors to banks has reduced the viable size of the traditional banking industry.

The dramatic increase in competition facing banks is apparent in the minimal extent to which business relied on domestic banks in 1990 for additional credit. Baer and Brewer (1991) report the following statistics. In 1990, business credit provided by domestic banks, finance companies, U.S. branches of foreign banks, offshore sources, and by nonfinancial commercial paper grew 7.3 percent. Domestic banks provided only a small fraction, 7 percent, of this growth in funding. The year 1990 was unusual in that many banks were attempting to increase their capital-to-asset ratios by restricting asset growth. The figures reflect, however, a longer-run decline in bank business lending. Over the decade of the 1980s, banks' share of short- and medium-term lending to businesses declined at an annual rate of 1.5 percent. Furthermore, as Baer and Brewer point out, the market is continuing to develop new substitutes for bank lending like asset-backed commercial paper (backed by trade receivables) and prime rate funds (backed by commercial loans). These sources, which are not included in the above sources, added about two percentage points in 1990 to growth in short-term business credit.

Beginning in the last half of the 1960s, a series of financial innovations eroded regulatory restrictions on competition in deposit gathering. High market rates of interest produced by high rates of inflation generated incentives to escape the low ceilings on deposit rates fixed by Reg Q and the prohibition of payment of interest on demand deposits. In the 1960s, the Eurodollar market developed as a way of allowing large depositors to put their deposits on banks' books in Europe, where Reg Q did not apply. In the 1970s, automatic teller machines allowed banks to evade some geographical restrictions on banking. Money market funds and NOW accounts allowed depositors with small accounts to avoid ceilings on deposit rates. Money market funds permit savers with small amounts of savings to bypass financial institutions and invest indirectly in commercial paper, which is issued only in large denominations. NOW accounts are checkable deposits that evade the prohibition of payments of interest on demand deposits through the technicality of being labeled a savings account.

Banks have lost their dominant role not only as collectors of relatively cheap funds from small savers but also as suppliers of loans to low-risk businesses. Many large corporations issue commercial paper directly to financial intermediaries like pension funds, rather than borrow from banks. By the end of 1989, money market funds, with more than 20 million accounts, held about $455 billion in assets, much of it commercial paper. Moreover, the Glass-Steagall Act, which forbids banks from underwriting corporate securities, has prevented banks from meeting the changing needs of their corporate clients by underwriting their debt issues. In addition, a variety of firms not regulated as banks lend to corporations and consumers. Subsidiaries owned by AT&T, Ford, General Electric, and Sears make commercial loans. Automobile companies finance car loans through financial subsidiaries. American Express, AT&T, and Sears finance consumer loans through their credit card divisions.

Regional banks retain a comparative advantage in making loans to companies too small to enter the money market. They are, however, losing their comparative advantage in gathering deposits. In particular, they rely on deposit insurance as an aid in competing with money market funds for the relatively large accounts of older depositors.

Securitization, the packaging of illiquid assets like mortgages and car loans into a security that can be sold, has eroded the former natural monopoly possessed by banks to transform a portfolio of illiquid assets into liquid liabilities. Securitization has increased the range of financial intermediaries that can hold the illiquid assets formerly held only by banks. Pension funds, insurance companies, mutual funds and individuals now hold assets that formerly were held chiefly by banks. In the decade of the 1970s, banks held 34.8 percent of the financial assets of financial intermediaries, which include, in addition to banks, other depository institutions, government-sponsored enterprises, insurance companies, pension and retirement funds, and money market and other mutual funds. By 1989, this figure had fallen to 26.6 percent [U.S. Treasury (1991), Ch. I, Table 7].

Government policies have also created competitors for banks. The sharp rise of market rates in 1972 in combination with fixed Reg Q ceilings on time and savings deposits produced an outflow of funds from thrifts and banks. In order to maintain the flow of funds to housing without raising Reg Q ceilings, the government expanded the financing activities of the Federal National Mortgage Association, or "Fannie Mae," and the Federal Home Loan Mortgage Corporation, or "Freddie Mac." Fannie Mae and Freddie Mac purchase mortgages and then either hold them for their own account or package them so they can be held by institutional investors. These federally sponsored credit agencies compete with banks and thrifts for the financing and warehousing of mortgages.

Tax laws have placed banks at a disadvantage in competing for the long-term savings of individuals. For example, certain laws make some portion of an employee's wages tax-exempt if placed in a long-term savings plan (such as a 401-K plan that allows the employee to defer taxes on interest income from investments). These laws encourage corporations and state and local governments to replace banks as deposit gatherers. Corporations and state and local governments then negotiate directly with pension and thrift funds. Because these funds typically are large enough to evaluate the risk of their assets, they can hold commercial paper and bonds issued by corporations. This financial intermediation completely bypasses banks.

C. The Extension of Deposit Insurance

Had the market forces described above been left unopposed, they would have forced a contraction of the banking industry in the 1980s. Contraction was postponed through the extension of deposit insurance coverage in the form of the policy of too big to fail. This extension provided a subsidy to banks by lowering their costs of funding relative to the costs they would have incurred if some holders of their liabilities had not been protected from loss. Too big to fail arose from pressures created by the lack of satisfactory institutional arrangements for closing banks rather than from a conscious decision on the part of policymakers.

The FDIC was created in 1933 to protect depositors holding small accounts. It was not created to keep insolvent banks in operation. That task was assigned to the Reconstruction Finance Corporation. [See Todd (1988), App. C, and Todd (1991).] The emergence of too big to fail is recounted in *Bailout* by Irvine Sprague, a former director of the FDIC. Sprague recounts the transformation of the FDIC from an agency charged with covering losses of insured depositors of *already failed* banks into a modern day Reconstruction Finance Corporation that *prevents* failures by protecting all creditors of large banks from loss.[3]

Beginnings From 1950 until 1982, Section 13(c) of the Federal Deposit Insurance

Act allowed the FDIC to prevent a bank from failing if the bank were judged "essential to provide adequate banking service in its community." Sprague points out that legislative history is an unclear guide to the intended use of the "essentiality" clause, but that "this authority was not intended for widespread use" [Sprague (1986), p. 28]. Probably, it was included to prevent the failure of banks in rural areas served by a single bank. In any event, as Sprague points out, the language effectively gave the FDIC complete discretion because "the courts have always upheld an agency's discretionary authority....No challenge has been successful. So there you have it. A bank can be bailed out if two of three FDIC board members determine it should be" (Sprague, p. 28). Since the passage of the Garn-St. Germain Act in 1982, the FDIC has had the additional authority to prevent failures by arranging purchase and assumption transactions if it determines that liquidation of the bank is a costlier alternative.

In 1971, Unity Bank in Boston became the first bank bailed out under the essentiality doctrine. One of the FDIC directors opposed the bailout on the grounds "that bailouts were bad public policy and doing the first one would lead to many more, possible an uncontrollable flood" (Sprague, p. 46). That director was persuaded not to vote while the other two directors, Sprague and Wille, voted to keep Unity afloat, even though it was mismanaged. Unity was saved because of a fear that the failure of a bank considered to be a black institution would set off riots in black neighborhoods. Sprague (p. 48) notes, "[M]y vote to make the 'essentiality' finding and thus save the little bank was probably foreordained, an inevitable legacy of [the riots in] Watts." At the time, Sprague reports he believed Unity could not set a precedent because it was "a unique case, one of a kind" (Sprague, p. 49). In fact, shortly thereafter, the FDIC bailed out Bank of the Commonwealth, a large, mismanaged bank in Detroit for the same reason.

In retrospect, Sprague identifies the bailout of Unity as the first step in establishing too big to fail as public policy. "[T]he important precedent was, of course, the irreversible turn we had taken with Unity, away from our historic narrow role of acting only after the bank had failed....Now we were in the bailout business, how deeply no one could then tell" (Sprague, p. 49). Sprague then goes on to describe how over time too big to fail became embedded in banking regulation through the precedent of saving one troubled bank at a time, rather than as a result of a conscious decision. By Chapter 15 of *Bailout*, Sprague says: "Of the fifty largest bank failures in history, forty-six—including the top twenty—were handled either through a pure bailout or an FDIC-assisted transaction where no depositor, insured or uninsured, lost a penny. In effect, the forty-six enjoyed 100 percent insurance protection. The four lonely exceptions...were the result of unusual circumstances" (Sprague, p. 242).[4]

Continental Illinois Because of its size, the bailout of Continental Illinois exemplified most clearly the transformation of the FDIC into a modern Reconstruction Finance Corporation. Although only 10 percent of Continental's deposits were insured, the FDIC protected all of its depositors. [The following draws on Sprague (1986), Part 4. See also Thomson and Todd (1990).] In the late 1970s and early 1980s, Continental grew rapidly by taking on high-risk loans. In particular, Continental purchased $1 billion in oil and gas loans from Penn Square, collateralized by drilling rigs and other assets made worthless when the oil drilling business collapsed. Continental's downfall began with the bankruptcy of Penn Square Bank in Oklahoma City in July 1982. On May 9, 1984, foreign depositors began to withdraw deposits from Continental. Initially, the Federal Reserve Bank of Chicago assisted it with discount window loans, which eventually totaled $7.6 billion.

Because no buyers could be found for Continental, the FDIC decided to keep it in operation through "open bank assistance." It purchased $1 billion in preferred stock from Continental's holding company, which lent the funds to Continental. This arrangement amounted to capital forbearance in that Continental was allowed to remain in operation with an amount of private capital below regulatory standards. (It also protected the creditors of the holding company, as well as the bank.)

Recent Developments Two recent bank failures illustrate the blanket coverage extended to uninsured depositors under the policy of too big to fail. On August 10, 1990, the Comptroller of the Currency closed National Bank of Washington and named the FDIC as receiver. Because of the lapse of time between the dissemination of information about the bank's problems and the closing of the bank, depositors at the Nassau branch had begun to withdraw funds beginning early in 1990. Discount window lending by the Fed might have permitted a sizable portion of these deposit withdrawals. The foreign deposits remaining when the bank was seized, although not formally insured by the FDIC, were protected. According to newspaper accounts, the FDIC protected Washington National's foreign deposits in order to provide assurance to foreign depositors at money-center banks that their deposits were protected (*American Banker*, 9/27/90). The policy of too big to fail has effectively extended insurance to deposits in banks' overseas branches.[5]

On January 6, 1991, the FDIC took control of the Bank of New England Corporation's banks—Bank of New England, Connecticut Bank and Trust, and Maine National Bank. The FDIC's initial estimate of the loss was $2.3 billion (*Financial Times*, 1/8/91). Newspaper commentary accompanying the rescue makes clear how broad the criteria have become for bailing out a bank's uninsured creditors (*Wall Street Journal*, 1/7/91):

> The arrangement will protect from loss all depositors, even those with accounts exceeding the $100,000 insurance ceiling. Mr. Seidman made it clear in an interview that the urgency of the rescue transcended the bank's difficulties. "We're looking at an eroding economy, particularly in New England," he said....Over the weekend, government officials stressed the need to improve credit conditions in New England to slow economic deterioration there.

At present, "too big to fail" appears to be a misnomer as even small banks are usually not allowed to fail with a loss to uninsured depositors. As William Seidman, former chairman of the FDIC, noted (*Wall Street Journal*, 6/5/92):

> Some people mistakenly believe that small-bank failures usually are resolved through a payout of insured deposits—a liquidation, where uninsured depositors and creditors suffer some loss. The reality is that, currently, about nine out of ten small-bank failures are resolved through "purchase and assumption" transactions. In a P&A [purchase and assumption transaction], all the deposits (including those over the $100,000 insurance limit) generally are assumed by a healthy bank. Of the 169 banks that failed in 1990, only 20 were resolved through a payout of insured deposits. The rest were resolved through P&As.

While deposit insurance expanded principally through growth of the policy of too big to fail, explicit increases in the size of covered deposits and regulatory actions also expanded its coverage. Regulators used increases in coverage per account to lower the cost of funds and to increase their availability to banks and thrifts when increases in market rates above Reg Q prompted disintermediation. Increases in coverage per account coincided with peaks in market rates: 1966, 1969, 1974, and 1980. FDIC-insured deposits as a fraction of total deposits increased from about 55 percent in 1965 to more than 70 percent in the 1980s [U.S. Treasury (1991), Conclusions and Recommendations, Figures 6 and 7].

During the 1980s, the FDIC also increased the kinds of bank liabilities protected from loss. It extended insurance to the deposits of pension plans by "passing through" the $100,000 insurance limit to the individual participants of the plans. It insured brokered deposits.[6] The FDIC also insured private parties to swap transactions with banks in receivership.

The current low rate of return to banking is consistent with the argument that the policy of too big to fail has kept the banking industry from contracting in response to increased competition. In the 1970s, the return on assets for insured commercial banks was .77 percent. From 1985 to 1989, this figure fell to .55 percent [U.S. Treasury (1991), Ch. I, Table 6]. The decline in the value of bank stocks relative to the S&P 500, which began in the late 1970s and became more pronounced beginning in 1986, reveals investor skepticism about the future profitability of the banking industry given its current size. Even with the rally in bank stocks in early 1991, the P/E ratio of money-center and large regional banks is only half that of firms in the S&P 500 (*American Banker*, 3/18/91).

D. Pressures to Postpone Closing Insolvent Banks

Regulators incur a variety of pressures to postpone closing a troubled bank. Closing a bank produces active disapproval from those affected adversely. In contrast, beneficiaries are unaware of the costs indirectly imposed on them by the relaxation of market discipline involved in keeping a troubled bank afloat. Beneficiaries include consumers who benefit from competition and potential entrants in the banking industry.

The ability of regulatory agencies to keep open a troubled bank inevitably invites political pressures. Congressmen pass on constituent discontent over the job losses and personal disruptions that accompany the closing of a bank. The case of the Keating Five is instructive. Beginning in 1987, five senators apparently intervened with the Federal Home Loan Bank Board in order to keep Lincoln Savings and Loan in operation. The Senate Ethics Committee found the intervention itself appropriate. The only issue was whether is was appropriate to accept money from Mr. Keating while intervening on his behalf with federal regulators. In summarizing the report of the Ethics Committee, *Congressional Quarterly* [Cranford (1991), p. 518] noted:

> Significantly, the committee found nothing intrinsically wrong with the intervention by these five senators with federal regulators in 1987 in behalf of Charles H. Keating....Each had ample information to justify contacting regulators about the fairness of the regulatory treatment Lincoln was receiving. The case has hung on the nexus between the five senators' intervention and the enormous political contributions that they collected from Keating.

Congressional Quarterly [Cranford (1991), p. 519] also reports Sen. DeConcini's reply to the report of the Ethics Committee:

> As the committee effectively acknowledges, in early 1987 I had strong reason to believe that a major Arizona company was being treated unfairly by the federal government. I further had reason to believe that 2,000 Arizona jobs were unfairly at stake.

Pressures on regulators to keep troubled banks afloat do not have to be political. Regulators may temporize because they are genuinely uncertain whether a bank is insolvent. It is often difficult to measure the market value of a bank's assets and, consequently, the market value of its capital. Regulators want to be fair, and they want to be perceived as fair in the media. Given the ambiguity of measures of capital, they naturally tend to close a bank only when it is clearly insolvent.[7] Their desire for fairness presents them with another dilemma over troubled banks: given a chance, some of these banks will recover. If regulators were to close a bank that is not obviously insolvent, they would inevitably be criticized for the "premature and unnecessary" closure of a bank that "if given a chance, would make it." They would receive especially heated criticism from small borrowers with special, ongoing relationships with the troubled bank.[8]

In the case of the Bank of New England, the Comptroller of the Currency only closed the bank when depositors actually began to run it. In an *American Banker* (1/9/91) article, Comptroller Clarke and FDIC Chairman Seidman were reported as having said that "they did not act until last weekend because only then was it certain that the Bank of New England Corp. had no chance to survive." In the same article, Karen Shaw, president of the Institute for Strategy Development, noted: "There was the hope, even if it was an errant hope, that the bank would survive. It had made it through several crises."

Rather than liquidate a large bank for failure to meet a capital standard, regulators are more likely to try to find a merger partner for the bank while allowing it to remain in business. Such partners, however, are hard to find. Possible merger partners have an incentive to wait until the condition of a troubled bank deteriorates to the point where it is actually taken over by the FDIC. They can then negotiate with the FDIC. In this way, banks not only avoid a possible costly court fight with the troubled bank's stockholders, but also open up the possibility that the FDIC will add incentives to make the acquisition more attractive.

An additional incentive to procrastination in closing a bank is the multiplicity of regulators. Understandably, each regulator would like for the other regulator to receive any criticism for closing a bank. For example, the Comptroller of the Currency has the responsibility for declaring national banks insolvent. The Comptroller, however, does not use its own resources to keep a troubled bank afloat. It has an incentive, therefore, to wait and hope that the Fed will effectively close the bank by pulling its discount window loan or that the FDIC will close the bank by refusing to grant a waiver for the bank to attract insured brokered deposits. Also, state regulators may have been reluctant to revoke the charters of insolvent state-chartered banks. Closing down a bank that they examine may appear as an admission of failure.

III. THE PROBLEMS WITH TOO BIG TO FAIL

Restrictions on the ability of market forces to close banks embodied in the policy of too big to fail started to cause problems when banks began to experience significant external competition in the 1970s and 1980s. The extension of deposit insurance in the form of the policy of too big to fail provided a subsidy to banks that kept the banking industry from contracting. It also encouraged risk taking. Kept from shrinking by an extension of the implicit subsidies of deposit insurance, banks responded to the loss of low-risk corporate customers by turning to riskier investments. Many banks also increased the subsidy from deposit insurance by holding riskier asset portfolios without increasing their capital.

A. FDIC Insurance as a Subsidy to Risk Taking

This section first explains why government-sponsored insurance subsidizes risk taking by failing to price risk. The remainder of the section documents the increase in the riskiness of the banking system since the 1960s. Banks have acquired increasingly risky asset portfolios, with no increase over this period in capital ratios.

Insurance offered by a private company pools individual risk by establishing a fund into which premiums are paid and from which losses are met. The insurance company is the residual claimant on the fund. It makes money when the fund grows and loses money when it declines. For this reason, the insurance company places restrictions on its policyholders that limit the risks they take. Private insurance cannot subsidize risk taking. It must price risk accurately or go out of business.

Although the FDIC uses the term "insurance fund," its fund is fundamentally different from the kind of fund maintained by a private insurance company. With the FDIC fund, there are no residual claimants whose money is at stake. The Treasury keeps a tally on the cumulative difference between incoming FDIC deposit premia and outgoing FDIC expenditures and includes interest on the positive balance. This tally is the FDIC "insurance fund." The FDIC fund can be depleted, but it cannot become insolvent. If the current receipts from the premia paid by banks are insufficient to cover current FDIC expenditures, then FDIC deposit insurance commits the taxpayer to pay the difference. It is this commitment that allows deposit insurance to be used to subsidize risk taking.

In contrast to a private insurance arrangement that limits risk taking, FDIC insurance encourages risk taking. The subsidy banks receive from the guarantee of their deposits by the government increases with the riskiness of their asset portfolio and decreases with the amount of capital they hold. FDIC deposit insurance does not lower the cost of funds appreciably for a conservatively managed, highly capitalized bank, but it does for a risk-taking, poorly capitalized bank. Both kinds of banks pay the same flat rate on their insured deposits.[9]

The encouragement given by deposit insurance to risk taking was kept in check as long as restrictions on competition gave banks a high franchise value. A high franchise value acts like a large amount of capital. It limits risk taking because stockholders bear significant losses if the bank fails. Increased competition in banking, however, has eroded the franchise value of banks, especially since the 1970s [Keeley (1990)].

B. Evidence of Increased Risk in the Banking System

Deposit insurance has allowed the banking industry to pursue riskier investment strategies in the 1980s without increasing its capital. In the early 1960s, insured commercial banks had a ratio of capital to total assets of about 8 percent.[10] In the 1980s, this ratio fell to about 6 percent [U.S. Department of Commerce (1965), Table 607, and U.S. Department of Commerce (1985), Table 826]. The 6 percent aggregate figure conceals significant variation among banks. At year-end 1989, the largest 25 banks had a ratio of capital to assets of only 4.8 percent [U.S. Treasury (1991), Ch. II, Table 2]. Barth,

Brumbaugh and Litan (1990, Table 3) report that, as of June 1990, 183 banks with assets of $11.2 billion were operating with capital-to-assets ratios of less than 3 percent. An additional 67 banks with combined assets of $80 billion had capital-to-assets ratios between 3 and 3.5 percent.

There is also evidence that, for troubled banks, capital based on the book value of assets overstates capital based on market values. Using cross section data to study the relationship between book and market values, Mengle (1991, p. 21) finds that, among banks that failed, capital based on book values significantly overstated capital based on market values. Mengle (1991, p. 19) also notes:

> Failures are far more common than book value insolvency numbers would suggest; in any given year, the number of failures far outstrips the number of book value insolvencies in either the current or the previous year....only 6 percent of the banks that failed in 1985 had reported themselves to be book value insolvent in 1985.

Moreover, the stock market values many banks less highly than the book value of their capital. Barth, Brumbaugh, and Litan (1991, Table 6) show that for 20 of the 25 largest U.S. banks, the market value of their equity is less than the book value.

While the ratio of book capital to assets has changed very little for the banking system over the last two decades, banks' asset portfolios have become riskier. The loss of blue chip corporate customers to the commercial paper market left remaining bank loan portfolios riskier. Particularly since the mid-1980s, bank lending has been concentrated in high-risk categories. From 1985 through 1990, 65 percent of the increase in bank loans was in real estate. Of the increase in real estate lending during this period, 43.5 percent was in commercial real estate [Board of Governors (March 1991), Table 1.25, "Assets and Liabilities of Commercial Banks" and Board of Governors (December 1991), Table 1.54, "Mortgage Debt Outstanding"]. Banks purchased large amounts of mortgage-backed securities, which present considerable interest rate risk, and became heavily involved in off-balance sheet activities such as loan commitments and standby letters of credit. In dollar terms, these latter activities grew from 58 percent of assets in 1982 to 116 percent in 1989 [U.S. Treasury (1991), Ch. 1, p. 27].

The increase in this riskiness of bank asset portfolios could not have occurred without the subsidy to risk taking provided by deposit insurance. Consider the contrasting management of the banks described in the following quotations:

> Long dependent on a regional economy that rises and falls with the auto industry's swings, banks in the region [Midwest] rarely stray far from the basics of opening checking accounts, backing small businesses and managing trust funds. Economic uncertainty has generally kept them from seeking quick gains through risky loans to commercial developers,

> junk bond artists or Third World nations (*Wall Street Journal*, 4/11/91).
>
> Each week, Walter Connolly [head of the Bank of New England Corp.] would survey the numbers from his banking empire, 450 branches that stretched from the top to the bottom of New England. If the numbers didn't look right—if a bank had lost even a bit of market share—Connolly would get the bank's president on the phone and demand to know what had happened. No matter what he was told, he had the same answer: "Grow it, grow it." "The whole culture was one of growth," said Donald J. Kauth...."Size was success to Walter," said one colleague. "He wanted to retire as the chairman of the biggest bank in Boston" (*Washington Post*, 1/9/91).

Deposit insurance subsidizes the risk-taking bank, not the conservatively managed bank. In particular, deposit insurance makes it possible for a bank to finance rapid growth with cheap deposits even if that growth is achieved by acquiring low quality and risky assets.

C. Systemic Risk

The policy of too big to fail is often defended as a response to inherent instability in the banking system. This section makes the opposite argument, namely, that deposit insurance and the policy of too big to fail have created instability in the banking system.

Because too big to fail entails closing banks without imposing losses on depositors, there is an ongoing possibility that the FDIC will have to ask Congress for funds to close insolvent banks.[11] The regressive character of the wealth transfers involved in bailing out the creditors of large banks, however, makes it difficult for Congress to appropriate funds for the FDIC. The ongoing possibility of a need for additional funding to operate the FDIC, combined with the uncertainties surrounding the congressional appropriations process, creates a potential for systemic instability. In a situation where many banks are poorly capitalized, a run on a large bank at a time when the deposit insurance fund is depleted could cause bank runs to spread uncontrollably. Under current institutional arrangements, therefore, regulators must maintain control over the timing of the closing of insolvent banks. This control can only be achieved by protecting all creditors of banks (including uninsured depositors) from loss. Current institutional arrangements make too big to fail an imperative.

Too big to fail, however, is part of a vicious circle. Protecting all creditors from loss limits incentives for creditors to monitor the riskiness of bank asset portfolios. Banks can then hold only minimal amounts of capital while making risky investments without increasing the rate they pay on deposits. This behavior, however, creates precisely the weakness in the banking system that makes too big to fail appear to be an imperative. Ironically, deposit insurance has produced the systemic instability it was supposed to prevent.

IV. THE WORLD WITHOUT TOO BIG TO FAIL

A. The New Legislation

The policy of too big to fail resulted in part from a lack of satisfactory institutional arrangements for closing insolvent banks in a timely way. The 1991 Deposit Insurance Reform Act addresses the problem of timely closure by requiring regulators to close a bank when its capital falls below a specified level. [The Shadow Financial Regulatory Committee (1988) has been the primary proponent of this approach.]

The new act requires bank regulators to establish five capital categories: well capitalized, adequately capitalized, undercapitalized, significantly undercapitalized, and critically undercapitalized. It requires regulators to classify as critically undercapitalized any bank with a capital-to-assets ratio of 2 percent or less. Regulators must close such a bank within 90 days. Furthermore, the act legislates a list of strictures that bank regulators must impose on banks in the undercapitalized and significantly undercapitalized categories.

The mandatory early intervention written into the new law probably derived from the political difficulty in introducing market discipline by explicitly limiting deposit insurance.[12] The law intends that regulators close troubled banks before insured deposits are put at risk. Consequently, the FDIC would not have to absorb a loss when a bank fails. It follows that the new law should remove the former subsidy to risk taking created by deposit insurance. Its intent is to make deposit insurance superfluous without explicitly limiting or repealing it.

Will the Deposit Insurance Reform Act end the policy of too big to fail through the prompt closing of troubled banks? Will banks begin to assume an optimal amount of risk? Answering these questions requires a benchmark against which the legislation can be judged. This benchmark is taken to be a banking system in which market discipline controls both the closure decision and the riskiness of bank asset portfolios. How would such a system work?

B. Market Closure

Such a system could apply the arrangements for corporate bankruptcy to the banking industry. Under corporate bankruptcy law, the timing of the closure decision of troubled firms is approximately right.[13] Although much of corporate bankruptcy law would not be applicable, it would be possible to recreate its major features for banks. First, bankruptcy law provides a market mechanism for placing corporations in receivership. That is, the decision to place a corporation in receivership is made by a firm's creditors or management rather than by public officials. Second, corporations in receivership are not allowed to fail catastrophically. Chapter 11 allows a bankrupt corporation to continue in operation while it is either reorganized or liquidated in an orderly fashion. Third, bankruptcy law provides a rule for apportioning losses among a firm's creditors. Fourth, although insolvent corporations are not liquidated abruptly, they are not kept in operation with government money. The individuals involved have the necessary incentives to close institutions that are not viable.

These features of corporate bankruptcy law could be approximated for banks.[14] First, the policy of too big to fail could be eliminated by rescinding the ability of any government agency to offer guarantees to bank creditors, including depositors. Bank creditors then would have their own money at risk in a bank failure. Analogous to corporate bankruptcy, bankruptcy of a bank would be triggered by failure to honor an obligation for payment.[15] Second, a petition for bankruptcy would put a bank into the kind of receivership provided for by Chapter 11 in corporate bankruptcy. Third, when a bank went into receivership its depositors would incur an immediate loss (haircut) on the amount of their deposits at the close of the day preceding the bankruptcy decision.[16] Regulators would set the size of the loss so that the failed bank would again possess positive net worth. Apart from the haircut, depositors would have complete access to their funds, unlike creditors in a corporate bankruptcy. Fourth, if necessary, banks in receivership could obtain new funds from debtor-in-possession financing, that is, financing in which new lenders receive priority in repayment over existing holders of subordinated debt.

C. A Proposal to Restructure Deposit Insurance

The provision of a Chapter 11 arrangement for banks, which would ensure that banks never failed abruptly, would protect the payments system. The issue remains, however, of whether allowing bank depositors to close a bank through a run could precipitate a system-wide run. In particular, economists differ over whether the ability of the Federal Reserve to undertake large-scale open market purchases of securities to supply reserves to the banking system would be sufficient to prevent a general run of the banking system.[17] This issue is likely to remain contentious. A system of deposit insurance, however, could be designed that would keep the closure decision in the hands of bank creditors while still protecting against bank panics. Deposit insurance, which currently is an entitlement granted whenever a bank creates a deposit, could be fixed in quantity and priced by the market.

Specifically, the Treasury would auction deposit insurance certificates to banks, which would sell them to depositors desiring to insure their deposits. The amount of these certificates, however, would be kept less than the total deposits in the banking system. In addition, individual banks would be able to offer insurance certificates only up to a fraction of their total deposits. In this way, all banks would have some depositors genuinely at risk in the event of a failure.[18]

An advantage of this proposal is that it is agnostic on the issue of whether instability is an inherent feature of banking. On the one hand, if policymakers believe that the banking system is prone to instability, they can maintain permanently a relatively high ratio of deposit insurance certificates relative to the total deposits of the banking system. On the other hand, they may believe that the best way to ensure a stable banking system is through market discipline that gives individual banks an incentive to hold high levels of capital and limit risk taking. They could then gradually eliminate the certificates.

V. BANK CLOSURE AND RISK TAKING WITH THE NEW LEGISLATION

Under the new law, how well will regulators approximate the results that would be achieved by competitive market forces? Will troubled banks be closed neither prematurely nor tardily? Will banks take the right amount of risk, neither too much nor too little?

A. Optimal Closure

The new law continues to rely heavily on the discretion of government regulators. Regulators still decide when to write down the book value of a bank's assets and, as a consequence, when to lower the credit category into which a bank falls. Fear of triggering a run could still make regulators reluctant to downgrade a large bank's capital category.

Alternatively, the new law could create political pressure to close troubled banks prematurely. It gives regulators a whole arsenal of weapons for limiting risk and restricting the activities of troubled banks. If a bank does fail with a significant loss to the FDIC, bank regulators could easily by accused of negligent supervision.[19] In order to avoid the criticism of negligence, regulators might write down the book value of a bank's assets at any sign of trouble. In the spirit of the new law, they might take strong action against any bank whose capital falls below even the most conservative capital categories.

B. Optimal Risk Taking

Even if banks are closed promptly when the book value of their capital falls below 2 percent, losses to the deposit insurance fund may remain large. Limiting losses to the insurance fund will also require limiting the riskiness of bank asset portfolios. The new legislation leaves uncertain whether limiting bank risk will occur through imposition of market discipline or through regulator intervention.

Consider, in this regard, the failure on August 10, 1990, of National Bank of Washington (discussed earlier). National Bank of Washington was the second bank closed under the powers granted by the Financial Institution Reform, Recovery, and Enforcement Act of 1989. These powers allow regulators to seize a bank before it becomes insolvent. On March 31, 1990, the bank had a capital-to-assets ratio of 5 percent (Consolidated Reports of Condition and Income). When seized four months later, it still had a capital-to-assets ratio of 1.4 percent. Measured by the book value of its assets, it was solvent. When National Bank of Washington was closed and sold to Riggs National Bank, however, the FDIC had to retain $539 million in its assets, one-third of the bank's $1.6 billion in assets. The FDIC's initial estimate of its loss was $500 million (*American Banker*, 9/27/90). National Bank of Washington was in fact deeply insolvent when it was closed.

The new law requires regulators to close within 90 days a bank with a capital-to-assets ratio of 2 percent or less. The experience with National Bank of Washington, which was closed when it had a book value capital ratio of 1.4 percent, suggests that the new law will not necessarily prevent failures that impose heavy losses on the FDIC.

A study by Alton Gilbert (1992, Table 4) of 1,000 banks that failed since 1985 puts the average loss ratio at 27 percent (the loss to the FDIC divided by the book value of the failed bank's assets). Under the system of bank regulation that existed prior to the Deposit Insurance Reform Act, the standard practice was for regulators to close banks when their book capital-to-assets ratio reached 0 percent. With the passage of the new act, they will close banks when this ratio reaches 2 percent. Given the magnitude of the historic loss ratio, 27 percent, the change from 0 to 2 percent should not be expected to have a significant effect in reducing FDIC losses.

Two other changes in the regulatory regime could, however, keep FDIC losses small in the future. First, the public could come to believe that federal regulators will allow large banks to fail with losses to uninsured depositors. Uninsured depositors would then begin to exert a discipline on bank risk taking by demanding a return on their deposits commensurate with the riskiness of banks' portfolios. Market discipline would force banks to price risk correctly by imposing higher interest rates on the uninsured deposits of banks with risky asset portfolios. Correct pricing by banks would limit the riskiness of their asset portfolios.

Second, bank regulators might be drawn heavily into limiting bank risk. Because of the difficulties in evaluating risk, this involvement would probably take the form of relatively crude quantitative limits on different kinds of investments. Attempts by regulators to restrict the riskiness of bank asset portfolios, however, could prevent banks from allocating capital efficiently by balancing risk and return. Reducing the riskiness of bank assets is not an end in itself. After all, banks exist because of the need to make risky loans. They are financial intermediaries that specialize in pricing risk and monitoring risky lending. If regulators are drawn into this second alternative, they could greatly harm the banking industry's ability to extend credit efficiently.

VI. CONCLUDING COMMENT

The new legislation may remove most of the subsidy offered by deposit insurance. Increases in the deposit insurance premium levied by the FDIC could even turn deposit insurance into a net tax. If implicit subsidies in deposit insurance kept banking from contracting in the 1980s, then the new legislation, by removing these subsidies, will precipitate a contraction of banking. The contraction may be particularly severe among large banks that lost corporate customers to the commercial paper market in the 1980s. The difficulties in achieving optimal closure and risk taking in banking discussed above are likely to be exacerbated by the need for the banking industry to contract. This contraction could be impeded by the tendency of failed banks to be merged rather than closed and by legal restraints that prevent banks from diversifying freely into other financial and commercial activities.

Banking is still different from other industries. There is no active market for corporate control in which raiders can acquire a bank and shrink it. There is no market-driven bankruptcy procedure. Consequently, there is no market mechanism to assure efficient shrinkage of the banking industry. It is important that this problem be understood and publicly debated.

ENDNOTES

1.The FDIC has argued that the policy of too big to fail has been imposed on it by statutory restrictions that require the least costly method of resolving a bank failure. Specifically, the FDIC can economically liquidate a small bank, but not a large one. Large bank failures, consequently, are handled by purchase and assumption arrangements, which avoid liquidation, but require the FDIC to inject enough funds into the sale of closed banks to restore their solvency and to avoid depositor losses. This situation reflects the absence of a Chapter 11 arrangement for banks that would allow either the market or regulators to close banks without forcing immediate liquidations.

2.Ironically, the European Common Market is using the U.S. federal model to promote open competition in banking. Starting in 1993, banks will be free to branch across national boundaries. Furthermore, in general, host-country regulators cannot place any restrictions on the activities of branches of foreign banks not imposed by the home-country regulator. [See Coleman and Hart (7/29/91).] The combination of guaranteed free entry and home-country regulation sharply curtails the ability of host-country regulators to limit competition in the banking industry.

3.Even when the too big to fail doctrine is applied, banks can fail in that their charters are revoked and their stockholders lose their investments. Too big to fail means that the FDIC and the Federal Reserve prevent a lack of funding from closing large, troubled banks while the FDIC arranges a takeover by another bank (a purchase and assumption transaction). The FDIC subsidizes the takeover so that bank depositors (uninsured as well as insured) do not incur any losses.

4.The major "lonely exception" was Penn Square, which was liquidated because the FDIC believed that the bank's negligent and possible fraudulent loan practices might create such extensive litigation as to render impossible a purchase and assumption transaction.

5.By the end of 1990, these deposits totaled about $300 billion and amounted to 51 percent of the deposits of the nine largest U.S. banks.

6.In 1984, the FDIC and FSLIC adopted regulations to deny deposit insurance to certificates of deposit purchased from a broker. The regulations, however, were overturned by a federal court, and Congress was unwilling to pass legislation allowing the regulatory agencies to prohibit brokered certificates of deposit.

7."Regulators, attuned to the necessities of congressional relations, and no more willing than other human beings to put other people out of work, will forbear until the death rattle is clearly audible" [Wallison (1991), p. 12].
8.Such criticism is unlikely to acknowledge the moral hazard problems of allowing a troubled bank to remain open. "History and what little we know of human nature suggest that as weak bank managements struggle to survive they will reach for more risky investments to pay for their more costly funds, obscure from examiners the dangerous condition of their enterprise, appeal to their elected representatives as needy constituents and surrender only when all hope is gone" [Wallison (1991), p. 12].
9.In principle, risk-based capital guidelines can offset the incentives deposit insurance creates for risk taking. In practice, however, such guidelines are hard to implement. They assign risk on the basis of broad categories, which do not differentiate between riskiness of assets within categories. Also, it is often hard to defend the relative assessment of risk across categories. For example, the 1988 Basle Agreements on risk-based capital guidelines stipulate that mortgage-backed securities, which are often subject to significant risk from interest rate fluctuations, require only one-fifth the capital of a commercial loan. The most important drawback to risk-based capital guidelines is their failure to reward risk reduction through asset diversification.
10.At the time, this capital ratio was adequate because restrictions on competition made banking relatively safe. The absence of any change in the bank prime rate from August 1960 through December 1965 used to be cited as evidence of the cartelization of banking.
11.At present, the FDIC possesses only a limited ability to generate additional revenue through increases in the premium it levies on deposits. Additional premium increases will reduce the ability of banks to compete with other financial intermediaries. Banks are already subject to the special tax imposed by noninterest-bearing reserve requirements. In the past, required reserves and FDIC deposit premia have collected similar amounts of revenue. For example, in December 1990, depository institutions held $57.5 billion in required reserves, and the three-month Treasury bill rate was 6.8 percent. At an annual rate, the reserve requirement tax was collecting $3.9 billion in revenue (.068 x $57.5). In 1989, FDIC assessment income came to $3.5 billion.
12.Direct attempts to limit deposit insurance, such as reducing the $100,000 deposit limit, limiting the number of allowable accounts per household, and providing for a depositor deductible, proved too controversial to include in the new law.
13.Dotsey and Kuprianov (1990) discuss relevant issues in the context of the problems with the S&L industry in the 1980s.
14.A detailed proposal is available from the author.
15.Although creditors could petition a bankruptcy court to close a bank that did not honor its debts, most petitions for bankruptcy would probably be voluntary petitions by bank management made to stop an incipient run.
16.The American Banker's Association (1990) and Boyd and Rolnick (1988) have advocated depositor haircuts.
17.Anna Schwartz argues that it would. She observes (personal communication to the author): "There were runs before the public could confidently count on a lender of last resort to nip them in the bud. I keep asking why Britain had its last run on banks in 1866, but the U.S. continued to experience them until 1933. In the first case, the lender of last resort had learned what to do to prevent a run, and the public knew it." Diamond and Dybvig (1983), in contrast, construct a model in which in principle it is possible to have bank runs that would not be offset by open market purchases.
18.For example, assume a depositor has $20,000 in deposits at the time his bank enters bankruptcy court and $15,000 in deposit insurance certificates. Assume also that depositors receive a haircut of 5 percent. The depositor, then, receives a haircut of 5 percent on the $5,000 of deposits not covered by his certificates. When a bank is placed into bankruptcy and its depositors incur haircuts, the bank submits the deposit insurance certificates registered with it to the Treasury. The Treasury becomes a claimant on the failed bank for an amount equal to the percentage haircut applied to the bank's certificates.

19. *Pratt's Letter* (December 20, 1991) commented: "When Senate Banking Committee Chairman Riegle prematurely (and unjustly) dispatched Comptroller Clarke to regulatory boot hill, he delivered a powerful message of his own: Mess up and I'll have your head. And now that Congress has legislatively signed what it perceives to be a $95 billion check for the FDIC and RTC, its proclivity for the Riegle-style witch hunt will increase."

REFERENCES

American Banker. "Banks Halt Their Binge in Mortgage Securities." May 9, 1990, p. 1.

__. "FDIC Vetoed Plan to Curb Its Coverage in DC Failure." September 27, 1990, p. 1.

__. "Regulators Defend Timing in Seizure of Boston Bank." January 9, 1991, p. 1.

__. "Even After a Five-Month Surge, Bank Stocks Remain Dirt Cheap." March 18, 1991, p. 1.

American Bankers Association. "Federal Deposit Insurance: A Program for Reform." March 1990.

Baer, Herbert and Elijah Brewer III. "The Credit Crunch and the Diminishing Role of Banks." Federal Reserve Bank of Chicago, July 1991, processed.

Barth, James R., Philip F. Bartholomew, and Michael G. Bradley. "Reforming Federal Deposit Insurance: What Can Be Learned from Private Insurance Practices?" Research Paper #161, Federal Home Loan Bank Board, June 1989.

Barth, James R., R. Dan Brumbaugh, Jr., and Robert E. Litan. "The Banking Industry in Turmoil: A Report on the Condition of the U.S. Banking Industry and the Bank Insurance Fund." Report to the Financial Institutions Subcommittee of the House Committee on Banking, Housing and Urban Affairs, 101st Cong., 2nd sess., December 1990.

Bartholomew, Philip F. *Estimating the Cost of Regulatory Forbearance During the Thrift Crisis*. Congressional Budget Office, 1991, processed.

Board of Governors of the Federal Reserve System. *Annual Statistical Digest*. Washington, D.C.: Board of Governors, March 1991.

__. *Federal Reserve Bulletin*. Washington, D.C.: Board of Governors, December 1991.

Boyd, John H. and Arthur J. Rolnick. "A Case for Reforming Federal Deposit Insurance." Federal Reserve Bank of Minneapolis *Annual Report*, 1988.

Butler, Henry Nolde. *Legal Change in an Interest-Group Perspective: The Demise of Special Corporate Charters*. Ph.D. Dissertation, Virginia Polytechnic Institute and State University, May 1982.

Coleman, Martin and Susan Hart. "Europe Can Teach U.S. a Few Lessons on Reform." *American Banker*, July 29, 1991, p. 4.

Cranford, John R. "Decision in Keating Five Case Settles Little for Senate." *Congressional Quarterly*, March 2, 1991, pp. 517-23.

Diamond, Douglas W. and Philip Dybvig. "Bank Runs, Deposit Insurance, and Liquidity." *Journal of Political Economy* 91 (June 1983): 401-19.

Dotsey, Michael and Tony Kuprianov. "Reforming Deposit Insurance: Lessons from the Savings and Loan Crisis." Federal Reserve Bank of Richmond *Economic Review* 76 (March/April 1990): 3-28.

Financial Times. "Lifeboat Rushes Into New England Storm." January 8, 1991, p. 17.

Gilbert, R. Alton. "Effects of Legislating Prompt Corrective Action on the Losses of the Bank Insurance Fund." January 1992, photocopy.

Kane, Edward J. *The S&L Insurance Mess: How Did It Happen?* Washington, D.C.: Urban Institute Press, 1989.

Kaufman, George G. "Banking Risk in Historical Perspective." Federal Reserve Bank of Chicago *Proceedings of a Conference on Bank Structure and Competition*, 1986, pp. 231-49.

Keeley, Michael. "Deposit Insurance, Risk and Market Power in Banking." *American Economic Review* 80 (December 1990): 1183-1200.

Mengle, David L. "The Case for Interstate Banking." Federal Reserve Bank of Richmond *Economic Review* 76 (November/December 1990): 3-17.

__. "Market Value Accounting and Bank Failures." Federal Reserve Bank of Richmond, June 1991, processed.

Mengle, David L. and John R. Walter. "How Market Value Accounting Would Affect Banks." Federal Reserve Bank of Chicago *Proceedings of a Conference on Bank Structure and Competition*, forthcoming 1991.

New York Times. "Numbers Crunch." June 10, 1990, p. E1.

Rolnick, Arthur and Warren E. Weber. "The Causes of Free Bank Failures: A Detailed Examination." *Journal of Monetary Economics* 14 (November 1984): 267-91.

Shadow Financial Regulatory Committee. "An Outline of a Program for Deposit Insurance Reform." Statement No. 39. Mid America Institute for Public Policy Research, Chicago, December 5, 1988.

Sprague, Irvine H. *Bailout*. New York: Basic Books, 1986.

Thomson, James B. and Walker F. Todd. "An Insider's View of the Politics of the Too Big to Fail Doctrine." Federal Reserve Bank of Cleveland Working Paper #9017, December 1990.

Todd, Walker F. "Lessons of the Past and Prospects for the Future in Lender of Last Resort Theory." Federal Reserve Bank of Chicago *Proceedings of a Conference on Bank Structure and Competition*, May 11-13, 1988, pp. 533-77.

__. "Banks Are Not Special: The Federal Safety Net and Banking Powers" in Catherine England (ed.), *Governing Banking's Future: Markets vs. Regulation*. Boston: Kluwer Academic Publishers, 1991.

U.S. Department of Commerce. *Statistical Abstract of the United States*. Washington, D.C.: 1965 and 1985.

U.S. Treasury. "Modernizing the Financial System." February 1991.

Wall Street Journal. "U.S. Recession Claims Bank of New England As First Big Victim." January 7, 1991, p. 1.

__. "Bruised by the S&L Fiasco, Lawmakers Now Try to Show They Are Born Again Bank Guardians." March 19, 1991, p. A26.

__. "In Great Lakes Region Many Bankers Prove Caution Can Pay Off." April 11, 1991, p. 1.

__. "The Facts About the FDIC." June 5, 1991, p. A12.

Wallison, Peter J. "Treasury Bank Plan: Strangle the Weak." *Wall Street Journal*, February 13, 1991, p. 12.

Washington Post. "Bank of New England Out-Paced Rivals." January 9, 1991, p. F1.

QUESTIONS

1. What were the major restrictions on competition within banking prior to the 1960s? What factors have increased banking competition since that time?

2. How did the FDIC's too big to fail policy evolve?

3. What is Hetzel's evidence for the claim that the policy of too big to fail has kept the banking industry from contracting in response to increased competition?

4. What pressures exist for postponing the closing of insolvent banks?

5. What evidence of increased risk in the banking system does Hetzel cite?

6. How will the Deposit Insurance Reform Act of 1991 affect the policy of too big to fail?

READING 22

The New Banking Law Toughens Regulation, Some Say Too Much

Kenneth H. Bacon

WASHINGTON—After starting out with a Bush administration plan aimed at rescuing the U.S. banking system, Congress has passed a law that many observers fear may undermine banks further.

The legislators rejected most of President Bush's proposals to expand banks' business horizons. Instead, they approved on Wednesday a much tougher regulatory system. And many bankers and analysts think that Congress went too far.

"This legislation creates a system of arbitrary, Draconian and inflexible regulatory criteria designed to ensure that no bank will ever again fail," says Karen Shaw, president of the Institute for Strategy Development, a financial consulting firm here. "In pursuit of this Quixotic goal, the legislation will ensure that while few banks ever fail, none will ever prosper."

THE LAW'S PROVISIONS

The new legislation will require regulators to move more quickly to correct problems and to close banks before they become insolvent. It will limit the Federal Reserve Board's ability to keep sick banks alive. And it will end the Federal Deposit Insurance Corp.'s authority to reimburse uninsured deposits—those over $100,000 and foreign accounts—when large banks fail. That change may make the Fed even more eager to protect major institutions.

The tougher regulation is a political quid pro quo for $70 billion needed to shore up the Bank Insurance Fund, which has been drained by more than 1,100 bank failures since 1984. Congress blames regulators for responding too slowly to emerging problems. "Very little corrective action was taken early in the game," says Senate Banking Committee

Chairman Donald Riegle, a Michigan Democrat.

The law's early-intervention provisions will force banks and regulators to address problems quickly. But bankers say the legislation will make it harder for them to lend, precisely when the administration is pressing them to spur the economy with easier credit.

Bankers also worry that, as more banks fail, the premiums that the survivors pay for deposit insurance will rise sharply to repay Bank Insurance Fund borrowings from the Treasury. "Every time you raise the fees is money off the bottom line," says John B. McCoy, chairman of Banc One Corp. in Columbus, Ohio.

CONSUMERS TO PAY

Consumers may end up paying much of the premium increases. "Next time you have a drop in auto rates, maybe you drop it nine-tenths of a point rather than a full point," he explains. The higher premiums "will increase the cost for consumers to do business" and thus could hurt banks and the economy, he says. "Maybe the consumer doesn't borrow the next time."

Over time, predicts Robert Litan of the Brookings Institution, the legislation will strengthen banks; but in the short term, he fears, it could exacerbate the credit squeeze. "We've got policies at the federal level going in opposite directions," he contends. "The Treasury says, 'Ease up'; the legislation says, 'Tighten up.'"

Yet Mr. Litan doesn't denounce the bill. "As taxpayers," he says, "we should feel that this is better than nothing at all. We got the money to protect deposit insurance. We got new regulations" to promote sounder banking. So, he thinks "this is modest good news for taxpayers."

QUICKER ON THE TRIGGER

In essence, the new law will force regulators to pull the trigger much sooner on sick banks. Regulation will be tied to bank capital, and when capital declines, regulators will be required to take "prompt corrective action"—such as caps on growth, reductions or suspensions of dividends, stock sales to raise capital, and management changes. And they even will be permitted to close banks when the institutions' ratio of capital to assets falls to 2%. At least 100 small and medium-sized banks could be closed down under this rule, one analyst estimates.

"The penalties are so severe if you drop below the top capital standards that banks will simply have to run at cushions above those levels," says Paul Homan, the chairman of First Florida Banks Inc. "I've discussed this with my board. We don't want to come under that tight scrutiny. All our plans are to move to a comfortable cushion" of capital.

The new law, which regulators must translate into rules, is likely to force many banks to boost capital—a difficult task when many are already suffering from low earnings and low stock prices. While strong banks such as NCNB Corp. and BankAmerica Corp. will be able to raise capital, weaker ones may have to look for merger partners. "Mergers will be the only way out," says Edward Furash, managing partner at Furash & Co., a consulting firm. "It's a Darwinian solution—only the stronger will survive."

Bank shareholders could be hurt in two ways. Some banks probably will have to sell more stock to raise capital, diluting the value of current holdings. And if capital falls to a critical level and regulators close a bank before it's insolvent, stockholders "will get wiped out earlier than they thought," Mr. Furash says.

The changes could hurt borrowers as well. Some weakly capitalized regional banks and large money-center banks will have difficulty lending to the fast-growing and midsized companies that rely primarily on banks for credit. And Steven Wechsler, president of the National Realty Committee, which represents real-estate interests in Washington, worries that the new rules "may very well compound the problem we're living with today"—the difficulty in rolling over existing loans or getting new credit.

Even big companies that are grappling with financial problems and reduced credit ratings will suffer, says Charles Peabody, a banking analyst at Kidder, Peabody & Co. "You're going to find that these rules and regulations are going to make banks think a little more about whether they want to fund these high-risk credits," he says.

But some bankers who have survived corrective regulation when their banks were in trouble don't object to the tough new standards. "People and institutions can and will respond to pressure," says A.W. "Tom" Clausen, who guided Bank of America out of trouble in the 1980s.

Forbearance is what got us into the S&L mess. We need the opposite," he says. "We need a clear-cut system of regulation that rewards banks with strong ratings by letting them enter new lines of business and expand their operations. And we need swift and certain sanctions for institutions with poor ratings. We also need a trigger level that will force quick, mandatory regulatory intervention to liquidate or to hold shotgun weddings for failing institutions."

But Congress is providing only half of the Clausen equation: the tough regulations, without commensurate rewards.

MANY PROPOSALS KILLED

Over the past 10 months, Congress killed most of an administration plan to modernize the banking system by allowing well-capitalized banks to set up nationwide branch systems and to become financial supermarkets offering a broad range of insurance and securities products and services. Such banks also would have been allowed to affiliate with commercial corporations, such as Sears, Roebuck & Co.

Treasury Secretary Nicholas Brady called the measure a "pale shadow" of what's needed to strengthen the banking system and criticized Congress for backing away from reforms designed to reduce the chances that taxpayers ultimately will have to bail out the Bank Insurance Fund.

But President Bush never fought hard for his plan, and the Treasury couldn't marshal broad support for it. Initially, the administration and large banks—those that would have benefited most from its proposals—assumed that the need to recapitalize the Bank Insurance Fund would pull through plans to modernize a web of Depression-era bank laws. But the need for funding had almost the opposite effect—it reminded lawmakers of the savings-and-loan bailout and made them anxious to tighten bank regulation but reluctant to allow banks into new business areas.

"Voting the money was so controversial that what we thought was the engine driving the train turned out to be the anchor dragging down the ship," says Rep. Barney Frank, a Massachusetts Democrat.

AN OLD POLICY DISCONTINUED

In addition, the proposals encountered insurmountable obstacles: internecine warfare between big and little banks; opposition from insurance, securities and consumer groups; and disputes between the Treasury and Michigan Democratic Rep. John Dingell, the House godfather of securities regulation, over combining banks and brokers.

So, in Mr. Homan's view, banks are "going to get the worst of both worlds: They're going to get these new regulations, and they're not going to get new powers."

But aside from the $70 billion loan to support deposit insurance, banks are getting something many have wanted for years: an end to the "too big to fail" doctrine. Under this policy, which never was codified in law, regulators have resolved bank failures in ways that end up protecting all depositors, even those outside the deposit-insurance safety net.

Although the policy bolstered confidence in the system during the recent wave of bank failures, banks complain that reimbursing uninsured depositors helped deplete the insurance fund and forced huge increases in their insurance premiums. Premiums have nearly tripled to 23 cents per $100 of domestic deposits in the past 18 months and could rise to 30 cents next year as the industry begins repaying the new loan to the fund. With every one-cent rise in those premiums costing the banking industry some $250 million a year, banks are anxious to slow the increase.

The banking package would bar the FDIC from paying off uninsured depositors after Dec. 31, 1994. To grant an exception, the Fed, the FDIC and the administration must decide that all depositors should be reimbursed to prevent a jolt to the financial system. In the process, they would elevate what now is a bureaucratic decision to a much more visible political level. This change is designed to discourage even limited use of "too big to fail."

DANGERS OF RIGIDITY

In addition, the new law limits the Fed's ability to keep sick banks alive with long-term loans from its discount window. This also shrinks the federal safety net for banks in an effort to slow the drain on the insurance fund. A House Banking Committee study found that many banks failed despite heavy borrowing from the Fed, thereby increasing the cost to the FDIC.

"The Fed will be tougher" on banks as a result of these changes, predicts Frederick Shultz, a former Fed vice chairman. With less flexibility to help banks once they get into trouble, it will work harder to keep them out of it, he says. Mr. Litan agrees: "The Fed is going to be very nervous about the banks walking too close to the edge. I think the Fed is going to end up being the primary regulator for the 50 largest banks," those whose problems could most easily set off financial turmoil.

Although Mr. Shultz applauds the changes, he worries about rigid regulation. "You want a regulator who is tough in good times and gives you some flexibility in bad times," he says, adding that the stricter rules from Congress "won't help."

Regulators, too, worry about the law trimming their discretion. It will create "a much more formulaic approach," says Susan Krause, senior deputy comptroller of the currency for supervision policy. "We would always prefer supervisory flexibility. We don't have as much mistrust in ourselves as the legislators do."

Regulators and bankers worked behind the scenes to build as much flexibility as possible into the new law, but they were operating from a politically awkward position. The prompt-corrective-action provisions were written largely in response to congressional concern about lax regulation. And banks found it difficult to oppose stiffer regulation when the insurance fund was getting a $70 billion line of credit.

Eventually, however, banks will benefit as the new law succeeds in reducing bank failures. Payments from the insurance fund should slow, easing pressure for premium increases. And John Medlin, the chairman of First Wachovia Corp., applauds provisions permitting regulators to take over, merge or sell banks before they become insolvent. "By allowing regulators to move in when a bank is still salable—when it has more meat on its bones—some money can be saved," he says.

The new regulatory plan is designed to encourage banks to operate safely and with ample capital to cushion against failure. "It will change bank decision-making and behavior," says Steven Roberts, partner at KPMG Peat Marwick. "You can't put off hard decisions."

But some observers doubt that the new law will make banks any safer. Says Mr. Furash of the consulting firm: "The bottom line is the bill doesn't help the outlook for banking one bit. It ignores 20 years of decaying earnings.... Congress walked away from the worst financial crisis the country has faced sine the 1930s."

HIGHLIGHTS OF THE BANKING LEGISLATION

The banking bill passed by Congress will bolster the deposit insurance fund, tighten bank regulation, slightly trim the scope of federal deposit insurance and give the Federal Reserve Board new authority to regulate foreign banks in the U.S.

Congress refused to adopt Bush administration proposals to allow banks to establish branches nationwide, affiliate with commercial companies or expand their ability to sell insurance and securities. President Bush is expected to sign the bill, but the administration intends to continue fighting for these changes.

In addition, Congress stripped from the bill a controversial measure to impose a floating cap on credit-card interest rates.

Here are highlights of the legislation:

FDIC FUNDING

The bill bolsters the shrinking bank deposit insurance fund with $70 billion in borrowing authority. It increases to $30 billion from $5 billion the amount the Federal Deposit Insurance Corp. can borrow from the Treasury to cover the costs of bank failures. The loans, plus interest, would be repaid by premiums that banks pay on domestic deposits over the next 15 years.

In addition, the bill allows the FDIC to borrow for working-capital needs. The money—about $45 billion—and interest would be repaid as the FDIC sells the assets of failed banks.

BANK REGULATION

The bill establishes a new regulatory regime by firmly linking supervision to bank capital. Regulators must set five capital levels for banks and thrifts, ranging from well-capitalized to critically undercapitalized. Regulatory action would be mandatory as capital fell. This corrective-action regime must be in place a year after the law is enacted.

In addition, regulators must draft a new set of non-capital measures of bank safety, such as underwriting standards and minimum earnings levels, to take effect Dec. 1, 1993. The legislation also requires regulators to perform annual, on-site bank examinations; place limits on real-estate lending by banks; and tighten auditing requirements.

DEPOSIT INSURANCE

The bill reduces the scope of federal deposit insurance. The most significant change would end the so-called too big to fail doctrine, under which the government protects all deposits, even those beyond the $100,000 insurance limit, in most banks. The FDIC's current ability to reimburse uninsured deposits—those over $100,000 and foreign deposits—would be sharply limited after 1994. The Federal Reserve Board's ability to keep banks alive with extended loans from its discount window also would be restricted, starting two years from enactment.

In addition, only the best-capitalized banks would be able to offer insured brokered deposits—large certificates of deposit sold through brokerage firms—or to insure accounts established under employee pension plans.

In an attempt to give banks an incentive to follow safer practices, the bill instructs the FDIC to change the way it assesses banks for deposit insurance, moving from flat premiums to fees that require banks engaging in risky practices to pay higher premiums than conservatively managed banks. The new system must be in place by Jan. 1, 1994.

FOREIGN BANKS

In response to the problems with Bank of Credit & Commerce International, the legislation would give the Federal Reserve new authority to police foreign bank operations in the U.S.

SECURITIES PROVISIONS

The legislation for the first time explicitly gives brokerage firms access to Federal Reserve discount window loans in times of financial crises. Currently, the Fed provides emergency liquidity to Wall Street through banks, but Morgan, Stanley & Co. and Goldman, Sachs & Co. argued that direct borrowing would make emergency credit lines more secure.

Another provision would protect plaintiffs' rights to proceed with billions of dollars of securities fraud suits filed before the Supreme Court's June decision in the Lampf case, which changed the statute of limitations.

MISCELLANEOUS PROVISIONS

The measure protects the rights of Citicorp and Bankers Trust Co. to underwrite insurance in Delaware but bars other bank affiliates from underwriting.

The bill relaxes the "qualified thrift lender test" for thrifts by allowing them to invest more of their assets outside of housing-related areas.

QUESTIONS

1. Under the new banking law:
   (a) How is additional funding provided for the Bank Insurance Fund? How will this be repaid?
   (b) How is regulation tied to bank capital? How is this expected to affect bank capital and bank lending?
   (c) How are the problems associated with regulatory forbearance and the too-big-to-fail policy lessened?

2. What proposed regulatory changes were excluded from the legislation? Why?

3. Chapter 11 in the text evaluates the Treasury plan for reforming the banking system. Do a similar evaluation for the law Congress actually passed.

READING 23

Deposit Insurance: Recapitalize or Reform?

Mark E. Levonian

Public dismay over the poor financial health of the Federal Deposit Insurance Corporation's Bank Insurance Fund (BIF) has grown in recent months. The FDIC makes payments from BIF if an insured bank fails or must be assisted. The resources of the fund reached an all-time high of $18.3 billion in 1987, but a General Accounting Office audit revealed that BIF had only about $4 billion at the beginning of 1991, and was projected to be at or near zero by the end of the year. The U.S. Office of Management and Budget has predicted a $22.5 billion shortfall by the end of fiscal year 1995.

Congress is considering two types of solutions to the problem: First, to pump more money into BIF in the short run to "recapitalize" the fund, and second, to undertake a more fundamental overhaul or "reform" of the U.S. deposit insurance system. In this *Letter*, I argue that both recapitalization and reform are appropriate solutions, but to two different types of financial problems. Determining the relative merits of the solutions therefore requires a thorough understanding of BIF's current difficulties.

ILLIQUIDITY OR INSOLVENCY

BIF could be having a simple cash flow problem: the fund may have plenty of money in the long run, but be strapped in the short run, a condition of *illiquidity*. Illiquidity appears to be at least part of BIF's financial trouble. Before 1988, income to the fund exceeded payouts, and the difference was either rebated to insured banks or added to insurance fund reserves every year. Since then, payouts have exceeded income due to an unusually large number of bank failures. On top of these losses, projected failures over the next few years are likely to cause payouts to exceed both premium collections and the remaining balance in BIF's reserve fund.

Illiquidity is a problem of timing: receipt of income is spread out over time, whereas spending needs are concentrated in the present. The straightforward solution is that BIF should borrow to cover the shortfall, and pay off the debt in future periods using future revenues. Borrowing is the fundamental financial tool for shifting resources between time periods. No opprobrium should be associated with borrowing under these circumstances: it is simply the flip side of BIF's usual practice of lending (by investing in securities) during less lean periods.

However, the shortfall might be so severe, and the amount of required borrowing so large (or the interest rate so high), that BIF might be unable to pay back both principal and interest out of future income. In that case, the fund is *insolvent*. (This is a financial, rather than legal, definition of insolvency; the requirement that the borrowing be repaid *with interest* makes this definition equivalent to looking at the "present value" of BIF's net worth.) Insolvency cannot be fixed by shuffling resources from one time period to another. The problem is like trying to cover oneself with a fig leaf: the leaf can be moved around some, but if it is too small for the area to be covered, then the situation demands more leaves. And insolvency demands that either expenditures be reduced, or that current and future income be increased. Borrowing adds nothing to BIF resources in the long run and pushes any insolvency problem into the future without resolving it.

At the very least, BIF suffers from illiquidity. Whether it is insolvent is harder to determine. Most projections for the fund focus on the next few years, but examining only these near-term cash flows is not sufficient to distinguish between the two types of problems. The real question is whether there is *any* time interval—and it could be quite long—over which BIF could borrow the needed funds and generate sufficient income to repay principal and interest.

Such a longer-run view of insolvency generally requires the use of economic models of insurance. Research using these models reveals that the fund may have been insolvent in the late 1980's, when premiums were relatively low. Premiums have been raised substantially since then, but by some estimates insolvency may still be a component of the current problem. If there are elements of both illiquidity *and* insolvency in BIF's current financial squeeze, each must be dealt with.

RECAPITALIZATION

One way to recapitalize BIF is through a large injection of cash, in a form that need not be repaid. The money could come from a supplemental insurance premium or special assessment, in effect a one-time tax on the banking system. Alternatively, taxpayer money could be injected into the insurance fund by the Treasury. The only significant difference between these two is the incidence of the tax. An injection of this type could solve the liquidity problem and at the same time make the fund solvent.

However, most recapitalization proposals implicitly assume that the problem is illiquidity, since most involve some type of borrowing to be repaid from collected premiums. Debate has revolved around the amount and source of the borrowing; suggested sources have included the U.S. Treasury, the Federal Reserve, and the banking industry itself.

The press often refers to borrowing from the Treasury as a government "bailout" of BIF. However, the term "bailout" would seem to imply a transfer, or outright gift. As long as the loan is repaid with interest, it is hard to discern a meaningful sense in which this borrowing constitutes a gift, except to the extent that borrowing at the government rate may understate the true economic cost of the financing.

The Federal Reserve has expressed reservations about lending to BIF, not on financial grounds, but rather because it sets a dangerous precedent: Such a loan might create expectations that the Fed would lend to equally troubled, but perhaps less creditworthy, borrowers in the future. This concern may be especially germane given the delicate financial health of a number of state and local government entities.

A typical proposal for BIF to obtain funding from the banking industry envisions preferred stock issued by BIF and purchased by insured banks. This scheme vividly illustrates the fact that resources are shifted rather than enhanced in such a recapitalization: any payments BIF makes to the banks as preferred stockholders would be funded by insurance premiums those same banks pay to BIF.

A more subtle proposal for borrowing from the industry would shift banks' reserve deposits from the Federal Reserve to BIF. Currently, banks use these legally required deposits as clearing balances and to maintain adequate liquidity, both of which are legitimate business functions. It is not clear how the funds ever could be used by BIF to pay for bank failures without creating further problems for banks in general.

REFORM

Most reform proposals address BIF insolvency by structurally changing some combination of the deposit insurance system, the regulatory system, or the banking system. Reforms aim to increase the flow of BIF income relative to expenditures over time; some incidentally may provide sufficient current funds to solve the liquidity problem. BIF income can be increased by raising the rate banks pay for deposit insurance or by broadening the base against which premiums are assessed. The premium rate already has increased several times over the past two years, to the current level of 23 cents per 100 dollars of deposits. As I argued in a previous *Letter* (91-3), a few banks could afford to pay—and in all fairness should pay—even higher rates. However, a general rate hike might lead to a counterproductive increase in failures, as healthy, low-risk banks would suffer financially under a higher rate.

Instead of (or in conjunction with) raising rates, the assessment base could be broadened to include more than just domestic deposits: Foreign deposits could be included in the deposit base, or premiums could be assessed against total bank assets. The effect is little different from an increase in the premium rate, although broadening the base might eliminate some of banks' bias toward funding sources, such as foreign deposits, that currently are not subject to premium assessment.

In a different vein, one proposal would require the Federal Reserve to pay interest on banks' reserve deposits into the insurance fund, thereby increasing BIF's income stream. The Fed currently pays no interest on these deposits, so such a policy would directly reduce the income of the Federal Reserve System. Since the Fed transfers its excess income to the U.S. Treasury each year, this proposal is equivalent to injecting taxpayer funds into BIF.

On the other side, expenditures can be trimmed by reducing payouts on bank failures. Proposals include reducing the coverage limit from the current level of $100,000, reducing the number of insured accounts per person, and instituting co-insurance, under which depositors would bear some fraction of any losses due to the failure of their bank. Other proposals would eliminate or reduce insurance coverage of brokered deposits, or would restrict BIF from choosing to cover any deposits beyond those that are legally insured.

These and similar steps to cut BIF expenses by reducing deposit insurance coverage should be taken only with extreme care. Deposit insurance was established to achieve important public policy goals, including protecting depositors and enhancing the stability of the banking and financial system. Reducing coverage makes these goals more difficult to attain. BIF may save money in the short run, but sacrificing the stabilizing effect of deposit insurance in a quest for solvency may not be a desirable tradeoff.

PERMANENT REPAIR OF THE SYSTEM

The best way to deal with any current insolvency and avoid future problems is to cut BIF expenditures by reducing the probability of bank failures. Several reform proposals could reduce failure costs without affecting the degree of protection and stability provided by deposit insurance. These include measures to restrict the range of bank activities, require more frequent examinations of banks, raise bank capital requirements, and link deposit insurance premiums to bank risk.

Additional restrictions on banks' freedom to engage in riskier activities could reduce the chances of insured bank failures from large, unexpected losses. But regulators would have to determine which bank activities constitute necessary parts of the banking business, a burden that markets are probably better suited to bear in a changing financial environment. If regulators are too restrictive, failures could become *more* likely as bank profitability declines.

Requiring annual on-site examinations would cut the expected cost of bank failures by reducing the leeway banks have for taking undue risk. Of course, examinations are themselves costly, and the increased costs of more frequent exams must be weighed against the likely reduction in costs to BIF.

Compelling banks to maintain higher capital also reduces the expected cost of bank failures by giving banks a larger cushion against financial shocks. Raising capital might be costly for some banks in the short run, but the industry may find this preferable to high flat-rate deposit insurance premiums, as argued by Pozdena (*FRBSF Letter*, 91-10). An important side benefit of higher capital is that it alters the incentives facing insured banks. Bank managers and stockholders ultimately have considerable control over the probability that a bank will fail; economic theory says that those with more capital invested have less incentive to take undue risk. Risk-based premiums would have similar incentive effects, by forcing banks to pay more for deposit insurance if they take greater risks. These measures that change the incentive structure are the surest road to long-run solvency for BIF.

CONCLUSION

The current policy debate on deposit insurance often fails to discriminate adequately between "reform" and "recapitalization." Proposals treat different aspects of the Bank Insurance Fund's current financial problems, with reform generally addressing insolvency and recapitalization addressing illiquidity. In the short run, illiquidity can be resolved through borrowing from any of several sources. In the longer run, proposals for reform are vastly more important, especially those that create a healthier set of incentives for insured banks. Recapitalization must not be viewed as an alternative to reform: Without meaningful reform, an endless succession of recapitalizations may loom.

QUESTIONS

1. How does Levonian differentiate between the illiquidity problem of the Bank Insurance Fund and the insolvency problem? Why do each of these problems occur?

2. What proposals have been advanced to recapitalize the Bank Insurance Fund? What shortcomings, if any, do they have?

3. What proposals have been advanced to reform the deposit insurance system? What are the advantages and disadvantages of each proposal?

4. What does Levonian suggest to reduce the probability of bank failures?

READING 24

Securitization: More than Just a Regulatory Artifact

Charles T. Carlstrom and Katherine A. Samolyk

Competitive and regulatory pressures have prompted banks and other financial intermediaries to participate in credit markets in ways that are not directly reflected on their balance sheets. This poses a problem for regulators, who must assess the risks of these off-balance-sheet lending activities. One such activity is the packaging of loans into marketable securities, which is known as asset-backed lending or securitization.

For example, banks and other loan originators often sell fixed-rate mortgages to government-sponsored agencies, which in turn package these loans with those acquired from other institutions into mortgage pools. The agency sells securities that are claims to these pools to investors in the bond market. In the past several years, securitization has spread beyond government-sponsored activity to private asset-backed pools that fund a wide range of loans.

The recent proliferation of asset-backed lending has raised questions about its impact on the performance of banks. This concern reflects the fact that banks are involved in many aspects of the securitization process, such as packaging, servicing, or enhancing the creditworthiness of these securities. Regulators must determine what risks securitization poses to the participating institutions and how these risks should be reflected in the assessment of bank capital requirements.

This *Economic Commentary* explores banks' incentives to engage in securitization. Part of the dramatic increase in this activity can be traced to banking regulations that raise the cost of funding loans with deposits. However, another important factor driving asset-backed lending by banks is the improvement in information technology that has made securitization cost effective. Indeed, the proliferation of asset-backed lending to nonbank firms indicates that this mode of funding has become efficient for firms not subject to these regulatory costs.

From this perspective, we contend that securitization itself is not undesirable, and in fact is an efficient response by banks to their changing financial environment. Securitization serves as a vehicle for institutions to mitigate both credit and interest-rate risks, while generating fee income for participating banks. Moreover, the securitization process enables banks to attract investors who would otherwise not hold bank liabilities. Nevertheless, securitization poses a challenge to regulators, as they must assess how this activity affects risk in the banking industry.

SECURITIZATION AND DIVERSIFICATION

As their name suggests, depository institutions, such as commercial banks and savings and loans (thrifts), have traditionally funded their lending activities by attracting deposits. However, until 1986, deposit-rate ceilings limited the ability of these institutions to attract funds when market rates rose above regulated maximums. Banks and thrifts also tended to operate in fairly localized markets because of information costs and regulations limiting the scale and scope of banking activities. Depositories were therefore vulnerable to local credit-market conditions, such as the health of the local real-estate market. This was particularly true of thrifts, which were required to hold a certain fraction of their portfolios as residential mortgages.

Indeed, asset-backed lending began as an outgrowth of the government's effort to increase the flow of funds to the mortgage market. In the late 1960s, government-sponsored credit agencies such as the Federal National Mortgage Association (Fannie Mae) and the Government National Mortgage Association (Ginnie Mae) were established to create a secondary market in which existing mortgages could be sold. These agencies operated as intermediaries, buying government-guaranteed mortgages and funding these acquisitions by issuing securities. In 1970, Ginnie Mae issued a new type of credit-market instrument: the mortgage "pass-through," which was a claim to the return on a specified pool of mortgages. Hence, securitization was born.[1]

Today, the asset-backed market is a viable entity in its own right. Pools of securitized mortgages currently fund nearly 40 percent of home mortgages outstanding (see figure 1). Although government-sponsored mortgage-backed securities account for the largest share of this market, the past decade has witnessed the growth of securitization by private firms packaging mortgages as well as other loans such as credit-card and auto receivables. Depository institutions and nonbank firms are now able to originate and sell a wide variety of loans to asset-backed pools, rather than funding them on their balance sheets.

Asset pooling increases the liquidity of the underlying loans to the point where they can be sold to investors who are willing to hold direct claims on a diversified portfolio (see box). Because these claims increase the diversification and liquidity of loan portfolios, the associated securities are often bought by banks as well as by other investors.

FIGURE 1 HOME MORTGAGES HELD BY MORTGAGE POOLS VS. COMMERCIAL BANKS AND THRIFTS

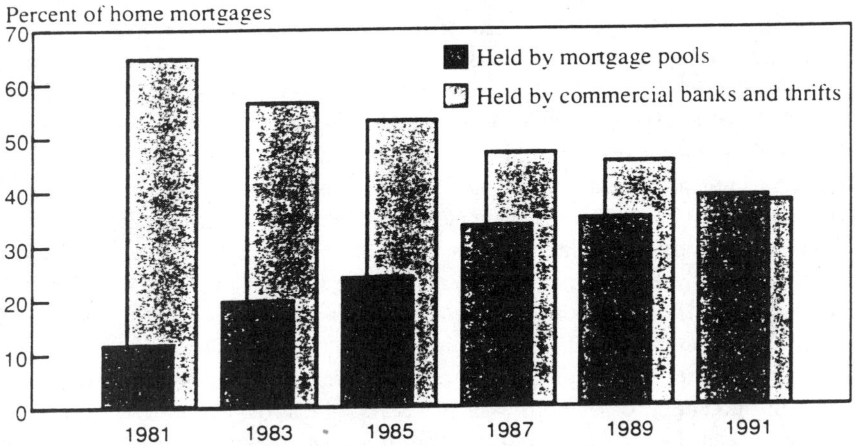

NOTE: All data are for the fourth quarter. The two categories do not add to 100 percent because other institutions, such as finance companies, also hold home mortgages.

SOURCE: Board of Governors of the Federal Reserve System.

Securitization allows banks to avoid the risks associated with deposit funding. When depository institutions fund loans with deposits, the liabilities they are issuing (deposits) have very different characteristics from the assets they are acquiring (loans). Individual loans, such as mortgages, are illiquid: They have a relatively long term to maturity and are generally not individually marketable to investors. Alternatively, deposit liabilities, such as checking and savings accounts, are short-term, liquid assets.

The differences in the maturity of banks' assets and liabilities cause depository institutions to be vulnerable to interest-rate risk. When interest rates rise, banks must pay higher deposit rates while being effectively locked into the return on their existing portfolios.[2] An unexpected increase in interest rates will therefore reduce their net income. This risk is asymmetric, however: When interest rates drop unexpectedly, banks do not gain by an equal amount. In this case, banks are not as locked into the return on their loan portfolios, because borrowers can often refinance their terms of credit.

Securitization in effect allows depository institutions to mitigate both the credit risks and the funding risks associated with lending, especially in the case of fixed-rate mortgages.[3] Indeed, an increasingly large number of home mortgages are being earmarked for sale into mortgage pools (see figure 1).

CREDIT ENHANCEMENT OF ASSET-BACKED POOLS

The growth of asset-backed lending other than government-backed mortgages raises the question of how securitization is able to market illiquid loans. Asset securitization involves the issuance of private-rated (asset-backed) securities as claims against a pool of assets held in a trust. In addition to relying on cash flows of the underlying assets to pay investors, the credit rating of the asset-backed pools is enhanced in any of several ways.

One such enhancement is a bank stand-by letter of credit (SLC). For a stipulated fee, banks will issue an SLC, in which they promise to insure the purchasing party up to a prespecified amount for any losses incurred on the securitizing loans. However, before loans are securitized, both the loans and the bank issuing the SLC are rated. Because the rating of a pool can be affected by the rating of the bank guaranteeing the loans, this form of enhancement has become somewhat less widespread.

An increasingly popular enhancement, the cash-collateral-account method, has the borrowers covering potential losses with cash placed in an escrow account.[a] Another method is for these securities to be overcollateralized. That is, extra loans are added to the pools so that the value of the loans exceeds the value of the securities that are claims to the pool.

[a]See suzanne Wittebort, "Asset-Backeds Come of Age," *Institutional Investor*, December 1991, pp. 77-80.

REGULATORY MOTIVES FOR ASSET SECURITIZATION

Although securitization can help banks to manage both credit risk and interest-rate risk, the recent surge in asset-backed lending has been more commonly attributed to the regulatory costs of traditional bank funding.

Capital requirements, which stipulate that depository institutions must back a certain fraction of their loans with equity capital, are an important regulatory incentive for securitization. Because they increase the amount of losses that equity holders can bear, capital requirements tend to reduce the risk of bank failure. Alternatively, nonbank lenders (such as finance companies) are not subject to regulated capital requirements. Instead, they evaluate the inherent risk of borrowers to determine the terms at which they are willing to extend credit.

The growth in asset-backed lending by banks can therefore be viewed as a response to increased competition from nonbank lenders. If the regulatory capital requirement on a particular class of loans is greater than merited by the inherent risk of the claims, then in order to compete with nonbank lenders, banks must securitize these loans—that is, move them off their balance sheets, where they are not subject to capital requirements. An unavoidable consequence, however, is that the loans which remain on bank balance sheets are likely to be those for which the market's assessment of risk premiums is greater than the regulated assessment.

Two other regulatory taxes that have been cited as potential inducements for asset-backed lending by depository institutions are fractional reserve requirements and flat-rate FDIC insurance premiums on deposit liabilities. These assessments are viewed as raising the cost of deposit funding, thus encouraging depository institutions to fund loans off-balance-sheet. However, securitization has continued to expand in spite of decreases in the reserve requirements set by the Board of Governors of the Federal Reserve System. In addition, deposit insurance is subsidized to the extent that flat-rate deposit insurance premiums are unlikely to be a major factor in the growth of securitization. But, since deposit insurance premiums are currently not risk based, they may still have the undesirable effect of causing banks to securitize their safest and most liquid loans.

It has also been argued that deposit insurance may increase the incentive for banks to issue standby letters of credit (SLCs) to enhance securitized loans, because SLCs are senior claims in the event of bank failure (see box).[4] This incentive to shift risk to the FDIC, however, may not be too important. Because the creditworthiness of both the loans being securitized and the bank issuing the credit-enhancing SLC affects the credit rating of the pool, banks that issue SLCs are generally lower-risk institutions.[5] Thus, it is doubtful that the current deposit insurance scheme is a major reason why banks issue SLCs, because the seniority of claims is important only in the event of bank failure.

SECURITIZATION AND LOAN FINANCING

While regulatory costs and portfolio risks associated with deposit funding may help to explain asset-backed lending by banks, the increase in securitization by nonbank firms is evidence that this financing method has become a viable alternative to other sources of credit—including bank finance. Indeed, nonbank securitization is just one example of the growing competition banks face from nonbank suppliers of credit.

A prominent factor underlying the evolution of the financial sector, especially that of asset-backed securities markets, has been the improvement in technology for producing information. This has enabled firms to transfer information about individual accounts, making securitization much more cost effective.

These innovations provide another important rationale for the growth of securitization, since asset-backed lending may reduce the costs associated with monitoring certain types of credit. The basic intuition is as follows. The cost of funding a portfolio is related to the costs of monitoring its performance. By issuing asset-backed securities through a separate subsidiary (called a special-purpose vehicle), a firm can separate these claims from other claims on its balance sheet. Investors, therefore, need assess only the performance of the asset pool rather than the general creditworthiness of the borrowing firm. If the assessment of the pool is less costly to monitor than that of the entire firm, the ability to separate these claims from the remainder of the firm's balance sheet enables the firm to obtain better credit terms on the pool.

For example, when Macy's extends consumer installment credit to its customers, it obtains credit-card receivables that it must finance. If the store funds these receivables on its overall balance sheet, the funding costs will reflect Macy's general creditworthiness. Alternatively, if Macy's securitizes its credit-card receivables through a special-purpose vehicle, it may be able to obtain lower financing costs, as the credit quality of these receivables alone may be less costly to assess.

CONCLUSION

The proliferation of asset-backed lending is merely one indication of how the financial scene is changing. As evidenced by the involvement of nonbanks in this market, securitization is clearly more than an artifact of banking regulations. Although off-balance-sheet lending by depository institutions may be more efficient than traditional bank intermediation for some types of loans, these activities may also impact the risk of banks' balance sheets. Because of the potential for increased FDIC exposure to bank failures, policy-makers are understandably concerned about the rapid growth of this practice.

In its role as an insurer, the government aims to maintain the solvency of the insurance fund by setting deposit insurance premiums and capital requirements. But it is precisely these assessments that can affect the risks undertaken by depository institutions. Such regulatory taxes create incentives for banks to shrink their balance sheets through securitization.

Unfortunately, when regulated capital requirements and deposit insurance premiums do not reflect the riskiness of a bank's portfolio, they create the incentive for banks to securitize their safest loans and to hold the riskier ones. Thus, risk is shifted to the FDIC (and ultimately to taxpayers). Regulatory changes that more accurately price an institution's risk will tend to diminish the adverse incentives for bank asset securitization.

The risk-based capital guidelines currently being implemented, as well as the risk-based deposit insurance premiums recently legislated by Congress, are attempts to link regulatory costs to an institution's risk. Risk-based capital standards will be phased in by year-end. Banks will then be charged different deposit insurance premiums depending on the overall quality of their asset portfolios.

Because the new risk-based guidelines stipulate higher capital requirements on all bank loans other than home mortgages, they may actually increase the volume of securitization.[6] However, the trend toward asset-backed lending is not entirely adverse for the FDIC. Depository institutions can earn fee income for participating in various dimensions of the securitization process, such as by enhancing asset-backed pools.

Moreover, with appropriate regulatory supervision of banks' off-balance-sheet activities, asset-backed lending can mitigate the rising costs of the federal safety net as it reduces the share of credit funded on the balance sheets of depository institutions. Thus, securitization is better viewed as an important innovation in the financial sector—one that allows new suppliers of credit to enter the market and existing ones to intermediate credit more efficiently.

ENDNOTES

1.See Christine Pavel, "Securitization," Federal Reserve Bank of Chicago, *Economic Perspectives*, vol. 10, no. 4 (July/August 1986), pp. 16-31.

2.The growth of variable-rate mortgages has also helped to reduce the dangers of interest-rate variability.

3.Consider the role of interest-rate volatility during the 1980s in the thrift crisis. The interest-rate increases in the early part of the decade, and the subsequent sharp drop in rates in the mid-1980s, severely weakened the position of thrifts and, to a lesser extent, banks. This volatility was further aggravated by interest-rate ceilings, such as Regulation Q.

4.Current banking regulations do not allow a bank to issue any claims senior to those of the FDIC: When a bank fails, no individual or institution can receive its funds ahead of the federal insurance agency. However, the SLCs used as credit enhancements in effect give asset-backed security holders a senior claim on the bank's assets, thus maximizing the subsidy that banks receive from deposit insurance. See Lawrence M. Benveniste and Allen N. Berger, "Securitization with Recourse: An Instrument that Offers Uninsured Bank Depositors Sequential Claims," *Journal of Banking and Finance*, vol. 11, no. 3 (September 1987), pp. 403-24.

5.See Robert B. Avery and Allen N. Berger, "Loan Commitments and Bank Risk Exposure," Federal Reserve Bank of Cleveland. Working Paper 9015, December 1990.

6.See Howard W. Albert, "Asset Securitization: Benefits for All Banks," *The Bankers Magazine*, vol. 174, no. 6 (November/December 1991), pp. 16-20.

QUESTIONS

1. The traditional view of banks or financial intermediaries is that banks accept funds from depositors and lend them to borrowers. How do securitization activities differ from this traditional view? Are banks still functioning as intermediaries when they engage in securitization?

2. How does securitization benefit banks?

3. How do regulations on bank capital and deposits promote securitization?

4. How has improved information technology promoted securitization?

READING 25

Path-Dependent Options

William C. Hunter and David W. Stowe

A relatively new class of options—the so-called path-dependent options—has become increasingly popular in recent years. Like other options, these contracts give their owners the right—but not the obligation—to buy or sell a specific quantity of an underlying asset (stock, bond, futures contract, commodity, and so forth) at a specified price, called the strike or exercise price, during a specific time period.

Since 1982 the use of path-dependent options has grown dramatically. A path-dependent option has a payout directly related to movements in the price of the underlying asset during the option's life. In principle, these options take many forms and can be contingent on virtually any statistic of the underlying asset's price path—for example, the high price, the low price, or the average price over some time period. Today path-dependent options are available on a host of assets including common stock, interest rate products, precious metals, commodities, foreign currencies, and stock indexes; they are often used with convertible securities issues and in merger transactions and have recently begun trading on two major exchanges.[1]

In many cases these options allow investors to limit their potential losses (and gains) and thus have a type of built-in insurance feature. They also allow investors with specialized knowledge about asset price volatility to exploit this information better in their investing and hedging activities. While factors such as cost or risk mean that path-dependent options will not satisfy every investor's needs, these options have generated interest by filling several voids or niches in derivative securities markets.

The sections that follow introduce the notion of path dependency, review the modern origins of path-dependent options, and give several examples of reasons that investors and institutions find these options attractive. The discussion also describes some essential features of three types of path-dependent options—the lookback option, the barrier option, and the average-rate or Asian option. A forthcoming article in the *Economic Review* will describe in detail the valuation and pricing of these options, illustrate how they are used by individual investors and firms, and discuss their advantages and disadvantages (risks) as investment vehicles.

THE AMERICAN PUT OPTION

A call option conveys to its owner the right to buy the underlying asset while a put conveys the right to sell the underlying asset. An option that allows its owner to buy or sell the underlying asset (exercise the option) at any time during the life of the option is called an American option. An option allowing the owner to exercise his or her right only at the option's expiration or maturity date is called a European option.

The payoff on a European call or put option written on a share of common stock that pays no dividends depends only on the market price of the underlying common stock at maturity. That is, if T is the maturity date of the option, t is the current date, X is the exercise price, and S is the market price of the underlying common stock at time $T>t$, then the payoff or intrinsic value at T is equal to the larger of the quantities (S - X) and zero for the call option and (X - S) and zero for the put option. Using standard options notation, the payoff on the European call at time T is written as $max(S - X,O)$ while the payoff on the European put at time T is equal to $max(X - S,O)$. Payoff at time T, $(T>t)$, on the European call or put option on a stock that pays no dividends is independent of the particular path taken by the stock price during the period between the times t and T. Such standard European call and put options on a nondividend paying stock are the simplest examples of what are called path-independent options.

In contrast, an American put option written on a share of common stock has a path-dependent payoff structure. (This happens to be the case irrespective of whether the stock pays a dividend or not). For example, looking forward from the perspective of date t, the payoff at time $T>t$ on the American put option depends not only on the price of the underlying stock at time T but also on the particular time path followed by the stock between times t and T.

An illustration will demonstrate the straightforward intuition behind the statement that the American put is an example of a path-dependent option. Assume that the underlying stock pays no dividend and that the put option is in the money—that is, the market price of the stock is less than the exercise price. The investor holding the put could exercise the option and receive an amount of cash equal to the exercise price minus the current price of the stock that he has just sold, X - S. It should be obvious that if the stock price is close enough to zero at the date the investor chooses to exercise early, he or she will be better off; the principal and interest received from investing the proceeds will exceed the difference between the exercise price and the stock price at the option's maturity date. In addition, the cases in which early exercise is optimal occur when the put is selling for X -

S so that selling it would be less profitable than exercising it and investing the proceeds. The key condition making early exercise preferable is that the stock price follows a path that drops close enough to zero over the life of the option to make the principal and interest earned by exercising the option greater than the exercise price minus the stock price at maturity. Thus, the payoff to the investor is seen as path dependent.

THE MODERN ORIGINS OF PATH-DEPENDENT OPTIONS: THE LOOKBACK OPTION

For both standard options and securities, specific examples having characteristics similar to path-dependent options can probably be traced back at least to the early 1800s. However, the modern treatment of these securities—the rigorous valuation or pricing of these claims on the basis of dynamic hedging principles—is a more recent phenomenon, set in motion in 1979 with publication of an article by M. Barry Goldman, Howard Sosin, and Mary Ann Gatto. The authors had derived an explicit valuation formula for a hypothetical option epitomizing the age-old finance dictum of buy low (cheap) and sell high (dear)—the so-called lookback option. To allow buying low and selling high, the exercise price on the lookback option is set at the expiration of the contract instead of at contract origination (as it is for standard options). That is, at expiration the owner could "look back over the life of the option" and choose as the exercise price the most favorable price that had occurred.

If a lookback call option were exercised, the owner would be able to buy the underlying asset at the lowest price that occurred during the life of the option. Similarly, the owner of a lookback put would be able to sell the underlying asset at its highest price realized over the life of the option. It is clear that the payoff on a lookback option depends not only on the underlying asset's price on the expiration date of the option but also on the particular path followed by the price of the asset over the life of the option, hence the path dependency.

Countering the argument that their research was a purely hypothetical exercise in contingent claims valuation, Goldman, Sosin, and Gatto (1979) argued that lookback options could be of value to investors as speculative and hedging instruments and could survive as traded securities. In less that two-and-a-half years the authors were proven correct. On March 16, 1982, Macotta Metals Corporation of New York introduced and began trading lookback options on gold, silver, and platinum. The lookback call gave an investor the right to buy gold, silver, or platinum at its ex post realized low price, and the lookback put allowed the investor to sell the precious metal at its ex post realized high price.

USES OF PATH-DEPENDENT OPTIONS

The choice of the particular price-path statistic on which a path-dependent option is based depends on the motivation of the option writer, ranging from wanting to control some particular risk to filling some niche in the market. Some specific examples illustrate this point.

On April 22, 1982, Manufacturers Hanover Corporation sold a $100 million note offering. The sale required holders to convert the securities at maturity in 1992 into shares of the company's common stock. The conversion price would be the lower of $55.55 and the average closing price of the common stock for the thirty-day period immediately preceding the notes' maturity. By making the conversion price dependent on the average price of the common stock, the company alleviated suspicions among investors that management would fraudulently manipulate the stock price upward just before the conversion date.[2]

The "capped" stock-index option is an example of an exchange-traded path-dependent option developed to fill a special niche or appeal to specific investors in the market. Capped stock-index options, fairly new examples of path-dependent options, are so named because they place ceilings on profitability. Because of these ceilings, capped options are cheaper than traditional stock-index options. Capped options were launched during the fall of 1991 on both the Chicago Board Options Exchange and the American Stock Exchange. Like other index options, they can be used to protect the values of stock portfolios by providing a cheaper way to obtain portfolio insurance.

Capped options trade off the Standard and Poor's (S&P) 100 and 500 Indexes on the CBOE and the Major Market and Institutional Indexes on the Amex. Like the standard call option, the value of a capped call option increases if its underlying index goes up, and a capped put option's value increases if the index declines. If the underlying index fails to attain the level specified by the option contract, known as the strike price, the options expire worthless and the sellers keep all of the premiums they collected. On the other hand, if the indexes reach the strike price, sellers must pay the optionholders the difference between the index level and the strike price but no more than a fixed cap value.

Each of these options has a cap price. For the options currently trading on the CBOE the cap price is set thirty points above the strike price for a call and thirty points below the strike price for a put, giving the options a cap value of $3,000 (thirty points times $100 per point). For those trading on the Amex the cap price is set at twenty points above and below the strike price, yielding a cap value of $2,000 (20 points times $100 per point). The purpose of the cap price is to force automatic exercise of the options. If the underlying index closes at or above the cap price for a call option or at or below the cap price for the put option, the options are automatically exercised and the cap buyers are paid the cap value two days after exercise.

The following scenario illustrates the mechanics of the capped option. An investor believes that the stock market will rally modestly from its closing value of 378 for the S&P 500 index on, say, January 12, 1992, and the third Friday in March 1992, the expiration date for the cap. The strike or exercise price on capped calls is 390, making the cap price 420 (390 plus the thirty points for the S&P 500 index). If the index closes at or above 420 between January 12 and the third Friday in March 1992, the capped call purchaser will be paid $3,000 (the net profit would be less by the amount of the premium). If the index closes at a figure less that 420 but greater that the strike price of 390—for example, 400—the purchaser will be paid an amount equal to the value of the index minus the strike price, in this case ten points times $100 per point or $1,000. On the other hand, if the index fails to reach the strike price of 390, the option expires worthless and the seller keeps the entire premium collected.

As is true for other exchange-traded options, the owners of capped options can sell them in the open market before maturity. Clearly, the payoff on the capped option depends on the particular path the underlying index follows over the life of the option; the option is path dependent. One appealing characteristic of the capped put or call option is that the seller's or writer's risk is limited to the cap amount or value while theoretically there is no limit to the risk faced by the writer or seller of a standard stock-index or -equity option. This feature of capped options, which is essentially a kind of built-in insurance, should make investors more willing to write options on the indexes offering them.

OTHER POPULAR PATH-DEPENDENT OPTIONS

The average-rate option and the barrier option are two other frequently used path-dependent options that are growing in popularity. Both are currently used most extensively in the foreign exchange markets. However, their structure is such that their use will most likely increase in domestic markets in the future. The capped option discussed above exhibits some of the essential features of a barrier option.

Barrier Options. Simple stated, a barrier option is a path-dependent option that is either canceled, activated, or exercised if the underlying instrument (the stock index in the case of a capped index option) reaches a certain level, regardless of the point at which the underlying asset is trading at maturity. Barrier options, also known as knock-out, knock-in, or trigger options, are typically straight European options until or from the time the underlying instrument reaches the barrier price.

There are four popular types of barrier options: up-and-out, up-and-in, down-and-out, and down-and-in. With the up-and-out barrier, the option is canceled should the underlying instrument rise above a certain level. The up-and-in option, on the other hand, is worthless unless the underlying instrument rises above a certain level or price, at which point it becomes a normal put option. Down-and-out options are canceled if the underlying instrument falls below a certain price. Down-and-ins are activated only when the underlying instrument's price falls to a certain level.

Because of these extinguishing or activating features, barrier options are cheaper than ordinary European options and are thus attractive to investors who are averse to paying large premiums. In addition, as illustrated in the case of the capped option, the sellers or writers of barrier options may be able to limit their downside risk.

Average-Rate Options. Average-rate or Asian options are path-dependent options, European in structure, for which the strike price is based on the average (geometric or arithmetic) price of the underlying instrument over a specified period of time, so the actual strike price is not determined until the exercise date on the contract. For foreign exchange average-rate options, the actual practice is for the average to be taken from the option's start date to a preagreed setting date. For example, suppose that a U.S. exporter buys an average-rate floating-strike call option to purchase a foreign currency for U.S. dollars at the average exchange rate over some given period, with the option expiring at the end of the period. If the average exchange rate over the period is less than the spot exchange rate at the time payment is due to the foreign importer, the exporter would profit more from exercising the option than transacting at the spot exchange rate. On the other hand, if the period's average exchange rate exceeds the spot rate, the exporter is better off converting dollars at the current spot exchange rate, in which case the option expires worthless. This example also shows that it is possible to use average rate options to hedge or limit the uncertainty associated with regular foreign cash inflows and outflows as a result of volatile exchange rates.

Many multinational corporations use average-rate put options on foreign currencies to hedge their estimated monthly foreign exchange income in an effort to achieve some budgeted average exchange rate for the year. Hence, the design of this particular option is of great value to these corporations that are in the market on a regular basis. Current accounting principles provide for foreign currency transactions to be translated at either the spot rate at the time of the transaction or the spot rate for the date of the firm's balance sheet. Any variations can be flowed through into the firm's income. For a path-dependent put, the option can be exercised if the balance-sheet rate is less than the strike (average) rate, resulting in the appearance of additional income. This additional income is calculated by multiplying the nominal amount by the difference between the strike rate and the spot rate and subtracting from this figure the amount of premium paid.

Large multinational commercial banks offer average-rate currency options to their multinational customers because these companies' usual spot dealings leave them with an average exchange rate on their books. By selling path-dependent average-rate currency options, the banks offset the average-rate foreign exchange risk exposure on their books. The premiums banks receive enhance yield by reducing their funding costs or by lowering their average exchange rate. In addition, these banks stand to earn management fees and commissions in other areas as a result of these activities, so it is worth the risk they take. Because average-rate options have lower volatility than standard European options, they are cheaper to purchase.

VALUATION OF PATH-DEPENDENT OPTIONS

This section attempts to offer some insights into the valuation of two path-dependent options—the lookback and the average-rate option.

Valuing the Lookback Option. As is the case for most options, the key condition required to price the lookback option in the modern tradition is that it must be possible to hedge its risk. That is, it must be shown that the cashflow obligation(s) of the writer of a lookback call option can be exactly met by the payoff from another portfolio (a hedge portfolio). Indeed, Goldman, Sosin, and Gatto (1979) showed that such a hedge portfolio could be constructed so that the lookback option can be valued without regard to the risk premium in the underlying asset's expected return. These authors showed that when the risk-free interest rate was equal to exactly one-half the underlying asset's variance, the lookback call option is identical to the purchase of a straddle (a portfolio of puts and calls on the same assets at the same strike price) on the asset. Therefore, the writers of lookback calls can simply hedge their obligation by purchasing a straddle on the same underlying asset. Because the lookback option can be hedged, it can be valued using the risk-neutral pricing technology associated with the Black-Scholes (1973) paradigm.

Valuing an Average-Rate (Asian) Option. There are two types of average-rate or Asian options: the fixed-strike and floating-strike options. The payoff on a floating-strike Asian call option at expiration is equal to the greater of either zero or the difference between the underlying asset's terminal spot price and the average value of the asset over the life of the option—that is, $max(S - Avg_s, 0)$. It is comparable to a lookback call option for which the strike price is the average value of the underlying asset as opposed to its minimum value. Because mathematical complexities have prevented development of a closed-form analytic model (such as the Black-Scholes equation) to price such an instrument, these options must be valued with a numerical approximation technique such as Monte Carlo analysis.[3]

The value of an Asian option can never be greater than the value of a regular lookback call option, for which the strike price is the achieved minimum of the asset. Thus, the price of a regular lookback option sets an upper boundary on the average-rate option's value (because the minimum value is an extreme and the average is never equal to an extreme value unless all of the values are equal).

For fixed-strike options, the second type of average-rate option, the terminal payoff is the maximum of either zero or the difference between the average value of the underlying asset and a fixed strike price—$max(AVG_s - X, O)$. The average can be computed using either the geometric average or the arithmetic average. Again, because of mathematical complexities no closed-form equation has been developed for pricing the average-rate option written on the arithmetic average.

Under the standard risk-neutral (Black-Scholes) pricing approach, it is assumed that the natural logarithm of stock price returns are normally distributed. In valuing an Asian option written on the geometric average of an asset's value over time, this standard assumption still holds because the product of the logarithm of stock price returns is normally distributed, and this option can be valued in closed form using the Black-Scholes approach. However, the assumption breaks down for an Asian option written on the arithmetic average because the sum of the logarithm of the stock price returns over time is no longer normally distributed. As a result, it is necessary to employ other valuation techniques for an average-rate option written on the arithmetic average of the underlying asset's price.[4]

CONCLUSION

It should be clear from this overview of path-dependent options that risk management is not a static field. New products and financial instruments are continuously being developed to meet new needs. While many risks can be managed with traditional hedging instruments such as standard options, futures contracts, and swaps, the rapid development of exotic options like the path-dependent options suggests that the market for innovative risk-management products is in no way saturated. The demand for these new instruments is likely to continue growing as long as risk-management techniques using traditional hedging vehicles require close monitoring, involve fairly high commissions or management costs, and fail to reduce risks in the way desired.

The development of path-dependent options is, however, only one response to the demand for innovative risk-management instruments. In addition, because these instruments build on existing standardized derivative products, they may not serve the needs of every investor or institution. Their future development is likely to tend toward greater customizing for specific situations.

It is well known that a portfolio of existing standard products can replicate the payoffs on most of the new derivative products such as those discussed here. Indeed, this very fact allows creation of risk-free hedge portfolios for these contracts and also makes it possible to price them using the familiar risk-neutral pricing technology. However, the management and effort required for existing products to duplicate the payoff from the newer contracts tend to be too expensive an alternative for individual investors. Thus, the financial services firms that produce these new contracts add value to the market. These products have made a place for themselves because they are tailored to meet specific risk-management and investment needs.

ENDNOTES

1.The Chicago Board Options Exchange (CBOE) and the American Stock Exchange (AMEX) both trade path-dependent options known as "capped options." These options are described in detail below.

2.Such suspicions on the part of investors were not totally unwarranted. In a separate case, two Merrill Lynch vice presidents were fired for allegedly artificially driving up the price of options on a portfolio under their management on Christmas eve of 1981 in an attempt to maximize their bonus, which was tied to the portfolio's December 24, 1981, closing value (*Wall Street Journal*, January 21, 1982, 4). This example also points out the advantage of making this type of path-dependent option contingent on the average price of the underlying asset over some extended period rather than the closing price on some particular day, as the chances for artificial manipulation are greatly reduced. The growing popularity of tying conversion prices or ratios to time averages of prices in mergers seems to reflect similar concerns.
3.Monte Carlo simulating is a numerical approximation technique that can be used to compute option values by simulating the path taken by the price of the asset underlying the option over time. By simulating numerous such price paths, the technique allows one to compute the expected value or price of the option with increasing precision as the number of iterations or runs of the simulation are increased. This technique is described in detail in the forthcoming *Review* article examining the valuation of path-dependent options.
4.A more thorough discussion of the valuation or pricing of the lookback and the average-rate options, including a brief tutorial on the basic tenets of option pricing using the modern risk-neutral pricing technology pioneered by Black and Scholes (1973), will appear in the forthcoming *Review* article referred to above. The article explains how Monte Carlo analysis can be used to price Asian options written on the arithmetic average as well as how these options can be used to hedge foreign exchange risks from the viewpoint of individual investors and multinational corporations. The reader interested in the basic of option pricing is referred to Hull (1990) and Kolb (1991).

REFERENCES

Black, Fischer, and Myron Scholes. "The Pricing of Options and Corporate Liabilities." *Journal of Political Economy* 81 (May/June 1973): 637-59.

Goldman, M. Barry, Howard Sosin, and Mary Ann Gatto. "Path-Dependent Options: Buy at the Low, Sell at the High." *Journal of Finance* 34 (December 1979): 1111-27.

Hull, John. *Options, Futures, and Other Derivative Securities.* Englewood Cliffs, N.J.: Prentice-Hall, Inc., 1989.

Hunter, William C., and David W. Stowe. "Path-Dependent Options: Valuation and Applications." Federal Reserve Bank of Atlanta *Economic Review* (forthcoming 1992).

Kolb, Robert W. *Options: An Introduction.* Miami: Kolb Publishing Company, 1991.

QUESTIONS

1. How does an American option differ from a European option? Why is the American option a path-dependent option?

2. How do capped stock-index options work? How does their risk compare with that of standard stock-index options?

3. What are the key features of barrier options and average-rate options?

4. How are average-rate options used in foreign exchange transactions?

READING 26

Managing Interest Rate Risk with Interest Rate Futures

Charles S. Morris

Increased interest rate volatility in the 1970s and 1980s has led to greater volatility in the returns on bonds and other fixed-income assets. Consequently, investors in bonds and financial institutions with fixed-income assets and liabilities on their balance sheets are now exposed to much greater risks from capital gains and losses. The problem is compounded because managing risks caused by interest rate volatility has traditionally been difficult and costly.

During the last 15 years, however, many new financial instruments have been developed to help investors manage risks caused by increased interest rate volatility. One of the most popular types of instruments is interest rate futures contracts. Interest rate futures allow investors to protect the value of their fixed-income investments by providing a hedge against interest rate changes. Interest rate futures are now an important tool for investors who want to protect themselves from interest rate volatility.

This article explains how interest rate futures, when properly used in a hedging strategy, allow investors to manage interest rate risk. The first section of the article defines interest rate risk, examines its impact on investors and institutions, and discusses how interest rate risk can be managed. The second section provides an introduction to interest rate futures and discusses why they are good assets for hedging interest rate risk. The third section shows how investors and institutions can use interest rate futures to manage interest rate risk and discusses some of the other risks involved in using interest rate futures.

INTEREST RATE RISK AND INTEREST RATE RISK MANAGEMENT

Bonds and other fixed-income assets have become riskier investments in recent years.

These assets are riskier, not because issuers are more likely to default on their obligations, but because interest rates have become more volatile. This section explains why increased interest rate volatility has increased the risk of fixed income assets, provides some examples of investors and institutions affected by greater interest rate volatility, and discusses methods of managing interest rate risk.

What Is Interest Rate Risk?

Investments in fixed income assets, such as bonds, are risky because the volatility of their prices can lead to unexpected capital gains and losses. The risk of an asset can be measured by the volatility of its returns, which is the sum of the income flows from the asset plus any changes in its price. Since the income flows from a fixed income asset, such as the coupon payments and maturity value of a coupon bond, are fixed, the riskiness of the asset depends only on its price volatility. For example, as the volatility of a bond's price rises, the bond's riskiness rises because unexpected capital gains or losses are more likely.

The primary cause of volatility in the price of a fixed-income asset is interest rate volatility.[1] Indeed, the volatility in prices due to interest rate changes is commonly termed "interest rate risk." For example when interest rates fall, the price of a bond rises; when interest rates rise, the price of a bond falls. The sensitivity of a fixed income asset's price to interest rates, that is, the degree of interest rate risk, depends largely on the asset's maturity. The longer to maturity, the larger the change in price due to a change in interest rates.[2]

Interest rate volatility has risen sharply in recent years. Chart 1 shows the volatility of interest rates on 1-year and 10-year Treasury securities from 1955 to 1988. Interest rate volatility in each year is measured by the standard deviation of the monthly interest rates during that year. The average standard deviation of 1-year interest rates over the 1979-88 period was more than twice that of the 1955-78 period, rising from 0.5 percent per month over the 1955-78 period to 1.2 percent per month over the 1979-88 period. The relative increase in the volatility of 10-year rates was even sharper. The average standard deviation of 10-year interest rates over the 1979-88 period was more than three times higher than that over the 1955-78 period, rising from 0.25 percent to 0.8 percent. The rise in interest rate volatility over those periods is not limited to 1-year and 10-year rates, but is typical of the volatility of interest rates at all maturities.

Who Is Affected by Rising Interest Rate Volatility?

Many investors and business firms are exposed to greater risks because of the increase in interest rate volatility in recent years. Examples include individual and institutional investors in government and corporate bonds, depository institutions such as banks and savings and loans (S&Ls), securities dealers, mortgage banks, and life insurance companies to name a few.

CHART 1
Interest rate volatility

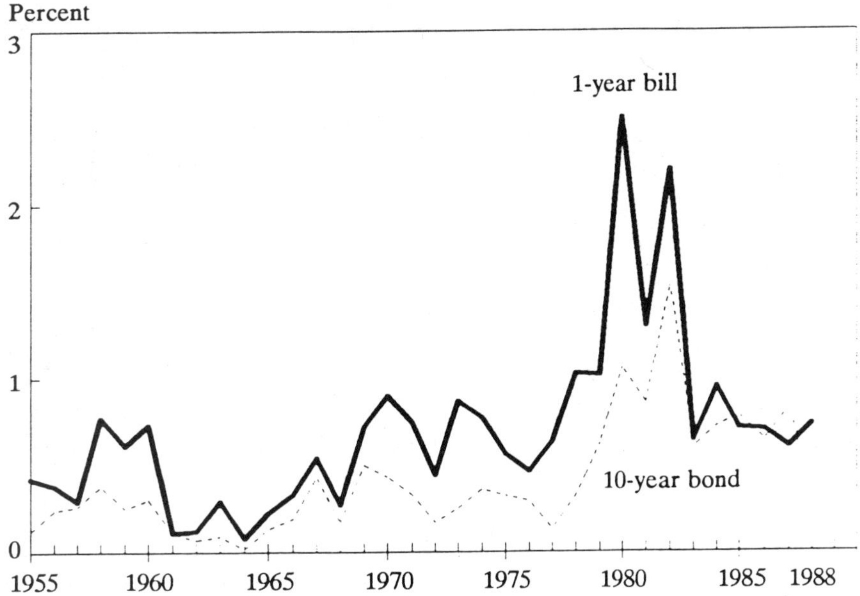

Note: Annual standard deviations of monthly constant maturity rates for 1-year U.S. Treasury bills and 10-year U.S. Treasury bonds.
Source: Board of Governors of the Federal Reserve System.

One group of investors exposed to greater risks is investors in bonds. The rising risk of holding bonds is clear from Chart 2, which shows the volatility of returns on U.S. Treasury bonds from 1950 to 1987. Bond market volatility in each year is measured by the standard deviation of the monthly percentage returns on a long-term U.S. Treasury bond index during that year.[3] Bond market volatility rose from an average annual standard deviation of 1 percent per month over the period from 1950 to 1965 to 2.25 percent over the period from 1966 to 1978. Bond market volatility rose further from 1979 to 1987, averaging 4.1 percent per month.

Rising interest rate volatility has also increased the risk exposure of depository institutions, such as banks and S&Ls. When interest rates rise, the market value of their net worth generally falls; when interest rates fall, the market value of their net worth generally rises. The market value of an

CHART 2
Bond market volatility

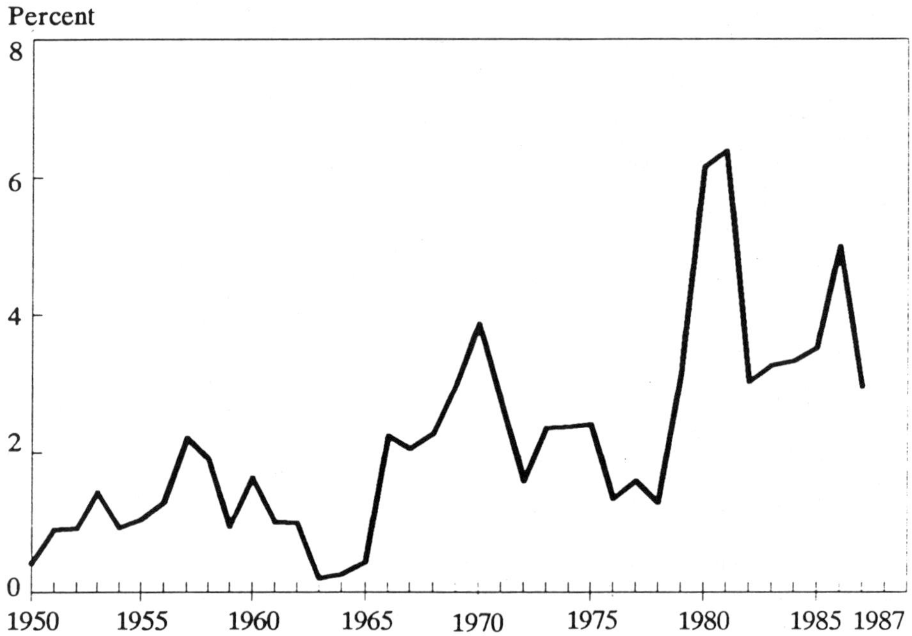

Note: Annual standard deviations of total monthly returns on a long-term U.S. Treasury bond index.
Source: Center for Research in Stock Prices.

institution's net worth is the difference between the market values of its assets and liabilities. The effect of a change in interest rates on the market value of a firm's net worth depends on the relative interest rate sensitivities of its assets and liabilities, which primarily depend on their relative maturities. Because the assets of banks and S&Ls generally take longer to mature than do their liabilities, the value of their assets is more sensitive to changes in interest rates than the value of their liabilities. As a result, when interest rates rise, for example, the net worth of a depository institution falls because the value of its assets falls more than the value of its liabilities.

Securities dealers are also exposed to greater risks due to rising interest rate volatility. When interest rates rise, securities dealers suffer losses like other bondholders because the value of the bonds they are holding in inventory falls.[4] Securities dealers can also suffer losses when interest rates fall, however, because they often commit themselves to delivering bonds at a future date for a fixed price when they do not have the bonds in inventory or the funds to purchase them immediately. If interest rates fall before a dealer purchases the bonds, he will suffer a loss because the price he has to pay for the bonds he has to deliver will be higher than he had expected when he made the initial commitment.

Mortgage banks are also exposed to greater interest rate volatility. A mortgage bank originates mortgages and then sells them to other investors. In general, mortgage banks hold very few mortgages on their balance sheet. They can suffer losses if interest rates rise, however, because they typically commit to a mortgage rate before the mortgage is actually closed and sold. If interest rates rise between the time they commit to a rate and the time the mortgage is sold, the value of the mortgage will fall; and mortgage banks will get a lower price than they had expected when they made the initial commitment.

A final example of a group of firms exposed to greater risk due to rising interest rate volatility is life insurance companies. For example, changes in interest rates affect life insurance companies because when interest rates fall the spread earned on Guaranteed Interest Contract (GIC) commitments falls. In recent years, life insurance companies have become heavy issuers of GICs, which are securities that guarantee a fixed interest rate on invested funds over a several-year period. GICs are generally purchased by long-term investors, such as pension funds and company thrift plans. Often, a life insurance company will commit to a rate on a GIC for a short time period before it receives the funds. Life insurance companies can suffer losses if interest rates fall during the commitment period because when they receive the funds from the GIC, they will have to invest the funds at a lower rate than they had expected when they committed to the GIC rate. As a result, the spread earned on the GIC falls.[5]

What Is Risk Management and Hedging?

Investors and business firms manage risk by choosing the amount of risk to which they want to be exposed. The choice of how much risk to bear varies with every investor. For example, some investors will choose to accept the increased price volatility of fixed-income investments of recent years, while others will take actions to reduce the riskiness of their fixed-income investments. In general, though, investors will not choose to minimize risk because there are costs to reducing risk. The most important cost is that the expected return on their investment also falls when risk is reduced.

Traditionally, investors have found it difficult and costly to reduce risks caused by interest rate volatility. Investors in bonds, for example, typically could reduce interest rate risk only by selling some of their bonds and buying short-term money market instruments. Financial institutions exposed to interest rate risk had to rely on balance sheet restructuring to reduce the mismatch between the maturities of their assets and liabilities.

In recent years new financial instruments—such as interest rate futures, options on interest rate futures, and interest rate swaps—have been developed that allow investors in fixed income assets to manage interest rate risk at a relatively low cost by hedging. In general, hedging is a risk management strategy in which investors choose assets such that changes in the prices of the assets systematically offset each other. Fixed income investors can hedge the interest rate risk of an asset, such as a Treasury bond, by buying or selling hedging assets whose values change in the opposite direction to the value of the Treasury bond when interest rates change. The interest rate riskiness of a hedged Treasury bond is lower than the interest rate riskiness of the unhedged bond because the change in the value of the hedging asset due to a change in interest rates offsets at least some of the change in the value of the bond. It is important to realize, however, that hedging reduces price volatility because it offsets increases as well as decreases in the price of the Treasury bond.

For any given fixed income asset, the best hedging instrument for reducing interest rate risk is the one whose price is most closely related to the price of the asset when interest rates change. The more closely the prices are related, the larger the reduction in risk that is possible because changes in the price of the hedging asset are more likely to offset changes in the price of the asset being hedged.

While hedging can reduce risk, it generally cannot completely eliminate risk. Hedging will completely eliminate risk only if the values of the portfolio and hedging asset are perfectly related. However, the prices of the assets being hedged and the hedging asset are rarely perfectly related because of differences in factors such as credit quality, liquidity, maturity, and call or prepayment options. Thus, as a practical matter, hedging is an activity that permits investors to manage, but not eliminate, risk.[6]

AN INTRODUCTION TO INTEREST RATE FUTURES

Of the variety of financial instruments used to hedge interest rate risk, one of the most popular is interest rate futures. This section describes interest rate futures, discusses the types of interest rate futures available, and explains why they are good hedging instruments.

What Are Interest Rate Futures?

An interest rate futures contract is an agreement between two parties to buy or sell a fixed income asset, such as a Treasury bond or Treasury bill, at a given time in the future for a predetermined price. For example, if in January a person buys March Treasury bond futures, he is simply agreeing to buy Treasury bonds in March. On the other hand, if in January he sells March Treasury bond futures, he is simply agreeing to sell Treasury bonds in March. Nothing is exchanged when the futures contract is written because it is only an agreement to make an exchange at a future date. The price of a futures contract is the price the buyer agrees to pay the seller for the asset when it is delivered.[7]

Delivery of the asset in a futures contract rarely occurs, however. The reason is futures traders can always close out the contracts they have bought or sold by taking an offsetting position in the same futures contract before delivery occurs. For example, rather than taking delivery, a buyer of ten March Treasury bond futures can settle his position by selling ten March Treasury bond futures. Similarly, a seller of ten March Treasury bond futures can settle his position by buying ten March Treasury bond futures. In 1988, Treasury bonds were delivered in less than 0.1 percent of all Treasury bond futures traded at the Chicago Board of Trade, which are one of the most widely traded interest rate futures.[8]

Since a futures trader who has settled an initial position has both bought and sold futures, his profit depends on the prices of the futures he has bought and sold. Just like any other trader, futures traders make a profit when they buy futures at a price lower than they sell futures, and they suffer a loss when they buy futures at a price higher than they sell futures. Whether a person makes a profit or suffers a loss, therefore, depends on two conditions: first, whether he initially bought or sold futures, and second, whether the price of the futures rises or falls between the time he enters the initial contract and the time he takes an offsetting position.

A buyer of futures makes a profit when the futures price rises and suffers a loss when the futures price falls. Suppose, for example, on January 10 a person buys a March Treasury bond futures contract for $95 per $100 face value of Treasury bonds, and on February 19 he settles his position by selling a March Treasury bond futures contract for $97. Under these circumstances, the person would make a profit of $2 per $100 face value of Treasury bonds because he has one agreement to buy Treasury bonds in March for $95 and another agreement to sell Treasury bonds in March for $97. On the other hand, if the price falls to $92 on February 15, he would lose $3 per $100 because he has one agreement to buy Treasury bonds for $95 and another agreement to sell Treasury bonds for $92.

In contrast, a seller of futures suffers a loss when the futures price rises and makes a profit when the futures price falls. This time, suppose on January 10 a person sells a March Treasury bond futures contract for $95, and on February 15 he settles his position by buying a March Treasury bond futures for $97. The person would suffer a loss of $2 because he has one agreement to sell Treasury bonds in March for $95 and another agreement to buy Treasury bonds in March for $97. On the other hand, if the price falls to $92 on February 19, he would make a profit of $3 because he has one agreement to sell Treasury bonds for $95 and another agreement to buy Treasury bonds for $92.

Interest rate futures are relatively new financial instruments. While futures on commodities have been trading on organized exchanges in the United States since the latter half of the 1860s, the first interest rate futures contract did not start trading until October 1975, when the Chicago Board of Trade (CBT) introduced futures on Government National Mortgage Association (GNMA) certificates.[9] Since then, futures on many different fixed income assets have been developed. However, there are still many fixed income assets, such as corporate bonds, on which no futures are traded.

The assets on which interest rate futures are traded span the maturity spectrum—interest rate futures on short-term, medium-term, and long-term assets are traded on several futures exchanges in the United States and abroad. The first futures contract on a short-term asset was the Treasury bill futures contract, which was introduced on the International Monetary Market (IMM) exchange in 1976. Since then, interest rate futures on other short-term assets, such as Eurodollar time deposits and 30-day interest rates, have begun trading on several exchanges, with the IMM Eurodollar futures being the most popular.[10] Interest rate futures on medium-term assets, such as Treasury notes, are also traded on several exchanges.[11] Finally, there are interest rate futures on long-term assets, such as Treasury bonds and a municipal bond index, with the CBT Treasury bond futures being the most popular.[12]

The success of interest rate futures is shown in Chart 3. One measure of activity in a futures market is a contract's open interest—the number of contracts not yet offset by opposite transactions or delivery. Chart 3 shows the open interest in the CBT Treasury bond futures contract from 1978 to 1988. Although open interest in Treasury bond futures is fairly volatile, the trend is clearly upward. Chart 3 also shows open interest rose sharply in 1980 and 1981—the two peak years in bond market volatility (Chart 2)—suggesting that investors took advantage of the futures market for managing risk.

Why Are Interest Rate Futures Good Hedging Assets?

Interest rate futures are good hedging assets for two reasons. First, the transaction costs of buying and selling them are relatively low. Second, interest rate futures prices are closely related to the prices of many fixed income assets when interest rates change.

The transaction costs of establishing a futures position are low because nothing is really being bought or sold—the contract is just an agreement to make a trade at a future date. When a position is established, the only outlays are broker fees and commissions and an initial margin deposit with the broker.[13] The fees paid to brokers and traders are quite small. For example, the cost of establishing and settling a position in a CBT Treasury bond futures contract, which is based on $100,000 face value of bonds, is about $41.[14] The initial margin is also very small—the margin on a CBT Treasury bond futures used for hedging purposes is $2,000—and the margin generally earns a market rate of interest.[15]

Interest rate futures hedge the interest rate risk of many fixed-income assets successfully because interest rate futures prices are closely related to the prices of many fixed income assets. The prices are closely related because interest rate futures prices are sensitive to changes in interest rates just like fixed income asset prices. The price of any futures contract—whether it is an interest rate, exchange rate, commodity, or any other type

CHART 3
Treasury bond futures open interest

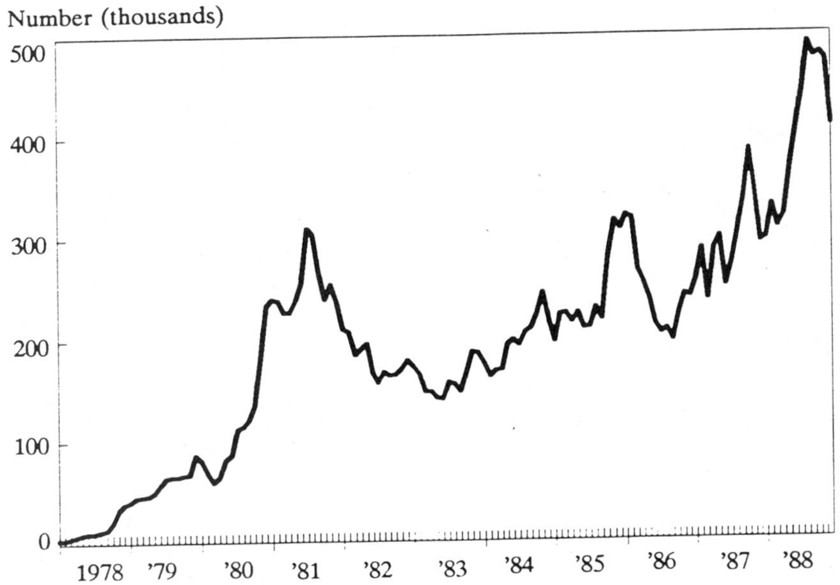

Note: Values are monthly averages of daily open interest in the Chicago Board of Trade Treasury bond futures contract with at least one month until expiration.
Source: Data Resources Inc.

of futures contract—is always very closely related to the price of the underlying asset.[16] Since interest rate futures are based on fixed income assets and the prices of these assets move in the opposite direction of interest rates, interest rate futures prices move in the opposite direction of interest rates.

Like any other hedging asset, though, the extent to which a given interest rate futures contract will provide an effective hedge for a fixed income asset depends on how closely the futures price is related to the price of the asset being hedged. Chart 4, for example, shows that the prices of a 30-year Treasury bond and the CBT Treasury bond futures are nearly identical.[17] The small differences that do exist are shown at the bottom of the chart. Because of this close relationship, Treasury bond futures should be very effective at hedging Treasury bonds against interest rate volatility.

In contrast, the price of the CBT Treasury bond futures is not as closely related to the price of a 30-year corporate bond as to the

CHART 4
Treasury bond futures and treasury bond price

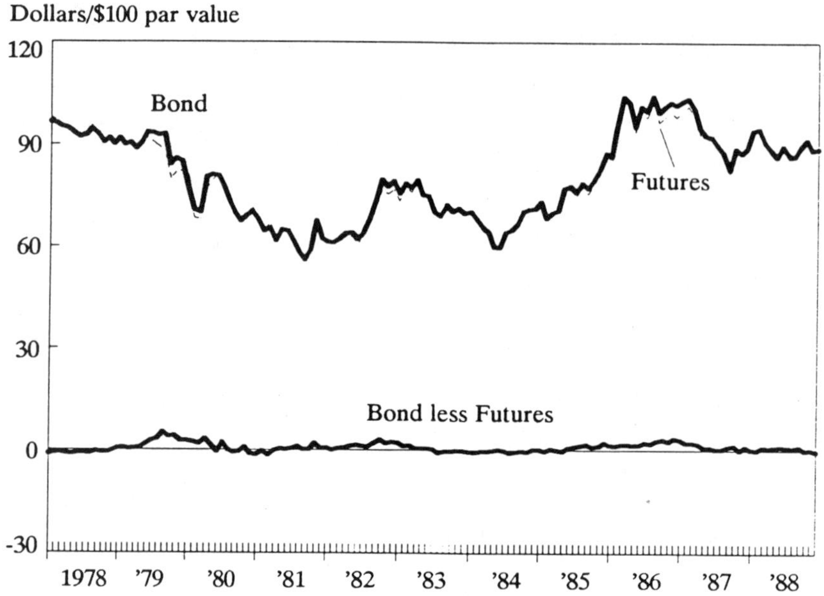

Note: The bond price is the price of the 9.25 percent 30-year Treasury bond that matures in November 2007. The futures price is the price of the nearest Chicago Board of Trade Treasury bond future with at least one month until expiration.
Source: Data Resources Inc.

price of the 30-year Treasury bond (Chart 5). The difference between the corporate bond price and the futures price is clearly more variable than the difference between the Treasury bond price and the futures price.

The prices of corporate bonds and Treasury bond futures are less closely related because corporate bond prices can change for a variety of reasons other than changes in the general level of interest rates. For example, the price of a corporate bond would fall if the issuer's credit rating fell or if adverse general economic conditions led investors to believe the chances of default were more likely. The price of a corporate bond could also fall if a large investor decided to sell his share of an issue. Since these factors would not affect the price of a Treasury bond, a Treasury bond futures contract would not hedge an investor against these price changes. As a result, Treasury bond futures should be a less effective hedge for a corporate bond than for a Treasury bond.[18]

CHART 5
Treasury bond futures price and corporate bond price

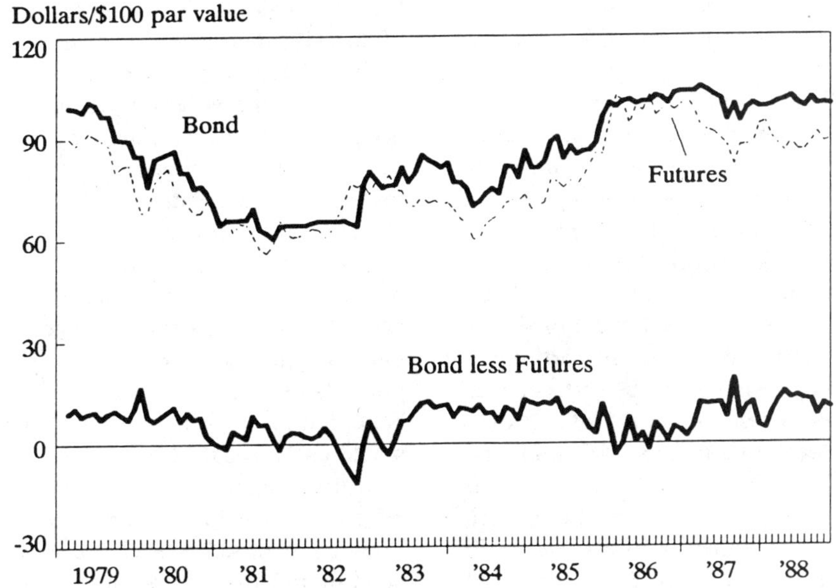

Note: Corporate bond is an A-rated 9.50 percent 30-year bond of a U.S. industrial firm. The futures price is the price of the nearest Chicago Board of Trade Treasury bond future with at least one month until expiration.
Source: Data Resources Inc.

MANAGING INTEREST RATE RISK WITH INTEREST RATE FUTURES

Businesses and investors use interest rate futures in a variety of ways to manage interest rate risk. Hedging strategies can be complex, however, and this can expose investors to new risks. This section provides some specific examples of how interest rate futures are used to hedge interest rate risk and then discusses some of the other risks involved in hedging with interest rate futures.

Hedging Interest Rate Risk with Interest Rate Futures

Investors can hedge interest rate risk by selling or buying interest rate futures. Whether an investor sells or buys futures depends on how changes in interest rates affect the value of his portfolio.

In general, an investor who suffers losses on his investment portfolio when interest rates *rise* hedges interest rate risk by *selling* interest rate futures.[19] When interest rates rise, interest rate futures prices fall. If an investor loses money on his portfolio when interest rates rise, then, he needs to make a profit from falling futures prices. That is, he needs the gain on his futures contract to offset the loss on his original investment portfolio. Since sellers of futures make a profit when futures prices fall, the investor would hedge by selling futures. Similarly, when interest rates fall, the losses on the futures offset the profits on the original investment portfolio.

Conversely, an investor who suffers losses on his portfolio when interest rates *fall* hedges by *buying* interest rate futures. When interest rates fall, interest rate futures prices rise. If an investor loses money on his portfolio when interest rates fall, he needs to make a profit from rising futures prices. Since buyers of futures make a profit when futures prices rise, the investor would hedge by buying futures. Similarly, when interest rates rise, the losses on the futures offset the profits on the portfolio.

Hedging a Treasury Bond Portfolio. Treasury bond prices fall when interest rates rise, so an investor in Treasury bonds would hedge his portfolio against changes in interest rates by selling interest rate futures. In this way, a gain or loss on the Treasury bonds would be offset by a loss or gain on the futures contracts.

An example of the reduction in price volatility that can be achieved by hedging is shown in Chart 6. This chart shows the price of a portfolio of unhedged Treasury bonds and the price of a hedged portfolio. The unhedged portfolio contains 30-year and 10-year U.S. Treasury bonds. The bonds are hedged using the CBT Treasury bond futures.[20] The value of the hedged portfolio of bonds is clearly less variable than the value of the unhedged portfolio. The volatility of the price of the hedged portfolio, measured by the standard deviation of the change in price, is 60 percent lower than the volatility of the price of the unhedged portfolio.

Hedging a Corporate Bond. An investor in corporate bonds would hedge his portfolio against changes in interest rates by selling interest rate futures because corporate bond prices fall when interest rates rise. Corporate bond futures do not exist, so the investor would use Treasury bond futures as a hedge. Treasury bond futures should be a less effective hedge for corporate bonds than for Treasury bonds, however, because Treasury bond futures prices are not as closely related to corporate bond prices as to Treasury bond prices.

An example of the reduction in the price volatility of a corporate bond that can be achieved by hedging is shown in Chart 7. This chart shows the prices of an A-rated 9-1/2 percent 30-year bond of a U.S. industrial company and the value of the hedged bond.[21] The value of the hedged bond is still quite variable, but less variable than the unhedged portfolio. The standard deviation of the change in the value of the hedged bond is 8 percent lower than that of the unhedged portfolio. As expected, Treasury bond futures are a less effective hedge for corporate bonds than for Treasury bonds.[22]

CHART 6

Hedging treasury bonds

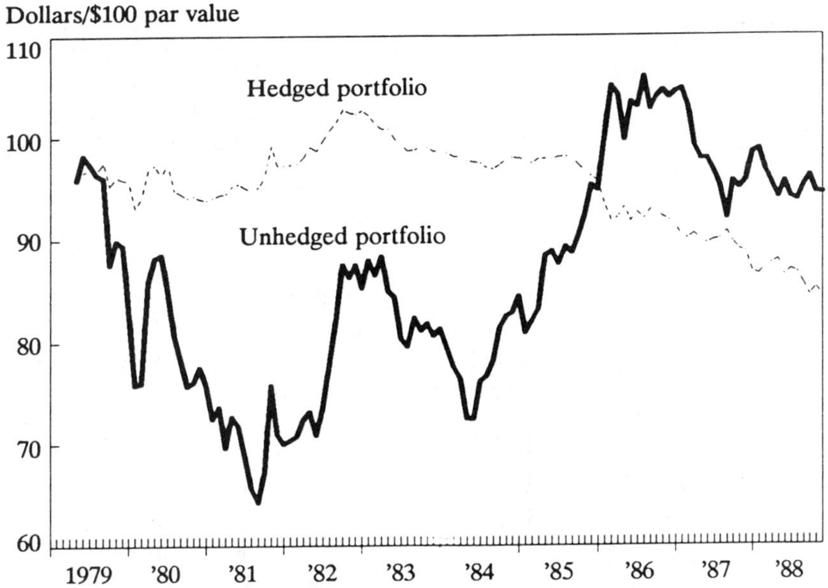

Note: The bond portfolio is an equally weighted portfolio of the 30-year U.S. Treasury bond that matures in November 2007 and the 10-year U.S. Treasury bond that matures in May 1989. The hedged price is the price of the minimum risk hedged portfolio of bonds using the nearest futures contract with at least one month until expiration.
Source: Data Resources Inc.

Depository Institutions. Depository institutions, such as banks and S&Ls, would hedge net worth against changes in interest rates by selling interest rate futures because their net worth generally falls when interest rates rise.[23] When interest rates rise, the net worth of a typical depository institution falls because the value of its assets falls by more than the value of its liabilities. For example, suppose an S&L has assets with a market value of $100 million and liabilities with a market value of $90 million, resulting in a net worth of $10 million. If interest rates rise, the value of the assets might fall by, say, $5 million to $95 million. Since the liabilities have shorter maturities, their value would fall by only, say, $4 million to $86 million, resulting in a net worth of $9 million. But interest rate futures prices also fall when interest rates rise. So if the S&L sells interest rate futures, the gain on the futures when interest rates rise would offset some of the $1 million decline in net worth due to the rise in interest rates.[24]

CHART 7
Hedging corporate bonds

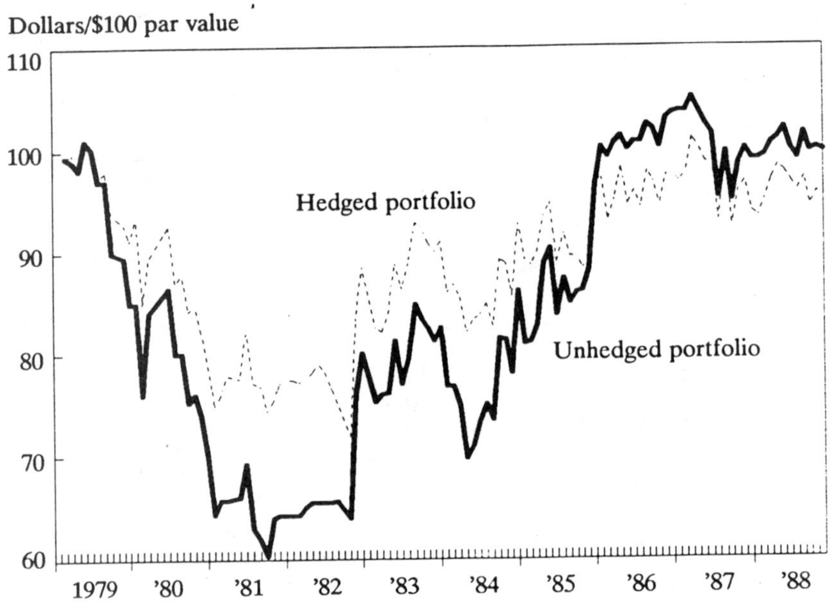

Note: Corporate bond is an A-rated 9.50 percent 30-year bond of a U.S. industrial firm. The hedged price is the price of the minimum risk hedged bond using the nearest futures contract with at least one month until expiration.
Source: Data Resources Inc.

Securities Dealers. Securities dealers hedge interest rate risk by selling interest rate futures sometimes and buying them at other times. Securities dealers would hedge the bonds they have in inventory against changes in interest rates like any other bondholder by selling interest rate futures. On the other hand, securities dealers would hedge bonds they are committed to deliver at a future date for a predetermined price against changes in interest rates by buying interest rate futures.

To understand when securities dealers would buy futures, consider the following example. Suppose a securities dealer has agreed to deliver $10 million face value of Treasury bonds for $90.00 per $100 face value of bonds in two months, and the current price of the bonds is $89.50 per $100. If the dealer had the bonds in inventory or the funds to buy them, he would make a profit of $0.50 per $100, or $50,000. If not, though, he faces the risk that interest rates will fall and bond prices will rise. For example, if interest rates fall and bond prices rise $0.25, he would have to pay $89.75 per $100 for the bonds, and the profit on the commitment would fall 50 percent to $25,000. However, if interest rates fall, the futures price should rise. Since a person who buys a futures contract makes a profit when its price rises, the profit on the futures should offset much of the decrease in the profit on the commitment when interest rates fall.

Mortgage Banks. Because the value of mortgage commitments falls when interest rates rise, mortgage bankers would hedge mortgage commitments against changes in interest rates by selling interest rate futures. For example, suppose a mortgage banker commits to a 10-percent interest rate on a $100,000 mortgage. If the mortgage closes in two months and interest rates do not change, the mortgage banker could sell the mortgage for $100,000. However, if interest rates rise, the value of the mortgage will fall. If, for example, the mortgage value falls to $98,000, the value of the mortgage commitment would fall $2,000. But since interest rates rose, interest rate futures prices would have fallen. Therefore, if the mortgage banker sells interest rate futures, the profit on the futures he sold would offset the loss on the mortgage commitment when interest rates rise.

Life Insurance Companies. Life insurance companies would hedge GIC commitments against changes in interest rates by buying interest rate futures. For example, suppose a life insurance company commits to a 10 percent interest rate on a GIC but will not receive the funds for two months. In addition, suppose the life insurance company expects to invest the funds in an 11 percent corporate bond. If interest rates do not change in the two-month period, the life insurance company would earn a spread of one percentage point. But if interest rates fall and the corporate bond rate falls to, say, 10.5 percent, the spread earned on the GIC would fall 50 percent to 0.5 percentage points. When interest rates fall, though, interest rate futures prices rise. Therefore, by buying futures, life insurance companies can offset declines in the spread on GIC commitments when interest rates fall.[25]

THE RISKS OF HEDGING WITH INTEREST RATE FUTURES

Although hedging with interest rate futures allows investors to reduce interest rate risk, it generally cannot completely eliminate risk. All hedges generally contain some residual, or base, risk. Moreover, hedging also introduces some new risks. Some of those risks are credit risk, marking to market risk, and managerial risk.

Basis Risk. The risk that remains after an investor hedges his portfolio is called basis risk. An investor who hedges his portfolio with interest rate futures bears basis risk because, when interest rates change, the change in the price of the futures contract does not perfectly offset the change in the price of the asset being hedged. Fixed income asset prices can change for reasons other than changes in interest rates. As a result, the basis risk in a hedge will be relatively high when factors other than interest rates are an important source of the changes in the price of the asset being hedged.

For example, an asset's price will fall if the issuer's credit rating falls or if the asset is relatively illiquid and a large amount is sold. Since these factors would not affect the prices of interest rate futures, such as Treasury bond futures, interest rate futures cannot offset price changes caused by such factors. In fact, that is why Treasury bond futures proved to be a less effective hedging instrument for the corporate bond than for the Treasury bond portfolio in the examples used in the preceding section.

Credit Risk. The credit risk in an interest rate futures hedge is not that the opposite party in the futures contract will default, but that the opposite party in the asset being hedged will default. Individuals do not have to be concerned about the opposite party defaulting on a futures contract because every futures exchange has a clearing organization that is a party to every futures contract in order to guarantee the integrity of the contract.[26] That is, the clearing house is the seller in every contract bought and the buyer in every contract sold. But the risk remains that an investor will end up with an unhedged open futures position if there is a default on the asset being hedged.

For example, suppose an investor in corporate bonds hedges his portfolio against changes in interest rates by selling interest rate futures. If interest rates fall, the prices of the bond and futures will rise. Since futures were sold, the investor would suffer losses on the futures, but those losses would be offset by the gains on the bonds. If the bond issuer defaults, though, the investor would have the losses on his futures position but no gains to offset the losses.

Marking to Market Risk. Marking to market risk is the risk investors will have to cover futures losses when the contract is marked to market at the end of each day. All futures exchanges require every unsettled futures position to be marked to market every night and settled daily. That is, at the end of each day, funds are transferred from individuals who lose on their contracts to individuals who gain on their contracts so that buyers and sellers actually realize the gains and losses from daily price changes as they occur. A problem could occur for those who suffer losses on their futures position, though, because they must make immediate cash outlays. Although losses on futures contracts are generally offset by gains on the asset being hedged, investors usually do not receive those gains as they occur. Therefore, investors would either have to liquidate other investments and lose the associated income flows or pay interest on borrowed funds to cover their futures losses as they occur.

Managerial Risk. Managerial risk, broadly defined, is the risk futures will be used inappropriately and result in greater, rather than less, risk. This is really a "catch all" category that accounts for anything else that can go wrong with a hedging program. One major reason managerial risk arises is interest rate futures can be used for speculative purposes. In addition to being good assets for hedging, futures are also good assets for speculating on price movements for two reasons. First, it costs very little to open a futures position, and second, an open unhedged futures position is as risky as the underlying asset. While speculators play an important and useful role in futures markets, an institution that wants to hedge with futures must have internal controls to make sure those responsible for hedging are not speculating.

Managerial risk also arises because futures hedging strategies are complicated. Because they are complicated, it is possible for managers to make incorrect decisions that significantly lower a firm's value. For example, suppose a manager wants to minimize the interest rate risk of his bond portfolio, but he overhedges by selling too many futures contracts. If interest rates were to fall, the losses on the futures position could be much greater than the gains on the bonds. Thus, when overhedged, the riskiness of a portfolio is greater than the minimum level of risk and the return is less than that associated with the minimum level of risk. In fact, the riskiness of an overhedged portfolio can be even greater than the riskiness of the unhedged portfolio. To control this risk, it is important that managers understand the complexities of hedging with interest rate futures, the capabilities and limitations of a hedging program, and the need to continually monitor hedging programs.

CONCLUSION

The riskiness of investments in bonds and other fixed income assets has increased in recent years because of increased interest rate volatility. The lack of traditional low-cost methods for managing this increase in interest rate risk led to the development of many new financial instruments that can be used to hedge interest rate risk. One of the most popular types of instruments is interest rate futures contracts. Interest rate futures are now trading on exchanges around the world, and they have become an important part of virtually every portfolio manager's tool kit for managing interest rate risk.

This article showed how interest rate futures can be used to manage interest rate risk. In many cases, interest rate risk can be substantially reduced. It must be remembered, though, that hedging with interest rate futures can be complex, and investors must thoroughly examine all aspects of interest rate futures and hedging techniques before implementing a hedging strategy.

ENDNOTES

1.The riskiness of a fixed income asset also depends on the volatility of other factors that affect its price, such as the creditworthiness of the issuer and the liquidity of the asset.

2.This assumes a uniform change in rates on all maturities. The interest rate sensitivity of a fixed income asset also depends on other factors, such as the size of the coupon payments and the dates the coupon payments are received.

3.Although the volatility of total returns is the same as price volatility for a given bond, the volatilities are not the same when the composition of a bond portfolio changes over time because the coupon payments change. Since the composition of the portfolio that underlies the index in Chart 2 changes, the volatility of total returns is shown.

4.Securities dealers make a profit on their bonds when interest rates fall. Indeed, all investors in fixed-income assets make a profit when interest rates move in one direction and suffer a loss when interest rates move in the other direction. In the remaining examples, the discussion will focus on how a change in interest rates in only one direction affects an investor. The direction of the change in interest rates that is used is the one that produces a loss for the investor.

5.Viewed another way, a GIC commitment is a fixed rate liability that is not matched by an asset. When interest rates fall, the value of the GIC commitment rises, but there is no asset whose value also rises. Therefore, the insurance company's net worth falls when interest rates fall.

6.The risk that remains after a portfolio has been hedged is called *basis risk*. If the riskiness of a portfolio is measured by the standard deviation of the change in its value, the minimum level of basis risk that can be achieved through hedging is

$$\sigma_h=\sigma_p\sqrt{(1-\rho_2)},$$

where σ_p is the standard deviation of the change in the value of the unhedged portfolio, and ρ is the correlation coefficient between the changes in the values of the portfolio and the hedging asset. The maximum percentage reduction in risk is

$$100(\sigma_p-\sigma_h)/\sigma_p=100(1-\sqrt{(1-\rho^2)},$$

which depends only on ρ, and risk will be completely eliminated only if ρ equals 1 or -1.

7.The delivery dates for most interest rate futures are in March, June, September, and December. The actual delivery date varies with the contract. For example, the seller of a Treasury bond contract at the Chicago Board of Trade can deliver Treasury bonds on any day in the contract month, although the last trading day is seven business days prior to the last business day of the month. Although some interest rate futures have contract months that extend out to three years, most of the contracts traded are contracts with the nearest delivery month.

8.For some interest rate futures, such as the Eurodollar time deposit futures on the International Monetary Market exchange, all contracts must be settled by taking an offsetting position. That is, delivery of the underlying instrument is not allowed.

9.Although the GNMA futures contract was initially successful, it stopped trading in December 1984.

10.Treasury bill futures are also traded on the MidAmerica Commodity Exchange in Chicago. Eurodollar futures are also traded on the London International Financial Futures Exchange. The 30-day interest rate futures contract is traded at the Chicago Board of Trade.

11.Treasury note futures are traded on the Chicago Board of Trade exchange, the MidAmerica Commodity Exchange in Chicago, and the Financial Instrument Exchange, a division of the New York Cotton Exchange.

12.Treasury bond futures are also traded on the MidAmerica Commodity Exchange in Chicago and the London International Financial Futures Exchange. Futures on the municipal bond index are traded at the Chicago Board of Trade.

13.The margin on a futures contract is "good faith" money deposited with a broker to assure him that losses can be covered in the event of adverse price movements.

14.See Arnold Kling, "Futures Markets and Transaction Costs," in Myron L. Kwast, ed., *Financial Futures and Options in the U.S. Economy: A Study by the Staff of the Federal Reserve System* (Washington, D.C.: Board of Governors of the Federal Reserve System. 1986), pp.41-54.

15.The minimum initial margin a person must deposit when establishing an open position in a futures contract and the minimum level that must be maintained is set by the exchanges and is changed from time to time. The margin level depends on factors such as the volatility of the price of the underlying instrument and the maximum daily change in the futures price the exchange allows. Margins also may depend on whether a person is just buying or selling futures alone or is buying or selling futures to establish a hedge. The margin on an outright purchase or sale of CBT Treasury bond futures is $2,500. Although interest is generally paid on the initial margin, interest is not paid on additions to the margin account because additions represent losses that have been transferred to the accounts of parties that have gained from price movements.

16.The relationship between the price of a futures contract and the price of its underlying asset is most easily seen on the last day of trading for a particular contract, at which time the two prices must be exactly equal. In general, if there are no transaction costs and capital markets are perfect, the difference between a futures price and the price of the underlying assets can be no larger than the net cost of holding the underlying asset in inventory--inventory costs less income flows from the asset--until the futures contract expires. This relationship between the price of a futures contract and the price of its underlying asset is known as the cost of carry theory of futures prices. Prices do deviate slightly from cost of carry, though, because of transaction costs and capital market imperfections. For a detailed discussion of the relationship between interest rate futures prices and bond prices, see James M. Little, "What are Financial Futures?" in Nancy H. Rothstein and James M. Little, eds., *The Handbook of Financial Futures* (New York. McGraw Hill Book Company, 1984), pp.35-66.

17.The closeness of these two prices should not be surprising. The CBT Treasury bond futures price should be very closely related to the price of its underlying asset, which is an 8 percent 20-year Treasury bond. Since 30-year Treasury bond prices and 20-year Treasury bond prices are closely related, the futures price, and the bond price in Chart 4 are closely related.

18.Viewed another way, Treasury bond futures are less effective in hedging the total risk of a corporate bond than a Treasury bond because (1) Treasury bond futures only hedge interest rate risk, and (2) interest rate risk accounts for a smaller share of the total risk of a corporate bond than of a Treasury bond. In terms of hedging only the interest rate risk of a corporate bond--that is, changes in the price of the corporate bond due to changes in interest rates--Treasury bond futures should be fairly effective.

19.Of course, an equivalent statement of this rule is that an investor who makes profits on his investment portfolio when interest rates fall hedges interest rate risk by selling interest rate futures.

20.This example assumes the investor wants to minimize risk. For simplicity, the value of the hedged portfolio ignores the effects of margin requirements, transaction costs, taxation, accounting practices, and regulatory requirements, all of which could affect the value of the hedge and the hedging strategy. The prices are end-of-month data, and the futures price is on the nearest contract with at least on month until expiration.

The example does not account for the possibility that risk could be reduced further by (1) using futures with contract months that are further out, and (2) estimating the number of contracts to sell over shorter time periods and then adjusting the number of contracts to account for the changes. On the other hand, the example could be overstating the degree of risk reduction because the number of contracts sold is estimated from actual price data over the hedging period, whereas investors must estimate the number of contracts using data from periods prior to the hedging period.

21.The qualifications and assumptions that applied to the hedge of the Treasury bond portfolio also apply to this example (see footnote 20).

22.Although Treasury bond futures did not provide a good hedge for a single corporate bond, they should provide a better hedge for a portfolio of corporate bonds. The corporate bond in this example had an A rating, which suggests that credit risk is at least partly responsible for the relatively poor relationship between the bond price and the futures price. A diversified portfolio of corporate bonds, however, would be exposed to less credit risk, and therefore its price would be more closely related to the futures price.

23.The best futures contract for hedging a depository institution's net worth is one whose price sensitivity to interest rate changes is as close as possible to the sensitivity of the institution's net worth to interest rate changes. The sensitivity of the institution's net worth to interest rate changes rises with the extent to which its asset and liability maturities are mismatched. Thus, institutions whose maturity structure is only slightly mismatched would choose futures contracts based on short-term assets, such as Treasury bills or Eurodollar time deposits. On the other hand, institutions whose maturity structure is highly mismatched would choose futures contracts based on longer term assets, such as Treasury bond and note futures.

24.Of course, when interest rates fall, the value of the S&L's assets will rise more than the value of its liabilities, but the gain in net worth will be offset by a loss on the futures. In other words, like any other hedging asset, futures offset capital gains as well as capital losses. In the remaining examples, the discussion will focus on how hedging with futures offsets capital losses, but it is important to remember that futures hedges also offset capital gains.

25.Recall that a GIC commitment is a fixed rate liability that is not matched by an asset. Therefore, net worth falls when interest rates fall because the increase in the value of the GIC commitment is not offset by an increase in the value of an asset. Since net worth falls when interest rates fall, the GIC commitment can be hedged against changes in interest rates by buying interest rate futures.

26.The exchanges are also protected because many exchanges have limits on the amount a futures price can change within a day. The limits are equal to the minimum margin deposit that individuals must have on deposit with their broker.

QUESTIONS

1. What is interest rate risk? How does it affect individual and institutional investors?

2. What are interest rate futures and how do they help investors manage interest rate risk?

3. What accounts for the innovation and widespread use of interest rate futures? Is this explanation consistent with the textbook's economic analysis of innovation?

READING 27

Will Increased Regulation of Stock Index Futures Reduce Stock Market Volatility?

Sean Becketti and Dan J. Roberts

On October 19, 1987, the Dow Jones Industrial Average plunged 508 points, the worst single-day loss ever for U.S. stocks. This episode, along with others, has caused policymakers and the public in general to focus their attention on stock market volatility. Many believe that large swings in stock prices have occurred more often and have become larger in recent years.

Some people blame stock index futures for the perceived increase in stock market volatility. Stock index futures might contribute to stock market volatility in two ways. First, futures and stock trading might interact to worsen individual stock market disruptions, such as the October 1987 collapse. Second, futures trading might produce a market environment generally more susceptible to stock market disruptions. Many studies have analyzed the interactions between futures and stocks in individual stock market collapses. This article is one of relatively few concerned with the second, more general way in which futures might increase stock market volatility.

To reduce the effect of futures on stock market volatility, regulations aimed at reducing the general level of futures activity have already been adopted or have been proposed. While these regulations may or may not reduce stock market volatility, they certainly will impose costs on participants in the stock index futures market. Because the regulations are costly, it is important to find out whether the stock index futures market actually contributes to stock market volatility.

This article finds that futures market regulations intended to reduce futures trading are unlikely to reduce stock market volatility. The first section of this article describes the market for stock index futures and explains why futures are blamed for stock market volatility. The second section discusses the costs of current and proposed futures market regulations. The third section presents evidence that stock index futures have not increased stock market volatility, whether measured by the frequency or the size of large swings in stock prices.

I. STOCK INDEX FUTURES AND STOCK MARKET VOLATILITY

Stock index futures are one of the most successful financial innovations of the 1980s. Two characteristics of stock index futures make them popular with investors. First, the price of these futures is closely related to the value of the stock market as a whole. Second, they are relatively inexpensive to trade. These two characteristics make stock index futures useful in a variety of investment programs. However, these characteristics also lead some observers to blame stock index futures for stock market volatility.

What Are Stock Index Futures?

A financial futures contract is an agreement to buy or sell a financial asset, such as a Treasury bond or a specified amount of a foreign currency, at a given time in the future. The price of the future transaction is determined when the agreement is made. Stock index futures are financial futures contracts in which the underlying financial asset is a basket of stocks. The several different stock index futures contracts are distinguished by the basket of stocks underlying the contract. The most popular of these is the Chicago Mercantile Exchange's contract based on the Standard & Poor's 500 Composite Stock Price Index.

No money is exchanged when a futures contract is traded. A futures contract is simply an agreement to make an exchange in the future. As it turns out, however, assets are not exchanged even in the future. Instead, buyers and sellers of stock index futures contracts are required to settle their positions by taking offsetting positions. For instance, investors who buy S&P 500 contracts must settle their positions by selling contracts by the original contracts' delivery date.[1]

An example may help clarify this process. The price of the S&P 500 futures contract is quoted as an index, in units that are comparable to the actual S&P 500 stock price index. The real price paid for an S&P 500 futures contract is $500 times the value of the index. Thus, if the index value is 300, an investor would pay $150,000 to buy one futures contract ($500 times the index value of 300). Sometime before the expiration date of the contract, the investor must offset this position by selling a contract at whatever the futures index value happens to be. For the purpose of this example, assume the investor sells a contract to offset his initial purchase when the futures index has increased to 303. At this index value, the investor would sell the contract for $151,500 ($500 times 303). Thus, the investor would make a profit of $1,500 ($500 times the three-point change in the futures index value).

Stock index futures were introduced in mid-1982 and were an immediate success (Chart 1). By 1984, the dollar value of S&P

Chart 1
Volume of Stock Index Futures Trading

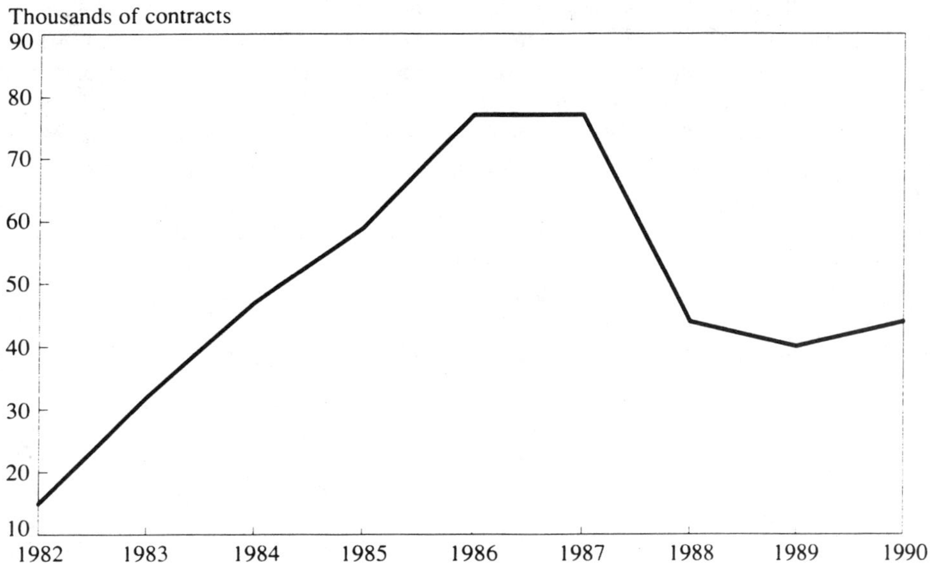

Note: This chart displays the typical daily stock index futures volume from April 21, 1982 through July 31, 1990. Futures volume is measured by the median daily number of S&P 500 futures contracts traded.

Source: Data Resources Inc., Lexington, Mass.

500 contracts traded exceeded the dollar volume of stocks traded on the New York Stock Exchange (Merrick 1987). Trading volume peaked in 1986 and 1987, when the median number of contracts traded each day was 77,000.[2] Volume declined after the stock market collapse in October 1987. In recent years, futures trading volume has averaged around 40,000 contracts a day.

Why Are Stock Index Futures Popular?

Stock index futures are popular among investors because they are an economical substitute for buying and selling a diversified portfolio of stocks. Futures prices are tied to the values of diversified portfolios rather than to the prices of individual stocks. As a result, investors can buy or sell futures rather than buying or selling many different stocks because the transactions costs of futures are low.

Investors who buy stock index futures contracts receive similar gains and losses as if they bought an equivalent amount of stock. The gains and losses are similar because the price of a futures contract is highly correlated with the price of the basket of stocks in the index that underlies the contract (Cornell and French 1983). In the example above, the 1 percent increase in the futures price, from 300 to 303, reflects a comparable increase in the value of the S&P 500 index. Thus, investors who buy contracts benefit if stock prices rise after they purchase their futures contracts. These investors receive the increase in the value of the index when they offset their position by selling contracts. Similarly, investors who sell contracts benefit if stock prices fall after they sell their futures contracts. To offset their position, these investors purchase contracts at the new, lower price.

Another important feature of stock index futures is their low transactions costs. Trading stock index futures contracts is less expensive than trading the equivalent basket of stocks because brokers' fees and margin requirements in the futures market are relatively low (Kling 1986). The brokerage cost at a discount broker of establishing and settling a position in an S&P 500 index futures contract is only $32. Since the value of a contract is $500 times the value of the index, this fee represents just over 0.02 percent of the underlying value of the contract when the S&P 500 index is 300. Brokerage fees for an equivalent stock purchase are many times higher.

The initial margin requirement for futures trading is also relatively small. A margin is the minimum amount of money an investor must pay to buy securities.[3] The margin on an S&P 500 index futures contract used for hedging is currently $8,000—less than 5.5 percent of the contract when the S&P 500 index is 300. Investors can earn interest on their initial margin by using U.S. government securities to meet the margin requirement. In contrast, the margin requirement for stock purchases is 50 percent of the value of the purchase, and the margin must be paid in cash.[4]

How Are Stock Index Futures Used?

The characteristics that make stock index futures popular also make them well suited to a number of different investment uses. Portfolio managers can sell stock index futures to hedge the value of a diversified stock portfolio against changes in the value of the stock market as a whole (Morris 1989). As stock prices change, losses (profits) on the stocks will be largely offset by profits (losses) on the futures contracts because futures prices are closely related to the value of a broad market index. For example, if stock prices fall, the value of the stock portfolio falls. At the same time, the price of the futures contract falls. When portfolio managers buy futures to offset their initial futures contract sales, they make a profit because they pay less than they received when they originally sold the futures. This profit on the futures trades can help offset the loss on the stocks and thus reduce the change in the value of the total portfolio.[5]

Many investment strategies require portfolio managers to adjust the proportion of stocks in the portfolio over time. Portfolio insurance, asset allocation, and market-timing strategies are just a few of the investment approaches that involve frequent changes in stock holdings (Petzel 1989). Portfolio managers frequently choose to make these adjustments by buying or selling futures rather than stocks.

Another investment strategy involving stock index futures is index arbitrage. This strategy is a form of program trading in that it involves the purchase or sale of a group of stocks.[6] While the price of stock index futures is highly correlated with the value of the underlying stock index, occasionally the price of the futures contract diverges from its usual relationship to the value of the stocks. These episodes provide arbitragers with opportunities to profit. For example, assume the price of the futures contract rises, while the price of stocks does not change. In this situation, arbitragers can guarantee a profit by selling the relatively expensive futures contract and buying the relatively inexpensive stocks. This arbitrage continues until the usual relationship between futures and stock prices is restored.

Finally, stock index futures are an attractive asset to stock market speculators. The availability of futures makes it possible for speculators to take positions that would not be economical if they had to buy or sell shares directly.

Why Are Stock Index Futures Blamed for Stock Market Volatility?

Stock market volatility can be divided into two types, normal volatility and jump volatility (Becketti and Sellon 1989). Normal volatility refers to the ordinary ups and downs in stock prices. Jump volatility, on the other hand, refers to occasional and sudden extreme changes in prices. The leading example of jump volatility is the market collapse in mid-October 1987. However, the market has endured many stock price jumps besides those in October 1987.

The type of stock market volatility that concerns legislators, regulators, and market makers is jump volatility.[7] Jumps in stock prices over a few hours or a day can temporarily disrupt capital markets and strain market mechanisms. In the most extreme example of jump volatility, the October 1987 market collapse, many stocks stopped trading for several hours. The execution of trades of other stocks also was delayed sometimes for hours, leaving investors with little idea of the prices that would prevail when their trades were executed. In addition, losses suffered by many stock market specialists threatened their continued participation in the market (U.S. Presidential Task Force on Market Mechanisms 1988).

Jump volatility also raises concerns about individual investors' access to, and participation in, the market. An increase in jump volatility may make it more important for investors to employ sophisticated strategies to protect the value of their portfolios. While institutional investors possess the expertise in, and the access to, futures and options markets necessary to execute these strategies, some observers fear that individual investors do not have the same expertise and access. As a result, these observers fear that individual investors will simply leave the stock market in reaction to an increase in jump volatility.[8]

The features of stock index futures that make them popular—low transactions costs and a close relationship to the value of the stock market—also explain why futures are blamed for volatility. For example, these features increase speculative activity. To the extent speculative activity tends to increase the volatility of futures prices, this futures market volatility then spills over into the stock market. In addition, low trading costs ensure that the fads and panics that occasionally afflict financial markets find little or no resistance in futures markets. The shifting moods of the financial community are translated immediately into violent oscillations in futures prices and then into stock prices.

Program trading is also believed to increase jump volatility. Some observers fear stock price jumps can set off a cascade effect, that is, a free-fall in stock prices that feeds on itself.[9] According to this view, a sudden drop in stock prices can trigger computer-driven futures trading strategies that drive stock index futures prices down. The drop in futures prices then feeds back to the stock market, and the cycle begins again.

II. COSTS OF REGULATIONS THAT REDUCE FUTURES MARKET ACTIVITY

Many people believe stock index futures contribute to jump volatility in the stock market. To reduce the effect of futures on jump volatility, regulations that reduce the general level of futures activity have been adopted or proposed. These regulations reduce futures activity because they make futures trading more costly.

One type of regulation that has already been adopted is circuit breaker rules. Circuit breakers are rules that temporarily suspend trading if price movements exceed certain thresholds. Proponents of circuit breakers believe that suspending trading prevents panics by giving traders time to reevaluate market conditions and to bolster their liquidity and credit (Morris 1990). Thus, one reason for circuit breakers is they halt trading during an incipient panic. Another reason for circuit breakers, however, is to reduce the general level of futures activity.[10]

One cost of circuit breakers is they make futures trading riskier. Circuit breakers raise the possibility that investors may not be able to trade at some time in the future. Because circuit breakers are triggered by events that cannot be predicted accurately, investors cannot effectively protect themselves against the possibility of these trading halts. From the point of view of investors, this uncertainty makes it riskier to trade in futures.

Another cost of circuit breakers is they can expose clearing houses to increased credit risk by implicitly extending margin credit to some traders (Moser 1990). Traders in futures are required to make additional margin payments when they suffer losses. If trading is halted because of a circuit breaker, the adequacy of margins is evaluated at the price of the last recorded trade. While trading is halted, the true market price, that is, the price that would prevail in the absence of the circuit breaker-imposed trading halt, may change substantially. Thus, some traders have trading losses that are not recognized while trading is halted. When trading resumes, if the losses are so large that these traders cannot fulfill their contracts, the clearing house may be forced to assume the failed traders' obligations.

Circuit breakers also may inadvertently increase stock market volatility. When circuit breakers are close to being triggered, market participants may buy or sell futures frantically to avoid being locked in. This panic trading may increase futures market volatility which, in turn, will increase stock market volatility. In addition, if circuit breakers suspend futures trading but not stock trading, stock market volatility may increase as frustrated futures investors shift their trading to the stock market (Morris 1989).

A regulation that has been proposed to reduce the volume of futures trading is higher margin requirements. Higher margins directly increase the transactions cost of trading futures by increasing the amount of money investors must post to make trades.[11] These increased costs reduce all futures trading, including hedging. The general reduction in trading represents a loss of liquidity to the market. In addition, the reduction in hedging makes investors more vulnerable to swings in the value of stocks than they would be if margins were lower and they hedged more completely.

III. DO STOCK INDEX FUTURES CAUSE STOCK MARKET VOLATILITY?

Futures market regulations that reduce the overall level of futures market activity thus impose substantial costs on investors. Imposing these costs is justified by the belief that reducing futures trading reduces jump volatility in the stock market. But without persuasive evidence that futures are responsible for stock market volatility, regulations intended to reduce volatility by reducing the overall level of futures trading are inadvisable.[12]

Have Stock Index Futures Increased the Frequency of Stock Price Jumps?

One way stock index futures might increase jump volatility is to make stock price jumps more likely. Researchers measure jumps by setting a band within which stock price movements are considered normal or ordinary. Movements outside the band are identified as jumps because they are considered exceptional. For example, some researchers identify jumps in daily data as price changes in excess of 1 or 2 percent, either up or down (Schwert 1990).

Using a statistical technique designed to highlight unusual values, this article defines a daily jump as any day in which the S&P index rises or falls more than approximately 1.75 percent.[13] At current price levels, this represents about a 40-to-50-point or more move in the Dow.[14] From July 1962 through August 1990, 4.5 percent (317 days) of all daily changes in the S&P 500 stock index were jumps. Forty-six percent of these jumps represented declines in the stock index. The median jump involved a change of slightly more than 2 percent, either up or down, in the S&P 500 index.

At first glance, the futures market appears to have made stock price jumps more likely because jumps in stock prices have been more frequent since stock index futures began trading. Trading in S&P 500 stock index futures began on April 21, 1982. From 1962 through April 20, 1982, 3.6 percent of daily returns were jumps. From April 21, 1982, through August 1990, 6.6 percent of daily returns were jumps. In other words, stock price jumps have been almost twice as frequent since the introduction of futures as in the preceding 20 years.

Closer examination, however, shows the increase in the frequency of jumps cannot be attributed to stock index futures because the frequency of jumps began increasing well before futures began trading (Chart 2). In the 1960s, only 1.1 percent of daily returns were jumps. By the early 1980s, jumps represented 7.4 percent of daily returns. In fact, compared with the early 1980s, stock price jumps have become slightly less frequent since the advent of stock index futures trading. Thus, it is not plausible to attribute the slow, steady increase in the frequency of jumps since the early 1960s solely, or even mainly, to the futures market.

Even though the frequency of jumps has decreased compared with the early 1980s, jump volatility might be even lower if stock index futures were not available. One way to test whether the futures market contributes to jump volatility is to see if jumps are more frequent when futures activity is high. If stock index futures are a source of additional jump volatility, then volatility should be high when futures activity is generally high and low when futures activity is generally low.

As it turns out, trading volume—the most common measure of futures activity—appears to be unrelated to the frequency of jumps. Chart 3 displays monthly observations of futures trading volume and hourly stock price jumps.[15] For this comparison, hourly jumps are a more appropriate measure of volatility than daily jumps.[16] The volume of futures trading grew steadily from 1982 then peaked in 1986-87 at around 77,000 contracts a day. In contrast, the frequency of hourly jumps showed no upward trend. In October 1987, the frequency of jumps rose sharply without a corresponding rise in futures volume. Both volatility and volume fell sharply after October 1987. Since the stock market collapse, there has been no upward or downward trend in either volatility or volume. Thus, the only period over which a close relationship appeared to exist is the several months of decline in volume and volatility just following the October 1987 collapse.

The lack of relationship between futures volume and the frequency of jumps apparent in Chart 3 is confirmed by statistical analysis. One statistic that measures the relationship

Chart 2
Frequency of Jumps in Daily Stock Returns

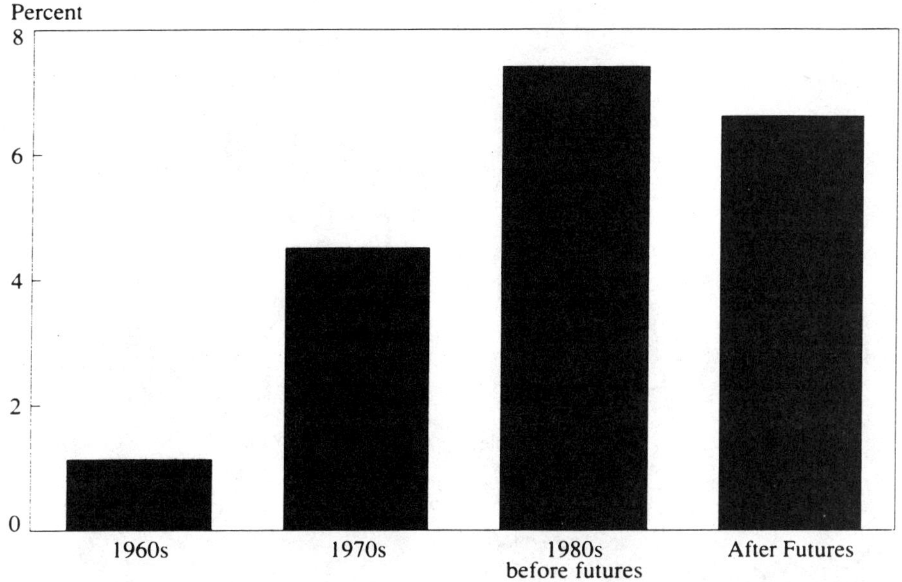

Note: This chart displays the frequency of stock price jumps in different periods. The frequency of jumps is measured by the number of daily jumps in the S&P 500 index divided by the number of trading days in the period. The bar labeled "1960s" includes data from July 3, 1962, through the end of the 1960s. The bar labeled "1970s" covers the entire 1970s. The bar labeled "1980s before futures" includes data from the beginning of 1980 through April 20, 1982. The bar labeled "After Futures" includes data from April 21, 1982 - the first day of trading for the S&P 500 futures contract - through August 10, 1990.

Source: Standard and Poor's Corporation.

between two variables is the correlation coefficient. The correlations between daily and hourly stock price jumps and futures trading volume are small, indicating little or no association between futures trading volume and the frequency of stock price jumps.[17] The correlation between daily stock price jumps and futures volume is only 0.14 and is not significantly different from zero at the 5 percent level. The correlation between hourly stock price jumps and futures volume is also small, 0.17. However, this correlation is significantly different from zero at the 5 percent level.

The statistical significance of the relationship between futures volume and hourly stock price jumps disappears, however, when other factors that might affect volatility are taken into account. One problem with correlation coefficients is they ignore the

Chart 3
Futures Volume and the Frequency of Stock Price Jumps

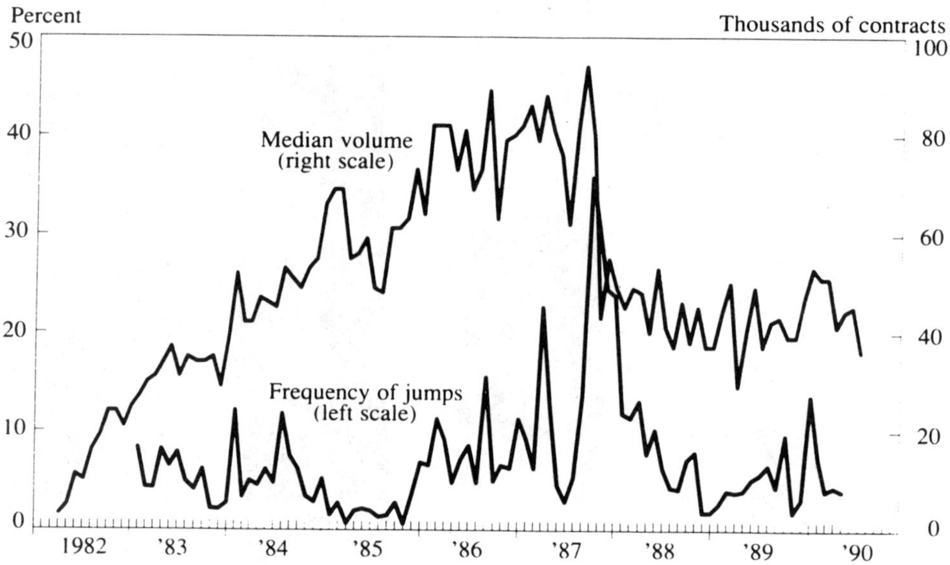

Note: This chart displays monthly measurements of stock index futures volume and the frequency of stock price jumps. Futures volume is measured by the median daily number of S&P 500 futures contracts traded. The frequency of stock price jumps is measured by the number of hourly jumps in the S&P 500 index divided by the number of trading hours in the month.

Source: Data Resources Inc., Lexington, Mass. (for futures volume) and Tick Data Inc., Lakewood, Colo. (for S&P 500 index).

impact of other variables that may be important. For example, stock market volatility may exhibit seasonal variation reflecting end-of-year tax-related trading strategies or the time pattern of dividend payments. In addition, stock market volatility today may be influenced by recent episodes of volatility. In other words, once volatility is high, it may stay high for a while. To test for these possibilities, the frequency of jumps was regressed on its own recent past and seasonal factors along with the volume of futures trading. When these other factors were taken into account, the relationship between jumps and futures volume was no longer statistically significant.[18]

Chart 4
Futures Volume and the Size of Stock Price Jumps

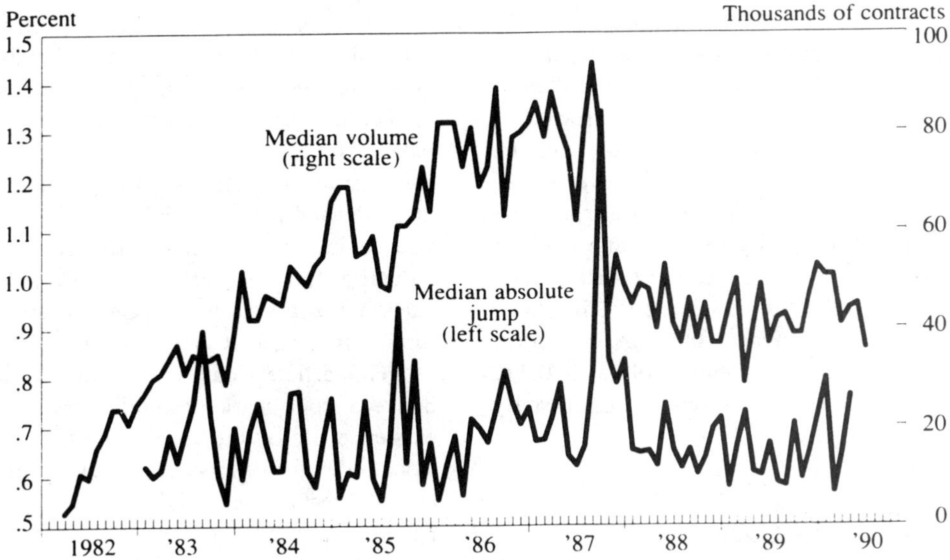

Note: This chart displays monthly measurements of stock index futures volume and the size of stock price jumps. Futures volume is measured by the median daily number of S&P 500 futures contracts traded. The size of stock price jumps is measured by the median hourly absolute percentage change in the S&P 500 index within each month.

Source: Data Resources Inc., Lexington, Mass. (for futures volume) and Tick Data Inc., Lakewood, Colo. (for S&P 500 index).

Have Stock Index Futures Increased the Size of Stock Price Jumps?

Another way that stock index futures might increase jump volatility is to increase the size of stock price jumps when they do occur. However, the size of the typical stock price jump has not increased markedly since futures began trading. From the beginning of 1962 through April 20, 1982, the median daily jump involved a 2.1 percent change in stock prices, either up or down. Since April 20, 1982, the typical jump has increased only 0.2 percent to 2.3 percent.

Even though the typical jump has not grown larger since stock index futures trading began, jumps might be even smaller if futures were not available. If stock index futures are responsible for this type of increase in jump volatility, then jumps should be larger when futures activity is generally high and smaller when futures activity is generally low.

As it turns out, however, the size of the typical hourly jump in stock prices appears to be unrelated to the volume of futures trading. Chart 4 shows that the median absolute hourly stock price jump essentially has been flat except for the October 1987 market collapse. In contrast, the volume of trading grew until October 1987, dropped sharply just after the market collapse, and has been flat ever since.

A correlation analysis confirms the impression given by the chart. The correlation between the size of daily stock price jumps and futures volume is only 0.03. The correlation between the size of hourly stock price jumps and futures volume is 0.11. Neither of these correlations is significantly different from zero.[19]

IV. CONCLUSION

The high correlation between stock index futures prices and stock prices, combined with the low cost of futures trading, has led some observers to blame high levels of stock index futures activity for recent bouts of volatility in the stock market. Circuit breakers were adopted partly to reduce futures activity in order to reduce stock market volatility. Higher margins also have been proposed to reduce futures activity. However, circuit breakers and higher margins impose costs on investors and may have adverse effects on the functioning of financial markets. Thus, reducing futures market activity to reduce stock market volatility makes sense only if futures trading is responsible for volatility.

This article finds little or no relationship between stock market volatility and either the existence of, or the level of activity in, the stock index futures market. As a result, while circuit breakers and higher margins may be useful for other reasons, their depressing influence on the volume of futures trading is unlikely to reduce stock market volatility.

APPENDIX

This article uses a statistical method designed to highlight potential outliers—abnormally small or large values—to identify stock price jumps. The method consists of constructing a band based on a robust measure of the dispersion of the observations in the sample. Observations that fall outside this band are identified as jumps.

The upper and lower ends of the band are calculated as follows:

upper end of band = 75th percentile + 1.5 (interquartile range)

lower end of band = 25th percentile - 1.5 (interquartile range)

(continued on next page)

The interquartile range is the difference between the 75th and 25th percentile of the distribution of stock returns. These percentiles are calculated for the entire sample of returns. The frequency of jumps is calculated as the number of jumps divided by the number of observations.

A similar measure of jumps is used and described in Becketti and Sellon 1989. This measure is particularly well suited to analyzing data that are approximately normally distributed except in the tails of the distribution. Stock returns fit this description exactly. The value *1.5* in the formulas above controls the frequency of jumps. For a normally distributed variable, this measure identifies less than 1 percent of a large sample as jumps.

This measure has the advantage of being able to identify multiple jumps when the maximum number of jumps is not known in advance. Because jumps are restricted to lie outside the interquartile range, up to half the observations could, in theory, be identified as jumps. Since the quartiles are the only order statistics used in constructing the cutoffs, the breakdown point of this measure is 25 percent; that is, up to a quarter of the observations could be replaced by arbitrary values without affecting the measure. This is a high breakdown point for a measure of dispersion. A detailed study of this measure and its statistical properties can be found in Hoaglin, Iglewicz, and Tukey 1987.

ENDNOTES

1.Physical delivery rarely occurs in most futures contracts, whether financial or commodity. In the case of stock index futures contracts, delivery is prohibited and cash settlement required because of the difficulty of assembling the precise basket of stocks that underlies the contract.

2.The median volume is the 50th percentile of the observed volumes; that is, half the observed volumes are less than the median and half are greater. As a measure of the central tendency or average value, the median is less sensitive to a few unusual observations than is the arithmetic mean.

3.For stock purchases, the margin is the down payment on a loan used to buy the stock. For futures purchases and sales, the margin in essentially a performance bond the investor posts to guarantee he will fulfill his side of the contract.

4.There are some exceptions and qualifications to the requirement that margins for stock purchases are paid in cash. Sofianos 1988 provides a thorough description of margin requirements.

5.An additional reason that stock index futures contracts are particularly useful for hedging is that short sales of stocks are often difficult and costly. Investors sell stocks short by borrowing shares and then selling the borrowed shares. Thus, to sell stocks short, investors must find current shareholders willing to lend their shares. This requirement limits the volume of short sales to the amount of existing shares. In addition, it can be difficult and time-consuming to find the desired number of shares to borrow.

In contrast, it is easy and economical to take the equivalent position by selling futures contracts. When a futures contract is sold, the seller is simply agreeing to sell the underlying asset at some future date. Since futures contracts are settled in cash rather than shares of stock, sellers never have to obtain the shares of stock. Thus, the amount of futures contracts that can be sold is limited only by the availability of buyers.

6.The New York Stock Exchange defines a program trade as the simultaneous purchase or sale of at least 15 stocks with a total trade value greater than $1 million. See Duffee, Kupiec, and White 1990 for an examination of program trading.

7.Most researchers have found that normal volatility in U.S. stock markets has, with the exception of the Great Depression, been stable since the mid-19th century (Schwert 1990; Shiller 1989).

8.Former Treasury Secretary Donald Regan expressed this viewpoint forcefully in testimony at a U.S. Senate hearing (1988). He said, "The public has every reason to believe that the present game is rigged. It is. Many would be better off in a casino since there people expect to lose but have a good meal and a good time while they're doing it."

9.Following the October 1987 market collapse, the Brady Commission (U.S. Presidential Task Force on Market Mechanisms 1988) identified some types of program trading as a contributing factor to the collapse. The Brady Commission also concluded that links forged by program trading between the futures and stock market have made the stock market vulnerable to disruptions emanating from the futures market. In the *Interim Report of the Working Group on Financial Markets*, another study of October 1987, then-chairman of the SEC David Ruder concurred that "certain futures-related trading strategies [i.e., program trading] have resulted in a dramatic increase in the size and velocity of institutional trading which, in turn, has resulted in substantially increased price volatility."

10.The Brady Commission (U.S. Presidential Task Force on Market Mechanisms 1988) emphasized this role of circuit breakers. Their report points out that circuit breaker mechanisms counter the illusion of liquidity by formalizing the economic fact of life...that markets have a limited capacity to absorb massive one-sided volume.... This makes it less likely in the future that flawed trading strategies will be pursued to the point of disrupting markets and threatening the financial system." (U.S. Presidential Task Force on Market Mechanisms 1988, p.66)

In other words, circuit breakers force investors to realize there will be times in the future when they will not be able to carry out some futures-related trading strategies. As a result, these investors will be less aggressive in pursuing these strategies in the present. Thus, the portion of futures trading due to these strategies will decline as a result of circuit breakers.

11.Noting that margins in the futures market are low compared with margins in the stock market, the Brady Commission proposed that margins be "harmonized" across markets. The Commission reasoned that the apparent disparity in margin requirements encourages excessive futures trading. David Ruder, in the *Interim Report of the Working Group on Financial Markets*, also called for higher margins on futures, in part to "decrease derivative market speculative activity."

12.Circuit breakers and higher margins might be ineffective even if stock index futures contribute to stock market volatility (Edwards 1988). In this case, of course, the regulations are inadvisable. This article, however, argues against regulations intended to reduce futures trading on the grounds the evidence does not support the notion that stock index futures are linked to stock market volatility. Of course, statistical evidence on the general relationship between futures activity and stock market volatility cannot determine whether futures trading was related to a specific historical event, such as the October 1987 market collapse.

13.The precise cutoffs for jumps are daily S&P 500 returns greater than 1.7865 percent or less than -1.7367 percent. The statistical technique used to determine these cutoffs is described in the appendix.

14.The New York Stock Exchange places restrictions on index arbitrage whenever the Dow Jones Industrial Average moves 50 points or more from its closing value on the previous trading day. While the exchange did not use the statistical method employed in this article in designing its restrictions, this exchange rule indicates that this statistical method highlights stock movements that the exchange also recognizes as potentially destabilizing.

15.Chart 3 displays monthly observations of the median daily volume of trading of S&P 500 index futures contracts and the frequency of hourly jumps in the S&P 500 index. Monthly observations are used because the hypothesis under examination relates the frequency of price jumps to changes in the general level of activity in the futures market. The median daily volume for the month is an indicator of the general level of activity in the futures market. Thus, the data displayed in Chart 3 show whether months with higher-than-average futures trading activity are also months with a higher-than-average frequency of jumps.

A related question, not considered in this article, is whether stock price jumps and high futures volume occur at precisely the same time. This question is concerned not with volatility, but with the ways new information is incorporated in securities prices. This latter question is addressed more appropriately with daily or hourly, rather than monthly, observations. Karpoff (1987) surveys studies that test whether increases in trading volume are related to price changes and discusses the significance of these studies.

16.It is difficult to appraise the relationship between daily stock price jumps and futures trading from a chart of monthly observations because there are many months with no daily jumps. The data on hourly stock prices cover the period from February 1983 through May 1990. Thus, the hourly data are available only after stock index futures began trading. For this reason, only daily stock price jumps could be used to assess whether stock price jumps increased after futures were introduced. In these data, hourly returns greater than 0.5386 percent or less than -0.5151 percent are considered jumps.

17.Correlations were calculated between monthly observations of the median daily volume of S&P 500 stock index futures trading and the frequency of daily and hourly jumps in the S&P 500 index. The correlation coefficient is Kendall's tau, a nonparametric statistic that takes on values between minus one and one. Values near minus one or one indicate pairs of variables with a strong association. Values near zero indicate pairs of variables with little or no association.

18.This result is obtained by regressing the log of the monthly frequency of hourly stock price jumps against 12 lagged values of stock price jumps, monthly dummy variables, and the log of the median monthly volume of daily futures trading. The regression is estimated using data from February 1984 through May 1990. The coefficient on the trading volume variable is 0.57 indicating that a 1 percent increase in trading volume is associated with a 0.57 percent increase in the frequency of jumps. This regression has an R-square of 0.55 and a F-statistic of 2.61 with 24 numerator and 51 denominator degrees of freedom.

This regression is representative of an extensive regression analysis performed to see if any relationship between futures trading activity and jump volatility could be discovered. A second measure of futures activity--the open interest in S&P 500 stock index futures contracts--was included. This analysis confirmed the lack of association between futures trading and jump volatility reported in this article. Details of this analysis are available on request.

19.Correlations were calculated between monthly observations of the median daily volume of S&P 500 stock index futures trading and the median absolute daily and hourly jumps in the S&P 500 index. As before, the correlation coefficient is Kendall's tau.

REFERENCES

Becketti, Sean, and Gordon H. Sellon, Jr. 1989. "Has Financial Market Volatility Increased?" Federal Reserve Bank of Kansas City, *Economic Review*, June.

Cornell, Bradford, and Kenneth R. French. 1983. "The Pricing of Stock Index Futures," *The Journal of Futures Markets*, Spring.

Duffee, Gregory, Paul Kupiec, and Patricia White. 1990. "A Primer on Program Trading and Stock Price Volatility: A Survey of the Issues and the Evidence," Finance and Economics Discussion Series no. 109, Board of Governors of the Federal Reserve System, January.

Edwards, Franklin R. 1988. "Studies of the 1987 Stock Market Crash: Review and Appraisal," *Journal of Financial Services Research*, June.

Hoaglin, David C., Boris Iglewicz, and John W. Tukey. 1986. "Performance of Some Resistant Rules for Outlier Labeling," *Journal of the American Statistical Association*, December.

Karpoff, Johnathan, M. 1987. "The Relation between Price Changes and Trading Volume: A Survey." *Journal of Financial and Quantitative Analysis*, March.

Kling, Arnold. 1986. "Futures Markets and Transactions Costs," in Myron L. Kwast, ed., *Financial Futures and Options in the U.S. Economy: A Study by the Staff of the Federal Reserve System*. Washington: Board of Governors of the Federal Reserve System.

Merrick, John J. 1987. "Price Discovery in the Stock Market." Working paper no. 416, Salomon Brothers Center for the Study of Financial Institutions, Graduate School of Business Administration, New York University, April.

Morris, Charles S. 1989. "Managing Stock Market Risk with Stock Index Futures," Federal Reserve Bank of Kansas City, *Economic Review*, June.

Morris, Charles S. 1990. "Coordinating Circuit Breakers in Stock and Futures Markets," Federal Reserve Bank of Kansas City, *Economic Review*, March/April.

Moser, James T. 1990. "Circuit Breakers," Federal Reserve Bank of Chicago, *Economic Perspectives*, September/October.

Petzel, Todd E. 1989. *Financial Futures and Options: A Guide to Markets, Applications, and Strategies*. New York: Quorum Books.

Regan, Donald. 1988. Testimony, U.S. Senate Hearing, Committee on Banking, Housing, and Urban Affairs, May 24.

Roll, Richard. 1988. "The International Crash of October 1987," *Financial Analysts Journal*, September/October.

Schwert, G. William. 1990. "Stock Market Volatility," *Financial Analysts Journal*, May/June.

Shiller, Robert J. 1989. "Causes of Changing Financial Market Volatility," in *Financial Market Volatility*, Federal Reserve Bank of Kansas City.

Sofianos, George. 1988. "Margin Requirements on Equity Instruments," Federal Reserve Bank of New York, *Quarterly Review*, Summer.

U.S. Presidential Task Force on Market Mechanisms. 1988. *Report of the Presidential Task Force on Market Mechanisms*, Washington, January.

Working Group on Financial Markets. 1988. *Interim Report of the Working Group on Financial Markets*, Washington, May.

QUESTIONS

1. What are stock index futures? How are they used and how do they benefit investors?

2. Becketti and Roberts argue that the use of stock market index futures has not increased volatility in the stock market. How do they support this position?

3. How is the use of stock index futures regulated and what are the costs of this regulation?

PART FOUR

THE MONEY SUPPLY PROCESS

The complete money supply model developed in Part IV of the text is an important tool for helping students identify the factors which determine the money supply and cause it to change. The two readings for Part IV illustrate the influence of depositor and bank behavior on the money supply which is discussed in Chapter 16 of the textbook.

The first one, Reading 28, is "Belying Forecasts, U.S. Prints More Cash" by Lindley H. Clark, Jr., and Alfred L. Malabre, Jr. This reading can be used to discuss the factors behind recent movements in the currency-checkable deposit ratio. Clark and Malabre present a number of reasons to account for the rapid growth of currency relative to other forms of money since the end of 1989 and suggest the implications of this increase in currency for money supply growth and the economic stimulus that growth generates.

Reading 29, "Coping with Bank Failures: Some Lessons from the United States and the United Kingdom", relates to Chapter 16's discussion of bank panics. Authors R. Alton Gilbert and Geoffrey E. Wood look to the nineteenth and early twentieth centuries to investigate the consequences of bank panics and to examine various efforts to prevent panics in the United Kingdom and the United States.

READING 28

Belying Forecasts, U.S. Prints More Cash

Lindley H. Clark Jr. and Alfred L. Malabre Jr.

For a society that only a few years ago some analysts were deeming soon to be "cashless," the U.S. is pumping out a remarkable amount of cash.

By about now, according to the disproven forecasts, credit-card plastic and payments-by-computer were to have virtually eliminated the need for greenbacks and coins. In fact, the currency component of the U.S. money supply has surged of late, outstripping the growth of such other major forms of money as funds held in checking and savings accounts.

The trend, which has gained impetus from the turmoil in the Middle East but predates it, is something of a mystery to economists, as well as a surprise. And, whatever its causes, it is serving to complicate the Federal Reserve's already-tricky task of setting a monetary course that will induce continued growth in a difficult time for the economy.

"Far from becoming a cashless society, the U.S. appears to be relying *more* on currency as means of payment," concludes a study by the Federal Reserve Bank of San Francisco.

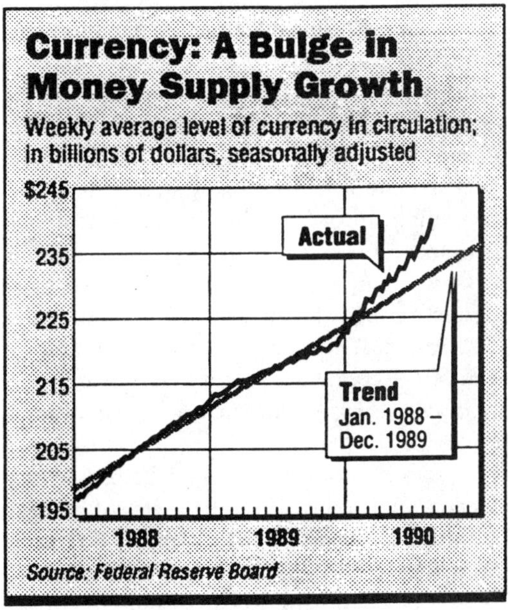

CIRCULATION IN FOREIGN COUNTRIES

A few statistics underline the trend. Since last December, currency—from pennies to $10,000 bills—has surged at an annual rate of about 12%, triple the 1989 gain of about 4%. By comparison, checkable deposits have risen only about 3% annually since December and savings deposits have risen only a little more.

In the past, surges in currency normally signaled accompanying surges in consumer spending. These developments "have almost always been contemporaneous," says David Meiselman, an economist at Virginia Polytechnic Institute. Lately, however, "there clearly hasn't been any surge in spending," he notes.

One reason for the unusual pattern can be seen in the estimate of a Federal Reserve official that roughly two-thirds of the more than $241 billion of currency in circulation is circulating abroad. This is sharply higher than the rate a few years ago, the official reckons, though he stresses there are no firm figures on the amount of expatriate cash. "This means," he adds, "as far as stimulating domestic economic activity is concerned, about two-thirds of our currency is simply not in play."

Cash, of course, has long helped in tax evasion and lubricated all sorts of illegal operations, particularly the booming international trade in illicit drugs. The swift spread of automatic teller machines—from about 10,000 in the late 1970s to nearly 100,000 across the U.S. now—also has given cash a new lease on life. But the political upheaval in Eastern Europe and the Soviet Union, as well as rampant inflation in Latin America, have intensified demand for U.S. currency.

An accelerating rise of U.S. currency in circulation was evident well before Iraq invaded Kuwait, notes Milton Friedman, a Nobel-laureate economist at the Hoover Institution. He attributes this speedup to "dollars in effect replacing domestic currencies" in some Latin and Eastern European countries.

Meanwhile, Fed Chairman Alan Greenspan has estimated that $5 billion to $7 billion in U.S. currency is circulating in just one Latin American nation, which he declines to name. Argentina, in fact, recently pondered adopting the U.S. dollar as its currency as a way to bring down inflation, but opted to stick with the austral.

Anatol Balbach, a senior vice president of the St. Louis Federal Reserve Bank, reports that "there is evidence that $1.5 billion of currency was shipped to Argentina, Brazil and Switzerland, for example, last December and January, and that much of the cash going to Switzerland was shipped on to points in Eastern Europe." There are currency dealers in New York, he adds, "who do little else but ship currency abroad."

(Exporting large amounts of currency is perfectly legal, but transactions involving more than $10,000 are supposed to be reported to the Treasury. However, analysts believe many of these transactions go unrecorded.)

DOLLAR AS A HAVEN

There are no firm figures on the impact of Iraq's invasion of Kuwait and the subsequent U.S. military buildup in Saudi Arabia, but most economists estimate that the Middle Eastern turmoil will further expand the outflow of cash.

Paradoxically, the dollar's international value has fallen against most major currencies in recent years, largely reflecting concern over America's huge, persistent deficits in the federal budget and foreign trade. Even so, backed by U.S. military might, the dollar has become "the rainy-day currency when there is real trouble somewhere in the world," says Richard Porter, assistant director of monetary affairs at the Federal Reserve Board.

As flattering as that may be for the dollar, the currency's outflow does complicate policy for the Federal Reserve, which attempts to guide economic activity in part by expanding or shrinking the money supply through buying or selling Treasury securities.

With the rising threat of a new recession, the Fed has been under mounting pressure to expand the money supply, and it has recently begun to do so. For example, the M2 version of the money supply—currency plus checking and most savings accounts—rose less than 1% annually between late April and late June, but since then increased more than 4% annually.

LIMITED STIMULUS TO ECONOMY

But much of this recent growth has been in the currency component, as we have seen, and analysts warn that such growth provides relatively little stimulus for the domestic economy. Moreover, dollars used abroad obviously generate little fuel for domestic business activity.

Even those dollars circulating at home, whether stashed under mattresses or spent at stores, generally provide less stimulus than similar sums of money on deposit at a bank, which in effect can be lent and relent so that $1 on deposit may ultimately support as much as $10 in loans.

Breaking down the money-supply data, Jerry Jordan, chief economist of First Interstate Bank of Los Angeles, concludes, "We need easier money, but I'm afraid the currency surge is persuading some people in the Fed that further easing isn't necessary." This is a mistake, he says, adding that he looks for "a very weak economy in coming months."

However weak the economy as a whole may prove to be, the surge in currency has produced a boom of sorts for workers at the Treasury Department's Bureau of Engraving and Printing.

All of the nation's paper currency is produced on presses at two adjoining buildings on Washington's 15th Street. As recently as 1987, the presses ran 24 hours a day, five days a week, turning out some six billion in individual notes, worth $62 billion, in denominations ranging from $1 up to $100;

the printing of larger denominations was ended soon after World War II.

But now the presses are operating six days a week and for the full year are expected to produce about seven billion in notes, worth some $80 billion. With an expected further rise in demand for currency, note output should reach eight billion in 1991, according to Ira Polikoff, a spokesman for the bureau.

QUESTIONS

1. What reasons are given in Reading 28 for the recent rapid growth of currency relative to other forms of money? Does this account of factors increasing the currency-checkable deposits ratio include any important influences not discussed in Chapter 16 in the text? Explain.

2. How does the rapid growth of currency in circulation affect: (a) how much money supply growth occurs; and (b) the degree to which this money supply growth stimulates economic activity?

READING 29

Coping with Bank Failures: Some Lessons from the United States and the United Kingdom

R. Alton Gilbert and Geoffrey E. Wood

The number of U.S. bank failures has risen dramatically in the past few years. Banks failed at the rate of about six per year from 1950 through 1981. In 1984, however, 79 banks failed, and 120 banks failed in 1985.[1] Yet this sharp rise in the rate of bank failure has not produced the kind of public "panic" that accompanied bank failures during much of U.S. history.

In a banking panic, the failure of one bank leads people to fear for the safety of their funds at other banks. Subsequent attempts to withdraw their deposits from other banks put these banks in jeopardy as well. Recent experience suggests that bank failures no longer cause banking panics. There are now well-established and frequently tested principles for preventing a bank failure from turning into a panic.

To fully appreciate the importance of these principles in preventing panics, it is necessary to review some episodes of history during which panics occurred. History illustrates the inherent vulnerability of the banking industry to panics, when there are no policies in place to prevent them; it also illustrates the adverse effects of panics on the operation of banking systems and economic activity.

To prevent banking panics, it is necessary to convince the public that the operation of the banking system will not be disrupted by the failure of one bank or even by the failure of several banks. The government policies that create this public confidence in the stability of the banking system reflect the history of each nation. This paper contrasts the experience with banking panics in the United Kingdom to that in the United States.

The last banking panic in the United Kingdom occurred in 1866. At that time the Bank of England acted to prevent the disruption of the banking system when banks failed and the public in England came to believe that the Bank of England had accepted that responsibility and would be successful in carrying it out.

The United States established a central bank in 1914, but the Federal Reserve System failed to prevent banking panics in the early 1930s. Thus, the public in the United States did not have the experience of observing a central bank successfully dealing with banking panics. The last banking panic in the United States (1933) occurred in the same year when the federal government established deposit insurance. This observation indicates that federal deposit insurance has been an important feature of the policies in the United States for preventing banking panics.

WHAT ARE BANKING PANICS AND WHY ARE THEY DANGEROUS?

Two features of the operation of commercial banks make the banking system vulnerable to disruptions when depositors lose confidence in their banks. First, a large part of the liabilities of banks is payable to depositors on demand. Second, the cash reserves of banks are a small fraction of their deposit liabilities. Thus, if large numbers of depositors suddenly wanted to convert their deposits to currency, the banking system would not immediately have enough cash on hand to honor their demands. When a banking panic occurs, people attempt to be among the first to convert their deposits to currency because they remember that during previous banking panics, only those who demanded currency early enough were able to get it.[2]

Microeconomic Effects of Banking Panics

Deposits and reserves of the banking system decline one-for-one as depositors withdraw currency. If total reserves were just equal to required reserves before the withdrawals of currency, reserves would be deficient after the withdrawals. Each bank responds to its reserve shortage by selling assets, producing a decline in demand deposits that exceeds the initial conversion of demand deposits to currency.

The vulnerability of the banking system to panics is illustrated in tables 1 and 2 by the use of balance sheets. Table 1 presents the hypothetical balance sheet of an individual bank that is required by some regulatory authority to keep a cash reserve of at least 10 percent of total deposits. Because of concern about the viability of the bank, customers withdraw $10 million in the form of currency, reducing the bank's cash reserves to zero. To raise cash reserves, the bank sells $9 million of its interest-earning assets.[3]

When the bank sells its assets to increase its cash reserves, however, it draws cash from other banks, causing their reserves and deposits to decline. These banks must now sell some of their assets to eliminate *their* reserve deficiencies. Thus, the initial withdrawal of currency by depositors produces a chain reaction of reductions in deposits payable on demand.

The effects on the banking *system* of the currency withdrawals are illustrated in table 2.

Table 1

Balance Sheet of an Individual Bank (millions of dollars)

Assets		Liabilities	
Before the banking panic:			
Cash	$ 10	Deposits payable on demand	$50
Interest-earning assets	100	Time deposits	50
		Net worth	**10**
After withdrawal of $10 million in currency:			
Cash	$ 9	Deposits payable on demand	$40
Interest-earning assets	91	Time deposits	50
		Net worth	**10**

Table 2

Balance Sheet of the Banking System (billions of dollars)

Assets		Liabilities	
Before the banking panic:			
Cash	$ 100	Deposits payable on demand	$500
Interest-earning assets	1,000	Time deposits	500
		Net worth	**100**
After withdrawal of $10 billion in currency:[1]			
Cash	$ 90	Deposits payable on demand	$400
Interest-earning assets	900	Time deposits	500
		Net worth	**90**

[1]In the banking panic, sales of interest-earning assets cause the prices of those assets to fall. In this illustration, banks reduce their net worth by $10 billion, recognizing that loss on the sale of assets that had a value of $100 billion before the panic.

Prior to the banking panic, the banking system has assets of $1.1 trillion and deposits payable on demand of $500 billion. As the banking panic begins, bank customers withdraw $10 billion in currency from their deposit accounts payable on demand. Given the 10 percent reserve requirement, total deposits must decline until the remaining cash reserves of $90 billion are 10 percent of total deposits.

This shrinkage in the assets of the banking system may reduce the confidence of the public in the banking system even more, inducing additional withdrawals of deposits in the form of currency. The additional loss of reserves would force even larger reductions in bank deposits, interest-earning assets, net worth of banks and number of banks.

Macroeconomic Consequences of Banking Panics

A banking panic causes a sharp reduction in the money supply (currency held by the public plus bank deposits payable on demand). Sharp and unexpected reductions in the money supply usually cause reductions in economic activity and, consequently, an increase in unemployment and business failures. The panic will end when the public becomes convinced that banks are safe and that it can withdraw currency from deposit accounts whenever it wishes. At that time, the public will again deposit part of its currency with banks.

HOW TO PREVENT BANKING PANICS—THE BRITISH EXPERIENCE

How can the failure of one bank be prevented from spilling over into the whole banking system with such catastrophic consequences? Only by removing the fear that *all* banks are in danger of failing. Can this be done in practice? It can, and the way to do it was discovered before the theory behind the method was developed.

The Bank of England

The history of the British approach to preventing banking panics involves the history of the Bank of England. The British government chartered the Bank in 1694 as a means of raising funds to fight a war with France. Those subscribing to the stock of the Bank made loans to the British government. In return, the Bank was given some exclusive rights to function as a commercial bank.[4]

Although the Bank was privately owned, there was always a close relationship between it and the government. Some aspects of the relationship, based on evolving traditions, were implicit rather than spelled out in the Bank's charter or other legislation. For instance, by the 1800s, the government expected the Bank to buy any part of its new debt issues not purchased by others.

The Bank of England maintained a large inventory of gold upon which it could draw in a panic to meet the public's demand for gold. Legislation in 1844 gave the Bank a monopoly on issuing bank notes and made the notes of the Bank legal tender. That legislation set a limit on the amount of the Bank's notes that could be outstanding, though it specified that the limit could be exceeded in an emergency. The limit on the notes of the Bank could be lifted at the discretion of the government. Thus, the Bank of England could expand the monetary base (currency plus reserves) in an emergency, since its notes were used as currency and were held as part of bank reserves.

One aspect of the policies that evolved over time was the Bank's response to a banking panic. The evolution of that policy is described in this section by discussing first, what happened during two banking panics that occurred in England during the 1800s and second, why no panics have occurred in the British banking system since 1866.

The Panic of 1825

In December 1825, a banking panic occurred in London after the failure of a bank (Sir Peter Pole and Company). As people fled from deposits at other banks to gold, gold reserves were drained from the Bank of England. To convince people that their bank deposits were safe, the Bank lent gold freely from its holdings.[5]

The panic was allayed when it became clear to the public that there was nothing about which to panic—that there was indeed sufficient gold to meet the public's increased demand for gold. As a result, the failure of one bank did not turn into a general financial crisis. Unfortunately, however, banking panics continued to occur in England after 1825 because the Bank of England had not made a public commitment to act as the "lender of last resort" in all financial crises. A lender of last resort acts to increase the monetary base if many people want to withdraw cash (gold and notes of the Bank of England) from their banks.

The significance of a lender of last resort in a banking panic can be illustrated by referring to the balance sheets in table 2. If depositors withdraw cash, the lender of last resort acts to increase the reserves of the banking system, thus preventing the contraction of the money supply that could be caused by a banking panic. Until the English public became convinced that the Bank of England would act to increase the monetary base (cash in the hands of the public plus bank reserves) in financial crises, many of them tended to withdraw cash from banks when there were problems in the financial system.

The Lesson of 1866

The last major banking panic in England occurred in 1866. Since then, although events have occurred that could have triggered banking crises (in 1873, 1890, 1907, 1914, 1931, and 1973), they did not do so.[6] What changed after 1866?

The panic of 1866 began with the failure of a major English bank. Overend, Gurney and Company was a large bank, founded early in the 19th century from the amalgamation of two banks that had been important and active in the 18th century. Hit by a variety of setbacks, Overend's was compelled to seek assistance from the Bank of England on May 10, 1866. The Bank refused to provide assistance and that afternoon Overend, Gurney and Company was declared insolvent.

The next day, there were runs on all banks. People scrambled for cash because no bank was trusted.[7] The Bank of England, which was being drained of notes, briefly made things worse by hesitating over whether to make its usual purchases of newly issued government debt. By the evening of Friday, May 11, however, the Bank gave assurance that it would provide support to the banking system, and, though demands for small bills continued for a week, the panic was essentially broken in one day.[8] The important consequence of this episode was that the Bank had implicitly accepted the responsibility of acting as lender of last resort and the public understood that the Bank had accepted that responsibility. For a discussion of the historical development of the concept of a lender of last resort, see the insert [on page 276].

HOW TO PREVENT BANKING PANICS—THE U.S. EXPERIENCE

The U.S. economy suffered the effects of banking panics long after the British discovered how to prevent them. The United States established the Federal Reserve as the central bank in 1914. There were eight major banking panics before then and additional financial crises that had more limited regional impact.[9] The formation of the Federal

The Lender of Last Resort and Walter Bagehot

The name and the work of Walter Bagehot recur continually in the discussion of banking and bank failures. His main proposal called for the Bank of England to *announce* that it was willing to act as lender of last resort and that it would do so unhesitatingly whenever necessary. By lender of last resort, he meant that the Bank would, in times of panic, "lend freely, at high interest rates." It would lend freely, so that banks could satisfy the demands of their customers for cash and thus allay panic. It would do so at penally high interest rates to ensure that the Bank was truly the lender of *last* resort; banks would come to it only when the whole banking system was short of cash. The policy of setting a high lending rate was designed both to prevent excessive monetary expansion in normal times and to guarantee that banks repaid their borrowings when interest rates dropped after the panic, so that the money stock was not permanently boosted by crisis borrowing.

Bagehot emphasized that the Bank should not only behave in this way, but also should announce in advance that it would do so whenever necessary. He saw this "precommitment," which the Bank had never made before the episode of 1866, as vital. A credible precommitment would give assurance that sound banks would not be allowed to fail as a result of the failure of some other bank. Once this assurance was given, panic would be less likely. Indeed, the Bank might not actually have to act as lender of last resort at all; merely standing ready to do so might be sufficient to provide stability.

[1]Bagehot was, among other things, a journalist. He became editor of *The Economist*, and wrote voluminously on many subjects (including *The British Constitution*). But he is most widely remembered and discussed for his book, *Lombard Street* (first published in 1873) (Bagehot, 1978), and for his campaign in *The Economist* to have adopted his recommendations for the conduct of the Bank of England.

[2]Although now traditional, Bagehot's recommendation was not accepted without demur. Thomson Hankey, a director of the Bank, was particularly critical of the proposal. After the Overend and Gurney affair, Hankey denied that the Bank had an unequivocal duty to lend freely in panics. He was concerned with what has become known as "moral hazard." If bankers know that the central bank will lend freely in a panic, he argued, they will take more chances: hold lower reserves, make riskier loans or pay higher dividends.

Hankey is plainly correct. The issue, however, is which is the lesser evil, slightly riskier banks or the prospect of a collapse in the money stock.

Hankey's criticism of Bagehot's principles for running a central bank did not represent the official views of the Bank. Officially the Bank neither accepted nor rejected Bagehot's principles but came to act in a manner consistent with these principles.

Reserve, however, did not end the problem of banking panics; the last panic occurred in 1933. The period since the last banking panic coincides with the period of federal deposit insurance.

Banking Until the 1860s (Civil War Period)[10]

Bank Structure and Regulation—After the Revolutionary War, the new U.S. government confined its monetary role to the minting of gold and silver coin. State governments assumed responsibility for chartering and supervising commercial banks. State banks issued bank notes, which circulated as currency, and had deposit liabilities against which customers could write checks. Both the bank notes and demand deposits were payable on demand in the form of the coins minted by the federal government.

The first banking panic occurred in 1814 during the War of 1812 with the British. In response to fears about the outcome of the war, many people attempted to redeem bank notes and convert their bank deposits into coin. The banking system responded by suspending coin payments, which kept the contractions of the money supply and bank assets from being as large as they would have been (see the insert [on page 278]). In all of the major U.S. banking panics through 1907, the banking system suspended cash payments to depositors and holders of bank notes.

The Panic of 1837—The panic described above was unusual in that it was triggered by anxieties about the war. Other banking panics in this period occurred when bank failures caused the public to lose confidence in the value of their bank notes and deposits. The panic of 1837 shows the nature of panics in this period before the U.S. Civil War.

The U.S. economy experienced an economic boom from 1834 through 1836, supported by large investments in the United States by Europeans. Many of these large investments were in railroads and purchases of public land by those moving to the western frontier.

The boom stopped in 1837. Gold flowed from the United States to Europe as European investors demanded payment of their loans and liquidated their U.S. investments. This outflow of gold reduced the cash reserves of banks, which, along with failures by business firms, caused some banks to fail. The Dry Dock Bank, a major bank in New York City, closed on May 8, 1837. All other banks in New York City experienced runs by depositors the next day. The New York City banks suspended coin payments on May 10, and Philadelphia banks followed suit on May 11. Within the next 10 days, banks in all the leading cities suspended coin payments.

New York City banks resumed coin payments to holders of bank notes and deposits on May 10, 1838, exactly one year after the suspension. Banks in the rest of the nation resumed coin payments between August 1838 and early 1839.

This episode illustrates the vulnerability of the banking system to disruption. Without a central bank, the supply of cash in the economy was determined by the coins minted by the federal government and international movements of precious metals. The bank runs following the failure of the Dry Dock Bank showed that the public's confidence in banks could be undermined quickly when an

Suspending Cash Payments

Commercial banks in the major urban areas in the United States suspended payments of cash to depositors and note holders during each of the major banking panics from 1814 through 1907. During suspensions, banks in an area would agree to act together in refusing to pay out cash. Until the 1860s, the form of cash demanded by depositors during panics was metal coins. In the early 1860s, the cash demand during panics included currency.

During these general suspensions of cash payments, banks remained open for business and permitted their customers to use deposits to make payments to others. Checks were cleared and deposit liabilities were transferred among banks. Nonredeemed bank notes continued to circulate as currency. When banking panics were over, banks resumed the payment on demand of coin for bank notes and deposits.

The significance of the suspension of bank payment in the form of coin or currency can be illustrated by referring to table 2, the balance sheet of the banking system. As soon as bankers realized that the public was attempting to convert its money holdings to coin or currency, the bankers as a group refused to meet this demand for cash. In this case, their cash reserves would stay at $100 billion, and with that cash available to meet reserve requirements, the banking system would not have to sell assets and reduce its liabilities. By suspending cash payments, the banks would prevent the contraction of the assets and liabilities of the banking system.

important bank went under. At this time, however, the U.S. banking system had no institution comparable to the Bank of England, which had a reputation for financial strength and an inventory of cash that could cut short a panic. Consequently, some banking panics in the United States, like the panic of 1837, were followed by long periods of suspended cash payments.

Money and Banking from the 1860s to the Formation of the Federal Reserve System in 1914[11]

The National Banking System—Reforms were begun in the 1860s to achieve two purposes: to establish a national currency, with all currency accepted at par value in exchange throughout the nation, and to make the banking system less vulnerable to panics. As a first step, the federal government began chartering national banks whose notes were to be the primary national currency. National banks were required to hold both collateral with the Treasury Department against their notes as well as cash reserves that were a percentage of their deposit liabilities and notes. The collateral and reserve requirements were imposed to restrain the growth of bank liabilities and to promote greater public confidence in the banking system.

The basic flaw in the design of the new system was the absence of a central bank with the power to increase the monetary base should the public lose confidence in the value of bank deposits. In this period, there were major banking panics in 1873, 1884, 1893, and 1907. Banks acted cooperatively during these panics to increase their reserves by creating clearing house loan certificates (see the insert [on page 280]). The creation of clearing house loan certificates, however, did not permit banks to meet the public demand for currency. During each of these panics they also suspended payments of coin and currency to depositors.

The Panic of 1907—The nature of banking panics in this period can be illustrated by the panic of 1907, which occurred in October and November of that year. This panic is interesting for several reasons. Its effects on the nonfinancial sectors of the economy were relatively severe, and its events provide a good illustration of how the loss of public confidence in one bank can lead to loss of confidence in the banking system. Finally, political reaction to this panic led to the formation of the Federal Reserve System.

For several years prior to 1907, gold flowed from Europe to the United States because Europeans invested heavily in the U.S. economy. In the fall of 1906, European investors began liquidating their U.S. investments, resulting in large gold outflows from the United States. This disinvestment was associated with sharp drops in U.S. stock prices in March and August 1907. The U.S. economy went into a recession after May 1907; the rate of decline in real economic activity was relatively low until the banking panic in the fall of that year, but relatively rapid after the panic.

The Panic of 1907 began with a depositor run on the Mercantile National Bank in New York City, which had suffered large losses. The New York clearinghouse came to the aid of the Mercantile National Bank in October 1907, after the bank was put under new management. This action, however, was insufficient to stem the panic. Depositor runs began at other institutions, reflecting a general loss of public confidence in the stability of the banking system. Within a few days, all depository institutions in New York City faced depositor runs. Banks in New York City suspended cash payments in November 1907, and the suspension of payments spread quickly to other cities. The panic and suspension of payments ended in early 1908, but only after a sharp decline in economic activity and a rise in bankruptcies in the nonfinancial sectors of the economy.

Banking Crises of the 1930s and the Beginnings of Federal Deposit Insurance[12]

After the long series of banking panics, culminating in the Panic of 1907, Congress finally responded by passing legislation in 1913 to establish the Federal Reserve System. There were no banking panics from 1914,

Increasing the Monetary Base by Creating Clearinghouse Loan Certificates

The banking system attempted to cope with the banking panics through emergency actions other than the suspension of cash payments. One approach involved the issuance of clearinghouse loan certificates. Clearinghouses were cooperative institutions established by banks to economize on the resources used in clearing checks and notes among themselves. Checks and notes drawn on other members of a clearinghouse were presented to the clearinghouse for collection, rather than being sent to each bank for collection. Banks deposited cash with their clearinghouses and, in turn, received certificates that were accepted by the other banks for covering net debit positions in clearinghouse settlements. Originally, the clearinghouse certificates were merely receipts for cash held by clearinghouses.

In each of the banking panics from 1857 through 1907, the banking system acted cooperatively to expand the monetary base by increasing the amount of clearinghouse certificates outstanding. The certificates issued during the panics were not simply receipts for cash held by the clearinghouses but were loans to banks with their assets pledged as collateral. The standard practice was for a clearinghouse association to accept some of the assets of a bank as collateral and issue certificates payable by the clearinghouse association. A bank that received such certificates would pay interest on them until they were redeemed after the panic was over. These transactions effectively converted the clearinghouses into fractional reserve banking institutions by creating certificates that exceeded their holdings of cash.

Initially, clearinghouse certificates circulated only among banks that were members of the clearinghouse. During panics, clearinghouse members agreed to accept these certificates in payment from other member banks, rather than insisting on payment in cash. The circulation of these certificates among banks in place of cash payments allowed the participating banks to use their cash to meet the cash demands of their depositors. In some panics, however, clearinghouse associations issued certificates in small denominations that banks offered to their depositors as substitutes for cash. These small-denomination

(continued on next page)

when the Federal Reserve System began its operations, until the early 1930s. Then, however, a series of banking crises resulted in the closing of all banks in the nation in March 1933.

certificates then circulated as currency. This use of clearinghouse certificates was not legal, but the government banking authorities did not challenge their use during panics.

[1]Gorton (1985a, b) and Timberlake (1984). The Aldrich-Vreeland Act of 1908 established a procedure for the emergency issuance of national bank notes that was copied after the procedures than banks had used for issuing clearinghouse loan certificates during panics. The panic of 1914 tested the effectiveness of this innovation just before the Federal Reserve System began operations. By issuing notes that were available for such an emergency, banks did not have to suspend cash payments. See Cagan (1963), pp. 26-28, and Sprague (1915).

The Federal Reserve did not respond to these banking crises as the Bank of England had nearly 70 years before. U.S. commercial banks came under liquidity pressures because of cash withdrawals by depositors and outflows of gold from the United States. Yet, except for a few months in 1932, the Federal Reserve did not increase the monetary base in response to these cash withdrawals from banks. Moreover, commercial banks did not act cooperatively to suspend cash payments to depositors as they had in earlier banking crises.[13] Consequently, the deposit liabilities of the banking system declined sharply.

Congress took various approaches to dealing with the general collapse of the banking system in the 1930s. The most significant legislation was the establishment of federal deposit insurance. There have been no general banking panics in the United States since 1933.

HAS DEPOSIT INSURANCE PREVENTED BANKING PANICS IN THE UNITED STATES?

The Pros and Cons of Federal Deposit Insurance

Recent experience indicates that large numbers of bank failures do not induce nationwide banking panics. A controversial issue, however, is whether federal deposit insurance could be eliminated without undermining public confidence in the banking system.

The British solved the problem of banking panics more than 100 years before they adopted a program of deposit insurance administered by the government.[14] Some argue that it is time to eliminate federal deposit insurance in the United States.[15] In their view, banking panics are best prevented by a credible lender of last resort, and they argue that the Federal Reserve has learned how to function as such. Federal deposit insurance gives depository institutions the incentive to assume greater risk than if deposit insurance were eliminated or offered by private firms.

An opposing view is that federal deposit insurance is essential for preventing banking panics. Since federal deposit insurance has been in effect for over 50 years, depositors rely on it, rather than on their assessment of the financial condition of their banks. In this view, banks would be vulnerable to runs by depositors as they had been prior to 1933 if federal deposit insurance were canceled.

The Importance of Credible Insurance: The S&L Experience

Developments in Ohio and Maryland in 1985 provide some evidence on the importance of federal deposit insurance in preventing banking panics in the United States. The deposits of 80 Ohio savings and loan associations (S&Ls) had been insured by the Ohio Depository Guarantee Fund (ODGF), a private deposit insurance fund founded by the S&Ls themselves to insure their deposits. On March 4, 1985, the largest S&L insured by the ODGF incurred losses because of the failure of a government securities dealer with which the S&L had large investments. These losses exceeded the capital of the S&L and the entire reserves of the ODGF. When these events were publicized, depositors at other ODGF-insured S&Ls began to withdraw their deposits. Their confidence in the safety of their funds was destroyed when the reserves of the ODGF were wiped out.[16] Eleven days later, the governor ordered all of the S&Ls insured by the ODGF closed. One of the conditions for reopening was that they obtain federal insurance for their deposits.[17]

The loss of confidence in the ODGF-insured institutions did not lead to a general loss of confidence in depository institutions. There were no runs on *federally* insured banks or S&Ls in Ohio.

Similar events transpired in Maryland in May 1985. A private fund insured the deposits of 102 Maryland S&Ls. Losses at the largest S&L insured by the private fund triggered runs by depositors on the privately insured S&Ls throughout the state. Once again, there were no runs on federally insured institutions. The Maryland state government required the privately insured S&Ls to obtain federal deposit insurance. In reaction to these developments in Ohio and Maryland, several other states have required their privately insured thrift institutions to obtain federal deposit insurance coverage.

SUMMARY AND IMPLICATIONS FOR THE UNITED STATES

The rate of bank failure in the United States is currently high relative to failure rates in most years since World War II. There have been many episodes in U.S. history when increased bank failures led to banking panics that disrupted the operation of the nation's banking system.

To prevent banking panics, it is essential that the public maintain confidence in the safety of their deposits even though *some* banks are failing. In the United Kingdom, public confidence in the stability of the banking system was established through the commitment of the Bank of England to act as the lender of last resort in financial crises. This policy was established in the banking panic of 1866, and the U.K. banking system has not experienced a banking panic since. The basic feature of that policy involves a commitment to increase the monetary base (currency held by the public plus bank reserves) when bank runs occur.

Policies in the United States reflect a different historical development. After various banking panics, the Federal Reserve was established in 1914 as the central bank with the responsibility of acting as the lender of last resort if a banking panic occurred. The Federal Reserve failed in that responsibility in the early 1930s, which resulted in a nationwide banking panic in the United States in 1933. There have been no banking panics in the United States since the federal government established deposit insurance in the 1930s. Runs by depositors on privately insured savings and loan associations in Ohio and Maryland during 1985 provide some evidence that federal deposit insurance is an essential feature of the policies in preventing banking panics in the United States.

ENDNOTES

1.A bank is declared to have failed when it is closed by the government authorities. The government authorities close a bank when its net worth falls close to or below zero.

2.Several recent studies develop theoretical models of the behavior of banks and their depositors to investigate the conditions that are likely to cause a banking panic. See Batchelor (1986), Bryant (1980), Diamond and Dybvig (1983), Gorton (1985a), Ho and Saunders (1980), and Jacklin and Bhattacharya (1986).

3.If many banks sell assets at the same time, the prices of bank assets may fall. In that case, the bank would have to sell additional assets and charge losses against net worth.

4.Clapham (1944), Fetter (1965) and Santoni (1984).

5.The actions of the Bank in the panic of 1825 are described vividly by Jeremiah Harman, director of the Bank, in Bagehot (1978), p.73:

> We lent it [gold]...by every possible means and in modes we had never adopted before; we took in stock on security, we purchased exchequer bills, we made advances on exchequer bills, we not only discounted outright, but we made advances on the deposit of bills of exchange to an immense amount, in short, by every possible means consistent with the safety of the Bank and we were not on some occasions over nice. Seeing the dreadful state in which the public were, we rendered every assistance in our power.

6.A succinct survey of the history of these episodes can be found in Schwartz (1986).

7."Panic, true panic, came with unexpected violence that day." (Clapham, 1944), p.263. "Terror and anxiety took possession of men's minds for that and the whole of the succeeding day." (*Bankers Magazine*, 1866). "No one knew who was sound and who was unsound." (*The Economist*, 1866).

8.A detailed description of the failure of Overend, Gurney, and Company and the events surrounding that failure can be found in Batchelor (1986).

9.The nine major banking panics occurred in 1814, 1837, 1857, 1861, 1873, 1884, 1893, 1907 and 1931-33.

10.This section is based largely on Hammond (1963).

11.This section is based largely on Cagan (1963), Robertson (1964), pp.302-30, Scroggs (1924), and Sprague (1910).

12.This section is based largely on Friedman and Schwartz (1963).
13.Friedman and Schwartz (1963, pp.311-12) argue that banks did not suspend cash payments because they thought the need to do so had been eliminated by the establishment of the Federal Reserve.
14.The British program of deposit insurance was introduced under the Banking Act of 1979. With few exceptions, all depository institutions are covered and must contribute to an insurance fund. Coverage is 75 percent of each account, with a maximum compensation of £10,000 for each depositor. This program was introduced in response to the secondary banking crisis of the early 1970s.
15.Ely (1985), England (1985), O'Driscoll and Short (1984), Short and O'Driscoll (1983), and Wells and Scruggs (1986).
16.Federal Reserve Bank of Cleveland (1985).
17.The Federal Reserve attempted to stop the depositor runs by lending cash to the privately insured S&Ls. Federal Reserve employees from throughout the System were put on special assignment to accept the assets of these S&Ls as collateral for the cash loans. This response, however, did not stop the depositor runs. This indicates that, in a nation in which depositors have come to rely on deposit insurance to maintain their confidence in the safety of their funds, the central bank may not be able to maintain that confidence by lending cash to depository institutions when the protection of deposit insurance is suddenly eliminated.

REFERENCES

Bagehot, Walter. *Lombard Street,* reprinted in Norman St. John-Stevas, ed., *The Collected Works of Walter Bagehot* (Hazell Watson and Viney Ltd., 1978).

Bankers Magazine, June 1866, pp.45-46.

Batchelor, Roy A. "The Avoidance of Catastrophe: Two Nineteenth-century Banking Crises," in Forrest Capie and Geoffrey E. Wood, eds., *Financial Crises and the World Banking System* (St. Martin's Press, 1986), pp.41-73.

Bryant, John. "A Model of Reserves, Bank Runs, and Deposit Insurance," *Journal of Banking and Finance* (December 1980). pp.335-44.

Cagan, Phillip. "The First Fifty Years of the National Banking System—An Historical Appraisal," in Deane Carson, ed., *Banking and Monetary Studies* (Richard D. Irwin, 1963), pp.15-42.

Clapham, Sir John. *The Bank of England: A History* (Cambridge University Press, 1944).

Diamond, Douglas W., and Philip H. Dybvig. "Bank Runs, Deposit Insurance, and Liquidity," *Journal of Political Economy* (June 1983), pp.401-19.

The Economist, June 1866, pp.15-16.

Ely, Bert. "Yes—Private Sector Depositor Protection is a Viable Alternative to Federal Deposit Insurance!" in Federal Reserve Bank of Chicago, Proceedings of a Conference on Bank Structure and Competition, held in Chicago, May 1-3, 1985, pp.338-53.

England, Catherine. "A Proposal for Introducing Private Deposit Insurance," in Federal Reserve Bank of Chicago, Proceedings of a Conference on Bank Structure and Competition, held in Chicago, May 1-3, 1985, pp.316-37.

Federal Reserve Bank of Cleveland. *1985 Annual Report.*

Fetter, Frank Whitson. *Development of british Monetary Orthodoxy* (Harvard University Press, 1965).

Friedman, Milton, and Anna J. Schwartz. *A Monetary History of the United States, 1867-1960* (Princeton University Press, 1963).

Gorton, Gary. "Bank Suspension of Convertibility," *Journal of Monetary Economics* (March 1985a).

____. "Clearinghouses and the Origin of Central Banking in the United States," *Journal of Economic History* (June 1985b).

Hammond, Bray. "Banking before the Civil War," in Deane Carson, ed., *Banking and Monetary Studies* (Richard D. Irwin, 1963), pp.1-14.

Ho, Thomas, and Anthony Saunders. "A Catastrophe Model of Bank Failure," *Journal of Finance* (December 1980), pp.1189-207.

Jacklin, Charles J., and Supipto Bhattacharya. "Distinguishing Panics and Information-Based Bank Runs: Welfare and Policy Implications," First Boston Working Paper Series 86-16 (February 1986).

O'Driscol, Gerald P., Jr., and Eugenie D. Short. "Safety-Net Mechanisms: The Case of International Lending," *Cato Journal* (Spring/Summer 1984), pp.185-204.

Robertson, Ross M. *History of the American Economy,* 2nd ed. (Harcourt, Brace and World, 1964).

Santoni, G. J. "A Private Central Bank: Some Olde English Lesson," this *Review* (April 1984), pp.12-22.

Schwartz, Anna J. "Real and Pseudo-financial Crises" in Forrest Capie and Geoffrey E. Wood, eds., *Financial Crises and the World Banking System* (St. Martin's Press, 1986), pp.11-31.

Scroggs, William O. *A Century of Banking Progress* (Doubleday, Page and Company, 1924).

Short, Eugenie D., and Gerald P. O'Driscoll, Jr. "Deregulation and Deposit Insurance," Federal Reserve Bank of Dallas *Economic Review* (September 1983), pp.11-22.

Sprague, O. M. W. *History of Crises under the National Banking System*, National Monetary Commission, Sen. Doc. No.538, 61 Cong. 2 Sess. (U.S. Government Printing Office, 1910).

___. "The Crisis of 1914 in the United States," *American Economic Review* (September 1915), pp.499-533.

Timberlake, Richard H., Jr. "The Central Banking Role of Clearinghouse Associations," *Journal of Money, Credit and Banking* (February 1984), pp.1-15.

Wells, Donald R., and L. S. Scruggs. "Historical Insights into the Deregulation of Money and Banking," *Cato Journal* (Winter 1986), pp.899-910.

QUESTIONS

1. What is a banking panic? Why is banking vulnerable to panics? What are the consequences of these panics?

2. How did suspending cash payments and the creation of clearinghouse loan certificates in the U.S. help banks to cope with banking panics?

3. The last major banking panic in England occurred in 1866; The U.S. continued to experience major panics until the early 1930s. Why?

4. Under what circumstances could federal deposit insurance be eliminated in the U.S. without making the banking system more prone to panics?

PART FIVE

THE FEDERAL RESERVE SYSTEM AND THE CONDUCT OF MONETARY POLICY

As the nation's central bank, the Fed plays a major role in determining the money supply. The relation between central bank independence and inflation rates, the policy role of Federal Reserve Bank presidents, debt monetization, and the conduct and goals of monetary policy are key issues to which the five readings for Part V relate.

Reading 30 is "The Independence of Central Banks" by Sun Bae Kim. Studies show that inflation is lower in countries with central banks that have greater legal independence. After examining the legal determinants of central bank independence and the inflation performances in Germany, the United Kingdom, and Japan, Kim concludes that a reputation for controlling inflation can be an effective substitute for legal independence. This reading can be used with Chapter 17's discussion of the independence of the Fed or with the discussion of credibility in Chapter 30.

Reading 31 is "Inflation Hawks: Fed Banks' Presidents Hold Private Positions But Major Public Role" by Alan Murray. This reading explores the differences on monetary policy questions among the Fed bank presidents and between them and Fed Chairman Alan Greenspan. Murray notes that the presidents' policy votes reflect a decidedly anti-inflation stance and that they are open to criticism from those disapproving their lack of public accountability. This reading is recommended for use with Chapter 17's discussion of the Fed's structure and independence.

Reading 32 is "Fed Assume Bigger Share of U.S. Debt" by Alfred R. Malabre, Jr. A sharp increase in Fed purchases of Treasury securities since 1990 draws attention to the relationship between debt monetization and inflation. Malabre suggests that the current episode of debt monetization is prompted by slow growth of the monetary aggregates which is seen as an impediment to a sustained economic recovery. The threat is that debt monetization will raise inflation in the future. This reading is suggested for use with Chapter 18's discussion of the budget deficit and the monetary base.

Reading 33 is "M2 and the Business Cycle" by Frederick T. Furlong and John P. Judd. Furlong and Judd explore the reliability of M2 as a target for monetary policy in the long run and in the short run and provide explanations for the recent slowdown in M2 growth. This reading is recommended for use with Chapter 20's discussion of the Fed's monetary policy targets and goals.

Reading 34 is "A Price Objective for Monetary Policy" by William T. Gavin and Alan C. Stockman. Gavin and Stockman propose that the Fed make an explicit commitment to price stability by targeting a long-run growth path for a particular price index and using it as a benchmark for setting annual monetary growth targets. They assert that this policy actually would improve the Fed's flexibility in pursuing other monetary policy goals. This reading goes with Chapter 20's discussion of monetary policy goals and targets.

READING 30

The Independence of Central Banks

Sun Bae Kim

What explains the difference in inflation rates among countries? According to widely cited studies by Bade and Parkin (1987) and Alesina (1988), countries with central banks that have greater *legal* independence in setting monetary policy tend to have relatively lower average inflation rates. For example, Switzerland and Germany are said to have the most legally independent central banks and also the lowest annual inflation rates among industrialized countries, each averaging about 3.5 percent between 1974 and 1990. Japan and the U.S. rank next in terms of central bank independence, with average inflation rates for the period of 5.1 and 6.3 percent, respectively. At the opposite end of the spectrum are the central banks of Italy and the U.K., with relatively little formal independence. Average annual inflation rates in Italy and the U.K. were 12.1 and 9.8 percent, respectively, during the same period.

These findings are consistent with the theory that inflation and the credibility of monetary policy are linked. According to this theory, governments are sometimes tempted to attain short-term political objectives by compromising long-term economic goals. For example, a government may try to win an election by printing money to increase output and reduce unemployment in the short-run. Repeated use of this approach, however, erodes the credibility of monetary policy and drives up the public's inflationary expectations, and hence prices, without any long-run effect on unemployment. Placing monetary policy under an independent authority that the public perceives as less prone to pursue such myopic policies provides an institutional mechanism to mitigate this credibility problem.

These findings have not gone unnoticed by policymakers. A growing number of countries plagued by high inflation rates in the past have sought to give their central banks more formal independence from the government in conducting monetary policy.

Chile and New Zealand enacted new legislation to this effect in 1989 (see *Weekly Letter* November 23, 1990), and similar proposals currently are being considered in Argentina and in a number of Eastern European countries, including Czechoslovakia and Poland. As the European Community (EC) moves closer to forming a monetary union, some member countries have been calling for greater national central bank independence within the Community, as a step to ultimately establishing an independent supernational central banking system.

This *Letter* discusses the three principal legal determinants of central bank independence—formal central bank objectives, appointment procedure for its policy board, and financial relations with the Treasury—by drawing on the experience of three countries: Germany, the U.K., and Japan. Germany and the U.K. represent the opposite ends of the spectrum of independence. Japan provides an interesting example where formal legal arrangements understate the actual degree of central bank independence. This suggests that the establishment of a legally independent central bank is not a necessary condition for credibility of monetary policy; a well-established reputation for controlling inflation can be an effective substitute.

FORMAL OBJECTIVES OF CENTRAL BANKS

In Germany, the Bundesbank Act of 1957 explicitly states that the Bank "shall be independent of instructions from the federal government." The Bundesbank is legally obliged to support the general economic policy of the German government "only insofar as this support does not undermine its assigned task of preserving monetary stability." This latter provision is fundamental to safeguarding the Bank's independent position.

At the other end of the spectrum, the Bank of England is subordinated by law to the Treasury. The Bank of England Act (1946) stipulates that the Treasury may issue directives to the Bank after consultation with the Governor. This legal provision ensures that, in the event of a disagreement, the government's position on monetary policy will prevail over that of the Bank of England (BOE). In practice, the Treasury has never actually issued directives, because monetary policy is formulated through close coordination between the Bank and the Treasury, with the latter having the upper hand.

Japan falls somewhere between these two examples. Legally, the Bank of Japan (BOJ) can independently determine discount rate policy and open market operations. In other respects, however, the BOJ's independence is significantly curtailed. For instance, any change in commercial banks' reserve ratios requires approval of the Ministry of Finance (MOF). In fact, the Bank of Japan Law (1942) empowers the Finance Minister to direct the BOJ to change its bylaws or to undertake any actions it deems necessary. This power, however, has never been exercised, and in practice, major monetary policy issues are determined through close cooperation between the BOJ and the MOF, which is facilitated by having a (non-voting)

MOF representative on the Bank's Policy Board.

APPOINTMENT OF CENTRAL BANK POLICY BOARDS

Governments may exercise leverage over central banks by controlling the appointment and dismissal of members of the monetary policy board. The degree of a central bank's independence can thus be enhanced by limiting these powers, for example, by making the terms of board members longer than the electoral cycle, or by limiting the proportion of policy board members that can be directly nominated or appointed by the government.

When the government is responsible for formulating monetary policy, it typically controls directly all appointments to the policy board of the central bank. In the U.K., the Governor, Deputy Governor, and the directors of the BOE are all appointed by the Crown, which in practice means by the Prime Minister acting on the advice of the Chancellor of Exchequer (Treasury). The Governor and Deputy Governor are appointed for renewable terms of five years; the directors have staggered four-year terms which are also renewable.

Although the Bank of Japan is considered to be a relatively independent central bank, all positions on its Policy Board are direct government appointments. The Board consists of seven members: the Governor, appointed by the Prime Minister's Cabinet for a five-year renewable term, two nonvoting members serving *ex officio* as representatives of the Ministry of Finance and of the Economic Planning Agency, and four voting members appointed for four years by the Cabinet with the consent of both Houses.

In Germany, the Central Bank Council determines the monetary and credit policies of the Bundesbank. It consists of the ten-member Directorate and the eleven Land (district) Central Bank Presidents. The Directorate, which includes the President and the Vice President, are nominated by the federal government and appointed by the President of the Federal Republic for a period of eight years. The President of the Federal Republic also appoints the eleven Land Bank Presidents for eight-year (renewable) terms. Their nomination, however, must come from the Bundesrat, the upper house of the parliament, which represents the various regions of the country. In making a nomination, the Bundesrat must follow the recommendation of the political authority in the Land concerned. This ensures that the federal government is not able to nominate directly a majority of the Central Bank Council. As a further check on the government's direct input in the appointment process, the Central Bank Council has the right to comment on the nomination of any Directorate member or Land Bank President.

FINANCIAL RELATIONS BETWEEN CENTRAL BANKS AND GOVERNMENTS

Budgetary autonomy would seem to be a natural feature of central bank independence.

But, in fact, many central banks along the entire spectrum of independence have complete budget autonomy. The Bank of Japan, along with the Bank of France and the Reserve Bank of New Zealand, are notable exceptions; all must obtain prior approval from the government for their budget expenditures. One possible reason why budgetary autonomy is not linked to monetary policy independence is that, unlike other government agencies, virtually all central banks generate revenue from seignorage or assets purchased by creating non-interest bearing (or low interest-bearing) liabilities against themselves.

A significant determinant of central bank independence is the extent to which the government can obtain financing directly from the central bank. The more power the Treasury has to demand direct financing from the central bank, the less latitude the central bank has in pursuing monetary policies aimed at maintaining long-term price stability. In Germany, direct central bank credit to the government is strictly limited, but the Bundesbank is allowed to acquire government paper in open market operations. The law explicitly states, however, that such secondary market purchases can be used only for monetary control purposes. In the U.K., the Treasury can cover current budget spending requirements with direct short-term loans from the BOE. Moreover, the law does not limit BOE purchases of government securities. In Japan, the BOJ is prohibited from direct purchases of new issues of long-term government securities, but there is no barrier to BOJ advances to the government or secondary market purchases of government debt.

LAW VERSUS REPUTATION

Formal legal arrangements of central banking in Germany and the U.K. give a fairly clear indication of the degree of their independence. And, the relative inflationary performance of both countries is consistent with the notion that independent central banks tend to generate lower inflation rates. In Japan, less formal arrangements and practices (which are more difficult to measure) also have been important; monetary policy generally has been more independent in practice than central bank legislation suggests. In other words, achieving low inflation has been possible in Japan without the benefit of a particularly *legally* independent central bank.

This achievement may be explained by the BOJ's trustworthy record of keeping inflation in check. Such a reputation may have provided an effective substitute for legal independence in establishing policy credibility. Of course, the two are not mutually exclusive, as the German case illustrates, where the Bundesbank's track record in controlling inflation has been even more impressive. No doubt, the collective memory of hyperinflation contributed to Germany's decision to buttress high central bank reputation with legal safeguards for its independence.

Establishing formal independence will be particularly important for a country attempting to build monetary policy credibility against an historical background of variable and insufficient monetary restraint. Perhaps it is not a coincidence that countries with particularly poor inflation records in the past, such as Argentina, Chile, New Zealand, and some of the Eastern European countries, are the very ones that have recently formalized, or are contemplating formalizing, the independence of their central banks. Formal central bank independence may offer the potential to provide a disciplinary check on monetary policy and thereby improve long-run inflation performance.

REFERENCES

Alesina, Alberto. 1988. "Macroeconomics and Politics." In *NBER Macroeonomic Annual*, 1988, Cambridge, Mass., MIT Press.

Bade, Robin and Michael Parkin. 1987. "Central Bank Laws and Monetary Policy." Unpublished mimeograph. Department of Economics, University of Western Ontario.

QUESTIONS

1. What is the relationship between central bank legal independence and inflation? What explains this relationship?
2. Based on the three determinants Kim discusses, describe the legal independence of the Bundesbank, the Bank of England, and the Bank of Japan.
3. What leads Kim to conclude that legal independence is not necessary for controlling inflation?

READING 31

Inflation Hawks: Fed Banks' Presidents Hold Private Positions But Major Public Role

Alan Murray

Richmond, VA — As a chief executive, Robert Black is doing fine. Just look at his financial statement:

Revenues: $2.04 billion.
Expenses: $0.12 billion.
Net: $1.92 billion.

Mr. Black's business: making money. Literally. As president of the Federal Reserve Bank of Richmond, he straddles an odd but awesome combination of public and private power.

He is paid like a private banker—$175,600 a year. His shareholders are private banks. His board members are private citizens. His budget is free of congressional scrutiny. He works in a spacious corner office atop a striking skyscraper with a fine view of the James River.

Once every six weeks, Mr. Black abandons these comforts and goes to Washington, where he assumes the role of a powerful government official. Mr. Black and his 11 fellow presidents of Fed district banks join with the seven Fed governors in Washington to set interest-rate policies that profoundly affect the nation's economy.

"I'm not aware of any other agency," says Rep. Lee Hamilton, an Indiana Democrat, "where such major policy decisions are made by individuals who are not government officials."

The bifurcated status of the 12 Fed bank presidents has periodically set off controversy ever since the central bank was founded 78 years ago. Advocates of this arrangement argue that it helps shield the Fed from political pressures. But it also hands enormous power to people who need not answer to the public or the government.

AN INBRED GROUP

On the surface, the presidents are strikingly similar. They are all male, all white. Eight hold Ph.D.s in economics. Nine have spend most or all of their careers at the Fed; three are former employees of three others. In short, they are an inbred group. In what other 12-man group would one-third be named Robert?

"It's a bureaucracy," comments Preston Martin, a former Fed vice chairman. "It may be the finest bureaucracy in government, but it is a bureaucracy. And a bureaucracy perpetuates itself."

In recent years, the presidents also have become increasingly powerful. Members of the Fed's secretive Federal Open Market Committee say the presidents, though not always voting as a bloc, have nonetheless become the Fed's leading anti-inflation hawks, advocating tight-credit policies that hold up short-term interest rates. Their tight-fisted stance was partly responsible for the Fed's slow response to the recession last year.

The presidents are "much like the West Germans," complains Sen. Pete Domenici, a New Mexico Republican. "They have a total fear of inflation. They write about it. They talk about it. Some of them, it seems, would like negative inflation."

BIG CHANGE PROPOSED

In response to recent publicity of the president's rising power, four influential Democratic legislators will today introduce legislation to eliminate the presidents from policy making. The bill—sponsored by Rep. Hamilton, Sen. Paul Sarbanes of Maryland, Sen. Jim Sasser of Tennessee and Rep. Byron Dorgan of North Dakota—would give all power over monetary policy to the board of governors in Washington.

Tight-Money Presidents
Dissenting votes in the Greenspan Fed

	Dissents for Tighter Money	Dissents for Easier Money
Fed Governors	2	21
Fed Presidents	18	2

Source: Policy records of the Federal Open Market Committee

A study to be released today by the congressional Joint Economic Committee, chaired by Sen. Sarbanes, finds that the Fed is unique among major industrial nations for the power it gives to central-bank officials who are neither elected nor appointed by elected officials. Even the German Bundesbank—often praised for its independence—has policy makers who are appointed either by the president or the upper house of parliament, the study says.

Yet the 12 Fed presidents, despite all their influence, toil in relative obscurity. Who are these quasi-private public-policy makers? Where do they come from? To whom are they accountable? The answers to these questions are clouded in the Fed's mystique and arcane traditions.

The district banks perform a wide variety of services for commercial banks, collecting and clearing checks, providing currency and coin, processing savings bonds and transferring money by wire. They earn money from the fees they charge for these services, from loans they make to financial institutions, and most important, from interest payments on the large portfolios of government securities they hold.

But the presidents' greatest power comes from their membership on the Open Market Committee, which sets targets for the federal funds rate—the rate banks charge one another for overnight loans—and thus influences other short-term rates.

On the committee, the presidents sit down with the seven Fed governors, who unlike them, are appointed by the White House and confirmed by the Senate. Because only five of the presidents may vote at each meeting, they normally have a minority of the votes. But all 12 may speak at meetings and thus help shape the consensus. And with two governor seats currently vacant, the presidents have had voting parity with the governors in recent weeks.

Because the committee usually strives for a consensus on policy decisions, official dissents by voting members are relatively rare. But of the 20 tighter-money dissents cast in committee meetings during Fed Chairman Alan Greenspan's four-year tenure, all but two have come from district presidents. And of 23 dissents for an easier policy—meaning lower short-term interest rates—only two came from presidents.

And dissents tell just part of the story. Mr. Black, though he has never dissented during the Greenspan years, is clearly one of the panel's leading anti-inflation "hawks." He and several other presidents have pushed Fed policy toward tighter credit—sometimes further than Mr. Greenspan, a formidable inflation-fighter himself, has wanted.

The presidents' hawkish views were on display in early July at the Fed's policy committee meeting, when a majority of them expressed a desire to reduce the 1992 target ranges for money supply growth, according to people attending the meeting. They were joined by Fed Governor Wayne Angell. But Mr. Greenspan argued against the change. The committee ultimately agreed to go along with the chairman, but only after being assured the issue would be revisited next February.

The presidents are named by the private-sector boards of directors of the district Fed banks, subject to the approval of the Fed board of governors in Washington. Once appointed, they can, in practice, stay in office as long as they choose. And even the district banks' directors say they have little or no influence over their presidents' actions on interest rates.

Last year, for example, the board of the Dallas Fed voted repeatedly to recommend cuts in the discount rate. But Robert Boykin, then the Dallas Fed's president, repeatedly went to Washington and argued against his own board's view. "It is a very unhappy position," says Bobby Inman, former chairman of the Dallas board and former deputy director of Central Intelligence. Mr. Inman is convinced that if the Fed "had moved reasonably decisively in April and May" of 1990, rather than waiting until late in the year to ease, "we would have, if not avoided the recession, had a shorter and shallower one."

'FINE-TUNING' DISPARAGED

Mr. Black denies that the Fed could have blunted the recession. He even rejects the notion that the Fed should try to ease recessions. "it's more fun to try and fine-tune" the economy, he says, "but we're not smart enough to fine-tune." His views reflect the Fed's experience in the 1970s, when efforts to fight recession led instead to double-digit inflation. It's better, in his view, for the Fed to focus on a single goal: price stability.

Moreover, many economists warn that persistent efforts to push short-term interest rates artificially low can boomerang: With the bond market fearing higher inflation, long-term rates can actually rise in response, harming the economy.

Mr. Black's background provides an interesting, if not altogether typical, look at the makings of a Fed hawk. A courtly Southern gentleman, he was born in Hickman, Ky., a small bluff town along the Mississippi River. His parents were strict and conservative "in every sense," he recalls. His father ran a number of small businesses; his mother was a teacher.

Mr. Black remembers sitting on his porch and listening to excursion boats, with their calliopes playing, on the river. "I always wanted to ride one," he says, "but my mother thought they were a den of iniquity because they had dancing, and maybe drinking."

Mr. Black encountered economics while at the University of Virginia and decided he wanted to teach it. But even before he had completed his doctoral dissertation, the Richmond Federal Reserve Bank made its claim on him. "I was making $120 a month teaching," he recalls. "They offered to pay me $300 a month to do my dissertation for the bank." Except for one year of teaching at the University of Tennessee, he has been at the Richmond Fed ever since. He became its president in 1973.

Today, Mr. Black runs the bank with polite efficiency. He travels by elevator down the 24 floors of his building to greet visitors at the door. While walking through the lunch room, he stops repeatedly to banter with employees. Everything about him speaks of an earlier era. He mocks the valuable modern art gracing the halls of his building; in a corner of his office he has mounted two large, black stones on a pedestal, with a plaque reading, "Frog Egg and Tadpole, by Henry Moore."

But there is little mistaking Mr. Black's hard views about monetary policy. He was one of the first at the Fed to call for tight control of growth in the money supply, and he got a reputation in the late 1970s and early 1980s as the Fed's leading hawk.

Today, Mr. Black has several competitors for that honor. Chief among them is Cleveland Fed President Lee Hoskins. But although the two men share similar economic views, they are a study in personal contrasts. Mr. Black is courteous, self-depreciating and eager to find a consensus. Mr. Hoskins is blunt, uncompromising and frequently dissents. Mr. Black loyally defends Chairman Greenspan; Mr. Hoskins is said to sometimes irk the chairman. A few years ago, Mr. Hoskins came close to open warfare with the chairman and the board when he opposed a board plan to provide back-up funding for failed thrifts.

Also pushing for tight credit are Thomas Melzer, president of the St. Louis Fed; Gary Stern of Minneapolis; Robert Parry of San Francisco and occasionally Roger Guffey of Kansas City, Mo. Mr. Boykin, recently retired in Dallas, often joined them. His successor, Robert McTeer, who trained under Mr. Black at Richmond, may fall into the hawk camp.

A MIDDLE GROUP

Another group of presidents is less adamant in battling inflation and more concerned about short-term economic growth. They include Richard Syron of the Boston Fed, Edward Boehne of Philadelphia and Silas Keehn of Chicago. New York Fed President Gerald Corrigan, the most powerful of the presidents because of his bank's role in implementing securities transactions for the system, is also usually placed in this camp.

In contrast, Robert Forrestal, president of the Atlanta Fed, has emerged as the lonesome dove among the presidents. Quiet and unassuming, a lawyer rather than an economist, Mr. Forrestal has made few waves during most of his seven years as a Fed policy maker. But in the past year, he has launched a muted rebellion against the anti-inflation group.

Born in 1931 in Manhattan, the son of Democratic supporters of the New Deal, he went to parochial schools, singing in the glee club and contemplating a career in music. At St. John's College in New York, he took economics, but only because it was a requirement. He served as a Naval officer in the Korean War, and then—giving up the idea of a music career—went to Georgetown Law School and joined a small law firm in Washington.

Unlike many of his economist colleagues, Mr. Forrestal ended up at the Fed by default. He was in constant conflict with his law firm's managing partner. Hearing that the Fed board was looking for an attorney, he applied and was hired, planning "to stay two, three or four years and then go back to a private law firm." Instead, he stayed on, moving to the Atlanta Fed as general counsel in 1969 and rising through the ranks until he became president in '83.

Because his Fed work had involved mostly matters such as bank regulation and check-clearing operations, Mr. Forrestal came to the Open Market Committee unversed in monetary policy. His discomfort with the subject shows; at committee meetings, he frequently appears to be reading his statements rather than delivering them extemporaneously. And until recently, he usually stayed quietly in the mainstream of policy decisions.

But early last year, months before Chairman Greenspan acknowledged the problem, Mr. Forrestal began speaking in meetings about the difficulties companies faced in getting credit. The only other voice then complaining of credit problems was former Governor Martha Seger.

"By May or June of last year, I began to suspect the downturn might be more critical than people thought at the time," Mr. Forrestal says. "It seemed serious enough, and the danger of a pronounced policy great enough, that I thought we should ease policy sooner than the others." He wasn't a voting member of the policy committee in 1990, but as soon as he became one, last February, he dissented in favor of an easier policy.

In some ways, Mr. Forrestal's revolt seemed a reaction against his fellow presidents' growing clout and focus on inflation. "While I certainly think inflation is a very important goal," he says, "there are costs to achieving that. I would have preferred to err on the side of easing." He adds that fighting inflation is "a long-term goal, and sometimes you have to adjust your tactics. I'm not willing to risk exacerbating a recession to get an inflation number in the short term." As for Mr. Black's notion that controlling inflation is the sole goal of monetary policy, Mr. Forrestal says: "I don't agree with that. Economic growth is one of our goals."

In Mr. Forrestal's view, the Fed's policy committee has too many economists. "People from other disciplines can bring a good deal of analytical ability" to Fed discussions, he says. "I think lawyers, businessmen, bankers would help." He admits that at times, non-economists are "at a disadvantage if you get into a lot of technical discussion." But that, he says, "is what you have a staff for."

Mr. Forrestal and Mr. Black agree that the presidents' role has changed. Mr. Black argues that their power over policy has increased "because they've become more persuasive." And Mr. Forrestal notes the presidents "have become more outspoken on issues and have gone public on issues more than they used to."

But neither of them wants to subject Fed presidents to presidential appointment and Senate confirmation. "I think it would politicize the position," says Mr. Black, who adds that "no president would ever appoint me to anything."

In a report earlier this year, four Democrats on the Senate Banking Committee advanced the notion that the presidents' role in making policy might violate the constitutional provision requiring that high government officials be appointed by the president and confirmed by the Senate. But a federal court ruled otherwise in 1986, holding that the government has the right to delegate certain powers.

Former Fed Chairman Paul Volcker also favors the status quo. "The organizational characteristics of the Federal Reserve are seemingly odd," he says, "but it somehow, in its peculiar way, reflects a pretty good balance. You get some continuity, professionalism and insulation from politics. And the way the presidents are selected contributes to all of those things."

QUESTIONS

1. What role do the Federal Reserve Banks' presidents play in making monetary policy?

2. Why are some legislators concerned over the rising power of the Fed bank presidents? What curbs on that power do they propose?

3. What are the various positions the Fed bank presidents take regarding inflation and monetary policy?

READING 32

Fed Assumes Bigger Share of U.S. Debt

Alfred L. Malabre, Jr.

More of the nation's huge debt burden is being shouldered by a customer with a broad back and very deep pockets: the Federal Reserve System.

The Fed has sharply increased its purchases of Treasury securities since 1990, apparently to allow for more borrowing in the private sector and help spur the economy. Fed Chairman Alan Greenspan and other board governors claim they will keep a lid on inflation. But a growing number of economists view the Fed's new willingness to take on more of the debt as inflationary in the long run.

The Fed's share of the mounting debt pile remains small—less that 3% of a total that's fast approaching $12 trillion. But this share has grown markedly since 1990, in contrast to a previous pattern of persistent shrinkage. Fed holdings of U.S. government securities have risen more than 33% in less than two years; in the same period, total debt rose less than 10% and federal debt about 20%.

Fed Holdings and Inflation

Comparison of percent of total debt held by the Federal Reserve and year-to-year change in consumer price index, quarterly data

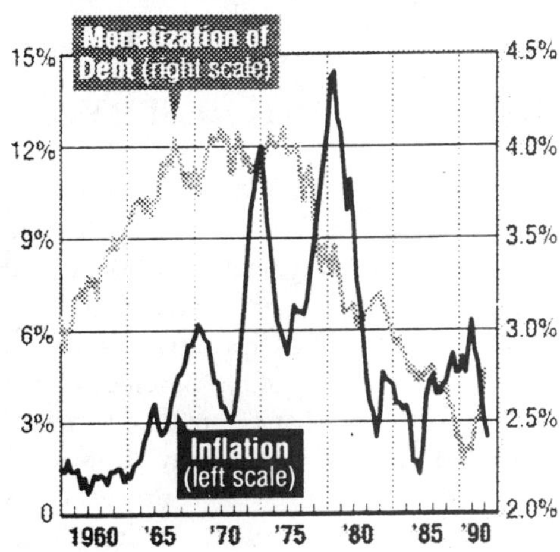

Sources: ISI Group Inc; Federal Reserve Board; Bureau of Labor Statistics

"The Fed's recent willingness to hold more of the debt signifies a sea change," says Edward S. Hyman, president of ISI Group Inc. He views the change as "a bad development" since it threatens ultimately to cause steeper price increases. But he also stresses that the lead times between Fed moves to hold more debt and increased inflation tend to be long.

"It's probably not too late for the Fed to change course and avert a new inflationary surge," he says.

For now, "by taking on more of the total debt itself, the Fed is allowing more room in the credit markets for private borrowers," says Robert H. Parks, an economic consultant in New York. Otherwise, interest rates would tend to be higher and less affordable, he says, adding, "The Fed in effect is financing Treasury borrowing with newly created money."

CREATING BANK RESERVES

To increase its debt holdings, the Fed may buy government securities directly from the Treasury, but more typically it does so in the open market. Bank reserves are created in the process, since the Fed can "pay" simply by crediting the amount of its purchases to the account of the bank involved in the transaction. As a result, money is born.

Economists call the process debt monetization. Without it, rising federal deficits tend merely to shuffle spending to the government sector from the private sector, rather than stimulate the economy as a whole.

For all the short-term benefits, a rising money supply, if it goes on long enough and is sharp enough, can eventually outstrip the available supply of goods and services and so fuel inflation. The government's most "potent financing technique" is for the Fed "to monetize the Treasury's debt by purchasing it," says William C. Melton, a former Fed official who now serves as chief economist of IDS Financial Services Inc.

The recent shift in the Fed's overall debt holdings, as opposed to how much of the total is in short-term or long-term securities, has received relatively little notice. Efforts to assess Fed policy have focused mainly on such familiar gauges as the federal funds rate, which banks charge one another on short-term loans, and on aggregates that gauge the money supply.

By and large, these well-publicized indicators suggest an effort by the Fed to loosen the monetary reins. But this endeavor has occasionally seemed halting and marked by caution. The federal funds rate, near 4%, is lower than three months ago, but slightly higher than a few weeks ago. M1, a relatively narrow measure of the money supply, has climbed briskly for many months. But the broader M2, M3 and M4 aggregates have not. Adjusted for inflation, all three are lower now than three years ago.

NO AMBIVALENCE

There's no such ambivalence in the Fed's recent assumption of more of the debt. In the first quarter of 1990, Fed holdings of U.S. government securities amounted to just over

$233.5 billion. The total has been rising sharply ever since, surpassing $312 billion in the final quarter of 1991.

As the chart indicates, substantial time often may elapse between shifts in the Fed's willingness to assume debt and developments on the price front. The Fed monetized a rising portion of debt from the early 1960s until nearly the end of the decade, and the trend continued at a slower, more erratic pace until 1976. Yet, inflation remained relatively dormant until the latter half of the 1960s.

A footnote: Unlike the present situation, the Fed's monetizing through the 1960s can hardly be viewed as an effort to relieve credit markets overburdened by federal deficits. Through most of the period, the federal budget was in or close to balance.

The pattern from 1976 to 1990 also shows a long lag between shifts in the Fed's debt share and price developments. The Fed's share of debt fell substantially, a process that economists call demonetization and regard as disinflationary, just as monetization is deemed inflationary. But inflation intensified sharply from 1978 to 1980, well after the Fed's share of debt had begun to fall. As demonetizing continued, inflation finally did abate.

Most economists look for the Fed to adopt a more restrictive policy once the recovery gains strength and the presidential election is over. Some believe that this policy shift may already be at hand. But the hazard is that this could squeeze hard-pressed private borrowers, especially with the federal budget deficit near $400 billion and the economy reviving. The upshot could be appreciably higher interest rates and, once again, a stalled recovery or a new recession.

"The Fed will find it very hard to reverse its recent policy of debt monetization," says Lacy H. Hunt, chief economist in New York for Hongkong Bank Group. He warns that any return to debt demonetization would be "catastrophic" for the recovery, which he believes finally got under way in February.

Some economists disagree with such assessments and caution that the inflationary die is already cast, whatever the Fed decides to do in coming months. "The Fed has already passed the flash point for inflation," claims H. Erich Heinemann, chief economist of Ladenburg, Thalmann & Co.

QUESTIONS

1. What is debt monetization?
2. What are the benefits and dangers of debt monetization?
3. Based on past relationships between debt monetization and inflation, are current fears of higher inflation justified?

READING 33

M2 and the Business Cycle

Frederick T. Furlong and John P. Judd

The role of the monetary aggregates as indicators or targets of monetary policy has waxed and waned over the past fifteen years. Emphasis on monetary targeting reached a high in 1979-1982, when the Federal Reserve explicitly targeted M1 in implementing its anti-inflation policies. After that, the aggregates were de-emphasized, based largely on the view that deregulation of the financial system had rendered the relationship between money and the economy unreliable, at least for an extended transition period.

In the past few years, interest in the aggregates, especially M2, has resurged. Two factors seem to have led to this development. First, recognition has grown that deregulation may not have interfered with the stable *long-run* relationship between M2 and total spending on goods and services (and thus with the price level). Second, the slow growth in M2 that preceded this recession has led some to argue that the Fed should have paid more attention to that signal.

In this *Letter*, we review the evidence on the reliability of M2 as a guide for monetary policy in general, and then assess the implications of the recent slowdown in M2 for future economic activity.

IN THE LONG RUN...

Is the relation between M2 and nominal GNP (that is, total spending on goods and services) stable in the long run? Chart 1 shows the velocity of M2 (referred to here as V2) over the past 30 years. V2 is measured as the ratio of nominal GNP to M2, and thus indicates how many times in a year a given stock of M2 is spent and respent on goods and services. As the Chart shows, V2 fluctuates widely in the short run, but in the long run, the series exhibits a stable trend, always returning to a constant level since the late 1950s. This suggests a stable long-run relationship between the *levels* of M2 and

Chart 1
Income Velocity of M2
(GNP/M2)

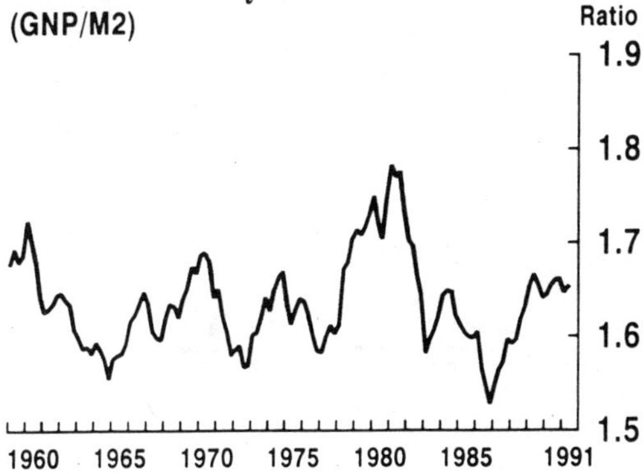

nominal GNP; specifically, the stock of M2 tends to be spent and re-spent about 1.64 times per year on goods and services. Statistical analyses (technically called cointegration tests) confirm this conclusion, and suggest that over the post-war period M2 has led GNP on average. These tests also suggest that the other monetary aggregates (M1, M1A, and M3) have *not* had such stable long-run relationships (Miller, 1991).

What do these results mean for monetary policy? They suggest that if the central bank knows the average level of M2 over a long period of time, it can predict nominal GNP over the same period fairly accurately. How long a period is required for this relationship to hold? Empirical estimates suggest that nominal GNP adjusts to a new level of M2 with very long lags. In fact, it appears to take around 4½ years for one-half of this adjustment to be completed.

Moreover, over periods this long, adjustment of nominal GNP translates into adjustment of the price level. In the long run, the level of output produced by the economy is determined by underlying supply conditions (such as the labor force and productivity) and is unrelated to M2. Thus the influence of M2 on nominal GNP translates fully into an influence on the aggregate price level.

In sum, the fact the V2 is stable in the long run means that persistent, excessive M2 growth will lead to excessive inflation. Or, put more positively, if monetary policy keeps M2 growth under control over a period of several years, it simultaneously would keep inflation under control.

IN THE SHORT RUN...

The wide fluctuations in V2 around its average level (Chart 1) show that there *is* no simple relationship between money and output, so M2 is a much less useful indicator of economic activity in the short run. Some of these fluctuations can be explained by the effects of interest rates and the lags in the response of GNP to money. For example, as market interest rates rise relative to those paid on M2 accounts, people economize on their holdings of M2 and its velocity increases. However, even after accounting for interest rate spreads and lagged responses, large errors remain in explaining V2.

In order to be more precise about the usefulness of M2 as a short-run, or cyclical indicator, we estimated a model of M2, prices, real GNP, and a market interest rate that incorporates the short-run relationships among changes in these variables, as well as the long-run relationships among their levels. This model (called a vector-error-correction model) is similar to the one estimated by Miller (1991). It is used to estimate the relative importance of M2 impulses to the short-run behavior of real GNP. (An M2 impulse can be though of as an unexpected one-time movement in M2 growth.)

We asked two questions of this model. First, what does M2 tell us about future movements in real GNP if we have information about contemporaneous interest rates, prices, and real GNP? The answer is: Not much. As shown in Chart 2, M2 impulses historically have accounted for a very small percentage of the total uncertainty (prediction error) in real GNP in our model. In other words, M2 does not contain much additional information about future real GNP over and above that contained in contemporaneous interest rates, prices, and real GNP.

The second question is, what does M2 tell us about real GNP when information on M2 is all we have? The answer is: A little more, but still not a lot. In this case, unexpected movements in M2 account for no more than about 16 percent of the overall uncertainty in real GNP. Thus, even if the "deck is stacked" in favor of a role for M2, the effect of an M2 impulse on output easily could be swamped by the effects of other factors.

Chart 2
Real GNP Forecast Error:
How Much Is Accounted for by M2 ...

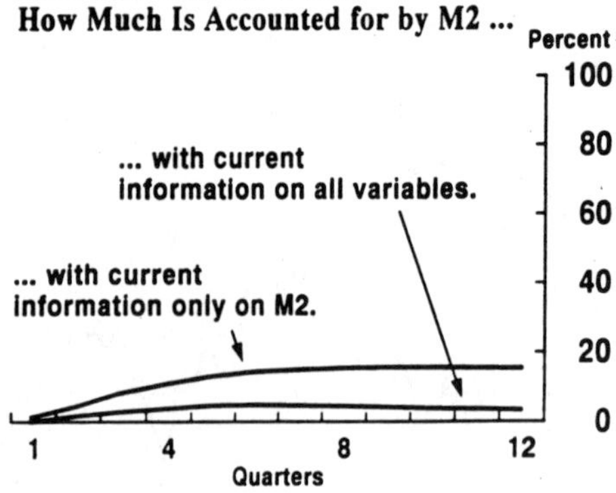

IN THE CURRENT CYCLE...

The analysis so far applies to the long-run and short-run relationships observed **on average** over the past 30 years. Undoubtedly, business cycles differ, and M2 is more important in determining real GNP in some cycles than in others. Is it likely that M2 is having a larger than average effect on economic activity in this cycle? Does the decline in M2 in recent months threaten to abort the business cycle recovery?

To answer these questions, we consider the possible sources of the recent decline in M2, and what they may imply for real GNP in the future. First, the weakness in M2 is not entirely explained by past and current movements in output, prices, and interest rates. Over the past several quarters, M2 has been well below the level predicted based upon its historical relationship with these other variables (see Chart 3). M2 moved outside the error band early last year, and since then the gap has widened. There is only a 5 percent chance that M2 would have fallen outside the error band if the historical relationship were still in place. This suggests that unusual factors most likely have accounted for the weakness in M2.

Chart 3
Actual and Predicted M2

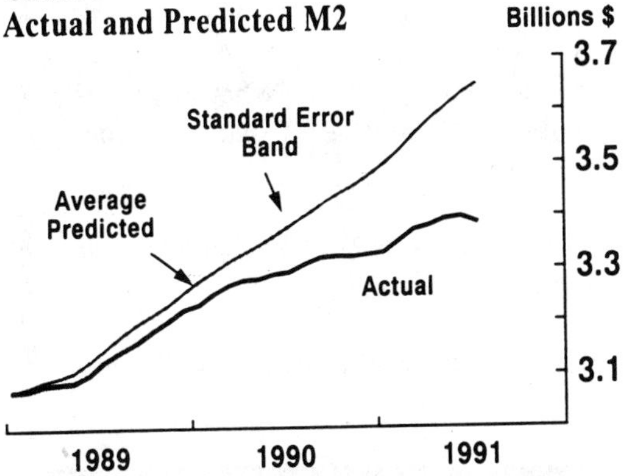

Monthly Estimation from Oct. 1978 to Dec. 1988.

Two categories of explanations have been put forth. First, the decline in M2 could reflect a portfolio shift into other assets. For example, the yield curve has steepened recently, meaning that rates of return on longer-term assets have risen relative to those on the comparatively short-term assets in M2. This may be why funds invested in stock and bond mutual funds have risen sharply while M2 has declined. It is generally agreed that such portfolio shifting should have little or no implication for future economic activity, and would therefore not call for a monetary policy response.

The second category, which has received the most attention, has to do with the role of reduced credit availability in determining M2 and economic activity: in other words, the so-called "credit crunch." It has been argued that credit availability has been restricted by the downsizing of the thrift industry, tougher capital standards for banks, and other factors, and that reduced credit has restricted both M2 and economic activity.

However, this view suggests that M2 may not be playing an independent role in the current business cycle. In other words, whether or not weak M2 is likely to precede weakness in the economy may depend more on whether or not there is a credit crunch than on the behavior of M2 itself.

In summary, M2 has not been a very reliable or significant cyclical indicator in the past. It is possible that its correlation with economic activity has been strengthened in the present cycle by a credit crunch. However, to the extent that this is the case, the real issues have to do with developments in the credit markets, not necessarily with M2.

The role of a credit crunch in the recent recession is an open issue, which will be discussed in a future *Letter*.

REFERENCE

Miller, Stephen J. 1991. "Monetary Dynamics: An Application of Cointegration and Error-Correction Modeling." *Journal of Money, Credit and Banking* (May) pp. 139-154.

QUESTIONS

1. Describe the long run relation between M2 and nominal GNP. What does this relation mean for the conduct of monetary policy? What does it imply for real output, the price level, and inflation over the long run?

2. Describe the short run relation between M2 and nominal GNP. What accounts for this relation? What does it mean for the conduct of monetary policy?

3. What explanations do Furlong and Judd offer for the recent slowdown in M2 growth?

READING 34

A Price Objective for Monetary Policy

William T. Gavin and Alan C. Stockman

The idea of monetary policy aimed at producing a stable price level has gained increasing support in the United States in recent years. In 1991, the Neal Resolution proposed to make such a policy objective law. Elsewhere, the notion of price stability has also become more popular. For example, the central banks of Canada and New Zealand recently adopted explicit multiyear targets for inflation, and a commitment to price stability is widely thought to be a necessary condition for successfully monetary union in the European Community.

During the past decade, inflation has been reduced significantly, and many observers believe that further moderation may be in store in the next several years. Nevertheless, price stability remains an elusive goal both here and abroad.[1] This *Economic Commentary* discusses some of the reasons why price stability is so difficult to achieve. One explanation lies in the nature of monetary targeting. Another is simply the absence of an explicit commitment to a long-term objective for the price level.

THE M2 TARGET

The Federal Reserve System was created in 1913 under the umbrella of a gold standard. Our currency was fully convertible into gold until 1933, and indeed, some vestiges of convertibility lingered on until 1971. But since 1971, the monetary standard has had no anchor other than the annual monetary targets.

The wide ranges assigned to the targeted aggregates and uncertainty about the income velocity of money have made the monetary targeting exercise problematic as a vehicle for achieving price stability. The uncertainty induced by the broad ranges is compounded by the practice of building the annual monetary targets on the previous year's *actual* fourth-quarter average of the money stock (assumed here to be M2) rather than on the midpoint of that year's target.[2] This procedure means that target misses are forgiven; consequently, the level of M2 will be highly unpredictable over long horizons.

To illustrate how the current practice causes uncertainty about the future money stock, consider that the M2 target range for 1992 is four percentage points wide (2.5 percent to 6.5 percent). Without knowing precisely where in this range we will end the year, and assuming that future M2 targets are also four percentage points wide, the potential target range has an eight percentage point spread at the end of 1993—from roughly 5 percent to 13 percent (see figure 1). In only five years hence, the range of uncertainty about the M2 level would be 20 percentage points wide (from 12.5 percent to 32.5 percent).

One way to narrow the range of possible outcomes for both M2 and prices would be to specify a multiyear path for M2. Such a path would not remove all of the questions about the aggregate's future growth, but it would limit the range of uncertainty to the 4 percent bands around the annual targets, regardless of the forecast horizon.

It may be risky to rely exclusively on an M2 path to achieve price stability, however, because of the potential for unexpected changes in its velocity trend. Among all of the monetary aggregates—currency, the monetary base, M1, M2, and M3—only M2 has exhibited a constant trend in velocity over the last 30 years.[3] However, there is no guarantee that this will continue. From 1869 until 1945, for example, M2 velocity declined at an average annual rate of 2 percent; it then rose at the same pace in the 10 years following the war.

FIGURE 1 GROWTH RANGES FOR M2

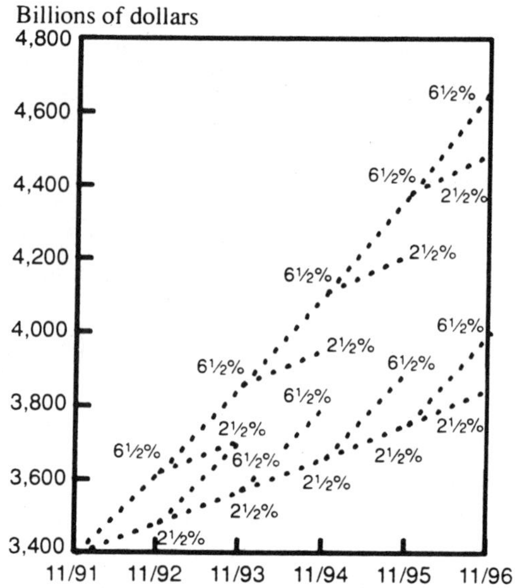

SOURCES: Board of Governors of the Federal Reserve System; and authors' calculations.

Although M2 velocity has been constant on average for the last 30 years, quarterly values fluctuate, sometimes widely: The standard deviation of quarterly growth has been an annualized 4 percent since 1960. The potential exists for both permanent and temporary shifts in velocity. In the past, temporary shifts have been associated with the rise and fall of interest rates or, more precisely, with the opportunity cost of holding M2 balances. (Opportunity cost is the difference between market interest rates and interest rates paid on deposits included in M2.)

Throughout the most recent recession, the opportunity cost of M2 fell, but, atypically, M2 velocity did not. This unusual behavior has raised the question of whether there has been a permanent shift in M2's velocity trend.[4]

Unfortunately, we cannot clearly recognize such a shift until well after a change has occurred. The length of time needed to distinguish a change in the trend depends on the relative size of the permanent and temporary shifts. In the case of M2 and the other monetary aggregates, the variance of temporary shifts is quite large relative to the variance of permanent shifts. For example, if the M2 velocity trend began to grow at 2 percent per year, it would take several years for analysts to be sure that this was not just a temporary fluctuation. By that time, the economy would have suffered the costs of a persistent unexpected shift in the price level (by an additional 2 percent per year). One way to hedge against the risks of an unexpected shift in velocity would be to specify the annual M2 targets in the framework of a multiyear path for the price level.

A PRICE-LEVEL OBJECTIVE

In December 1983, then Federal Reserve Chairman Paul Volcker defined price stability as a condition that exists when people make decisions "...on the basis that 'real' and 'nominal' values are substantially the same over [a suitably long] planning horizon..."[5] This sentiment was echoed more recently by current Chairman Alan Greenspan: "For all practical purposes, price stability means that expected changes in the average price level are small enough and gradual enough that they do not materially enter business and household financial decisions."[6]

We can make this definition of price stability operational by specifying a time path for the trend in a specific price index that extends indefinitely into the future. For example, suppose that policymakers decide to stabilize the Consumer Price Index (CPI). The Federal Reserve could specify a target path for prices that would gradually decelerate until the price-level trend became horizontal. Price stability would be achieved if the actual CPI moved along this path.

Price-level targets should also include bounds around the target path to let the public know how far the index will be allowed to stray before action is taken to bring it back in line. An example of such an operational definition of price stability is shown in figure 2. The target path is based on the actual CPI in December 1989 growing 5.5 percent that year, 5 percent in 1990, and then declining half a percent each year until the path becomes horizontal in the year 2000. We have set bounds of plus and minus 3 percent around this trajectory.[7]

To our knowledge, there is only one case in which a central bank based its policy actions on a price-index target. This was a six-year episode in the 1930s when the Swedish central bank, the Riksbank, targeted that nation's CPI at around 100. Figure 3 shows that the actual price level stayed well within 3 percent of this figure throughout all six years, crossing the price target twice. Although this was a rather brief period in

FIGURE 2 A PRICE-LEVEL OBJECTIVE

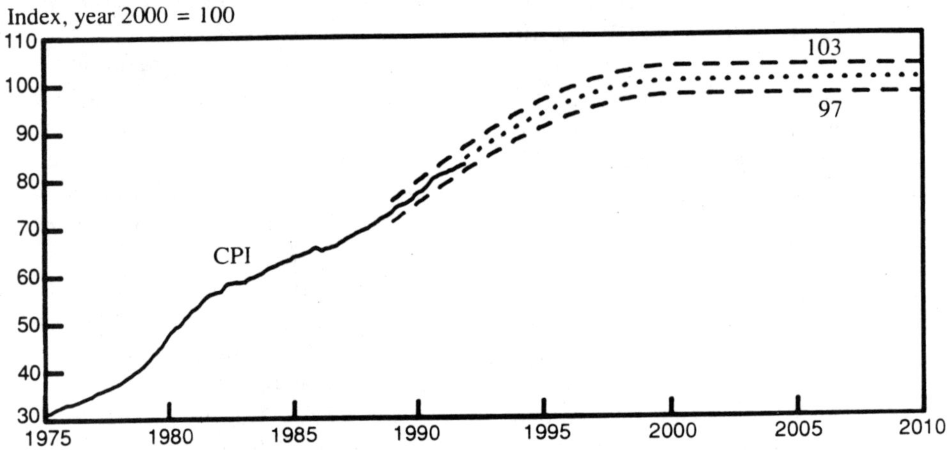

SOURCES: U.S. Department of Labor, Bureau of Labor Statistics; and authors' calculations.

FIGURE 3 SWEDEN'S CONSUMER PRICE INDEX, 1931–41

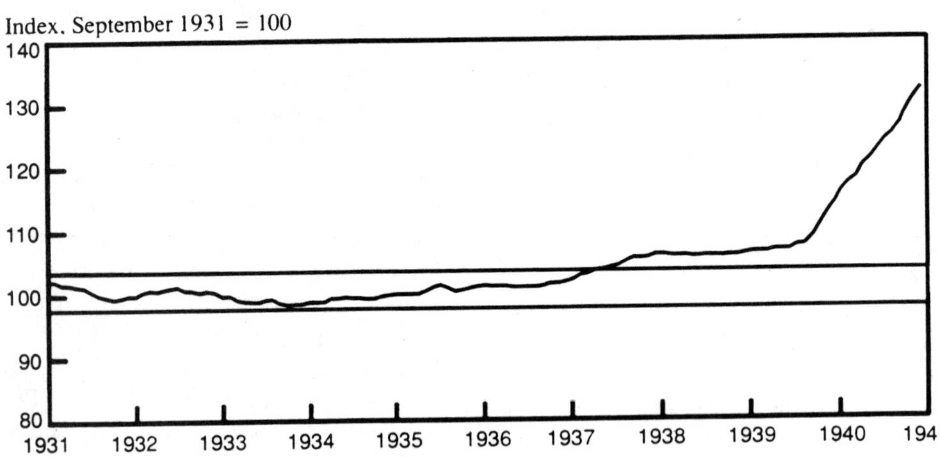

NOTE: The band was imposed on the historical data by the authors.
SOURCE: *Sveriges Riksbank 1940*. Stockholm: Riksbankens Sedeltryckeri. 1941.

history, it illustrates that a measurable objective for price stability can be achieved.[8]

WHY NOT AN INFLATION TARGET?

Part of the opposition to a price-level target may stem from confusion about the way price information is used to guide policy actions. The price level can be thought of as the sum of two components: a trend determined by the monetary authorities and a transitory component associated with real shocks to the economy. Many economists oppose price-level targeting because real shocks, such as oil shortages, droughts, and changes in the tax system, dominate short-run fluctuations in the price level.

In 1968, for example, Milton Friedman advocated monetary targets rather than price-level targets as short-run guides for policy because

> Of the three guides listed [exchange rates, price index and money stock], the price level is clearly the most important in its own right. Other things the same, it would be much the best of the alternatives...But other things are not the same...We cannot predict at all accurately just what effect a particular monetary action will have on the price level and, equally important, just when it will have that effect. Attempting to control directly the price level is therefore likely to make monetary policy itself a source of economic disturbance because of false stops and starts.[9]

A long-term price-level objective would not require the Federal Open Market Committee (FOMC) to react to the highly variable monthly inflation reports on a short-term basis. Since any one month's report contains information mainly about transitory effects, it may tell us very little about the monetary trend. Yet, when the monthly price-level changes are added up over extended periods, the transitory effects offset each other and the monetary trend is revealed.

Analysts often look back to multiperiod averages of inflation in order to discern the underlying trend. The longer the period of averaging, the less important are the transitory effects of real shocks. Thus, in discussing long-term trends, analysts may look at inflation averages going back as far as two to five years. In a sense, the price level is the longest average of all, inasmuch as it is the accumulation of all monthly price changes dating back to the beginning of the index. Unlike the inflation rate, which is highly variable around its trend, the price level maintains a steady relationship vis-a-vis its trend. Thus, the behavior of the price level, when observed against the backdrop of a target path, should provide a steady signal about the thrust of future policy.

Admittedly, the relationship of the current price level to its long-term target path would not tell us what policymakers should do today. Intermediate targets for money or other short-term indicators of policy are still needed to make these near-term decisions. The value of the price-level target is that it would provide a benchmark for long-run decision making. For example, consider the decision that the Federal Reserve must make at the beginning of a new year when the monetary targets are set. If in the previous year the price level was below the long-term path and M2 came in below the midpoint of its target range, the price-level objective would provide clear guidance for raising the M2 path. In the absence of an explicit long-term objective, the FOMC cannot make such a decision without increasing long-run inflation expectations.

THE (NON) PROBLEM OF MULTIPLE OBJECTIVES

There is little doubt that a path for the price level would provide an anchor for the dollar. Some analysts fear, however, that such a path would limit the Federal Reserve's flexibility in meeting its additional responsibilities (such as conducting countercyclical policy and acting as the lender of last resort during financial crises). We believe such fears are unwarranted. Currently, the public cannot clearly distinguish a countercyclical policy action from one that leads to a higher inflation trend. This confusion limits the Fed's ability to conduct countercyclical policy because it induces, at least temporarily, a trade-off between the short-run growth objective and expectations of higher inflation rates in the future. The presence of an explicit path for the price level would enhance the System's ability to communicate policy intentions accurately and, more important, would provide a benchmark against which to judge this communication.

Under the present system, the Federal Reserve is often constrained by financial market expectations. These constraints show up when the market confuses a short-term policy action with a permanent change in long-term goals. For example, in 1982, 1986, and 1991, the System implemented a series of discount-rate cuts in response to weakness in the economy. In each case, the final cut was associated with a subsequent *increase* in the long-term bond rate. In no instance did the Fed consciously adopt a higher inflation objective with its last discount-rate cut, yet the market responded as if it had. Such responses reduce the efficacy of policy actions and would be less likely to occur if the System committed to an explicit path for the price level.

Moreover, a price-level objective would not interfere with the Federal Reserve's flexibility in responding to financial crises. Consider the policy response to the stock market crash of October 19, 1987. To prevent a systemic crisis in the nation's financial system, the Fed immediately eased policy by providing all the liquidity the market needed. The time horizon for maintaining liquidity in the market is much shorter than that for stabilizing the price level. Thus, there was plenty of time following the crash for the FOMC to mop up the excess liquidity that had been pumped into the market.

Perhaps an even more important consequence of achieving price stability is that it would reduce the incidence of financial crises. As economist Anna Schwartz has documented, high and uncertain inflation greatly increases the risk of bank failures and bank runs.[10] That is, financial crises usually occur when prices are falling relative to trend. A price-level objective would enhance financial stability and make such incidents less likely.

CONCLUSION

Price stability is not an end in itself. The reason for seeking price stability is to raise living standards and the quality of life for all Americans. Monetary targeting was effective in containing the runaway inflation of the 1970s, but it has not brought about the end of inflation.

Committing to a long-term trend for a particular price index would help to provide guidance for adjusting monetary targets and maintaining price stability. Such a policy would reduce relative price uncertainty as well as increase the system's flexibility in responding to short-term events. Achieving price stability would create an environment less prone to financial crises and at the same time give the Federal Reserve more latitude in dealing with such emergencies when they arise.

ENDNOTES

1.For a description of the uncertainty inherent in the U.S. price level, see Jeffrey J. Hallman. "Uncertain Inflating and Price-Level Rules," Federal Reserve Bank of Cleveland, *Economic Commentary*, January 15, 1992.

2.The practice of forgiving target misses leads to a phenomenon known as "base drift." For a thorough discussion of base drift in the early years of monetary targeting, see Alfred Broaddus and Marvin Goodfriend, "Base Drift and the Longer Run Growth of M1: Experience from a Decade of Monetary Targeting," Federal Reserve Bank of Richmond, *Economic Review*, vol. 70, no. 6 (November/December 1984), pp. 3-14.

3.See Jeffrey J. Hallman, Richard D. Porter, and David H. Small, "Is the Price Level Tied to the M2 Monetary Aggregate in the Long Run?" *American Economic Review*, vol. 81, no. 4 (September 1991), pp. 841-58.

4.See John B. Carlson and Susan M. Byrne, "Recent Behavior of Velocity: Alternative Measures of Money," Federal Reserve Bank of Cleveland, *Economic Review*, vol. 28, no. 1 (1992 Quarter 1), pp. 2-10.

5.See Paul A. Volcker, "We Can Survive Prosperity," speech presented at the joint meeting of the American Economic Association-American Finance Association, San Francisco, December 38, 1983.

6.See Alan Greenspan, statement before the Committee on Banking, Housing and Urban Affairs of the U.S. Senate, February 21, 1989.

7.This particular target is described more completely in William T. Gavin and Alan C. Stockman, "A Flexible Monetary-Policy Rule for Zero Inflation," Federal Reserve Bank of Cleveland, unpublished manuscript, June 1989.

8.The price-index target was abandoned by the Riksbank in favor of exchange rate targeting in April 1937. For a more detailed description of this episode, see Susan Black and William T. Gavin, "Price Stability and the Swedish Monetary Experiment," Federal Reserve Bank of Cleveland, *Economic Commentary*, December 15, 1990.

9.See Milton Friedman, "The Role of Monetary Policy," *American Economic Review*, vol. 58, no. 1 (March 1968), p. 15.

10.See Anna J. Schwartz, "The Lender of Last Resort and the Federal Safety Net," *Journal of Financial Services Research*, vol. 1 (1987), pp. 77-111.

QUESTIONS

1. Why does the Fed's current practice of setting annual target ranges for money supply growth create uncertainty about future price levels?

2. If the Fed adopted a price level objective as Gavin and Stockman suggest, would month-to-month variations in the inflation rate make monetary policy too erratic? Why?

3. Why do Gavin and Stockman argue that a long-run price level objective gives the Fed more flexibility to use short-run countercyclical policy and to deal with financial crises?

PART SIX

INTERNATIONAL FINANCE

In a world characterized by increasing economic integration and interdependence, the operation of foreign exchange markets and the international financial system have become increasingly important. The five readings for Part VI discuss various aspects of international finance.

Reading 35, "Big MacCurrencies", uses the prices of Big Macs around the globe to estimate the implied purchasing power parity value of the dollar in terms of a number of foreign currencies. It is intended for use with Chapter 21's discussion of long run exchange rate determination.

"Currencies on the Verge of a Nervous Breakdown," Reading 36, supplements Chapter 21's discussion of short run exchange rate determination. It examines the German mark's role as the anchor currency of the European exchange rate mechanism and questions whether the mark can maintain that position in light of rising inflation and budget deficits in Germany.

Reading 37 is "Understanding Latin American Currency Pegs to the Dollar" by William Gruben and John H. Welch. Gruben and Welch explain how exchange rate pegging works and the motivations for pursuing fixed exchange rates. They emphasize that in order for pegging to work, a foreign country must match its monetary policy to that of the U.S. This reading will supplement the discussions of exchange rate determination in Chapter 21 and fixed exchange rates and monetary policy in Chapter 22.

"U.S. Foreign Exchange Rate Operations" by Kristina Jacobson is Reading 38. Jacobson describes how the goals and methods of U.S. foreign exchange operations have evolved under the Bretton Woods fixed exchange rate system and, since 1973, under the floating exchange rate system. Her detailed look at foreign exchange operations can be discussed with either Chapter 21's treatment of intervention in the foreign exchange market or the coverage of the evolution of the international financial system in Chapter 22.

Reading 39 is "European Monetary Union: How Close Is It?" by Michael J. Chriszt. Chriszt reviews the evolution of the European Monetary System, explains how the exchange rate mechanism works, and describes the European Community's recent moves towards monetary union. This reading may be used with Chapter 22's discussion of fixed exchange rates and monetary policy.

READING 35

Big MacCurrencies

The *Economist's* Big Mac index was first launched in 1986 as a ready reckoner to whether currencies are at their "correct" exchange rate. It is time for our annual update.

The case for munching our way around the globe on Big Macs is based on the theory of purchasing-power parity. This argues that the exchange rate between two currencies is in equilibrium when it equalises the prices of an identical basket of goods and services in both countries. Advocates of PPP argue that in the long run currencies tend to move towards their PPP.

Our basket is simply a Big Mac, one of the few products that is produced locally in a great many countries. Many of our readers ask why we do not simply derive our PPPs from different cover prices of *The Economist*. But because the magazine is not printed in every country, local prices would be distorted by transport and distribution costs.

The Big Mac PPP is the exchange rate that leaves hamburgers costing the same in each country. Comparing the current exchange rate with its PPP gives a measure of whether a currency is under- or overvalued.

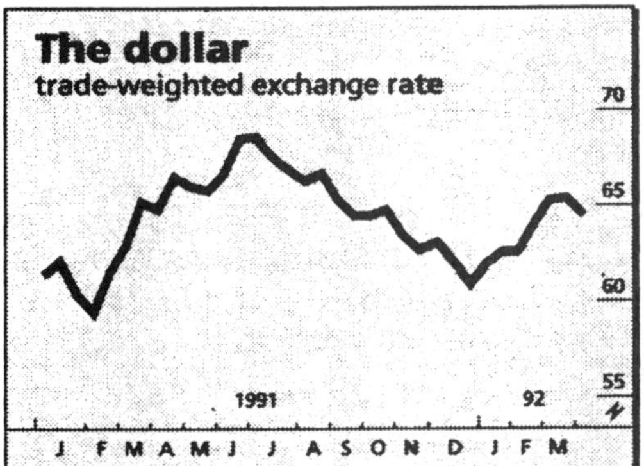

For example, the average price of a Big Mac in four American cities is $2.19. In Japan our Big Mac watcher had to fork out ¥380 ($2.86) for the same gastronomic delight. Dividing the yen price by the dollar price gives a Big Mac PPP of $1=¥174. On April 10th the actual dollar exchange rate was ¥133, which implies that on PPP grounds the dollar is 24% undervalued against the yen.

On similar sums, the dollar is 20% undervalued against the D-mark, with an estimated PPP of DM2.05. The dollar has moved further away from its PPP over the past year: in April 1991 it was undervalued by only 13%. How can the dollar have become more undervalued when its actual exchange rate has barely budged? The answer lies in price movements. Big Mac prices have fallen by an average of 3% in America over the past 12 months; in Germany they have risen by 5%.

As the table shows, the dollar seems to be undervalued against most currencies. The exceptions are the currencies of countries where Big Macs cost less in dollars than in America: the Australian dollar, the Brazilian cruzeiro, the Chinese yuan, the Hong Kong dollar, the Hungarian forint and last, but by no means least, the rouble. Moscow is the best place for burger-bargain hunters: a Big Mac costs only 59 cents at the market exchange rate. In other words, the rouble is undervalued by 73% against the dollar.

An addition to our table this year are three Latin American currencies. The Big Mac index signals, for example, that the Argentine peso is overvalued against the dollar (though much less so against other currencies). Brazil's cruzeiro, however, looks cheap.

Looking at cross rates within Europe suggests that most of the ERM currencies are overvalued against the D-mark on PPP grounds. For example, sterling's PPP is DM2.59, compared with its central rate of DM2.95. This supports those who argue that sterling joined the ERM at too high a rate. Other estimates, however, put sterling's PPP at up to DM3.10.

The hamburger standard

Big Mac prices

Country	Prices* in local currency	Implied PPP** of the dollar	Actual exchange rate 10/4/92	% over(+) or under(-) valuation of dollar
Argentina	Peso3.30	1.51	0.99	–34
Australia	A$2.54	1.16	1.31	+13
Belgium	BFr108	49.32	33.55	–32
Brazil	Cr3,800	1,735	2,153	+24
Britain	£1.74	0.79	0.57	–28
Canada	C$2.76	1.26	1.19	–6
China	Yuan6.30	2.88	5.44	+89
Denmark	DKr27.25	12.44	6.32	–49
France	FFr18.10	8.26	5.55	–33
Germany	DM 4.50	2.05	1.64	–20
Holland	Fl 5.35	2.44	1.84	–24
Hong Kong	HK$8.90	4.06	7.73	+91
Hungary	Forint133	60.73	79.70	+31
Ireland	I£1.45	0.66	0.61	–8
Italy	Lire4,100	1872	1,233	–34
Japan	¥380	174	133	–24
Russia	Rouble58	26.48	98.95†	+273
Singapore	S$4.75	2.17	1.65	–24
S.Korea	Won2,300	1,050	778	–26
Spain	Ptas315	144	102	–29
Sweden	SKr25.50	11.64	5.93	–49
United States††	$2.19	—	—	—
Venezuela	Bs 170	77.63	60.63	–22

Source: McDonald's * prices may vary locally, ** Purchasing-power parity: local price divided by dollar price, † Market rate, †† New York, Chicago, San Francisco and Atlanta

Some readers find the Big Mac index hard to digest. To be sure, hamburgers are primitive predictors of exchange rates. Local price differences may be distorted by taxes, property costs or trade barriers. Nevertheless, the Big Mac can provide a rough and ready guide to how currencies might move over the long term. Experts who calculate PPPs by more sophisticated means come up with results that are not radically different. Indeed, many of them suggest that the dollar is even more undervalued than the hamburger standard indicates.

The message, therefore, is that the greenback should rise in the future. But when? Exchange rates can deviate significantly from PPPs for long periods.

Yet other economic fundamentals now seem to point in the same direction. Most currency-watchers expect interest rates to rise in America over the next 12 months as the economy picks up steam. Germany's interest rates may fall as its economy continues to stall. If so, interest-rate differentials will move in favour of the dollar and the greenback will rise. It has already gained almost 10% against the yen and the D-mark since January, and most forecasters are betting it will climb further this year.

The snag is that forecasters used the same arguments about relative interest rates a year ago, and that expectation helped to push the dollar up by 27% against the D-mark in the five months to July. As America's recovery faltered, the Fed cut interest rates again, and inflation fears caused Germany's Bundesbank to raise its rates further. The dollar slid, to end the year little higher than it began.

Forecasts of a firmer dollar are therefore only as firm as forecasts of economic recovery. Wise investors will not hold their breath—and will grab those cut-price Big Macs while they can.

QUESTIONS

1. Why does The Economist use a Big Mac to measure the purchasing power parity exchange rate for the dollar?

2. How is the implied PPP of the dollar derived? How is the percent over or under valuation of the dollar derived?

3. The Economist says that the dollar should rise in the future. What is the basis for this prediction?

READING 36

Currencies on the Verge of a Nervous Breakdown

The European exchange-rate mechanism (ERM) has been dominated by the D-mark almost since its birth in 1979. Decades of sound money in West Germany made its currency the ideal anchor for the system. No longer. With inflation, government borrowing and strikes on the rise, united Germany is hardly the iron man of Europe.

The ERM was designed as a multilateral system. In theory, if one country's currency hit its floor against another's, both governments had to take action. But in practice it was weak-currency countries that sprang into action, raising interest rates to keep their currencies in touch with the rock-solid D-mark.

Many countries saw pegging their money to the D-mark—in effect, handing monetary control to the Bundesbank, Europe's most independent central bank—as the best route to low inflation. But Germany no longer has the lowest inflation in the ERM: in seven of the other ten member countries prices are rising at less than Germany's 12-month rate of 4.8%. And the German government has abandoned sound finance: its huge budget deficit, equal to around 6% of GNP, has forced the Bundesbank to push interest rates to their highest level since 1945.

This causes two worries about the ERM. The first is whether a relatively high-inflation currency can continue to anchor the system. The risk in a drifting anchor is that inflationary expectations in all ERM countries will drift upwards with it. But replacements for the D-mark are thin on the ground. Denmark currently has the lowest inflation rate in the ERM, at 2.3%, but its economy is too small to act as an anchor. The French franc is the strongest candidate: France's inflation is 3.2% and its budget deficit one of the smallest in the EC. The snag is that its low-inflation virtue is relatively recent. And France's central bank, unlike the Bundesbank, is not independent of its government; if French unemployment continues to rise, politicians might be tempted to cut interest rates in order to spur growth.

The markets still believe the D-mark is the best anchor, and back the Bundesbank to

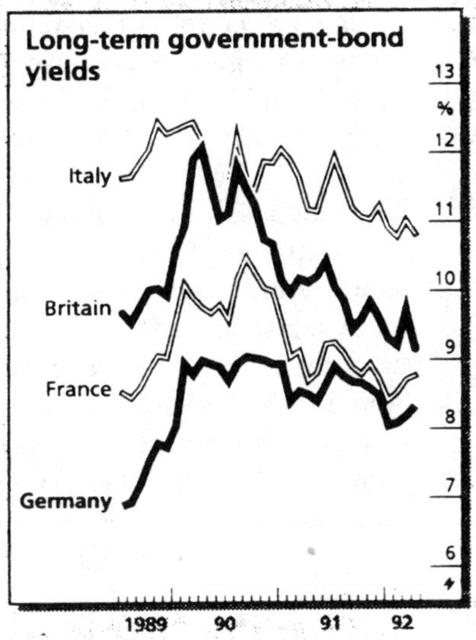

Inflation rates, %

	1979-88 annual average	Latest
Denmark	7.1	2.3
Belgium	5.0	2.7
Luxembourg	4.8	2.8
France	7.7	3.2
Ireland	9.7	3.7
Britain	7.3	4.0
Holland	3.0	4.2
Western Germany	**2.9**	**4.8**
Italy	11.6	5.6
Spain	10.6	6.9
Portugal	18.0	8.0

Source: OECD

beat inflation. This is shown by the fact that Germany's long-term government-bond yields remain the lowest in the ERM; they have actually fallen over the past 18 months, and are now only half a percentage point higher than just before the collapse of the Berlin Wall, in November 1989.

But it is hard to see yields falling much further. Recent pay rises in Germany have been excessive. Broad money, M3, grew by an annualised 9.7% in the first quarter of this year, well above its target range of 3½ - 5½%. The Bundesbank is unlikely to cut rates for some time. It may even raise them. That gives rise to the second ERM worry: for how long will German interest rates depress growth in the rest of Europe?

Interest-rate differentials between Germany and other countries have narrowed over the past three years. In 1989 France's short-term interest rates were three percentage points above Germany's; today they are only a quarter of a point higher. But German short rates—now 9.8%—nonetheless set a floor for those in the rest of the ERM. Other countries must stick to higher real interest rates than their sluggish economies need.

The gap between two countries' interest rates reflects the expected future movement in their exchange rates. Take France as an example: the markets have traditionally kept French interest rates above Germany's, to make up for the greater risk that the franc might be devalued. As French inflation has dwindled, so has that risk, and with it the devaluation premium included in French interest rates. But French rates cannot actually fall below Germany's for long, unless investors expect the D-mark to be devalued against the French franc. Alone among the ERM's eight original currencies, the D-Mark has never been devalued against another currency. This looks unlikely to change.

The best way to lower European interest rates would be for Germany to cut its budget deficit, so letting the Bundesbank ease monetary policy. This is unrealistic at present. An alternative is to revalue the D-mark against all other ERM currencies.

Had the D-mark been revalued in 1990, at the time of unification, it would have helped dampen Germany's economic boom, and inflation could have been kept in check at lower interest rates. Other ERM countries would now have lower interest rates than they do, and their exports would have grown to meet Germany's demand.

Now, however, the benefits to be had from revaluing the D-mark are less clear. A big revaluation (more than 10%, say) would help to reduce inflationary pressures in Germany and so allow the Bundesbank to cut interest rates a bit sooner than it now looks likely to do. But it would not, as some argue, help other ERM economies to cut their rates. On the contrary, these might well rise relative to Germany's, because any realignment, after so long a period of stability, would most likely increase the perceived risk of future devaluations of non-German currencies. Speculation about realignment has caused most countries' bond yields to rise against Germany's since the autumn.

A stronger D-mark would, at least in the short term, make other countries' exports more attractive. But the revaluation would have to be large to make much difference. And there's the rub. France's support for any general realignment is crucial, and France would not accept a big one—or indeed any devaluation of the franc against the D-mark. It is committed to its *franc fort*—strong franc—policy.

There are other problems too. Purchasing-power parities suggest that the D-mark is already overvalued against the other big member currencies. Indeed, with wage costs in France rising less than half as fast as in Germany, French exports have already become more competitive. Governments may remain opposed to a nominal revaluation of the D-mark, but its real exchange rate (allowing for inflation) is already rising.

QUESTIONS

1. Why are German interest rates at post-World War II high levels? Predict how this will affect the currencies of the other member countries of the European exchange-rate mechanism and illustrate with a diagram of exchange rate equilibrium.

2. "The gap between two countries' interest rates reflects the expected future movements in their exchange rates." Explain this in terms of the interest parity condition.

3. What has happened in recent years to the interest rate differentials between Germany and other ERM countries? If German interest rates rise above French interest rates, what is implied about the expected exchange rate for the mark?

4. The reading argues that if the German mark were revalued upward by 10%, interest rates in the other ERM countries might rise. Explain and illustrate with a diagram of exchange rate equilibrium.

READING 37

Understanding Latin American Currency Pegs to the Dollar

William C. Gruben and John H. Welch

Latin American countries have been making major changes in their economic policies in recent years, but one reform of particular importance to U.S. monetary policy has been scarcely noticed in the United States. Argentina, Chile, Bolivia and Mexico have begun to peg their currencies to the U.S. dollar. (See the box titled "A Glossary of Exchange Rate Regimes.")

When a country pegs its currency to the dollar, that country's government sets a limit on the price of its currency relative to the dollar. If the amount of that country's currency required to buy a dollar rises above the limit, the government uses its reserve of dollars to buy its own currency in an effort to bid the exchange rate back to the limit.

For example, Argentina has established an exchange rate peg with a limit of one peso per dollar. If the amount of pesos required to buy a dollar rises above one, the Argentine government purchases pesos with U.S. dollars to bring Argentina's exchange rate within the limit.

By fixing their exchange rates to the dollar instead of allowing them to fluctuate freely, Latin American countries are effectively importing U.S. monetary policy. Thus, these new Latin American currency ties increase the importance of U.S. monetary stability because the effects of instability will be amplified in other parts of the world.

A simple explanation of why countries peg their currencies to the dollar is to facilitate investment and trade and to hold down inflation. This article explains how exchange rate pegging works, why exchange rate pegs amount to importing U.S. monetary policy and what motivates countries to import U.S. monetary policy instead of pursuing their own.

HOW EXCHANGE RATE PEGGING WORKS

If a foreign country pegs its exchange rate to the dollar, the consequences of failing to follow U.S. monetary policy can be severe. Suppose a country that pegs its exchange rate to the dollar launches a highly expansionary monetary policy, but the United States does not. The inflation rate in the pegging country will probably be higher than in the United States because inflation, by definition, is too much money chasing too few goods.

When a country's exchange rate is pegged to the dollar, the price of dollars in the other country's currency is supposed to remain fixed, no matter what. As the prices of goods produced in the foreign country rise faster than prices of U.S. products, U.S. buyers will purchase fewer of the foreign country's products. For the same reason, the foreign country's buyers will import more products from the United States and will purchase fewer products from home.

As demand in the foreign country falls off, unemployment rises there. Ultimately, unemployment rises because the combination of exchange rate pegging and a high rate of monetary expansion make the country's products increasingly expensive relative to products from the United States, where inflation is lower. (The box titled "Prices and Inflation in Countries with Flexible Exchange Rates" describes the effects of inflation and rising prices in countries without currency pegs to the dollar.)

In sum, an exchange rate peg to the dollar amounts to importing U.S. monetary policy because a foreign country with a currency peg can suffer highly punitive consequences by failing to match its monetary policy to that of the United States. Furthermore, this country will eventually lose all of its dollar reserves and will ultimately have to abandon its attempts to peg to the dollar. That is, it will no longer be able to defend its fixed exchange rate by purchasing its currency with dollars.

WHY COUNTRIES IMPORT MONETARY POLICY

With such severe consequences, why would anyone want a pegged currency? For Latin American countries, the answer is that they want to establish stable, anti-inflationary monetary policies, and to make them credible to potential investors and other observers.

Credibility is an important issue because a government's stated policy is not always a credible policy. Latin American countries have often shifted far from stated policies of monetary stability; new policies that emphasize stability are often met with fears that they will not last.

Latin American countries want price stability because it facilitates trade and stimulates investment by improving firms' abilities to predict selling prices and the costs of doing business. A stable monetary policy, like that of the United States, goes a long way toward establishing price stability.

During the early 1980s, many Latin American countries moved away from stable monetary policies. These moves cause Latin America a good deal of difficulty and

A Glossary of Exchange Rate Regimes

Exchange rates can be determined by several methods. At one extreme is a *pegged*, or *fixed, exchange rate* policy, in which the central bank fixes the price of its currency at a constant value and exchanges a foreign currency, such as the U.S. dollar, for the local currency at the constant value. The central bank becomes the main supplier of foreign exchange to the market. The central bank's ability to support its own currency's exchange value depends on the size of central bank dollar holdings.

At the other extreme is a *floating*, or *market-based, exchange rate* policy, in which exchange rates are determined completely in the market, with little or no intervention by the central bank. If the market for foreign exchange is not well-developed, small movements in the demand for and supply of dollars causes large exchange rate movements.

Any exchange rate that is not fixed through a currency peg is considered a *flexible exchange rate*. Numerous arrangements fall between the extremes of fixed and market-based exchange rates. The most common type in Latin America is a *crawling peg*. In a crawling peg regime, the central bank increases the price of the dollar over time to maintain the competitiveness of domestic goods in international markets. In this sense, crawling pegs resemble market-based exchange rate regimes. On the other hand, the central bank buys and sells dollars at an announced exchange rate and continues to be the main source of foreign exchange, making the crawling peg more like the fixed rate regime.

aggravated pre-existing problems that stemmed from events in the 1970s.

In the 1970s, many Latin American countries had borrowed money to develop new industries or to expand existing ones. Historically, most Latin American countries have been large exporters of raw materials, and during the 1970s, raw materials prices were high. These countries expected that continued high prices would allow them to pay off their loans.

When interest rates rose and raw materials prices fell sharply in the early 1980s, Latin American countries began to have difficulty making their debt payments. The declines in raw materials prices led to falling incomes and serious government revenue problems for many Latin American countries.

To expand exports and contract imports, these countries began to devalue their currencies against the dollar. To address their revenue problems, these countries would then print money at very expansionary rates. As the resulting inflation put new pressures on their exchange rates, these countries would again devalue. Protracted cycles of devaluation, inflation and more devaluation began to appear in some countries—and their business communities soon began to expect such cycles and to suspect government claims that the cycles would stop.

Prices and Inflation in Countries with Flexible Exchange Rates

Countries that do not peg the value of their currency to the dollar are pursuing a flexible exchange rate policy and, thus, are not importing U.S. monetary policy. If a country with a flexible exchange rate pursues a monetary policy that is more expansionary than the United States', exchange rate adjustments will eventually push domestic and foreign demand for traded goods back to their pre-inflation relationships. With pegged exchange rates, this adjustment does not occur.

How does this adjustment process take place with flexible exchange rates? Just as in the case of pegged exchange rates, rising prices in the foreign country discourage demand for this country's products. Because foreign buyers want to purchase fewer of the country's goods, their demand for the country's currency also declines. The increased prices in the foreign country will mean that both its citizens and U.S. buyers will choose to purchase more U.S. products and, therefore, demand more U.S. dollars.

Because of the reduced demand for the foreign country's currency and of the increased demand for U.S. currency, the price of U.S. currency in terms of the foreign currency will rise. For the same reason, the price of the foreign currency in terms of U.S. currency decreases. That is, everyone must now exchange more of the foreign currency to buy a dollar.

Consequently, flexible exchange rates counteract the effects of higher inflation in the foreign country. As prices rise in the foreign country, the value of its currency in terms of dollars falls. There is no longer any extra incentive to purchase U.S. goods over home-country goods.

The cycles of devaluation and inflation only aggravated economic uncertainty that had already emerged. For Latin America, the 1980s came to be called *the Lost Decade.* Both income and investment shrank. Technology in developed countries continued to advance rapidly, however, and the drop-off in Latin American investment resulted in increasing technological backwardness in the region.

Meanwhile, the depression of raw materials prices persisted, and many Latin American leaders realized that they would have to concentrate more on manufactured exports and less on the export of raw materials. To facilitate low-cost manufacturing production by allowing imported inputs, to hold down inflation and also to placate rising protectionist pressures in the large U.S. market, Latin American countries began to lower their trade barriers. These countries also began to privatize their publicly owned industries and to pursue stable fiscal and monetary policies.

These measures alone might have achieved what Latin American governments wanted, if these governments had not had histories of reneging on new policies. But these histories created a credibility problem. If no one believes a reform will persist, even the most well-designed and well-intentioned policy can fail.

Latin American governments can only regain full credibility by maintaining stable monetary and financial policies over a protracted period. But there are ways of accelerating credibility.

One way for a government to enhance credibility is to let the business community see easily and quickly if the government is cheating. Currency pegging is one such signal. Currency pegging can lead to a stable monetary policy, and it can allow the business community to identify deviations from stable policy.

Currency pegging can hasten credibility because of the consequences of pursuing a highly expansionary monetary policy when a government is trying to maintain a fixed exchange rate. If a country with a peg to the dollar begins to print enough money to make inflation a good deal higher at home than in the United States, people will want less of that country's currency and more dollars as that country prices its products out of the market. If that happens and the government wants to maintain its fixed exchange rate, the government must spend its foreign currency reserves to buy back its own currency. That is the only way the government could keep its currency's exchange rate at the old levels. If the government did not spend these reserves in this way, the international price of its currency would fall, which means that the exchange rate would no longer be fixed.

But as the government intervenes in the foreign currency markets, it runs down its foreign currency reserves. The loss of such reserves would be easily noticeable, and the business community might suspect that this meant the country had been expanding its domestic currency stock imprudently. Investors who were bringing money into the country would pull out in fear of a devaluation and further inflation. Those who were planning to invest might change their minds.

If the country ran out of reserves, it would have to devalue. The devaluation would aggravate inflation by sharply increasing the price of imports. And a new round of inflation, bad in and of itself, would trigger yet another round of economic decline. In sum, a country with a fixed exchange rate has an added incentive to limit inflation, and the private sector knows it.

WHY LATIN AMERICA MAY NOT ALWAYS WANT TO IMPORT U.S. MONETARY POLICY

Latin American economies differ a good deal from ours. Economic shocks that affect the United States in one way may affect some Latin American countries in quite another way. As a result, the optimal path of monetary growth for the United States or Argentina or Chile or Mexico will not always be the same, even if all these nations are working in earnest to preserve economic stability.

Ultimately, when the business community takes for granted a Latin American government's commitment to hold down inflation, that country might safely uncouple its currency from the dollar. With a credible, demonstrated commitment to keep inflation low, a government can pursue a stable monetary policy on its own and allow its exchange rate to adjust to external market forces. This independence would allow the rate to accommodate price movements that are not tied to excessive internal monetary expansion. After all, not every price movement is solely a result of monetary expansion.

QUESTIONS

1. What is meant by "pegging" a currency? How will Latin American countries benefit from pegging their currencies to the dollar?

2. Explain what a foreign country must do to keep its currency pegged to the dollar if U.S. is pursuing an expansionary monetary policy? What if the U.S. is pursuing a restrictive monetary policy? What happens if the foreign country does not match the U.S. monetary policy?

3. Must a country match U.S. monetary policy if exchange rates are flexible? Explain.

4. What economic events during the 1970s and 1980s led Latin American countries to peg their currencies to the dollar?

READING 38

U.S. Foreign Exchange Operations

Kristina Jacobson

The volume of U.S. official foreign exchange operations has grown substantially in recent years. In 1989, the total volume of U.S. transactions in the exchange market was over $20 billion, the highest ever. At the same time, because recent U.S. operations have usually involved the purchase of foreign currency, U.S. foreign currency balances have grown to record levels, reaching nearly $45 billion in December 1989.[1]

Such changes in U.S. foreign exchange operations reflect the evolving nature of U.S. exchange rate policy over the postwar period. During the Bretton Woods system of fixed exchange rates, which lasted from 1947 to 1973, the primary goal of U.S. operations was to maintain the dollar price of gold, chiefly through official transactions with foreign authorities. With the shift to floating exchange rates in the early 1970s, the focus of U.S. operations has been to counter disorderly conditions, primarily through direct intervention in the market.

This article describes how the goals and methods of U.S. foreign exchange operations have changed over time. The first section reviews the institutional framework for U.S. foreign exchange operations. The second section discusses the role of the United States in the Bretton Woods system of fixed exchange rates and U.S. exchange rate policy goals and methods during that time. The third section discusses the goals and methods of U.S. operations during the floating-rate regime.

I. FRAMEWORK FOR OPERATIONS

The U.S. Treasury and the Federal Reserve System cooperate in formulating and implementing U.S. exchange rate policy. In a broad sense, because foreign economic policy falls under the Treasury's domain, the Treasury is ultimately responsible for exchange rate policy. However, the Fed consults with the Treasury on deciding exchange rate policy and directly implements that policy.

The foreign exchange desk at the Federal Reserve Bank of New York conducts all U.S. foreign exchange operations, using Treasury and Federal Reserve funds. Since 1978, the Fed and the Treasury have generally shared equally in financing operations. The Treasury pays for its portion of operations with its Exchange Stabilization Fund (ESF).[2] The Federal Reserve System pays for its operations with an account owned by all 12 Federal Reserve banks. The Federal Open Market Committee (FOMC), the Fed's principle policymaking body, regulates operations for the Fed's foreign exchange account.[3]

The Treasury reports the U.S. foreign exchange policy goal in general terms to the International Monetary Fund (IMF). The IMF is an international organization designed to promote cooperation in international monetary and payment issues. Currently, the goal of U.S. foreign exchange operations as reported to the IMF is to counter disorderly market conditions or to act when "otherwise deemed appropriate" (International Monetary Fund 1986). The Federal Reserve recognizes the Treasury's goal and ensures that operations for the System foreign exchange account will follow the Treasury's commitment to the IMF.

The FOMC manages the System account through three formal documents: the Foreign Currency Directive, the Authorization for Foreign Currency Operations, and the Procedural Instructions. These documents require that Fed operations be "conducted in close and continuous consultation and cooperation with the United States Treasury" (Board of Governors 1989). The documents also provide guidelines on financing arrangements between the Fed and foreign authorities or the U.S. Treasury. The FOMC also formally and informally monitors the size of System foreign currency balances. For any operations not falling within the guidelines, the foreign desk must seek approval from the entire FOMC or a delegated subcommittee of the members.

Each day, the foreign desk must decide whether and how to intervene within the guidelines agreed upon with the Treasury. To provide the desk with up-to-the-minute information, staff members at the New York Fed continuously watch the 24-hour, worldwide foreign exchange market and convey significant developments to the Treasury and the Fed's Board of Governors in Washington, D.C. Treasury and Board staffs also study the market, but the New York Fed follows developments most closely. Each morning, New York staff members call various commercial banks to obtain the latest exchange rate quotes and to get a "feel" for the market. New York staff members may also call foreign central banks to coordinate foreign exchange operations. If the desk plans to conduct operations, the manager of the foreign desk determines exactly when and how to act. In making intervention decisions, the manager consults officials at the Treasury and the Board.

The rest of this article reviews the goals and methods of U.S. foreign exchange operations, first during the fixed-rate regime and then during the floating-rate regime.

II. FIXED-RATE REGIME: GOALS AND METHODS

The Bretton Woods system of fixed exchange rates lasted from 1947 to March 1973. The U.S. dollar was the center of the system and the value to which other countries pegged their currencies. The role of foreign authorities was to intervene in the foreign exchange market to maintain the value of their currency relative to the dollar. For example, if it was deemed necessary to cause the pound to rise against the dollar, British authorities bought pounds, increasing the demand for the pound and pushing up its price. Alternatively, to cause the pound to fall against the dollar, British authorities sold pounds, increasing the supply of pounds and pushing down the pound's price.

In contrast to the role of foreign authorities, the role of the United States was to maintain the dollar price of gold at $35 an ounce. The United States stood ready to sell gold to foreign authorities who wished to convert dollars acquired through foreign exchange operations. The annual U.S. notification of its exchange rate goal to the IMF stated this commitment.[4]

The allowable limits of exchange rate fluctuation were small during the fixed-rate regime, except for occasional currency devaluations or revaluations.[5] For example, in the mid-1960s, the pound was frequently under downward pressure in part because of a large British trade deficit. The downward pressure continued despite efforts of global monetary authorities to maintain the currency's value. Consequently, in 1967, British authorities devalued the pound (Chart 1).

Although exchange rate fluctuations were generally small during the fixed-rate period, exchange rate pressures surfaced in other ways. Because authorities used their reserves to intervene in the market to maintain fixed exchange rates, pressure on exchange rates was evident through changes in the size of official reserves, such as dollar holdings of foreign officials and the U.S. gold stock. For example, the U.S. gold stock dropped substantially during the 1960s, as the United States upheld its obligation to sell gold for dollars obtained by foreign authorities through their foreign exchange operations (Chart 2). In addition, as a result of exchange rate pressures, governments sometimes changed monetary and fiscal policy.[6]

Operations to Protect the U.S. Gold Stock

The convertibility of dollars into gold was the foundation of the Bretton Woods regime. Foreign authorities were willing to hold dollars because the United States assured their convertibility into gold at a fixed price. During the 1960s, however, the fixed-rate system showed signs of strain. The dollar was under downward pressure, largely because of the U.S. current account deficit. To counter downward pressure on the dollar, foreign authorities bought dollars in the market and consequently built up large dollar reserves. As foreign authorities exchanged their excess dollar balances for gold and the U.S. gold stock fell, concern grew about whether the United States could continue to

Chart 1
The Bretton Woods Period: Foreign Exchange Value of the Dollar
(Foreign currency units per dollar)

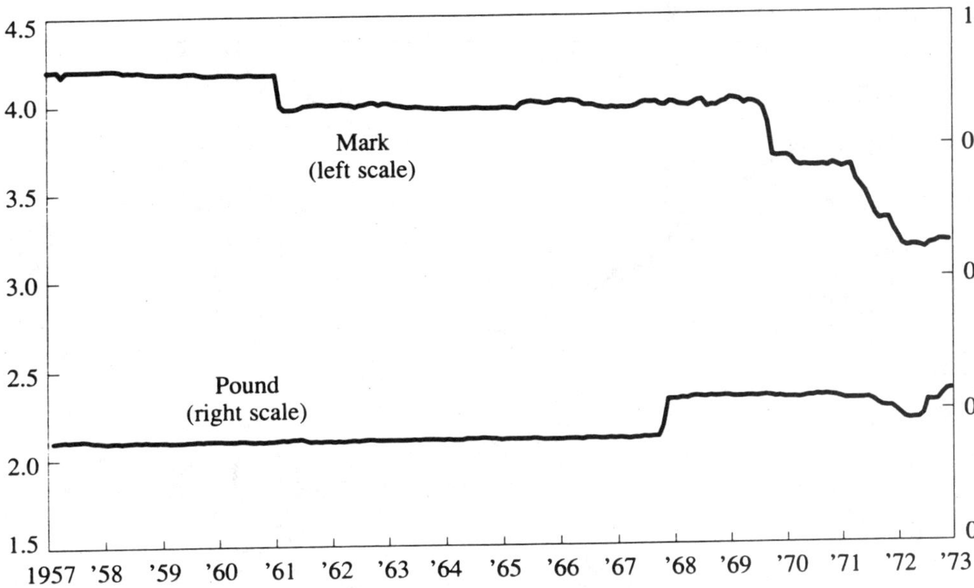

Source: *Federal Reserve Bulletin*, various issues.

convert dollars into gold. Early in the decade, with downward pressure on the dollar intensifying, the United States began to act to protect its gold stock and the global monetary system. Four basic methods were used in this effort.

First, the United States borrowed foreign currency through a swap network. The swap network is a mechanism through which U.S. and foreign authorities may temporarily exchange domestic and foreign currency. The swap network consists of a series of reciprocal credit agreements between U.S. and foreign authorities.[7] In effect, each country agrees to exchange its currency for foreign currency on demand, up to an agreed-amount. The country initiating the exchange is the borrower; the other country is the creditor. The borrower purchases foreign currency from the creditor and agrees to sell the currency back at the same exchange rate on a specified date, usually in three months. The borrower may extend the swap if both parties agree.[8]

During the fixed-rate regime, the United States borrowed through the swap network

Chart 2
The Bretton Woods Period: U.S. Gold Stock

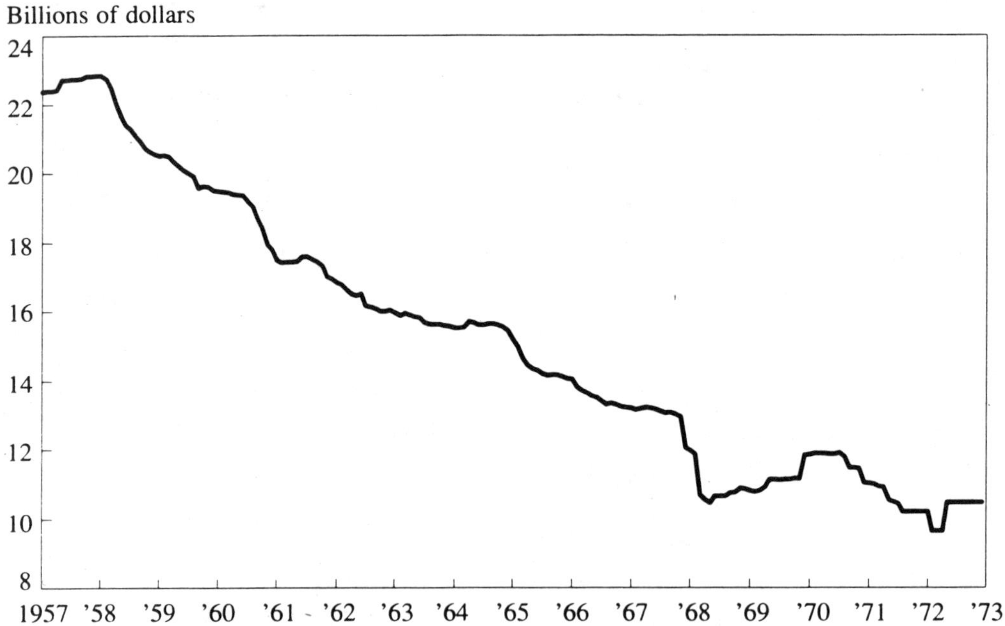

Source: Data Resources, Inc.

primarily to relieve exchange rate risk on dollars held by foreign authorities. Because the dollar was frequently under downward pressure, foreign authorities holding large amounts of their reserves in dollars were at risk that the dollar would be devalued, causing their reserves to lose value. Through the swap network, the United States borrowed foreign currency to purchase a portion of the dollars held by foreign authorities, decreasing the dollar holdings of the foreign authorities. In this way, U.S. authorities hoped to limit the amount of dollars foreign authorities converted into gold. By absorbing some of the dollars foreign authorities did not want, the Unites States hoped to buy time for exchange market conditions to stabilize.

The United States also loaned dollars to foreign authorities through the swap network. For example, with the pound under downward pressure in the mid-1960s, the United States loaned dollars to the Bank of England so it could intervene to maintain the pound's value.

A second method U.S. authorities used during the fixed-rate regime was to sell foreign-currency-denominated bonds, called "Roosa bonds," to foreign authorities.[9] These bonds served as a source of foreign currency to purchase the dollar reserves of foreign authorities and to repay swap debt. For example, in May 1963, the United States sold $30 million equivalent of Belgian-franc-denominated bonds to the Belgian authorities and used the proceeds to buy surplus dollars held by the Belgian authorities. Also, in August 1963, the United States sold a $50 million two-year mark bond to the West German authorities and used the proceeds to repay earlier U.S. borrowing of marks through the swap network. In this way, the United States limited how long a swap remained outstanding (Coombs 1963).

The third method used to protect the gold stock involved drawing on the U.S. reserve position in the IMF. The United States and other IMF members pay quotas, or membership fees, to the IMF. These quotas provide most of the resources the IMF lends to member countries in pursuit of its goals. The United States drew down from its reserve position at various times during the Bretton Woods period. For example, in 1965, the United States drew foreign currency to buy excess dollars from foreign authorities and to pay off swap borrowing. Paying off swap borrowing by drawing from the IMF provided another way to limit how long a swap was outstanding.

Finally, as a fourth method to protect the U.S. gold stock, U.S. and foreign authorities cooperated to keep the market price of gold from rising above the official $35 rate. The United States was concerned that a high market price for gold would induce foreign authorities to exchange their dollar reserves at the U.S. gold window. To keep the market price of gold from rising above the official price, the United States and other nations formed an organization called the gold pool, which sold gold in the London market from 1961 to 1968. However, this effort met with limited success.

Operations in the Foreign Exchange Market

Although the chief role of the United States during the fixed-rate period was to maintain the fixed price of gold, U.S. authorities also on rare instances intervened directly in the foreign exchange market. At times, the intervention was undertaken to reduce pressure on foreign authorities to buy dollars—by limiting the number of dollars bought and held by foreign authorities, the United States hoped to decrease the amount of gold it would have to sell. At other times, the intervention was undertaken to calm financial markets. For example, after the assassination of President Kennedy in 1963, U.S. authorities entered the exchange market to counter speculative pressures and provide assurance that U.S. international financial policy had not changed. Two other notable episodes of U.S. intervention came in 1965 and in 1967, both in response to downward pressure on the British pound. In these episodes, the United States purchased pounds to help British authorities maintain the value of the pound. Although U.S. intervention was infrequent during the fixed-rate period, U.S. authorities did undertake various types of intervention. In conducting its direct intervention, the desk had several choices on how to approach the market, depending on exchange market conditions and the goal of the intervention. For example, the desk at times dealt directly with a commercial bank. The commercial bank in turn was free to inform other market participants as it saw fit. The market may have interpreted such operations as a signal about how U.S. officials viewed exchange rates.

At other times, the desk preferred to approach the market indirectly by asking a commercial bank to act on its behalf. The commercial bank would act just as it would act for any other customer and would be precluded from revealing on whose behalf it was acting. Also, the desk on occasion chose to act passively, responding to an offer privately placed in the market rather than initiating an operation at a certain rate. The desk might have used this approach when trading was thin in order to restrain the impact that an aggressively pursued transaction might have had on the market.

Intervention by the foreign desk, no matter what the approach, has had implications for the operations of the domestic desk at the Federal Reserve Bank of New York. The domestic desk automatically offsets, or sterilizes, the effect of any U.S. exchange market intervention on the U.S. money supply. It does so by buying or selling U.S. Treasury securities as part of its "open market operations."[10] For example, when the foreign desk sells dollars for foreign currency to counter upward pressure on the dollar, the U.S. money supply increases as the dollars enter the U.S. banking system. To offset this intervention, the domestic desk sells Treasury securities to drain the dollars created by the intervention.

Because the United States sterilizes all of its intervention, the end result of a U.S. exchange market intervention is a change in the relative supplies of U.S. and foreign bonds held by the public. In the above example, the domestic desk's sale of Treasury securities adds to the supply of Treasury securities held by the public; hence, the relative supply of U.S. Treasury securities increases as a result of the sterilized intervention.

Sterilized intervention is generally thought to affect exchange rates less than nonsterilized intervention does. Nonsterilized intervention changes the size of the U.S. money supply because no offsetting purchase or sale of Treasury securities occurs. A change in the U.S. money supply directly affects the exchange rate because the supply of dollars relative to foreign currency changes. Also, a change in the U.S. money supply may influence U.S. interest rates and U.S. economic activity, which in turn may affect the exchange rate. Sterilized intervention, on the other hand, does not change the size of the U.S. money supply. However, to the extent investors regard foreign and domestic bonds as imperfect substitutes, the change in relative bond supplies may cause some exchange rate adjustment. In addition, sterilized intervention may influence the exchange rate by signaling a change in U.S. economic policy.[11] Nevertheless, most research suggests that sterilized intervention—in the absence of a fundamental change in U.S. economic policy—probably does not have a lasting effect on the foreign exchange value of the dollar.[12]

III. FLOATING-RATE REGIME: GOALS AND METHODS

Despite efforts by U.S. and foreign authorities, the Bretton Woods system remained under pressure in the 1960s and early 1970s. This pressure resulted mainly from imbalances in international payments positions of several countries. Concern about U.S. ability to maintain convertibility of the dollar also persisted. In 1971, the U.S. Treasury suspended converting dollars into gold and foreign currency. Although efforts to maintain the Bretton Woods regime continued over the next two years, the fixed-rate system collapsed by March 1973. Fixed exchange rates between the dollar and most major currencies no longer were in effect, and exchange rates moved in response to market forces.[13]

During the floating-rate regime, from March 1973 to the present, the United States has conducted foreign exchange operations primarily to counter disorderly markets. The U.S. report to the IMF has reflected this goal.[14] At times, U.S. authorities have interpreted the objective narrowly, focusing market operations on efforts to counter short-term market disorder. At other times, U.S. authorities have interpreted the objective more broadly, acting to adjust exchange rates considered out of line with economic fundamentals. In 1985, the United States officially broadened its foreign exchange market goal to include both countering disorderly markets and entering the market when "otherwise deemed appropriate" (International Monetary Fund 1986). During the floating-rate regime, the focus of U.S. operations has been direct intervention in the foreign exchange market in response to movements in exchange rates. The dollar's value has varied substantially over the period (Chart 3). This section reviews the changes in U.S. foreign exchange market goals and methods during the floating-rate regime.

Narrow Interpretation: 1973 to 1977

In the years immediately after the Bretton Woods system broke down, the United States directed most of its foreign exchange market intervention toward countering disorderly markets in the narrow sense. Narrowly defined, characteristics of a disorderly market include sharp exchange rate movements, thin trading, and wide spreads between the rates at which market participants are willing to buy (bid rates) and the rates at which they are willing to sell (ask rates). The volume of U.S. intervention from 1973 to 1977 was relatively small. The dollar rose and fell during these years in response to changing market perceptions of economic fundamentals. When the dollar fell sharply, U.S. authorities frequently bought dollars to stabilize market conditions. The United States paid for these purchase by using its foreign currency reserves and by borrowing through the swap network. To accommodate this borrowing, U.S. authorities expanded swap lines with

Chart 3
The Floating-Rate Period: Trade-Weighted Value of the Dollar

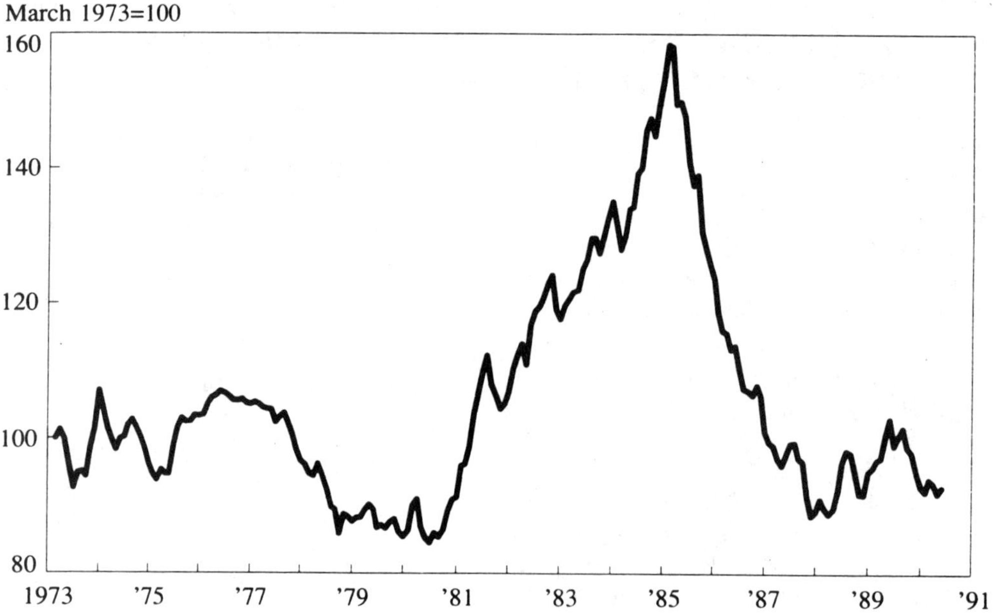

Source: Board of Governors of the Federal Reserve System.

several countries. During periods when the dollar rose, U.S. authorities took the opportunity to purchase foreign currency to repay debts.

An example of U.S. operations during this period was the purchase of dollars in July 1973 to "assist the market in finding solid footing" (Coombs 1973). At the time, the dollar was under downward pressure, in part because of rising interest rates in Europe and market concern about inflationary pressures in the United States. The foreign exchange market showed signs of disorder, including wide bid-ask spreads and thin trading. Trading became so disorderly at times that some New York banks withdrew from the market.

Another notable episode of U.S. intervention was in February 1975, when the United States, Germany, and Switzerland purchased dollars in the first major concerted intervention during the floating-rate period. The dollar was falling because of a severe U.S. recession, a decline in U.S. interest rates relative to foreign rates, and rising inflation in the United States relative to several other countries. These developments had a strong impact because the market doubted whether U.S. economic policy could contain inflationary pressures.

Broad Interpretation: 1978 to 1980

In the late 1970s, the dollar declined sharply, prompting authorities to act more forcefully. The trade-weighted value of the dollar declined 20 percent from June 1976 to October 1978, largely because of market concern about economic imbalances among major industrial nations (Chart 3). The U.S. economy was experiencing rising inflation and a worsening current account deficit. In contrast, other countries, such as Japan and Germany, were experiencing weak economic growth and substantial current account surpluses. Initially, U.S. authorities purchased dollars "to deal...with the disorder in the exchange market" (Holmes 1978).

The United States began a series of steps to stop the dollar's fall in 1978. In January, the Federal Reserve and Treasury began to participate equally in financing intervention. This was a notable change in tactics because most intervention had previously been for the Fed account. In addition, the Treasury and the Bundesbank agreed to set up a swap arrangement, augmenting U.S. resources for foreign exchange intervention. Over the following months, the Treasury borrowed under this agreement, obtaining marks to use for dollar purchases in the market. During 1978, the Federal Reserve also tightened domestic monetary policy, which increased U.S. interest rates and helped strengthen the dollar.

On November 1, 1978, U.S. authorities announced a major plan to halt the dollar's decline. This plan included, among other efforts, the purchase of dollars in the exchange market. The United States had decided the dollar's decline "had gone beyond what could be justified by underlying economic conditions" (Holmes 1979, p.67). The plan was the first major departure from a narrow interpretation of the U.S. exchange rate objective. Increases in Federal Reserve swap agreements with various central banks helped finance the intervention, and tighter monetary policy bolstered the move. The United States also used several financing arrangements to increase the Treasury's resources for intervention.

The Treasury drew on the resources available from the IMF. For example, in 1978, the Treasury drew from its position at the IMF to obtain foreign currency to purchase dollars. The Treasury also obtained foreign currency by selling Special Drawing Rights (SDRs) to foreign authorities. An SDR is an international reserve asset the IMF began creating in 1970 to supplement other world reserve assets like the dollar and gold. IMF member nations receive SDR allocations according to the size of their quotas. In 1978, the Treasury sold SDRs for marks, yen, and Swiss francs.

The Treasury also issued foreign-currency-denominated securities, or "Carter bonds." In contrast to the Roosa bonds sold to foreign authorities during the fixed-rate regime, the Carter bonds were sold to the public. The Treasury issued nearly $2.8

billion equivalent of Carter bonds by January 1979 and ultimately issued over $6 billion equivalent before it began redeeming the bonds in 1981 (Holmes 1979, p.203, and Cross 1981). In addition, the Treasury increased gold sales to obtain foreign currency.

The Treasury also made use of financing arrangements with the Federal Reserve. Warehousing, for example, is a method of exchanging dollars in return for foreign currency not needed at the time. The Fed buys foreign currency from the Treasury and simultaneously agrees to sell the currency back at the same exchange rate as in the purchase at some specified date in the future. The FOMC regulates System warehousing of foreign currency for the Treasury and in 1978 the FOMC broadened its warehousing authorization, allowing the System to warehouse foreign currency for the general Treasury account as well as for the ESF.[15] In this way, the System could warehouse the foreign currency proceeds of the Carter bonds until the Treasury used them.[16]

Narrow Interpretation: 1981 to 1984

With the arrival of the Reagan Administration in 1981 and a more hands-off approach to government, U.S. authorities once again interpreted the goal of countering disorderly markets narrowly. From 1981 to 1984, the United States rarely intervened in the foreign exchange market. This policy stance reflected the view of the Treasury during the first Reagan term that the market should determine exchange rates. The new policy limited intervention to extreme circumstances, such as after the shooting of President Reagan in March 1981. Furthermore, the administration questioned whether intervention could have much effect on the exchange rate.[17]

The dollar rose dramatically during the early 1980s (Chart 3). This rise has been attributed to the strong U.S. economy, large budget deficit, tight U.S. monetary policy, and high real interest rates relative to the rest of the world. From July 1980 to its peak in February 1985, the dollar's value increased over 85 percent. As the dollar rose, the domestic business community began to complain that the dollar's strength limited the competitiveness of U.S. products against foreign competitors.

Broad Interpretation: 1985 to Present

In 1985, against the backdrop of a very strong dollar, the Treasury during the second Reagan term returned the United States to a broad interpretation of its exchange rate policy goal. Since then, the United States has intervened both to calm disorderly markets and to correct apparent inconsistencies between exchange rate levels and economic fundamentals. In pursuit of its goals, the United States has intensified cooperation with foreign authorities on international economic policy. Also, in contrast to operations during most of the postwar period—which had largely consisted of dollar purchases—recent U.S. intervention has consisted mostly of dollar sales, resulting in record U.S. holdings of foreign currency.

During 1985, the United States intervened more heavily than it had for several years. From January to March 1985, U.S. authorities sold over $650 million in the foreign exchange market. These actions were taken to prevent a further rise in the dollar's value, thus reflecting a broader interpretation of U.S. intervention goals. During 1985, official intervention goals as reported to the IMF were broadened to include intervening "to counter disorderly conditions in the exchange markets or when otherwise deemed appropriate" (International Monetary Fund 1986). The major episode of U.S. intervention in 1985 occurred after the meeting of the five industrialized G-5 nations at the Plaza Hotel in September.[18] At this meeting, G-5 officials agreed that appreciation of foreign currencies was desirable because exchange rates did not reflect economic fundamentals. Officials were also concerned about the threat of rising protectionism in the United States. In the weeks after the Plaza Accord, the United Sates sold dollars in the largest U.S. intervention since the late 1970s. Foreign authorities also sold substantial amounts of dollars. The volume of U.S. intervention from September to October exceeded $3 billion, nearly five times the volume of the U.S. intervention earlier in the year. As the dollar continued to fall throughout the rest of 1985 and 1986, further U.S. intervention became unnecessary.

By early 1987, the dollar had fallen to its lowest level in seven years. The weak dollar reflected a growing U.S. trade deficit and signs of a weakening U.S. economy. At a meeting in February at the Louvre in Paris, G-7 officials decided that exchange rates reflected economic fundamentals.[19] As a result, these officials decided to "cooperate closely to foster stability of exchange rates around current levels" (Bank for International Settlements 1987). This agreement, the Louvre Accord, has guided international cooperation in exchange rate policy to the present. The Louvre Accord also signaled a shift in U.S. policy from encouraging the appreciation of foreign currencies to fostering exchange rate stability.

During the rest of 1987, the dollar generally fell and U.S. intervention consisted primarily of dollar purchases. The dollar's continued decline reflected in part large U.S. trade deficits. The October stock market crash and the associated easing of monetary policy by the Federal Reserve also placed downward pressure on the dollar. In 1987, the United States conducted an even higher volume of intervention than in 1985. This intervention largely consisted of dollar purchases to stop the dollar's slide. Foreign officials cooperated with the U.S. effort and in December 1987, G-7 officials restated their Louvre commitment to cooperate in the foreign exchange market. In an effort to calm the market, these officials also announced that "either excessive fluctuation of exchange rates, a further decline of the dollar, or a rise in the dollar to an extent that becomes destabilizing to the adjustment process, could be counterproductive by damaging growth prospects in the world economy" (U.S. Department of the Treasury 1987).

The next major increase in the volume of U.S. intervention came in 1989. This intervention again was consistent with the G-7 commitment to exchange rate stability. The bulk of U.S. intervention in 1989 was during the first half of the year. For example, the dollar came under upward pressure at times during the spring and summer because of political uncertainty abroad and interest-rate differentials favorable to the dollar. In response, U.S. authorities sold dollars.[20] Also, after their September 23 meeting, G-7 officials issued a communique stating that the dollar's rise was inconsistent with longer run economic fundamentals (Bank for International Settlements 1989). During the last months of the year, upward pressure on the dollar subsided and the dollar fell.

Recent U.S. intervention has resulted in the largest U.S. holdings of foreign currency ever. Total holdings of the Federal Reserve and the Treasury combined have risen from $8 million in 1973 to nearly $45 billion in December 1989.[21] The growth of these balances reflects the fact that recent intervention has usually involved dollar sales.

IV. SUMMARY

The goals and methods of foreign exchange operations have changed over time. Under the Bretton Woods regime, the role of the United States was to convert officially held dollars into gold. In the 1960s, concern for the U.S. gold stock grew, as foreign monetary authorities accumulated large amounts of dollars. To protect the gold stock, the United States borrowed foreign currency to buy dollars from foreign authorities. The United States also on rare occasions intervened directly in the foreign exchange market.

The primary objective of U.S. exchange rate policy during the floating exchange rate period has been to counter disorderly market conditions. Over time, U.S. authorities have interpreted this objective both narrowly and broadly. Major episodes of U.S. intervention occurred in the late 1970s, in 1985, and from 1987 to the present. In the late 1970s, U.S. authorities intervened to support the weak dollar and, in 1985, to counter the strong dollar. From 1987 to the present, U.S. operations have been mixed, with the underlying goal to maintain exchange rate stability. Direct intervention was particularly heavy in 1989, totaling over $20 billion, the highest volume ever.

ENDNOTES

1.Data on the size of U.S. foreign currency holdings in 1989 were obtained from Board of Governors of the Federal Reserve System 1990a. Data on the volume of U.S. transactions in the foreign exchange market were taken from various issues of the Federal Reserve Bank of New York's *Quarterly Review*.

2.The ESF fund was established by the Gold Reserve Act of 1934 to be operated by the Treasury to stabilize the exchange value of the dollar. The Treasury maintains its ESF and its general accounts at the Federal Reserve, which acts as the government's banker.

3.The FOMC is made up of seven members of the Board of Governors and five of the 12 district Federal Reserve Bank presidents.

4.During the fixed-rate regime, the United States was committed to buying gold at $35 an ounce "for settlement of international balances and other legitimate monetary purposes" (International Monetary Fund 1967).

5.During the fixed-rate regime, the foreign exchange value of a country's currency was officially set by that country's government. Countries occasionally revalued (officially raised) or devalued (officially lowered) their currencies against the dollar. For more information, see Federal Reserve Bank of New York 1983.

6.For example, in the early 1960s, the United States undertook "Operation Twist," which was designed both to limit outflows of short-term capital by keeping short-term interest rates high and to foster economic growth by keeping long-term interest rates low (Salvatore 1983).

7.The Bank for International Settlements (BIS) also may participate in swaps.

8.The Federal Reserve conducts most swaps for the United States. The Treasury has conducted swaps infrequently for relatively small amounts. The FOMC monitors Federal Reserve swap arrangements and in 1963 decided the Fed should not extend its borrowing through the swap network for more than one year.

9.These bonds were named after Robert Roosa, Undersecretary for Monetary Affairs, U.S. Treasury, 1961-64.

10.For a discussion of open market techniques, see Roth 1986.

11.These two ways that sterilized intervention may affect the exchange rate are more formally called the portfolio balance channel and the signaling channel. The portfolio balance channel operates if interest rates and the exchange rate adjust to reestablish equilibrium in the bond market because foreign and domestic bonds are not perfect substitutes. In the example in the text, for instance, market participants initially may not want to hold the additional U.S. Treasury securities added to the market by the sterilization. But, if the dollar's value falls, market participants may become willing to purchase the new "cheaper" dollar-denominated securities. If domestic and foreign bonds are perfect substitutes, however, sterilized intervention (operating through the portfolio balance channel) is ineffective. The signaling channel operates if the intervention signals the market about a change in macroeconomic policy, which obviously would affect the exchange rate. For further discussion, see Edison 1990.

12.A 1983 G-7 study, for example, found that from 1973 to 1981, sterilized intervention "did not generally have a lasting effect, but that intervention in conjunction with domestic policy changes did have a more durable impact" (Jurgensen 1983). For a discussion of other studies, also see Edison 1990, and Frenkel 1990.

13.During a floating-rate regime, currencies either appreciate or depreciate in response to market forces. The terms revalue and devalue apply only in fixed-rate systems. For more information, see Federal Reserve Bank of New York 1983.

14.During the floating-rate regime, the goal of U.S. policy has generally been "to counter disorderly conditions in the exchange markets" (International Monetary Fund 1988).

15.For information about the effect of warehousing on the money supply and for information about other aspects of U.S. foreign exchange operation, see Meulendyke 1989.

16.Another type of financing arrangement between the Fed and the Treasury is for the Fed to monetize SDRs and gold. If the ESF wishes to supplement its dollar balances, it may ask the Fed to monetize SDRs. The Fed does this by purchasing SDRs from the ESF for dollars. More precisely, the Fed purchases SDR certificates, which represent the Fed's claim on a specified amount of SDRs. If the ESF wishes to use monetized SDRs, it must first repurchase them from the Fed. Monetizing gold is similar to monetizing SDRs except, instead of SDR certificates, the Fed purchases gold certificates, representing the Fed's claim on a specified amount of the Treasury's gold.

17.Beryl Sprinkel, then Chairman of the President's Council of Economic Advisers, expressed this view in his 1981 Congressional testimony, saying that he was "not at all certain that intervention in a market as massive as our dollar exchange market can have much effect, certainly not in the longer run" (International Economic Policy 1981).

18.The G-5 includes the United States, Japan, West Germany, France, and the United Kingdom.

19.The G-7 includes members of the G-5 plus Canada and Italy.

20.Over time, the ESF has increased the amount of SDRs it has asked the Federal Reserve to monetize. In 1989, the ESF increased the amount of SDRs monetized by the Federal Reserve to $8.5 billion, a 70 percent increase over the year before, to supplement its resources for foreign currency operation. These figures were taken from various issues of the *Federal Reserve Bulletin*.

21.Over time, the FOMC has increased the limit on the amount of foreign currency the Federal Reserve may hold. The current maximum, is $25 billion. The Federal Reserve also continues to warehouse foreign currency for the Treasury to supplement the Treasury's resources for foreign currency operations. At its March 1990 meeting, the FOMC increased the amount of foreign currency the Fed may warehouse for the Treasury to $15 billion. The previous increase in the limit was from $5 billion to $10 billion in September 1989. Such increases reflect the Treasury's need of dollars for foreign currency purchases rather than foreign currency for dollar purchases (Board of Governors 1990b).

REFERENCES

Abrams, Richard K. 1979. "Federal Reserve Intervention Policy," *Economic Review*, Federal Reserve Bank of Kansas City, March.

Balbach, Anatol B. 1978. "The Mechanics of Intervention in Exchange Markets," *Economic Review*, Federal Reserve Bank of St. Louis, February.

Batten, D.S., and Mack Ott. 1984. "What Can Central Banks Do about the Value of the Dollar?" *Economic Review*, Federal Reserve Bank of St. Louis, May.

Bank for International Settlements. 1987. "Chronology of Economic Policy Developments: February and March 1987," April 15, p.8.

___. 1989. "Chronology of Economic Policy Developments: September and October 1989," November 15, p.11.

Board of Governors of the Federal Reserve System. 1962. *Federal Reserve Bulletin*, September.

___. 1963. *Federal Reserve Bulletin*, September.

___. 1970. *Federal Reserve Bulletin*, March.

___. 1988. *75th Annual Report 1988*, BOG.

___. 1989. *76th Annual Report 1989, BOG, p.75.*

___. 1990a. *Federal Reserve Bulletin*, May, Table 3.12.

___. 1990b. "Record of Policy Actions of the Federal Open Market Committee, Meeting Held on March 27, 1990," press release, May 18.

Coombs, Charles A. 1962. "Treasury and Federal Reserve Foreign Exchange Operations," *Federal Reserve Bulletin*, Board of Governors of the Federal Reserve System, September.

___. 1963. "Treasury and Federal Reserve Foreign Exchange Operations," *Federal Reserve Bulletin*, Board of Governors of the Federal Reserve System, September.

___. 1970. "Treasury and Federal Reserve Foreign Exchange Operations," *Federal Reserve Bulletin*, Board of Governors of the Federal Reserve System, March, p.227.

___. 1973. "Treasury and Federal Reserve Foreign Exchange Operations," *Federal Reserve Bulletin*, Board of Governors of the Federal Reserve System, September, p.216-17.

Cross, Sam Y. 1981. "Treasury and Federal Reserve Foreign Exchange Operations," *Federal Reserve Bulletin*, Board of Governors of the Federal Reserve System, September.

Destler, J.M., and C.R. Henning. 1989. *Dollar Politics: Exchange Rate Policymaking in the United States*. Washington: Institute for International Economics.

Edison, Hali J. 1990. "Foreign Currency Operations: An Annotated Bibliography," *International Finance Discussion Papers*, May.

Federal Reserve Bank of New York, 1983. "Fedpoints 38, Currency Devaluation and Revaluation."

___. 1981. *Statfacts, Understanding Federal Reserve Statistical Reports*, November.

Frenkel, Jacob A., Morris Goldstein, and Paul R. Masson. 1990. "International Dimensions of Monetary Policy: Coordination Versus Autonomy," *Monetary Policy Issues in the 1990s*, Federal Reserve Bank of Kansas City, pp.201-02.

Holmes, Alan R., and Scott E. Pardee. 1975. "Treasury and Federal Reserve Foreign Exchange Operations, February-July 1975," *Monthly Review*, Federal Reserve Bank of New York, September.

___. 1978. "Treasury and Federal Reserve Foreign Exchange Operations," *Quarterly Review*, Federal Reserve Bank of New York, Spring, p.56.

___. 1979. "Treasury and Federal Reserve Foreign Exchange Operations," Quarterly Review, Federal Reserve Bank of New York, Spring.

International Economic Policy. 1981. Hearing before the Joint Economic Committee, U.S. Congress, 1 Sess. Washington: Government Printing Office, p.19.

International Monetary Fund. 1967. *Eighteenth Annual Report, Exchange Restrictions*, Washington, p.667.

___. 1986. *Exchange Arrangements and Exchange Restrictions, Annual Report*, Washington, p.523.

___. 1988. *Exchange Arrangements and Exchange Restrictions, Annual Report*. Washington, p.500.

Jurgensen, P. 1983. *Report of the Working Group on Exchange Market Intervention*, March, p.17.

Meulendyke, Ann-Marie. 1989. *U.S. Monetary Policy and Financial Markets*, Federal Reserve Bank of New York, pp.144-47, 222-24.

Roth, Howard L. 1986. "Federal Reserve Open Market Techniques," *Economic Review*, Federal Reserve Bank of Kansas City, March.

Salvatore, Dominick. 1983. *International Economics*. New York: Macmillan Publishing Co., Inc., p.517.

U.S. Department of the Treasury. 1987. Press release. Washington, December 22.

QUESTIONS

1. What options were available to the U.S. to protect its gold stock under the Bretton Woods system of fixed exchange rates? Explain how each worked to reduce pressure on the dollar.

2. How is U.S. intervention in foreign exchange markets "sterilized"? What does this mean regarding the effects of such intervention?

3. Why did the dollar rise in the early 1980s and then fall in the latter half of the 1980s? What foreign exchange operations did the U.S. undertake during this period, and why were these operations performed?

READING 39

European Monetary Union: How Close Is It?

Michael J. Chriszt

Many attempts to establish monetary unions across national borders have failed, but a few successful unions still exist today.[1] A monetary union is a formal arrangement in which two or more independent countries agree to fix their exchange rates or to employ only one currency to carry out all transactions. One of the most ambitious efforts to date is now under way in the European Community (EC, or the Community), whose twelve member countries are striving toward European Monetary Union (EMU).[2] When full union is achieved, these nations, which account for nearly 40 percent of world trade, will carry out transactions with one currency through one central bank and will be subject to one monetary policy.[3] One big obstacle to European Monetary Union is that it will require EC member states to forgo national monetary policies, instead subordinating themselves to a single monetary policy concerned with the interests of the European Community at large.

The EC's readiness to establish monetary union owes much to the European Monetary System (EMS) and, in particular, its exchange rate mechanism (ERM). Established in 1979, the EMS has provided exchange rate stability and the degree of economic convergence among EC member states necessary as a foundation for full monetary union. The purpose of this article is to explain the development of the European Monetary System, describe how its exchange rate mechanism works, and recount the EC's recent moves in the direction of monetary union.

A RATIONALE FOR FIXED EXCHANGE RATES AND MONETARY UNION

From a nation's point of view, there are economic and political reasons both for and against pursuing monetary union. One widely held explanation of why independent nations would choose to adopt a fixed exchange rate regime is that doing so has a number of positive welfare effects.[4] A currency union can increase and stabilize the income level within a country by reducing uncertainty surrounding its currency's value. The fact that the zone of fixed exchange rates can be considered as one entity for purposes of producing goods and services allows resources to be allocated more efficiently. In addition, fixed rates may promote price stability because random shocks can be better absorbed by a group of countries with a broader, more diverse production base (natural resources, capital, and labor) than by a single country's economy. Moreover, eliminating individual countries' potential use of exchange rate management as a nontariff trade barrier should increase economic efficiency over the longer run. The fact that the need for foreign exchange transactions is reduced in a currency union also helps its member countries save the resources they would otherwise use for foreign exchange market transactions.

Countries may use monetary union or steps toward it to further political goals. Establishing a union would offset the influence of a larger country that might be brought into the group, in effect diluting the larger nation's economic power through the collective political power of the union participants' shared economic objectives. In addition, each of the member nations, even the more dominant ones, would gain economic influence vis-a-vis countries outside the union merely by being part of a federation that is stronger than any one member nation. Formal bonds among union members would also reduce the likelihood of a large outside state's dominating either the union as a whole or any single member country.

However, monetary union also carries costs for its members. The most fundamental potential cost has to do with agreeing to a fixed exchange rate. By floating its exchange rate, a country can use its currency's value as a policy instrument, actively influencing or passively allowing appreciation or depreciation. As mentioned earlier, monetary union requires that an individual country relinquish control over its exchange rate, thereby abandoning an important tool for maintaining economic and political sovereignty.

EVOLUTION OF THE EUROPEAN MONETARY SYSTEM

The concept of economic and monetary union is inherent in the Treaty of Rome, establishing the European Economic Community in 1957. The treaty states that "the Community shall have as its task, by establishing a common market and progressively approximating the economic policies of member states,... a harmonious development of economic activities" ("Treaty Establishing the European Economic Community" 1987, 125). This idea was expanded in the Single European Act of 1987, which states that to "ensure the convergence of economic and monetary policies which is necessary for the further development of the Community, member states shall...take account of the experience acquired in cooperation within the framework of the European Monetary System" ("Single European Act" 1987, 549). Economic "convergence" has been identified with the improvement and cooperation necessary to harmonize living and working conditions in all EC member states (Horst Ungerer et al. 1990). The European Monetary System and the Exchange Rate Mechanism can be viewed as a means to achieve convergence, which is a necessary condition for economic and monetary union.

At the EC's inception, monetary unification was not an issue: the international monetary system was working well in 1958. During the 1960s, however, dollar and international payments crises led EC leaders to give serious consideration to formal monetary integration. Large fluctuations in member states' exchange rates were beginning to jeopardize gains from earlier progress toward more efficient and profitable commercial transactions among members; monetary cooperation and integration began to seem essential if the economic benefits of being an EC member were to be preserved and fostered.

Community heads of state initiated efforts to establish a monetary union in 1969, asking the EC Commission to prepare a plan for economic and monetary union. The resulting blueprint, known as the Werner Report (after Luxembourg's Prime Minister Manfred Werner), concluded that the first step would be to reduce exchange rate fluctuations among member states. Complete monetary union was scheduled to be in effect by 1980.

The EC's initial approach to exchange rate stabilization was structured within the Bretton Woods system (established by delegates from many nations in 1945 at Bretton Woods, New Hampshire, at a conference to plan postwar economic arrangements). Bretton Woods required participating countries to maintain their currencies' exchange rates within a 1 percent range against the U.S. dollar, whose value was fixed to gold at $35 per ounce. Under this arrangement, EC currencies were held within 2 percent of each other. The Bretton Woods system collapsed in 1971, however. A new international monetary agreement—the Smithsonian Accord—emerged later the same year, allowing currencies to vary 4.5 percent against the dollar. This arrangement meant that EC currencies could move as much as 9 percent against other members' monies.

This range was considered by some EC countries to be too wide and unstable. To regain exchange rate stability, Belgium, Luxembourg, France, Italy, the Netherlands, and West Germany devised the European Joint Float Agreement in April 1972. This arrangement involved maintaining 2.25 percent fluctuation margins around established rates for EC currencies, while permitting the 4.5 percent margins against the U.S. dollar established by the Smithsonian Accord.

The Joint Float is better known as "the snake in the tunnel." If the exchange rates between each EC currency and the U.S. dollar were charted over time and the charts overlaid each other, the image of a snake would appear: the exchange rates among EC members would fluctuate within a narrow band (the snake's body) that would never exceed 2.25 percent in width, while the body would squirm up and down in relation to the dollar within a 4.5 percent band (the tunnel) (Richard W. Edwards 1985, 537). When the Smithsonian agreement was abandoned in March 1973 and exchange rates were allowed to float, the snake lost its tunnel; the 2.25 percent margins were maintained, however, among EC currencies.

The Joint Float was meant to encompass all EC currencies, but within two years of its inception five of the EC's members—Denmark, France, Ireland, Italy, and the United Kingdom—had withdrawn for a variety of reasons. The economic turbulence of the 1970s and the limited progress toward economic and monetary convergence made keeping these members' currencies within the 2.25 percent band unfeasible. There were various unsuccessful attempts to restore these parameters throughout the decade, but EC leaders realized that the Joint Float guidelines could not achieve exchange rate stability. For the moment, plans to establish a monetary union were shelved.

Two main factors may explain why movements toward European Monetary Union failed at first. One significant development was the introduction of the ambitious Werner Plan at a time of turmoil for the world's economies. The collapse of Bretton Woods and the oil crisis of 1973 created tremendous pressures—strains that could not be addressed without affecting exchange rates. Besides these external forces, among themselves member states failed to coordinate domestic macroeconomic policies to the extent necessary to bring about economic convergence (Dennis Swann 1984).

ESTABLISHMENT OF THE EUROPEAN MONETARY SYSTEM

The European Monetary System succeeded the Joint Float as a monetary plan in 1978 but did not begin formal operations until March 1979. All EC countries at the time became participants in the EMS, although the Italian lire was allowed a wider fluctuation margin; Britain chose not to participate in any of the arrangements, apart from actual membership, largely because of fears about losing monetary sovereignty.

The goal of the European Monetary System was to establish a greater measure of monetary and exchange rate stability in the Community. Its designers regarded the EMS as a central ingredient of a more complete strategy aimed at lasting economic growth and stability, a return to full employment, the harmonization of living standards, and a lessening of the EC's regional disparities ("European Council Resolution" 1978). Community leaders saw the EMS as a route to an effective long-term program for close economic cooperation and a zone of monetary stability—requirements for monetary union.

The EMS included an exchange rate mechanism to stabilize movements among EC currencies. The system also established financing arrangements to fund intervention in the currency markets as well as consultation procedures to ensure cooperation and clarity among EC states' monetary policies. Finally, the European Currency Unit (ECU) was installed as the exchange rate mechanism's denominator, or "benchmark."

All EC member states embrace the European Monetary System, but not all participate in its exchange rate mechanism. For instance, Portugal and Greece have access to the ECU and its benefits because they belong to the EMS, but neither country fixes its exchange rate to the ECU—a requirement for ERM participation. The United Kingdom remained outside the ERM until October 1990.

Table 1
Composition of the ECU

Currency	Weight (percent)
Belgian/Luxembourg Franc	8.1
French Franc	19.3
Guilder	9.7
Mark	9.6
Danish Krone	30.4
Punt	2.5
Peseta	1.1
Drachma	5.2
Pound Sterling	0.7
Escudo	12.6
	0.8

Source: Commission of the European Community

HOW THE EXCHANGE RATE MECHANISM WORKS

The European Currency Unit serves as the basis for determining exchange rate parities, or central rates, among EMS members. The ECU can best be described as a basket made up of fixed amounts of all EC currencies. Each currency's weight is decided by the relative importance of that country's GNP in total Community output and the overall share of each state's intra-EC trade. Weights are normally revised every five years. See Table 1 for the current composition of the ECU.

In addition to possessing bilateral central rates against each other, every EMS currency has a central rate against the ECU. For example, the deutsche mark's central rate against the French franc is FF 3.35, and its ECU central rate is ECU 2.06. Table 2 shows official cross and ECU rates used to track currency fluctuations in the EMS.

Maximum deviations from bilateral parity grid rates permitted in the EMS agreements are defined by intervention points that are 2.25 percent above or below each bilateral central rate.[5] For example, if the mark strengthens against the france, its upper limit in relation to the French currency would be roughly FF 3.43 [(3.35 x .0225) + 3.35]. Should the mark depreciate against the franc, the lower limit would be FF 3.27 [3.35 - (3.35 x 0.225)].

The European Council Resolution establishing the EMS states, "Intervention in participating currencies is compulsory when the intervention points defined by the fluctuation margins are reached" ("European Council Resolution" 1978, 10). When this

TABLE 2
EUROPEAN MONETARY SYSTEM RATES AS OF JULY 1, 1991*

	Spot	ECU	Position versus Weakest ERM Currency (percent)
Peseta	114.02	128.490	5.14
Belgian Franc	37.33	42.0674	1.90
Lira	1356.00	1528.08	1.77
Guilder	2.0565	2.3175	1.05
Pound Sterling	1.6155	0.6976	1.00
Mark	1.8265	2.0583	0.97
Punt	1.4650	0.7692	0.86
Danish Krone	7.0035	7.8923	0.45
French Franc	6.1855	6.9705	0.00

* *Comparisons of individual currencies within the Exchange Rate Mechanism (ERM) of the European Monetary System (EMS). The first two columns of figures show conversion rates per dollar (except the pound sterling, which is expressed in dollars per pound) and the European Currency Unit (ECU), respectively. Column three shows the position of each against the weakest ERM currency.*

Source: Reuters News Service

occurs, the central banks involved must engage in reciprocal buying and selling of their currencies on the exchange markets. For example, if the mark appreciates to a standing at FF 3.43, the Bundesbank must sell marks in exchange for francs and the Banque de France must buy francs for marks.

Although central banks usually make foreign exchange market interventions in participating currencies, early interventions—before compulsory intervention limits are reached—are often made using third currencies, especially the U.S. dollar. Rather than letting their currencies fluctuate within the entire allowable range, the authorities in some EMS countries try to maintain their currencies' position within a narrower band. Carrying out the more frequent interventions necessary to remain within these self-imposed margins using EMS currencies would be a cumbersome process for the central bank of the country maintaining its narrow margins; each intervention would require consulting with the central banks whose currencies would be involved in the transaction. Because the United States has not required any such concurrence involving foreign exchange intervention, a large part of intramarginal EMS interventions are made in dollars. In addition, because the dollar is a leading reserve currency, EMS central banks usually have ample dollar reserves with which to carry out interventions.

The EMS includes a device to ensure that one currency's strength or weakness does not put unmanageable strain on the system. This "divergence indicator" measures a currency's deviation from all parity grid rates by comparing the currency's exchange rate with its ECU central rate. If a currency deviates from the central rate by three-fourths of its permitted fluctuation range, it has crossed a "threshold of divergence" ("European Council Resolution" 1978, 10). According to the European Council Resolution,

> When a currency crosses its "threshold of divergence," this results in a presumption that the authorities concerned will correct the situation by adequate measures, namely:
>
> (a) diversified intervention;
> (b) measures of domestic monetary policy;
> (c) changes in central rates;[6]
> (d) other measures of economic policy ("European Council Resolution" 1978, 10)

When a currency reaches its threshold of divergence against its ECU rate, only the issuer of that currency must take corrective action. (The EMS provides credit facilities for members with insufficient foreign reserves.) The divergence indicator is a signal for policy action to commence. If the central bank in question refuses to take adequate measures, it must give reasons for its inaction to other EMS central banks. Further consultations will, if necessary, take place in the appropriate European Community bodies in order to alleviate the situation.

RECENT MOVES TOWARD EUROPEAN MONETARY UNION

Although economic and monetary cooperation and union were alluded to in the EC's establishing treaty, member states were unwilling to embrace any major commitment to this goal before the late 1980s. The Madrid summit in June 1989 unanimously adopted the first phase of a three-phase plan by Jacques Delors, President of the European Commission, to push the EC toward economic and monetary union.

The first phase calls for closer cooperation between member state governments in economic and monetary policy. Phase Two foresees the establishment of new Community institutions, including the European System of Central Banks (see the box for a detailed look at the envisioned EC central bank), and Phase Three would institute a single currency and a single monetary policy decided and implemented by the EC central bank.

The Community is in Phase One now; conflict over timing and implementation has impeded progress on Phases Two and Three. At the October 1990 summit in Rome, however, eleven of twelve EC heads of state approved a text establishing a timetable for the final phase, with only Britain's Prime Minister Margaret Thatcher dissenting. The text states that on January 1, 1994, the agreed-upon start for the second phase, a new Community institution will be established to strengthen the coordination of monetary policies, to develop the instruments and procedures needed for the future conduct of a single monetary policy, and to oversee development of the ECU.

Within three years from the start of the second phase, the European Commission and the council of the new monetary institution will report on progress made so that provisions can be arranged for the start of the third phase.

Recent developments may have made the Rome summit's timetable appear too ambitious. The painful economic adjustments required by the former East Germany following German economic and monetary union have shown Community leaders that a European-wide monetary union may have some perils, especially for the countries that are not as economically well-off. The initial impact of the Persian Gulf crisis and its effect on oil prices also reminded EC members that coordination is difficult during times of economic distress, when it is tempting to use sovereign discretionary policies to address domestic conditions. The current work of EC leaders forging EMU is now focused more on fostering economic and monetary convergence within the Community, rather than establishing schedules for eventual union.

The outcome of the June 1991 European Council summit leaves the twelve EC members facing difficult negotiations on economic and monetary union. The members have not reached agreement on the future shape of the European Community and on how much sovereignty they should have to relinquish to achieve monetary union. The EC summit's official communiqué said that at the next European Council summit, in December 1991, the draft texts, which contain all the necessary factors for the implementation of EMU, should be finalized. A phrase was added indicating that Britain maintained its reserve on the goal and timetable of the monetary union. The remainder of the report stressed the need for satisfactory and lasting progress on economic convergence beginning immediately, during the first stage of EMU.

Although most members agree on the EMU goal, they are still at odds on whether to set up a European central bank in 1994 or 1996 and on how independent it should be from political influence. Britain's position appears to be that a single currency should emerge when and if the economics of such a move permit it and not through imposed timetables (Ralph Atkins and David Marsh 1991). An alternative plan under consideration would create a two-tiered monetary union: a core group—Germany, France, and the Low Countries—would proceed rapidly to union, to be joined by other European Community members when their economies had developed sufficiently, thus avoiding a painful adjustment process. Although this two-tiered plan has all but been dismissed, it nonetheless reflects the multifaceted nature of the ongoing European Monetary Union negotiations.

CONCLUSION

The European Monetary System and its exchange rate mechanism are operating as planned, even though members have not entirely agreed on the timing or characteristics of a monetary union.[7] The EC's Single Market Program—EC 1992—is likely to encourage continued economic convergence, which would ease the progress toward union. In addition, relaxing the timetable for EMU should allow member countries to plan for and apply the market forces as a prelude to concentrating their efforts on monetary integration.

THE PROPOSED EUROPEAN CENTRAL BANK

A common central bank has been deemed crucial for the European Community to achieve its established goal of monetary union. To this end, a committee of EC central bank governors—the counterparts to the chairman of the Federal Reserve System—drafted statutes in November 1990 for the European System of Central Banks and the European Central Bank (ECB). The EC's present Intergovernmental Conference on Monetary Union is expected to finalize the plan by the end of 1991.

Organizational Features

According to the plan, the European System of Central Banks will consist of the ECB and the central banks of the member states. EC members are obliged to ensure that national laws, including the statutes of their national central banks, are compatible with ECB legislation and existing EC treaties.

The decision-making bodies of the ECB will be its executive board and council. The board will comprise a president, a vice-president, and four other members, all chosen by EC heads of state after consultation with the European Parliament, while the council will incorporate the board and the twelve member-state central bank governors.

The execution of routine operations will be handled through the central bank system's federative structure. The structure is modeled on the principle of subsidiarity, which holds that functions should be performed by the agency that can most effectively handle them, at a position as low within the hierarchy as possible and thus nearest to the constituency affected by such functions. National central banks will be used as operational arms of the ystem, while the executive board will address matters of policy.

The system's structure meets two important requirements for making policy with Community-wide goals. Because monetary policy decisions will be placed in the hands of the central decision-making bodies, national self-interests are likely to be subordinated to ECB goals. Yet member states will continue to play an important role in executing the system's day-to-day tasks through both the ECB and the individual central banks.

The Basic Principles

Price stability will be the system's primary objective. However, this goal does not mean that monetary policy will be carried out without regard to other Community economic policy objectives. The system will also support the Community's general economic policy as established by the relevant EC institutions. objective. However, this goal does not mean that monetary policy will be carried out without regard to other Community economic policy objectives. The system will also support the Community's general economic policy as established by the relevant EC institutions.

The statues' authors hope to ensure the ECB's democratic legitimacy and accountability through its formation process and reporting requirements. Democratic legitimacy is conferred by the statue's requirement that member states' governments approve the statute before it may be implemented. Accountability is addressed through the statute's calls for an annual report to be presented to EC heads of state, the Council of the European Community, and the European Parliament. In addition, the ECB will report regularly on the system's activities and must publish their financial statements. Further accountability is established by authorizing the president of the Council of the European Community and a Commission member to attend ECB Council meetings.

More Work Ahead

Although the draft statute for the European System of Central Banks and the ECB deals fully with organizational provisions, the statute still needs work in two major areas. First, the plan does not yet address transitional arrangements: the decisions on the necessary steps to be implemented in Stage Two, the transition to Stage Three, the ECB's start-up procedures, and the implications of full participation in the system by some member states at different dates than others—the so-called "two-speed" Europe, in which poorer EC states do not immediately participate in monetary union because of economic differences. Second, certain technical questions—especially those relating to income distribution—some legal questions, and the location of the ECB's headquarters are still under consideration.

Also unresolved are questions concerning the responsibility for exchange rate policy, the exact procedure for giving operational powers to the executive board, and the need for collateral in lending to credit institutions. The Committee of Governors intends to complete work in these areas in the course of the ongoing Intergovernmental Conference.

ENDNOTES

1.See Graboyes (1990) for a detailed discussion of past and present monetary unions.
2.European Community members are Belgium, Denmark, France, Germany, Greece, Ireland, Italy, Luxembourg, the Netherlands, Portugal, Spain, and the United Kingdom.
3.Statistics on world trade (in 1989) were found in International Monetary Fund (1990).
4.For a more detailed discussion of this explanation, see Grubel (1981, 512-27, 641-63).
5.The upper and lower rates are actually 2.2753 percent and 2.2247 percent, respectively. These bands ensure that the buying rate for central bank A of currency B is equal to Central bank B's selling rate of currency A because they represent the exact arithmetical inverse. As the total allowable fluctuation remains 4.5 percent (2.25 + 2.25 = 2.2753 + 2.2247), the difference is insignificant.
6.A change in central rates, or a parity grid realignment, which means currency revaluation or devaluation, is considered a drastic solution to exchange rate digressions. Central rate changes are infrequent, and none have been made since 1987. (See issues of *Financial Times* for a table that shows parity grid realignments).
7.See Ungerer et al. (1990, tables 17-24) for a detailed look at competitiveness and convergence measures.

REFERENCES

Atkins, Ralph, and David Marsh. "Kohl, Major in EMU Accord." *Financial Times*, June 10, 1991, 1.
Edwards, Richard W. *International Monetary Collaboration.* Dobbs Ferry, N.Y.: Transnational Publishers, Inc., 1985.
"European Council Resolution." *Bulletin of the European Communities* no. 12 (1978).
Graboyes, Robert F. "The EMU: Forerunners and Durability." Federal Reserve Bank of Richmond *Economic Review* 76 (July/August 1990): 8-17.
Grubel, Herbert G. *International Economics.* Homewood, Ill.: Richard D. Irwin, Inc., 1981.
International Monetary Fund. *Direction of Trade Statistics 1990 Yearbook.* Washington, D.C.: IMF, 1990.
"Single European Act." In *Treaties Establishing the European Communities*, abridged ed., 523-76. Luxembourg: Office for Official Publications of the European Communities, 1987.
Swann, Dennis. *The Economics of the Common Market.* 5th ed. New York: Penguin Books, 1984.
"Treaty Establishing the European Economic Community." In *Treaties Establishing the European Communities*, abridged ed., 115-383. Luxembourg: Office for Official Publications of the European Communities, 1987.
Ungerer, Horst, Jouko J. Hauvonen, Augusto Lopez-Claros, and Thomas Mayer. *The European Monetary System: Developments and Perspectives.* Occasional Paper 73, International Monetary Fund, November 1990.

QUESTIONS

1. What is a monetary union? How can participation in a monetary union benefit a nation? What costs can a monetary union impose on member nations?

2. Briefly describe these exchange rate stabilization efforts: the Bretton Woods system; the Smithsonian Accord; the Joint Float Agreement.

3. How does the European Monetary System's current exchange rate mechanism work? What must central banks do if exchange rates approach the maximum allowable deviations?

4. What is the proposed structure for the European System of Central Banks and the European Central Bank? Compare this to the structure of the Federal Reserve System.

PART SEVEN

MONETARY THEORY

How the money supply and the Fed's monetary policy affect interest rates, aggregate spending and output, employment, and the price level is the subject of monetary theory. The six readings for Part VII discuss some central topics and controversies of monetary theory: the demand for money and stability of money's relationship to gross national product; the relationship between budget and trade deficits; the relative effectiveness of monetary and fiscal policy; inflation; rational expectations and efficient markets; and the activist/nonactivist policy debate.

Reading 40 is "Understanding the Behavior of M2 and V2" by David H. Small and Richard D. Porter. Small and Porter investigate the relationships among M2, nominal GNP, and the opportunity cost of holding M2 balances and explain why velocity is stable over the long run but exhibits substantial variability in over shorter intervals of one to two years. This reading is for use with the discussion of money demand in Chapter 23.

"Investigating U.S. Government and Trade Deficits" by Ellis W. Tallman and Jeffrey A. Rosensweig is Reading 41. The "twin" deficits" have received much attention in recent years from economists, policymakers, and the media. Tallman and Rosensweig discuss the casual evidence and theoretical support for the existence of a causal linkage between these deficits, review recent empirical studies of this linkage, and present their own research which suggest that government budget deficits are a cause of trade deficits. This reading can be used with Chapter 25's discussion of monetary and fiscal policy.

Reading 42 is "Monetary vs. Fiscal Policy: New Evidence on an Old Debate" by Peter E. Kretzmer. Which is more important to the economy, monetary or fiscal policy? This question, disputed by Monetarists and Keynesians in the 1960s and 1970s, has continued relevance in the 1990s as the economy responds sluggishly to lower interest rates. Kretzmer reviews the debate over the relative importance of monetary and fiscal policy, discusses how the effects of monetary and fiscal policy may have changed in recent years, and presents evidence that monetary policy has become less effective in recent years but is still more effective than fiscal policy. This reading is recommended for use with Chapter 26's discussion of policy effects in the aggregate demand and supply model or with Chapter 27's coverage of the Monetarist-Keynesian debate on money and economic activity.

In Reading 43, "Public Preferences and Inflation," Carl E. Walsh offers an explanation for differences in inflation rates across countries based on differences in public willingness to tolerate inflation. To support this explanation, Walsh presents data for the U.S. and New Zealand on public attitudes toward inflation and unemployment, and the relationship between inflation and unemployment and elected politicians' popularity ratings. This reading is recommended for use with the discussion of inflation in Chapter 28.

Reading 44 is "Challenges to Stock Market Efficiency: Evidence from Mean Reversion Studies" by Charles Engel and Charles S. Morris. Engel and Morris first discuss the expected behavior of stock prices in an efficient market. They then explain mean reversion of stock prices in an inefficient market and review the evidence from a number of studies of stock prices and returns.
They conclude that, despite some evidence that stock prices are mean reverting, more evidence is needed before concluding the stock market is inefficient. This reading supplements the discussion of efficient markets theory in Chapter 29.

Reading 45 is "Activist Monetary Policy for Good or Evil? The New Keynesians vs. the New Classicals" by Tom Stark and Herb Taylor. This reading delineates the essential elements of these two schools and explains why their positions on activist policy differ. It ties in with Chapter 30's discussion of New Classical and nonclassical rational expectations models. (Alternatively, instructors may wish to use this reading with the coverage of the activist/nonactivist debate in Chapter 28.)

READING 40

Understanding the Behavior of M2 and V2

David H. Small and Richard D. Porter

As part of its responsibility of reporting to the U.S. Congress, the Federal Reserve System establishes ranges for the growth of various monetary aggregates over the coming year. These ranges are set so as to foster the ultimate objectives of the Federal Reserve, mainly stable economic growth and stable prices. The relations between these aggregates and income and prices, therefore, bear both upon the appropriate width of the target range set for each aggregate and upon the proper response of policy should one of them deviate from its range.

This article focuses on the properties of the M2 aggregate and of its velocity, V2, the ratio of gross national product to M2. The time frame is the intermediate run—the one-to two-year intervals that are associated with monetary targeting and over which V2 has fluctuated by substantial amounts. The article shows that much of the intermediate-run variability in this velocity measure can be explained by changes in the opportunity cost of holding M2 balances, defined as a market interest rate less the average rate paid on M2 deposits. Those changes, in turn, depend upon the rate-setting behavior of depository institutions: the more quickly and the more fully deposit rates adjust to changes in market rates, the more stable will be the opportunity cost of M2 and, therefore, the more stable will be V2 itself. Empirically, the average rate on M2 deposits tends to respond sluggishly to changes in market rates, so that opportunity costs vary significantly over the intermediate run but vary far less in the long run as deposit rates adjust.

Given the history of market rates, these two relations—between V2 and M2's opportunity cost and between the opportunity cost and market rates—account for much of the past variability of V2. Nonetheless, predictions about the relationship of movements in M2 and in gross national product still embody much uncertainty. While the forecasts from models of M2 demand and deposit rates developed by the staff of the Federal Reserve Board are reasonably accurate, the interval since the deregulation of deposits in M2 has not been long enough for confidence to have been built in specific estimates of these relationships. Moreover, even if the links among market rates, deposit rates, GNP, and M2 demand were stable and fully understood, uncertainty about shocks elsewhere in the economy, and about the interest rate changes needed to offset them, would still necessitate judgement in setting the appropriate path for M2.

To shed light on these issues, this article first reviews the recent behavior of V2 and its determinants. It then examines the Board's formal model of M2 demand, which explicitly traces the relations between M2 on the one hand and income, prices, interest rates, and its other determinants on the other; and it reports simulations of that model to quantify the importance of the relationships governing the determination of M2 demand and deposit rates and of the uncertainty surrounding them. An appendix provides a brief exposition of the model.

1. V2 and leading velocity

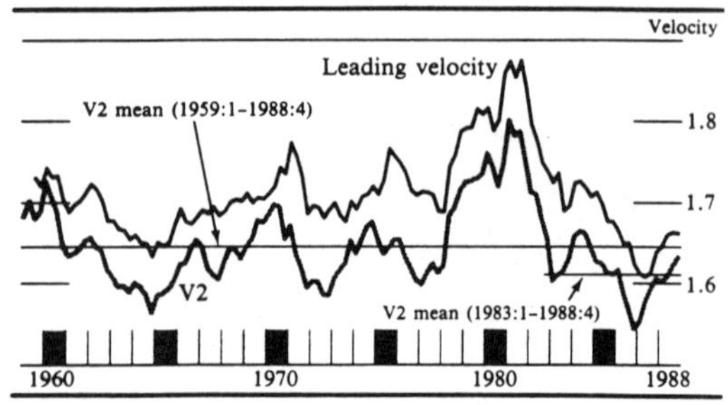

2. Velocity and the opportunity cost of M2

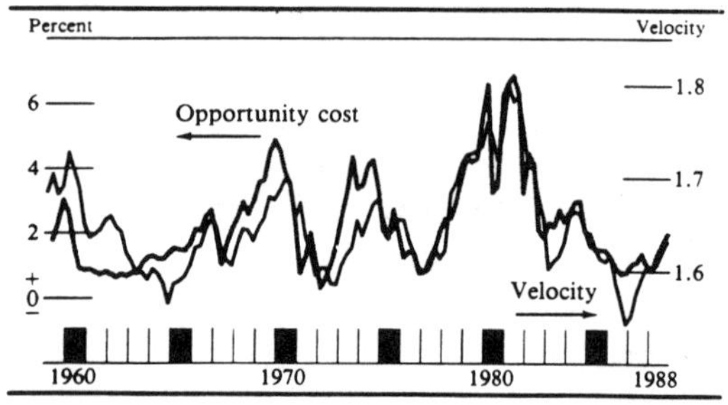

HISTORICAL BEHAVIOR OF V2, OPPORTUNITY COSTS, AND DEPOSIT RATES

The velocity of M2, V2, has fluctuated about a generally flat trend over the last three decades (chart 1).[1] However, some evidence suggests that the introduction of money market deposit accounts at the end of 1982 had a once-and-for-all depressing effect on the average level of V2. With their transaction features and attractive offering rates, MMDAs apparently drew in funds that previously had been held outside M2 and thereby lowered V2.

Changes in M2's opportunity cost appear to be the main factor causing V2 to deviate from its trend (see chart 2).[2] The relation between V2 and the opportunity cost of M2 seems reasonably stable, even after the extraordinary initial growth of MMDAs.[3] Indeed, the simple correlation between V2 and M2's opportunity cost is 0.78 over the period from 1959:2 to 1988:4.

The opportunity cost of M2, in turn, moves less than market interest rates because

3. Opportunity cost of M2 and its components

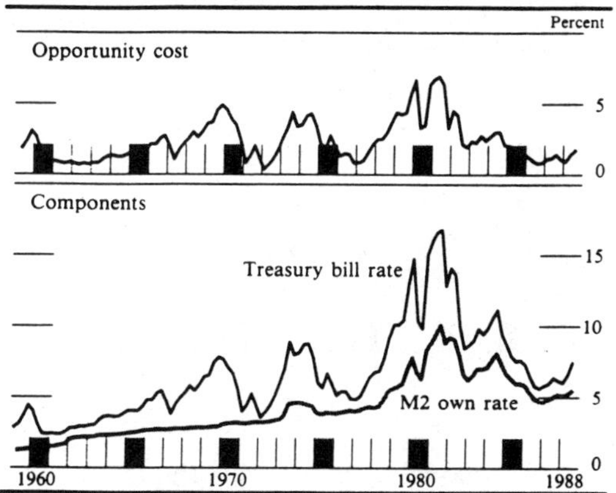

4. The federal funds rate and M2 deposit rates

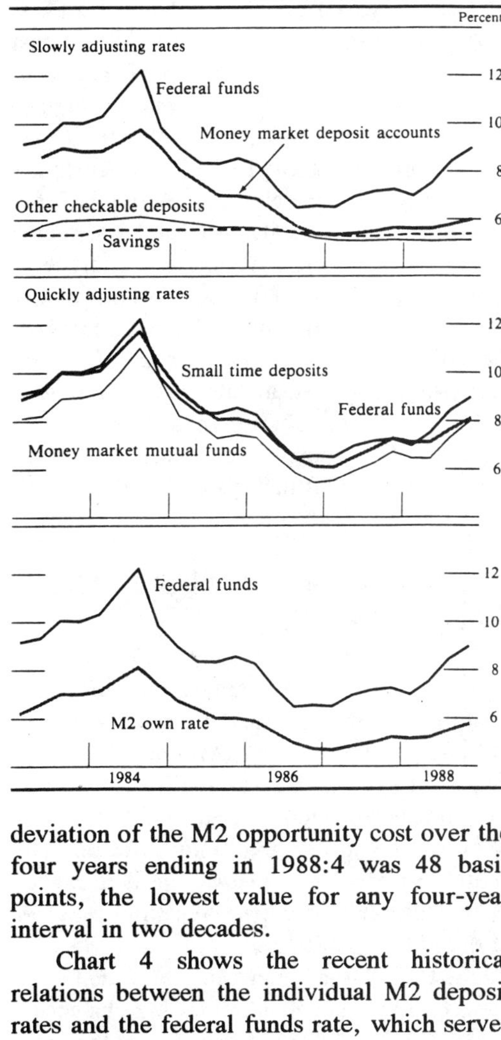

the average rate on M2 deposits—the M2 own rate—is adjusted in the wake of changes in the Treasury bill rate; obviously, greater adjustment tends to stabilize opportunity costs more.[4] From 1959:2 to 1988:4, the standard deviation of the Treasury bill rate was 3.23 percentage points while that of the opportunity cost of M2 was only 1.53 percentage points. In the 1960s and 1970s, most of the adjustments made to the M2 deposit rate involved changes in rates that were under Regulation Q; these adjustments were generally made in lagged response to the upward trend in open market rates. However, since the deregulation of deposit rates began in mid-1978, the rate on M2 has generally responded more sensitively to changes in market rates. As a result, the M2 opportunity cost has been considerably more stable since 1983 than it was during the late 1960s and most of the 1970s, even though the variability of market rates was roughly the same in the two periods (see chart 3). The standard deviation of the M2 opportunity cost over the four years ending in 1988:4 was 48 basis points, the lowest value for any four-year interval in two decades.

Chart 4 shows the recent historical relations between the individual M2 deposit rates and the federal funds rate, which serves as a proxy for short-term open market rates. The first panel relates the funds rate to the more slowly adjusting M2 deposit rates—the rates on other checkable deposits, savings deposits, and MMDAs; the second panel shows the relation with the more quickly adjusting rates on small time deposits and on money market mutual funds; and the last shows the M2 own rate. Much of the recent responsiveness of the M2 own rate to changes in market rates, and therefore much of the increase in the stability of the M2 opportunity cost, stems from the closeness with which the rates on small time deposits and on money market mutual funds have followed short-term open market rates. When short-term market rates have risen, that closeness has promoted the stability of V2 in two ways: first, by permitting those instruments to retain deposits; and, second, by making them attractive to funds in other components of M2 that might otherwise have left the aggregate altogether.

MODELING M2 DEMAND AND DEPOSIT RATES

To explore the implications of these relationships for setting the target range for M2 and for dealing with deviations from that range, the Federal Reserve staff has developed an econometric model of the relationship of M2 to GNP and to market interest rates. The model has two components: the demand for M2 by the public and the rate-setting behavior of depository institutions.[5]

The relation between V2 and the opportunity cost of holding M2 balances, which is exhibited in chart 2, forms the basis of the staff econometric model of the demand for M2. In the model, the ratio of M2 demand to GNP (that is, the reciprocal of V2) is affected primarily by the opportunity cost of

5. Response of M2 to increases of 1 percent in the scale variables and in the opportunity cost of M2

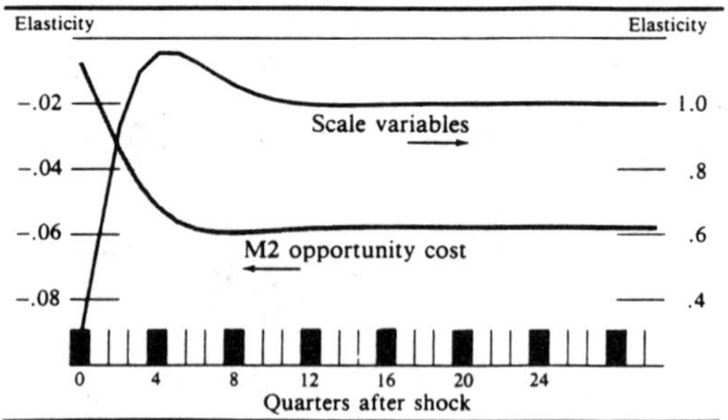

M2.[6] The model also specifies the short-run dynamics by which M2 demand, and hence V2, adjusts toward its long-run level; these adjustments include, among other things, current and lagged responses to changes in nominal GNP, personal consumption expenditures, and M2 opportunity cost, and to previous changes in M2 itself.

The estimated behavioral responses of M2 demand to increases in the scale variables, nominal GNP and personal consumption expenditures, and in the M2 opportunity cost unfold fairly smoothly and nearly monotonically over time, although they exhibit some overshooting of their long-run values (see chart 5).[7] As estimated, the demand for M2 takes slightly less than a year to respond fully to shocks to GNP, but needs about a year and a half to respond fully to shocks to opportunity costs. The long-run elasticity with respect to changes in opportunity costs is estimated to be -0.057; that is, a 1 percent increase in opportunity costs induces a 0.057 percent decrease in the level of M2.

The response of M2 demand to a change in market rates is more complex because the lagged adjustments of offering rates result in changes in opportunity costs long after the initial movement in market rates. The staff model links deposit rates to the federal funds rate. After allowing for costs of servicing accounts, deposit rates are assumed to adjust one for one with the funds rate in the long run.[8] The speed of this adjustment varies significantly across the different types of M2 deposits; the rates on the more liquid accounts adjust more slowly, as chart 4 makes evident. In addition, as tests conducted with the staff model indicate, apart from rates on small time deposits, offering rates adjust downward faster than they adjust upward.

Chart 6 shows the estimated responses of the M2 own rate and the M2 opportunity cost to changes of plus and minus 100 basis points in the federal funds rate. During the first quarter following the rise in the funds rate, the Treasury bill rate is estimated to increase about 90 basis points. But, because rates on small time deposits and on money market mutual funds respond relatively quickly, the average M2 offering rate moves up about 40 basis points (top panel), leaving a net increase in the opportunity cost of about 50 basis points (lower panel). After two quarters, the Treasury bill rate has completed its adjustment and the opportunity cost starts to decline as M2 deposit rates continue to adjust upward, albeit sluggishly.

Combining the model of M2 demand with that of deposit rate setting produces a model of the monetary sector in which M2 demand is tied to GNP and the federal funds rate. The response of M2 demand to a change in the funds rate follows a humped profile, as shown by the black lines in chart 7. The opportunity cost initially falls after a decrease in the funds rate (as in chart 6), working to increase M2 demand. However, as the deposit rates continue to decline, the opportunity cost begins to rise and the demand for M2 weakens, though remaining above its original value. As chart 7 shows, the short-run elasticity peaks seven quarters after the shock in the funds rate at -0.14, about twice the absolute value of the long-run elasticity of -0.073.[9]

6. Response of M2 own rate and opportunity cost to increases and decreases in the federal funds rate

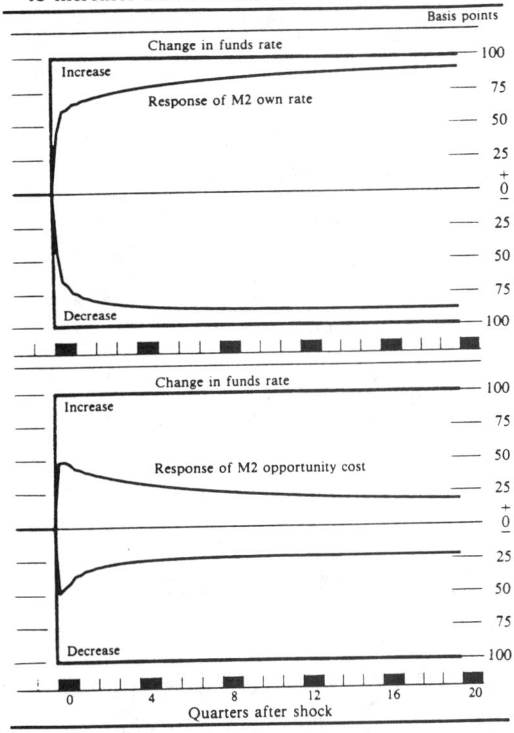

7. Response of M2 with respect to an increase of 1 percent in the federal funds rate

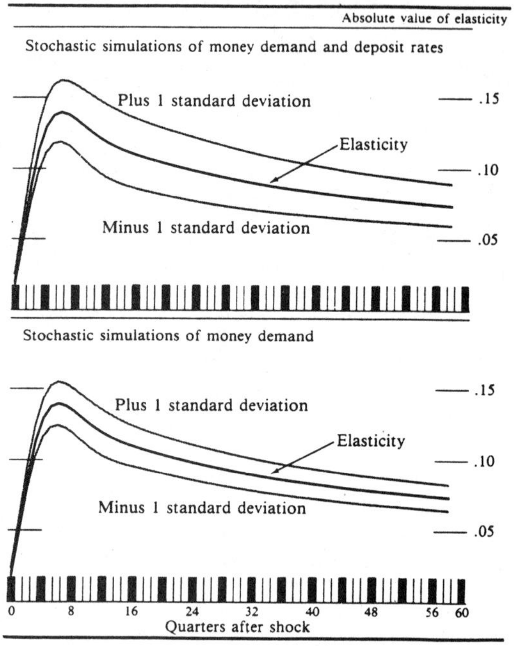

STABILITY OF THE DEMAND FOR M2 AND ASSOCIATED TARGETING ISSUES

The usefulness of M2 as a guide to monetary policy depends not only on the strength of M2's relationships to income and interest rates, but also on the stability and predictability of those relationships. An impression of the stability of the equation for M2 demand can be gleaned from the forecasts of the annual growth rates of M2 shown in table 1. These forecasts are mainly within the model's estimation period—1964:1 to 1986:2; they represent dynamic simulations of the model, in which past values of GNP and the M2 opportunity cost are exogenous.[10]

As indicated by the correlation of 0.907 between the actual and forecasted growth rates, the model captures the swings in M2 growth reasonably well. The table also shows that changes in the M2 opportunity cost make the more significant contributions to short-run swings in M2 growth (column 4), while changes in GNP and personal consumption expenditures account for more of the slowly evolving changes in trend M2 growth (column 5).

8. Actual and simulated velocity of M2

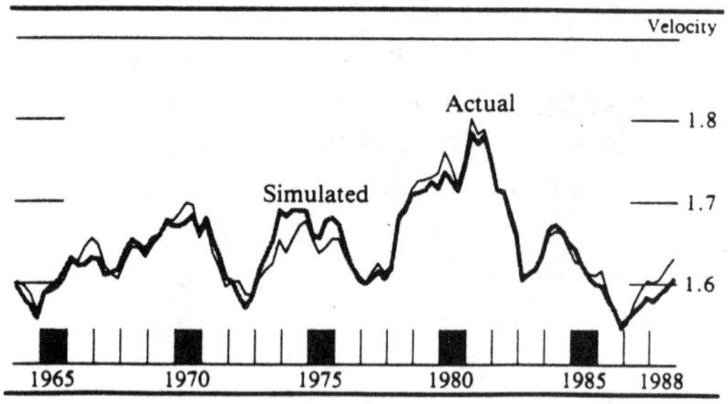

The implied forecasts of V2 using the forecasted levels of M2 and historical values of GNP that are shown in chart 8 indicated the model's ability to track the relation between V2 and opportunity costs. However, the divergence of the actual and simulated values starting in 1987 is as pronounced as any in the estimation period and largely reflects the overprediction by 1.8 points of M2 growth in 1987 (see table 1). This forecast is relatively large, and it is somewhat disturbing, coming as it does in the first full out-of-sample year. However, the forecast of M2 growth in 1988 was quite accurate; therefore, the simulated

1. Forecasts of annual growth in M2, 1964–88

Percent change, fourth quarter to fourth quarter, except as noted

Year	Actual (1)	Forecast (2)	Forecast error (1–2) (percentage points) (3)	Contribution to forecasted M2 growth (percentage points): Opportunity costs (4)	Contribution to forecasted M2 growth (percentage points): Scale variables (5)
1964	7.9	8.6	−.6	.0	5.8
1965	8.0	6.8	1.3	−.9	8.4
1966	4.8	7.1	−2.3	−2.3	9.5
1967	9.1	6.8	2.3	1.0	5.9
1968	7.8	8.1	−.3	−1.9	10.0
1969	4.4	5.2	−.8	−2.6	7.8
1970	6.1	5.4	.7	.0	5.6
1971	13.5	13.0	.5	5.6	7.9
1972	12.8	13.7	−.9	3.6	10.6
1973	7.2	4.8	2.4	−6.7	11.0
1974	5.9	7.4	−1.5	−2.6	9.9
1975	12.1	11.2	.9	2.8	8.7
1976	13.3	14.7	−1.4	3.8	11.5
1977	11.2	12.1	−.9	1.2	11.2
1978	8.0	7.9	.1	−4.7	12.2
1979	8.2	8.9	−.7	−3.7	12.4
1980	8.9	8.2	.7	−.7	8.9
1981	9.3	8.8	.4	−1.3	10.1
1982	9.1	8.7	.4	3.4	5.9
1983	12.1	12.2	−.1	2.4	6.4
1984	7.7	7.7	.0	−.6	9.4
1985	8.9	10.0	−1.1	2.3	8.2
1986	9.3	8.1	1.2	3.0	5.5
1987	4.2	6.0	−1.8	.3	5.9
1988	5.3	5.5	−.3	−1.7	7.3
Summary statistic					
Root mean squared error	...	...	1.2	...	...
Mean absolute error	...	...	1.0	...	...
Mean error (bias)	...	...	.0	...	...
Correlation of actual and forecasted annual growth	...	.907	...	...	...

and actual velocities plotted in chart 8 parallel one another in 1988.

These results lend some credence to future forecasts of the M2 demand model, at least to forecasts over such annual intervals and conditional on actual values of income and opportunity costs; but they fail to incorporate any uncertainty associated with forecasting opportunity costs. This issue is addressed in forecasts of M2 growth based on endogenous deposit rates (table 2, column 2).[11] These forecasts start in 1984:1, about the earliest these deposit-rate equations are applicable.[12] For comparison, the forecasts in column 4 also start in 1984:1, but they take past opportunity costs as given.

Although the summary statistics in columns 3 and 5 suggest that the use of forecasted rather than historical deposit rates has no appreciable effect on the forecasts of M2 growth, behind these statistics there is a noticeable difference between the two sets of forecasts for the period from 1987:4 to 1988:2. Over this period, the simulated

2. Alternative forecasts of quarterly growth in M2, 1984:1–1988:4, based on forecasted and actual deposit rates

Year and quarter	Actual growth (1)	Forecasted deposit rates: Forecasted growth (2)	Forecasted deposit rates: Error (3)	Actual deposit rates: Forecasted growth (4)	Actual deposit rates: Error (5)
1984:1	7.5	6.9	.6	6.9	.6
2	7.3	7.3	−.1	7.3	−.1
3	6.3	7.1	−.8	7.1	−.8
4	8.9	8.2	.7	8.3	.7
1985:1	12.0	9.2	2.9	9.3	2.8
2	6.1	9.7	−3.6	9.8	−3.7
3	9.7	10.5	−.8	10.2	−.5
4	6.7	9.2	−2.5	8.6	−1.9
1986:1	5.5	8.0	−2.5	7.4	−1.9
2	9.9	7.8	2.1	7.1	2.8
3	11.0	9.3	1.7	9.0	2.1
4	9.6	8.5	1.0	8.2	1.4
1987:1	6.1	6.4	−.3	6.3	−.2
2	2.1	5.7	−3.5	5.8	−3.7
3	3.4	5.4	−2.0	5.8	−2.4
4	4.9	4.7	−.2	5.6	−.7
1988:1	6.2	5.4	.7	6.5	−.4
2	6.9	5.7	1.2	6.2	.7
3	3.8	5.5	−1.7	5.1	−1.4
4	3.8	4.5	−.7	3.8	.0
Summary statistic					
Root mean squared error	...	...	1.8	...	1.8
Mean absolute error	...	...	1.5	...	1.4
Mean error (bias)	...	...	−.4	...	−.3

deposit rates result in M2 growth rates that are around 1 percentage point lower than those based on historical rates. In 1987 and early 1988, the actual M2 own rate rose more than the simulated rate (chart 9), producing higher M2 growth for the forecast using historical deposit rates.

Table 2 also shows that the relatively accurate *annual* forecasts reported in table 1 mask relatively large *quarterly* errors that tend to offset one another over the course of a year. These annual and quarterly forecast results reflect all errors in the various aspects of the model: possibly omitted variables and other misspecifications of the model, as well as uncertainties about the estimated values of the coefficients and about the behavior of the additive residuals in the model. These last uncertainties are especially important in evaluating the M2 growth rates that are likely to be associated with alternative paths for

9. Actual and simulated own rates for M2

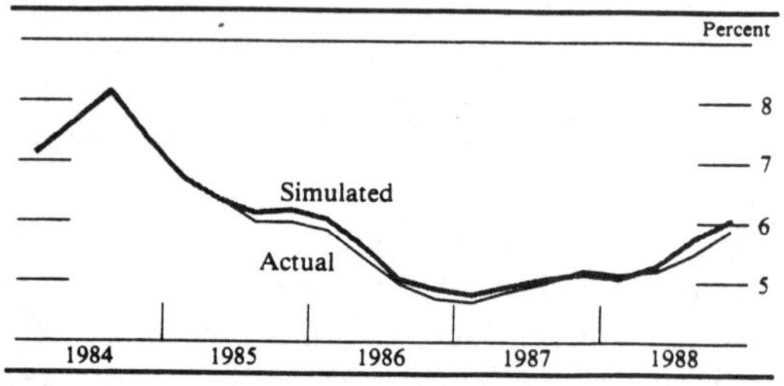

3. Responses of M2 to changes in the federal funds rate

Quarters after change	Uncertainty in money-demand and rate models		Uncertainty in money-demand model only	
	Estimate	Standard deviation	Estimate	Standard deviation
	Elasticity of M2 with respect to the federal funds rate[1]			
0	−.020	.005	−.020	.004
1	−.054	.009	−.054	.006
2	−.087	.013	−.087	.008
3	−.113	.017	−.113	.011
4	−.129	.019	−.129	.013
5	−.138	.021	−.138	.015
6	−.140	.022	−.140	.015
7	−.138	.023	−.138	.015
8	−.134	.023	−.134	.016
9	−.130	.024	−.130	.016
10	−.126	.025	−.126	.016
11	−.122	.026	−.122	.016
12	−.118	.026	−.118	.016
24	−.098	.022	−.098	.012
36	−.086	.019	−.086	.011
48	−.078	.016	−.078	.010
60 (long run)	−.073	.015	−.073	.009
	Change in annualized quarterly growth rates of M2 after increase of 100 basis points in the federal funds rate (percentage points)			
0	−.86	.19	...	...
1	−1.37	.18	...	...
4	−.30	.15	...	...
8	.20	.11	...	...
12	.14	.05	...	...
24	.05	.02	...	...
36	.03	.01	...	...
48	.02	.01	...	...
60 (long run)	.01	.01	...	...

1. Evaluated for a 1 percent increase in the federal funds rate.

GNP or interest rates.

Table 3 and chart 7 cast light on this issue. Table 3 displays confidence intervals for the elasticity of M2 with respect to the federal funds rate.[13] It provides estimated standard deviations for the elasticity of M2 with respect to the funds rate, after allowing for uncertainties in coefficients and error terms in the equations for both M2 demand and the deposit rates; and chart 7 shows the confidence intervals around the estimated elasticity of M2 in terms of a band of one standard deviation about the estimated values. The elasticity follows the humped pattern discussed earlier, reaching its largest values after six quarters. The standard deviation around the elasticity peaks somewhat later, about twelve quarters after the shock, but then it too begins a steady decline. Table 3 also lists the implied estimated changes in quarterly M2 growth rates, and their standard deviations, following an increase of 100 basis points in the federal funds rate.

In light of the degree of uncertainty that table 3 and chart 7 reveal, the separate contributions of the equations for M2 demand and the deposit rates are especially interesting. when we allow for uncertainty only in the equation for M2 demand, the standard deviation of M2's elasticity with respect to the funds rate falls approximately 40 percent from its level when uncertainty is allowed for in the equations for both M2 demand and the deposit rates.

The remaining coefficient uncertainty involves the elasticity of M2 demand with respect to GNP. Here, our measures of uncertainty are necessarily biased downward because, in formulating the model, a long-run elasticity of unity was imposed and thus no uncertainty arises in this regard. Nonetheless, the speed with which the model converges to this long-run elasticity is a function of freely estimated parameters, and the associated uncertainty can be computed. One standard deviation of the estimated elasticity is about one-sixth of the estimated value during the first few quarters following a change in GNP (see table 4). Over longer horizons, the standard deviation falls, reflecting the long-run constraint of a unitary elasticity and the implied convergence of the standard error to zero.

4. Elasticity of M2 with respect to scale variables[1]

Quarters after change	Estimate	Standard deviation
0	.272	.067
1	.607	.089
2	.933	.059
3	1.097	.035
4	1.155	.042
5	1.153	.054
6	1.124	.055
7	1.087	.047
8	1.054	.035
9	1.029	.024
10	1.012	.017
11	1.002	.016
12	.997	.015
24	1.000	.001
36	1.000	.000
48	1.000	.000
60 (long run)	1.000	.000

1. The scale variables are nominal GNP and personal consumption expenditures.

CONCLUSION

This article examines the empirical linkages among M2, nominal GNP, and the opportunity cost of M2 balances. M2 is apparently rather closely tied to nominal GNP in the long run, as indicated by the long-run stability of V2; but changes in market rates can have significant short-run effects on M2 and V2 through their effects on the opportunity cost of holding M2 balances. The equation for M2 that was used to characterize the behavior of that aggregate is rather standard in terms of variables used to explain M2—mainly, income and opportunity costs. But the resulting behavior that is imparted to M2 by the sluggish adjustment of deposit rates to changes in market rates is not always recognized.

This sluggish adjustment process for deposit rates produces swings in the opportunity cost for M2 deposits that initially widen when market rates increase but that gradually narrow as deposit rates adjust upward. M2 has, therefore, a greater response to changes in market rates in the short run than in the long run. However, the experience with deregulated rates for most M2 deposits is limited to the 1980s, and therefore the uncertainty concerning their behavior and effects on M2 is probably greater than is conveyed in the model presented here.

ENDNOTES

1.This observation refers to "contemporaneous velocity"--that is, the current level of GNP divided by the current level of M2. An alternative measure of the link between M2 and the gross national product is "leading velocity," in which current GNP is divided by a past level of M2. Using previous values of M2 allows for lags between changes in M2 and their effect on GNP and thereby potentially provides a more stable measure of velocity. The use of leading rather than contemporaneous velocity appears to smooth some of the variations in V2, but it does not affect the major swings in velocity, including those of recent years (see chart 1). The mean level of contemporaneous velocity is lower than that of leading velocity because, for any given period, the latter uses a smaller number--that is, an earlier value of M2--in the denominator. Here, M2 is lagged two quarters. Hereafter, the concept of velocity used throughout this article is the contemporaneous measure.

2.The opportunity cost of M2 is the three-month Treasury bill rate less the average rate paid on M2 deposits. These rates and all other rates used in this article are effective annual yields.

3.In view of the relatively attractive rates paid on MMDAs, the introduction of these accounts may have decreased the long-run equilibrium opportunity cost of M2 balances, increasing the demand for this aggregate and lowering its velocity. After their introduction in December 1982, MMDAs (not seasonally adjusted) promptly grew to 13 percent of M2 (seasonally adjusted) on average during 1983:1.

4.The M2 own rate is defined as the deposit-weighted average of the observed rates paid on M2 deposits; each type of deposit is weighted by the value of its ratio to M2, lagged one quarter. Currency and demand deposits are assumed to earn no explicit interest.

5.For a full discussion of this and other models, see George R. Moore, Richard D. Porter, and David H. Small, "Modeling the Disaggregated Demands for M2 and M1 in the 1980s: The U.S. Experience," in Board of Governors of the Federal Reserve System, *Financial Sectors in Open Economies: Empirical Analysis and Policy Issues* (the Board, forthcoming, 1989).

6.The long-run demand for M2 also includes a time trend and a dummy variable to account for the introduction of MMDAs. These variables are only marginally significant and drop out altogether when the sample period starts in 1960:1 rather than in 1964:1, for example.

7.In computing the scale variable elasticity, the two scale variables entering the M2 demand model are changed in tandem by the same percentage amounts.

8.In "Modeling the Disaggregated Demands," Moore and his colleagues provide some evidence that this assumption is warranted.

An exception to the one-for-one adjustment is the rate on other checkable deposits, which is subject to a "reserve tax" on the margin. The reserve tax is assumed to be 12 percent, equaling the marginal reserve ratio for OCD balances in excess of the low-reserve tranche. For the other non-M1A deposit rates, the reserve tax should reflect the 3 percent marginal reserve ratio applicable to nonpersonal time and savings accounts at institutions with too little vault cash to avoid being bound by reserve requirements. But since this requirement is not applied to all nontransaction accounts, the average tax is generally considerably less than 3 percent. For simplicity, the model assumes it is zero.

9.Strictly speaking, this elasticity depends both upon the level of interest rates at which it is evaluated and upon the associated magnitude of the change in interest rates. However, in experiments testing federal funds rates of 4 percent to 16 percent, the elasticity varied by only 0.002.

10.Whether to use dynamic or static simulations is an issue in models such as the staff's model of M2 demand, in which there are lagged dependent variables. Static simulations use historical values for the lagged dependent variables, while dynamic simulations use model forecasts of the variables.

11.The deposit-rate models use the historical values of the rates on federal funds and on Treasury bills.

12.Rates on all deposit categories except passbook savings accounts were deregulated by this period. Rates on passbook accounts were deregulated in 1986:2, but they move so sluggishly in response to changes in market rates that using simulated rather than historical values would not substantially affect the forecasts.

13.In principle, these confidence intervals can be computed directly from the model's underlying estimated coefficients, after some distributional assumptions concerning the estimated coefficients have been made. In practice, direct computation is fairly difficult when the model is viewed as a dynamic system and because of the way we have estimated it. Thus, we have used a stochastic simulation technique to construct the confidence intervals, where random parameter values are drawn from multivariate normal distributions using the estimated variance-covariance matrixes of the parameters.

QUESTIONS

1. What is V2? Is is constant? Is it stable? Why is the stability of velocity an important issue for monetary theory and policy?

2. What is the opportunity cost of M2? Why does it vary over time? How does the behavior of M2's opportunity cost explain the long run and intermediate run behavior of V2?

3. What examples do Small and Porter give that illustrate the impacts of financial innovation and depository institution behavior on velocity?

4. According to Small and Porter, the Federal Reserve Board uses a model in which "M2 demand is tied to nominal GNP and the federal funds rate." Is such a model more similar to Keynes' or Friedman's approach to money demand? Explain.

READING 41

Investigating U.S. Government and Trade Deficits

Ellis W. Tallman and Jeffrey A. Rosensweig

The 1980s witnessed record-sized deficits of more than $150 billion on both the U.S. government and trade accounts. The development of these deficits during approximately the same time span prompted frequent allusions to them in business, policy-making, and academic circles as "twin deficits."

For much of the decade, trade imbalances and government budget deficits were major news topics in the business press (see John Greenwald 1984, Mike McNamee et al. 1988, and "Some of My Best Friends Are Deficits" 1990). The media put forward an image of the United States as a debtor nation, borrowing domestically and internationally to support extravagant spending behavior by the government as well as the private economy. Meanwhile, the issue of growing debt, both the government's and the nation's as a whole, also became central in policy debates as numerous analysts questioned the long-term viability of economic progress with a growing external debt. With the change in status of the United States from net foreign creditor to debtor nation, policymakers and economists face the challenge of dealing with a possible decline in living standards.

By 1983 a casual explanation directly linking the two mushrooming deficits—the twin deficits story—was gaining wide exposure.[1] The notion suggests that the two series' large movements in the same direction occurred because of an underlying interrelationship. A combination of existing theory on international economics and what appeared to be compelling empirical facts observed primarily in the United States during the 1980s gave rise to the idea. The validity of the hypothesized relationship between these two deficits is a crucial issue as the United States faces ongoing massive fiscal deficits into the 1990s and the foreseeable future.

Following a presentation of some of the visual evidence that prompted the twin deficits explanation, this article includes a more rigorous examination of existing theory and of scholarly investigation into the linkages between government and trade deficits. It concludes with a discussion of how the authors' original research contributes to this academic and policy debate.

ORIGINS OF THE TWIN DEFICITS IDEA

Briefly, the twin deficit story as it pertains to a flexible exchange rate regime (it will be treated more fully in a later section) claims that an increased government deficit places incipient upward pressure on real, or inflation-adjusted, interest rates, attracting foreign capital in search of these higher returns. This increased flow of capital into the United States prompts the real exchange rate to appreciate, raising the dollar's foreign exchange value. In turn, the higher exchange rate inhibits exporting by making U.S. products costlier abroad. A higher-valued dollar also results in relatively less expensive—and therefore more attractive—imported goods. Falling exports and rising imports eventually move the trade balance toward deficit.[2]

The twin deficits hypothesis is one possible explanation of the comovements portrayed in data such as that shown in Charts 1 and 2. However, such an informal method of inference does not provide sufficient evidence of a fundamental underlying relationship. Further cursory analysis, performing straightforward statistical analysis (standard correlation techniques) on these two deficit series to explore basic relationships among the data, reveals that the two series have positive correlation contemporaneously, with correlation coefficients of approximately 0.7 in level terms and 0.34 in ratios to nominal GNP (see Table 1). These findings suggest that the variables move together to some extent over time, consistent with the comovement displayed in Charts 1 and 2.

Chart 1 shows the gross facts regarding the two deficits, facts that underlie the initial appeal of the hypothesized relationship between them. The two data series—net foreign investment balance and total government budget balance—both moved dramatically into deficit during the 1980s; the government balance turned radically into unprecedented deficits (in nominal magnitudes) prior to similar movements in the trade measure.[3]

The striking aspect of Chart 1 is the apparently extreme magnitude of both deficit measures during the 1980s. However, because these deficits are measured in level terms in current face-value or nominal dollars, observed associations between these deficit magnitudes may not be based on a structural interrelationship between the data series.

Many macroeconomic series tend to grow over time because of inflation as well as economic growth. Therefore, economists often scale or normalize nominal dollar totals by dividing them by a nation's nominal gross national product (GNP). Taking each deficit series as a ratio to nominal GNP accounts for economic growth and removes any inflationary bias from using nominal magnitudes, allowing clear focus on the specific relationship between the deficits. Most of the study uses deficit measures scaled as a ratio to GNP.

Chart 1
Total Government Budget Balance and Net Foreign Investment in Current Dollars

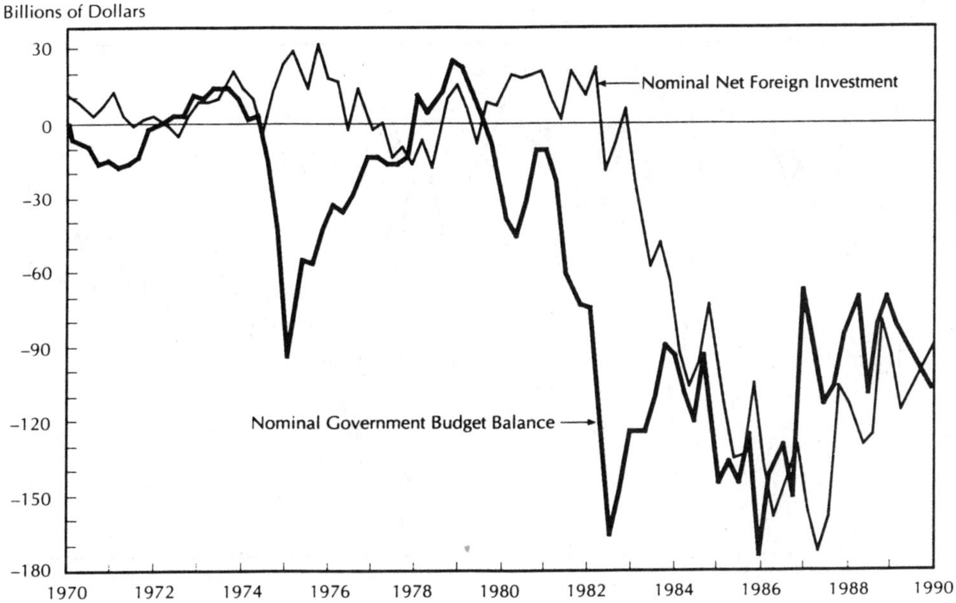

Source: All charts and tables were calculated by the authors using data from the National Income and Produce Accounts (NIPA), U.S. Department of Commerce, Bureau of Economic Analysis.

Does the apparent relationship of the two deficits remain after adjusting them for GNP? Chart 2 plots the two measures as ratios to GNP; the fiscal and trade deficits still appear to be related, although the similarities in movement are less striking. What is noteworthy, however, is the lengthy duration of substantial deficit in the 1980s that the two series have in common.[4]

Consistent with Chart 1, Chart 2 shows that the government budget balance ratio to GNP turns sharply into deficit immediately before the similar downturn in the trade balance ratio (to GNP) during the early 1980s. This empirical observation likely enhanced the popularity of the twin deficit explanation for the conjunction of record-sized deficits. The explanation not only refers to a relationship between the deficits but suggests a causal impact running from the government to the trade deficit.

To investigate the possibility of lead-lag relationships, cross-correlation techniques, which measure the linkage of one variable's movement with that of another a number of periods before or after observation of the initial variable, have been used. Table 1 presents the cross-correlations for various

Chart 2
Total Government Budget Balance and Net Foreign Investment Relative to Nominal GNP

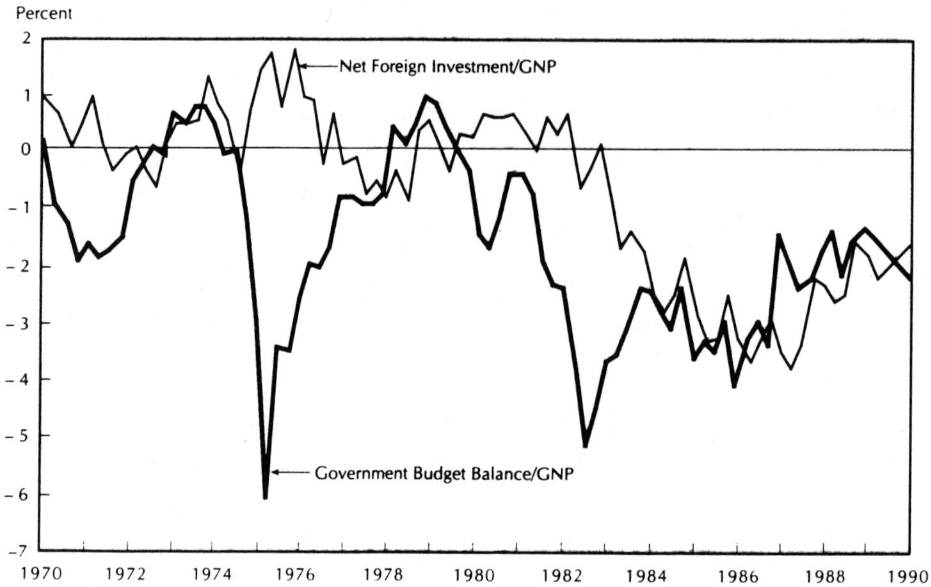

quarterly lags and leads spanning twelve periods in either direction. The table indicates large positive correlations of movements in trade and those in the government budget deficit several quarters earlier. The largest correlations exist roughly at the point when the government deficit measure is lagged seven quarters relative to the trade deficit: 0.87 for deficits measured as nominal levels and 0.72 for deficits as ratios to nominal GNP. To compare movements in the government balance with succeeding movements in trade, Chart 3 shows the government deficit ratio lagged seven quarters in relation to the trade deficit ratio.

As expected, given the pattern found in the cross-correlations, Chart 3 shows an even stronger relationship between the two deficit series than Charts 1 and 2 indicate. However, like the visual and statistical evidence presented earlier, this information is still only casual evidence that increased government deficits may lead to larger trade deficits.

THEORETICAL SUPPORT

In addition to the suggestive casual evidence, there are theoretical frameworks that support the existence of a twin deficits relationship. Combined, these two factors

Table 1
Correlations and Cross-Correlations of U.S. Government Deficits and Trade Deficits

Cross-Correlations of Trade Deficits with Quarterly Leads (–) and Lags of Government Deficits*		
Lead/Lag	Levels	Ratios
–12	.161	.067
–11	.202	.079
–10	.255	.083
– 9	.313	.093
– 8	.346	.092
– 7	.375	.092
– 6	.424	.109
– 5	.488	.168
– 4	.529	.210
– 3	.558	.245
– 2	.611	.270
– 1	.662	.306
0	.698	.339
1	.707	.389
2	.756	.458
3	.815	.559
4	.832	.608
5	.837	.662
6	.854	.685
7	.867	.724
8	.844	.709
9	.813	.690
10	.794	.660
11	.776	.648
12	.731	.582

* *Cross-correlations at 0 are contemporaneous correlations.*

have provided ample motivation for further inquiry into the validity of a twin deficit notion, which has been the focus of recent academic research.

The frequently hypothesized relationship between the two deficits is often buttressed by the presence of both deficits in a variant of the core savings/investment identity from the National Income and Product Accounts (NIPA):

$$\text{Gross National Savings} = \text{Gross Investment by the Nation.} \tag{1}$$

This identity can be disaggregated into a familiar form:

$$S_p + S_g = I + NFI \tag{2}$$

where, S_p is private savings, S_g is government savings (total government budget balance), I is private domestic investment, and NFI is the nation's net foreign investment. The additive inverse of NFI is net foreign borrowing, which in this research is considered a theoretically pleasing broad measure of the trade deficit. Thus, net foreign borrowing ($-NFI$) is used as the trade deficit measure, $TDEF$. Employing the additive inverse of government savings ($-S_g$) as the government deficit ($GDEF$), the following relationship suggests the twin deficits relationship:

$$TDEF = GDEF + (I - S_p). \tag{3}$$

The identity above provides a useful framework for analyzing the proposed twin deficits relationship. While the framework does not indicate any behavioral or temporal relationships, it predicts that any government deficit increase not offset by changes in the private-sector savings/investment balance will affect the trade deficit. The trade deficit may

Chart 3
Government Budget Balance (with Seven Lags) and Net Foreign Investment Relative to Nominal GNP

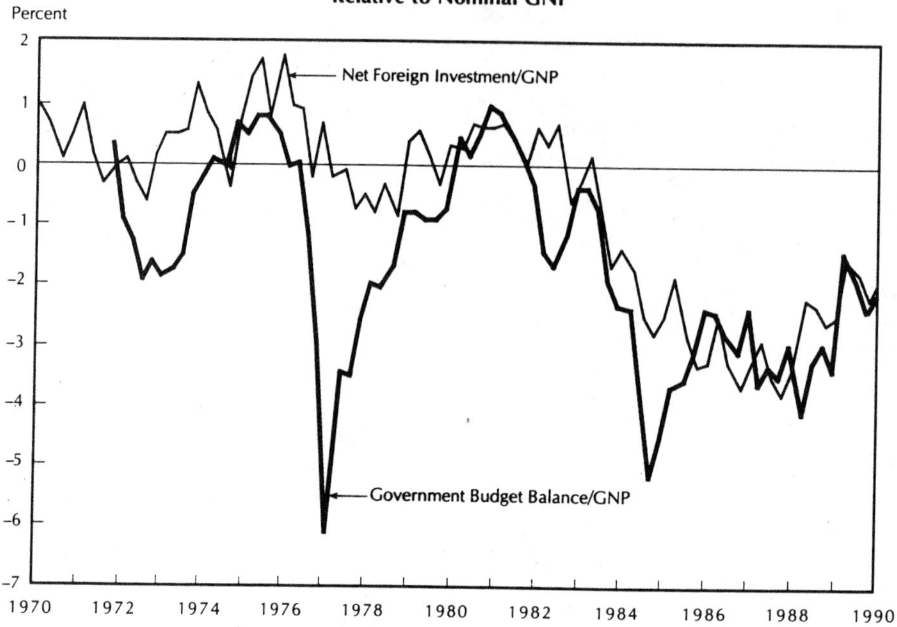

not respond if private savings changes to offset government deficit movements. The crucial question is whether or not government deficit changes are fully offset by private savings responses.

A model of international economics proposed by Robert Mundell and J. Marcus Fleming in the early 1960s provides one theoretical perspective that may help justify the twin deficits notion. In a world of capital mobility and flexible exchange rates the Mundell-Fleming model predicts that increased government budget deficits put incipient upward pressure on domestic interest rates, inducing capital inflows that lift the foreign exchange value of the dollar. After a time lag, the higher value of the dollar retards exports and stimulates imports.

According to the Mundell-Fleming model, a positive relationship exists between government deficits and trade deficits because, it is assumed, people implicitly perceive government bonds issued to finance deficit expenditures as increasing their net wealth. Thus, they do not see a need to increase their current private savings to cover future tax liabilities arising from the deficit financing.

Recent theoretical work concerning government fiscal policy suggests that private savings behavior may change in the presence of increased budget deficits. Robert J. Barro (1974) reintroduced a concept, referred to as Ricardian equivalence (in acknowledgement of the contribution by David Ricardo), suggesting that people recognize that financing tax cuts by bonds merely alters the time profile of taxation. In this view, rational people realize that a tax cut financed by bonds does not increase their net wealth: while current taxes are reduced, future tax liabilities, in "present value" terms, increase by the same amount. As a result, a tax cut resulting in a government budget deficit may induce rational individuals to save an additional portion of their income.[5] The Ricardian equivalence proposition suggests that the net private savings term in the savings/investment identity increases to offset government deficit movements. If Ricardian equivalence holds, then private savings rather than the trade deficit (net foreign borrowing) finances the increased government deficit. There is no anticipation of a twin deficits linkage in this framework.[6]

The implications of the Mundell-Fleming approach contrast clearly with those of Ricardian equivalence in regard to the relevance and validity of a twin deficits relationship. Among the numerous theoretical approaches to open-economy macroeconomics, these two were selected as frameworks for interpreting the empirical analysis because of their prominence in the discipline and their sharply contrasting conclusions.

RESEARCH FINDINGS

Recent economic research has produced a substantial body of empirical literature employing rigorous econometric estimation techniques to test the validity of the twin deficits hypothesis. Nonetheless, the current body of evidence does not yield a consensus on the relationship between government and trade deficits. Some studies using a Mundell-Fleming framework indicate that the twin deficit notion is consistent with the data. In contrast, other studies, finding no underlying relationship between government and trade deficits, are consistent with the predictions of Ricardian equivalence.

How did the empirical work lead to such diametrically opposed conclusions? The following summaries of selected, representative empirical studies include some possible explanations for such varying results and implications. Clearly, certain issues are of primary importance—for example, the choice of appropriate data series and data samples (periods) for examination. These and other important issues are emphasized in the following discussion of existing empirical research into whether the twin deficits notion fits the evidence.

Stephen M. Miller and Frank S. Russek's (1989) empirical work is concentrated on two subperiods of post-World War II U.S. data—one subsample associated with the fixed exchange rate period (1946:Q1 to 1971:Q2) and the other generated during years of flexible exchange rates (1971:Q3 to 1987:Q2). The researchers use measures of the trade and government deficits in nominal levels as well as in ratios to nominal GNP. Only in the flexible exchange rate period do their results support the twin deficit notion for *both* deficit levels and deficit ratios. Thus, Miller and Russek present evidence suggesting a causal impact of government deficits on trade deficits during the floating rate era.[7]

Despite rigor and attention to detail in their study, Miller and Russek, using bivariate analysis of two deficit measures, do not address the interrelationships between government and trade deficits and other relevant explanatory variables. The observed relationship between the two deficit measures does not necessarily reflect an underlying twin deficits structure because one or more other variables may explain the apparent comovements in both series.[8] Research into the twin deficits story requires explicit examination of the entire set of variables that may relate meaningfully to trade and government deficits behavior. A number of other studies estimate relationships between a selection of additional variables that appear relevant for the twin deficits story.

B. Douglas Bernheim (1988), using annual data from the Organisation of Economic Cooperation and Development for the United States and several of its major trading partners, investigates the possibility that fiscal deficits lead to trade deficits.[9] The data sample spans the period from 1960 to 1984, and the estimations employ broad measures of the deficits relative to the relevant nominal gross domestic product (GDP) measures for each country. Bernheim explicitly estimates a regression in which the government deficit affects the trade deficit, but not the reverse, an assumption that restricts his specification.

The effect of budget deficits on trade deficits is likely to be less in the presence of unemployed resources, according to Bernheim.[10] He argues that in weakened economic conditions it is possible for additional government expenditures or a tax cut—both of which may increase the fiscal deficit—to increase private income and private savings, thereby minimizing the effects of the increased government deficit on the trade deficit. To account for business-cycle effects, Bernheim uses the current as well as last period's growth rate in GDP. The estimation results for the United States suggest that the fiscal deficit does significantly affect the trade deficit. Evidence for the trading partners—except for Japan, where no relationship appears to exist—is also consistent with the twin deficits story.

While it provides some evidence for the existence of a twin deficits relationship across nations, the Bernheim study is limited by the absence of additional potentially important variables, namely the real exchange rate and the real interest rate. Because they are not included as explanatory variables in Bernheim's estimations, some aspects of a twin deficit investigation remain unresolved.

Another criticism of earlier studies, aside from excluding important variables from the estimations, is that there is no explicit theoretical structure generating the empirical models for estimation. Rather, those previous studies are centered on a proposed relationship suggested by the Mundell-Fleming framework. The lack of a formal structure as a foundation for the empirical work leaves researchers with few hypotheses that can be rejected.

Recent research by Paul Evens (1989) uses an abstract model economy in which people (agents) make decisions rationally and over a lifetime horizon; his model and theoretical framework provide a more rigorous structure for empirical estimation than has been seen in prior research. Primarily, the model generates a testable hypothesis about the relationship between fiscal deficits and trade deficits—specifically, that in a world incorporating a Ricardian view of taxes and deficits no clear relationship between the deficits should be observed.

Evans (1989) estimates an empirical model that is specified in first-difference form (variables measured as changes from the previous period) and that includes a real (inflation-adjusted) interest rate, real government spending, and real government debt as explanatory variables.[11] The empirical results using data from Canada, France, West Germany, Italy, Japan, the United Kingdom, and the United States suggest that Ricardian equivalence is a reasonable abstraction in the real world.

While Evans's study is more rigorous than earlier work, it is open to criticism on certain empirical grounds that may hinder interpreting the results. For the purposes of this discussion the most relevant criticisms are that there is no variable to account for the effect of real exchange rate variability and that the estimations employ data measures in first difference form. Evans estimates the model in first differences because his theoretical model specifies data in that form. Recently, much empirical literature has focused on testing statistically to determine whether data are more appropriately modeled in levels than in first differences. The issue becomes most relevant when results achieved by using first-differenced data have implications different from those of tests involving data specified in levels. In Evans's case the use of first-differenced data is simply intrinsic to the model, but, as discussed below, the question of whether it is more appropriate to model in levels or in differences can be addressed explicitly and prior to estimation of an empirical model, as in Jeffrey A. Rosensweig and Ellis W. Tallman (1991). The topic is addressed more fully in the next section.

Walter Enders and Bong-Soo Lee (1990) follow Evans in modeling more rigorously the economic behavior underlying the observed relationship between the trade and government deficits.[12] Using quarterly data on the United States from 1947:Q3 to 1987:Q1 for real consumption, real government spending, real public debt, real interest rates, the external current account, and the exchange rate, the researchers apply an estimation methodology known as vector autoregression (VAR). Through techniques that account for dynamic interaction among variables, the methodology allows estimation of relationships without imposing very restrictive assumptions on the specification. Essentially, a VAR specifies that each variable in a system or model is determined by its own lagged values (an autoregression) and the lagged values of all other variables in the system. Despite what appears to be an important effect of the changes in the real public debt on the current account, the model suggests no direct relationship. An explicit test of the Ricardian equivalence proposition with the data cannot reject the hypothesis that budget deficits do not affect the current account.

The criticism of Enders and Lee's (1990) research is similar to that lodged against Evans (1989). First, the estimates are performed on data specified in first differences. The specification in first differences is only a criticism if statistics suggest that such a transformation is inappropriate for the data. However, Enders and Lee do not provide statistical evidence to support the first difference transformation. An additional shortcoming is that, although the nominal exchange rate is among the explanatory variables included in Enders and Lee's work, their measure of this variable exhibits no movement for the fixed exchange rate period from 1947:Q3 until 1973.

THE APPROPRIATENESS OF FIRST-DIFFERENCED DATA

One vein of recent empirical literature focuses on statistical tests that examine whether data are more appropriate for model estimation in first differences or in level form. Statistical techniques are used to determine whether data are stationary in levels—that is, whether the data series' statistical properties, such as means and variances, do not change over time. That quality is an important one to identify because nonstationary data employed in estimation techniques produce statistics that should not be analyzed in the same way as those generated from stationary data. In many cases, estimations using nonstationary data series produce results that lead to incorrect statistical inferences.

Clearly, the answer to the question of whether data used in an examination of twin deficits should be in levels or in first differences is more pertinent if estimation results using first-differenced data lead to inferences that are different from those drawn from data in level form. Among the empirical studies surveyed above, those that support the twin deficits notion tend to have either deficit levels or deficit ratios to GNP as the main variables under study. On the other hand, researchers who found no twin deficits relationship were more often investigating data transformed into first differences.[13] These patterns suggest that the particular data transformation does significantly color the results of inquiry into the twin deficits phenomenon; the choice of data transformation influences whether evidence supports or contradicts the twin deficits story.

The research discussed below, detailed in Rosensweig and Tallman (1991), explicitly considers which is the appropriate form (levels or differences) for representing the data in estimation. Statistical tests guide the choice of data transformation.

ADDITIONAL EVIDENCE

Rosensweig and Tallman (1991) examine the empirical relationship between the U.S. government and trade deficits using a data set that includes a real interest rate measure as well as a real exchange rate measure. The additional variables capture common movements in trade and government deficits that result from these two variables. Like Enders and Lee (1990) and John D. Abell (1990), Rosensweig and Tallman employ vector autoregression methodology.[14] Additional evidence presented below concerning support for the twin deficits story corroborates the results in Rosensweig and Tallman. The research focuses on the idea that movements in the government deficit have a causal impact on the trade deficit.

The data set employed consists of quarterly observations on the variable measures listed above from the period of flexible exchange rates, 1971 to 1989. The trade and government deficit variables are measured as ratios to GNP to account for growth and inflation, as discussed above.

Despite contrasting evidence from typical Dickey-Fuller tests for stationarity, the Rosensweig and Tallman (1991) study shows that there is statistical support for estimating the VAR in level form rather than as differences.[15] Hence, in the research reported here, levels of the four variables (with the deficit series as ratios to GNP) in a VAR with eight lagged quarterly values of each series have been used.[16] Each part of the investigation takes place within the paradigm of VAR, employing the set of four variables described above.

According to the twin deficits notion, movements in the government deficit precede similar changes in the trade deficit, implying that past government deficits would explain a substantial portion of the movements in subsequent trade deficits. This assertion is tested using VAR, which is well suited for such inquiries, by determining whether the statistical evidence supports the hypothesis that the other variables are unaffected by past movements in the government deficit.[17] If the statistics suggest that the movements in other variables are not affected by past movements in the government deficit, the implication would be that the government deficit movements do not precede the movements in the other variables.

The estimated statistics imply rejection of the proposed hypothesis at conventional significance levels, as shown in Table 2, indicating that the government deficit has an important explanatory role and appears to precede statistically the movements in the trade deficit. The implications of these statistics are consistent with evidence from the simpler single-equation estimations also presented in Table 2, where the F-statistics show that *GDEF* is important for explaining *TDEF* movements.

For completeness, the importance of lagged values of *TDEF* on the remaining system of variables is examined by testing statistically for whether the model's other variables respond to trade deficit (as ratio to GNP) movements. The twin deficits story suggests that past movements of the trade deficit should show no impact upon subsequent movements of the other variables.

If the statistical evidence suggests that past trade deficits do have substantial effects on the other variables' subsequent values, then the inferences from the finding that government deficit movements precede trade deficit changes is weakened. Instead, the indication would be that the trade and government deficit variables each affect the other. In formal terms, if the statistics imply rejection of the hypothesis that lagged values of the trade

Table 2
Block-Exogeneity Tests and Single-Equation Block F-Tests

Tests of the Multivariate Hypothesis

GDEF (ratio to GNP) lags are unimportant to the VAR system

χ^2 (24) = 41.75
Critical Value 36.415 at 5 percent significance level.
Reject the null hypothesis. *GDEF* lags are important to the VAR system.

TDEF (ratio to GNP) lags are unimportant to the VAR system

χ^2 (24) = 27.94
Critical Value 36.415 at 5 percent significance level.
Cannot reject the null hypothesis that *TDEF* lags are unimportant for the VAR system.

Single-Equation Block F-Tests*

Variable	F-Statistic on 8 lags	Significance Level
	Dependent Variable - *GDEF*	
GDEF	8.34	.00
REALI	.66	.72
REALEX	1.32	.26
TDEF	.84	.57
	Dependent Variable - *REALI*	
GDEF	2.08	.07
REALI	4.71	.00
REALEX	.42	.90
TDEF	1.98	.08
	Dependent Variable - *REALEX*	
GDEF	1.73	.13
REALI	2.22	.05
REALEX	15.77	.00
TDEF	1.70	.13
	Dependent Variable - *TDEF*	
GDEF	3.06	.01
REALI	1.07	.40
REALEX	.97	.47
TDEF	4.98	.00

* *REALI indicates real interest rates; REALEX indicates real exchange rates.*

deficit have no impact on the other variables, then the statistics would suggest bidirectional causality.

The statistics generated from the test on the trade deficit measure suggest that past trade deficits do not affect subsequent movements in other variables.[18] Results from tests of the single-equation restrictions (tested by F-statistics and presented in Table 2) coincide with those of the multivariate test. Overall, the evidence suggests that trade deficits have little effect on the subsequent behavior of the system's variables. Both the statistical evidence presented above and the findings of Rosensweig and Tallman's (1991) empirical work point toward the existence of a twin deficit relationship in U.S. data.[19]

CONCLUSION

The movement of both the U.S. fiscal and external trade accounts into substantial, persistent coinciding deficits has become an often noted or bemoaned phenomenon. This joint, precipitous slide into deficits during the 1980s, combined with an apparent temporal relationship whereby fiscal changes precede trade balance movements, led to the development of a popular "twin deficits" story. This explanation has relied on casual evidence to assert a causal influence of the government deficit on subsequent trade deficits.

The notable gross facts of dual deficit expansion underlying the widely popular twin deficit hypothesis has been further backed up by certain economic frameworks that lend theoretical underpinnings to the notion.

However, other frameworks, stemming from a Barro-Ricardian theory, are less supportive of the possibility that there is a truly causal linkage between the deficits. The crucial nature of large and persistent deficits in the U.S. government budget and external accounts, the seemingly compelling evidence of their coincidence during the 1980s, and the uncertainty arising from theoretical alternatives about their potential causal linkage have stimulated intensive empirical scrutiny of the twin deficit notion's validity.

The evidence from a range of detailed studies has been mixed or inconclusive. Those starting from a Ricardian framework (such as Evans 1989 and Enders and Lee 1990) find Ricardian results; that is, they find little support for a clear link between the two deficits. However, many of these studies that fail to support the twin deficits idea use particular data transformations (first differences). In contrast, other studies (for example, Bernheim 1988 and Miller and Russek 1989) present evidence in favor of a twin deficit explanation.

The original research reported here was based on an extensive data set and a relatively unrestricted vector autoregression methodology. Further, the deficits data were examined in levels form (as ratios of GNP). This crucial choice of data transformation—versus first differences—was motivated by tests for stationarity of the data. The results provide clear evidence favoring the validity of a twin deficits notion.[20] Clearly, if, as the evidence suggests, government deficits lead or influence subsequent trade deficits, then fiscal policy could well have an important role to play in any attempt to bring the U.S. trade accounts toward balance.

ENDNOTES

1.See, for example, Feldstein (1983), Laney (1986), and Volcker (1984).

2.Feldstein (1983), Laney (1986), and Volcker (1984) are useful references for the story.

3.The two data series are net foreign borrowing (additive inverse of net foreign investment), a broad measure of the trade deficit, denoted as *TDEF*, and the total government deficit series, denoted as *GDEF*. These series are examined on a quarterly basis for the period 1971:Q1 to 1989:Q4, from essentially the beginning of the flexible exchange rate regime under which the large trade and government deficits of the 1980s developed.

4.In ratio form, the government deficit reached 6 percent of nominal GNP in 1975 during the deep recession in 1974-75. In 1982 the deficit-to-GNP ratio approached 5 percent again during a recessionary period, then remained in the 3 percent to 4 percent range throughout the recovery and expansion years as well. Government budget deficits are likely during recessions because, as incomes shrink, tax revenues decline and government outlays for unemployment compensation and the like rise. These "automatic stabilizers" increase the government deficit in ways that may have little to doe with the trade deficit and its movements. This recessionary phenomenon is likely to appear again during 1991.

5.In a simple economic model, the Ricardian equivalence proposition predicts that agents will save the tax cut so that the interest proceeds will cover increased tax liabilities in the future.

6.The Ricardian view does not imply that a twin deficit phenomenon cannot be observed in data. The proposition suggests, though, that there are no behavioral or structural underpinnings to the observation of twin deficits. The main empirical difficulty in distinguishing between Mundell-Fleming and Ricardian implications is that if government deficit movements are correlated with changes in government spending behavior, the twin deficits may appear to be consistent with Mundell-Fleming and also to behave consistently with a Ricardian view. This situation, referred to as observational equivalence, may arise because of the Ricardian view that government spending behavior affects private consumption decisions by reducing the amount of output available for private consumption. Government choice of financing method—debt versus taxes—does not alter the amount of output available for private consumption and therefore does not affect perceived wealth.

7.The researchers present empirical evidence about whether the government deficit "Granger causes" the trade deficit. Granger causality is a statistical notion that innovations in one variable precede innovations in another variable. The inferences drawn from Granger causality tests can be controversial. However, the statistical evidence is consistent with the theoretical implications presented in the Miller and Russek article.

8.Darrat (1988) finds bidirectional Granger causality between the government deficit and the trade deficit in estimates that use an assortment of additional explanatory variables. Also, he estimates the relationship using one data sample that mixes data generated during both the fixed and flexible exchange rate regimes.

9.The countries he studies are Canada, Japan, Mexico, West Germany, the United Kingdom, and the United States.

10.This point relates to the argument above that business-cycle downturns affect the government budget deficit in ways that probably do not influence the trade deficit.

11.The model includes the real government spending variable because the theory suggests that government spending rather than the method of financing government spending affects private consumption decisions (see note 5). Also, Evans (1989) discussed measurement error in the existing current account data that fails to account for the increased market value of U.S. investment abroad. For more detail on this issue see Dewald and Ulan (1990).

12.Abell (1990) estimates a VAR system with several relevant explanatory variables. Using first-differenced data, he finds little support for the government deficit as a primary explanatory variable for the trade deficit measure. The results suggest the absence of the causal underpinnings of the twin deficit story. It is notable that the data sample—monthly observations from 1979 to 1985—presents only a limited picture of the historical behavior of the two deficits and the related variables.

13.It is also important to note that Evans (1989) and Enders and Lee (1990) employ government spending variables and measures of the real public debt rather than only measures of the fiscal deficit, as in the previous studies. The model implications suggest the relevance of the government spending measures for the estimates.

14.Runkle (1987) criticizes the use of VAR techniques without providing some mechanism to infer statistical significance of the results. Rosensweig and Tallman (1991) provide confidence intervals for the relevant statistical output.

15.Rosensweig and Tallman (1991) employ Monte Carlo integration techniques to estimate a Bayesian posterior probability for the stationarity of the data in level form. Results suggest that the model should be specified in levels.

16.A VAR with six lags produced statistics with the same inferences as those presented in the text.

17.A block exogeneity test, a multivariate test that examines whether the regressions for all the remaining variables are (statistically) significantly changed by removing the lagged values of the government deficit (to GNP) ratio from all regressions, is used. The chi-square statistic with 24 degrees of freedom of 40.9 suggests rejection of the null hypothesis that *GDEF* lags are unimportant at the 5 percent significance level.

18.The chi-square statistic for 24 degrees of freedom of 27.94 does not allow rejection of the null hypothesis at the 5 percent significance level.

19.See Rosensweig and Tallman (1991) for more detailed attention to issues like the percentage of variance explained, the direct impact on particular variables of shocks to other variables,and the dynamic effects of shocks.

20.These findings do not contradict Ricardian equivalence because the specification does not allow a direct test of Ricardian hypotheses.

REFERENCES

Abell, John D. "Twin Deficits during the 1980s: An Empirical Investigation." *Journal of Macroeconomics* 12, no. 1 (1990): 81-96.

Barro, Robert J. "Are Government Bonds Net Wealth?" *Journal of Political Economy* 82 (November/December 1974): 1095-1117.

Bernheim, B. Douglas. "Budget Deficits and the Balance of Trade." In *Tax Policy and the Economy*, edited by Lawrence H. Summers. Cambridge, Mass.: MIT Press, 1988.

Darrat, Ali F. "Have Large Budget Deficits Caused Rising Trade Deficits?" *Southern Economic Journal* 54 (April 1988): 879-87.

Dewald, William G., and Michael Ulan. "The Twin-Deficit Illusion." *Cato Journal* 9 (Winter 1990): 689-707.

Enders, Walter, and Bong-Soo Lee. "Current Account and Budget Deficits: Twins or Distant Cousins?" *Review of Economics and Statistics* 72, no. 3 (1990): 373-81.

Evans, Paul. "Do Budget Deficits Affect the Current Account?" Ohio State University Working Paper, July 1989.

Feldstein, Martin. "Domestic Saving and International Capital Market Movements in the Long and Short Run." *European Economic Review* 21 (1983): 129-51.

Greenwald, John. "Smooth Waters Now, But Rapids Ahead: Budget and Trade Deficits Trouble the Second-Term Outlook." *Time*, November 19, 1984, 96-98.

Laney, Leroy. "Twin Deficits in the 1980s: What Are the Linkages?" *Business Economics* 21 (April 1986): 40-45.

McNamee, Mike, Paul Magnusson, Catherine Yang, Tim Smart, and Howard Gleckman. "The Economic Drama: New Cast, Old Script; Can Bush and Congress Make Headway against the Daunting Deficits They Inherit?" *Business Week*, December 26, 1988, 94-97.

Miller, Stephen M., and Frank S. Russek. "Are the Deficits Really Related?" *Contemporary Policy Issues* 7, no. 4 (1989): 91-115.

Rosensweig, Jeffrey A., and Ellis W. Tallman. "Fiscal Policy and Trade Adjustment: Are the Deficits Really Twins?" Federal Reserve Bank of Atlanta Working Paper 91-2, March 1991.

Runkle, David E. "Vector Autoregressions and Reality." *Journal of Business and Economic Statistics* 5, no. 4 (1987): 437-42.

"Some of My Best Friends Are Deficits; America's Twin Deficits have so far failed to trigger the long predicted economic crunch." *The Economist*, January 20, 1990, 73.

Volcker, Paul A. "Facing Up to the Twin Deficits." *Challenge* 27 (March/April 1984): 4-9.

QUESTIONS

1. What is the "twin deficits" problem? Explain the supposed causal link between these deficits.

2. Explain the identity $S_p + S_g = I + NFI$. What does it imply about the relationship between the government budget deficit and the trade deficit?

3. What are the differences between the Mundell-Fleming model and the Ricardian equivalence model regarding the possibility of a causal link between the twin deficits?

4. Compare Rosensweig's and Tallman's research methods and results to those of the earlier studies they cite. What policy implications do their findings have?

READING 42

Monetary vs. Fiscal Policy: New Evidence on an Old Debate

Peter E. Kretzmer

The economy's apparently sluggish response to lower interest rates during 1991 has led some analysts to speculate that monetary policy may be less effective than in the past. These analysts argue that fiscal stimulus is necessary to combat the recent slow growth of the economy. In response, the President and Congress are debating the shape of a fiscal stimulus package.

Questions about the relative effectiveness of monetary and fiscal policy are not new. The issue was at the heart of the Monetarist-Keynesian debate of the 1960s and early 1970s. The monetarists held that monetary policy was much more important to the economy than fiscal policy, while the Keynesians argued that fiscal policy was dominant.

Evidence from this debate, however, is of limited help to today's policymakers. First, the debate was never fully resolved. Moreover, numerous changes in the U.S. economy have occurred in the last two decades.

This article revisits the monetary-fiscal policy debate. The first section reviews the dispute between the monetarists and the Keynesians. The second section discusses how the effects of monetary and fiscal policy on the economy may have changed in recent years. The final section presents evidence indicating that while monetary policy has become less effective over the years, it is still relatively more effective than fiscal policy.

THE MONETARY-FISCAL POLICY DEBATE

The debate over the relative importance of monetary and fiscal policy was originally waged by two philosophically opposed groups of economists. The monetarists believed the money supply played a central role in determining economic performance. They used evidence from their empirical studies to show that changes in the money supply had a larger effect on the economy than changes in fiscal variables. The Keynesians believed that to stabilize the economy, fiscal policy was essential. They claimed that methodological problems invalidated the conclusions of the monetarist studies.

The first empirical study that attempted to determine which of the two positions was correct was conducted by Milton Friedman and David Meiselman in 1963. They examined simple correlations between consumption and money and between consumption and fiscal variables. Friedman-Meiselman found that consumption was correlated to a much larger extent with money than with the fiscal variables. They interpreted this piece of evidence as consistent with the monetarist belief that monetary policy is more important than fiscal policy.

In 1965, Keynesians Albert Ando and Franco Modigliani argued that Friedman and Meiselman's evidence failed to show that monetary policy was more important than fiscal policy. First, Ando-Modigliani attacked Friedman-Meiselman's choice of sample periods on the grounds that the results may be sensitive to the inclusion of the World War II years. Second, Ando-Modigliani criticized Friedman-Meiselman's focus on contemporaneous relationships, reasoning that any complete study of the effectiveness of policy must account for lags in the effect of policy changes.

Ando-Modigliani's most serious criticism, however, was that Friedman-Meiselman failed to allow for feedback from the economy to the measures of monetary and fiscal policy. One example of this problem arose in the way in which Friedman-Meiselman measured their fiscal variable (called autonomous expenditures). Ando-Modigliani pointed out that the monetarists' measure of autonomous expenditures included the fiscal deficit, which moves inversely with economic activity. To see why this is a problem, suppose the government increases autonomous expenditures to increase economic activity. The increase in economic activity will reduce the deficit by generating tax revenue, thereby offsetting part of the initial rise in autonomous spending. As a result, the correlation between economic activity and autonomous spending would appear weak even if the initial increase in spending had a strong effect on output.

A 1968 study by Leonall Andersen and Jerry Jordan responded to some of the Ando-Modigliani critique.[1] Andersen-Jordan regressed U.S. nominal GNP on current and lagged measures of money and two fiscal variables.[2] They made a key improvement over the Friedman-Meiselman study by including lagged effects of the monetary and fiscal variables. They also used fiscal policy measures that corrected for the problem of feedback from the economy. Andersen-Jordan found that the coefficients on the monetary variable were statistically significant, while the coefficients on both fiscal variables were not. Thus, despite changes in methodology, the Andersen-Jordan results continued to support the Friedman-Meiselman conclusion that monetary variables dominate fiscal variables in explaining the U.S. macroeconomy.

But the Andersen-Jordan study, and similar studies that followed, still had problems. A remaining central flaw, noted in

1974 by Alan Blinder and Robert Solow, was a failure to control for the feedback from the real economy to the conduct of monetary policy. Blinder-Solow argued that such feedback could lead to incorrect conclusions about the relative importance of monetary and fiscal policy.

This feedback problem arises from the way in which the Federal Reserve has conducted monetary policy during much of the post-World War II era. With some exceptions, the Fed has carried out a policy of stabilizing interest rates over the short term. Suppose an increase in investment demand pushes interest rates and output upward. If the Fed is stabilizing interest rates, it will increase the money supply to limit the increase in interest rates. In other words, the increase in output causes the increase in the money supply, not the reverse. Failure to allow for the effect of output on money could have led to positive coefficients on money in the Andersen-Jordan study even if changes in money do not cause changes in output. Thus, not accounting for the potential feedback from output to money may render the monetarist conclusion unwarranted.[3]

By the mid-1970s, the debate between the monetarists and the Keynesians subsided without either side being able to convert the other. Monetarists continued to believe monetary policy was dominant, while Keynesians continued to believe the flaws in the studies were serious enough to invalidate the monetarists' conclusions.

RECENT CHANGES IN THE EFFECTS OF MONETARY AND FISCAL POLICY

The uncertainty surrounding the results of the early studies makes it difficult for policymakers to draw firm conclusions on the effects of monetary and fiscal policy. But even if the debate had been resolved, would the results be of value today? Probably not, because the economic impact of monetary and fiscal policy is likely to have changed since the mid-1970s.

Monetary Policy

Monetary policy in the United States is conducted primarily through Federal Reserve open-market operations. Open-market operations, which are purchases or sales of Treasury securities by the Fed, change the quantity of reserves held by the banking system. Open-market operations also affect the federal funds rate, the interest rate at which banks lend reserves to one another for short periods of time. Changes in the federal funds rate in turn can affect real output. For example, a decrease in the federal funds rate can lead to a decrease in other interest rates, thereby raising both consumption and investment demand.[4]

Recently, however, structural changes in the U.S. economy may have changed the impact of monetary policy on real output. These changes include the removal of interest rate ceilings on bank deposits, the development of more nonbank sources of financing for firms, and the growth of the foreign sector.[5]

Prior to their removal in the 1980s, interest rate ceilings on bank deposits tended to reinforce the effect of higher interest rates on economic activity. When market rates rose above the ceilings, disintermediation—the flight of funds from the banking system—took place. With a smaller pool of funds available to banks, bank credit for purchases such as homes and consumer durables became less available, reinforcing the effects of higher interest rates. The removal of interest rate ceilings on bank deposits, therefore, has probably reduced the real effects of monetary policy.

The growth of more nonbank sources of financing for firms has also probably weakened the effect of monetary policy. Investment by firms that depend largely on bank loans is sensitive to their availability. But now that more firms can turn to the commercial paper market, the convertible bond market, or the swap market to help finance their investment, interest rate increases may have less effect on business investment.

The growth in the foreign sector has also impacted the effect of monetary policy. As world capital markets have become more integrated and the U.S. share of the world economy has shrunk, monetary policy has become less effective because it is more difficult for the Federal Reserve to alter U.S. interest rates relative to other countries' interest rates. For example, assume the Federal Reserve sells Treasury securities in an effort to increase U.S. interest rates. The higher interest rates will now immediately attract foreign investors. As the foreign investors purchase the securities, U.S. interest rates are pushed back down. Thus, it has become more difficult for the Federal Reserve to alter U.S. interest rates.

On the other hand, with a larger foreign sector, the exchange rate has become more important for output determination because it affects the levels of both exports and imports. If expansionary monetary policy causes the value of the dollar to fall, exports should increase and imports should decrease, thereby expanding real output. Now that the foreign sector is larger, the output effect will be larger. Thus, the exchange rate channel for monetary policy has become more important, potentially making the economy more sensitive to monetary policy.

Fiscal Policy

Fiscal policy refers to expenditures by federal, state, and local governments and to the taxes levied to finance these expenditures. The U.S. economy has recently changed in several ways that may have altered the impact of fiscal policy on real output. First, transfer payments have grown and defense spending has shrunk as shares of the federal budget. Second, federal individual income tax rates dropped sharply in the 1980s. And third, budget deficits have been large in recent years.

Defense and transfer payments. The balance between defense spending and transfer payments as shares of the economy has changed rather dramatically over the past few decades. Defense spending proposed by President Bush's latest budget (FY 1993) continues a long-term decline, falling from over 10 percent of GNP in the early 1950s to about 5 percent today.[6] At the same time, transfer payments—payments from the government to a group of people defined by a characteristic such as age or income—have increased from about 3 percent of the economy in the 1950s to over 10 percent today.

This change in the makeup of the budget may have reduced the potency of fiscal policy. In the 1950s, a 1 percent change in government spending across the board would have included larger changes in defense spending than in transfer payments, because defense spending was a larger share of the budget.[7] Today, however, a 1 percent change in spending would include larger changes in transfer payments. Because defense spending is stimulative while many types of transfer payments are not, the effect of proportional changes in government spending on output may have weakened over the years.

Increases in defense spending are likely to stimulate aggregate demand. To understand why, first consider another form of government spending that affects the economy differently than defense spending. For example, when the government buys food products to serve meals to its employees, the purchases presumably substitute for about an equal amount of private meal purchases (by the same employees) that would otherwise have been made. Thus, there is little or no net increase in aggregate demand. However, when the government buys military equipment, the purchase is not a good substitute for private spending on goods and services. Thus, an increase in defense spending is likely to generate a net increase in aggregate demand.[8]

Transfer payments affect aggregate demand only if the spending patterns of the group receiving the transfer payments differ from the spending patterns of taxpayers in general. To illustrate, consider government aid to students. This program takes money from taxpayers and redistributes it to students. As long as the spending patterns of students are similar to the spending patterns of the general population, expanding aid to students should have no effect on aggregate demand.

Tax rates. Tax rates fell substantially in the 1980s, potentially increasing the effectiveness of fiscal policy. When the government buys goods and services, it creates income for the producers of the goods and services. The income is consumed in an amount that depends, among other things, on how much of the income remains after taxes. With lower tax rates, more after-tax income is earned, more consumption takes place, more after-tax income is generated, and so on. The size of this "multiplier" for government expenditure thus depends on tax rates. Lower tax rates in the 1980s may have increased the output effect of government expenditures, making fiscal policy more potent.

Budget deficits. The large budget deficits of recent years may have forced policymakers to rely less on fiscal policy to influence the economy. A great deal of public attention has focused on the size of the deficits and their possibly harmful effects. In this environment, it has become more difficult to propose new expenditure programs or engage in other aggressive fiscal policy, making fiscal policy a less important factor in the 1980s. Furthermore, fiscal policy could lose even more importance in the 1990s, since the 1991 budget agreement forces Congress to offset expenditure increases or tax reductions so that the budget deficit does not grow.[9]

NEW EVIDENCE ON THE MONETARY-FISCAL POLICY DEBATE

This section presents evidence on the monetary-fiscal policy debate that attempts to account for the methodological problems of previous studies and for the changes in the U.S. economy. The results suggest that while monetary policy has become less effective over the years, it is still more effective than fiscal policy.

Empirical Model

One of the remaining problems with the earlier studies is that they did not completely account for the feedback from the economy to the policy variables. To account for the feedback, a vector autoregression (VAR) is used to analyze the data. In a VAR, each variable is regressed on its own lags and the lags of each of the other variables in the data set. In this way, the procedure allows each variable to be affected by its own history and the history of each of the other variables. For example, output is regressed on lags of policy variables in one equation, while the policy variables are regressed on lags of output in other equations.

The variables in the VAR are quarterly measures of real output, inflation, two monetary policy variables, and two fiscal policy variables.[10] Output is measured by the growth rate of industrial production.[11] Inflation is measured by the growth rate of the CPI. The monetary policy variables are the growth rate of the monetary base and the 90-day Treasury bill rate.[12] The fiscal policy variables are the change in total government expenditures (net of interest payments) as a fraction of GNP and the government budget deficit as a fraction of GNP.[13]

VARs are run for two 30-year subsamples. The results are then compared in order to identify changes over time in the potency of monetary and fiscal policy.[14] The first subsample extends from the second quarter of 1950 through the fourth quarter of 1979. The second subsample extends from the second quarter of 1962 through the fourth quarter of 1991.

Results

Using the results of a VAR, there are several ways to evaluate the effects of monetary and fiscal policy on output. The three used here are causality tests, variance decompositions, and impulse response functions. Causality tests focus on the statistical significance of monetary and fiscal policy variables in affecting real output. Variance decompositions compare the relative contributions of the monetary and fiscal variables in explaining output. Impulse

Table 1

Causality Tests

Sample period	Monetary	P-value	Fiscal	P-value
1950:Q2–1979:Q4	1.64	.07	1.05	.42
1962:Q2–1991:Q4	1.76	.05	1.46	.13

Note: Column 2 reports F-statistics for the hypothesis that monetary variables do not affect output. Column 4 reports F-statistics for the hypothesis that fiscal variables do not affect output. Columns 3 and 5 report the associated significance levels for the hypotheses tests.

Table 2

Variance Decompositions of Output

Sample period	Monetary	Fiscal
1950:Q2–1979:Q4	28	15
1962:Q2–1991:Q4	23	17

Note: Column 2 reports the estimate for the percentage of output variance explained by monetary policy variables. Column 3 reports the estimate for the percentage of output variance explained by fiscal policy variables.

response functions show the estimated responses of output to hypothetical changes in policy.

Causality tests. Causality tests are used to determine whether the effects of the policy variables on output are statistically significant. For example, if the coefficients on the monetary policy variables are significant but the coefficients on the fiscal policy variables are not, the test would suggest that monetary policy is more effective than fiscal policy.

The effects of monetary policy on output, while not that strong, probably exceed the effects of fiscal policy (Table 1). The coefficients on the monetary policy variables are statistically significant, at the 10 percent significance level in the first subperiod and at the 5 percent significance level in the second subperiod. In contrast, the fiscal policy variables do not have a statistically significant effect on output in either subperiod.

Variance decompositions. While the causality tests indicate whether policy variables have a statistically significant effect on output, they do not show the relative size of these effects. The variance decomposition of output, however, can be used to compare the size of the monetary policy effect with the size of the fiscal policy effect, and to see how the size of the effects has changed over time. Specifically, the variance decomposition shows the percentages of the variability of output that are explained by the monetary and fiscal policy variables.[15]

The variance decompositions results appear in Table 2. The first column, the estimated effect of monetary policy, shows the percentage of the variance of output explained by monetary base changes and Treasury bill rate changes. The second column, the estimate of the effect of fiscal policy, shows the percentage of the variance of output explained by government expenditure changes and budget deficit changes.[16]

Table 2 indicates that the effect of monetary policy is greater than the effect of fiscal policy in both subperiods. For example, in the first subperiod, the variation in output

Chart 1
Effect of Monetary Base Shock on Output

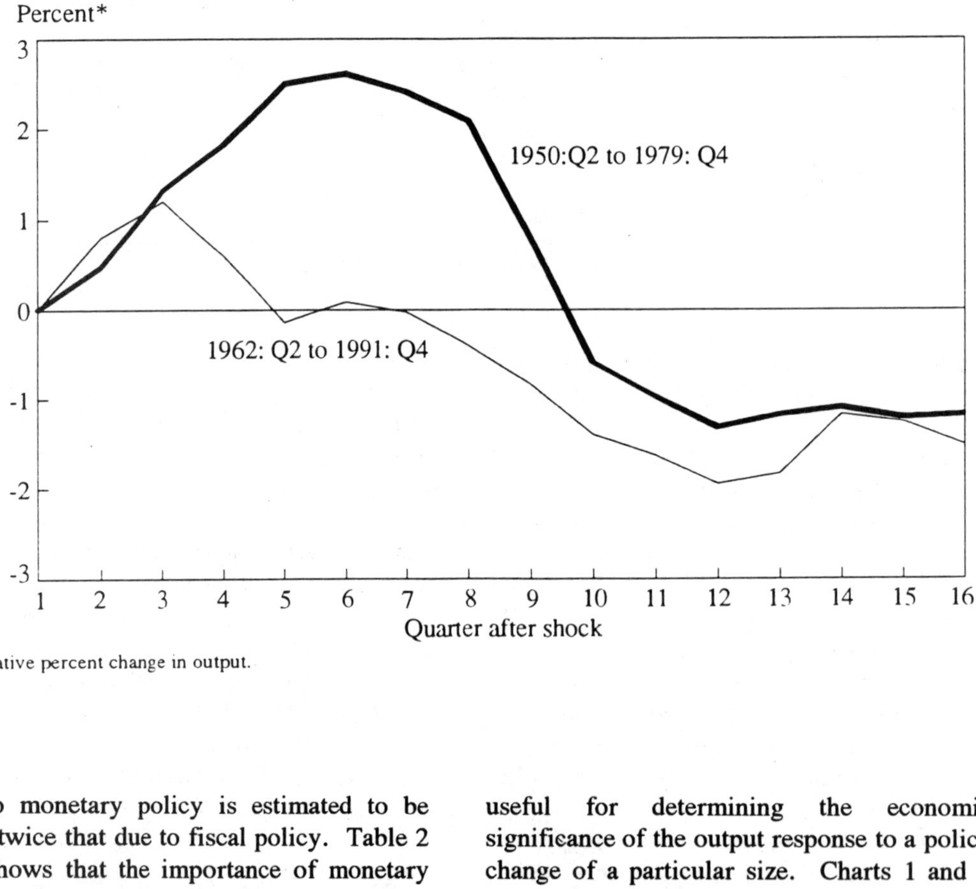

* Cumulative percent change in output.

due to monetary policy is estimated to be about twice that due to fiscal policy. Table 2 also shows that the importance of monetary policy fell somewhat from the first to the second subperiod, while the importance of fiscal policy remained about the same.

Impulse response functions. The impulse response function shows the estimated response of output to a permanent change in monetary or fiscal policy.[17] It is particularly useful for determining the economic significance of the output response to a policy change of a particular size. Charts 1 and 2 show the output responses to changes in the monetary policy variables, while Chart 3 shows the output responses to changes in the fiscal policy variables.

Chart 1 compares the response of output to a 1 percent increase in the monetary base in the two subperiods. The increase in output is

Chart 2

Effect of Interest Rate Shock on Output

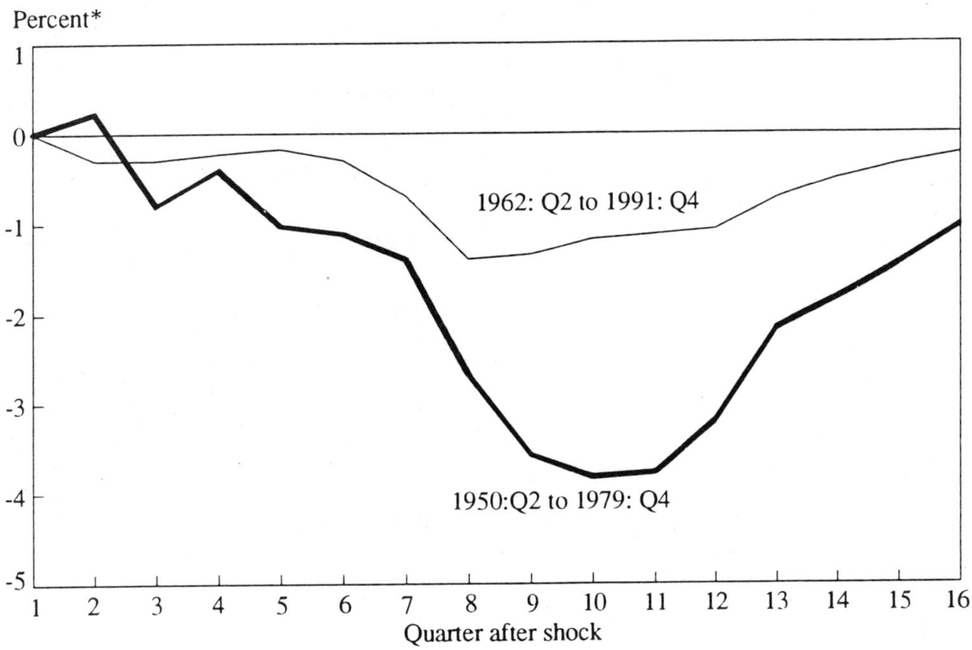

* Cumulative percent change in output.

larger in the first subperiod than in the second subperiod. For the first subperiod, the peak response of output to a 1 percent base increase is between 2 and 3 percent.[18] For the second subperiod, the peak response of output is just over 1 percent.

Chart 2 compares the response of output to a one-percentage-point increase in the Treasury bill rate in the two subperiods. The decline in output following an increase in the Treasury bill rate is larger for the first subperiod than for the second subperiod. For the first subperiod, output falls almost 4 percent after a one-percentage-point increase in the Treasury bill rate. For the later subperiod, the response is much smaller—output falls between 1 and 2 percent.[19]

Chart 3 shows how output responds when government expenditures and the budget

Chart 3
Effect of Expenditure and Deficit Shocks on Output

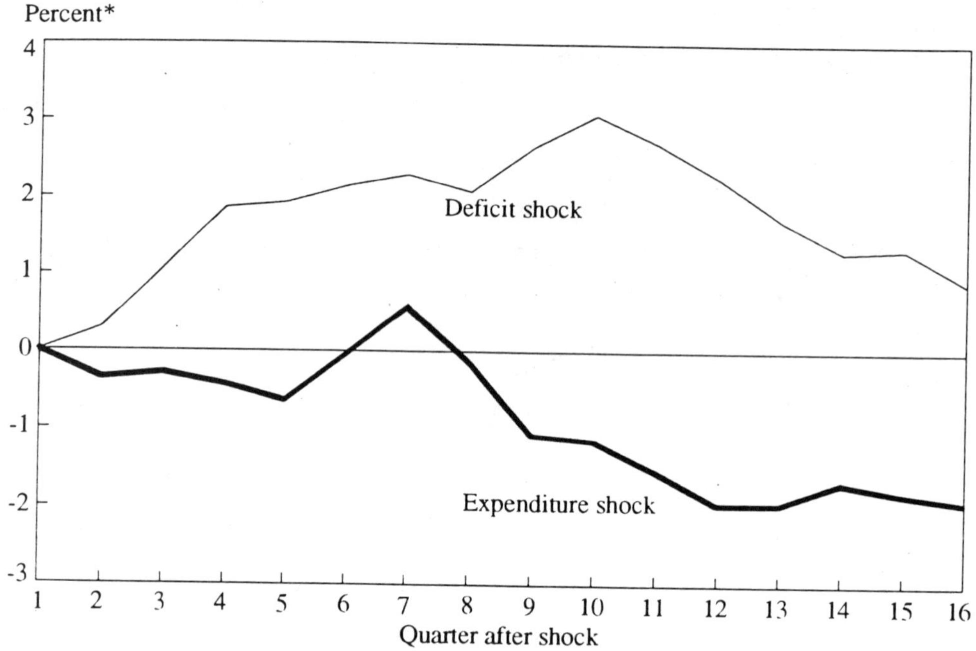

* Cumulative percent change in output.
Note: Sample period is 1962: Q2 to 1991: Q4.

deficit increase by 1 percent of GNP. Only the second subperiod is shown for these fiscal policy changes because the causality tests clearly showed that fiscal policy was statistically insignificant in the first subperiod. The response of output to the increase in government expenditures is slightly positive after about two years but appears to be negative in the longer run. Output responds more strongly to the increase in the budget deficit, rising by about 3 percent.

CONCLUSIONS

Monetarists and Keynesians debated the relative importance of monetary and fiscal policy throughout the 1960s and 1970s. Yet the evidence from this period is of limited help to today's policymakers, since these studies had methodological flaws and many changes in the U.S. economy have occurred in the last two decades.

This article corrects the flaws of the early studies and finds that monetary policy has become less effective over time, but is still more effective than fiscal policy. The effects of both money and interest rates on output appear to have fallen over the years. As a result, more monetary stimulus may now be necessary to achieve a particular change in output than in the past.

The study also suggests that the fiscal stimulus packages being debated by Congress may be of limited help. While the effect of fiscal policy on output is not statistically significant over the sample period, there is some evidence that increases in the budget deficit may increase output. The fiscal packages under consideration, however, leave the deficit unchanged, as required by the 1991 budget agreement.

ENDNOTES

1.The Anderson-Jordan study was the first, and perhaps the most important, of the St. Louis studies, so-called because the studies were prepared by the research department of the Federal Reserve Bank of St. Louis.

2.The monetary variable was M1 or the monetary base, and the fiscal variables were full-employment expenditures and full-employment tax receipts. The sample period extended from the first quarter of 1952 through the second quarter of 1968.

3.More precisely, the bias in the estimated coefficient on money arises if output shocks are contemporaneously correlated with money through the feedback mechanism or if output shocks cause future changes in money and there is autocorrelation in the output shocks.

4.Newly created reserves, through increasing the money supply, may make households and corporations feel wealthier. This perceived increase in wealth may also stimulate consumption and investment demand.

5.Kahn discusses a similar set of factors as reasons for the changing interest sensitivity of the U.S. economy.

6.The decline in defense spending was only partially offset by the Reagan defense buildup during the first half of the 1980s.

7.This example assumes that the 1 percent change affects all categories of expenditure proportionately, leaving each category's share of the government budget unaffected. It is not difficult to imagine an expenditure proposal that violates this assumption. The measure of expenditures used in the empirical section of this article does not differentiate among different types of government spending.

8.The effect defense spending has on the aggregate supply of goods and services depends on the degree to which the spending affects the productivity of the private economy. There is substantial debate over the effect of defense spending on productivity. One argument is that defense spending spurs innovation and scientific progress that add to the productivity of the nondefense sector. Others argue the defense industry is a drag on productivity, since it diverts scientific talent from nondefense to defense jobs. There is currently no clear consensus on the effects of defense spending on productivity and aggregate supply.

9.Congress must compensate for any tax reduction by cutting expenditures or raising other taxes; any expenditure increase must be offset by an expenditure cut elsewhere or a tax increase.

10.Similar data sets have been analyzed by authors such as Sims and Litterman and Weiss, but usually without the fiscal variables.

11.The empirical work was repeated using the growth rate of real GNP as an alternative output measure.

12.The monetary base was chosen over M1, since its movements are more likely to indicate Fed monetary policy. Movements in M1 are also influenced by bank behavior as well as the liquidity preferences of the public.

The federal funds rate is considered by many to be the optimal interest rate for the analysis of monetary policy because it has often been the Fed's main policy instrument. The short-term Treasury bill rate is substituted in its place because a longer series is readily available for the Treasury bill rate than for the funds rate. Both interest rates yield similar results.

Using both the interest rate and money variables tends to exaggerate the importance of monetary policy, since interest rate innovations can also reflect other nonmonetary shocks to the economy. Sims, and Litterman and Weiss assume that only money stock innovations reflect the effects of monetary policy, an assumption that almost surely underestimates the true importance of monetary policy. This research treats the combined effect of monetary and interest rate innovations as reflecting an upper bound on the possible influence of monetary policy. By ordering the interest rate last in computing the variance decompositions and impulse response functions, the degree of exaggeration in this measure of the effect of monetary policy is minimized. See Kretzmer (forthcoming) for further details.

13.The budget deficit is measured as the difference between government expenditures, net of interest payments, and total government receipts, including inflation tax revenue. The deficit is used as the second fiscal variable, rather than receipts, in order to impose on the VAR the cointegration of government expenditures and government receipts. See Bohn and Kretzmer (forthcoming) for more details on this issue.

14.The subsample length of 30 years is judgmental, based on the tradeoff between statistical power and the ability to infer when changes in the effects of policy actually occurred. There are six variables and ten quarters of lags included in the VAR. Thus, each equation has 61 regressors. At least 120 observations, twice the number of regressors, are needed to obtain a reasonable degree of precision.

15.The estimated variance decompositions and impulse response functions (the third technique) are unique only if the innovations in the variables are mutually uncorrelated. In the absence of this condition, it is necessary to model the relation among the contemporaneous innovations. Typically, an ordering is determined, where first in the ordering means "most exogenous" and last in the ordering means "most endogenous." In this setup, innovations in X, for example, are maintained to be related only to the innovations in the variables that precede X in the ordering.

16.Innovations in the two fiscal policy variables are strongly positively correlated. As a result, it is difficult to separate out the individual influences on output of expenditure innovations and deficit innovations with any degree of confidence. Equivalently, the ordering of the two variables substantially affects the individual results. However, the sum of the influences is quite unaffected by the ordering.

17.In order to compute the impulse response function, it is necessary to invert the VAR, expressing each variable as a function of lagged innovations in itself and the other variables. Then, the coefficients on the lagged innovations measure the response over time of the dependent variable to a unit shock in that independent variable. Thus, the change is permanent in the sense that it is not actively reversed by policymakers.

18.Recall that the results reported here use industrial production as the output measure. Industrial production is more responsive to money than is real GNP. This result is consistent with Kretzmer (1989) who finds that output of service industries is less responsive to money than output of durable manufacturing industries. The result using real GNP are qualitatively similar to the results reported for industrial production.

19.The reduced sensitivity of output to interest rate innovations is consistent with the results presented in Kahn.

REFERENCES

Anderson, Leonall C., and Jerry L. Jordan. 1968. "Monetary and Fiscal Actions: A Test of Their Relative Importance in Economic Stabilization," Federal Reserve Bank of St. Louis, *Review*, November, pp. 11-24.

Ando, Albert, and Franco Modigliani. 1965. "The Relative Stability of Monetary Velocity and the Investment Multiplier," *American Economic Review*, September, pp. 693-728.

Blinder, Alan S., and Robert M. Solow. 1974. "Analytical Foundations of Fiscal Policy," in *The Economics of Public Finance*. Washington: Brookings Institution.

Bohn, Henning. 1991. "Budget Balance through Revenue or Spending Adjustments? Some Historical Evidence for the United States," *Journal of Monetary Economics*, June, pp. 333-59.

Friedman, Milton, and David Meiselman. 1963. "The Relative Stability of Monetary Velocity and the Investment Multiplier in the United States, 1897-1958," in *Stabilization Policies*. Englewood Cliffs: Prentice Hall.

Kahn, George A. 1989. "The Changing Interest Sensitivity of the U.S. Economy," Federal Reserve Bank of Kansas City, *Economic Review*, November pp. 13-34.

Kretzmer, Peter E. Forthcoming. "How Important Are Monetary and Fiscal Policy in Explaining Postwar U.S. Data? A Vector Autoregression Approach," Federal Reserve Bank of Kansas City, working paper.

__. 1989. "The Cross-Industry Effects of Unanticipated Money in an Equilibrium Business Cycle Model," *Journal of Monetary Economics*, March, pp. 275-96.

Litterman, Robert B., and Laurence Weiss. 1985. "Money, Real Interest Rates, and Output: A Reinterpretation of Postwar U.S. Data," *Econometrica*, January, pp. 129-56.

Sims, Christopher A., 1980. "Comparison of Interwar and Postwar Business Cycles: Monetarism Reconsidered," *American Economic Review*, May, pp. 250-57.

QUESTIONS

1. What were the fundamental positions of the monetarists and the Keynesians in the debate over the relative importance of monetary and fiscal policy? What evidence and arguments did each side present to buttress its stand?

2. What structural changes in the U.S. economy does Kretzmer suggest may have altered the effects of monetary policy? Have these changes increased or lessened monetary policy's impacts on real output?

3. How has the effectiveness of fiscal policy been influenced in recent years by changes in the government budget?

4. What does Kretzmer conclude from his empirical work about the relative importance of monetary and fiscal policy? What are the implications of his findings for policymakers?

READING 43

Public Preferences and Inflation

Carl E. Walsh

Inflation rates vary enormously from country to country. Between 1977 and 1989, for instance, inflation averaged 6.2 percent in the U.S., 2.8 percent in Japan, and 40 percent in Iceland. Even within the European Common Market inflation rates in this period ranged from 3.0 percent in Germany to 19.1 percent in Greece.

What accounts for these differences? Is it because countries with high inflation experienced stronger inflationary shocks, from either external or internal sources, than low inflation countries? Is it because differing institutional structures in each country lead nations to respond differently to common worldwide economic events?

Recent theories imply that differences in inflation may simply reflect public attitudes in a country, in particular, a willingness to tolerate inflation in return for short-run economic expansion and reduced unemployment. According to these theories, an economy's average rate of inflation reflects the weight society places on inflation relative to unemployment. Countries that weigh the costs of inflation heavily should have lower average rates of inflation. Conversely, countries that place low weight on maintaining low inflation should have higher average inflation. These theories are based on the notion that central banks have an incentive to engage in expansionary policies in order to achieve a temporary reduction in unemployment at the cost of higher inflation. If society places little weight on the costs of the higher inflation, the incentive will be great to attempt to reduce unemployment. As a result, inflation will tend to be higher.

Recent work comparing household surveys of attitudes in the U.S. and New Zealand provides some interesting evidence on the role of social attitudes in affecting a nation's inflation experience. Since 1977, inflation has averaged 6.2 percent in the U.S. and 12.1 percent in New Zealand. The surveys are consistent with the hypothesis that New

Zealanders are less averse to inflation than Americans; New Zealand's higher rate of inflation may reflect the political process which supplies the rate of inflation the public demands.

MEASURING ATTITUDES TOWARDS INFLATION

Survey data allow the construction of a measure of average attitudes towards inflation. However, it is important to keep in mind that attitudes towards inflation are usually complex and vary with each individual's own personal economic situation. One of the major real costs of inflation, particularly when the inflation was not fully anticipated or indexation is incomplete, is an arbitrary redistribution of wealth. An unexpected rise in the rate of inflation tends to distribute wealth away from creditors and towards debtors; an unexpected decline in inflation has the opposite effect. It should not be surprising, therefore, that attitudes towards inflation vary widely across the population. Broad measures of average views on inflation can hide this diversity of opinion but may still be useful in assessing the general attitude of the population.

In order to construct a measure of society's preference for inflation, it is necessary to focus explicitly on the costs and benefits of inflation. In the abstract, most people would probably prefer zero inflation. Such an observation is relatively unhelpful though, since it fails to provide any information on the price society would be willing to pay to achieve zero inflation. Since the major cost of reducing inflation is usually considered to be the resulting temporary rise in unemployment, the appropriate way to measure society's preference for inflation is to focus on the trade-off the public is willing to make between inflation and unemployment.

Smyth and Woodfield (1991) examine this trade-off by constructing an index based on the survey responses to the question: "What is the single most important problem facing New Zealand now?" The index is equal to the number citing inflation expressed as a fraction of the number citing either inflation or unemployment as the most important problem. By relating this index to actual inflation and unemployment, Smyth and Woodfield can calculate the preferences of a hypothetical "median voter," represented by the point where the number of people who would cite inflation as the most important problem is the same as the number who would cite unemployment. They then compare the results with similar evidence from U.S. surveys.

The results of the comparison are quite interesting and consistently reveal that New Zealanders have a greater tolerance for inflation. The contrast in attitudes with Americans can be illustrated by considering the following questions: How much inflation will the median voter accept? The answer will depend on the level of unemployment, but at an unemployment rate of 6 percent, often taken as a rough estimate of the sustainable average rate of unemployment in the U.S., the critical rate of inflation is 4.2 percent. As inflation rates rise above this figure, more survey respondents cite inflation than unemployment as the most serious problem. The corresponding critical inflation rate at 6 percent unemployment for New Zealand is estimated by Smyth and Woodfield to be in the range of 30-34 percent, eight times the value for the U.S.

This comparison may be misleading since New Zealand has traditionally had much lower rates of unemployment than the U.S. Thus, 6 percent unemployment may be "normal" in the U.S., but it represents unprecedented unemployment relative to New Zealand's historical experience. Perhaps it is not surprising then that inflation would need to be at very high levels indeed to be considered as serious as 6 percent unemployment in New Zealand.

Currently, New Zealand is suffering from high rates of unemployment, and recent major structural changes in its economy make it difficult to estimate what might be the normal rate of unemployment. If, however, one assumes a normal unemployment rate of 3 percent, the contrast in attitudes towards inflation is still quite remarkable. At an unemployment rate of 3 percent, the critical rate of inflation exceeds 13 percent. According to this study, New Zealanders are clearly more tolerant of inflation than Americans are.

POLITICAL POPULARITY

A second way to measure the public's preferences towards inflation is to examine how inflation and unemployment affect the popularity of elected politicians. In the U.S., the proposition that Presidential popularity depends on the state of the economy is well established and forms the basis of political models of the business cycle. These models attribute business cycles to the manipulation of the economy by administrations striving to be reelected. Political business cycle models, and the evidence that they can explain economic fluctuations, are critically reviewed in Huh (1990).

Smyth and Woodfield (1991b) examine results from a New Zealand survey in which respondents were asked whether they approved or disapproved of the overall performance of the government. They then estimate the impact of inflation and unemployment on the government's approval rating using data from the end of 1985 to the beginning of 19990, a period characterized by government attempts to reduce inflation. The results indicate that increases in either inflation or unemployment significantly reduce the approval rating the public gives the government.

Smyth and Woodfield estimate that at an initial unemployment rate of 3 percent and an inflation rate of 12 percent, a rise in unemployment to 4 percent would require a drop in inflation to less than 7 percent to prevent the New Zealand government's approval rating from falling. The implicit trade-off between inflation and unemployment rates that would hold government approval constant places much more weight on unemployment than appears to be the case in the U.S. This is consistent with the survey evidence on public identification of the most serious economic problem.

DO OTHER COUNTRIES FOLLOW THE SAME PATTERN?

According to the Smyth and Woodfield studies, New Zealanders seem more willing to trade off inflation for unemployment reductions than Americans, and New Zealand has generally experienced much higher inflation than has the U.S. Is the experience of other countries also consistent with this pattern?

Nordhaus (1989) reports estimates of the impact of unemployment and inflation on governmental popularity as measured by opinion polls from the mid-1950s to the 1970s for the U.S., Germany, and the U.K. His estimates suggest that a 1 percentage point rise in the unemployment rate together with a 4 percentage point fall in inflation would leave the government's popularity unchanged in the U.S. In Germany, in contrast, the negative impact of such a rise in unemployment would be offset by a drop in inflation of just 1.3 percent. The U.K. falls at the opposite extreme—inflation would need to decline by 8.6 percent to offset a rise in the unemployment rate of 1 percent if the government's popularity were to remain unchanged. Thus, one can interpret this as evidence to rank the three countries according to their preferences for inflation relative to unemployment: Germany gives greatest importance to low inflation, then the U.S., then the U.K. Countries that weigh inflation heavily, like Germany, should have low average rates of inflation. This is, in fact, exactly what the data reveal. From 1960 to 1979, the average rates of inflation in Germany, the U.S., and the U.K. were, respectively, 3.7 percent, 4.7 percent, and 8.0 percent.

AN ALTERNATIVE INTERPRETATION

So far, the discussion has suggested that some countries, like New Zealand, have had more inflation than the U.S. because their citizens have been willing to tolerate higher rates of inflation. But there is an alternative interpretation. Perhaps countries that have high inflation simply learn to live with it. Social institutions and economic arrangements may adjust so as to reduce the costs of inflation. Indexation of wages, financial contracts, and taxes, for example, can reduce the distortionary income and wealth redistribution that inflation can cause. Inflation may be viewed as a less serious problem in high inflation countries simply because those countries have adjusted in ways that help ameliorate the consequences of inflation.

This interpretation, however, is consistent with the general view that a country's inflation rate settles at a level that balances the perceived costs of inflation with the perceived short-run gains. Adjustments that help to eliminate or reduce the perceived costs—such as indexation of wages, social security payments, financial instruments, and so forth—will result in a rise in inflation until costs again balance the perceived gains.

REFERENCES

Huh, Chan Guk. 1990. "Political Business Cycles." Federal Reserve Bank of San Francisco *Weekly Letter* (December 14).

Nordhaus, William D. 1989. "Alternative Approaches to the Political Business Cycle." *Brookings Papers on Economic Activity* 2, pp. 1-49.

Smyth, David J., and Alan E. Woodfield. 1991a. "Inflation-Unemployment Choices in New Zealand and the Median Voter Theorem." *Economic Letters* 35 (April) pp. 397-400.

Smyth, David J., and Alan E. Woodfield. 1991b. "Inflation, Unemployment and Macroeconomic Policy in New Zealand: A Public Choice Analysis." *Public Choice.* Forthcoming.

QUESTIONS

1. Why do studies of attitudes toward inflation focus on the trade-off the public is willing to make between inflation and unemployment?

2. Describe the index Smyth and Woodfield construct to measure public attitudes toward inflation in the U.S. and New Zealand. What differences do they note between attitudes toward inflation in the two countries? Are these differences in attitudes consistent with differences in actual inflation rates in these countries?

3. How do the findings Walsh reports on politicians' popularity ratings shed light on public attitudes toward inflation?

4. Predict what would happen to the inflation rate in a country if widespread indexation reduces the perceived costs of inflation. Why do you make this prediction? Can you think of other institutional changes that would alter the public's preferred rate of inflation?

READING 44

Challenges to Stock Market Efficiency: Evidence from Mean Reversion Studies

Charles Engel and Charles S. Morris

Analysts have traditionally regarded the stock market as an efficient market because they believe stock prices reflect the market value of future dividends. Dividends, in turn, depend on a company's profits. As a result, stock prices should change only in response to new information about future profits. For example, a company's stock price will rise if it patents a new way to harness solar power because future profits will rise. Conversely, its stock price will fall if its chief competitor discovers the new way first.

In recent years, however, many analysts have begun to question the efficiency of the stock market. What information, they ask, could have possibly caused the profitability of the companies in the Dow Jones Industrial Average to fall 23 percent on October 19, 1987? These analysts claim the stock market is inefficient because many traders pay attention to information unrelated to future profits. For example, some traders may jump on the bandwagon and buy stocks only because past returns were high. While prices will ultimately reflect true values, such behavior causes prices to overshoot true values in the short run. The tendency for prices to overshoot but eventually revert to true values is called *mean reversion*.

Is the stock market efficient? This article surveys the mean reversion evidence. The article finds that stock prices might be mean reverting, but the evidence is not strong enough to rule out market efficiency. The first section of the article discusses the features of an efficient stock market. The second section shows why prices may be mean reverting in an inefficient stock market. The third section shows that the evidence on mean reversion is mixed. Thus, more evidence is needed before declaring the stock market inefficient.

EFFICIENT MARKETS

The efficient market theory describes how prices are determined in a securities market. In an efficient stock market, a stock's price reflects the current market value of its expected future income stream. If a stock's price is less than the value of its expected income stream, investors will quickly buy the stock. As they do, the price will rise until it equals the current value of the income. Conversely, if a stock's price is above the current value of expected income, selling pressure will quickly drive down the price to its current value.[1]

The income from a stock can be divided into two parts. One part is the dividends that are paid over the investment horizon. The second part is the price for which investors can sell the stock at the end of the investment horizon.

The market value of the expected income from a stock depends on the size of the income stream relative to the return on other investments that are equally risky. The return on equally risky investments can be represented by the inflation-adjusted, or real, interest rate on such investments. The real interest rate on a risky investment is the sum of the real interest rate on a riskless investment, such as Treasury bills, and a risk adjustment factor that rises with the riskiness of an investment. Thus, the current price of a stock, P_0, is

$$P_0 = \frac{ED_1 + EP_1}{1 + r}$$

where, ED_1 is the dividends that investors expect to be paid at the end of the investment period, EP_1 is the expected end-of-period price, and r is the real interest rate.[2] Thus, a stock will have a high price if it is expected to pay high dividend (high ED_1), if it is expected to appreciate rapidly (high EP_1), or if it is not very risky (low r).[3]

One feature of an efficient stock market is that highly profitable companies will have higher stock prices than unprofitable companies. In an efficient market, stock prices reflect the market value of future dividends, which ultimately depend on profits. Thus, stock prices reflect the market value of a company's future profits—that is, the company's *fundamental* value.

The economy benefits when stock prices reflect fundamental values because investment funds flow to their most valuable uses. Companies with profitable investment opportunities have high fundamental values, while companies without such opportunities have low fundamental values. As a result, companies with profitable investment opportunities can sell their stock for a higher price, and therefore get more investment funds, than companies without such opportunities.

A second feature of an efficient stock market is that expected real returns on stocks should be constant and equal to the real interest rate (Figure 1). Like most stock price indexes, such as the Dow Jones Industrial Average, the price in the figure includes the returns from dividends so that the percentage change in price is the total return.[4] If the real interest rate is constant over time, prices will grow along a straight line with a slope

Figure 1
Stock Prices in an Efficient Market

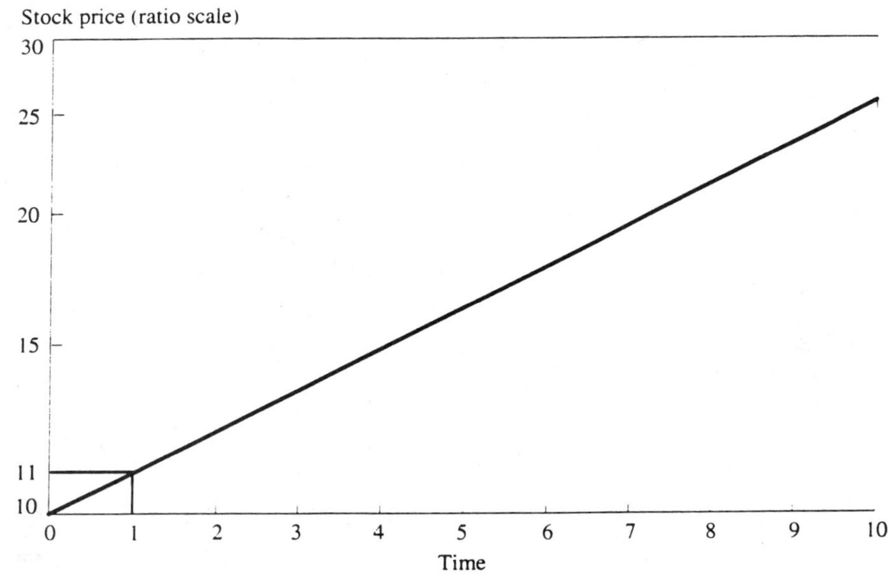

equal to the interest rate. The slope of the line is just the percentage change in price.[5] Thus, because the percentage change in price is the total return, the expected return on the stock is constant and equal to the real interest rate.

A third feature is that only new information about future profits causes real stock returns to deviate from the real interest rate. Because stock prices already reflect everything that investors expect about future profits, prices should rise more or less than expected only if investors get new information about future profits. For example, suppose the interest rate is 10 percent and the stock price is $10 (Figure 2). At the end of period one, the stock price can be expected to rise to $11. But if the company announces it will pay higher dividends with the profits from a new discovery, the stock is a bargain at $11. As investors buy more of the stock, the price might rise to $13. Thus, while the expected return on the stock was only 10 percent, the unexpected news led to a 30 percent return.

A final feature of efficient markets is that when actual returns differ from what was expected, investors should still expect future returns to be constant and equal to the real interest rate. In other words, if prices rise more than expected, investors should not expect prices to continue to grow faster just because they did so in the past. Furthermore,

Figure 2
Stock Prices in an Efficient Market: Change in Dividends

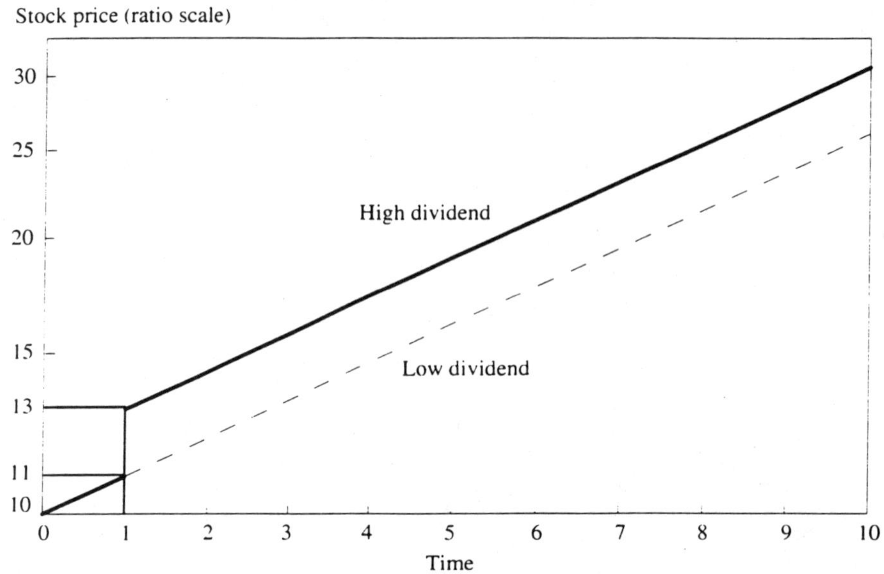

investors should not expect prices to grow slower to offset the unexpected increase. For example, in Figure 2, the stock price rose 20 percent more than expected over the first period. The unexpected increase reflected the *entire* value of the increase in future dividends. As a result, the stock price should resume growing at the old rate. This is shown in Figure 2 by the high-dividend path having the same slope as the low-dividend path.

INEFFICIENT MARKETS

Many analysts claim the stock market is inefficient because they believe prices often overreact to new information and overshoot fundamental values in the short run. If stock prices do not always reflect fundamental values, the stock market will not direct investment funds to where they are most valuable. Moreover, expected returns will vary over time because prices will be mean reverting. Finally, stock prices that overreact to new information are excessively.

Why Might the Stock Market Be Inefficient?

In an efficient market, stock prices reflect the current value of the future income that stocks generate because prices depend on *future* dividends, prices, and interest rates. If other factors, such as *past* prices and dividends, affect the value investors place on stocks, stock prices will deviate from fundamental values. When prices deviate from fundamental values, the market is inefficient.

One theory of why stock prices deviate from fundamental values is that many traders pay attention to recent trends in returns (Cutler, Poterba, and Summers). These "feedback traders" believe that if a stock's returns have been high in the recent past, they are likely to be high in the future. As feedback traders buy the stock to capture the excess returns, the price will rise above the stock's fundamental value. Likewise, if returns have been low in the recent past, feedback traders will sell the stock, driving the price below its fundamental value. Thus, in the short run, increases in stock prices are followed by further increases and decreases are followed by decreases.

According to the theory, however, stock prices will ultimately return to fundamental values. Arbitragers and traders who pay attention to fundamental values will discover which stocks are overvalued and which are undervalued. As they sell the overvalued stocks and buy the undervalued stocks, prices eventually reach their fundamental values.

An example may clarify how stock prices in an inefficient stock market differ from prices in an efficient stock market (Figure 3). Suppose a company's stock price jumps when it announces it will pay higher dividends with the profits from a new discovery. Because the return over the first period is 30 percent instead of 10 percent, feedback traders buy the stock. The upward pressure on the price drives the price above its fundamental value (shown by the dashed line segment). Traders who pay attention to fundamentals will then begin selling the overvalued stock, putting downward pressure on its price and causing the average return to fall over the next few periods. With lower past returns, fewer feedback traders buy the stock. Indeed, some may start selling the stock, producing even greater downward pressure on the price. Eventually, the price returns to its fundamental value. Prices that follow such a pattern of rising above their fundamental trend and then returning are said to be *mean reverting*.

Implications

In contrast to an efficient stock market, an inefficient stock market does not direct investment funds to their best use because prices do not necessarily reflect fundamental values. For example, feedback traders may irrationally drive the stock prices of companies with low fundamental values too high. Conversely, stock prices of companies with high fundamental values may be too low. As a result, companies with low fundamental values may be able to raise a lot of capital, while companies with high fundamental values may find it difficult to raise capital.

A second implication of an inefficient stock market is that mean reverting prices cause expected returns to vary. For example, although the average return in Figure 3 from the end of period one to the end of period five

Figure 3
Stock Prices in an Inefficient Market

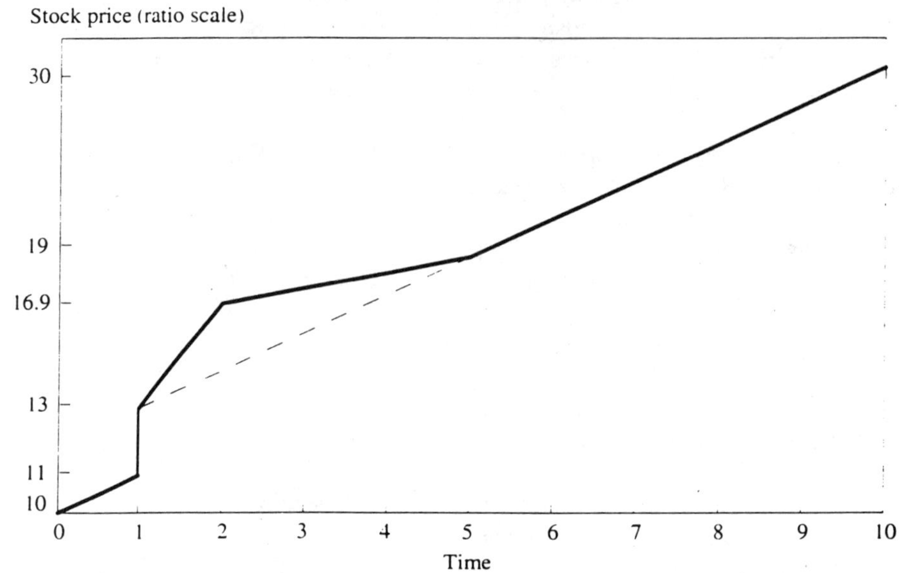

is 10 percent, the return is far from constant. As the price rises above the fundamental value, the return is 30 percent. But as the price reverts to the fundamental value, the average return is just 4 percent. Thus, greater than average returns are followed by less than average returns, while less than average returns are followed by greater than average returns.

A third implication is that prices are excessively volatile in the short run. Stock prices are volatile in an efficient market because new information causes unexpected changes in prices. However, prices are even more volatile in an inefficient market because prices will change by more than the value of the new information. In the long run, though, prices are not excessively volatile because they eventually revert to their fundamental trend. In other words, as shown in Figure 3, the long-run change in stock prices in an inefficient market is the same as in an efficient market.

IS THE STOCK MARKET EFFICIENT?

The evidence is mixed on whether the stock market is efficient. Some recent studies have found that stock prices are mean reverting, leading some analysts to conclude that the stock market is inefficient. Other studies cast doubt on this conclusion.

Evidence That Stock Prices Are Mean Reverting

After years of testing the efficient market hypothesis, financial economists have generally agreed that the stock market is efficient. In recent years, however, new research strategies have shown that stock prices are mean reverting over long investment horizons. The strategies rely on new statistical techniques that are potentially better able to detect regularities in stock prices. In addition, some researchers have begun to pay more attention to the long-run behavior of stock prices.

Variance-ratio tests. In the long run, stock price volatilities are the same whether or not prices are mean reverting. Short-run volatilities, however, are greater if prices are mean reverting than if they are not. As a result, the ratio of long-run volatility to short-run volatility is smaller if prices are mean reverting. The new statistical techniques use ratios of long-run volatilities to short-run volatilities to determine whether stock prices are mean reverting.

An example may help clarify this point. Suppose a stock's price will either rise 20 percent a year or fall 10 percent a year (solid lines in Figure 4). One measure of the volatility of this stock is the difference between the best and worst possible returns over the investment horizon. For a one-year investment, the best return is a 20 percent gain and the worst a 10 percent loss, so the volatility is 30 percent (20 percent less a negative 10 percent). For a two-year investment, the best return is 40 percent—20 percent in each of the two years—and the worst is a negative 20 percent, so the volatility is 60 percent. Thus, the volatility of the two-year investment is twice that of the one-year investment. More generally, the volatility of a k-year investment will be k times the volatility of a one-year investment if the market is efficient.[6]

The volatility of a k-year investment will be less than k times the volatility of a one-year investment, however, if prices are mean reverting. Because prices overshoot fundamental values in the short run but not the long run, prices are excessively volatile only in the short run. For example, prices might either rise 30 percent or fall 20 percent so that the volatility is 50 percent in the first year (dashed lines in Figure 4). If the price returns to its fundamental value by the second period, the best two-year return is 40 percent and the worst is a negative 20 percent, so that the volatility is 60 percent—just as in the efficient market. Thus, the volatility of the two-year investment is much less than twice the volatility of the one-year investment.[7]

Poterba and Summers have argued that the efficient market theory can be tested by looking at whether volatility rises proportionally to the investment horizon. They measured volatility by the variance of stock returns. If the market is efficient, the variance of k-year returns (r_k) should equal k times the variance of one-year returns (r_1).

Figure 4
Investment Risk

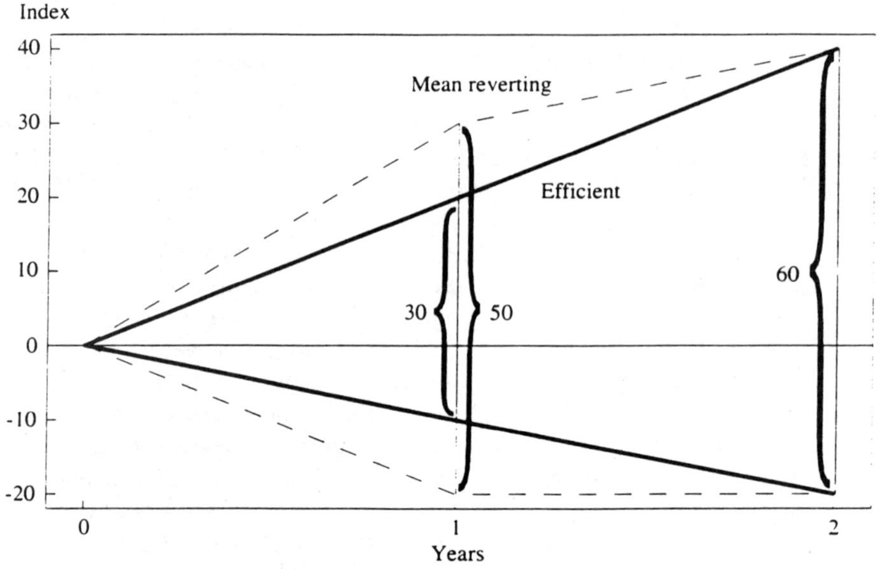

$$Variance(r_k) = k \times Variance(r_1)$$

or

$$\frac{Variance(r_k)}{k \times Variance(r_1)} = 1$$

Thus, the ratio of the variances at all investment horizons should equal one if the market is efficient, but should be less than one if prices are mean reverting.

Poterba and Summers concluded that the stock market is inefficient because prices are mean reverting. They calculated variance ratios for investment horizons of two to eight years. The data were excess returns on the New York Stock Exchange (NYSE) from 1926 to 1985, measured as monthly NYSE returns less U.S. Treasury bill returns. The variance ratios were less than one for all investment horizons greater than two years. For example, eight-year returns should be eight times more variable than one-year returns if the stock market is efficient. Poterba and Summers found, however, that eight-year returns are only three-and-a-half times more variable than one-year returns. In addition, the eight-year variance ratio is significantly less than one in a statistical sense. Finally, Poterba and Summers showed that mean reversion is stronger for stocks of small firms than of large firms.[8]

Regression tests. Another way to test the efficient market theory is to regress stock returns on past stock returns. If stock prices rise at a constant rate as suggested by the efficient market theory, returns should be constant over time and, therefore, unrelated to past returns. That is, in a regression of stock returns on a constant term and past returns, the constant term should be positive, but the slope coefficient on past returns should be zero. On the other hand, if prices grow faster than trend initially but slower as they return to trend, returns should be above and then below normal. Thus, if prices are mean reverting, the slope coefficient should be negative.

Many researchers have regressed stock returns on past returns to test the efficient market theory. Most of the studies used returns over very short investment horizons, such as daily or weekly returns. Although the slope coefficients were generally found to be statistically significant, they were not economically significant because they were so close to zero. Thus, in a review of many of the early studies, Fama concluded that the stock market is efficient.

More recent studies have extended the early research by using multiyear returns in the regressions. Fama and French (1988a) tested for mean reversion by regressing multiyear returns on past multiyear returns for investment horizons of one to ten years. They used monthly data adjusted for inflation from the NYSE and various industry groups over the period from 1926 to 1985. For example, for a four-year horizon, the return from March 1935 to March 1939 was regressed on the return from March 1931 to March 1935.

Fama and French concluded that stock prices are mean reverting. They found that the coefficients on past returns became negative for two-year returns, reached a minimum for three-to-five-year returns, and then approached zero as the investment horizon increased to eight years. For example, the coefficient on past NYSE returns for the four-year horizon was -0.36 and statistically significant. Thus, for example, if returns were 10 percent above average over the past four years, they are likely to be 3.6 percent below average over the next four years. Finally, like Poterba and Summers, Fama and French found that mean reversion is stronger for stocks of small firms than of large firms.[9]

Another way to use regressions to test for efficient markets is to regress stock returns on the difference between stock prices and a measure of fundamental values.[10] If stock prices are mean reverting, returns should be negatively related to past differences between prices and fundamental values. For example, if a stock price is above its fundamental value, future returns should be small as the price returns to the fundamental value.

Fama and French (1988b) found that stock prices are mean reverting when dividends are used to measure fundamental values. Dividends are a measure of fundamental values because stock prices should be proportional to dividends in an efficient market (see equation 1). Thus, if prices are mean reverting, returns should be negatively related to the difference between prices and dividends. Using inflation-adjusted NYSE returns from 1926 to 1986, Fama and French found that two-year to four-year returns are negatively related to the difference between stock prices and dividends.[11]

Campbell and Shiller found that prices are mean reverting using dividends and earnings to measure fundamental values. Because dividends ultimately depend on earnings, earnings can also be used to measure fundamental values. Using excess returns and inflation-adjusted returns on the Standard and Poor's 500 stock index from 1871 to 1987, they found that prices are mean reverting over one-year, three-year, and ten-year horizons.

Why the stock market might still be efficient

Despite the evidence that stock prices are mean reverting, the stock market might still be efficient for two reasons. First, some critics argue the evidence for mean reversion is weak, either because the data samples are too small or because the evidence depends entirely on the behavior of stock prices before World War II. Second, some critics argue that mean reverting stock prices are, in fact, simply a characteristic of more sophisticated versions of the efficient market theory.

Small sample size. Some researchers argue there are not enough data to conclude that stock prices are mean reverting. In general, the tests used to determine whether a statistic is significant assume that the statistic is calculated from an infinite number of observations. Because a finite number of observations are actually used in any test, the tests are only an approximation. The larger the number of observations, however, the better the approximation. The problem with mean reversion tests is that the data sets are very small. For example, from 1925 to 1985, there are only 12 independent observations of five-year returns (60 years divided by five).

Using statistical tests that account for the relatively small number of observations, several studies have found that previous work overstated the statistical significance of the mean reversion evidence (Mankiw, Romer, and Shapiro; Nelson and Kim; Kim, Nelson, and Startz; and McQueen). In general, these studies have found that the evidence on mean reversion is only marginally, if at all, statistically significant. Thus, while the evidence is suggestive, it is not strong enough to conclude that stock prices are mean reverting.

Mean reversion is due to pre-World War II data. Some researchers argue that stock prices may have been mean reverting in the past, but not anymore. According to these critics, stock prices were mean reverting only before World War II—stock returns were high in the late 1920s, low after the 1929 Crash and during the Great Depression, and then high during and right after the war. Since the war, however, they argue that such regularities in stock returns have largely disappeared.

Some recent studies show that mean reversion does disappear when the early years are excluded. Using NYSE returns from 1947 to 1986, Kim, Nelson, and Startz found that stock prices are not mean reverting. Indeed, for large-firm stocks, prices move away from the mean at long horizons.[12] Fama and French (1988a) found that mean reversion

Chart 1

Variance Ratios

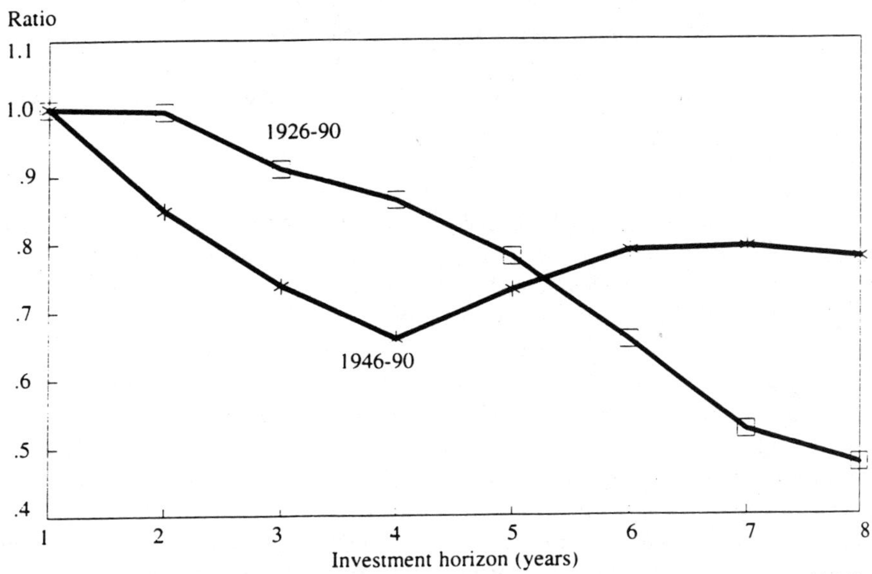

Note: Returns are monthly returns on the equal-weighted New York Stock Exchange portfolio less monthly returns on U.S. Treasury bills from 1926 to 1990 and 1946 to 1990. The variance ratio for a k-year investment horizon is calculated as the variance of the k-year return divided by k times the variance of the one-year return. The variance ratios are adjusted for small-sample bias as discussed in Poterba and Summers.

Source: Center for Research in Security Prices.

disappears for all of their groups when returns from 1941 to 1985 are used.[13]

Critics of the studies of postwar data might argue that the studies omit the second half of the 1980s—a period in which stock prices appear to have been mean reverting. For example, the return on the Dow Jones Industrial Average over the three years prior to the October 1987 collapse was 112 percent, while the return over the three years after the collapse was just 30 percent.[14]

Updating the postwar sample through 1990 does not significantly affect the results, however. The effect of updating the data is shown by calculating variance ratios over the 1946-90 period and comparing them with variance ratios calculated over the 1926-90 period (Chart 1). Mean reversion at long horizons has been weaker since 1946 than before 1946, although mean reversion at short horizons has been stronger over the postwar period. But because the sample is so small, these variance ratios are probably no more than marginally significant. Thus, overall, the postwar evidence casts doubt on the mean reversion evidence.

Sophisticated efficient market theories. Even if stock prices are mean reverting, the stock market might still be efficient. Mean reversion implies that the simple efficient market theory described earlier—where the real interest rate is assumed to be constant over time—is incorrect. In the simple theory, expected real returns are constant over time because the real interest rate is assumed to remain constant. But if real interest rates vary over time, returns should also vary over time in an efficient market. Indeed, if real interest rates are mean reverting, stock prices will also be mean reverting.

Real interest rates could vary for a variety of reasons. For a given riskless interest rate, changes in the riskiness of stocks or in investors' tolerance for risk would cause the risk adjustment factor, and therefore the interest rate, to change. Alternatively, for a given risk-adjustment factor, the riskless interest rate may change over time. Several researchers have developed sophisticated examples in which changes in risk tolerance and the riskiness of stocks cause interest rates, and therefore stock prices, to be mean reverting (Fama and French 1988b; Black; and Cecchetti, Lam, and Mark).

The basic idea underlying the sophisticated models is illustrated in Figure 5. Suppose that interest rates fall at the end of the first period. The decline could be due to a fall in the riskless interest rate, in the riskiness of stocks, or in the risk averseness of investors. According to equation 1, a decline in interest rates causes the current stock price to rise. At the same time, the lower interest rate implies that future prices will grow at a slower rate. As the figure shows, the stock price first jumps above the old trend and then slowly reverts to the old trend just as in the inefficient market theory. Indeed, Figure 5 looks very similar to Figure 2. Thus, if interest rates are mean reverting, perhaps because they fall during recessions and rise during recoveries, stock prices may appear mean reverting even if the stock market is efficient.

Poterba and Summers argue, however, that changes in the riskiness of stocks or the risk tolerance of investors cannot explain the mean reversion found in the data for two reasons. First, the degree of mean reversion in stock price data implies changes in the riskiness of stocks or in risk tolerance that are implausibly large. Second, although the behavior of stock prices in the feedback trader model and sophisticated efficient market theories are similar, they are not exact. Specifically, prices should move away from trend in the short run if they are mean reverting. In other words, as shown in Figure 2, if prices grow faster than normal, feedback traders should cause them to continue to grow faster than normal in the short run. In the sophisticated models (Figure 5), however, prices should immediately begin to grow slower than normal after a fall in interest rates. Lo and MacKinlay, and Poterba and Summers find that prices move away from trend for investment horizons of two years or less, which supports the feedback trader model.

Figure 5

Stock Prices in an Efficient Market: Change in Interest Rates

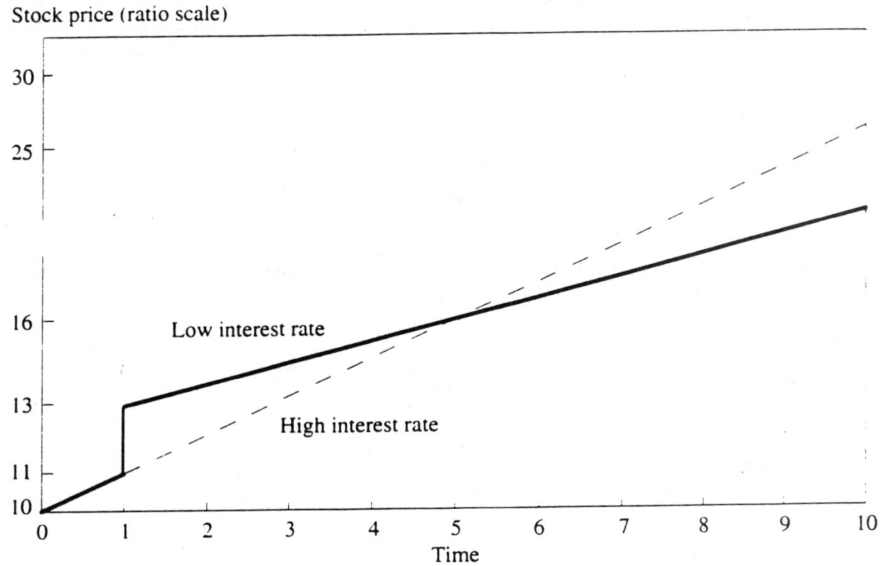

CONCLUSIONS

Analysts have traditionally regarded the stock market as an efficient market. More recently, some analysts have argued that feedback traders cause the market to be inefficient. The major problem for the economy of an inefficient market is that investment funds are not directed to where they are most useful.

This article reviewed the mean reversion evidence on stock market efficiency. Some studies of stock prices suggest prices are mean reverting. However, it is too early to conclude that the stock market is inefficient for two reasons. First, other studies indicate that stock prices are not mean reverting. Some show that the statistical tests are relatively inaccurate due to a lack of long-horizon stock returns, while others show that the evidence in favor of mean reversion is much weaker if pre-World War II data are excluded. Second, even if stock prices are mean reverting, it may be that one of the more sophisticated efficient market theories is correct.

ENDNOTES

1.Investors cannot get higher than average returns by following simple investment strategies, however. In an efficient market, arbitragers work so quickly that investors cannot take advantage of any mispricing of securities.
2.Because the real interest rate is used in equation 1, the price and dividend terms are also real values. Equation 1 would also hold if all values were expressed in nominal terms. Real terms are used to avoid changes in values induced by inflation. For expositional purposes, "real" will not be used as a modifier unless it is necessary for clarity.
3.More formally, the efficient market theory says that the price of a stock should equal the present value of all future dividends.

$$P_0=\sum_{i=1}^{\infty}\frac{ED_i}{(1+r)^i}=\frac{ED_1}{1+r}+\sum_{i=2}^{\infty}\frac{ED_i}{(1+r)^i}$$

The expected price of a stock one period in the future is just the present value of all dividends from that time on.

$$EP_1=\sum_{i=2}^{\infty}\frac{ED_i}{(1+r)^i-1}$$

Dividing EP_1 by $1 + r$ gives

$$\frac{EP_1}{1+r}=\sum_{i=2}^{\infty}\frac{ED_i}{(1+r)^i}$$

which is just the summation term in the second line of the P_0 equation. Thus, substituting $EP_1/1+r$ into the P_0 equation gives equation 1 in the text.
4.The dividend-inclusive price, q_t, is constructed so that the percentage change in price equals the total return from dividends and price appreciation. That is,

$$(q_t - q_{t-1})/q_{t-1} = (D_t + P_t - P_{t-1})/P_{t-1}.$$

One way to think of the dividend-inclusive price is that it is what the price of the stock would be if the stock did not pay dividends so that the total return comes from price appreciation.
5.The slope of the line is the percentage change in price instead of just the change in price because the vertical scale of the figure is a ratio scale. The slope equals the risk-adjusted interest rate because the dividend-inclusive price is constructed such that the percentage change in price equals the total return including dividends (see endnote 4). That is,

$$slope = (q_t - q_{t-1})/(q_{t-1} = (D_t + P_t - P_{t-1})/P_{t-1} = r,$$

and r is assumed to be constant over time in the simple efficient market theory described in the text. More sophisticated efficient market theories allow r to vary over time. In those theories, expected returns will vary overtime with r. These theories will be discussed later in the article.

6.If risk is measured by the variance of returns, the variance of the return on a k-year investment is just k times the variance of the return on a one-year investment. For example, if p_t is the log of the dividend-inclusive price, the two-year return is

$$(p_t - p_{t-1}) + (p_{t-1} - p_{t-2}) = p_t - p_{t-2}.$$

The variance of the two-year return is

$$var(p_t - p_{t-2}) = var(p_t - p_{t-1}) + var(p_{t-1} - p_{t-2}) \\ + 2cov(p_t - p_{t-1}, p_{t-1} - p_{t-2}).$$

If the market is efficient, the covariance between the current one-year return and the lagged one-year return is zero. Assuming the variance of one-year returns is constant over time, the two-year variance becomes $2var(p_t - p_{t-1})$.

7.If risk is measured by the variance of returns, the variance of the return on a k-year investment is less than k times the variance of the return on a one-year investment. For example, if p_t is the log of the dividend-inclusive price, the two-year return is

$$(p_t - p_{t-1}) + (P_{t-1} - p_{t-2}) = p_t - p_{t-2}.$$

The variance of the two-year return is

$$var(p_t - p_{t-2}) = var(p_t - p_{t-1}) + var(p_{t-1} - p_{t-2}) \\ + 2cov(p_t - p_{t-1}, p_{t-1} - p_{t-2}).$$

If prices are mean reverting, the covariance between the current one-year return and the lagged one-year return is negative. Thus, assuming the variance of one-year returns is constant over time, the two-year variance is less than $2var(p_t - p_{t-1})$.

8.Poterba and Summers report results for both value-weighted and equal-weighted NYSE returns. Value-weighted returns are calculated from a weighted-average price index for all stocks on the NYSE, where the weight on a stock's price is the market value of the firm's outstanding shares divided by the market value of all shares on the NYSE. Equal-weighted returns are calculated from a price index in which all stock prices have the same weight. The primary difference between the two measures of returns is that value-weighted returns are dominated by large-firm stocks.

The variance ratios for both types of returns are less than one for all horizons over two years. However, the equal-weighted statistics generally are smaller than the value-weighted statistics. For example, eight-year equal-weighted returns are three-and-a-half times more variable than one-year returns, while eight-year value-weighted returns are five-and-a-half times more variable than one-year returns. Because smaller firms carry a larger weight in equal-weighted returns than in value-weighted returns, these results suggest mean reversion is more prominent for stocks of small firms than of large firms.

Poterba and Summers report Monte Carlo estimates of the standard errors of the variance ratios for all horizons, but they report the statistical significance only for the eight-year horizon. The eight-year variance ratio is statistically different from one at the 8 percent level for the value-weighted returns and at the 0.5 percent level for the equal-weighted returns. It should be noted, however, that none of the variance ratios are more than two standard deviations from one.

The data used by Poterba and Summers end before the October 1987 stock market collapse. Extending the data through 1990, however, does not change the results.

9.Fama and French report results for value-weighted and equal-weighted NYSE returns, equal-weighted returns for groups of NYSE firms of similar size, and equal-weighted returns for various industries. In general, the coefficients for the three-to-five-year horizons are the most negative for all groups. Moreover, for most of the groups, the coefficients are more than two standard errors from zero only for the three-to-five-year horizons. The exceptions are the large-firm portfolios and the value-weighted returns, which are not more than two standard errors from zero at any horizon. Thus, like the Poterba and Summers results, mean reversion is more prominent for stocks of small firms than of large firms.

10.If the stock market is efficient, any difference between prices and a measure of fundamental value must be due to errors in measuring fundamental values. Because the measurement errors should cancel each other out over time, however, returns should not be systematically related to such measurement errors.

11.Fama and French actually regress returns on the log of dividends minus the log of prices and find that the slope coefficients are positive. This implies that the coefficient on prices minus dividends should be negative as discussed in the text. They report results for value-weighted and equal-weighted real returns. In general, the slope coefficients are larger in the equal-weighted regressions than in value-weighted regressions. Thus, they also find that mean reversion is more prominent for stocks of small firms than of large firms.

12.Kim Nelson, and Startz use the term "mean aversion" to describe the tendency of prices to move away from the mean. Like mean reversion, mean aversion is not consistent with the efficient market theory. However, no one has come up with a story that explains why prices should be mean averting over long horizons.

13.Poterba and Summers find that mean reversion does not disappear when returns from 1936 to 1985 are used. These results are apparently due to the fact that the sample still includes returns from the Great Depression.

14.The return over the three years prior to the 1987 collapse was calculated from monthly averages of the Dow Jones Industrial Average from September 1984 to September 1987. The return over the three years after the 1987 collapse was calculated from monthly averages of the Dow Jones Industrial Average from November 1987 to November 1990.

REFERENCES

Black, Fischer. 1990. "Mean Reversion and Consumption Smoothing," *Review of Financial Studies*, pp. 107-14.

Campbell, John Y., and Robert J. Shiller. 1988. "Stock Prices, Earnings, and Expected Dividends," *Journal of Finance*, pp. 661-76.

Cecchetti, Stephen G., Pok-Sang Lam, and Nelson C. Mark. 1990. "Mean Reversion in Equilibrium Asset Prices," *American Economic Review*, pp. 398-418.

Cutler, David M., James M. Poterba, and Lawrence H. Summers. 1990. "Speculative Dynamics and the Role of Feedback Traders," *American Economic Review*, pp. 63-68.

Fama, Eugene F. 1970. "Efficient Capital Markets: A Review of Theory and Empirical Work," *Journal of Finance*, pp. 383-417.

Fama, Eugene F., and Kenneth R. French. 1988a. "Permanent and Temporary Components of Stock Prices," *Journal of Political Economy*, pp. 246-73.

__. 1988b. "Dividend Yields and Expected Stock Returns," *Journal of Financial Economics*, pp. 3-25.

Kim, Myung Jig, Charles R. Nelson, and Richard Startz. 1991. "Mean Reversion in Stock Prices? A Reappraisal of the Empirical Evidence," *Review of Economic Studies*, pp. 515-28.

Lo, Andrew W., and A. Craig MacKinlay. 1988. "Stock Prices Do Not Follow Random Walks: Evidence from a Simple Specification Test," *Review of Financial Studies*, pp. 41-66.

Mankiw, N. Gregory, David Romer, and Matthew D. Shapiro. 1991. "Stock Market Forecastability and Volatility: A Statistical Appraisal," *Review of Economic Studies*, pp. 455-77.

McQueen, Grant. 1990. "Long Horizon Mean Reverting Stock Prices Revisited." Department of Finance, Marriott School of Management Brigham Young University.

Nelson, Charles R., and Myung J. Kim. 1990. "Predictable Stock Returns: Reality or Statistical Illusion?" Working Paper 3297. Cambridge, Mass.: National Bureau of Economic Studies.

Poterba, James M., and Lawrence H. Summers. 1988. "Mean Reversion in Stock Prices: Evidence and Implications," *Journal of Financial Economics*, pp. 27-59.

QUESTIONS

1. Why is stock market efficiency an important issue?
2. According to efficient market theory, what determines a stock's price and the behavior of its price over time?
3. What is meant by "mean reversion" of stock prices? Why might this occur?
4. Describe the tests for mean reversion and the results of those tests.
5. Why do Engels and Morris claim that it is too early to declare the stock market inefficient?

READING 45

Activist Monetary Policy for Good or Evil? The New Keynesians vs. the New Classicals

Tom Stark and Herb Taylor

Economic analysts and policy practitioners argue endlessly about how long it takes for monetary policy actions to affect output or employment, how long the effects will last, or how large they will be. But underneath it all, the truth is that economists cannot agree on how monetary policy affects the real economy in the first place. Theoreticians are offering two different explanations, each with its own implications for the way monetary policy ought to be conducted.

Perhaps the most popular explanation for money's impact was first proposed about 15 years ago by a group of economists now known as the New Classicals. These economists see episodes of money affecting economic activity as temporary aberrations that occur only when monetary policy actions happen to catch the public by surprise. Because they see these episodes as harmful, the New Classical economists think that central banks should avoid such surprises. They think that a central bank should just announce a simple money growth plan and stick to it. Such a policy, they say, would minimize economic disruptions and make inflation predictable.

In the last few years a group of economists labeled the New Keynesians has begun mounting a challenge to the New Classical view. The New Keynesians claim that under the right circumstances even widely publicized monetary policy actions can have a sustained impact on output and employment. And they claim that this impact can be used to help counteract what they see as the ecomomy's tendencies toward excessive volatility and unemployment. So the New Keynesians think that a good central bank conducts an activist monetary policy—it actively manages the supply of money and credit to keep the economy close to full employment.

Which side is right? Is an activist monetary policy good or evil? Neither side has all the answers, but both command serious attention in a very important policy debate.

THE NEW CLASSICALS' CASE AGAINST ACTIVIST POLICY

Like the great Classical economists of the last century, the New Classicals see the market system naturally bringing the economy to its peak level of efficiency. They see markets as a network of competitive auctions in which prices respond quickly and completely to changes in economic conditions. Basing their decisions on these market prices, households and firms automatically deploy the economy's real resources—its labor, raw materials, factories, and equipment—fully and efficiently. Activist monetary policy has no place in this world. Policy actions designed to alter the pattern of economic activity are ineffective and unnecessary.

Competition among many small households and firms makes the Classical economy efficient. In the Classical system, overall supply and demand conditions determine the prices people pay and the wages they earn. No business or individual is big enough to manipulate market conditions to its own advantage. Any firm that tried to charge above-market prices for its product would lose all of its customers to competing producers. Any worker that held out for above-market wages would lose his or her job to competing workers.

This environment may sound harsh, but it gives firms the incentive to perform at peak efficiency. Given the wage-price structure, each firm faces just one basic decision: how much to produce. And in its quest for profits, the firm will automatically choose a production level that balances consumer preferences with resource availability.

Consider the typical firm. For each unit it produces, it gets the market price. It also incurs costs equal to the price of the requisite labor and materials. The more it produces, the more it is prone to operating inefficiencies that push up per-unit production costs. At some point, the cost of producing another unit would exceed the product's market price. Expansion beyond that point would cut into profits, so the firm expands no further. Following this strategy not only maximizes the firm's own profits, it promotes overall economic efficiency as well. The product's market price measures its worth to the consumer. Wages and other input prices measure workers' and resource suppliers' valuation of their time and materials. So, in effect, the firm is producing only the units whose benefits to the consumer justify the burden their production imposes on workers and other resources.

Of course, economic conditions are constantly changing . Consumers' preferences shift away from one product and toward another; a new production technology comes along and displaces an old one. But in the Classical view, market prices and wages adjust quickly to changes in supply and demand, providing firms with the incentives to keep the economy's resources fully and efficiently employed. With the market system allocating resources so effectively, there is no reason to use monetary policy to alter the level of economic activity. But it's just as well. Because in the Classical world, any attempt at activist policy would fail.

The Classical economists developed the theory that money has no effect on economic activity. Clearly, prices are crucial to people's economic decisions in the Classical system. And usually we think of prices being quoted in terms of money. Yet the Classical economists maintained that changing the money supply would have no impact on output or employment. How can this be?

The Classicals claimed that when the money supply changed, all prices and wages would change in equal proportion, leaving the relationships among them unchanged. Consequently, households and firms would stick by their original employment and production decisions, leaving the real economy unaffected.[1]

Suppose, for instance, that the central bank pumps up the money supply. This increases the overall demand for goods and services, pushing up market prices. But workers recognize that higher prices erode the purchasing power of their wages. So they are willing to work the same hours and expend the same effort only if they get wage increases commensurate with the increase in market prices. Firms, competing for workers, agree to pay for the raises out of their inflated sales revenues, and they maintain their original level of employment and output. All that remains of the money supply increase are higher prices and wages.

The Classical economists recognized that, as a practical matter, these adjustments to a change in the money supply would not always proceed as smoothly as their theoretical analysis might suggest. But their message comes through clearly enough: the money supply ultimately affects the level of prices, not the level of economic activity.

The New Classical economists reinvigorated the Classical argument that monetary policy is generally ineffective. The Classical perspective on money's role in the economy was among the casualties of the Great Depression. The Keynesian Revolution swept through the economics profession and gave birth to the activist monetary policies of the postwar period. But in the early 1970s, some economists resurrected the Classical viewpoint. In fact, by combining parts of the Classical tradition with the notion of "rational expectations," these New Classical economists emerged with an even stronger position: monetary policy cannot systematically affect the real economy. Instances in which monetary policy actions alter employment or output levels are occasional, random events.

The New Classical analysis of money's impact on the economy is a variation on the old adage "knowledge is power." In keeping with their Classical tradition, the New Classicals maintain that markets are competitive enough to drive the economy to full employment, and responsive enough to keep it there in the face of shifting economic conditions. To this they simply add that a key element in markets' responsiveness is market participants acting upon rational expectations about where the economy is headed. The New Classicals assume that market participants understand the underlying structure of the economy and use the available data on current economic conditions to formulate accurate forecasts about future economic performance. Presumably, participants' actions in the marketplace today reflect those rational expectations.

The New Classicals go on to argue that market participants pretty much know what to expect from the monetary authority. Competitive market prices and wages automatically reflect those expectations, thus neutralizing the impact of any anticipated policy actions on output and employment. Admittedly, policy actions that take people by surprise can affect economic activity. But, the New Classicals point out, such "surprises" must, by definition, be occasional and without pattern. So the monetary authority cannot systematically influence the level of output or employment.

The New Classicals emphasize that even when a monetary policy action does take people by surprise, its impact is temporary. It lasts only as long as it takes for the markets to find out what the central bank has done and respond. And in the interim, people—particularly workers—are not necessarily better off.[2]

Textbook versions of the New Classical view assume that product prices respond to sudden shifts in economic conditions more quickly than wages do. For one thing, wage agreements, whether formal or informal, may cover several months, a year, or even several years—all periods much longer than it takes for product prices to change. Even where wages are set more frequently, workers usually agree to a certain wage without the benefit of complete information on the prices of the products they intend to buy. Consequently, when an unexpected monetary expansion comes along and pushes up product prices, firms find they can retain, and perhaps even expand, their work force without raising wages very much. And they make the most of the opportunity. They pay a slightly higher wage, hire more workers, produce more output, and sell it at the new, higher prices. Hence the expansionary monetary policy boosts aggregate employment and output.[3]

Of course, the workers eventually catch on. They shop. They see the higher product prices. And the next time they negotiate a wage, they demand compensation for their loss in purchasing power. Once wages rise as much as prices have, firms revert to their original hiring and production patterns. So money is, in the last analysis, neutral.

Overall, the New Classical analysis of money's impact on the economy casts activist monetary policy in a very dim light. First of all, the New Classicals see the economy exhibiting a strong tendency toward full employment that makes it unnecessary for the monetary authority to focus on the level of economic activity. But even beyond that, attempts to conduct an activist policy do more harm than good. An expansionary policy anticipated by the public simply creates instant inflation. If, as occasionally happens, the policy is not anticipated by the public, it affects output and employment essentially by tricking people into producing at a pace they would not have chosen if they were fully informed.

Given this perspective, the New Classicals' advice to policymakers is straightforward: do not try any surprise moves. Choose a simple money growth plan consistent with your inflation goals. Announce the plan far enough in advance to allow markets to react. Then just follow the plan.[4]

THE NEW KEYNESIANS' CASE FOR AN ACTIVIST POLICY

The New Keynesians don't see things quite the way the New Classicals do. The New Keynesians see an economy in which firms face only limited competition. These imperfectly competitive firms restrict their output to keep prices high and respond only partially to shifting demand conditions. As a result, the economy shows the tendencies toward underemployment and price "stickiness" that are very much a part of the traditional Keynesian perspective. The New Keynesians believe that in this world, regardless of how people form their expectations, monetary policy can and should be used to expand the level of economic activity.

Without strict market discipline, firms are less likely to achieve maximum economic efficiency. The difference between the Classical competitive firm and the imperfectly competitive firm is simple: the competitive firm must take the market price of its product as a given, whereas the imperfect competitor has the power to set price to its own advantage. And the right price structure for the imperfect competitor is not necessarily best for the overall economy.

In the competitive market, each firm is small and its output is nothing special. So its decision about how much to supply has no appreciable impact on the market price. If Farmer Jones decided to withhold some of his wheat from the market, how far could he drive up the price of wheat? If he tried to charge extra for Farmer Jones Wheat, who would pay the premium? No one.

Imperfect competitors have larger operations. Their product may have some special characteristic—real or imagined—that differentiates it in the mind of consumers. For these firms, size or special niche gives them some power over the price of their products. If General Mills were willing to cut its supply of breakfast cereal, cereal prices would rise. And if it decides to increase the price of Wheaties, some people would be willing to pay the premium.

In short, the imperfectly competitive firm has some advantage that frees its pricing structure from the strict discipline of the market. Of course, the firm is still subject to the Law of Demand: the higher the price it sets, the fewer units it will sell. So it must choose between setting a high price and selling to a limited number of customers, or setting a low price and grabbing the lion's share of the market. But one thing is for sure: it will not set as low a price as a Classical competitive market would establish. It will always find it profitable to set a higher price and maintain it by keeping output below competitive levels.

Exercising market power may make individual firms more profitable, but it imposes costs on society as a whole. From the social standpoint, imperfect competitors' prices are too high and their production is too low. Society would be better off if these firms would cut their prices to levels more consistent with resource costs. This would expand sales, production, and employment to more socially desirable levels.

Neither the notion of imperfect competition nor its impact on social welfare are original to the New Keynesians.[5] But the analysis offers them a rationale for their belief that the economy tends to underemployment. And it offers them something more—a jumping-off point for a new theory of how monetary policy can help alleviate the problem.

The New Keynesians believe monetary policy can work on imperfect competitors. Traditional theories of imperfect competition can explain underemployment, but they cannot explain why monetary policy should be effective in combating it. As long as prices and wages respond flexibly, the monetary authority is still powerless to affect firms' output and employment decisions. But the New Keynesians add a new wrinkle to the theory of imperfect competition: imperfectly competitive firms' prices are not as flexible as competitively established market prices. So real activity may respond to monetary policy actions.

In the Classical world, competitive markets adjust prices quickly and completely to every shift in economic conditions. In a world of imperfect competition, firms must set prices. When demand shifts are relatively small, these firms may not find changing prices worthwhile. It may be more profitable to maintain current prices and adjust production accordingly.

Economists have labeled the costs firms bear when they change their product prices "menu costs." That name captures the most obvious cost of repricing: printing new menus and catalogs and changing price tags and signs. But there are other costs as well. To find the new profit-maximizing price, the firm must estimate the likely nature, magnitude, and duration of the shift in customer demand. That kind of research and analysis uses up resources. In addition, frequent price changes may alienate customers and cost the firm some of its good will.

It's difficult to say how large menu costs are. It may seem that, as a practical matter, the cost of changing prices ought to be relatively small. But the New Keynesians emphasize that the benefits to changing prices can be small for imperfect competitors, too. So even small menu costs can thwart a price change.

When the demand for an imperfect competitor's product increases, the firm can respond in any number of ways. At one extreme, it can take the opportunity to raise its prices without losing sales. At the other extreme, it can hold the line on prices and take the opportunity to pick up sales volume. If the demand shift that the firm is experiencing is large, then choosing the right strategy can have a substantial impact on profits. But if the demand shift is relatively small, there is little advantage to choosing one over the other. A firm that simply maintains its original prices will not get as much as it could on each unit, but it will sell more units. So its profits will not be substantially compromised.[6] Once menu costs—even small ones—enter the equation, they can tip the scales in favor of maintaining current prices. Thus the profit-maximizing imperfect competitor may choose to accommodate a small demand shift without changing the price of its product.

This tendency for prices to be sticky in an imperfectly competitive environment affords the central bank some opportunity to influence overall output and employment. Suppose the central bank increases the money supply and thereby boosts overall demand for goods and services. Further suppose that individual firms decide that the demand increase is too small to make a price adjustment profitable. Instead, they decide to hold the line on prices and fully accommodate the increased demand for their products. In order to increase their output, they begin to hire more workers. So both output and employment pick up. Meanwhile, since product prices are not rising, workers are not demanding an inflation adjustment to their wages, so both wages and prices remain relatively constant.[7]

The New Keynesians recognize that the central bank's ability to raise output and employment in this way is circumscribed. If monetary policy actions create too large a demand shift, firms are more likely to raise prices than increase output. Furthermore, every firm faces different demand conditions and menu costs. Some will have lower thresholds for changing prices than others. So almost any policy action is likely to affect aggregate prices as well as aggregate output. In short, the New Keynesians acknowledge that a central bank cannot engineer dramatic or persistent increases in output and employment without driving up prices and wages. Nonetheless, New Keynesian analysis suggests that an activist policy can be successful, if used judiciously.

Overall, the New Keynesians see the potential for an activist monetary policy to improve the performance of an imperfectly competitive economy. Monetary policy may not be a cure-all, but it can help offset what New Keynesians see as the economy's chronic bias toward underproduction and underemployment in modern, imperfectly competitive economies.

Add to this underlying bias the fact that the economy is subject to sudden shifts in overall demand, and the New Keynesians' case for an activist monetary policy seems even stronger. For if price stickiness accentuates the impact of monetary policy on economic activity, it also accentuates the impact of other demand shifts as well. Thus a sudden decline in overall demand could drop the economy well below its potential level of performance. This suggests that monetary policymakers should be alert to these shifts and stand ready to offset them.[8]

WHO'S RIGHT?

Both the New Classicals and the New Keynesians offer explanations for monetary policy's impact on the economy. But the New Keynesian approach certainly casts activist monetary policy in a more positive light. Which explanation should we believe? One way to evaluate competing theories is to "let the data decide." But at this point, empirical tests do not provide a clear answer.

The New Classical theory has been around longer and been subjected to more empirical study. The results are not favorable to the hard-line New Classical view that only unexpected policy actions affect real activity. Statistical analyses seem to show output and employment responding to anticipated policy actions too. But, ironically enough, these kinds of results have prompted some New Classicals to support a theory that attributes even less potency to monetary policy actions: the *real business cycle* theory. According to this theory, monetary policy never causes fluctuations in economic activity. Rather, anticipated fluctuations in the economy cause the public to increase or decrease their demand for money. The central bank and financial system simply accommodate these demand fluctuations.[9]

The New Keynesian theory is relatively new, and empirical evidence is scantier. There is some supportive evidence, however. In countries where inflation is relatively low, which would suggest that expansionary monetary policies have not been pursued too aggressively, policy shifts seem to have more impact on real activity—as the New Keynesians would predict. But tests of the New Keynesian model are really in too early a stage to provide a convincing case one way or another.[10]

Empirical issues aside, there are unsettling aspects to both the New Classical and the New Keynesian models. Perhaps the most unsettling theoretical aspects have to do with the functioning of the labor market. Both groups admit they have trouble explaining why monetary policy actions that affect output have such a large effect on employment and such a small effect on wages. According to the New Classical theory, an unexpected increase in product demand induces firms to produce more because it pushes the product price up before wages have had a chance to rise in response. But firms need more workers in order to expand production. Won't that increased demand for labor itself push up wages?

The New Classicals' answer: some, but not much. True to their Classical perspective, they maintain that labor markets are competitive. They simply assume that labor supply is very sensitive to wage changes. Thus when labor demand increases, it evokes many more hours of work at only a slightly higher wage. The problem is that, as a practical matter, willingness to work does not seem to be all that sensitive to wage changes.

New Keynesians face a similar conundrum. According to them, when firms face a small increase in product demand, they hold the line on prices and expand output. Again, to expand output, firms need more workers. Granted, product prices are not increasing, so there is no inflation pressure on wages. But won't firms have to raise the wage they pay in order to induce more people to work? The New Keynesians' answer is no. True to the Keynesian tradition, they claim that there is a pool of involuntarily unemployed workers from which firms can always draw workers at the going wage. But to explain the involuntary unemployment, they must resort to some unconventional theories of the labor market.

Imperfectly competitive firms charge high prices, which restricts both output and employment. Nonetheless, the New Keynesians claim, these firms tend to pay the people they do employ relatively high wages. Different economists offer different reasons for this tendency. Proponents of the "efficiency wage" theory emphasize that by paying workers more than they would expect to earn if they had to go look elsewhere for a new job, the firm gives the worker the incentive to perform more effectively. Proponents of the "insider/outsider" theory emphasize that employees whose experience on the job is valuable to the firm can exact wage concessions from the firm. In either case, with wages high and employment opportunities limited, there is routinely a pool of willing workers unable to get jobs. Whenever firms want to expand output, they can tap this pool for workers without increasing the wage they pay.[11]

In short, both the New Classicals and the New Keynesians have a long way to go before either can proclaim their approach to be theoretically complete.

THE ACTIVIST POLICY DEBATE RENEWED

When the New Classical economics came on the scene in the early 1970s, it jolted academic economists and policymakers as well. The New Classicals were trying to explain precisely why monetary policy actions affect real activity. They concluded that money temporarily affects output and employment by tricking people into deviating from their preferred activity levels. This conclusion hardly cast activist monetary policy in the most favorable light, but there was little theoreticians could offer in rebuttal.

Now the New Keynesian school is offering an alternative explanation for money's impact on economic activity. That analysis, based on theories of imperfect competition, looks more favorably on activist monetary policy. The New Keynesians conclude that the economy tends toward underemployment and that an activist policy can help overcome the problem.

The New Keynesians can hardly claim to have overcome the New Classical paradigm. But they have reinvigorated the battle over the efficacy of an activist monetary policy.

ENDNOTES

1.To see this, suppose that initially bread costs $1 and workers earn $6 an hour, making a loaf of bread worth 10 minutes' work. If both prices and wages double, bread goes to $2 and wages go to $12, but a loaf of bread still trades for 10 minutes' work.

2.Thomas Sargent and Neil Wallace, in their article "'Rational' Expectations, the Optimal Monetary Instrument and the Optimal Money Supply Rule," *Journal of Political Economy* (April 1975) pp. 241-54, present a clear statement of the New Classical notion that expected monetary policy actions have no effect on economic activity.

3.Analyses stressing the role of wage contracts in limiting short-run wage flexibility can be found in Stanley Fischer's "Long-Term Contracts, Rational Expectations, and the Optimal Money Supply Rule," *Journal of Political Economy* (February 1977) pp. 191-205, and John Taylor's "Aggregate Dynamics and Staggered Contracts," *Journal of Political Economy* (1980) pp. 1-24. The idea that wages adjust imperfectly because workers are not completely aware of

current product prices is more consistent with the original New Classical formulation by Robert Lucas in "Some International Evidence on Output-Inflation Tradeoffs," *American Economic Review* (June 1973) pp.326-34.
4.The New Classical argument for this approach to monetary policy has most recently been articulated by Bennett McCallum in *Monetary Economics: Theory and Policy* (Macmillan, 1989).
5.The term "imperfect competition" is used here as a convenient expression for "monopolistic competition" a market model that can be traced back to the work of E.H. Chamberlin in the 1930's. Texts such as Paul Samuelson's *Economics* (McGraw-Hill) provide readable discussions of this market type.
6.This idea is sometimes called the PAYM insight because it emerged from the work of economists Michael Parkin, George Akerlof, Janet Yellen, and N. Gregory Mankiw. Specific references are to Parkin's "The Output-Inflation Tradeoff When Prices Are Costly to Change," *Journal of Political Economy* (1986) pp.200-24; Akerlof and Yellen's "Can Small Deviations From Rationality Make Significant Differences to Economic Equilibria?" *American Economic Review* (September 1985) pp.708-21; and Mankiw's "Small Menu Costs and Large Business Cycles: A Macroeconomic Model of Monopoly," *Quarterly Journal of Economics* (May 1985) pp.529-37.
7.Olivier Blanchard and Nobuhiro Kiyotaki develop this argument formally in "Monopolistic Competition and the Effects of Aggregate Demand," *American Economic Review* (September 1987) pp.647-66.
8.Prospects for this kind of policy get some theoretical support in Lars Svensson's "Sticky Goods Prices, Flexible Asset Prices, Monopolistic Competition, and Monetary Policy," *Review of Economic Studies* (1986) pp.385-405.
9.Frederic Mishkin provides a more complete discussion of the evidence on the New Classical hypothesis in *A Rational Expectations Approach to Macroeconometrics* (University of Chicago Press, 1983). For a good discussion of the real business cycle view and its monetary policy implications, see "Monetary Policy with a New View of Potential GNP," by John Boschen and Leonard Mills, this *Business Review* (June/July 1990) pp.3-10.
10.This New Keynesian result is presented by Laurence Ball, N. Gregory Mankiw, and David Romer in "The New Keynesian Economics and the Output-Inflation Trade-Off," *Brookings Papers on Economic Activity* (1988:1) pp.1-65. For an up-to-date discussion of the empirical evidence on the New Keynesian economics, as well as a good evaluation of its theoretical underpinnings, see Robert Gordon, "What Is New Keynesian Economics?" *Journal of Economic Literature* (September 1990) pp.1115-71.
11.Lawrence Katz provides an excellent overview of these modern labor market theories in "Some Recent Developments in Labor Economics and Their Implications for Macroeconomics," *Journal of Money, Credit, and Banking* (August 1988, Part 2) pp.507-30.

QUESTIONS

1. Compare the positions of the New Classicals and New Keynesians regarding: (a) market competition; (b) flexibility of prices and wages; and (c) speed of price and wage adjustments.

2. According to the New Classical view, what can be accomplished with an activist monetary policy? Why? How would New Keynesians respond to the New Classical views?

3. If the New Classical view is correct, how should the Fed conduct monetary policy?